Michael Noel
Colin Spence

Microsoft®
SharePoint
2010

UNLEASHED

SAMS | 800 East 96th Street, Indianapolis, Indiana 46240 USA

Microsoft® SharePoint 2010 Unleashed

ISBN-13: 978-0-672-33325-5

ISBN-10: 0-672-33325-2

Library of Congress Cataloging-in-Publication Data:

Noel, Michael.
  Microsoft SharePoint 2010 unleashed / Michael Noel, Colin Spence.
    p. cm.
  ISBN 978-0-672-33325-5
  1. Microsoft SharePoint (Electronic resource) 2. Microsoft Office SharePoint server. 3. Intranets (Computer networks) 4. Web servers. I. Spence, Colin. II. Title.
  TK5105.875.I6N64 2011
  006.7'8–dc22

                              2010040172

Printed in the United States of America

First Printing: October 2010

Trademarks

Warning and Disclaimer

Bulk Sales

Pearson offers excellent discounts on this book when ordered in quantity for bulk purchases or special sales. For more information, please contact:

U.S. Corporate and Government Sales
1-800-382-3419
corpsales@pearsontechgroup.com

For sales outside of the U.S., please contact:

International Sales
+1-317-581-3793
international@pearsontechgroup.com

Editor in Chief
Karen Gettman

Executive Editor
Neil Rowe

Development Editor
Mark Renfrow

Managing Editor
Sandra Schroeder

Senior Project Editor
Tonya Simpson

Copy Editors
Apostrophe Editing Services
Keith Cline

Indexer
Brad Herriman

Proofreader
Water Crest Publishing, Inc.

Technical Editor
Guy Yardeni

Contributing Writers
Ágnes Molnár
Alpesh Nakar
Ayman Mohammed El-Hattab
Ben Nadler
Brian P. Culver
Chris Chung
Conan Flint
Joel Oleson
Kim Amaris
Muhanad Omar
Toni Frankola
Ulysses Ludwig

Publishing Coordinator
Cindy Teeters

Book Designer
Gary Adair

Composition
Mark Shirar

Contents at a Glance

Table of Contents

About the Authors

Michael Noel, MS-MVP, MCITP, is an internationally recognized technology expert, best-selling author, and well-known public speaker on a broad range of IT topics. He has authored 17 major industry books that have been translated into more than a dozen languages worldwide. Significant titles include *SharePoint 2007 Unleashed*, *Exchange Server 2010 Unleashed*, *Windows Server 2008 R2 Unleashed*, *Forefront Unleashed*, and many more. Currently a partner at Convergent Computing (www.cco.com) in the San Francisco Bay area, Michael's writings and extensive public speaking experience across six continents leverage his real-world expertise helping organizations realize business value from information technology infrastructure.

Colin Spence, MCP, MCTS SharePoint, is a partner at Convergent Computing (www.cco.com) and has worked with SharePoint technologies for nearly a decade. He has worked with hundreds of clients architecting, implementing, configuring, and supporting SharePoint solutions that meet their unique business requirements. Colin has authored several bestselling books on SharePoint products for the Sams Publishing *Unleashed* series, including *SharePoint 2003, 2007*, and now *2010*. He contributes to numerous blogs and publications and speaks regularly on SharePoint technologies.

Dedications

I dedicate this book to my wife Marina. You are my reason for living and the love of my life.

—Michael Noel

My work is dedicated to my beautiful, supportive, and patient wife Nancy, who always gives the right amount of support and input during the creative process.

—Colin Spence

Acknowledgments

Michael Noel: One has to wonder why I continue to torture myself with these books, and to be honest with you, it's a very good question. The amount of time that one spends writing a book like this does not translate to fame or riches, as unfortunately I'm not in the business of writing bestselling murder mystery novels. On the contrary, it typically leads to headaches, ulcers, and some missing hair on your head.

So why spend the time? Why work in a lab for weeks and months, learning new software from every angle? Why spend the wee hours of the morning screenshooting a software platform that will be obsolete when the next edition comes out in three years?

Honestly, there are no logical answers to this, but I do know that it makes me feel good that I can impart some knowledge on the IT workers of the world who just want to come home at a decent time and spend time with their families instead of hugging a keyboard. I hope this book provides for this, and I'd like to think it can help my fellow IT geeks have the opportunity to get some daylight every once in a while.

That said, I must first and foremost thank my wife Marina, my daughter Julia, and my in-laws Val and Liza for all their emotional support during the late nights when things looked like they would never return to normal. You guys are amazing, and I could not have done this without you!

Thanks as well to my co-author, Colin Spence, who slaved over this one for months on end, producing some wonderful content in the process. It is a joy and pleasure to work with you again on another one of these crazy books, even if we lose ourselves and our sanity in the process!

We also had an amazing group of contributing writers from around the world involved in this project that worked long and hard to provide an incredible depth and breadth of knowledge into the book. This includes such great writers as Ágnes Molnár, who provided some excellent content on SharePoint Search, and Ayman Mohammed El-Hattab, who wrote brilliantly on SQL Server maintenance. It also includes some fantastic backup and restore guidance from Alpesh Nakar, some bulletproof guidance on extranets from Brian Culver, and an amazing PowerShell chapter and scripts from Toni Frankola. Finally, I also had help writing and testing some brilliant scripts from Muhanad Omar and Conan Flint. The work performed by these phenomenal authors really helps this book shine. Thanks, everyone!

Thanks to all the conference attendees around the globe who have attended my sessions over the years, to my clients, and to the book readers—over a quarter million strong—who have read my books over the ages. I really do appreciate the trust you show in me and my colleagues.

And finally, thanks to Neil Rowe at Sams Publishing for all your help getting this one out the door, and in the great relationship you've developed with me over the years. You are a great guy and a tenacious editor.

Colin Spence: To start at the beginning (not of time but of my involvement in the technical writing world), I'd like to thank Rand Morimoto, who got me involved in the writing process all those years ago, and Michael Noel, who jumped in to the first *SharePoint*

Unleashed book with me and helped ensure the success of the franchise. Neil Rowe at Sams Publishing continues to make the process a breeze logistically and can always be counted on for a kind word, such as "knucklehead," to spur me on to meet deadlines.

Because all this work needed to be done after hours from my home office (affectionately known as "the cave"), my wife needed the patience of a saint to deal with my permanent status of unavailability for normal activities (such as walking the dog and dinner), mood swings, rants, and diatribes. Sometimes I think the writing process is tougher for her than me, so I thank her from the bottom of my heart!

It is no exaggeration to say that becoming involved in technical writing at this level does change your life, not only from the amount of time and sweat it takes to produce the finished product, but also in the way one's perspective of the technology changes. Because this is the third SharePoint Unleashed book I've co-authored, I have a pretty good understanding of the vast assortment of tools and features in the product. This often makes "simple" questions difficult to answer. For example, when someone asks me "What is SharePoint?," I have to rein in my mental processes to condense the answer into a sentence or two, as the questioner will rarely sit still while I whip out a whiteboard and discuss .NET, IIS, web applications, site collections, lists, and libraries. I've found it's more important to understand the motivation behind the questions, and specifically the goals the person or organization has in mind when asking about SharePoint technologies.

Fortunately, I've had the pleasure of working with hundreds of companies in the design and implementation process since the SharePoint 2003 product line and have countless case studies and examples of how the features can be mapped to organizational requirements. More important, the lessons learned over the years of tools and features that may overly complicate the solution rise to the surface and give me ammunition to rein in clients' enthusiasm where needed. Hopefully this combination of deep knowledge of the product and real-world experience comes across in the format and content of this book.

It was a great experience working with a number of contributing writers for this volume, several of whom enabled us to confidently expand the scope of the book to cover the "hot" topics of application development and business intelligence in more detail. Ulysses Ludwig and I have worked together for a couple of years now, and the real-world projects we worked on together contributed greatly to the approach taken on the application development chapter. Likewise, Ben Nadler's expertise with PerformancePoint and Business Connectivity Services were very welcome, especially when we realized we'd need two chapters to provide a reasonable overview of the topics involved.

Additionally, Joel Oleson and Chris Chung provided guidance and content for the governance chapter, which was surprisingly challenging to write, due to the scope of the topic. Kim Amaris also assisted on the Office 2010 integration chapter; so thanks very much for your help as well. Thanks also to the team at Sams Publishing/Pearson Education who assisted with the editing, formatting, and fine-tuning of the content.

I hope I'm not forgetting others who contributed ideas, thoughts, and content, but if I am, please let me know, and I'll buy you a drink at Starbucks.

We Want to Hear from You!

As the reader of this book, you are our most important critic and commentator. We value your opinion and want to know what we're doing right, what we could do better, what areas you'd like to see us publish in, and any other words of wisdom you're willing to pass our way.

As an executive editor for Sams Publishing, I welcome your comments. You can email or write me directly to let me know what you did or didn't like about this book—as well as what we can do to make our books better.

Please note that I cannot help you with technical problems related to the topic of this book. We do have a User Services group, however, where I will forward specific technical questions related to the book.

When you write, please be sure to include this book's title and author as well as your name, email address, and phone number. I will carefully review your comments and share them with the author and editors who worked on the book.

Email: feedback@samspublishing.com

Mail: Neil Rowe
             Executive Editor
             Sams Publishing
             800 East 96th Street
             Indianapolis, IN 46240 USA

Reader Services

Visit our website and register this book at informit.com/register for convenient access to any updates, downloads, or errata that might be available for this book.

Introduction

When we sat down to write the original *SharePoint 2003 Unleashed* book, we had a hunch that the technology would be popular but did not anticipate how quickly the product would take off, and how much interest the IT industry would end up taking in SharePoint products and technologies. In the interim years, as we worked with implementing the product in companies of all sizes, we learned what the product did well and what it didn't do so well, and further refined our knowledge of SharePoint best practice design, deployment, and administration.

Our exposure to the latest version of SharePoint started well over a year before its release, in the pre-beta stages when SharePoint v14 was still being developed. We developed experience through our company, Convergent Computing (CCO), deploying it for early adopters through our close relationship with Microsoft as a Gold Partner. In addition, we also collaborated with and provided input to the SharePoint development team and the broader SharePoint community through Microsoft's Most Valuable Professional (MVP) program. The richness of features and the capabilities of what became the SharePoint 2010 version became evident to us during this time, and we used our hands-on experience with the beta stages of the product to begin designing this book, which provides a comprehensive look at SharePoint 2010 functionality, administration, and infrastructure.

A major challenge of this book was trying to identify and cover the most important tools, topics, practices, and skills that the range of our readers will find valuable in their interactions with SharePoint 2010. To do this, we drew upon our experiences over the last decade with hundreds of different organizations and distilled out the most common requirements in the areas of design, architecture, integration, and customization.

We endeavored to provide value to readers who may never have used SharePoint products before and those who are well versed with the products and may currently be using SharePoint 2010. You might be IT managers, IT architects, SharePoint administrators, SharePoint power users and, of course, SharePoint end users. Therefore, we carefully crafted the book to cover what we felt would add the most value to our audience. A key piece of this strategy is to expand beyond the out-of-the-box features of SharePoint 2010 and share our experience on some of the most common integration points of SharePoint 2010, such as SQL Server, Exchange Server, antivirus, Edge Security products, and tools such as SharePoint Designer 2010 and Visual Studio 2010. In this way, the book becomes more than a treatise on what SharePoint 2010 can do in a vacuum, but what it can do in a complex technology ecosystem.

This book is the result of our experience and the experiences of our colleagues at Convergent Computing and our clients in working with SharePoint 2010 products and technologies, both in the beta stages and in production deployments. We wrote this book to be topical so that you can quickly browse to a particular section and follow easy-to-understand, step-by-step scenarios. These exercises, instead of just giving simple examples of a feature, are designed to give examples of real-world applications of the technologies and tools that provide you with business value. In addition, if you need a good overview on SharePoint 2010, the book can be read in sequence to give you a solid understanding of the higher levels of security and functionality SharePoint can provide. Topics in the book are divided into four sections, each with topics in similar categories.

How This Book Is Organized

This book is organized into the following sections:

- ▶ Part I, "Planning for and Deploying SharePoint Server 2010," provides an introduction to the products in the SharePoint 2010 stack and includes prescriptive advice for how to architect and implement them. In addition, it covers upgrade advice from legacy versions of SharePoint and also details advanced installation scenarios with SharePoint 2010.

- ▶ Part II, "Administering and Maintaining SharePoint Server 2010," focuses on the day-to-day administration and monitoring required for a SharePoint backend environment. It details how to use new tools, including Windows PowerShell, for SharePoint 2010 Administration and covers backup and restore. It also focuses in particular detail on how to administer and maintain the SQL databases used by SharePoint.

- ▶ Part III, "Securing, Protecting, and Optimizing SharePoint Architecture," covers security concepts in detail that focuses on edge, transport, and content security. Topics such as SQL Transparent Data Encryption, SSL Certificates, IPsec encryption, Active Directory Rights Management Services, antivirus, and more are detailed. In addition, this section also includes information on how to virtualize a SharePoint 2010 farm using server virtualization technology.

▶ Part IV, "Using SharePoint 2010 Technologies for Collaboration and Document Management," starts with a comparison of SharePoint Foundation and SharePoint Server 2010 and then moves to the tools and capabilities provided by libraries and lists, to cover customization of libraries and lists, and then to managing the sites and pages that house these components. One chapter is dedicated to metadata and content types, another chapter discusses social networking tools, and another covers the process of SharePoint 2010 governance.

▶ Part V, "Leveraging Office Applications with SharePoint," focuses on the Office 2010 applications most used with SharePoint 2010 products, including Word 2010, SharePoint Workspace 2010, and Outlook 2010 and key collaboration tools that can be leveraged with SharePoint 2010. Next, topics including Excel Services, Access Services, Visio Graphics Services, Office Web Apps, and out-of-the-box as well as SharePoint Designer 2010 workflows are covered.

▶ Part VI, "Extending the SharePoint Environment," dedicates one chapter to the topic of application development with SharePoint Designer 2010 and Visual Studio 2010, one chapter to PerformancePoint Services, and one chapter to Business Connectivity Services.

If you, like many out there, were recently tasked with administering a SharePoint environment, or are looking for ways to bring document management and collaboration to the next level and need to understand how SharePoint 2010 can fit into your IT ecosystem, this book is for you. We hope you enjoy reading it as much as we've enjoyed creating it and working with the product.

CHAPTER 1

Introducing SharePoint 2010

It is rare for a technology product to attract as much attention as SharePoint has in recent years. True, every technology has its fan base, but SharePoint has attracted a massive following over the years. A huge percentage of all organizations today, of every shape and size, use some form of SharePoint within their organization.

This is no fluke. SharePoint is popular because of its capability to provide a platform for the creation of flexible, powerful, and intelligent business solutions. It provides for comprehensive document and records management, team collaboration, web content management, and extranet capabilities, all from an easy-to-understand and customizable interface.

Microsoft has further upped the ante with this latest release of SharePoint products and technologies, collectively referred to as SharePoint 2010. New features are included, such as a more scalable service application model, enhanced user interface (UI) with ribbon support, external data integration with Business Data Connectivity Services, and many more. Microsoft has listened to customer feedback and improved the platform significantly, providing for an intelligent platform that can grow with all types of organizations.

This chapter introduces the SharePoint 2010 products, giving a high-level overview of the features and functions in the platform. It lists the changes and features in SharePoint 2010 and serves as a jumping-off point to the other chapters in this book, indicating which particular areas of the book give more information about individual features and technologies.

Understanding the Capabilities of SharePoint 2010

Answering the question "What is SharePoint 2010?" is not an easy task. This is primarily because, unlike many of the other Microsoft tools on the market, SharePoint is designed to be a platform that can be molded and shaped to fit the needs of virtually any organization. One SharePoint environment may look drastically different than another SharePoint environment and may be used for completely different tasks.

Indeed, SharePoint is designed to be customized to solve individual business problems and to satisfy specific organizational needs. It is built to serve as a full-fledged document management solution, collaboration portal, team site workspace, public-facing website, extranet partner collaboration environment, or all these things at the same time.

SharePoint 2010 has evolved over the years from a disparate set of small-scale tools into a complex and capable tool in use at a large proportion of organizations in the world. But where did SharePoint 2010 come from? Before understanding what this version is, it is first important to gain a better understanding of the history of SharePoint products and technologies and how we got where we are today.

Exploring the SharePoint 1.0 Wave: SharePoint Team Services and SharePoint Portal Server 2001

SharePoint as we know it today had its roots in two distinct products developed by two different teams at Microsoft. These products overlapped in many areas, but during the development phases, they were seen as completely different products and were expected to have different names upon release. It was only as the release date approached that Microsoft decided to give each the name SharePoint, even though they were different in many ways.

The first of these two products became SharePoint Team Services and was seen as a team collaboration product with limited document management functionality. This product was released as an add-on to the FrontPage media, which is how many administrators stumbled upon it eventually. Although unique in approach, it wasn't very scalable and was limited in functionality. The letters STS still can be found in today's product line, such as in the STSADM tool.

The second product developed by Microsoft eventually became SharePoint Portal Server (SPS) 2001 and was seen as an extension to public folder functionality in Microsoft Exchange Server. The storage engine for SPS 2001 was the Microsoft Exchange jet engine database, which was completely different than the SQL Server based back-end of SharePoint Team Services.

Although innovative and providing some interesting and powerful features, these two versions of SharePoint did not see too much use in most organizations, aside for the occasional team site put together by scattered departments and an occasional portal.

Exploring the SharePoint 2.0 Wave: Windows SharePoint Services 2.0 and SharePoint Portal Server 2003

Microsoft's first real attempt to marry these two tools into a single product line and create a true collaboration environment was born out of the second wave of SharePoint technologies, SharePoint 2003, as shown in Figure 1.1. SharePoint Team Services was rebranded as Windows SharePoint Services (WSS) 2.0, and the portal product became SharePoint Portal Server 2003. Both products were built on the same SQL Server database engine, and Microsoft positioned the features to be an extension of each other. WSS was the "free" product, available with every license of Windows Server, whereas the SPS 2003 product became the fully featured portal that incorporated WSS sites into its topology.

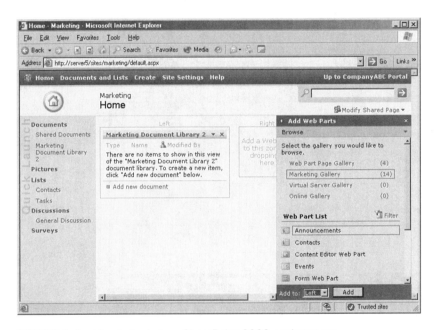

FIGURE 1.1   Viewing a legacy SharePoint 2003 environment.

Although it was a great effort, and a much more mature product than the 2001 line of SharePoint products, growing pains were still visible in the software. For many people, it wasn't quite clear whether to use SPS 2003 Areas or WSS Sites, and the integration was loose. This wave saw the first strong adoption of SharePoint, however, as many organizations deployed it for the first time.

Exploring the SharePoint 3.0 Wave: Windows SharePoint Services 3.0 and Microsoft Office SharePoint Server 2007

The point at which Microsoft SharePoint products and technologies really took off was the 3.0 wave. This wave saw the tightest integration between the new versions of the two products. WSS became WSS 3.0, and SPS 2003 was renamed Microsoft Office SharePoint

Server (MOSS) 2007. In addition, Microsoft combined its Content Management Server product with SharePoint, integrating it into MOSS 2007.

MOSS 2007 and WSS 3.0, as shown in Figure 1.2, saw massive adoption across the board, and many organizations started to deploy for collaboration, document management, intranets, and extranets. In addition, major industry websites started to move to SharePoint 2007, with tens of thousands of public-facing sites deployed on SharePoint within the first few years. This version saw true comprehensive document management, enterprise search, and collaboration capabilities as well, and many organizations deployed it to improve their efficiency and communications capabilities.

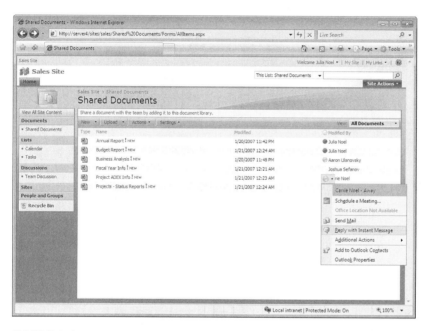

FIGURE 1.2   Viewing a legacy SharePoint 2007 environment.

SharePoint 2007's success was one of its disadvantages as well, unfortunately, as the growth of SharePoint sites led in some cases to a proliferation of siloed SharePoint farms and sites in many spots across organizations. There was a general lack of governance of the SharePoint environments, and this ended up hurting many companies as it created redundancy of data and inefficiencies. In addition, there were certain features that were asked for that were not part of the product, and other annoyances that people complained about that Microsoft sought to fix. Organizations looked to Microsoft to further improve its product, and Microsoft busily gathered information on what people liked and didn't like to include those new features in the next release of the product.

Exploring the Latest SharePoint 4.0 Wave: SharePoint Foundation Server and Microsoft SharePoint Server 2010

Early in 2010, Microsoft released its next wave of SharePoint products: SharePoint 2010. WSS was renamed once again, this time to SharePoint Foundation Server, and the Office in MOSS was dropped, with the product simply renamed Microsoft SharePoint Server 2010. A significant number of new features found their way into these two products, as will be demonstrated in this book. Organizations looking to effectively leverage the capabilities of SharePoint should first gain a good understanding of what those features are and understand how they can be matched to address specific business needs within their organization.

Using SharePoint for Collaboration and Document Management

SharePoint 2010 is many things to many people, so it is difficult to narrow the focus onto specific features and functionality. Two areas that are typically focused on, and help business decision makers better understand how SharePoint 2010 can be used, are in the areas of collaboration and document management functionality. SharePoint 2010 integrates extensively with the Office 2010 product line, so it becomes an extension of the business productivity tools that knowledge workers already know like the backs of their hands and therefore enhances collaboration between employees. SharePoint 2010 provides for road-tested and robust enterprise content management, document management, and records management for organizations of all different shapes and sizes. Organizations can store their documents within SharePoint document libraries and take advantage of version control, check-in/check-out, and new features such as the Managed Metadata Service, which can help control the type of metadata that documents in SharePoint have. SharePoint lists store data rather than files and can be leveraged in many ways, because each is a self-contained database that can be used in many of the same ways that a spreadsheet can.

Integrating Deeply with Microsoft Office Applications

Digging deeper into the concepts of collaboration and document management, SharePoint 2010 provides the highest level of integration with Office 2010 products but supports users of Office 2007 and to some extent Office 2003 applications. The integration is most extensive with Word, Excel, Outlook, Access, PowerPoint, Visio, and tools essentially designed for using with SharePoint 2010: SharePoint Designer 2010 and SharePoint Workspace 2010. This integration serves as the cornerstone for the collaborative capabilities of SharePoint 2010. Chapter 25, "Using Office 2010 Applications with SharePoint 2010," digs deeper into the topic of Office integration, as does Chapter 26, "Extending SharePoint 2010 with Excel Services, Access Services, and Visio Graphics Services."

An example of enhanced collaboration that many organizations are seeking is to reduce reliance on email as a primary collaboration tool. SharePoint offers an ideal solution because it enables users to simply email a URL that is a link to a SharePoint document in a document library instead of emailing the entire document. Then users can access the document in the document library, programmatically check out the document, make changes, and check the document back in. SharePoint can create a new version of the document to allow for access to the historical versions of the document. And the end result is one document title and one URL for the document, as opposed to the "old way of doing things" in which users had to try to locate the document on a file share or in a public folder, and then locate the proper document while trying to figure out why "ABC Proposal v1.0csmn.docx" was newer than "ABC Proposal v2.0mncs.docx."

Libraries and Lists as Data Management and Collaboration Tools

It is revealing to understand how SharePoint 2010 stores data, and the main repositories are libraries and lists. Some of the advantages provided by a SharePoint document library include the tools provided to the library administrator to control "who can do what" within the library, in terms of adding, deleting, editing, or just reading documents. In addition, versioning tools are available to track major and minor versions of files, as are alerts that inform users of changes, check-in and check-out controls, document templates available from the library, and powerful tools to create metadata that is added to the documents stored in the libraries.

Libraries are used for many purposes, one of which is to reduce reliance on file shares, which only offer a small subset of the features of SharePoint libraries. SharePoint libraries are typically managed by power users and IT staff, so more control can be put in the hands of the people using the tools every day. In addition, any text-based, Office, or index-supported file uploaded to a SharePoint library is indexed, making the contents available for searching, while still maintaining security trimming on the file. Many other features are available in libraries, such as enhanced navigation tools, workflows, and the ability to rate documents and add tags and notes, which greatly enhance collaboration within the libraries.

Alerts in SharePoint libraries and lists generate informative emails to users when certain types of changes occur, which means users don't have to religiously visit their lists and libraries every day to see what has changed, because SharePoint is "smart" enough to let them know. Workflows can be triggered manually or automatically when certain conditions are met, such as a user indicating that a document should be published to a major version, which sends an email with instructions to a manager to review and approve a document, for example.

Document libraries are one set of repositories in SharePoint 2010, and the other main set of repositories are called lists, which store data in rows and columns much like Excel spreadsheets. Most organizations immediately start moving data from Excel spreadsheets to SharePoint lists when the product is available. Consider the example of the spreadsheet used by sales for forecasting. Historically, each salesperson updates it the night before team meetings. The manager must then frantically collate the information into a "single source of the truth." When this manager moves the data to a SharePoint list, he can retire the spreadsheet, and each user simply adds or modifies rows of data in the list, and multiple users can access the list at the same time. Even better, the list tracks versions of the data in each row (a feature not offered by Excel) and time stamps each change and the identity of the user who made it, for powerful auditing capabilities. SharePoint lists enable users to export data to Excel or Access, edit data in the user-friendly datasheet view, and create different views to show subsets of the total data.

A sampling of the templates available for list and library creation follows:

- ▶ Document Library
- ▶ Picture Library
- ▶ Report Library
- ▶ Announcements
- ▶ Discussion Board
- ▶ Calendar
- ▶ Project Tasks
- ▶ Survey
- ▶ Blog

Several chapters are dedicated to exploring these subjects and providing step-by-step examples to help new and experienced SharePoint users put concepts into action in small amounts to time. Chapter 19, "Using Libraries and Lists in SharePoint 2010," starts with a ground-up approach to inform users, managers, designers, and architects about the range of capabilities in these repositories. Chapter 20, "Customizing and Managing Libraries and Lists to Meet Business Requirements," addresses the tools that power users and SharePoint site administrators will want to understand more fully to better meet end user requirements. Chapter 22, "Managing Metadata and Content Types in SharePoint 2010," covers the vitally important topic of metadata and how it can be leveraged within the SharePoint ecosystem to help organizations better manage their data and provide value to knowledge workers.

Organizing Collaborating with SharePoint Site Collections and Sites

Building upon the power of the repositories previously discussed (lists and libraries), SharePoint 2010 provides a powerful framework of sites and site collections to manage these repositories and provides additional management tools. The sites and site collections enable IT to build a framework that provides working spaces for departments, groups, teams, programs, divisions, offices, and any other type of business grouping. These sites can be branded with appropriate logos and color schemes and have web parts added to .aspx pages that perform many tasks, from simply displaying rich text, graphics, and charts to stock tickers, information about the weather, or data pulled directly from corporate databases.

Site collections are collections of sites that can be managed as a unit. A wide range of templates are available that make it quick and easy to create functionally specific site collections, such as the following:

▶ Team Site

▶ Document Workspace

▶ Blog

▶ Meeting Workspace

▶ Document Center

▶ Records Center

▶ Business Intelligence Center

▶ Publishing Portal

▶ Enterprise Wiki

For the sites created within the site collection, many other templates are available, including the following:

▶ Assets Web Database

▶ Basic Meeting Workspace

▶ Blog

▶ Contacts Web Database

▶ Document Center

▶ Enterprise Search Center

▶ Enterprise Wiki

▶ FAST Search Center

▶ Group Work Site

▶ Issues Web Database

▶ Projects Web Database

▶ Publishing Site with Workflow

▶ Records Center

▶ Team Site

▶ Visio Process Repository

Chapter 21, "Designing and Managing Pages and Sites for Knowledge Workers," focuses on other templates, tools, and capabilities of sites and site collections.

These features help collaborative teams work more efficiently and share data better. In addition, extranet capabilities, such as the ones discussed in Chapter 13, "Deploying

SharePoint for Extranets and Alternate Authentication Scenarios," can be used to collaborate with remote partners.

Deploying SharePoint Websites with Comprehensive Web Content Management

In addition to the document management and collaboration features in SharePoint, SharePoint 2010 is also ideally positioned to allow for web content management capabilities, enabling for complex and useful public-facing websites to be created that are very Web 2.0 in nature. Because SharePoint is a platform, these websites can take multiple forms and be customized visually, allowing for a large degree of personalization to suit the needs of the organization. Microsoft has also improved its Internet-facing licensing model for SharePoint 2010, making it a more attractive candidate for web content management.

Outlining Improvements in SharePoint 2010

Microsoft has spent considerable time gathering input from customers on previous versions of SharePoint. This input was directly used by the development team to create new functionality and features in this version of SharePoint. The product team delivered a huge range of services and functionality. For SharePoint administrators familiar with SharePoint 2007, it is important to gain a better understanding of what those changes are and how they can be used to build a better collaboration environment for your organization.

Understanding the Scalable Service Application Model in SharePoint 2010

One of the most significant architectural changes in SharePoint 2010 is the change to a service application architecture from the shared services provider architecture of SharePoint 2007. Service applications in SharePoint 2010 are independent services that can be shared across web applications or across farms.

Service applications in SharePoint 2010 include the Business Data Connectivity Service, which allows for connection to an external data source, the Managed Metadata Service, which enforces common metadata across a farm, and the Search Service, which is critical for Enterprise Search functionality. In total, there are more than a dozen service applications available out-of-the-box in SharePoint 2010, and Microsoft enables third-party service applications to be created as well.

Service applications enable a SharePoint 2010 environment to be more scalable because they can be easily shared across multiple servers. SharePoint architects can define which servers run which service applications, and which service applications apply to what farms. By separating the functionality in SharePoint onto this highly flexible service application tier, it becomes easier to scale up the environment with the needs of the individual environment. For example, Figure 1.3 illustrates a very large farm with multiple servers running individual service applications. Although most organizations will be served by smaller farms, it shows the scalability of the service application model. Service applications are covered in more detail in Chapter 2, "Architecting a SharePoint 2010 Deployment."

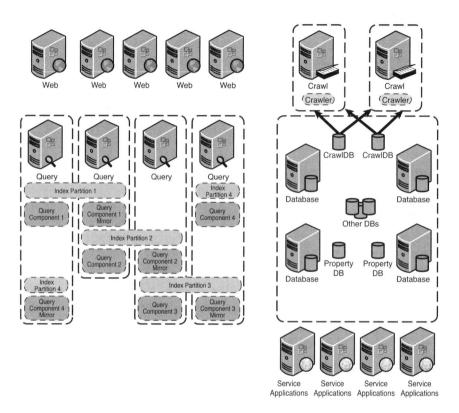

FIGURE 1.3   Viewing a large distributed SharePoint 2010 farm.

Outlining Search Improvements in SharePoint 2010

Another area of significant improvement in SharePoint 2010 is SharePoint's built-in Enterprise Search functionality. Rebuilt as a service application, SharePoint's native search tool has been rearchitected to enable the following:

▶ Redundant index functionality, now providing for index redundancy and high availability, something not possible in SharePoint 2007.

▶ Content sources can now be divided among multiple index partitions, such as what is illustrated in Figure 1.3. This allows for a greater load to be distributed between multiple servers.

▶ Improved search relevancy.

In addition to improvements in SharePoint 2010's native search, Microsoft also offers a different tool for SharePoint search: FAST Search Server 2010. FAST Search has all of the improvements available with the native SharePoint 2010 search but adds additional features, such as thumbnail previews, click-through relevance, and automatic metadata tagging. You can find more details on SharePoint 2010's search in Chapter 8, "Leveraging and Optimizing Search in SharePoint 2010."

Accessing the Improved Administration, Monitoring, and Backup Tools

There are two major improvements in the area of administration for SharePoint. The first comes in a revamped SharePoint Central Administration tool, shown in Figure 1.4. The second comes with the addition of Microsoft PowerShell as a scripting administration interface.

FIGURE 1.4   Examining the revamped SharePoint Central Administration tool.

Administrators familiar with SharePoint 2007 will recall the SharePoint Central Admin tool, a web-based interface used to administer SharePoint functionality. SharePoint 2010 greatly improves this interface, organizing functional tasks within specific pages, adding

support for the SharePoint Ribbon to make tasks easier to perform and adding new func-
tionality that previously was unavailable. More information on the use of the SharePoint
Central Administration Tool can be found in Chapter 6, "Managing and Administering
SharePoint 2010 Infrastructure."

The addition of Microsoft PowerShell as a SharePoint administration tool enables administrators to have a robust and comprehensive scripting interface that allows for automation
of manual tasks, scripted installations, and remote administration support. Microsoft
created more than 500 commandlets for PowerShell specific to SharePoint, some of which
are shown in Figure 1.5. Detailed information on PowerShell administration for
SharePoint can be found in Chapter 7, "Leveraging PowerShell for Command-Line
SharePoint Administration and Automation."

FIGURE 1.5   Using PowerShell for SharePoint 2010 Administration.

Using the Improved Backup and Restore Tools

Backup and Restore in the SharePoint admin interfaces in SharePoint 2010, shown in
Figure 1.6, has been improved over SharePoint 2007's available out-of-the-box options.
New improvements include progress bar indicators, granular site recovery options, and the
capability to recover data out of unattached content databases.

Although these tools improve the administration available in SharePoint 2010, they do
not necessarily provide comprehensive enterprise backup and restore capabilities. In
certain cases, it may become necessary to use a third-party product or an enhanced
Microsoft tool such as System Center Data Protection Manager. These options are
discussed in more detail in Chapter 10, "Backing Up and Restoring a SharePoint
Environment."

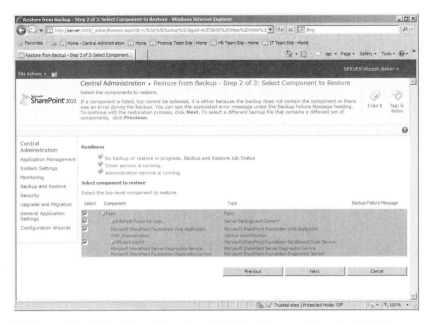

FIGURE 1.6   Using SharePoint Central Admin's improved backup interface.

Gaining Storage Flexibility with the Remote BLOB Storage Option

SharePoint 2010 now has the capability to natively support the storage of database BLOBs (binary large objects)—essentially the actual documents in the database, outside of the SharePoint content database, using a concept known as Remote BLOB Storage (RBS). Because the space consumed within SharePoint content database is approximately 80 percent BLOB content, using RBS can have a significant effect on the size and maintenance of content databases. More information on configuring RBS for SharePoint 2010 can be found in Chapter 9, "Managing and Maintaining SQL Server in a SharePoint Environment."

Using the Improved Interface and Ribbon Integration

The Office Ribbon, introduced with the Office 2007 client tools, presented a completely different way of working with Office documents, placing commonly used tasks across a tabular ribbon that remained at the top of the product. The success of this Ribbon meant that it found its way into SharePoint and is an integrated part of the SharePoint Web Experience, even at the top of the SharePoint Central Admin tool in some interfaces, as shown in Figure 1.7.

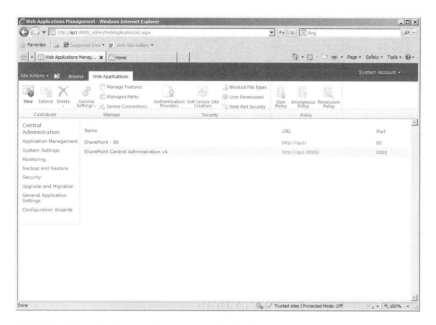

FIGURE 1.7   Viewing the SharePoint 2010 Ribbon.

By integrating the Ribbon into the out-of-the-box experience in SharePoint 2010, Microsoft made it easier to perform common tasks. By integrating the Ribbon within the SharePoint Central Admin tool, it makes administration tasks easier and more intuitive to perform.

Securing SharePoint 2010 with New Security Enhancements

Out-of-the-box, SharePoint provides for a secure interface, restricting access to documents and sites with comprehensive security down to the item level. In addition, SharePoint Search is security-trimmed, enabling users to see search results only from files to which they have access.

Although these security measures are robust, several layers of security aren't configured by default in a SharePoint farm, including transport security, storage-level encryption, or rights management. Fortunately, it is not too difficult to configure these items, and this book covers each topic in step-by-step detail.

Protecting SharePoint 2010 with Transport Security Options

A SharePoint environment provides two types of transport-level encryption. The first and most critical are Secure Sockets Layer (SSL) Certificates. These certificates protect the traffic between clients and the servers by encrypting the packets using Public Key Infrastructure

(PKI) encryption. The second type of transport-level encryption useful for SharePoint 2010 is IPsec encryption between servers in a SharePoint farm, such as between a SharePoint role server and the SQL Database server. Both of these options are discussed in more detail in Chapter 17, "Safeguarding Confidential Data in SharePoint 2010."

Protecting SharePoint Data with Storage Security Options

By default, SharePoint databases that store all content are not encrypted. The data within them is stored in a format that can be viewed if an administrator or backup operator has access to them. Indeed, if a content database is taken to a different farm, all content can be easily viewed simply by the administrator resetting the security credentials for the site collections.

This presents a challenge for many organizations that need to demonstrate that the data stored within SharePoint is properly secured and encrypted, and that if backup tapes are lost or stolen, the data will not be at risk of compromise. For these types of scenarios, Microsoft provides for a SQL encryption option known as Transparent Data Encryption (TDE), which allows for the databases to be fully encrypted on the SQL server without the application—in this case, SharePoint—being aware that there is any encryption at all. TDE is covered in more detail in Chapter 17.

Protecting SharePoint Web Access on the Edge Using Advanced Tools

Providing access to a SharePoint 2010 environment is not a task that should be taken lightly. Multiple security exploits and viruses on the web are constantly attacking web-based servers. Although SharePoint 2010 is built to be secure, it is not specifically designed to fend off these types of attacks. Subsequently, a more effective application layer inspection utility such as those provided by Microsoft's Forefront Edge line is ideal for securing a SharePoint 2010 environment. The two Microsoft Forefront Edge products include Forefront Threat Management Gateway (TMG) 2010 and Forefront Unified Access Gateway (UAG) 2010. Each of these products can be used to better secure an Internet-facing SharePoint portal or extranet environment, and the steps to do so are covered in detail in Chapter 14, "Protecting SharePoint with Advanced Antivirus and Edge Security Solutions."

Protecting SharePoint Content with Antivirus Options

By default, SharePoint 2010 does not contain any integrated antivirus scanning options. That said, it does include access to a comprehensive Antivirus Application Programming Interface (API) that enables third-party products to directly integrate with SharePoint to provide for antivirus protection of SharePoint content. In addition to these third-party options, Microsoft provides its own antivirus product for SharePoint, known as Microsoft Forefront Protection for SharePoint (FPS) 2010. This product is covered in more detail in Chapter 14.

Leveraging Metadata and Content Types

Simply stated, metadata is data about data, and it plays an even more important role in the SharePoint 2010 ecosystem than in previous versions with the implementation of Managed Metadata. Without leveraging metadata, SharePoint libraries aren't reaching their full potential, and a number of the powerful capabilities of SharePoint can't be leveraged. To fully leverage SharePoint 2010 tools, IT should create a plan for standard columns that are added to lists and libraries of different types and should leverage managed metadata as well.

With Managed Metadata Services, IT creates a term set and the terms it contains, which are then immediately available for use in libraries and lists. If the term set is then made available in a document library, when a SharePoint user adds a document, she can easily choose the metadata from managed metadata. Figure 1.8 shows an example in which the organization has defined specific document types that every uploaded document should be tagged with. By establishing a basic taxonomy of document types, the organization help ensure standards that help users to quickly find the specific type of document they are looking for and aids in navigation.

FIGURE 1.8   Choosing a managed metadata value for a document.

Content types are essentially "wrappers" that are applied to a list or library item that then bring tools and functionality with them. For example, a content type can have metadata columns associated with it (such as the document type managed metadata just discussed) and a document template, workflow settings, information management policy settings, and other settings. Although these might seem confusing initially, with some testing and experience, their value becomes very apparent. Chapter 22, "Managing Metadata and Content Types in SharePoint 2010," discusses both metadata and content types in more detail.

Social Networking Tool Advances

My Site personal websites have often been derided for not providing particularly useful tools and features (with user abandonment a direct corollary). However, Microsoft has completely revamped My Site websites and the social networking tools in SharePoint 2010, so they now provide an extremely powerful set of tools to enhance collaboration between SharePoint users and encourage interaction with the SharePoint environment. To point out a few examples, users can provide ratings to items in lists and libraries that enable them to determine as a group the most valuable assets in that list or library using one to five stars. Users can also post their own tags or use centrally managed tags, or post notes as shown in Figure 1.9. Again, this toolset separates the functionality available in SharePoint from that of the basic file share and encourages collaboration between users, and just as important, interaction with the data.

FIGURE 1.9   Note board in use in a document library.

My Site websites have undergone a dramatic makeover, as shown in Figure 1.10, where a slew of new tools are visible, including My Newsfeed, My Content, Tags and Notes, and tools familiar to SharePoint 2007 users, such as Organization, Colleagues and

Memberships. Chapter 22 provides additional insights into the value of these enhanced tools to the organization.

FIGURE 1.10   Updated look and feel and features of My Site.

Working with Office Web Apps

Office Web Apps are a new set of tools available in SharePoint 2010 that provide a browser-based viewing and editing experience for SharePoint 2010 users who need to collaborate on Word, Excel, PowerPoint, or OneNote documents. Office Web Apps provide a subset of functionality of the full client applications and should be tested thoroughly so that the organization understands the capabilities and limitations of the browser-based editing tools. Office Web Apps also provide some innovative features that are explored in Chapter 27, "Office Web Apps Integration with SharePoint 2010," such as enabling multiple users to edit an Excel document simultaneously and enabling the broadcast of PowerPoint slide decks using the browser. These tools add an entirely new way for users to interact with documents stored in SharePoint who may not have access to the full client applications.

Creating Powerful and Flexible Workflows

Workflows are even more powerful in SharePoint 2010 than in SharePoint 2007 products, and the integration with SharePoint Designer 2010 gives almost complete control over these workflows to power users and developers. Workflows are no longer as constrained as they were in SharePoint 2007 where custom workflows were essentially locked to a specific list or library, unless they were packaged as solutions. Chapter 28, "Out-of-the-Box Workflows and Designer 2010 Workflows," provides a detailed walk-through of the process of designing and using workflows in SharePoint 2010, whereas Chapter 29, "Application Development with SharePoint Designer 2010 and Visual Studio 2010," delves into some of the possibilities of application development with SharePoint Designer 2010.

Some of the highlights of SharePoint Designer 2010 include impersonation steps, where workflows can run under the context of another user other than that of the executing user. In addition, a workflow created at the top level of a site collection can be used by any subsite, whereas a workflow created in a specific subsite can be reused within that subsite. Workflows can also be exported from one site collection and then uploaded and activated in another site collection. Association Columns enable required columns to be automatically added to a list or library when a reusable workflow is associated to that list or library. Site workflows are associated to a site, rather than to a list, library, or content type. Standard workflows included with SharePoint Server (Approval, Collect Feedback, and Collect Signatures workflows) are now "declarative workflows," which means they are customizable in SharePoint Designer 2010.

Developing Applications Using Visual Studio

One appealing feature of SharePoint is that it supports application development in many shapes and forms. Because SharePoint is built on the .NET platform, developers can theoretically create applications to perform any set of functions required by the organization. SharePoint 2010 is intended to partner with SharePoint Designer 2010 and Visual Studio 2010 to make it even easier for developers to create powerful and stable applications. Additional enhancements in the development arena include

▶ A new client object model enabling code to be run on a client that was once relegated to running only on the SharePoint server.

▶ Rest APIs allowing for standards-based XML over HTTP communication with SharePoint.

▶ LINQ support allowing for integrated, object-like access to SharePoint data from familiar .NET languages such as C# and VB.Net.

▶ Sandboxed solutions are solutions safely deployed to a SharePoint site and are limited from doing harm to the farm through code access security (CAS). This has obvious implications for multi-tenancy hosting environments.

▶ Import, modify, and extend solution packages (.wsp).

▶ Develop SharePoint solutions with SharePoint project type templates and SharePoint project item templates.

▶ Create web parts and application pages for a SharePoint site.

Chapter 29 provides step-by-step instructions on how to create a Visual Studio web part that leverages LINQ to render a SharePoint list in a custom format.

Leveraging Business Intelligence Tools in SharePoint 2010

SharePoint 2007 made great steps to provide so-called business intelligence tools with the Excel Services Business Data Catalog and the PerformancePoint tool set, but a general concern was the learning curve required to leverage these tools to create interactive dashboards that enabled SharePoint users to quickly and efficiently gain access to the specific views of data they needed to do their jobs.

The Business Intelligence tools in SharePoint 2010 are complex enough and powerful enough that two full chapters are dedicated to the concept: Chapter 30, "Business Intelligence in SharePoint 2010 with PerformancePoint Services," illustrates the capabilities of the PerformancePoint service application, whereas Chapter 31, "Business Intelligence in SharePoint 2010 with Business Connectivity Services," delves into the capabilities of Business Connectivity Services. Excel Services, which enables end users to publish content to SharePoint libraries that can be exposed via the Excel Web Access web part is covered in Chapter 26, "Extending SharePoint 2010 with Excel Services, Access Services, and Visio Graphics Services." Figure 1.11 gives an example of a dashboard that Chapter 30 provides full instructions for creating.

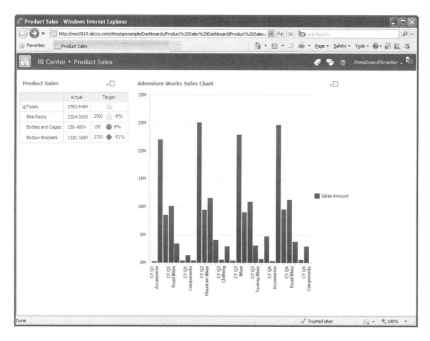

FIGURE 1.11   PerformancePoint dashboard.

Governing the SharePoint Environment

An overarching concern for IT has always been answering the question "Now that we have SharePoint and people are using it, how do we govern it?" Chapter 24, "Governing the SharePoint 2010 Ecosystem," provides insight and recommendations on the steps needed to ensure that the SharePoint 2010 environment meets the goals and vision set forth by IT and the needs of the end users. Although every organization is unique, and its goals and purposes for deploying SharePoint 2010 will also be unique, the range of tools and process discussed in this chapter can have value for all different types of organizations and businesses.

Summary

SharePoint 2010 provides for comprehensive document management, collaboration, web content management, and extranet capabilities in a powerful and capable set of products. Microsoft has invested a significant amount in SharePoint 2010 and has added a scalable service application infrastructure, newly revamped search, improved administration tools, and an abundance of improvements to the end user interface.

Each of these improvements and capabilities are discussed in detail throughout this book. Refer to the table of contents or the index to locate a specific topic, tool, or concept.

Best Practices

▶ SharePoint 2010 is a complex product line that can be many things to many different companies, but IT should have a clear understanding of how SharePoint will be leveraged and which tools will be provided to the user community.

▶ Help leverage SharePoint 2010 in your organization by understanding the integration points with the Office 2010 products, and learning more about compatibility with Office 2007 and previous versions.

▶ Only deploy those service applications that are required to satisfy individual business requirements of the project.

▶ Become familiar with the new SharePoint 2010 Administration tools, especially PowerShell scripting, as it is critical for administration of a SharePoint environment.

▶ Gain a familiarity with the incredible range of tools and capabilities in SharePoint 2010 by reviewing the topics covered in this book and following the step-by-step exercises to learn how to leverage the technologies.

▶ Focus on key technologies in SharePoint 2010, such as the managed metadata service, workflows and business intelligence to meet business challenges and requirements.

## CHAPTER 2

Architecting a SharePoint 2010 Deployment

Many organizations have made the decision to use SharePoint for one or more reasons but are not sure how to start deploying the infrastructure needed by the platform. There are many misconceptions about SharePoint, and further confusing the issue is that the architecture and terminology of SharePoint 2010 has changed dramatically from the previous versions of the technology.

Many SharePoint 2010 products and technologies are extremely powerful and scalable, but it is critical to properly match the needs of the organizations to a design plan. Matching these needs with a properly planned and implemented SharePoint farm is highly recommended and will go far toward ensuring that deployment of SharePoint is a success.

This chapter covers SharePoint 2010 design and architecture. The structural components of SharePoint are explained and compared. Server roles, database design decisions, and application server placement are discussed. This chapter focuses specifically on physical SharePoint infrastructure and design. Logical design of SharePoint user components, such as site layout and structure, are covered in the chapters in Part IV, "Using SharePoint 2010 Technologies for Collaboration and Document Management."

Understanding the SharePoint Server Roles

What an end user of a SharePoint environment sees on a SharePoint page is the result of a complex interaction that occurs on one or more servers performing varying tasks.

Information is stored in complex databases, web rendering is displayed courtesy of the web role, and searches and processes are driven by the Search service application role on servers.

Depending on the size of the environment, these roles may be on one or many servers. In very small environments, all roles may exist on a single server, whereas in very large-scale farms, the roles may be spread across tens or even hundreds of servers. These server roles are the base architectural elements in a SharePoint farm, or collection, of servers that provide for SharePoint services in an environment. It is subsequently critical to understand what these server roles are and how they are used in a SharePoint farm.

NOTE

There may be more than one SharePoint farm per organization. Best practices stipulate that there should be at least one farm used for testing in any environment. Chapter 4, "Advanced SharePoint 2010 Installation and Scalability," deals with scenarios in which more than one farm is deployed.

Understanding the Database Server Role

Nearly all SharePoint content is stored in databases, including all document library content, list items, document metadata, and web parts. There are only two exceptions to this. The first is if the database server uses a concept known as Remote BLOB Storage (RBS), which allows for the storage of the documents, or BLOBs (binary large objects), in another storage medium such as a file server or an archive. This concept is discussed in detail in Chapter 9, "Managing and Maintaining SQL Server in a SharePoint Environment." The other exception to this rule is the full-text search index, which is stored in flat-file format (see the following sections on the Search Service Application role). In some rare cases, certain web part solutions may store flat files on web frontends as well, which is a good idea in any case, but in reality the vast majority of SharePoint content is stored on the database server role, making it highly critical both for High Availability (HA) and for Disaster Recovery (DR).

The only supported database format for SharePoint is Microsoft SQL Server, and at least one SQL Server database role server must exist in a farm for SharePoint to function.

Supported versions of SQL Server for SharePoint 2010 are as follows:

- ▶ SQL Server 2005 SP3 x64
- ▶ SQL Server 2008 x64
- ▶ SQL Server 2008 R2 x64

CAUTION

Although SQL Server 2008 Express is supported, it is not recommended for most modern SharePoint environments because it does not scale well. Any production SharePoint environment should consider using either the full Standard or Enterprise editions of SQL Server.

There may be more than one database server role in a SharePoint farm, because a SharePoint administrator can define where a particular SharePoint database resides. In large environments, for example, there may be multiple SharePoint database role servers, each serving multiple databases as part of the farm.

Understanding the Web Server Role

2

The Web Server Role is the most obvious of the SharePoint roles, as most people understand the concept of a server running an application that serves up web pages to users that request them. In SharePoint's case, that application is Windows Server's Internet Information Services (IIS) application. A SharePoint farm member running the Web Server Role is responsible for rendering SharePoint content, including web parts, page layout, and all other information displayed to the user.

A SharePoint Web Server Role runs on either Windows Server 2008 x64 IIS 7.0 or, preferably, Windows Server 2008 R2 x64 IIS 7. In both cases, SharePoint 2010 requires specific roles to be installed in advance of installation, including the following components:

▶ Application Server Role

▶ Web Server (IIS) Role

▶ Microsoft SQL Server 2008 Native Client

▶ Windows Identity Foundation (KB974405)

▶ Microsoft Sync Framework Runtime v 1.0 (x64)

▶ Microsoft Chart Controls for Microsoft .NET Framework 3.5

▶ Microsoft Filter Pack 2.0

▶ Microsoft SQL Server 2008 Analysis Services ADOMD.NET

▶ Microsoft Server Speech Platform Runtime (x64)

▶ Microsoft Server Speech Recognition Language—TELE

Each of these components can be installed using the SharePoint 2010 media by clicking the Install Prerequisites link on the initial splash screen. This operation requires Internet connectivity. If Internet access is not available, each individual component needs to be manually installed.

TIP

Multiple web role servers may be set up in a SharePoint environment to scale out the number of users that can use the platform or to provide for high-availability access to the environment. In this case, load balancing of the connections made to a SharePoint environment allows for a larger number of users to access the content. Load balancing can be either hardware-based or software-based using Windows Network Load Balancing (NLB), fully supported for SharePoint web role servers.

Service Application Roles

The most significant architectural change in SharePoint 2010 is the addition of service applications, which replace the SharePoint 2007 concept of Shared Services Providers (SSPs). Service applications are independent services that can be shared across web applications or, in some cases, across farms.

Table 2.1 lists the service applications available with SharePoint 2010 and which version of SharePoint 2010 software they are available in.

TABLE 2.1   Examining a List of SharePoint 2010 Service Applications

	SharePoint Foundation 2010	SharePoint Server 2010 Standard Edition	SharePoint Server 2010 Enterprise Edition	Office Web App Services (Can Be Added to SharePoint Farm)
Business Data Connectivity Services	X	X	X	
Usage and Health Data Collection Services	X	X	X	
SharePoint Foundation Subscription Settings Service	X	X	X	
Managed Metadata Service		X	X	
Search Service		X	X	
Secure Store Service		X	X	
State Service		X	X	
User Profile Service		X	X	
Web Analytics Service		X	X	
Word Automation Services		X	X	
Access Services			X	
Excel Services			X	
PerformancePoint Service			X	

TABLE 2.1   Continued

	SharePoint Foundation 2010	SharePoint Server 2010 Standard Edition	SharePoint Server 2010 Enterprise Edition	Office Web App Services (Can Be Added to SharePoint Farm)
Visio Graphics Services			X	
Excel Calculation Services				X
PowerPoint Service				X
Word Viewing Service				X

Service applications can be resource-intensive and are often deployed on their own dedicated servers to separate their impact from the web role servers.

NOTE

Just because you've purchased access to a service application does not mean that you should turn it on. Every service application running on a server consumes a significant percentage of that server's resources, and turning on all the available service applications is a bad idea unless you've planned accordingly. Turn on only those service applications that need to run a service that satisfies a specific business need.

Search Service Application Role

One of the most commonly used service application role in SharePoint 2010 is the search service application role, because it is responsible for running the Enterprise search functionality that enables you to search both within and outside of SharePoint.

The search service application is different than the way it was in SharePoint 2007. Gone is the need to separate the indexing from the Query capability; in SharePoint 2010, these roles are combined into one. In addition, SharePoint 2010 has the capability to have multiple redundant indexes, something that was not possible in SharePoint 2007. For detailed information on configuring search in SharePoint 2010, refer to Chapter 8, "Leveraging and Optimizing Search in SharePoint 2010."

NOTE

The native search service application in SharePoint 2010 is different than Microsoft's other search offering, known as FAST Search Server 2010 for SharePoint. FAST Search Server enables thumbnail views on search results and automatic metadata tagging, among other improvements. The architecture of FAST Search Server is vastly different than the native search. Refer to Chapter 8 for more information on this topic.

Notice a few key things when architecting for the SharePoint search service application role. First, the index corpus used to store the full-text copy of all documents crawled can grow large in size based on the amount of content being indexed. The size of the corpus is directly related to the size of the actual document data being crawled. Depending on what is being indexed, and how much actual text is included in that data, the index corpus can range from 5 percent to 30 percent of the size of content being indexed, so be sure to include a large enough index disk drive for your index server.

There are a few things to note about SharePoint search:

▶ Search in SharePoint is security-trimmed for supported content, excluding some external content sources. This means that end users will get search results only from content that they have rights to access. This is a highly useful feature that prevents users from seeing content to which they don't have access.

▶ Although search is security-trimmed, the permissions are reevaluated only after performing a full crawl of content. Subsequently, if someone is removed from having permissions to a document, she can still see the text of that document as part of a search until a full, not an incremental, crawl has been performed.

▶ Because SharePoint 2010 allows for redundant search and indexing capability, any one server being down does not take down the entire environment, assuming the search service application is running on more than one server.

Inbound Email Server Role

For scenarios where SharePoint is configured to be email-enabled, various SharePoint servers can be assigned to the inbound email server role. Servers with this role have the SMTP service installed directly on them and are configured to enable inbound emails to be sent directly into SharePoint document libraries and lists. This functionality is critical for an environment looking to use SharePoint for records management or enterprise content management. For more information on how to configure SharePoint for inbound email functionality, reference Chapter 16, "Configuring Email-Enabled Content, Presence, and Exchange Server Integration."

TIP

Don't forget to load balance the SMTP Service across multiple inbound email role servers in environments with HA requirements! If this is not done, inbound email functionality will not be redundant and will be down for users if an outage of the primary server occurs.

SharePoint Central Admin Server Role

Although more of a minor role, the server or servers that hold the SharePoint central administration service, the main management application for SharePoint, are also considered a server role. In some large environments, this role may be separated onto dedicated servers to provide for central administration functionality without affecting existing server functionality.

> **TIP.**
>
> It is best practice to make the central administration role highly available by installing it on multiple servers, typically on multiple servers that also run the web role. Not doing this runs the risk of a server outage causing a loss of access to the tools necessary to troubleshoot the outage.

Understanding the Reasons for Deploying Multiple Farms

A SharePoint farm is fundamentally a collection of SharePoint role servers that provide for the base infrastructure required to house SharePoint sites and provide for other services, such as enterprise search. The farm level is the highest level of SharePoint architecture, providing a distinct operational boundary for a SharePoint environment. Each farm in an environment is a self-encompassing unit made up of one or more servers, such as web role servers, service application role servers, and SharePoint database servers.

In many cases, a single SharePoint farm is not enough to provide for all the needs of an organization. Some deploy multiple SharePoint farms to provide for test environments, farms where development can occur, or farms for extranet users or Internet use. You need to define how many farms are required for an organization when beginning the design process, because the number of farms created can directly reflect on the physical architecture of the servers in a SharePoint environment. Generally speaking, the more farms required, the more hardware is needed, so a full understanding of what can be gained by deploying multiple farms is first required.

Deploying Test Farms

Any production SharePoint environment should have a test environment in which new SharePoint web parts, solutions, service packs, patches, and add-ons can be tested. This applies to all organizations, regardless of size. It is critical to deploy test farms, because many SharePoint add-ons could potentially disrupt or corrupt the formatting or structure of a production environment, and trying to test these new solutions on site collections or different web applications is not enough because the solutions often install directly on the SharePoint servers themselves. If there is an issue, the issue will be reflected in the entire farm.

Because of these reasons, many organizations create a smaller SharePoint farm just for testing. The farm should be similar to the existing environments, with the same add-ons and solutions installed and should ideally include restores of production site collections to make it as similar as possible to the existing production environment. All changes and new products or solutions installed into an environment should subsequently be tested first in this environment.

> **NOTE**
>
> The SharePoint server or servers used for a test farm or even a production farm do not necessarily need to be installed on physical hardware; many scenarios with SharePoint servers installed on virtual server infrastructure are possible. Refer to Chapter 12, "Virtualizing SharePoint Components," for more information on this topic.

Deploying Development Farms

Developers in an organization that makes heavy use of SharePoint often need environments to test new applications, web parts, solutions, and other SharePoint customization. These developers often need a sandbox area where these solutions can be tested, and potentially one with different characteristics from production. These environments are also typically quickly provisioned and deprovisioned, so test environments are not the best location for them.

For these organizations, it may make sense to deploy one or more development farms so that developers have the opportunity to run their tests and develop software for SharePoint independent of the existing production environment. When developed, these applications can first be tested in the test farm and then finally deployed into production. For information on automating the creating of test farms using virtual host management software, refer to Chapter 12.

Deploying Extranet or Intranet Farms

Another reason to deploy multiple farms is for security. For security reasons, it is not generally recommended to have an internal SharePoint document management or intranet environment directly accessible from the Internet unless it is secured by an advanced reverse proxy platform such as Microsoft's Forefront Edge line that includes the Threat Management Gateway or Unified Access Gateway products.

Even for environments properly secured for inbound access, there may be scenarios in which SharePoint content needs to be made accessible by external users, such as in anonymous Internet portal scenarios or for extranet partner scenarios. Because a SharePoint farm requires high connectivity between farms members, it subsequently becomes necessary in these cases to deploy dedicated SharePoint environments in the DMZ of a firewall or in another isolated network.

> **NOTE**
>
> SharePoint Content Deployment can be used to push site content from one farm to another, for example, when content from an internal farm is pushed to an external extranet farm on a regular basis. The extranet farm remains secure and cannot access content on the internal farm, but users can still access required content that has selectively been chosen for publishing.

Deploying Global or Distributed Multifarm Environments

For environments with multiple geographical locations, it may make sense to deploy multiple farms in different geographical locations. This enables SharePoint content to be consumed locally and is what is recommended in scenarios in which WAN links are not as robust. Consider several key points before deciding where to deploy geographical farms:

- ▶ A single SharePoint farm should not span a WAN link and should ideally be limited to one geographical location. In some organizations, in which the definition of WAN includes at least 1GB of bandwidth with less than 1ms of latency between offices located relatively close to one another, it may be possible to stretch a farm across locations, but this is the only scenario in which this would be supported. If you need to consume content locally, it must be part of a separate farm.

- ▶ There is no native way to do two-way replication of content between farms with SharePoint 2010. However, several third-party companies on the market enable this type of functionality, which can be advantageous in disaster recovery scenarios in which content is replicated to multiple farms.

- ▶ For many organizations, it may make more sense to deploy a single, centralized SharePoint farm in one location rather than to deploy siloed SharePoint farms in multiple locations. Clients access SharePoint using the latency tolerant HTTP/HTTPS protocols, so access to a centralized infrastructure may make sense. It also has the advantages of providing a single URL to access SharePoint and keeps data in one location. Organizations need to decide if the level of service accessing SharePoint across a WAN is sufficient for this to be a possibility.

Planning for Multiple Farms

Consider several key points when designing a SharePoint environment to include multiple farms:

- ▶ All SharePoint server roles, with the exception of the database role, can only be a member of a single farm. You cannot have a SharePoint server reside in more than one farm at a time.

- ▶ A single database server can contain databases from multiple farms, though it is generally recommended to limit the number of content databases on a single SQL instance to no more than 50.

- ▶ If deploying multiple farms on a single SQL server, be sure to use a common naming convention for each farm database so they can be logically organized on the SQL server. For example, naming all databases with the prefix SP_Farm1, SP_Farm2, and so on can help identify which databases belong to which farm.

- ▶ All farm members must have near-full network connectivity (1Gb+ Bandwidth, <1ms latency) to all other farm members, with a large number of open ports with nearly all of them open. This effectively limits scenarios in which firewalls separate farm members, unless all ports are open between hosts.

▶ Although not required to have a test environment exactly match production in terms of the number of servers or the type of server roles, it is critical that the web role servers in each environment match each other so that more effective testing can take place.

Choosing the Right Hardware for SharePoint

When farm architecture has been outlined, it is critical to properly size the hardware environment that makes up your SharePoint farm. Each SharePoint server role has different hardware requirements, however, so it is important to first understand what those requirements are before beginning the procurement process.

Hardware Requirements for the SQL Database Role Servers

The heaviest hitter of all the SharePoint roles is the SQL database server role. This server role houses the SharePoint databases, where nearly all content in a SharePoint environment is stored. The databases house document libraries, documents, lists, sites, site collections, and their contents. For obvious reasons, this server is highly critical for SharePoint and requires a significant amount of hardware resources. Following are several key hardware requirements for the SQL database role:

▶ **Disk space**—Because SharePoint content is stored in the databases, the SQL database role server requires a large amount of disk space. How much disk space depends on how much content is stored in SharePoint, but assume the worst—when document versioning is turned on, SharePoint can consume much more space than people realize.

▶ **Processor**—The SQL database role works best when multiple processor cores are allocated to the database role. SQL Server is built to be multithreaded and can use whatever you give it. Today's multicore processors are the perfect fit for SharePoint.

▶ **Memory**—Server memory requirements are also high for the database role. The same general rule of thumb applies...the more memory allocated, the better a SQL server will perform. The total amount of memory recommended will vary depending on how heavily utilized the server is, but it is common to have SQL servers with 12GB, 16GB, 32GB, or more.

Hardware Requirements for Service Application Roles

The service application roles, depending on how many run on an individual server, can have serious hardware requirements. The search service application role, for example, which is responsible for creating a full-text searchable index for search, is the heaviest hitting of the SharePoint roles, excluding, of course, the database role. Search service application servers typically consume more memory and processor capacity because they are constantly engaged in the process of crawling content and making it searchable. Depending on the number of content sources crawled, there can be significant memory requirements, and index servers have been known to use at least 8GB, 12GB, or 16GB of memory and take advantage of multiple processor cores as well.

Other service application role servers may require an equal amount of memory and processor cores allocated as well. It's a general rule of thumb that SharePoint 2010 memory and processor requirements are much higher than for SharePoint 2007, and many people underestimate the required resources.

In addition to its processor and memory requirements, the search service application role also requires enough drive space to physically store the index files, which are essentially copies of all text that has been crawled across all data sources. The size of this index can range from 5 percent to 30 percent of the total size of the searchable content being crawled. For example, if SharePoint is configured to search a file share, and that file share contains 100GB of office documents, the index size will total between 5GB and 30GB, depending on how much actual text is stored in the documents. Large, graphical documents with little text will not bloat the index by much, but simple text files can consume a much larger percentage.

> **NOTE**
>
> Remember to calculate your index size based on the total size of all crawled content. Because SharePoint is an enterprise search application, the total size of all content may include not only documents in SharePoint, but also file servers, Exchange public folders, and websites.

Hardware Requirements for Web Role Servers

The web role server is the most utilitarian role, requiring a reasonable amount of memory and processor power, but nothing excessive. Indeed, better performance can often be gained by adding additional web role servers to a farm rather than by increasing the size of memory and processor power added to a system. Typically web role servers will have between 8GB and 12GB of RAM in most cases, and at least two cores allocated to it.

Determining Optimal Operating System Configuration

The core of a functioning SharePoint environment is the operating system that SharePoint runs on. All servers in a SharePoint farm require the Windows Server operating system. The following versions of Windows Server are supported:

▶ Windows Server 2008, Standard or Enterprise, x86 or x64

▶ Windows Server 2008 R2, Standard or Enterprise, x86 or x64

Windows Server 2008 R2 Operating System for SharePoint

The most optimal, secure, and performance-tuned operating system for SharePoint is Windows Server 2008 R2, which has built-in security enhancements to Kerberos and also handles client/server communications traffic better than previous versions of Windows, making it ideal to host SharePoint servers. For any new SharePoint farm deployments, you should highly consider the use of Windows Server 2008 R2 for these reasons where possible. An alternative to Windows Server 2008 R2 is Windows Server 2008 SP1.

Planning for Database and Additional Software

In addition to OS, a SharePoint farm requires software for the database, and preferably other add-ons such as backup and antivirus software. Although these are the most common software add-ons, there can be multiple third-party and other add-ons installed into SharePoint, depending on the needs and scale of the deployment. Consult with third-party vendors to determine any potential needs for your farm.

Database Software

The only supported database for SharePoint is Microsoft SQL Server. SharePoint databases must be installed on 64-bit SQL servers, and they can be successfully installed on the following types of SQL servers:

▶ SQL Server 2005 x64 SP3, Standard or Enterprise

▶ SQL Server 2008 x64 SP1, Standard or Enterprise

▶ SQL Server 2008 R2 x64, Standard or Enterprise

It is highly recommended to consider SQL Server 2008 R2 for the SharePoint database role because it provides for the most robust, capable, and secure platform for SharePoint. In addition, it includes features that are useful for SharePoint, such as PowerPivot and Transparent Data Encryption (TDE), which enables the SharePoint databases to be stored in encrypted format. SharePoint is unaware of the encryption, and application functionality is not affected because SQL handles the encryption. Note that SQL TDE is only available with the Enterprise edition of SQL server, however.

This type of functionality can be highly useful in scenarios in which, for compliance reasons, the data must be stored in encrypted format. For this reason and others, SQL Server 2008 R2 for SharePoint is highly recommended.

With so many new features to discuss and so little space, this section focuses on a number of different components that, together, make up the entire new SQL Server 2008 R2 product. This discussion introduces SQL's many components and purpose. The components consist of the following:

▶ **Database engine**—The database engine component is the heart of SQL Server. It is responsible for storing data, databases, stored procedures, security, and many more functions, such as full-text search, replication, and high availability.

▶ **Analysis services**—Analysis Services delivers online analytical processing (OLAP) and data mining functionality for business intelligence applications. Analysis Services allows organizations to aggregate data from multiple heterogeneous environments, transform this data into meaningful information that can then be analyzed and leveraged to gain a competitive advantage in the industry.

▶ **Integration services**—Provides businesses the opportunity to integrate and transform data. Businesses can extract data from different locations, transform data that may include merging data together, and move data to different locations, such as relational databases, data warehouses, and data marts. Integration services is the official SQL server extract, transform, and load (ETL) tool.

▶ **Reporting services**—Includes tools such as Report Manager and Report Server. This component is built on standard IIS and .NET technology and enables businesses to design report solutions, extract report data from different areas, customize reports in different formats, manage security, and distribute reports.

▶ **Notification services**—Consists of a notification engine and client components meant for developing and deploying applications that generate and send notifications to subscribers. Notifications are generated when they are either prompted by an event or triggered by a predefined or fixed schedule. Notifications can be sent to email addresses or mobile devices.

Backup Software

Although SharePoint 2010 products include built-in backup capability, the tools used are not enterprise level and do not have built-in scheduling, item-level restore, or robust alerting capabilities. It is subsequently recommended to purchase and install enterprise backup software. This may include software from a number of third-party vendors, or it may include a solution from Microsoft such as System Center Data Protection Manager (DPM) 2010. Backup and restore is discussed in more detail in Chapter 10, "Backing Up and Restoring a SharePoint Environment."

Antivirus Software

SharePoint 2010 includes an antivirus API that enables all documents to be scanned for viruses by a compliant antivirus engine. It is highly recommended to include SharePoint-specific antivirus as part of a SharePoint deployment, because client-specific antivirus cannot disinfect documents in SharePoint, and alternatively viruses could be uploaded into SharePoint if the client antivirus is missing or out of date.

There are multiple third-party antivirus vendors in the SharePoint space. In addition, Microsoft has its own antivirus product for SharePoint, ForeFront Protection for SharePoint (FPSP), which provides for multiengine antivirus scanning and optimal performance specifically geared toward SharePoint. For more information on antivirus products for SharePoint, reference Chapter 14, "Protecting SharePoint with Advanced Antivirus and Edge Security Solutions."

Index iFilters

The most common add-on for SharePoint search are iFilters. Index iFilters provide specific knowledge for the SharePoint indexer on how to break open specific file types and index the text content within them. For example, PDF iFilters are a common add-on because many organizations use PDF files extensively and require the ability to search against their contents. It is subsequently important to determine which file types will be stored in SharePoint and to determine whether iFilters are available for those file types so that the files can be properly indexed.

Examining Real-World SharePoint 2010 Deployments

Conceptually speaking about a SharePoint environment is not the same as actually viewing some real-design scenarios with the product. Therefore, the last section of this chapter focuses on viewing some sample real-world deployment scenarios that are supported and give insight into the architecture and design concepts surrounding SharePoint 2010.

Viewing a Sample Single-Server SharePoint Deployment

The most straightforward deployment of SharePoint 2010 is one that involves a single, all-in-one server that runs the database components and the web and all service application roles. This type of server deployment, shown in Figure 2.1, has the distinct advantage of being simple to deploy and administer.

Web/Query/
Service Applications
Database

FIGURE 2.1   Viewing a sample single-server SharePoint farm.

In this type of deployment, the server takes on all the roles of the environment, including the following:

▶ SharePoint Central Administration tool

▶ Content databases and other SharePoint databases

▶ All site collections and sites

▶ All service application roles

This environment works well for those environments with a small number of users. Its biggest disadvantage is that there is a great deal of contention between the database role and the SharePoint roles, which can cause performance constraints.

Viewing a Sample Small SharePoint Farm

For those organizations with a greater number of users or whose users are more active and require a separate server, the next step up in SharePoint design is a small farm model, as shown in Figure 2.2.

Web/Query/
Service Applications

Database

FIGURE 2.2   Viewing a sample small SharePoint farm.

In this type of deployment, two servers would be set up. The first would hold all the databases and would essentially be a dedicated SQL server box for SharePoint. The second server would run the SharePoint roles. By separating the database role from the SharePoint roles, significant performance increases can be obtained.

Viewing a Sample Mid-Sized SharePoint Farm

As an organization's document management and collaboration needs to grow, the SharePoint farm needs to grow with it. Figure 2.3 illustrates a mid-sized SharePoint farm with six total servers.

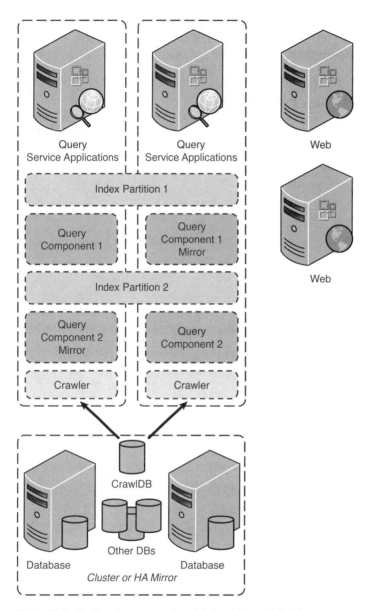

FIGURE 2.3   Viewing a sample mid-sized SharePoint farm.

In this configuration, the web role is now separate from the service application roles, which increases performance. In addition, Network Load Balancing (NLB) is used between the web role servers to provide for availability, and the SQL servers are clustered to provide for HA and DR of the database tier. This type of environment can easily scale into the tens of thousands of users.

Viewing a Sample Large SharePoint Farm

SharePoint operates under design principles that are massively scalable if needed. Using redundancy and load-balancing techniques such as the Microsoft Cluster Services and network load balancing, more performance can be obtained from an environment, simply through the addition of other servers to provide redundancy and load balancing to specific roles. For example, in a large farm, such as the one shown in Figure 2.4, multiple servers in cluster and NLB configurations enable the environment to be scaled into a large numbers of users. In addition, multiple search service servers and striped index partitions enable the search infrastructure to scale into the tens of millions of documents indexed.

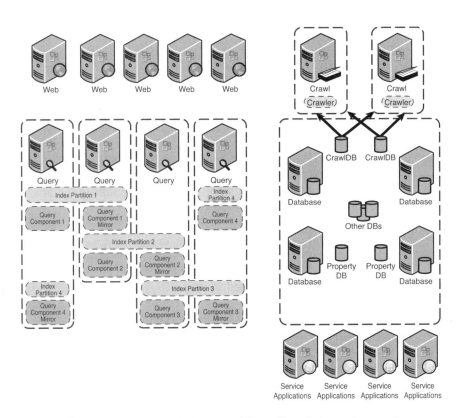

FIGURE 2.4   Viewing a sample large, multifarm SharePoint environment.

Addressing Common Business Issues with SharePoint Features

SharePoint 2010 was designed to address business needs and issues that commonly arise in organizations. This section pulls together the information about SharePoint features described in other chapters of this book to summarize some of the common business issues and how features of SharePoint can address those issues. Scenarios that represent these issues are described, along with the specific SharePoint technologies that can address the issues.

Addressing the Redundant Re-creation of Documents with SharePoint

In many organizations, users duplicate efforts or reinvent the wheel creating documents or gathering information previously used by someone else in the organization either because they didn't know the information existed or couldn't find it. This results in an inefficient use of time.

SharePoint solution—Full-text indexing and search of SharePoint document libraries, workspaces, metadata information, and lists.

SharePoint Search Service Application indexing of SharePoint 2010 sites enables indexing and searching site content so that users can quickly find the documents or information they need.

Addressing the Inability to Efficiently Search Across Different Types of Content

Users need information, and often the only way they can get it is to perform multiple different types of searches on multiple content sources and then manually consolidate the results. This results in the possibility of content not being searched (either because it is overlooked or just takes too much time) and an inefficient use of time.

SharePoint solution—SharePoint 2010 content sources that can be indexed and searched.

Adding frequently used sources of information as content sources in a SharePoint 2010 environment provides a means for users to perform one search request and have the results from many different content sources displayed together. For example, a single SharePoint search request could span other SharePoint sites, websites external to the organization, file shares, and Microsoft Exchange public folders. This enables users to easily search across many sources to find the information they need.

Addressing Inefficient Means of Document Collaboration with SharePoint Document Libraries

A team of people need to collaborate on a project and produce a set of documents to be sent to a client. User A works on the first document and saves it as Doc1. User A emails User B to let User B know the document is available for review. User B makes changes and additions and saves the document as Doc1 R1. User B creates an email with a list of ideas about additional changes that could be made and emails User A and User C. User C replies to User A and User B about User B's email about proposed changes, makes her own changes, saves it as Doc1 R2, and emails User A and B to let them know changes have been made. User A also replies about the proposed changes, makes "final" changes to the document, saves it as Doc1 Final, and emails the document to the client. Two days later, the client emails back with the list of changes the client wants to see in the document. User A edits the document again and saves it as Doc1 Final R1. The process continues until there are suddenly 10 versions of the document and 16 emails floating around about what should be in the document. At this point, the team isn't sure what changes have been made; the folder where the document is stored is cluttered with various versions of the document (and taking up a lot of space), and nobody knows which versions were sent to the client.

SharePoint solution—SharePoint team site with a shared document library, document-versioning enabled, and document discussions.

Rather than having multiple versions of multiple documents floating around with different names, a team site for the project with a shared document library could be used. Each client document would be stored in the library, and by using versions and entering version comments, the team would know who made changes, be provided with a brief overview of what or why changes were made, and know which one was sent to the client. By using document discussions in place of emails to have an online discussion of the document, all comments are stored in one place, with the document right there for easy access as opposed to sifting through multiple emails.

Addressing the Excessive Use of Email Attachments/Ability to Know When Documents Have Been Modified

A user emails an attachment to a group, revises the attachment, and then emails it to the group again, and so on. This results in excess email traffic, excess storage, and the potential that recipients won't see the current version of the attachment if it is modified after the email is sent.

SharePoint solution—Document workspaces/libraries and alerts.

Use document workspaces and libraries storing documents in a centralized document library, accessible by all team members. Alerts set up by team members notify them when the document changes. Team members know where the most current version of the document is located and are notified automatically when the document changes.

Addressing Difficulty Organizing or Classifying Content

In a traditional file system environment, a user creates a document. For future reference, should the document be stored in a folder based on the subject of the document, in a folder based on document type, in a folder based on the client the document was created for, or in all three places? Decisions of this type need to be made all the time, weighing the consequences of storing the document in one place versus another versus storing multiple copies of the document.

SharePoint solution—Use of topics, global document metadata using the managed metadata service search.

When using SharePoint, using document metadata and topics prevents the document creator from having to worry about where the document is stored. Metadata or specific fields of information that can be stored with the document can be used for information such as subject, client, and document type. Metadata can be enforced across all documents in a farm using the managed metadata service available in SharePoint 2010.

Because these fields are searchable, a document can be easily found regardless of what folder it is in.

Addressing Access to Line-of-Business Application Information

An organization may use a business application such as SAP or Microsoft Dynamics. Some individuals in the organization need to access information stored in these applications, but it would be costly to install and maintain the application on each desktop and to train all the users.

SharePoint solution—ASP.NET web parts, single sign-on.

ASP.NET web parts can be developed and used to access and display information from other applications and data sources. Single sign-on can also be enabled to provide seamless integration with the application. This provides the user with an easy, usable method for accessing information, and the IT department can maintain the code centrally and not have to worry about desktop deployment and specific training for the line-of-business applications. SharePoint 2010 also supports web parts, which opens it to the ability to view content from multiple third-party software and web part vendors.

Using SharePoint for Sharing Information with Partners, Vendors, and Clients

An organization needs to collaborate with another organization; for example, a marketing company doing research and developing collateral for the organization, or a client that the organization is working with on a specific project. The users from both organizations email documents and other information back and forth. Typically, these emails are sent to *all* people involved with the project so as to not leave anyone out. This can result in excess email traffic and emails being sent to users that they may not need (or want) to see.

SharePoint solution—Team site with extranet access.

The SharePoint team site template fits the needs of groups of people working collaboratively. The site can be set up for extranet access, enabling outside parties to participate as team members. Using a team site over a traditional email-based method of communication provides all kinds of benefits, including giving people the ability to review only what they want to review, set up alerts to be notified when specific information changes, set up a process for approving final documents, participate in online real-time discussions, and look at prior document versions.

Deploying a Team Collaboration Solution with SharePoint

A team collaboration site is used by a group of people working together for a common end result, or to complete a project. The success of the team or project depends on the effectiveness of the team and its ability to efficiently collaborate to complete the project. Therefore, the site is designed to facilitate team communications and sharing project information.

Typically, a team collaboration site is an internal, decentralized site that has a relatively small number of members. However, it can be configured to provide access for members external to the organization. When the site is implemented, it replaces the traditional file share–based storage, use of email, and use of other traditional applications the organization may have for storing and accessing documents and other information.

Outlining Business Needs for the Team Collaboration Solution

The general categories of business needs for this group are communications, project management, and document management. These needs can be mapped to SharePoint features, as presented in this section:

▶ **Communications**—Interacting with other team members electronically using workspace instant-messaging capabilities. Finding out when information has changed through the use of alerts. Having discussions on issues or documents using the general or document discussion components.

▶ **Project management**—Assigning major project tasks to individuals using a tasks list. Tracking and following up on tasks using a tasks list and various views of the list. Centralizing and distributing information such as objectives, agendas, and decisions for project meetings in one place using meeting workspaces. Providing status reports to management based on information in task items.

▶ **Document management**—Having a common place for storing documents by using shared document libraries. Managing document revisions using the check-in/check-out and version retention features. Controlling document publication using content approval. Enhancing the ability to find and feature specific documents by assigning them to topics and best-bets classifying documents for retrieval using metadata attached to the document.

Implementing a Team Collaboration Solution with SharePoint

The team collaboration site is implemented using a SharePoint team site. A shared document library is created in the team site for document management and a tasks list for assigning responsibilities. Content approval is enabled for the document library with the project manager assigned the role of approver. Document workspaces are also used for individual documents to incorporate direct access from SharePoint 2010 applications. The team uses document discussions to communicate ideas about document contents and a general discussion for items relating to the project. The team site is part of a SharePoint implementation that has content sources defined for searching relevant information and archived documents.

Outlining Ideas for Using the Team Collaboration Solution

This section includes some ideas to incorporate into the team site solution with the elements previously discussed. The major project milestone tasks can be entered into a tasks list, assigned to individual team members, and then tracked by the project manager. The tasks list can also be used for status reporting.

Users can initially create documents using Microsoft Office 2007/2010 applications and then save them to a document workspace. The document workspace can be used by the team members as a conduit for instant messaging on project-related issues. Discussions within the document can be used for providing feedback and recommendations for document content.

When the document is ready for publishing, it can be moved to the shared library where it is reviewed by the approver. The approver can set up an alert to be notified when the new documents are added or modified within the library.

Deploying a Corporate Intranet Solution with SharePoint

The corporate intranet is used for communicating information to employees and providing them with access to corporate line-of-business applications. The primary goals of a corporate intranet are to provide resources to employees that can help improve performance and to provide employees with centralized electronic access to corporate-based information for things such as policies, procedures, and roles and responsibilities. The benefits of the corporate intranet include providing an electronic means of accessing information as opposed to reliance on human intervention, providing an easier way of finding information, automating processes, and eliminating duplication of effort. The end result is a reduction in operational costs.

Meeting Business Needs with the Corporate Intranet Solution

The general business needs of this group include searching for information, corporate communications, workflow processing, management of web-based content, and application integration. These needs can be mapped to SharePoint features as presented in this section.

Corporate communications:

▶ Notifying employees about company events using an events list

▶ Notifying employees about changes in policies and procedures using announcements

▶ Obtaining feedback from employees using discussion boards and surveys

▶ Providing access to company policies, procedures, and forms through shared document libraries

▶ Providing access to company-maintained information, such as employee directories, using lists such as the contacts list

Searching:

▶ Finding location-specific information by having the ability to search across local sites, division-based sites, and the corporate portal

▶ Having a means for searching content external to the SharePoint infrastructure, such as external websites, file systems, and other internal application databases, and

SharePoint-based information and displaying the results together by using content sources and source groups

Workflow processing:

▶ Requiring documents to be approved before publishing using content approval

▶ Notification of outstanding items using alerts

▶ Simplifying processing using approve/reject views

Managing Web content:

▶ Providing non-IT staff with the ability to create team-based sites when necessary through the self-service site creation

▶ Standardizing the look and feel of sites by creating site templates

▶ Enabling users to create a place for collaboration when needed through the use of shared document workspaces

▶ Providing a way to make meetings more effective and meaningful by using meeting workspaces

▶ Removing the dependency on IT departments for updating sites and site content by using the web-based customization features and document library concept

▶ Enabling users to tailor the view of the intranet to accommodate their specific needs using personal sites

Application integration:

▶ Providing a single interface for intranet capabilities and access to applications by using link lists

▶ Providing a way for users to view application data without having to load the application on the desktop by creating web parts that retrieve and display application data

▶ Minimizing the problems associated with providing multiple user accounts and passwords for various applications by using single sign-on for application access

Implementing the Corporate Intranet Solution

The corporate intranet site is implemented using SharePoint 2010 sites. Features used on the site home page include announcements, links (to other major corporate sites and applications), search, events, and discussions. In the quick launch area are links to lists such as the corporate directory and to shared libraries including policies and procedures, newsletters, training, and benefits. Areas can be configured for operational groups within the organization and geographical groups within the organization, depending on the organizational requirements. Content sources that contain information useful to employees for doing their job can be added for indexing and search. Security and content approval can be implemented to enable controlled creation of sites and site content by a wide group of users. Integration can be provided for SharePoint-compatible applications by using preexisting integration web parts and developing custom web parts. Single sign-on can also be used for making it easier for users to access applications from within the site collection.

Ideas for Using the Corporate Intranet Solution

This section includes some ideas to incorporate into the corporate intranet site solution with the elements previously discussed.

Disseminate important corporatewide information such as policy and procedure changes using announcements. Put an expiration date on the announcements. If users see the same ones day-in and day-out, they have a tendency to ignore them.

Use a general discussion for obtaining employee feedback on policies, procedures, events, and other items of interest to employees. Moderate the discussion; have the human resources department or legal department responsible for approving all items submitted to the discussion group to ensure they are appropriate. Maintain a separate discussion forum for noncompany-related items, such as employees selling candy for their child's youth group. This type of discussion should not take up valuable home page space but provide a link to it from the home page. Surveys can also be used to get specific input on a topic.

Maintain a corporate events list in a calendar view to provide visual impact for upcoming events. Depending on the corporate climate, things such as birthdays and vacations can be maintained on the corporate calendar and company events and holidays.

Store company policies, procedures, and forms in shared document libraries for ease of maintenance and for accessibility. The department responsible for maintaining the documents should also be responsible for the publishing of documents (approve contents), and read access provided to other users.

Create content source groups for logical breakdown of content for searching to prevent an inordinate amount of time from being spent performing searches.

Using Active Directory as the basis for the company directory assists in keeping the SharePoint-viewed company directory synchronized with it. A customized view of the directory can be created that filters and displays only relevant columns of information.

Using an application such as Infopath 2010 or Infopath Forms Services, InfoPath forms can be created, filled out, and stored in document libraries for access and processing. Alerts can be set up in the library for people who need to process the documents so that when something is submitted, they are notified and can review the items. Approval processing can also be used to approve and reject the documents. This concept could be used for things such as expense reports and other workflow documents. For an end-to-end solution, application code can be developed to feed the data from the form documents into the appropriate external application (for example, the accounting system) for final processing.

Because there is generally a great deal of information on a corporate intranet, users should take advantage of the ability to create and customize their own personal site to include information they find useful. By using web parts that interface with Microsoft Outlook 2007/2010, the WSS personal site can become the primary user interface.

Deploying a Customer Extranet Solution with SharePoint

The primary purpose of the customer extranet portal is to service the needs of customers. The customer extranet enables customers to find information about products and services, and place help desk calls. In some customer extranets, client access is provided for things such as invoice payment and viewing account status and payment history. The customer extranet can also be used for document collaboration and managing joint projects with the customer. The content for this type of portal can originate from internal and external sources.

Meeting the Business Needs of the Customer Extranet Solution

The business needs of this group include searching for information, aggregating content from multiple sources, providing a dynamic view of relevant business information, collaborating on documents, sharing documents, managing joint projects, resolving issues, and providing a means for business transactions. The SharePoint features used to meet these needs are outlined as follows:

Searching:

- ▶ Providing customers with a means for viewing information about their account by using web parts that access line-of-business applications to retrieve and display customer-related information

- ▶ Enabling customers to find product/service information using the search features of SharePoint without having to speak with a service representative

- ▶ In addition to searching, providing the ability to view the results in a variety of ways depending on the needs using the filtering and sorting features of SharePoint

Content aggregation:

- ▶ Combining information from various sources into a single source for searching using content sources

- ▶ Accessing information from multiple business applications into one view using web parts

Dynamic views:

- ▶ Using filters to display subsets of information such as product-specific or location-specific data

- ▶ Using sort capabilities to present the information in a different order

Document collaboration:

- ▶ Sharing documents with clients using shared document libraries

- ▶ Controlling publication of documents using content approval

- ▶ Categorizing documents so that they can be easily found using document metadata

▶ Finding documents on a specific subject by searching the document text or the metadata attached to the document

Working on joint projects:

▶ Assigning/delegating tasks between parties using a tasks list

▶ Following up on overdue tasks by using views such as the Due Today view

▶ Sharing project-related information using a team site

▶ Discussing and resolving project issues using discussion boards

▶ Managing the overall project and reporting on status using a recurring event or multiple meeting workspace site

Resolving issues:

▶ Submitting issues/questions to a help desk using the issues list

▶ Responding to issues in a timely manner by using the alert feature on the issues list

▶ Having the ability to check the status of outstanding issues by using the my issues view

▶ Managing and tracking issue resolution using views of the issues list

Business interaction:

▶ Providing clients with access to business information such as invoice/payment status using customized web parts

▶ Enabling clients to perform business transactions by providing links to web-based application interfaces and/or customized web parts

Implementing the Customer Extranet Solution

The customer extranet site is implemented using SharePoint 2010 Sites. In addition, integration for SharePoint-compatible applications can be provided using existing web parts, developing custom web parts, and providing links to web-based frontends to business applications. Single sign-on can also be implemented to make it easier for users to access applications.

Features available on the extranet portal home page include a links list, announcements, discussion board, and search. The quick launch area can contain links to lists such as a limited corporate directory (with the listings for the salespeople and other people who customers typically deal with, such as accounting personnel) and frequently accessed shared libraries such as newsletters, training documents, and product information. Areas can be configured for support, product/service information, and billing information. A content source group can be created for the content in each area to make searches more targeted.

Document workspaces can be used to collaborate on documents. Team sites can be used when working with the customer on a joint project. Content sources can be created for product/service documentation and historical accounting information.

Security needs to be tight to ensure the integrity of customer-specific information. Restrictions need to be in place to prevent one customer from obtaining access to another customer's data.

Outlining Ideas for Using the Corporate Extranet Solution

This section includes some ideas to incorporate into the customer extranet site solution with the elements previously discussed. In addition to providing standard content, use audiences to target specific content to an individual or group of users.

Use the support area for linking to an issues list and a document library containing technical information. Links to supporting websites could also be in this area. Other possibilities would be to include a top-10-issues list and a download library.

Include a shared library with documents relating to products and services offered and links to corporate or other websites that have this information in the product/service information area. There could also be a discussion board on this area page so that clients could submit product- or service-related questions or requests and provide their ideas and feedback on products and services. When there is a need to get specific client feedback, a survey can be used.

Use team sites when working on projects with the customer. Include a tasks list to document division of responsibility, a contacts list for maintaining the contact information for members from both sides of the team, a custom punch list to document items yet to be completed, and a general discussion area as an alternative to email for documenting project-related correspondence in a central location, and create a weekly status meeting event or use a multiple meeting workspace for tracking and managing project status.

Summary

Microsoft SharePoint Server 2010 is a powerful tool that can enable knowledge workers to become more productive with a wide array of built-in tools and web parts. To take advantage of these features, however, the SharePoint environment must be properly designed and all the SharePoint components fully understood by the administrator in charge of designing the environment.

With SharePoint 2010 design knowledge, an administrator can properly scope and scale the infrastructure to handle anywhere from a handful of users to a large, distributed deployment of hundreds of thousands of users, enabling those users to take full advantage of the productivity gains that can be realized from the platform.

Best Practices

▶ Become familiar with SharePoint 2010 design terminology as it has changed significantly from SharePoint 2007. Note the concept of service applications.

▶ Use the latest version of SQL Server, SQL Server 2008 R2, whenever possible, particularly to take advantage of features such as PowerPivot, which are only provided with that version of SQL Server.

▶ Consider separating the service application roles from the web role servers to improve performance.

▶ Separate the database role from the SharePoint roles whenever possible to improve performance.

▶ Take an in-depth look at virtualization technologies, at a minimum for development and test farms, and potentially for production farms.

▶ Consider best-practice security approaches such as SQL Server Transparent Data Encryption (TDE) for storage security, IPsec and SSL Certificates for transport security, and Active Directory Rights Management Services (AD RMS) for Data Loss Prevention.

▶ Consider database mirroring for the content databases to provide for both high-availability and disaster recovery of SharePoint content.

▶ Remember to purchase and install any necessary third-party web parts, iFilters, backup, and antivirus software, or use some of the Microsoft offerings such as ForeFront Protection for SharePoint and System Center Data Protection Manager 2010.

▶ Allocate a significant amount of memory and processor cores to SharePoint servers, because they are resource-intensive.

▶ Be sure to allocate enough hard drive space for the Search Service Application roles for the index corpus; allocate 5 percent to 30 percent of the size of the data being indexed.

▶ Consider FAST Search Server for complex search requirements. See Chapter 8 for more information on how and why to deploy FAST Search server.

▶ Use clustering and network load balancing to scale the SharePoint server environment and provide redundancy.

## CHAPTER 3

Installing a Simple SharePoint Server 2010 Farm

After SharePoint architecture has been established, the actual SharePoint infrastructure must be installed and servers must be deployed. For the most part, installation of SharePoint 2010 is straightforward, particularly with the free SharePoint Foundation Server. The full Microsoft SharePoint Server 2010 product, on the other hand, requires more thought and involves the installation of more components.

This chapter covers the specifics of how SharePoint 2010 is installed for a simple, single server farm. Although these examples outline a simple farm, the concepts can be extended to multiserver farm deployments. After reviewing this chapter, it is highly recommended to review the subsequent chapter (Chapter 4, "Advanced SharePoint 2010 Installation and Scalability") for more complex farm configurations.

It is recommended to review the design chapter (Chapter 2, "Architecting a SharePoint 2010 Deployment") before beginning installation of a production environment. However, installation of a SharePoint server for testing can be easily performed with only this chapter as a guide.

Examining SharePoint Installation Prerequisites

Before installing SharePoint 2010, several prerequisites must first be satisfied, including both hardware and software prerequisites.

Defining Hardware Prerequisites for SharePoint 2010

A server that will be running all SharePoint roles, including the database role, should have the following minimum requirements:

- ▶ 64-bit four core (minimum) processor
- ▶ 8GB to 16GB of RAM (8GB for evaluation or testing, 16GB for production)
- ▶ 80GB of drive space for the system drive (plus twice as much space as the amount of RAM in the system)

> **NOTE**
>
> The move toward virtualization of servers has been gaining strength in recent years, and SharePoint server roles can all be virtualized within certain guidelines. Refer to Chapter 12, "Virtualizing SharePoint Components," for specific guidance on designing and deploying SharePoint using server virtualization technologies.

The server that holds the SharePoint database, whether on the same box (an all-in-one server) or on a dedicated server or existing SQL implementation, should generally be designed toward the high level on the hardware scale, because some of the more intensive activity is centralized on that server role.

As a rule of thumb, it is always recommended to deploy SharePoint on multiple servers, and at a minimum to deploy SharePoint on at least two servers: one for the database and one for the other SharePoint-specific roles. For more information on supported farm topologies, refer to Chapter 2.

Examining Software Requirements for SharePoint 2010

SharePoint 2010 requires either Windows Server 2008 SP2 or Windows Server 2008 R2. More specifically, the following Windows OS editions are supported:

- ▶ Windows Server 2008 R2 (x64) Standard, Enterprise, Datacenter, or Web Server Editions
- ▶ Windows Server 2008 SP2 (x64) Standard, Enterprise, Datacenter, or Web Server Editions

In nearly all scenarios, it is recommend to use the latest version of the Windows Server operating system (in this case, the R2 edition), though in the future, it is highly likely that SharePoint will use newer editions as well. For most deployments, the Standard edition of Windows Server is sufficient, except in certain scenarios when the Enterprise Edition is required for running SQL Server Enterprise Edition. The Datacenter edition, while supported, is not required, and the Web Server edition, while supported, is not recommended.

Service Account Requirements

It is strongly recommended that you create multiple service accounts for SharePoint. Although doing so might seem tedious, SharePoint will not be secure unless multiple service accounts are used. And in any situation, do NOT use a domain admin account for any SharePoint service.

The following provides a recommended list of service accounts that should be created. This should not be considered to be an exhaustive list; more might be needed depending on the requirements of the individual deployment:

- **SQL admin account**—SQL Server should be administered with a separate set of credentials than those used for SharePoint.

- **Installation account**—Used to install the SharePoint binaries on the SharePoint role servers. This account requires local admin rights on each SharePoint server and DBCreator and SecurityAdmin rights on the SQL Server.

- **SharePoint farm admins**—Used to administer the farm; should be configured. Typically, one account for each physical admin is created.

- **Application pool identity accounts**—Needed for each app pool. Generally speaking, it is good practice to have a separate app pool for each application. These accounts must be separate from farm admin accounts.

- **Default content access account**—The default account used to crawl SharePoint and other content. It must not be a farm admin, or the search results will include unpublished data in the results. There may be additional content access accounts created for other data sources that are crawled as well.

- **Search service application account**—This account is used to run the search service application.

- **Additional service application accounts as needed**—May require a separate service application account in certain scenarios.

Outlining Additional Prerequisites

In addition to the base Operating System, SharePoint also requires the hotfixes referenced in KB articles 976462 and 979917. These hotfixes are installed automatically when using the SharePoint installer. The SharePoint installer also installs the following server roles:

- Web Server (IIS) role

- Application server role

- Microsoft .NET Framework version 3.5 SP1

- Microsoft Sync Framework Runtime v1.0 (x64)

- Microsoft Filter Pack 2.0

- Microsoft Chart Controls for the Microsoft .NET Framework 3.5

- ▶ Windows PowerShell 2.0
- ▶ SQL Server 2008 Native Client
- ▶ SQL Server 2008 Analysis Services ADOMD.NET
- ▶ ADO.NET data services update for .NET Framework 3.5 SP1
- ▶ Windows Identity Foundation (WIF)

Database Role Prerequisites

For the database role, it is recommended to deploy the latest version of SQL Server, SQL 2008 R2. The following versions of SQL Server are directly supported:

- ▶ SQL Server 2008 R2 x64, Standard or Enterprise Editions
- ▶ SQL Server 2008 x64 (x86 cannot be used) with SP1 and Cumulative Update 2 or CU5 (or later than CU5—CU3 and CU4 are not recommended), Standard or Enterprise Editions
- ▶ SQL Server 2005 with SP3 x64 (x86 cannot be used) and CU3

In addition, depending on whether advanced SQL functionality is required, the following components may also be needed:

- ▶ SQL Server 2008 R2, if working with PowerPivot workbooks.
- ▶ SQL Server 2008 R2 Reporting Services add-in for Microsoft SharePoint Technologies 2010 (SSRS) to use Access Services for SharePoint 2010.
- ▶ Microsoft Server Speech Platform for phonetic name matching to work correctly for SharePoint Search 2010.
- ▶ If using the standalone server install option (not recommended), SQL Server 2008 Express with SP1, which is installed automatically.

FAST Search Requirements

If a FAST Search server for advanced SharePoint Search is required, different installation procedures and prerequisites apply. For more information on this topic, refer to Chapter 8, "Leveraging and Optimizing Search in SharePoint 2010."

Installing the SharePoint Server Operating System

After the edition of the server OS has been chosen, it must be installed on the SharePoint server. As previously mentioned, this step by step assumes that a single all-in-one SharePoint server will be set up and deployed.

The Windows Server 2008 R2 operating system encompasses a myriad of new technologies and functionality, more than can be covered in this book. If additional reading on the capabilities of the operating system is wanted, the recommended reference is *Windows Server 2008 R2 Edition Unleashed*, from Sams Publishing.

NOTE

It is highly recommended to install SharePoint 2010 on a clean, freshly built operating system on a reformatted hard drive. If the server used for SharePoint were previously running in a different capacity, the most secure and robust solution would be to completely reinstall the operating system using the procedure outlined in this section.

Installing Windows Server 2008 R2

This chapter assumes installation of SharePoint on the latest version of Windows Server, the 2008 R2 version. Installation of Windows Server 2008 R2 is extremely straightforward and takes approximately 30 minutes to 1 hour to complete. Microsoft has built the installation process to be nearly touch-free. Simply accept the defaults for any SharePoint server—there is no need to choose any custom installation settings. The high-level steps involved are as follows:

▶ Install Windows Server 2008 R2 with the defaults.

▶ Activate the server.

▶ Install any server-specific tools required.

▶ Patch and update the operating system.

▶ Add the server to an Active Directory domain.

▶ Copy the SharePoint 2010 binaries local to the server (recommended).

▶ Copy the SQL Server 2008 R2 binaries local (if installing the database role).

Installing SQL Server 2008 R2

The SharePoint databases need to reside in a SQL Server implementation. The version of SQL must be either SQL Server 2008 or higher, or SQL Server 2005. The SQL server component can either reside on a separate server or installed on the SharePoint server itself, for smaller, single server deployments.

NOTE

For testing or development, the Express version of SQL Server can be used, which is included in a standalone installation option of SharePoint. The standalone version of SharePoint and the Express version of SQL are NOT recommended for production environments.

This chapter assumes that the full SQL Server 2008 R2 product will be installed on a single SharePoint all-in-one server. Installation steps are subsequently illustrated for this scenario. The same concepts can be used for installing a two-server farm as well, with SQL Server on a single server and all SharePoint roles on another server. For more advanced installation scenarios, including scenarios where SharePoint is installed from PowerShell, refer to Chapter 4.

Installing SQL Server 2008 R2

From the SQL 2008 R2 binaries, perform the following steps to install:

1. Run setup.exe from the SQL binaries.

2. SQL Server 2008 R2 requires the .NET Framework; click OK to install it.

3. From the SQL installation center, shown in Figure 3.1, click on the installation link in the navigation bar, and choose the link for new installation or add features to an existing installation.

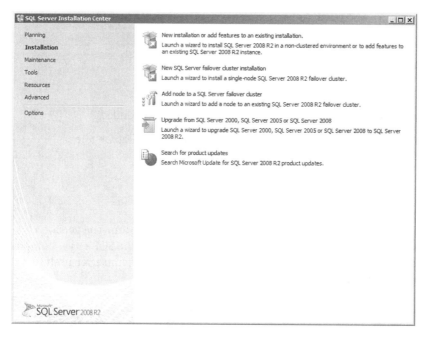

FIGURE 3.1   Starting a SQL Server 2008 R2 install.

4. Click OK on the Setup Support Rules dialog box.

5. From the dialog box specifying the edition to install, enter a valid product key, and click Next to continue.

6. Check the box to accept the license terms, and click Next to continue.

7. Click Install to install the Setup Support Files.

8. Review the warnings, as shown in Figure 3.2, and click Next to continue.

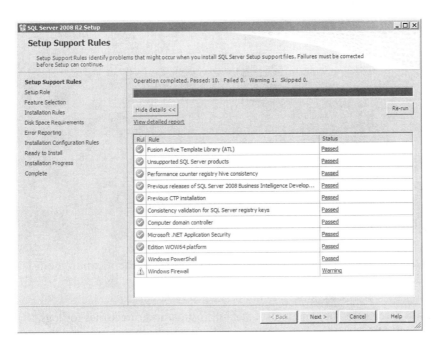

FIGURE 3.2   Reviewing setup warnings from SQL Server.

9. Select SQL Server Feature Installation from the Setup Role dialog box; then click Next to continue.

10. From the Feature Selection dialog box, click the Select All button, and click Next to continue. In a distributed environment, some SQL services may run on separate servers, but for a single SQL Server environment, all services may be installed.

11. Click Next at the Installation Rules dialog box.

12. Choose to install the Default instance, and click Next to continue.

13. Review disk space requirements, and click Next to continue.

14. From the Server Configuration dialog box, choose Service Accounts for each service. In most cases, you'll want to use the NT AUTHORITY/SYSTEM accounts for each service, as shown in Figure 3.3. In certain other cases, you may need to specify service accounts. After setting the service accounts, click Next to continue.

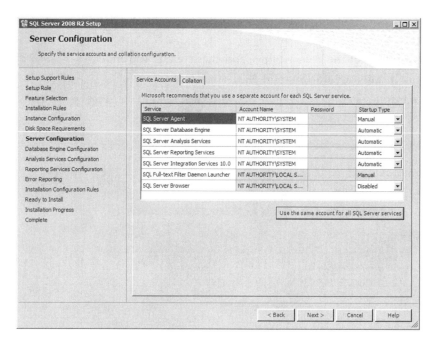

FIGURE 3.3   Setting SQL Service Accounts.

15. Under the Database Engine Configuration, choose Windows authentication mode. Click the Add Current User button to add the installation account as a SQL Administrator. (Or add an account that will be logged in later.)

16. Click the Data Directories tab, and choose default installation directories for logs, database files, and backup files. It is recommended to do this in advance and to separate SQL Logs from the databases from the beginning. Click Next to continue.

17. For Analysis Services configuration, add the Current User as an Administrator, and click the Data Directories tab. Select directory locations for data and logs, separating them on separate drive spindles when possible. Click Next to continue.

18. For the Reporting Services integration, select to install the SharePoint integrated mode default configuration, as shown in Figure 3.4. This enables Reporting Services to be integrated with SharePoint 2010. Click Next to continue.

19. Accept the defaults for Error Reporting, and click Next to continue.

20. After the installation configuration rules have run, click Next to continue.

21. At the summary page, review the settings and click Install.

22. When the install is complete, review the summary log file and click Close to finish.

Post-installation tasks should be conducted after SQL Server has been installed. Some of these post-installation tasks will validate whether the installation was successful, whereas other tasks are required to ensure that the server is secure and operational. The post-installation tasks include the following:

1. Review installation logs.

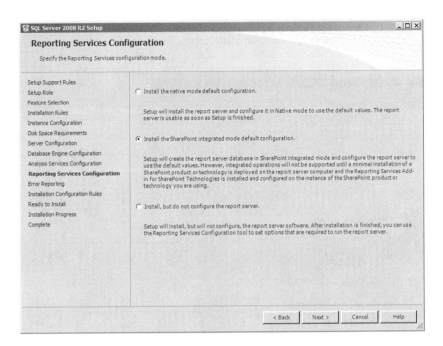

FIGURE 3.4   Installing SQL Reporting Services in SharePoint integrated mode.

2. Review event logs.

3. Obtain and apply the latest SQL Server service packs and critical updates.

4. Verify the server components that were installed.

It is also critical to rerun Microsoft Update to apply any necessary SQL Server patches. Running Microsoft Update will display the patches necessary for SQL.

> **NOTE**
>
> Remember to use Microsoft Update, and not the default Windows Update, because only Microsoft Update can detect the non-Windows patches, including SQL Server and SharePoint patches.

Creating a Windows Firewall Port Exception for SQL Server

The Windows firewall is highly recommended for security reasons, and it is not recommended to simply turn it off. By default, however, to get SQL services to run, you must create a manual Windows firewall port rule that enables port 1433, the SQL port, to be open on the server, as shown in Figure 3.5. If this port is not open, SharePoint cannot connect to the SQL server if it is installed on a separate server from the SharePoint server.

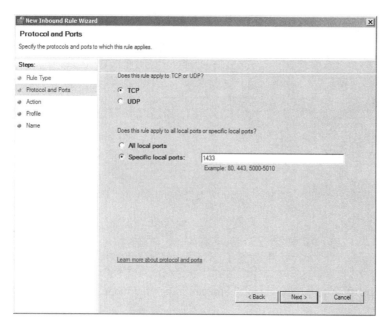

FIGURE 3.5   Creating a SQL port exception for the Windows firewall.

Enabling TCP/IP in SQL Configuration Manager

By default, some SQL Server installations do not have TCP/IP enabled for remote access. This is required for use by a remote SharePoint server. To enable TCP/IP, simply open SQL Server Configuration Manager (Start, All Programs, Microsoft SQL Server 2008 R2 – Configuration Tools, SQL Server Configuration Manager) and navigate to SQL Server Network Configuration, Protocols for <INSTANCENAME>. Change the TCP/IP to Enabled, as shown in Figure 3.6. If this is not done, SharePoint cannot connect to the SQL Server.

Installing Microsoft SharePoint Server 2010

Installation of SharePoint 2010 is deceivingly simple, but be sure you understand the process.

Running the Prerequisite Check for SharePoint 2010

The SharePoint team at Microsoft has done an excellent job in creating a prerequisite check and installation utility that can be run in advance of a SharePoint installation to turn on all server roles required and install all prerequisites automatically. Simply by running a wizard, SharePoint administrators can automate the installation of the SharePoint binaries and position the server to be ready to join or create a new farm.

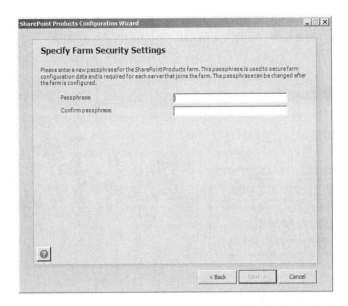

FIGURE 3.6   Enabling TCP/IP support in SQL Configuration Manager.

The Prerequisite check can be run directly from the splash screen, shown in Figure 3.7, displayed when running the setup from the SharePoint binaries. Click Install Software prerequisites, accept the license terms, and follow the prompts to install all necessary components.

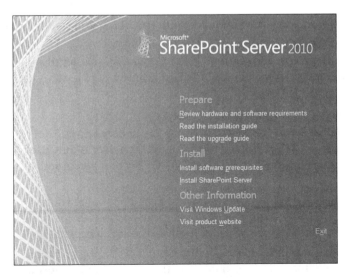

FIGURE 3.7   Starting the SharePoint 2010 installation process.

When done and the roles and hotfixes required are installed, as shown in Figure 3.8, click Finish to reboot the server. The server is now ready for installation of the SharePoint 2010 binaries.

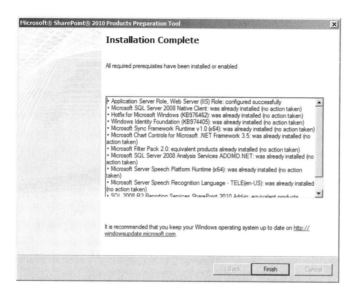

FIGURE 3.8   Reviewing the results of the prerequisite check and component installer.

Installing the SharePoint 2010 Binaries

The following steps are used to install the SharePoint 2010 binaries after the prerequisite checks have been run and all necessary software components have been installed:

1. While logged in as the Install account, run Setup.exe, and from the splash screen, click Install SharePoint Server.

2. Enter a valid SharePoint 2010 License Key. Note that the Standard and Enterprise edition license keys are separate, and installing a Standard license key only turns on Standard edition services.

3. Accept the license terms and click Continue.

4. From the Installation type dialog box, as shown in Figure 3.9, choose Server Farm as the type of installation. DO NOT SELECT Standalone, unless the server is only used as a demo box. The Standalone version installs a copy of SQL Server Express and should not be used in production.

5. From the Server Type dialog box, choose Complete. DO NOT SELECT Standalone because this has the same effect as selecting Standalone in the previous dialog box— it will install a single server with SQL Express Edition. Always select Complete.

6. Select the File location tab and specify a location for index files, as shown in Figure 3.10. Ideally, these files will be stored on a separate drive than the OS and SharePoint binaries. If you choose this option now, you won't have to go through the complex process of moving the index later. Click Install Now to start the installation process.

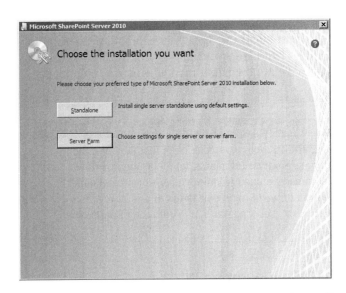

FIGURE 3.9   Installing SharePoint 2010 using the Server Farm option.

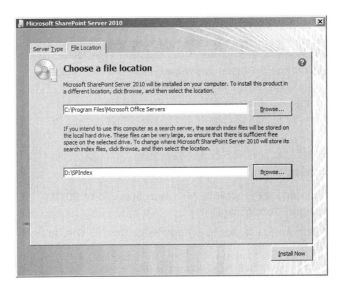

FIGURE 3.10   Specifying the location of the index files during a SharePoint 2010 install.

7. After the installation has completed, you can choose to run the Configuration Wizard now or later. It is recommended to not run the Configuration Wizard immediately but to first exit the application and check for any updates or patches before proceeding.

Patch SharePoint 2010 with any necessary patches, bearing in mind that there may be cumulative updates that are not reflected in Microsoft Update. It is important to install any service packs and cumulative updates first before continuing with the SharePoint installation, because it is much easier to patch now rather than when farm components are already configured.

NOTE

This point in the installation process, after the binaries have been installed and the system patched, is an ideal spot to create server templates from, for use in virtual server environments. These templates can be used to quickly provision SharePoint farm members, allowing for the creation of new SharePoint farms in a matter of minutes. For more information on this concept, see Chapter 12, "Virtualizing SharePoint Components."

Running the SharePoint 2010 Configuration Wizard

The SharePoint 2010 Configuration Wizard is the component that enables a server to either be added to an existing SharePoint 2010 farm or to create a new SharePoint farm from scratch.

NOTE

You can use Windows PowerShell to run the Configuration Wizard. Indeed, PowerShell is the only supported method of provisioning SharePoint with custom database names, so it is recommended for many scenarios. Installation using PowerShell is covered in Chapter 4.

In this example, we create a new farm using the following steps:

1. Start the Configuration Wizard (Start, All Programs, Microsoft SharePoint 2010 Products, SharePoint 2010 Configuration Wizard).

2. Click Next at the Welcome screen, and click Yes to acknowledge that IIS will be reset during the process.

3. Select to Create a New Server Farm, and click Next to continue.

4. For the Configuration Database settings, enter the name of the database server and select a name for the Config database. Consider the use of a SQL alias for the database server name so that it can be easily changed in the future. If the database server is the same as the one that is used for SharePoint, enter the local server name. Enter a Database Access Account that has DBCreator and Securityadmin rights on the SQL Instance. Click Next to continue.

5. Enter a farm passphrase into the subsequent dialog box, shown in Figure 3.11. Keep this passphrase in a safe place; it is needed to add any additional servers to the farm in the future. Click Next to continue.

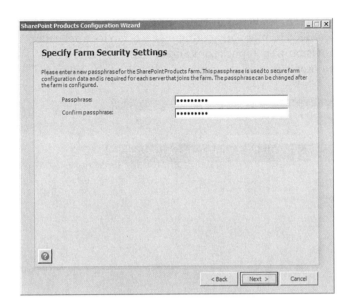

FIGURE 3.11   Entering a farm passphrase.

6. Specify a port for the SharePoint Central Admin Web Application. It is recommended to choose an easily remembered port name initially. You also have the opportunity to choose NTLM or Kerberos. Kerberos is the recommended setting for the long term, but for the initial installation, choose NTLM to ensure that you can gain access initially. For long-term production support, however, Kerberos, SSL, and a default port of 443 are highly recommended for the SharePoint central web application. More information on changing to Kerberos and configuring SSL and a default port for the central web application can be found in Chapter4. Click Next to continue.

7. Review the settings and click Next to start the Configuration Wizard.

8. Click Finish when the wizard is complete.

Running the Initial Farm Configuration Wizard

After the Configuration Wizard has run, the newly provisioned SharePoint central web application will start automatically. You may need to provide credentials to the site; use the farm installation credentials to start the application.

By default, SharePoint is configured to run the Initial Farm Configuration Wizard upon the first time using the central admin web application. This wizard will complete all other farm tasks, including installing and configuring service applications. For simpler environments, this farm can be used to get SharePoint to a condition where it is more or less ready for use. For more complex provisioning scenarios, see Chapter 4.

Use the following steps to run the Initial Farm Configuration Wizard:

1. Select whether to join the Customer Experience Improvement Program from the initial dialog box and click OK.

2. From the wizard introduction screen, as shown in Figure 3.12, select whether to run the wizard. If it is not run, you need to manually configure each service application component and manually provision web applications and site collections. In this scenario, we use the wizard to provision the components. Click Start the Wizard.

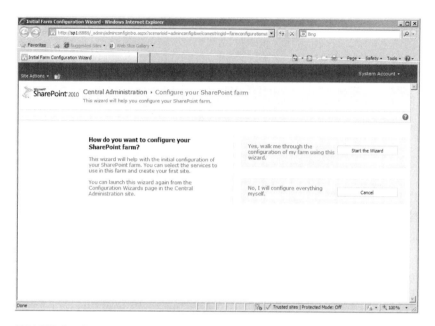

FIGURE 3.12   Choosing whether to run the Initial Farm Configuration Wizard.

3. From the subsequent screen, enter a service account that will become a managed service account for the farm. This should be different than the farm account.

4. Check the service applications that will be installed, from the list shown in Figure 3.13. Only install those service applications that supply required functionality for the site, because each service application uses a significant amount of resources on the server.

5. After selecting which service applications to install, click Next to start the provisioning process. This process may take a while to complete, depending on the resources of the server.

6. After the service application provisioning process has completed, the wizard will prompt you to create a web application and root site collection as the main site collection for the portal. You can skip this step or have the wizard provision it for you. Enter a title and choose a template, as shown in Figure 3.14. Click OK to continue.

7. Click Finish to close the wizard. You now should have a fully provisioned SharePoint 2010 environment.

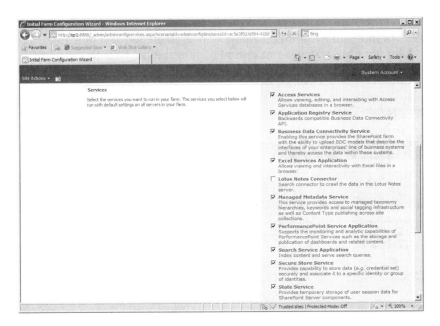

FIGURE 3.13   Selecting service applications to install.

FIGURE 3.14   Provisioning a site collection for the root web application using the wizard.

SharePoint central administration, as shown in Figure 3.15, will open and allow for additional configuration. For more information on additional configuration and how to administer a SharePoint farm using SharePoint central administration, refer to Chapter 6, "Managing and Administering SharePoint 2010 Infrastructure."

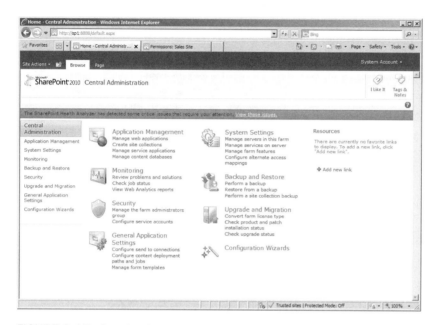

FIGURE 3.15   Running SharePoint central administration for the first time.

Summary

Installation of SharePoint 2010 products and technologies has been streamlined and is fairly straightforward, as long as necessary prerequisites are met and attention to detail is observed. With the proper precautions in place and the scenarios in this chapter followed, administrators can immediately take advantage of the advanced feature set available in SharePoint 2010.

Best Practices

▶ Review Chapter 2 before installing SharePoint 2010 into a production environment.

▶ Create multiple service accounts for use by SharePoint. Do not use a single service account, and do not use any domain admin accounts for SharePoint.

▶ Do not use any of the standalone installation options for a production environment.

▶ Use the latest version of Windows Server and SQL Server whenever possible. At the time of publishing, this included Windows Server 2008 R2 and SQL Server 2008 R2.

- ► Seriously consider deploying SQL Server on a separate server from SharePoint. Review the supported farm topologies from Chapter 2.

- ► Patch the operating system with all critical updates before installing SharePoint.

- ► Patch SharePoint 2010 with all the latest service packs and cumulative update patches before running the configuration wizard.

- ► Enable only those service applications that supply required functionality for the farm.

- ► Review Chapter 4 for more complex installation scenarios, including scenarios involving provisioning using PowerShell.

3

Advanced SharePoint 2010 Installation and Scalability

The needs of most organizations are not going to be met by a simple single-server SharePoint farm. Indeed, the power of SharePoint 2010 is in its scalability, and the majority of organizations are going to want to take SharePoint to the next level in terms of functionality.

This chapter covers the more advanced installation scenarios that aren't covered in Chapter 3, "Installing a Simple SharePoint Server 2010 Farm." It is meant to build upon the simple farm deployment examples illustrated in the previous chapter, but take you into the realm of tasks that are often performed during the installation of larger and more complex environments, including Kerberos, SSL configuration, and scripted installations of an entire farm using PowerShell.

In addition, this chapter focuses on techniques and information necessary to scale a SharePoint implementation to organizations of varying sizes. Specific components that can be scaled are described and contrasted. In addition, examples of scalability in organizations of different sizes are presented.

Creating an Installation Checklist

Installation of a large and complex SharePoint environment can be a complicated task, and various subtasks and routines must be run before the environment is production ready. It is subsequently important to create a mental and physical checklist of the types of tasks required for rollout of a farm.

The following list of tasks represents a common large farm deployment routine and can be used as a starting point for determining the task list that is required for installation of your specific environment. It is not a definitive list of all tasks, and the order of tasks performed may vary depending on the environment.

Conceptualizing and Architecting a SharePoint Farm

The following list denotes the high-level steps that should be followed before architecting a SharePoint environment:

1. Define the business needs that should ideally be met by the project.
2. Map business needs to technical solutions in SharePoint 2010.
3. Define the number of farms required to satisfy business and technical needs and to provide for publishing and other features.
4. Define the number and scale of intranet versus extranet environments, using guidelines from Chapter 13, "Deploying SharePoint for Extranets and Alternate Authentication Scenarios."
5. Define the physical architecture that will be required to deploy the technical solutions.
6. Define the security requirements, including number of service accounts and the rights they require.
7. Define the number of third-party and other MS solutions to properly secure and deploy.

Refer to Chapter 2, "Architecting a SharePoint 2010 Deployment," for more information on these tasks.

Installing SharePoint 2010

The following high-level checklist should be used for advanced SharePoint installations:

1. Build the SQL Database environment for SharePoint.
2. Build the SharePoint Server environment, including all role servers, from an OS perspective and also by installing the SharePoint binaries.
3. Create the SharePoint farms using the Configuration Wizard or (preferably) using PowerShell (as demonstrated in this chapter).

Refer to Chapter 3 for more information on these tasks.

Configuring SharePoint 2010

The following high-level checklist should be used to continue the installation of an advanced SharePoint environment:

1. Create Web Applications required, configuring them for Kerberos, SSL, and Load Balancing (all best practices).
2. Configure Managed Paths and Content Database structure, based on the parameters defined during the design phase.
3. Configure My Site functionality.

4. Configure the SharePoint Central Administration Web Application as a load-balanced, SSL, and Kerberos-enabled web application for performance, security, and high availability.

5. Configure all service applications required for the farm, using either the web-based wizard or (preferably), PowerShell, as demonstrated in this chapter.

6. Configure the User Profile Service to pull information into User Profiles.

7. Configure inbound mail settings, and configure them to be load balanced for availability of the service.

8. Configure outbound mail settings for alerts and other messages to be sent from SharePoint.

9. Configure search (covered in more detail in Chapter 8, "Leveraging and Optimizing Search in SharePoint 2010," including third-party iFilters such as PDF iFilters, and FAST Search if needed.

10. Configure backup (third-party, Microsoft DPM, or integrated backup.) Refer to Chapter 10, "Backing Up and Restoring a SharePoint Environment," for more details.

11. Configure edge security and antivirus (third-party or Microsoft Forefront products, covered in Chapter 14, "Protecting SharePoint with Advanced Antivirus and Edge Security Solutions").

12. Configure data and transport security options (covered in Chapter 17, "Safeguarding Confidential Data in SharePoint 2010").

13. Configure SQL maintenance and optimization, using concepts defined in Chapter 9.

14. Configure third-party product functionality as necessary.

15. Test, test, and retest before deploying into production.

16. Migrate content into SharePoint using third-party tools (if necessary).

Installing SharePoint 2010 Using PowerShell

PowerShell is a critical tool for SharePoint administrators that actually allows for options not available in the standard central administration GUI. For example, PowerShell is the only method that enables the creation of custom names for many of the databases created by SharePoint during the installation. In addition, creating a custom PowerShell script for installation of a new farm enables that farm to be repeatedly created, such as in the case of development farms.

Examining a PowerShell Script for Provisioning a Farm

When SharePoint binaries are installed in an environment, PowerShell can be used to provision any farm. The following script illustrates a way to have PowerShell create a new farm based on input from the end user and have all databases from that farm use the name of the farm in the database name, to enable multiple farms to be created in a single environment:

```
- - - - - - - - - - - - - - - - - - - - -.
$configType = read-host "Do you wish to join an existing Farm? (Y/N)"
if ($ConfigType -eq "Y") {
    $DatabaseServer = read-host "Preparing to join existing farm. Please specify the
    ➥name of your SQL Server";
    $ConfigDB = read-host "Next, specify the name of your Farm Configuration
    ➥Database";
    $Passphrase = read-host "Finally, please enter your Farm passphrase" -
    ➥assecurestring
} else {
    $DatabaseServer = read-host "Preparing to create a new Farm. Please specify the
    ➥name of your SQL Server";
    $FarmName = read-host "Please specify a name for your Farm (ex. SP2010Dev)";
    $ConfigDB = $FarmName+"_ConfigDB";
    $AdminContentDB = $FarmName+"_Admin_ContentDB";
    Write-Host "Please enter the credentials for your Farm Account (ex.
    ➥COMPANYABC\SP_Farm)";
    $FarmAcct = Get-Credential;
    $Passphrase = read-host "Enter a secure Farm passphrase" -assecurestring;
    $Port = read-host "Enter a port number for the Central Administration Web App";
    $Authentication = read-host "Finally, specify your authentication provider
    ➥(NTLM/Kerberos)";
}
if ($ConfigType -eq "Y") {
    Add-PSSnapin Microsoft.SharePoint.PowerShell;
    Connect-SPConfigurationDatabase -DatabaseName $ConfigDB -DatabaseServer
    ➥$DatabaseServer -Passphrase $Passphrase
} else {
    Add-PSSnapin Microsoft.SharePoint.PowerShell;
    Write-Host "Your SharePoint Farm is being configured..."
    New-SPConfigurationDatabase -DatabaseName $ConfigDB -DatabaseServer
    ➥$DatabaseServer -AdministrationContentDatabaseName $AdminContentDB -Passphrase
    ➥$Passphrase -FarmCredentials $FarmAcct
}
Initialize-SPResourceSecurity
Install-SPService
Install-SPFeature -AllExistingFeatures
New-SPCentralAdministration -Port $Port -WindowsAuthProvider $Authentication
Install-SPHelpCollection -All
Install-SPApplicationContent
Write-Host "Your SharePoint 2010 Farm has been created!"
if ($ConfigType -eq "N") {
    $WebAppCreation = read-host "Would you like to provision a Web Application using
    ➥the default Team Site Template? (Y/N)";
    if ($WebAppCreation -eq "Y") {
        $HostHeaderQ = read-host "Would you like to specify a host header? (Y/N)";
        if ($HostHeaderQ -eq "Y") {
```

```
            $HostHeader = read-host "Please specify a host header for your Web
            ➥Application (ex. intranet.contoso.com)";
            $URL = "http://"+$HostHeader;
            Write-Host "Creating your Web Application...";
            New-SPWebApplication -Name "SharePoint 2010 Team Site" -Port 80 -
            ➥HostHeader $FQDN -Url $URL -ApplicationPool "Content_AppPool" -
            ➥ApplicationPoolAccount (Get-SPManagedAccount $FarmAcct.UserName) -
            ➥DatabaseServer$DatabaseServer -DatabaseName $FarmName +
            ➥"_TeamSite_ContentDB_01";
            New-SPSite $URL -OwnerAlias $FarmAcct.UserName -Language 1033 -Template
            ➥"STS#0" -Name "Team Site";
            Write-Host "Configuration completed.";
        }
        else {
        Write-Host "Creating a Web Application using the default Team Site
        ➥Template..."
        }
    }
    else {
        Write-Host "Configuration completed.";
    }
}
Write-Host "Press any key to continue..."
$x = $host.UI.RawUI.ReadKey("NoEcho,IncludeKeyDown")
```
— — — — — — — — — — — — — — — — — —

Using concepts such as those demonstrated in this script, you can automate the creation
of an entire custom farm and have more control over the entire farm creation process.
Modifying variables and customizing the commandlets illustrated in the script can enable
further customization.

PowerShell for Provisioning Service Applications

Service application provisioning is a much more complex process than the installation of a
single farm. Consequently, a PowerShell script to provision all service applications in a
farm can be much longer and more complex. The following script can be used to provision
nearly all available SharePoint 2010 service applications, and it walks the end user through
the process and enables them to choose which service applications they want to install:

— — — — — — — — — — — — — — — — — —·
```
cls
if((Get-PSSnapin ¦ Where {$_.Name -eq "Microsoft.SharePoint.PowerShell"}) -eq
➥$null) {
    Add-PSSnapin Microsoft.SharePoint.PowerShell;
}

function Start-SPService($ServiceInstanceTypeName) {
```

```
$ServiceInstance = (Get-SPServiceInstance | Where {$_.TypeName -eq $ServiceIn-
➥stanceTypeName})

if($ServiceInstance.Status -ne "Online" -and $ServiceInstance.Status -ne "Pro-
➥visioning") {
    $ServiceInstance | Start-SPServiceInstance
}

$i = 0;
while(-not ($ServiceInstance.Status -eq "Online") -and $i -lt 10) {
    Write-Host -ForegroundColor Yellow "Waiting for the $ServiceInstanceTypeName
    ➥service to provision...";
    sleep 10;
    $ServiceInstance = (Get-SPServiceInstance | Where {$_.TypeName -eq
    ➥$ServiceInstanceTypeName})

    $i += 1;

    if($i -eq 10) {
        $continue = Read-Host "Service $ServiceInstanceTypeName has not yet been
        ➥provisioned. Would you like to wait? (Y/N)"

        if($continue -eq "Y") {
            $i = 0;
        }
    }
}
}


Function Configure-SPSearch  {
    PARAM($AppPool, $FarmName, $SearchServiceAccount)

    $searchServiceInstance = Get-SPEnterpriseSearchServiceInstance -local
    Start-SPEnterpriseSearchServiceInstance -Identity $searchServiceInstance

    $dbName = $FarmName + "_SearchServiceApplication"

    $searchApplication = New-SPEnterpriseSearchServiceApplication -Name "$FarmName
    ➥Search Service Application" -ApplicationPool $AppPool -DatabaseName $dbName
    $searchApplicationProxy = New-SPEnterpriseSearchServiceApplicationProxy -name
    ➥"$FarmName Search Service Application Proxy" -SearchApplication
    ➥$searchApplication

    Set-SPEnterpriseSearchAdministrationComponent -SearchApplication
    ➥$searchApplication   -SearchServiceInstance $searchServiceInstance
```

```
$crawlTopology = New-SPEnterpriseSearchCrawlTopology -SearchApplication
➡$searchApplication
$crawlDatabase = Get-SPEnterpriseSearchCrawlDatabase -SearchApplication
➡$searchApplication

New-SPEnterpriseSearchCrawlComponent -CrawlTopology $crawlTopology
➡-CrawlDatabase $crawlDatabase -
➡SearchServiceInstance $searchServiceInstance

while($crawlTopology.State -ne "Active")
{
    $crawlTopology | Set-SPEnterpriseSearchCrawlTopology -Active -ErrorAction
    ➡SilentlyContinue
    if ($crawlTopology.State -ne "Active")
    {
        Start-Sleep -Seconds 10
    }
}

$queryTopology = New-SPenterpriseSEarchQueryTopology -SearchApplication
➡$searchApplication -partitions 1
$searchIndexPartition = Get-SPEnterpriseSearchIndexPartition -QueryTopology
➡$queryTopology
New-SPEnterpriseSearchQueryComponent -indexpartition $searchIndexPartition -
➡QueryTopology $queryTopology -SearchServiceInstance $searchServiceInstance

$propertyDB = Get-SPEnterpriseSearchPropertyDatabase -SearchApplication
➡$searchApplication

Set-SPEnterpriseSearchIndexPartition $searchIndexPartition -PropertyDatabase
➡$propertyDB

while ($queryTopology.State -ne "Active")
{
    $queryTopology | Set-SPEnterpriseSearchQueryTopology -Active -ErrorAction
    ➡SilentlyContinue

    if ($queryTopology.State -ne "Active")
    {
        Start-Sleep -Seconds 10
    }
}
}
```

```
function Start-SPTimer {
    $spTimerService = Get-Service "SPTimerV4"

    if($spTimerService.Status -ne "Running") {
        Write-Host -ForegroundColor Yellow "SharePoint 2010 Timer Service is not
        ➥running. Attempting to start the timer."
        Start-Service "SPTimerV4"
        $spTimerService = Get-Service "SPTimerV4"

        while($spTimerService.Status -ne "Running") {
            Start-Sleep -Seconds 10
            Start-Service "SPTimerV4"
            $spTimerService = Get-Service "SPTimerV4"
        }

        Write-Host -ForegroundColor Green "SharePoint 2010 Timer Service is running."
    }
    else {
        Write-Host -ForegroundColor Green "SharePoint 2010 Timer Service is running."
    }
}




Function Get-SPServiceApplicationPoolByName($SPApplicationPoolName,
➥$ManagedAccount) {

    $appPool = Get-SPServiceApplicationPool | Where {$_.Name -eq
    ➥$SPApplicationPoolName}

    if($appPool -eq $null) {
        $appPool = New-SPServiceApplicationPool -Name $SPApplicationPoolName
        ➥-Account $ManagedAccount
    }

    Return $appPool
}

Function Get-SPManagedAccountByName($AccountName) {
    $managedAccount = Get-SPManagedAccount | Where {$_.Username -eq $AccountName}

    if($managedAccount -eq $null) {
        Write-Host "Please enter the credentials for your Managed Account
        ➥($AccountName)";
        $managedAccountCredential = Get-Credential;
```

```
        $managedAccount = New-SPManagedAccount $managedAccountCredential
    }

    Return $managedAccount
}

Function Get-SPServiceApplicationByType($TypeName) {
    $serviceApplications = Get-SPServiceApplication | Where  {$_.TypeName -eq
    ➥$TypeName}

    if($serviceApplications -ne $null) {
        $true;
    }
    else {
        $false;
    }
}

Function New-SPStateServiceApplicationGroup($FarmName){
        $dbName = $FarmName + "_StateService"

        Write-Host -ForegroundColor Yellow "Installing State Service Application..."

        New-SPStateServiceDatabase $dbName | New-SPStateServiceApplication -Name
        ➥"$FarmName State Service Application" | New-SPStateServiceApplication-
        ➥Proxy -Name
        ➥"$FarmName State Service Application Proxy" -DefaultProxyGroup
        sleep 10;

        Write-Host -ForegroundColor Green "State Service Application installed..."
}

Function New-SPUsageApplicationAndProxy($FarmName) {
    Write-Host -ForegroundColor Yellow "Installing Usage and Health Data Collection
    ➥Service..."

    $dbName = $FarmName + "_UsageandHealthDataCollectionService"
    New-SPUsageApplication "$FarmName Usage and Health Data Collection Service" -
    ➥DatabaseName $dbName
    $usageApplicationProxy = Get-SPServiceApplicationProxy | where{$_.Name -eq
    ➥"$FarmName Usage and Health Data Collection Service"}

    if($usageApplicationProxy.Status -eq "Disabled") {
        $usageApplicationProxy.Status = "Online";
        $usageApplicationProxy.Update();
    }
```

```
    Write-Host -ForegroundColor Green "Installing Usage and Health Data Collection
    ➥Service installed."
}

Function Rename-SQLDatabase {
    param (
            [string] $ServerName,
            [string] $SourceDb,
            [string] $DestDb
)

    $connection = New-Object System.Data.SqlClient.SqlConnection
    $command = New-Object System.Data.SqlClient.SqlCommand

    $connection.ConnectionString = "Server=$ServerName;Integrated Security=True;"

    $command.CommandText = "ALTER DATABASE [$SourceDb] SET OFFLINE WITH ROLLBACK
    ➥IMMEDIATE;ALTER DATABASE [$SourceDb] SET ONLINE;EXEC sp_renamedb [$SourceDb],
    ➥[$DestDb];"
    $command.Connection = $connection

    $command.Connection.Open();
    $command.ExecuteNonQuery();
    $command.Connection.Close();
}

Function New-SPPerformancePointApplicationAndProxy($AppPool, $DBServer, $FarmName) {
    Write-Host -ForegroundColor Yellow "Installing PerformancePoint Service..."

    $ppApp = New-SPPerformancePointServiceApplication -Name "$FarmName
    ➥PerformancePoint Services" -ApplicationPool $AppPool

    $temp = $ppApp.SettingsDatabase.split("\");
    $dbName = $temp[$temp.Length-1];

    $newDBName = $FarmName + "_PerformancePointServices"

    Rename-SQLDatabase -servername $DBServer -sourceDb $dbName -destDb $newDBName;
    Set-SPPerformancePointServiceApplication "$FarmName PerformancePoint Services" -
    ➥SettingsDatabase "$DBServer\$newDBName";

    New-SPPerformancePointServiceApplicationProxy -ServiceApplication "$FarmName
    ➥PerformancePoint Services" -Name "$FarmName PerformancePoint Services Proxy" -
    ➥Default
    Write-Host -ForegroundColor Green "PerformancePoint Service installed."

    Start-SPService "PerformancePoint Service"
```

```powershell
}

$serviceAppConfiguration = read-host "Would you like to configure SharePoint Service
➥Applications? (Y/N)"
if ($serviceAppConfiguration -eq "Y") {
    # Starting SP Timer Service
    Start-SPTimer

    $appPoolName = Read-Host "Please specify a name for ServiceApp application pool
    ➥(eg. ServiceAppPool)"

    $managedAccountName = Read-Host "Please enter service account (eg.
    ➥CompanyABC\sp_service)"
    $managedAccount = Get-SPManagedAccountByName $managedAccountName

    $appPool = Get-SPServiceApplicationPoolByName $appPoolName $managedAccount

    #$DatabaseServer = read-host "Preparing to join existing farm. Please specify the
    ➥name of your SQL Server";
    $FarmName =  Read-Host "Please enter your farm name";


    $decision = read-host "Would you like to install State Service Application?
(Y/N)"
    if ($decision -eq "Y") {
        New-SPStateServiceApplicationGroup $FarmName
    }

    $decision = read-host "Would you like to install Usage and Health Data Collec
    ➥tion Service Application? (Y/N)"
    if ($decision -eq "Y") {
        New-SPUsageApplicationAndProxy $FarmName
    }

    $decision = read-host "Would you like to install Access Services? (Y/N)"
    if ($decision -eq "Y") {
        Write-Host -ForegroundColor Yellow "Installing Access Services..."
        Start-SPService("Access Database Service")
        New-SPAccessServiceApplication -Name "$FarmName Access Services" -
        ➥ApplicationPool $appPool -Default
        Write-Host -ForegroundColor Green "Access Services installed."
    }

    $decision = read-host "Would you like to install Business Data Connectivity
    ➥Service? (Y/N)"
```

4

```
    if ($decision -eq "Y") {
        Write-Host -ForegroundColor Yellow "Installing Business Data Connectivity
        ➥Service..."
        Start-SPService("Business Data Connectivity Service")

        $dbName = $FarmName + "_BusinessDataConnectivityService"

        New-SPBusinessDataCatalogServiceApplication -Name "$FarmName Business Data
        ➥Connectivity Service" -ApplicationPool $appPool -databaseName $dbName

        Write-Host -ForegroundColor Green "Business Data Connectivity Service
        ➥installed."
    }

    $decision = read-host "Would you like to install Search Service? (Y/N)"
    if ($decision -eq "Y") {
        Write-Host -ForegroundColor Yellow "Installing Search Service..."

        $newAccount = Read-Host "Would you like to use $managedAccountName as the
        ➥search service account? (Y/N)"
        if($newAccount -eq "N") {
            $searchAccountName = Read-Host "Please enter search account (eg.
            ➥CompanyABC\sp_search)"
            $searchAccount = Get-SPManagedAccountByName $searchAccountName
        }
        else {
            $searchAccount = $managedAccount
        }

        if(-not (Get-SPServiceApplicationByType("Usage and Health Data Collection
        ➥Service Application"))) {
            $decision = Read-Host "Usage and Health Data Collection Service
            ➥Application needs to be installed to run Search Service. Would you
            ➥like to install
it now (Y/N)?"
            if ($decision -eq "Y") {
                New-SPUsageApplicationAndProxy $FarmName
            }
        }

        Configure-SPSearch $appPoolName $FarmName $searchAccount

        Write-Host -ForegroundColor Green "Search Service installed."
    }

    $decision = read-host "Would you like to install Excel Services? (Y/N)"
    if ($decision -eq "Y") {
```

```powershell
    Write-Host -ForegroundColor Yellow "Installing Excel Services..."
    Start-SPService("Excel Calculation Services")
    New-SPExcelServiceApplication -Name "$FarmName Excel Services" -
    ➥ApplicationPool $appPool -Default
    Write-Host -ForegroundColor Green "Excel Services installed."
}

$decision = read-host "Would you like to install Managed Metadata Service? (Y/N)"
if ($decision -eq "Y") {
    Write-Host -ForegroundColor Yellow "Installing Managed Metadata Service..."
    Start-SPService("Managed Metadata Web Service")

    $dbName = $FarmName + "_ManagedMetadataService"

    $MetaDataServiceApp = New-SPMetadataServiceApplication -Name "$FarmName
    ➥Managed Metadata Service" -ApplicationPool $appPool -DatabaseName $dbName
    $MetaDataServiceAppProxy = New-SPMetadataServiceApplicationProxy -Name
    ➥"$FarmName Managed Metadata Service Proxy" -ServiceApplication
    ➥$MetaDataServiceApp -DefaultProxyGroup
    Write-Host -ForegroundColor Green "Managed Metadata Service installed."
}


$decision = read-host "Would you like to install PerformancePoint Service? (Y/N)"
if ($decision -eq "Y") {
    Write-Host -ForegroundColor Yellow "Installing PerformancePoint Service..."

    $dbServer = Read-Host "Please enter the name of your database server (e.g.
    ➥""SQLSERVER"" OR ""SQLSERVER\INSTANCE"")"
    New-SPPerformancePointApplicationAndProxy $appPool $dbServer $FarmName

    Write-Host -ForegroundColor Green "PerformancePoint Service installed."
}

$decision = read-host "Would you like to install Secure Store Service? (Y/N)"
if ($decision -eq "Y") {
    Write-Host -ForegroundColor Yellow "Installing Secure Store Service..."
    Start-SPService("Secure Store Service")
    $dbName = $FarmName + "_SecureStore"
    $secureStoreServiceApp = New-SPSecureStoreServiceApplication -Name
    ➥"$FarmName Secure Store Service Application" -ApplicationPool $appPool -
    ➥DatabaseName $dbName -AuditingEnabled:$true
    New-SPSecureStoreServiceApplicationProxy -ServiceApplication
    ➥$secureStoreServiceApp -Name "$FarmName Secure Store Service Application
    ➥Proxy" -DefaultProxyGroup
    Write-Host -ForegroundColor Green "Secure Store Service installed."
```

4

```
    }

    $decision = read-host "Would you like to install Visio Graphics Service? (Y/N)"
    if ($decision -eq "Y") {
        Write-Host -ForegroundColor Yellow "Installing Visio Graphics Service..."
        Start-SPService("Visio Graphics Service")
        New-SPVisioServiceApplication -Name "$FarmName Visio Graphics Service" -
        ➥ApplicationPool $appPool
        New-SPVisioServiceApplicationProxy -Name "$FarmName Visio Graphics Service
        ➥Proxy" -ServiceApplication "$FarmName Visio Graphics Service"
        Write-Host -ForegroundColor Green "Visio Graphics Service installed."
    }

    $decision = read-host "Would you like to install Word Automation Services? (Y/N)"
    if ($decision -eq "Y") {
        Write-Host -ForegroundColor Yellow "Installing Word Automation Services..."
        Start-SPService("Word Automation Services")

        $dbName = $FarmName + "_WordAutomationServices"

        New-SPWordConversionServiceApplication -Name "$FarmName Word Automation
        ➥Services" -ApplicationPool $appPool -DatabaseName $dbName -Default
        Write-Host -ForegroundColor Green "Word Automation Services installed."
    }

    $decision = read-host "Would you like to start Microsoft SharePoint Foundation
    ➥Sandboxed Code Service? (Y/N)"
    if ($decision -eq "Y") {
        Write-Host -ForegroundColor Yellow "Configuring Microsoft SharePoint
        ➥Foundation Sandboxed Code Service..."
        Start-SPService("Microsoft SharePoint Foundation Sandboxed Code Service")
        Write-Host -ForegroundColor Green "Microsoft SharePoint Foundation Sandboxed
        ➥Code Service configure."
    }

    iisreset
}
    Write-Host -ForegroundColor Green "Installation completed."
— — — — — — — — — — — — — — — — — — — —·
```

Scripts like the ones previously displayed can be modified by administrators and customized as needed. The power of PowerShell is in this flexibility, because custom scripts can be used by administrators to build entire farms from scratch or simply perform everyday tasks.

For more information on using PowerShell with SharePoint 2010, refer to Chapter 7, "Leveraging PowerShell for Command-Line SharePoint Administration and Automation."

Understanding Scalability for SharePoint

The first step in scaling a SharePoint environment is to understand the level of usage it will receive, both presently and in the future. After the level of usage is determined, understanding which specific components can be extended is vital to structuring the system to match the desired user load. The key is to match SharePoint functionality to the specific identified need.

Mapping SharePoint Functionality to Business Needs

When deploying SharePoint, the primary concern for scalability is how many users will use the system. For departmental collaboration, the numbers may be small. For large, publicly accessible portals, on the other hand, the numbers could scale up quickly. Scaling a SharePoint implementation based on the number of users is simplistic but can be used as a starting point. In addition to total number of users, the following factors should be identified to more fully understand the load placed on a SharePoint server:

▶ Number of users

▶ Pages per user per work day

▶ Length of work day (hours)

▶ Type of work performed and level of office integration

▶ Size of document repositories

Collecting this information and understanding who will be accessing a SharePoint environment is the first step toward properly scaling the environment.

Gauging Content Growth

In addition to the amount of data that initially is loaded into SharePoint, an understanding of how fast that content will grow is critical toward properly scaling an environment. Running out of storage space a year into a SharePoint deployment is not an ideal situation. You need to understand how quickly content can grow and how to control this inevitable growth.

Proper use of site quotas in SharePoint is an effective way to maintain control over the size that a SharePoint database can grow to. Implementing site quotas as they are created is a recommended best-practice approach and should be considered in most situations. It is easy to bloat SharePoint with unnecessary data, and site quotas help local site administrators to make judicious use of their available space.

SharePoint's SQL database can grow in size dramatically, depending on how heavily it is used and what type of content is included in it. Use of the Remote BLOB Storage API, covered extensively in Chapter 9 can help to keep the size of content databases under control by taking documents out of the database and storing them in other file formats.

Scaling Logical SharePoint Components

The key to SharePoint's success is its capability to intelligently present information needed for each individual user, giving them quick and easy access to that information. SharePoint accomplishes this through various logical mechanisms that exist to help organize this content, structuring it in a way that pulls unstructured data together and presents it to the user. For example, a file server simply holds together a jumbling of documents in a simple file structure. Multiple versions of those documents further confuse the issue. SharePoint contains mechanisms to organize those documents into logical document libraries, categorized by metadata, which can be searched for and presented by the latest version.

In addition to the most obvious logical components, SharePoint enables sets of data to be scaled out to support groups of users. For example, by utilizing different site collections with their own unique sets of permissions, SharePoint can be configured to host different groups of users on the same set of machines, increasing flexibility.

Scaling Out with Site Collections

Building on the success of previous versions of SharePoint, SharePoint sites in SharePoint Foundation enable various teams or groups of users to have access to particular information relevant to them. For example, sites can be set up for each department of a company to enable them to have access to information pertinent to their groups.

Sites can be scaled out to support various site collections for each group of users. This enables the data to be distributed across a SharePoint environment logically, allowing a much larger population of users to be distributed across a SharePoint server environment. Each site collection can be administered by a unique owner designated within the site structure, similar to the one shown in Figure 4.1. This allows for security to be scaled out across a SharePoint site.

Scaling Out with Web Applications

SharePoint stores its data in SQL content databases but serves up access to that data via HTML and web services. The access to this data is served up to the user via the Windows Server Internet Information Services (IIS) service. IIS is composed of various logical structures known as *websites*, which are entry points to web content. Each website can be configured to point to various sets of information located on the web server or extended via SharePoint to be unique SharePoint web applications.

Utilizing unique web applications with SharePoint can help to further scale the functionality of an environment, allowing the flexibility to grant access to SharePoint using Secure Sockets Layer (SSL) encryption, or across different ports. In addition, deploying multiple virtual servers enables the use of multiple host headers for a SharePoint organization, such as sharepoint.companyabc.com, docs.companyabc.com, info.companyabc.com, sp.organizationa.com, and so on.

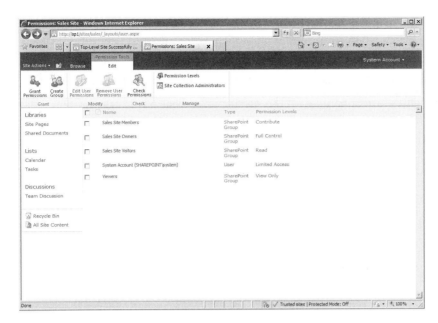

FIGURE 4.1 Scaling out with SharePoint 2010 sites.

Summary

Although SharePoint 2010 is deceptively easy to install, it is also a sophisticated product that can be complex to install and configure. Using techniques such as scripted installations using PowerShell, installation checklists, and scalability options can help to ensure the longevity of SharePoint architecture and can make it easier to grow a SharePoint 2010 environment.

Best Practices

▶ Create installation checklists to manage the installation process for a complex SharePoint 2010 environment.

▶ Use best practices for web applications, including configuring web applications for Kerberos security, Secure Sockets Layer (SSL) encryption, and load balancing using Windows NLB or hardware-based load balancers.

▶ Manage content growth through site quotas and monitoring solutions, such as System Center or third party products.

▶ Use site collections to scale SharePoint to varying groups with different security needs.

▶ Use IIS websites mapped to SharePoint web applications to manage varying types of web-based access to SharePoint sites, such as SSL-encryption or different host headers.

▶ Use a different SharePoint farm for the ultimate layer of security for a SharePoint environment, beyond what is provided by different site collections or web applications.

▶ Map SharePoint's functionality with the specific user needs of the organization.

## CHAPTER 5

Migrating from Legacy SharePoint to SharePoint Server 2010

Many organizations have existing SharePoint products and technologies deployed in production environments but are interested in taking advantage of the new features in SharePoint 2010. Many of these organizations have significant investments in the existing infrastructure, however, and need to ensure site functionality throughout the upgrade process.

SharePoint 2010 includes two built-in migration options that seem deceivingly simple, and the process itself is not actually complex. That said, the process is limited to migrations directly from SharePoint 2007, and some components will not migrate easily. In addition, the two Microsoft upgrade options are drastically different in approach, so it is important to explore the pros and cons of each option before making a decision.

This chapter covers upgrade and migration options from legacy versions of SharePoint to SharePoint 2010. Supported methodologies are compared, and the in-place and database attach options are listed and compared. In addition, advanced migration concepts and third-party migration options are explored.

Formulating a Migration Strategy

Migration from SharePoint 2007 to SharePoint 2010 for small environments is relatively straightforward and can be performed with minimal risk. For organizations with a complex or large SharePoint 2007 environment, however, migration to SharePoint 2010 can be a daunting task. Fortunately, the migration tools built into SharePoint 2010 enable a gradual migration approach, in which groups of sites are migrated slowly over time, allowing for reduced risk of failure or downtime and enabling administrators to test site functionality before finalizing individual site migrations.

The most difficult part of a migration subsequently becomes the validation portion, in which an assessment of existing SharePoint 2007 site functionality and whether it will migrate successfully is determined. This can be even more difficult for those environments with a heavy investment in third-party add-ons to SharePoint 2007. It is subsequently critical to formulate a migration strategy before beginning the process.

> **NOTE**
>
> There is no direct supported migration path to SharePoint 2010 from the 1.0 or 2.0 versions of SharePoint technologies, including SharePoint Portal Server 2001, SharePoint Portal Server 2003, SharePoint Team Services, or Windows SharePoint Services 2.0. The only way to migrate these environments to 2010 using Microsoft techniques is to first upgrade the servers and sites to SharePoint 2007, and then follow one of the migration paths demonstrated in this chapter.

Microsoft provides for two out-of-the-box upgrade options: the in-place upgrade and the database-attach options. Each options has its particular pros and cons, and it's important to understand first what each migration option is before committing to one or the other. No matter what option you choose, it is critical to test the migration process first before beginning.

Examining the In-Place Upgrade Scenario

The first and most straightforward option for upgrading to SharePoint 2010 is the in-place upgrade option. With this option, an existing SharePoint 2007 server is upgraded in place to SharePoint 2010. The advantage to this approach is that it is easy to perform and utilizes existing hardware and preserves custom farm settings such as Audiences or Search customization. The main disadvantage to this approach is that the hardware must be SharePoint 2010-capable and there is no going back when the migration starts.

The key to this approach is that the existing servers must be SharePoint 2010-compliant, which means they must be running the following minimum levels of OS and software:

▶ Windows Server 2008 x64 or Windows Server 2008 R2 x64.

▶ SQL Server 2005 x64, SQL Server 2008 x64, or SQL Server 2008 R2 x64 for the database.

▶ Service Pack 2 for WSS 3.0 and MOSS 2007, if using those products. For a list of other compatible upgrade versions of SharePoint, reference Table 5.1.

More on this option, including step-by-step instructions on how to perform an in-place upgrade, are provided later in this chapter.

Examining the Database Attach Scenario

The database attach upgrade process works off of a completely different concept. With this approach, you build the new SharePoint 2010 environment on completely different hardware and configure it to best practices. You have the option of completely rebuilding all farm aspects and can even have the new SharePoint environment serve as a farm target for multiple source farms of various versions (WSS, MOSS Standard, MOSS Enterprise). When the migration is ready to take place, it is done one content database at a time and is performed by attaching the database (or a restore of the database) to the new farm and upgrading it on that farm.

The significant advantage to this approach is that it is much more forgiving if there are errors, and it allows for easy fallback to the old farm if the migration fails. In addition, for larger and more complex environments, it allows for a phased-migration process, rather than the need to do a "big-bang" upgrade. The main disadvantage to this approach is that it migrates only content and does not migrate any farm settings, such as audiences or custom search settings. More on this scenario is presented in later sections of this chapter.

Examining Alternative Approaches and Third-Party Migrations

Although the in-place upgrade and database attach upgrade approaches are the only two direct Microsoft supported migration scenarios, various other approaches can be used, including the following:

▶ **Third-party migration tools**—These tools typically do not have limitations to what versions can be migrated from and also allow for splicing and splitting of site collections and content databases, something not supported in the Microsoft approaches. They also typically handle exceptions better.

▶ **STSADM exports or backups/restores**—Although STSADM, the command-line tool, can only export or back up/restore to the same version, it can be used to export SharePoint content to a farm of the same version level and then run the upgrade process on that farm. You can use this same concept with database restores as well.

▶ **Manual content move**—Some organizations simply prefer to build a new SharePoint 2010 environment and then show their users how to move content from the old farm to the new farm. This is particularly useful if there is a great deal of abandoned or useless data in the older farms.

Determining which approach to use is critical during the planning phase of an upgrade or migration project.

Planning for an Upgrade to SharePoint 2010

Before planning for an upgrade to SharePoint 2010, you must first examine the various supported upgrade scenarios and examine the existing environment using tools provided by Microsoft.

Understanding Supported Upgrade Scenarios

The in-place upgrade process or the gradual migration process has limitations to which versions of SharePoint can be migrated, and which version of SharePoint 2010 they can be migrated to. Table 5.1 indicates which versions of various SharePoint products can be upgraded directly using the in-place upgrade process provided by Microsoft.

TABLE 5.1   Supported Direct In-Place Upgrade Targets for Various SharePoint Versions

	SharePoint Foundation 2010	SharePoint Server 2010 Standard Edition	SharePoint Server 2010 Enterprise Edition
SharePoint Team Services			
SharePoint Portal Server 2001			
Windows SharePoint Services 2.0			
SharePoint Portal Server 2003			
Windows SharePoint Services 3.0 with SP2	X		
Microsoft Office SharePoint Server 2007 Standard Edition		X	
Microsoft Office SharePoint Server 2007 Enterprise Edition			X
Search Server 2008		X	X
Forms Server 2007		X	X
PerformancePoint Server 2007		X	X
Project Server 2007 with WSS 3.0 SP2 or MOSS 2007 SP2			X (with Project 2010)
SharePoint Foundation 2010		X	X
SharePoint Server 2010 Trial		X	X

As indicated in Table 5.1, the older versions of SharePoint are not supported for direct upgrade and must be first upgraded to a supported version if using the Microsoft tools. If this is not an option, third-party tools are available from major SharePoint manufacturers that enable direct upgrade between versions.

5

> **NOTE**
>
> If the source SharePoint 2007 farm is running SQL Server Express, it can only be upgraded to the equivalent SharePoint 2010 edition running with SQL Server 2008 Express Edition. To get around this issue, use the database attach upgrade process instead.

One exception to this list in terms of the database attach upgrade process involves WSS 3.0 migrations directly to SharePoint Server editions, which are supported on a database-by-database basis. In other words, you can take multiple WSS 3.0 farms, pull the content databases from those farms, and migrate their contents directly into a new SharePoint 2010 Server environment that has been freshly built. For more information about this option, see the "Examining the Database Attach Scenario" section of this chapter.

Assessing Site Migration Readiness with the Pre-Upgrade Check Tool

The most critical task that an administrator needs to perform before beginning a migration is to assess the state of the current site structure. Multiple factors can affect how a site migrates, so they need to be taken into account and tested in advance. Microsoft anticipated this when it created Service Pack 2 for SharePoint 2007 because SP2 includes a pre-upgrade check utility that enables administrators to check the readiness of their environment for upgrade to SharePoint 2010.

This pre-upgrade check runs as an extension to the STSADM command-line tool, included in the \Program Files\Common Files\Microsoft Shared\Web Server Extensions\12\BIN folder on a SharePoint 2007 Server (either WSS or MOSS). When an environment is completely upgraded to SP2, this tool can be run without risk because it is read-only and makes no modifications to any of the files on the server.

Run the pre-upgrade check by typing `stsadm -o preupgradecheck`, as shown in Figure 5.1.

The pre-upgrade check tool runs through a battery of tests and checks your environment for compliance with SharePoint 2010 variables. It produces a detailed report, such as the one shown in Figure 5.2, that outlines what areas of the existing farm are ready for upgrade, and which ones are in need of remediation before they can be upgraded.

Creating a Prototype Test Environment

As previously mentioned, it is critical to test the migration process in a lab environment. Doing so requires the current SharePoint 2007 environment to be restored onto a separate server, and then upgraded via either the gradual or in-place migration options described in this chapter. By doing this, the actual production environment remains untouched, and a full discovery of the types of issues that might be experienced during the migration can be uncovered.

It is ideal to have knowledge workers for each site test out the migrated site on the prototype server in advance. By giving the prototype server a different Fully Qualified Domain Name (FQDN), both the legacy 2007 site and the migrated 2010 version can co-exist so that functionality can be validated by the end users.

FIGURE 5.1   Running the pre-upgrade check tool in STSADM.

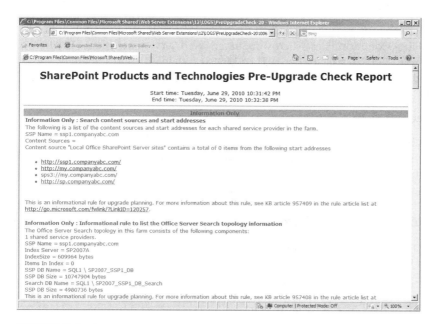

FIGURE 5.2   Viewing the Pre-Upgrade Check Report.

For example, if the sales department team site is normally accessed by https://sp.compa-nyabc.com/sites/sales, the prototype sales site that has been migrated can be accessed by http://sp-pilot.companyabc.com/sites/sales. This way, if there are errors experienced during the upgrade, they can be addressed in advance of the actual move.

Ideally, during this prototype phase, a hold would be placed on any type of serious site modification, such as custom web parts, SharePoint designer modification, and any types of activities that fit outside the scope of standard SharePoint document management functionality. This would limit the risk that a site customization made after the prototype server is built would cause issues not seen during the actual testing process.

SQL Database Upgrade Considerations

The database technology used by both SharePoint 2007 and SharePoint 2010 is Microsoft SQL Server, but x64-bit versions only, and only SQL Server 2005 SP3, SQL Server 2008, or (preferably) SQL Server 2008 R2. If the SQL database is upgraded, there is no effect on the SharePoint environment (aside from downtime from the migration process), and a SharePoint migration has no effect on a SQL server.

That said, some organizations use the opportunity afforded by a SharePoint environment to also migrate their SharePoint databases to SQL 2008 R2, which provides for the best set of options for SharePoint 2010, including PowerPivot functionality. This is typically done in scenarios where new hardware is utilized for the new 2010 environment.

Examining SharePoint 2010 Migration Paths

Although the SharePoint migration tools seem to enable only two types of migrations, there are actually several different approaches to migration that can be considered, depending on the needs of the environment. Some of the migration options enable migration to new hardware, whereas others reduce the risk of a migration approach by using multiple servers and migrating site by site.

Performing an In-Place Upgrade of a SharePoint Environment

The most straightforward path from SharePoint 2007 to SharePoint 2010 is to choose the in-place upgrade approach. This approach is typically used on small to mid-sized SharePoint deployments, because it involves an immediate upgrade of all site collections to SharePoint 2010, using the existing databases.

As previously mentioned, the main advantage to this migration approach is the simplicity of it and the fact that it preserves farm settings, such as Audiences. However, it is also the riskiest approach because it requires a full commitment to the upgrade process and, if it fails, the only way to recover is from backup.

Installing SharePoint 2010 Prerequisites

After the pre-upgrade check tool has run and you have remediated any potential noncompliant features, the first step toward upgrading a SharePoint 2007 environment is to install all those components that SharePoint 2010 requires as prerequisites. These components can be easily installed using the SharePoint 2010 media. When inserting the media, the autorun screen prompts for an option to install prerequisites. These install all necessary components that SharePoint 2010 requires directly on the box running SharePoint 2010. If the operating system is not Windows Server 2008 or Windows Server 2008 R2, or if the server is not x64 bit, you will immediately know at this point because the prerequisite installation process will fail.

If you need to manually install prerequisites, such as in the case when there is not Internet access to the system, the following roles and tools are required:

▶ Application Server Role

▶ Web Server (IIS) Role

▶ Microsoft SQL Server 2008 Native Client

▶ Hotfix for Microsoft Windows (KB976462)

▶ Windows Identity Foundation (KB974405)

▶ Microsoft Sync Framework Runtime v 1.0 (x64)

▶ Microsoft Chart Controls for Microsoft .NET Framework 3.5

▶ Microsoft Filter Pack 2.0

▶ Microsoft SQL Server 2008 Analysis Services ADOMD.NET

▶ Microsoft Server Speech Platform Runtime (x64)

▶ Microsoft Server Speech Recognition Language—TELE

▶ SQL 2008 R2 Reporting Services SharePoint 2010 Add-In

Running the Upgrade

After installing the prerequisites, simply click on the Upgrade button to start the in-place upgrade process. The wizard, as shown in Figure 5.3, will list information about the upgrade process and what is modified. After reviewing the information, click the Install Now button to initiate the process.

The installation process should continue without prompts until it finishes, at which point you can click Close. By default, it launches the Configuration Wizard, which continues the upgrade process and is required to continue.

Running the Configuration Wizard

The Configuration Wizard, when run, prompts you to upgrade the SharePoint farm immediately, as shown in Figure 5.4. Click Next to start the upgrade process. You will be prompted to restart the IIS and SharePoint services; click Yes when prompted to continue with the upgrade.

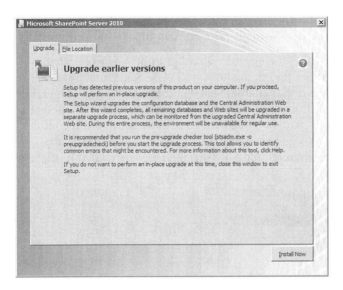

FIGURE 5.3   Performing an in-place upgrade.

5

FIGURE 5.4   Performing an in-place upgrade.

The one additional prompt that you receive when upgrading is a prompt that asks for a passphrase to be specified for the farm. This farm passphrase is used for all new server additions to the farm, so be sure to store it in a safe place. The purpose of the passphrase is to avoid servers being added to the farm without prior consent of an administrator.

After prompting for the farm passphrase, the upgrade wizard prompts you to decide how you want to handle the visual upgrade options, as shown in Figure 5.5. Visual upgrade is a useful process that Microsoft developed that enables SharePoint Site Collections to retain their 2007 look and feel, even though the backend has been migrated to SharePoint 2010. Visual upgrade works for either an in-place or a database attach upgrade and is recommended because it enables your users to get used to the new SharePoint 2010 visuals before they commit to them. More information on a visual upgrade is provided in the subsequent section of this chapter.

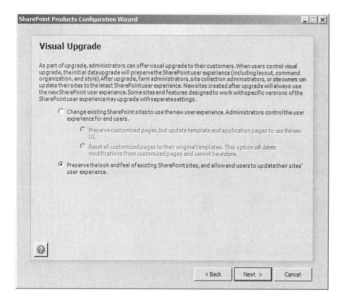

FIGURE 5.5   Selecting visual upgrade settings.

Choose a visual upgrade option from the list and click Next to continue. The Configuration Wizard gives you one more chance to review settings on the subsequent dialog box, before clicking Next to continue. The Configuration Wizard prompts you with a dialog box that states that you must install the same version of SharePoint 2010 on all members of the farm. Leave the Configuration Wizard, bring all farm members to the same point with the upgrade, and only then continue. If you continue before all farm members are upgraded, the upgrade process may fail.

The upgrade process may take a while, depending on your environment. When it is done, the Configuration Wizard prompts that the configuration is successful but that the upgrade itself is in progress. At this point, you can open the SharePoint Central Admin (SPCA) tool and view the upgrade status from the Upgrade and Migration area, as shown in Figure 5.6. When the upgrade is complete, this area lists a status of Succeeded.

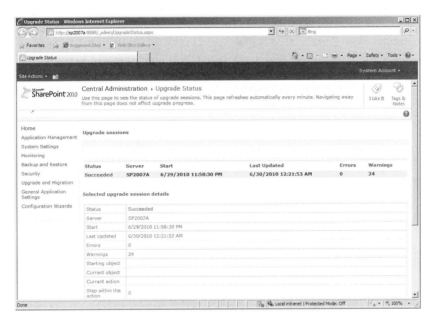

FIGURE 5.6   Viewing migration status.

If you choose to allow for previewing of the visuals first, you need to go through the visual upgrade steps, outlined in later sections of this chapter. Skip the "Performing a Database Attach Upgrade" section and proceed to the "Using Visual Upgrade" section for the next steps involved in the upgrade process.

Performing a Database Attach Upgrade

The database attach process is a much more risk-averse migration process and is subsequently more likely to be used for most environments. It has the significant advantage of enabling SharePoint administrators to create new best-practice SharePoint 2010 environments and simply move the databases to a new farm and upgrade them there.

Understanding the Steps to Perform a Database Attach Upgrade

The high-level steps involved with a database attach upgrade are as follows:

1. Create a new SharePoint 2010 farm to best practices and validate all functionality in the farm. Test functionality with a pilot on sample data and prepare users for the transition.

2. Back up the original SharePoint 2007 databases.

3. Set the SharePoint 2007 databases to read-only mode if the migration is expected to take a longer period of time.

4. Restore a copy of the SharePoint 2007 content databases to the SQL Server for SharePoint 2010. Attach the databases to SQL Server.

5. From the Manage Content Databases area of the SharePoint Central Admin tool on the SharePoint 2007 server, as shown in Figure 5.7, select each individual database.

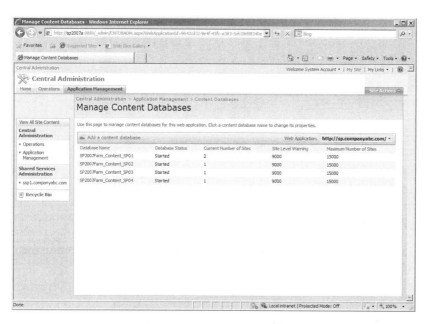

FIGURE 5.7   Selecting SharePoint 2007 content databases to be upgraded.

6. Check the remove content database box, as shown in Figure 5.8. Note that this will not delete the content database but simply detach it from SharePoint 2007.

7. Create a new web application in SharePoint 2010, if not already created, such as the one shown in Figure 5.9. For a seamless migration, this web application should match the name of the SharePoint 2007 web application. This new web application will be used to house the migrated databases.

8. In SharePoint Central Admin, on the new SharePoint 2010 server, be sure that there are no existing content databases in the newly created web application, as shown in

Figure 5.10. Depending on how you create the web application, there may be one created there by default. Simply remove it in advance of the migration.

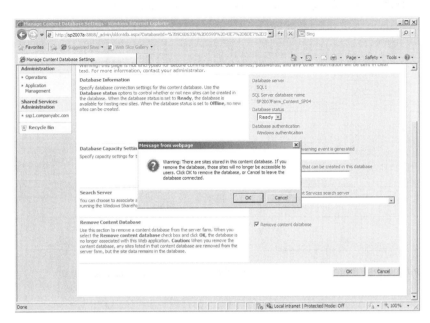

FIGURE 5.8   Detaching content databases from SharePoint 2007 so they can be upgraded.

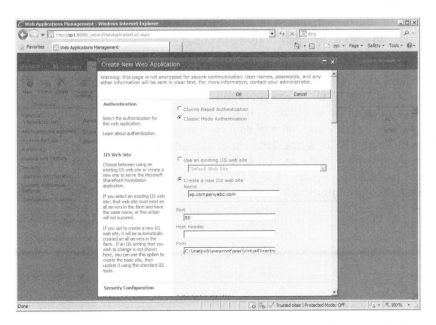

FIGURE 5.9   Creating a new web application for the migrated content databases.

FIGURE 5.10   Verifying that there are no content databases in the new web application.

9. From PowerShell, run commands to attach the content databases to the web applica-
   tion, as illustrated in Figure 5.11. You cannot add the databases from the GUI; they
   must be added either by the deprecated STSADM command-line tool or (preferably)
   PowerShell. When added, each database starts the upgrade process, also illustrated in
   Figure 5.11. You can watch the upgrade from the SPCA tool in the "Upgrade and
   Migration" section of SPCA.

The exact syntax to use when upgrading is Mount-SPContentDatabase –Name
DBNAME–DatabaseServer DBSERVER –WebApplication
http://yourwebapp.companyabc.com (where DBNAME, DBSERVER, and http://
yourwebapp.companyabc.com are all names of your databases, servers, and webapps,
respectively). Note in Figure 5.11 that one database has already been attached and
upgraded, and the second one is in the process of being upgraded. Depending on the size
of the database, this may take some time to upgrade. When a database is upgraded, it can
immediately be used, though until the Visual Upgrade process is done, it will still have the
same look and feel of the old site. For the visual upgrade process, refer to the subsequent
section of this chapter.

FIGURE 5.11   Attaching content databases and monitoring the upgrade process.

Using Visual Upgrade

The visual upgrade process can be used either with an in-place upgrade or a database attach upgrade, as previously mentioned. It enables the local site administrators to define when they would like to start using the new look and feel for SharePoint sites.

> **CAUTION**
>
> Visual upgrade is not available when upgrading My Site. When upgraded, My Site imme-diately assume the new SharePoint 2010 visuals.

Previewing the SharePoint 2010 Visuals in a Site

After migration, the site collection looks and feels exactly like a SharePoint 2007 site, assuming the option was chosen to keep the existing visuals temporarily during the upgrade process. Site administrators need simply to click on Site Settings to see the new visual upgrade option available to them, as illustrated in Figure 5.12.

When the visual upgrade action is chosen, administrators are given the dialog box, shown in Figure 5.13, which enables them to choose whether they want to keep using the previ-ous user interface, whether to preview the new interface, or whether to finalize and update the user interface. Be aware that when you update the user interface, there is no going back (without a restore), so be sure to properly test out the visuals and functionality before committing to the new visuals.

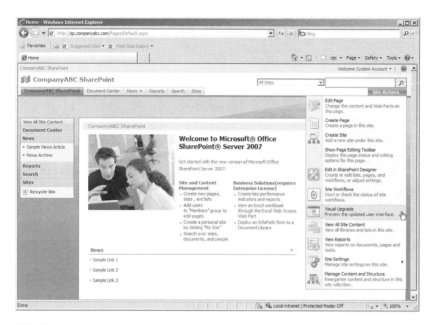

FIGURE 5.12   Choosing to preview the new SharePoint 2010 visuals on a migrated SharePoint 2007 site.

FIGURE 5.13   Choosing to preview the new SharePoint 2010 visuals on a migrated SharePoint 2007 site.

The new SharePoint 2010 visuals will then be shown for the individual site, as shown in Figure 5.14. You have the option at that point to click on Site Settings (which has moved to the left side, per SharePoint 2010 conventions) and commit the visuals after you are satisfied with the look and feel of the site.

FIGURE 5.14   Viewing and committing the new SharePoint 2010 visuals.

Repeat for any and all sites within the content database to commit the changes to SharePoint 2010 and make all sites adopt the new look and feel and added functionality.

Understanding the My Site Automatic Visual Upgrade

Unlike with standard content databases, when My Site content databases are upgraded, all visuals for SharePoint 2010 are automatically upgraded, as shown in Figure 5.15. It is subsequently doubly important to test out the upgrade process in a lab before running the upgrade in production.

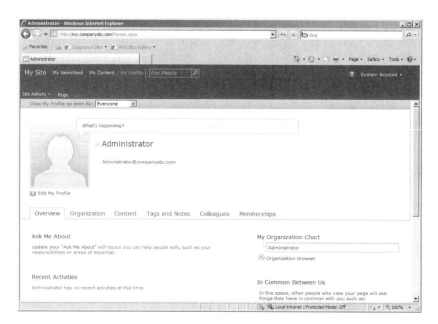

FIGURE 5.15   Viewing a migrated SharePoint 2007 My Site with the new SharePoint 2010 visuals.

Summary

SharePoint 2010 products and technologies give organizations an unprecedented amount of new features and capabilities. For those organizations with legacy SharePoint 2007 environments, the temptation to migrate quickly to SharePoint 2010 is strong. It is important to review migration options, however, as different migration approaches may not work for all organizations.

Choosing between the in-place upgrade or the database attach upgrade process is just one of the steps. Proper migration technique involves testing the selected process in a prototype lab environment and involving knowledge workers into a pilot of the migrated environment. Using these techniques, the overall risk of a SharePoint 2010 migration is greatly reduced, and the benefits of SharePoint's document management and collaboration platform can be more easily realized.

Best Practices

▶ Review the pre-upgrade scan results files and address issues documented by the tool before beginning the upgrade process.

▶ Perform the chosen migration technique in a prototype lab environment before running it in the production environment.

▶ Use the in-place upgrade process only for those environments that are smaller than 30GB and for those environments without a large amount of customized web parts or other complexities.

▶ Examine third-party and custom designed web parts for interoperability with SharePoint 2010, checking the Microsoft Software Development Kit for the types of code supported in a SharePoint 2010 environment.

▶ Reset unghosted sites to standard SharePoint site definitions where possible to ensure consistency across sites.

▶ Use the STSADM utility to export and import sites from one server to another for the creation of a prototype server or to support an advanced migration scenario.

▶ Use the visual upgrade process to ease the transition to the new SharePoint 2010 visuals.

▶ Consider the use of an application layer inspection-capable HTTP filter device such as TMG Server 2010 to provide for the ability to split HTTP traffic to multiple servers, thus enhancing the ability to migrate a single namespace to a new server using a phased approach.

CHAPTER 6

Managing and Administering SharePoint 2010 Infrastructure

IN THIS CHAPTER

▶ Operations Management with the SharePoint Central Administration Tool

▶ Administering Site Collections and Sites

▶ Using Additional Administration Tools for SharePoint

Administration of a SharePoint 2010 infrastructure can be complex and intimidating. Fortunately, the complexity of the SharePoint line of tools was simplified and streamlined within a comprehensive management tool known as the SharePoint Central Administration tool. It is subsequently important for a SharePoint administrator to become familiar with the tools and tasks available within the platform.

This chapter gives an overview of the SharePoint administrative tools, including a step-by-step look at all the major links and tasks included in the SharePoint Central Administration tool. Administration from the command line using PowerShell is covered in the subsequent Chapter 7, "Leveraging PowerShell for Command-Line SharePoint Administration and Automation." Considerable emphasis is placed on common tasks performed by administrators using the SharePoint Central Administration tool. In addition, this chapter takes a look at the other administration interfaces a SharePoint administrator may run into, such as the developer dashboard, the STSADM command-line tool, SQL Server Management Studio, and IIS Manager.

Operations Management with the SharePoint Central Administration Tool

The single most important tool to a SharePoint administrator is the SharePoint Central Administration tool (SPCA), shown in Figure 6.1. This tool, run on a dedicated IIS virtual server using a unique port (such as 14199), is installed on the first server in a farm. The tool can be invoked from the server console from the Start menu or, because it is web-based and is effectively just a SharePoint site collection within a dedicated web application, it can be invoked from any workstation. It is actually preferable from a security perspective to access the SharePoint Central Administration tool from a different workstation. If doing so, be sure to note what the hostname and port is for the SharePoint central web application when created.

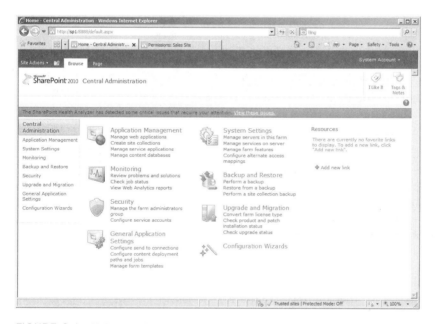

FIGURE 6.1   Using the SharePoint Central Administration tool.

NOTE

Although the default is to choose a custom port for the SharePoint Central Administration tool, it is recommended to instead change this to the default HTTPS port of 443, so that an SSL certificate can be easily added and a unique name for the SPCA tool can be used. For example, https://spca.companyabc.com would be an example of a best-practice way of accessing the SharePoint Central Administration tool from another workstation. This has the added advantage of enabling SPCA to be easily load balanced using network load balancing, either hardware-based or software-based, between two servers running the SPCA service.

The SPCA tool is divided into a home page, shown in Figure 6.1, which provides a launching point for some of the most commonly used tasks in SPCA. More detailed sets of tasks can be launched by clicking the links listed in the left pane of the page. These links take you to specific pages for each category of administration, including the following:

- ▶ Application Management
- ▶ System Settings
- ▶ Monitoring
- ▶ Backup and Restore
- ▶ Security
- ▶ Upgrade and Migration
- ▶ General Application Settings
- ▶ Configuration Wizards

Each of these categories and the tasks that can be performed within them are listed in subsequent sections of this chapter.

Administering Application Management Tasks in SPCA

The Application Management page, shown in Figure 6.2, contains those tasks directly related to the management of site collections, sites, web applications, and service applications. It is subsequently a page where an administrator can spend a great deal of time during the initial configuration of SharePoint 2010.

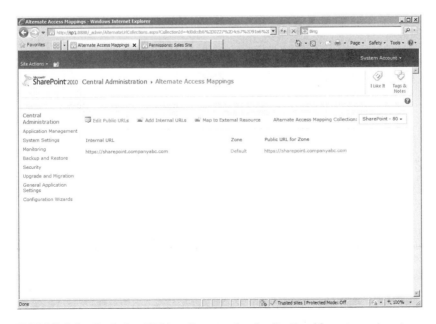

FIGURE 6.2 Exploring SPCA options on the Application Management page.

Web Applications

The first category on the page deals specifically with web applications and includes the following links:

▶ **Manage Web Applications**—Simply lists the web applications in the farm and their URLs and port. This area also enables the configuration of various web application settings.

▶ **Configure Alternate Access Mappings**—This highly important area controls Alternate Access Mappings (AAM), shown in Figure 6.3. AAMs are needed to indicate different server host header values for the machine. For example, in the diagram, http://intranet is the URL used to access the server internally, whereas https://share-point.companyabc.com is the URL used for external access. If an AAM is configured, SharePoint automatically translates all links to the host header value used by the client to access site content. This reduces the chance of links not working externally. For more information on configuring AAMs for remote access, reference Chapter 14, "Protecting SharePoint with Advanced Antivirus and Edge Security Solutions."

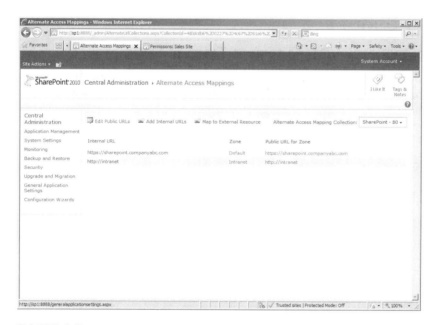

FIGURE 6.3   Using Alternate Access Mappings.

Site Collections

Within the second category on the Application Management page, labeled Site Collections, all the options for creating, deleting, and managing individual site collections are listed. Site collections provide the highest-level administrative object entity within SharePoint, with the exception of web applications and the farm. The links provided within the Site Collections category include the following:

▶ **Create site collections**—This link allows for the creation of new site collections from within SPCA, as shown in Figure 6.4. Site collections can be created from a default list of templates, or via custom templates created by the organization and added into SPCA using PowerShell or the STSADM command-line tool.

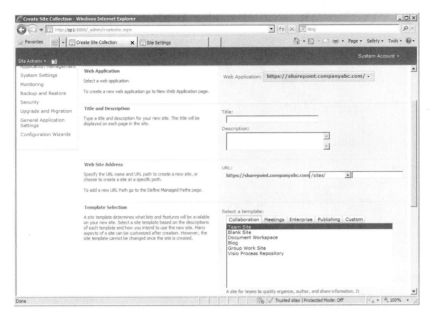

FIGURE 6.4   Creating new site collections.

▶ **Delete a site collection**—Enables an administrator to delete specific site collections. Note that when deleted, it is not easy to recover an entire site collection.

▶ **Confirm site use and deletion**—Leads to a page that enables the configuration of automatic site collection deletion of unused sites. This functionality is meant to help to control the growth of SharePoint content by removing site collections no longer in use and enables administrators to define warnings that are sent to site collection administrators.

▶ **Specify quota templates**—Enables administrators to create and modify quota templates for site collections. Individual size limits can be defined for site collections and applied to the individual site collections as they are created or at a later time. Site collection administrators are notified if their sites grow above a warning limit or if they are above the maximum size limit, which will result in new content not being added to the site.

▶ **Configure quotas and locks**—Takes the administrator to settings shown in Figure 6.5 that define whether a site collection is locked; effectively not allowing any content to be added because of the result of exceeding a template or simply because the content was locked into read-only mode for one reason or another.

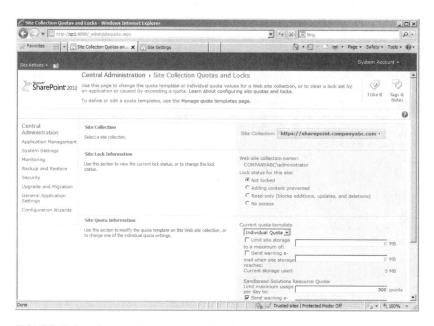

FIGURE 6.5   Viewing site quotas and locks.

▶ **Change site collection administrators**—Clicking this link in SPCA enables the administrator to define who the primary and secondary site collection administrators are for a site collection.

▶ **View all site collections**—All site collections within a specific content database can be viewed from within this link.

▶ **Configure self-service site creation**—Enables administrators to turn Self-Service Site Creation on or off for a web application. This concept enables users with the Use Self-Service Site Creation permission to create sites in defined URL namespaces. Be cautious when enabling this, because it can lead to a proliferation of sites within a site collection very quickly.

Service Applications

Within the third category on the Application Management page, labeled Service Applications, the tasks related to the critical service applications in SharePoint 2010 can be modified. For more detailed information about individual service applications, reference the chapters in which they are discussed. For example, for the Managed Metadata Service, refer to Chapter 22, "Managing Metadata and Content Types in SharePoint 2010," and for many other service apps, refer to Chapter 26, "Extending SharePoint 2010 with Excel Services, Access Services, and Visio Graphics Services."

▶ **Manage service applications**—This link takes administrators to the Service Applications page, shown in Figure 6.6. This page is the main administrative point to all the service applications, such as the Managed Metadata Service, PerformancePoint, Excel Services, and others.

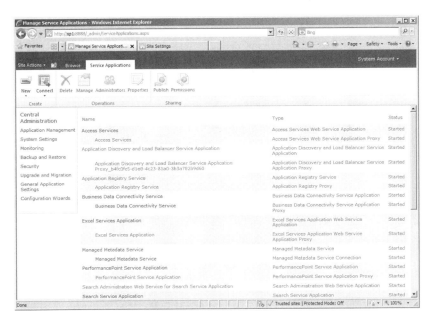

FIGURE 6.6   Viewing service applications within SPCA.

▶ **Configure service application associations**—Configuring service application associations enables them to be "tied" to an individual web application so that they can be used by the site collections within those web applications. Administrators can modify which web applications these service applications are tied to from within this interface.

▶ **Manage services on server**—This link takes administrators to the page shown in Figure 6.7, which enables individual services to be started or stopped on servers. Configuration information for those specific services can be accessed by clicking the blue links for services that enable settings to be modified.

Databases

Within the fourth category on the Application Management page, labeled Databases, all the tasks associated with SharePoint content databases are made accessible. This includes the following links:

▶ **Manage content databases**—This link presents a list of all content databases, similar to what is shown in Figure 6.8. As a side note, by modifying the maximum number of sites that can be created within a content database, you can control which content database a site collection is installed in. This can also be controlled from within PowerShell when creating a site collection.

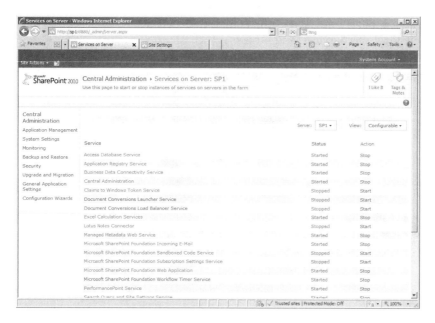

FIGURE 6.7   Modifying services on servers.

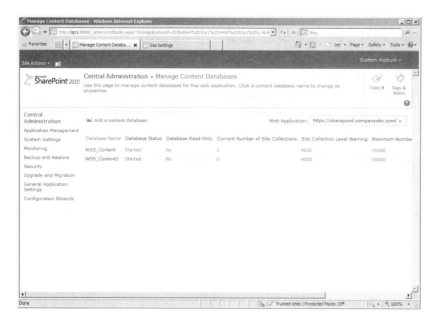

FIGURE 6.8   Administering content databases.

▶ **Specify the default database server**—The default database server used for all new databases can be specified in this section of SPCA. In addition, if using SQL Server authentication (not recommended) to connect to the SQL Server, the SA account and password can be designated here.

▶ **Configure the data retrieval service**—Data retrieval services such as OLEDB, SOAP Passthrough, CML-URL, or SharePoint Foundation can be enabled or disabled on individual web applications in this area of SPCA.

Administering System Setting Tasks in SPCA

The System Setting page, shown in Figure 6.9, consolidates tasks related to servers and the farm. This page is often referenced while setting up the infrastructure components of a farm during the initial configuration.

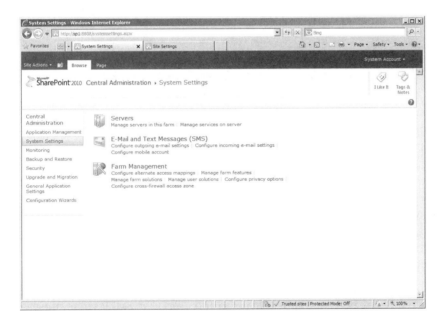

FIGURE 6.9   Viewing the system settings area of SPCA.

Servers

The first category on the page deals specifically with the servers used by SharePoint and includes the following links:

▶ **Manage servers in this farm**—Simply lists the servers in the farm, as shown in Figure 6.10, and which services they have running. This area also enables the removal of a specific server from the farm.

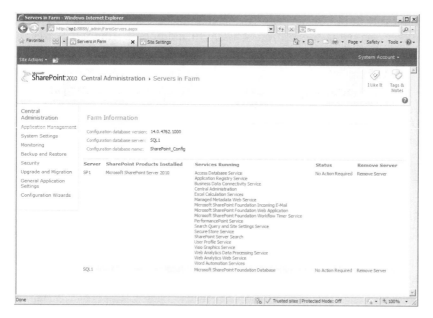

FIGURE 6.10   Managing servers in a farm.

▶ **Manage services on server**—This link takes you to the same services view as is linked to from the Application Management area of SPCA. It enables modification of individual service settings, and for starting and stopping services on individual servers.

Within the second category on the System Settings page, labeled E-Mail and Text Messages (SMS), all tasks related to messaging in the new environment, including outbound and inbound email to SharePoint, are displayed. For more detailed information on this area, including step by steps for enabling messaging functionality, refer to Chapter 16, "Configuring Email-Enabled Content, Presence, and Exchange Server Integration." This particular area includes the following links:

▶ **Configure outgoing email settings**—Enable an SMTP server to be defined that will be used to forward alerts and other emails to end users. The SMTP server must be configured to accept connections and allow relaying from the SharePoint server.

▶ **Configure incoming email settings**—Enables mail to be received directly by the SharePoint server and delivered into email-enabled distribution lists and email-enabled discussion groups. This powerful piece of functionality that integrates SharePoint with email platforms is also covered in detail in Chapter 16.

▶ **Configure mobile account**—If using a web-based text messaging service, it can be configured within this area of SPCA. This allows for monitoring alerts to be generated even if an outage in the email platform occurs.

Farm Management

Within the third category on the System Settings page, labeled Farm Management, tasks related to functions that apply to all servers in the farm are listed. These include the following:

▶ **Configure alternate access mappings**—Link to the same Alternate Access Mapping (AAM) list that the Application Management area linked to. AAMs define how links are translated when users access SharePoint using a specific FQDN, such as https://sharepoint.companyabc.com or http://sharepoint.

▶ **Manage farm features**—Enables specific farm features, such as the ones shown in Figure 6.11, to be turned on or off. It is the first area that should be referenced when trying to determine why a feature doesn't show up as an available option within a SharePoint site.

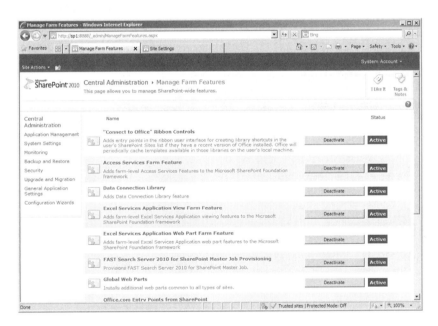

FIGURE 6.11   Managing farm features.

▶ **Manage farm solutions**—List any custom solutions, such as third-party products, which are added into the farm.

▶ **Manage user solutions**—Although not obvious from the title of its link, this area allows management of sandbox solutions and enables administrators to define whether specific solutions are blocked for end users.

▶ **Configure privacy options**—Private settings, such as whether to sign up for the Customer Experience Improvement Program (CEIP) or error reporting that is sent to Microsoft is defined in this area of SPCA. This area also enables administrators to define whether external web-based help is available for users within sites.

▶ **Configure cross-firewall access zone**—Defines which zone generates URLs that are generated when alerts and other messages are sent from the web application. For example, any administrator can define that all URLs are generated from the Internet zone settings, which have a URL of https://sharepoint.companyabc.com.

Administering Monitoring Tasks in SPCA

The Monitoring page in SPCA, as shown in Figure 6.12, deals with all built-in monitoring tools and concepts in SharePoint 2010. For more detailed information on configuring monitoring with SharePoint 2010, refer to Chapter 11, "Monitoring a SharePoint 2010 Environment."

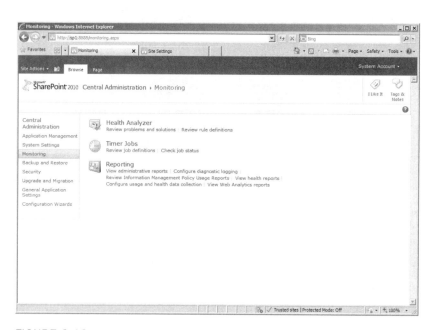

FIGURE 6.12   Exploring the monitoring options in SPCA.

The first category on the page deals specifically with the Health Analyzer, which determines the overall health of the SharePoint farm. This section includes the following links:

▶ **Review problems and solutions**—Takes the administrator directly to a list of configuration issues that exist in the farm based on the rules that are set up by the Health Analyzer.

▶ **Review rule definitions**—The rules that are run by the Health Analyzer can be modified in this area, as shown in Figure 6.13.

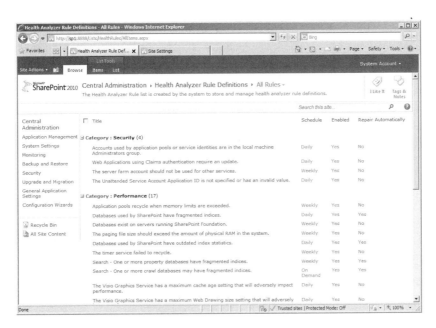

FIGURE 6.13   Modifying Health Analyzer rules.

Timer Jobs

Within the second category on the System Settings page are the tasks related to Timer Jobs. Timer Jobs, as shown in Figure 6.14, are extremely important services that run on a regularly scheduled basis to perform specific tasks, such as maintenance, analysis, synchronization, and other farm-critical tasks that must be performed on a regular basis. The links available within this field include the following:

▶ **Review job definitions**—This area of SPCA, as shown in Figure 6.14, enables the current timer job settings to be viewed and their schedules to be modified, if necessary.

▶ **Check job status**—The job status area of SPCA is where administrators should go to check on the status of current timer jobs and see when the next time they are scheduled to run.

Reporting

Within the third category on the Monitoring page, labeled Reporting, are links to all those administrative areas directly related to reporting, including diagnostic logs, usage reports, and health reports. The following key links are included in this area:

▶ **View administrative reports**—This area focuses on those reports that are related to administrative tasks. For example, search reports, such as the one shown in Figure 6.15, can be accessed from within this area.

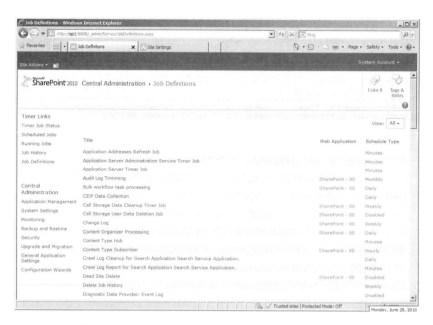

FIGURE 6.14   Exploring Timer Jobs.

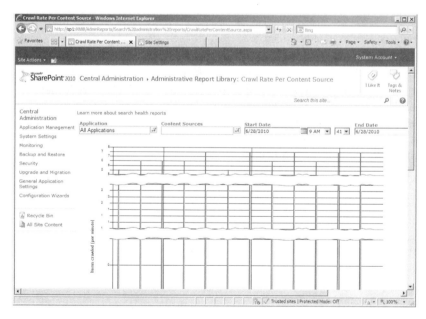

FIGURE 6.15   Accessing search reports.

▶ **Configure diagnostic logging**—Diagnostic logs are not turned on by default in SharePoint 2010, but can be enabled from within this area of SPCA. Logs can be generated for each category of service, as shown in Figure 6.16. In addition, settings related to event log flood protection and trace logs can be modified in this area. It is highly recommended to place all logs on a separate volume from the drive where SharePoint binaries and the OS are installed to avoid running out of disk space.

FIGURE 6.16   Configuring diagnostic logging.

▶ **Review information management policy usage reports**—These types of reports are used for information management policy reports, which are related to Information Rights Management and Data Leak Prevention (DLP), concepts discussed in more detail in Chapter 17, "Safeguarding Confidential Data in SharePoint 2010."

▶ **View health reports**—Health reports, such as the one shown in Figure 6.17, provide information such as what pages are the slowest, and who are the top active users in a site.

▶ **Configure usage and health data collection**—This area is critical because it allows for the configuration of the usage data logs, which can determine what areas of SharePoint are being used. It also enables the location of the usage logs to be set. As with all logs in SharePoint, it is highly recommended to store these on a separate data partition than SharePoint and the OS are installed on.

▶ **View web analytics reports**—Web analytics reports, such as the one shown in Figure 6.18, can determine top visitors to pages, number of page views, and other useful metrics in the SharePoint environment.

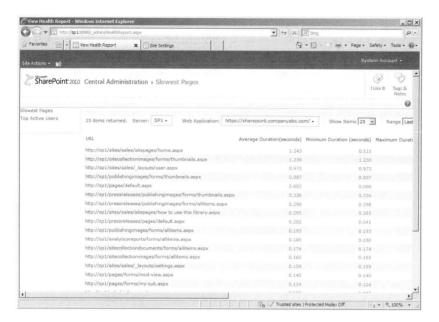

FIGURE 6.17   Viewing health reports.

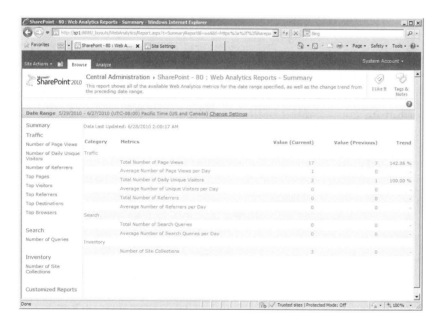

FIGURE 6.18   Viewing web analytics reports.

Reviewing Backup and Restore Settings in SPCA

The Backup and Restore page in SPCA, as shown in Figure 6.19, contains all relevant links that provide for integrated backup and restore functionality. This includes old options such as farm backup and restore, and new options such as granular backups. For detailed information on these options, refer to Chapter 10, "Backing Up and Restoring a SharePoint Environment."

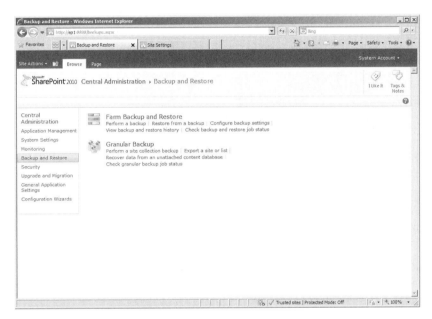

FIGURE 6.19   Viewing the Backup and Restore page in SPCA.

Farm Backup and Restore

Within the first category on the Backup and Restore page, labeled Farm Backup and Restore, the following links are included:

▶ **Perform a backup**—Enables administrators to perform a full farm backup or a backup of individual components in a farm using the wizard shown in Figure 6.20. This can back up all components needed to restore a farm, including content databases and indexes.

▶ **Restore from a backup**—Enables restores of the farm or farm components from the backups performed using the previous area of SPCA.

▶ **Configure backup settings**—Enables the number of backup and restore threads to be chosen and a default backup file location to be set.

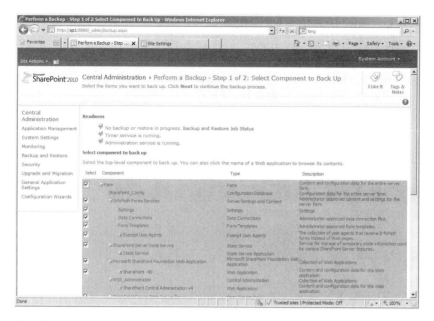

FIGURE 6.20   Backing up the farm using SPCA.

▶ **View backup and restore history**—History of backup and restore jobs can be viewed in this area of SPCA.

▶ **Check backup and restore job status**—Enables currently running backup and restore jobs to be viewed in real time.

Granular Backup

Within the second category on the Backup and Restore page, labeled Granular Backup, the options to back up individual site collections or subcomponents to site collections are provided. This type of functionality was available in SharePoint 2007 but required use of the command-line STSADM tool and was not an option within the GUI.

▶ **Perform a site collection backup**—Enables an entire site collection to be exported to a full-fidelity flat file copy that can be exported to a different location within the farm, to the same location, or to a new location in a different farm.

▶ **Export a site or list**—Enables content within a site collection to be exported using the settings shown in Figure 6.21. Note that these type of exports are not full fidelity, and some settings such as individual document permissions can be lost using the export option.

▶ **Recover data from an unattached content database**—This option, new in SharePoint 2010, is powerful, because it enables content to be recovered out of databases that are not attached to a SharePoint farm, although they do need to be attached to a SQL Server.

FIGURE 6.21   Exporting content using SPCA.

▶ **Check granular backup job status**—Enables administration to check on the status of an existing granular backup job.

Reviewing Security Settings in SPCA

The Security page in SPCA, as shown in Figure 6.22, contains all security-related items available for configuration in SPCA. For a detailed discussion on security in SharePoint 2010, refer to Chapter 15, "Implementing and Validating SharePoint Security."

Users

Within the first category on the Security page, labeled Users, all security settings related to not only users, but also specific user groups are listed. This includes the following:

▶ **Manage the farm administrators group**—Enables full farm administrators to be defined.

▶ **Approve or reject distribution groups**—Distribution groups automatically added by the Directory Management Service are listed in this area if the farm is configured to require administrator approval for new distribution groups. The Directory Management Service is enabled from within the incoming email settings in SPCA.

▶ **Specify web application user policy**—Permission for an individual user or a group to override security within a web application can be set in this area. For example, the Search Crawling Account can be configured to have read access to all content within the entire web application to enable it to be crawled.

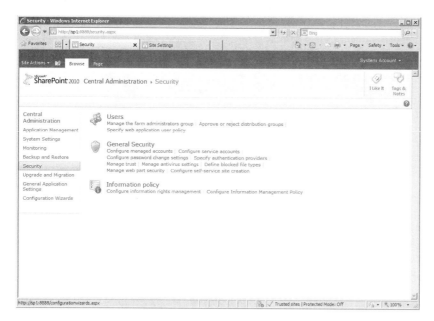

FIGURE 6.22   Viewing the security items in SPCA.

General Security

Within the second category on the Security page, labeled General Security, all other security settings that don't fit into either the first or third category are listed, including the following:

▶ **Configure managed accounts**—This area is highly useful for SharePoint admins, because it allows for the concept of a managed account to be configured. A managed account is a service account that can be set to automatically have its password changed, as shown in Figure 6.23. Managed accounts can be set for all SharePoint service accounts, such as the Crawl account, Search account, accounts for \service applications, and App Pool identity accounts.

▶ **Configure service accounts**—Enables specific services in Windows Server to be updated with the credentials of a specific managed account used as the service account. This enables services that run with the credentials of a user to be automatically updated per best practices.

▶ **Configure password change settings**—Enables administrators to determine what the individual settings for password changes are, such as who is notified via email of the changes and how many seconds to wait before notifying services of the change.

▶ **Specify authentication providers**—Enable administrators to define more than one authentication directory to use to gain access to SharePoint content, as shown in Figure 6.24. This complex topic is covered in great detail in Chapter 13, "Deploying SharePoint for Extranets and Alternative Authentication Scenarios."

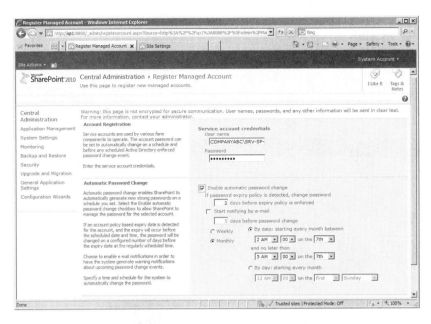

FIGURE 6.23   Creating a new managed account in SPCA.

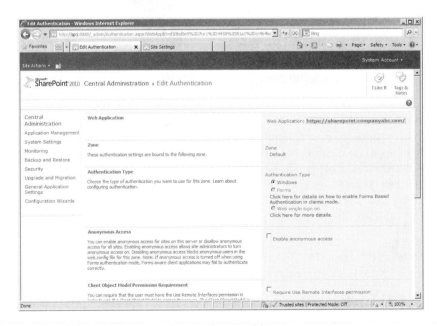

FIGURE 6.24   Modifying authentication providers.

▶ **Manage trust**—Within this area, different farms can be "trusted," allowing for their content to be intermingled with the farm and allowing for sharing of information between the farms. The trust relationships to other farms must be set up using PKI certificates and requires a common trusted root certificate when creating the trust, as shown in Figure 6.25. Trusts are required to consume information from another farm.

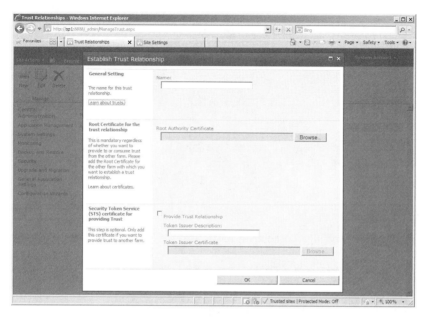

FIGURE 6.25   Adding a trust to a different farm.

▶ **Manage antivirus settings**—Antivirus settings are provided in SPCA as part of the built-in antivirus Application Programming Interface (API). Note that just because the API is there does not mean that antivirus functionality is available out-of-the-box. To enable antivirus, a supported antivirus product, such as Microsoft's Forefront Protection 2010 for SharePoint, must be installed. For more information on the antivirus settings in SharePoint and using antivirus products for SharePoint, refer to Chapter 14, "Protecting SharePoint with Advanced Antivirus and Edge Security Solutions."

▶ **Define blocked file types**—The default list of file type extensions that are blocked in SharePoint is defined in this area. It can be modified as necessary.

▶ **Manage web part security**—The security settings related to web parts, such as whether users can create connections between web parts, are listed in this area.

▶ **Configure self-service site creation**—Also linked to from the Application Management area of SPCA, enables specific users with the proper rights to create their own subsites.

Information Policy

Within the third category on the Security page, labeled Information Policy, information about enabling Information Rights Management (IRM) to enable document libraries to be secured using Active Directory Rights Management Services (AD RMS) is provided. For more information on IRM in SharePoint and AD RMS, refer to Chapter 17.

▶ **Configure information rights management**—Enables IRM settings to be enabled or disabled within SharePoint, depending on whether AD RMS is already deployed within the AD forest or whether SharePoint should manually address the server, as shown in Figure 6.26.

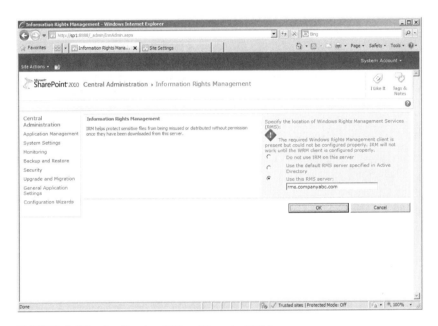

FIGURE 6.26   Configuring IRM settings in SPCA.

▶ **Configure information management policy**—Individual IRM policies for SharePoint, such as policies for labels, barcodes, auditing, and retention, can be defined within this area.

Reviewing Upgrade and Migration Settings in SPCA

The Upgrade and Migration page in SPCA, as shown in Figure 6.27, contains all settings related to an upgrade of SharePoint and also includes some links to useful information such as the patch status of systems in a farm. For detailed information on upgrading or migrating to SharePoint 2010, refer to Chapter 5, "Migrating from Legacy SharePoint to SharePoint Server 2010."

FIGURE 6.27   Viewing the upgrade and migration options in SPCA.

Upgrade and Patch Management

Within the only category on the Upgrade and Migration page, labeled Upgrade and Patch Management, the following links are included:

▶ **Convert farm license type**—Enables sites to input a license key to upgrade them from a standard license key to an enterprise license key, which would give them access to enterprise features in SharePoint 2010.

▶ **Enable enterprise features**—When an enterprise key has been enabled, enterprise features can be enabled from within this area. For a farm with an enterprise key enabled from the beginning, these settings are grayed out.

▶ **Enable features on existing sites**—For sites that were provisioned with standard edition features, the enterprise feature set can be enabled on them from within this area.

▶ **Check product and patch installation status**—This area, shown in Figure 6.28, provides useful information on the exact version number of all components on individual servers.

▶ **Review database status**—This area, useful only during a database attach upgrade, enables administrators to check on the upgrade status of individual databases.

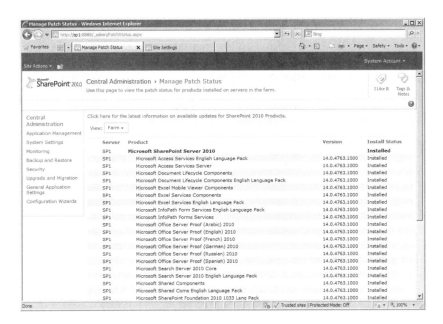

FIGURE 6.28   Checking patch status in SPCA.

▶ **Check upgrade status**—This final area is only used during an upgrade and is used to monitor the status of existing upgrade sessions.

Reviewing General Application Settings in SPCA

The General Application Settings page in SPCA, as shown in Figure 6.29, is perhaps the most complex of the various areas within SPCA. It includes all other settings in SPCA that didn't fit well into other categories, such as Content Deployment, Site Directory, InfoPath Forms Services, and others.

External Service Connections
Within the first category on the General Application Settings page, labeled External Service Connections, the following links are included:

▶ **Configure send to connections**—Enables administrators to choose whether to allow hosted site subscriptions to set up connections to sites outside their subscription. These settings are done on a per web application basis.

▶ **Configure document conversions**—As shown in Figure 6.30, enable administrators to define whether documents such as infopath forms, word documents, or XML pages can be converted to HTML pages so they can be viewed by browsers. A document conversions server must first be set up from within the services on servers area of SPCA for this to work properly.

InfoPath Forms Services
Within the second category on the General Application Settings page, labeled InfoPath Forms Services, all settings related to InfoPath Forms Services, a valuable tool that allows

for custom forms to be created and used in SharePoint, are discussed. This includes the following settings:

> **Manage form templates**—Displays the default form templates used by InfoPath Forms Services, such as the ones shown in Figure 6.31.

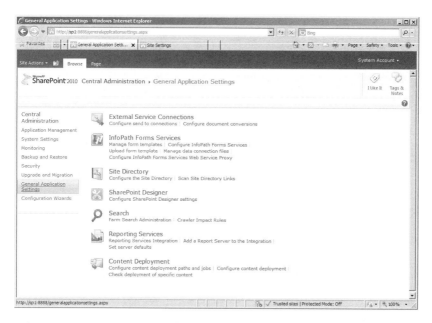

FIGURE 6.29   Viewing the general application settings in SPCA.

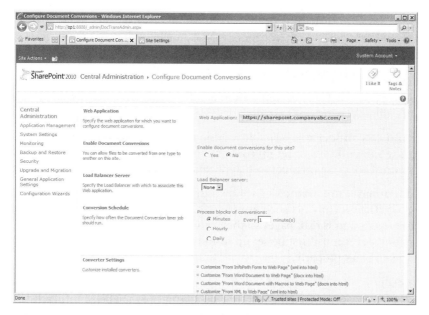

FIGURE 6.30   Configuring the document conversions service.

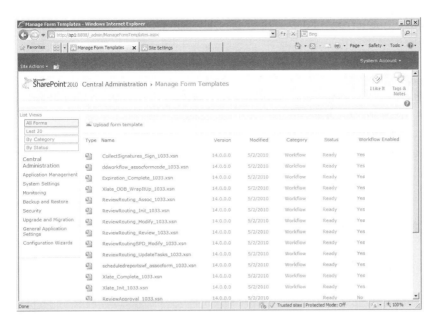

FIGURE 6.31   Using default form templates for InfoPath Forms Services.

▶ **Configure InfoPath Forms Services**—Settings unique to InfoPath Forms Services can be configured from within this area of SPCA, including whether the service is enabled for use by users within the farm.

▶ **Upload form template**—New form templates can be uploaded using this area of SPCA.

▶ **Manage data connection files**—Data connection files used with InfoPath can be uploaded using this interface.

▶ **Configure InfoPath Forms Services Web Service Proxy**—If a proxy is used between InfoPath Forms Services forms and web services, this functionality can be enabled in this area.

Site Directory

Within the third category on the General Application Settings page, labeled Site Directory, settings relating to the legacy site directory service are provided. The site directory was a lesser-used feature in older versions of SharePoint that would dynamically list all sites within a specific farm. If upgrading from SharePoint 2007, these settings will be relevant. If starting from scratch with SharePoint 2010, the site directory is not a recommended feature, and even though these settings show up in SPCA, you will not immediately see the site directory when creating new sites. It can be added if needed, but it is not recommended because it has been officially deprecated by Microsoft in SharePoint 2010:

▶ **Configure the Site Directory**—Enables the Site Directory Path to be created and what type of Site Creation Metadata is required.

▶ **Scan Site Directory Links**—Enables the legacy Site Directory to be scanned for broken links.

SharePoint Designer

Within the fourth category on the General Application Settings page, labeled SharePoint Designer, a single link is included, as follows:

▶ **Configure SharePoint Designer settings**—This area, shown in Figure 6.32, allows for SharePoint Designer access to be turned on or off for an individual site collection. Because SharePoint Designer is quite powerful and can cause problems for the uninitiated, some administrators turn it off, at least initially.

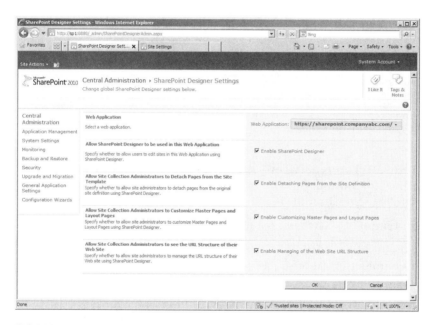

FIGURE 6.32   Enabling SharePoint Designer access within a web application.

Reporting Services

Within the fifth category on the General Application Settings page, labeled Reporting Services, settings related to running SharePoint together with a SQL Server Reporting Services instance are listed. This includes the following:

▶ **Reporting Services Integration**—Provides for the ability to turn on Reporting Services integration and to define the settings of the Reporting Services server.

▶ **Add a Report Server to the Integration**—Enables a specific report server to be designated within the farm.

▶ **Set Server Defaults**—When Reporting Services has been enabled, this area enables for specific server defaults for the farm to be set.

Content Deployment

Within the sixth and final category on the General Application Settings page, labeled Content Deployment, all settings related to Microsoft's concept of content deployment are listed. Content deployment is a one-way push of site content from one farm to another, typically done to publish content from internal farms to extranet farms or to push content out to remote locations. The settings related to content deployment in SPCA include the following:

> ▶ **Configure content deployment paths and jobs**—Focuses on setting up the individual content deployment jobs and paths used by those jobs.

> ▶ **Configure content deployment**—Takes administrators to a page shown in Figure 6.33, where content deployment can be enabled or disabled for the farm.

FIGURE 6.33   Enabling content deployment.

> ▶ **Check deployment of specific content**—Used to check on the status of content deployment jobs.

Using the Configuration Wizard's Page in SPCA

The final page, as shown in Figure 6.34, has one link that takes administrators to the wizard that can be used to configure the SharePoint farm for the first time, or to enable individual service applications. This wizard is covered in more detail in Chapter 3, "Installing a Simple SharePoint Server 2010 Farm."

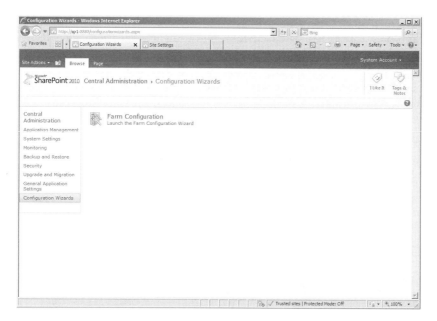

FIGURE 6.34   Viewing the SPCA launch link for the Farm Configuration Wizard.

You need to explore the various options and areas within the SharePoint Central Administration tool and understand how to perform certain administrative tasks. Combined with a good knowledge of PowerShell, SPCA is one of the most important tools available for the SharePoint administrator.

Administering Site Collections and Sites

Administration of individual site collections is different from administration of the backend of SharePoint. Indeed, Microsoft broke these two administrative tasks into two areas to enable the site collections to be administered by the people "closer to the ground" with SharePoint, typically the ones who use it on a regular basis for document management and collaboration.

These administrators have the ability to perform their own set of administration that affects only their specific site collection. The administrative tasks that they can perform are outlined in this section of the chapter, and apply to site collections created within SharePoint Foundation or full SharePoint Server 2010. These sets of administration options, as shown in Figure 6.35, are not visible to standard site members that do not have admin access to the site but are available to each site administrator, by clicking on the Site Actions link and selecting Site Settings.

Each administrative tasks is organized within the Site Settings tool by category, with categories such as Users and Permissions and Look and Feel. For more information on administration of site collections and site settings, refer to Chapter 21, "Designing and Managing Pages and Sites for Knowledge Workers."

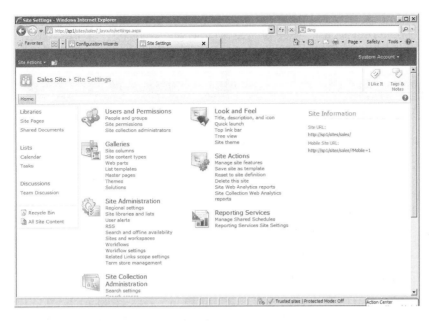

FIGURE 6.35   Administering SharePoint sites.

Using Additional Administration Tools for SharePoint

Although the vast number of administrative tools are stored within either the SharePoint Central Admin tool and individual Site Settings Administration, there are some additional tools that can be used by SharePoint administrators to fully administer a SharePoint environment. These include the critical PowerShell scripting tool, the legacy command-line STSADM tool, and specialty admin tools such as the IIS Manager and the SQL Server Management Studio.

Command-Line Administration of SharePoint Using the STSADM Tool

The STSADM tool has a long history with SharePoint products and technologies. Indeed, the acronym itself refers to SharePoint Team Services (STS) administration, which was the 1.0 version name of the SharePoint Foundation product, originally released with older version of the FrontPage (now SharePoint Designer) web authoring tool.

With SharePoint 2010, the STSADM tool is still used and supported, but Microsoft is switching focus of command-line administration to its PowerShell tool, which now supports more than 500 commandlets specifically built just for SharePoint. Administrators should first learn how to use PowerShell before using STSADM, because it is the preferred method of administering SharePoint. More information on PowerShell administration for SharePoint can be found in Chapter 7, "Leveraging PowerShell for Command-Line SharePoint Administration and Automation."

It's not intuitive to find the STSADM tool, unfortunately, because it is buried in the C:\Program Files\Common Files\Microsoft Shared\web server extensions\14\BIN folder on a SharePoint front-end server, where C:\ is the drive where SharePoint was installed.

TIP

It is convenient to add the C:\Program Files\Common Files\Microsoft Shared\web server extensions\14\BIN folder to the PATH statement on a SharePoint server so that STSADM can be run from any location in the command prompt window.

STSADM can create sites, delete sites, back up sites, restore sites, add users, remove users, change timer job intervals, change roles, and perform many other tasks. You should review the entire list of options available.

Working with the Internet Information Services Manager Tool

Occasionally, some administration of the Internet Information Services (IIS) application is required that cannot be performed using the SharePoint Central Admin tool. This includes installing the Secure Sockets Layer (SSL) certificates and changing authentication settings. The IIS Manager tool, as shown in Figure 6.36, can be used for this functionality and can be invoked by clicking on Start, All Programs, Administrative Tools, and Internet Information Services (IIS) Manager.

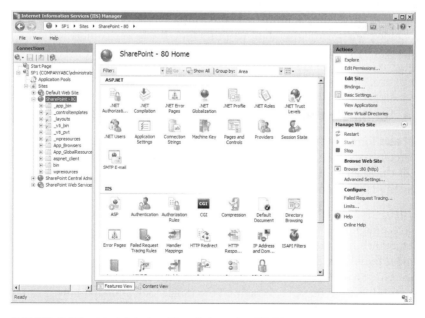

FIGURE 6.36   Administering SharePoint using IIS Manager.

Some SharePoint administration tasks can only be performed from within IIS Manager, including IP address assignment for web applications, SSL certificates, bindings, and some authentication settings. It is subsequently critical to become familiar with this tool for administration of a SharePoint 2010 environment.

SQL Server Administration for SharePoint

Administration of the SharePoint databases needs to be performed using the SQL Server Management Studio with SQL Server 2005, SQL Server 2008, or SQL Server 2008 R2. The SQL Server Management Studio, as shown in Figure 6.37, is discussed in more detail in Chapter 9, "Managing and Maintaining SQL Server in a SharePoint Environment."

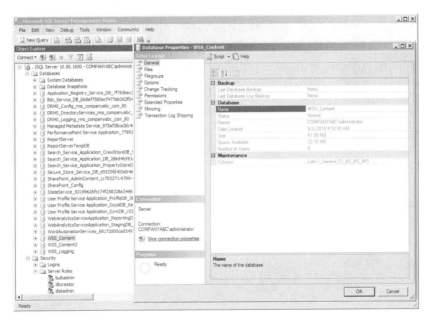

FIGURE 6.37   Administering SharePoint using SQL Server Management Studio.

Summary

Administration of SharePoint products and technologies can be complex, but fortunately Microsoft has centralized the vast number of administrative functions into a small number of highly powerful tools. Familiarity with these tools, and in particular with the SharePoint Central Administration tool, is subsequently a must for a SharePoint administrator.

In addition to the SharePoint Central Administration tool, powerful command-line administration using PowerShell and the legacy STSADM tool is available, and database and IIS-specific administration tools provide for additional administrative functionality. Through the use of these tools, administration of a SharePoint environment becomes more streamlined and capable.

Best Practices

▶ Become familiar with all the tasks in the SharePoint Central Administration tool.

▶ Let individual site administrators become more aware of the site settings administration options that are available in each site.

▶ Enable usage analysis processing to get a better idea of how sites are used and which ones are more popular.

▶ Consider the use of auto-site deletion for stale sites to reduce the overhead on the environment generated by unused sites.

▶ Use the IIS Manager tool for SSL certificate generation and to change authentication settings on individual IIS websites used by web applications in SharePoint.

▶ Use PowerShell for command-line administration, and only use the legacy STSADM tool for specific scenarios when legacy command-line functionality is needed.

▶ Review the powerful options in the PowerShell or the STSADM command-line tool, but be cautious about using them because they do not warn before making changes.

## CHAPTER 7

Leveraging PowerShell for Command-Line SharePoint Administration and Automation

Microsoft originally introduced Windows PowerShell in 2003 as an automation scripting engine to help administrators use various products across the Microsoft stack. Unlike other command-line tools that accept and return text, PowerShell works with .NET Framework objects, which enables it to be more flexible for administration of bulk changes and automation.

With the release of SharePoint 2010, Microsoft released 500+ PowerShell commandlets (cmdlets) designed to help automate and administrate SharePoint environments. These commandlets enable administrators to administer a SharePoint 2010 environment entirely from the command line, if needed. Indeed, SharePoint 2010 administration is positioned as PowerShell-first rather than GUI-first, and many tasks can only be performed from the command line. It is subsequently critical that SharePoint administrators have at least a basic understanding of PowerShell and how it can be used to administer a SharePoint farm.

This chapter focuses on introducing PowerShell to SharePoint administrators. It focuses first on a general overview of how PowerShell works, and then branches off to demonstrate how specific PowerShell commandlets can automate and administer SharePoint. Specific examples of common SharePoint administration tasks in PowerShell are illustrated.

Understanding Windows PowerShell Concepts

Before understanding how to use PowerShell to manage SharePoint, an administrator must first understand how PowerShell functions and must conceptualize the concepts used with PowerShell.

Getting Started with Windows PowerShell

PowerShell is available on all new Microsoft operating systems, and administrators can begin learning PowerShell even when SharePoint 2010 is not installed. To make sure that the latest version of PowerShell is installed, check the Microsoft PowerShell scripting center (http://technet.microsoft.com/en-us/scriptcenter/default.aspx). All the examples in this book were written with PowerShell 2.0.

To start working with PowerShell, go to Start, All Programs, Accessories, Windows PowerShell and run Windows PowerShell. This starts the PowerShell shell that can be used for typing PowerShell commands and executing scripts. The default PowerShell shell is shown in Figure 7.1.

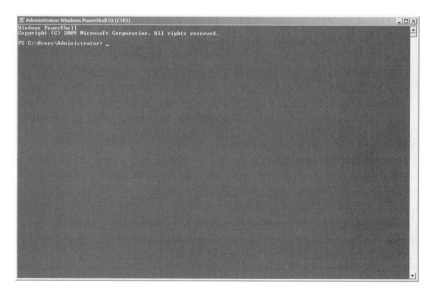

FIGURE 7.1   Viewing the default PowerShell shell on Windows 2008 Server.

On a computer with SharePoint installed, a SharePoint 2010-branded PowerShell shell with preloaded SharePoint cmdlets is installed. To start this shell, go to Start, All Programs, Microsoft SharePoint 2010 Products, SharePoint 2010 Management Shell. The shell also supports both standard command-line commands and the legacy STSADM command-line tool.

Using PowerShell to Display "Hello World!"

A common task performed when learning a new language is how to display "Hello World!". Creating such an application with PowerShell is simple. Type the following into a shell (you can omit lines starting with #. Everything after # is a comment) and press Enter:

```
# To comment in PowerShell use a Hash tag followed by your comments.
Write-Host "Hello World!" # you can also put comments after your command
```

PowerShell scripts can also be saved to a file and executed. Save this Hello World sample to HelloWorld.ps1. Use the standard command-line cd command to navigate to folder in which HelloWorld.ps1 is saved. To execute the script, type the following to the shell:

```
.\HelloWorld.ps1
```

Using the Integrated Scripting Environment

PowerShell comes with an integrated scripting environment to ease the creation and testing of scripts and functions. The scripting environment is available in Start, All Programs, Windows PowerShell 2.0, Windows PowerShell ISE. PowerShell ISE is shown in Figure 7.2.

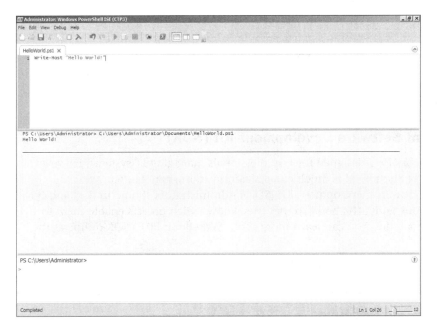

FIGURE 7.2 Viewing the "Hello World" sample from within the PowerShell-integrated scripting environment.

Before running any PowerShell cmdlet, make sure you have loaded the appropriate snap-in. The following code checks if SnapIn has been loaded and loads it if necessary:

```
if((Get-PSSnapin | Where {$_.Name -eq "Microsoft.SharePoint.PowerShell"}) -eq
➡$null) {
Add-PSSnapin Microsoft.SharePoint.PowerShell;
```

However, if you will be running these samples from the SharePoint 2010 Management Shell, the SharePoint PowerShell snap-in will be preloaded for you, and you can bypass this step.

Site Collections, Sites, and Webs

Cmdlets for SharePoint implement a different naming convention from the one used in the user interface. Table 7.1 shows the names of the most important SharePoint UI objects and the names of their respective GUI objects.

TABLE 7.1   Overview of the Most Important
SharePoint Objects Naming Conventions

Object Name in UI	Object Name in PowerShell
Web Application	SPWebApplication
Site Collection	SPSite
Site	SPWeb

Most of the samples in this chapter reference the preceding given objects, and you need to understand the difference between the two naming conventions.

The SharePoint Software Development Kit (SDK)

PowerShell is a technology designed for IT professionals managing IT systems. However, the management of SharePoint is much easier if administrators are familiar with the SharePoint 2010 Software Development Kit (SDK): Administrators should understand how SharePoint functions under the hood so that they know which objects enable them to retrieve certain properties. You can learn more about SharePoint 2010 SDK online at the following URL:

http://msdn.microsoft.com/en-us/library/ee557253(office.14).aspx

Get-Command and Get-Help

PowerShell comes with numerous cmdlets, Microsoft released more than 500 just for SharePoint, and this number grows with each new release or service pack. Memorizing all these commands would be a challenge.

There are two cmdlets that come to the rescue and help administrators understand what the individual commandlets are. Type the following in your SharePoint PowerShell shell:

`Get-Command`

This command lists all available SharePoint commands. Because there are so many cmdlets, they cannot fit on one screen. To check only specific sets of commands related with one object—for example, Site—type the following:

`Get-Command *Site*`

The preceding command lists all SharePoint cmdlets that have Site in their name. Depending on your SharePoint version, you will probably get the following or similar results, as shown in Figure 7.3.

FIGURE 7.3   Viewing the results of **Get-Command** cmdlet in SharePoint 2010 Management Shell.

As you can see, commands usually start with a verb (get, set, backup, and so on) and end with a noun. All the commands listed in Figure 7.3 enable you to work with SharePoint sites collections either for retrieving properties (Get- commands) or modifying site collection properties with Set- commands.

Most SharePoint commands require input before you can run them. In case you run a command without all the required properties, you will be prompted to enter these. To familiarize yourself with a PowerShell cmdlet, type the following:

```
Get-Help Get-SPSite
```

This command can give you detailed help for the `Get-SPSite` cmdlet. You can also type the preceding command with the following parameters: `-examples` or `-detailed` to check out more info on this command. SharePoint cmdlets are well documented and provide a great learning starting point.

The First SharePoint Cmdlet

The easiest way to start working with SharePoint cmdlets is to start the SharePoint 2010 Management Shell. On a computer with SharePoint 2010 installed, go to Start, All Programs, Microsoft SharePoint 2010 Products, SharePoint 2010 Management Shell. The shell loads; then type the following command into the command prompt:

```
Get-SPSite
```

The preceding command lists all site collections in the current SharePoint farm. Sample results are shown in Figure 7.4.

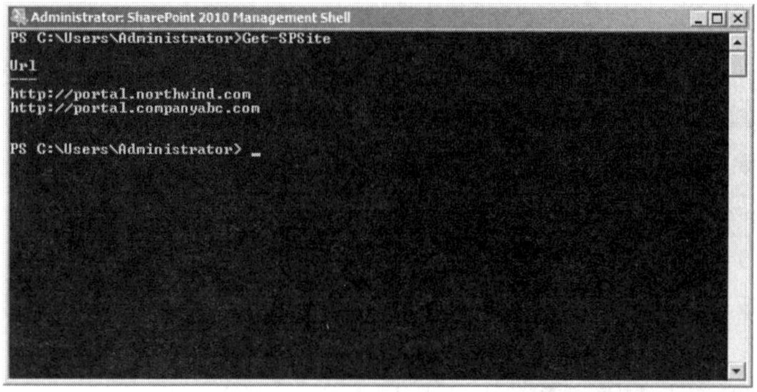

FIGURE 7.4   **Get-SPSite** cmdlets displays a list of SharePoint site collection URLs.

Verbs and Nouns

Every built-in PowerShell cmdlet is composed of a verb and noun (Verb-Noun)—for example, `Get-SPSite`. The verb part of a cmdlet indicates an operation that will be performed, and the noun indicates the object on which the operation will be performed. The `Get-SPSite` command gets a `SPSite` object (SharePoint site collection object).

The other common PowerShell operations (verbs) are `Set-` (modifies object), `Remove-` (deletes object), and `New-` (creates a new object).

Most SharePoint cmdlets come with these four verb-noun combinations. However, some objects might have more or less cmdlets depending on the object type—for example, the SPSite object also comes with Backup-, Move-, and Restore- cmdlets.

Working with Variables, Function, and Cmdlets

You can use PowerShell variables to store results from any executed command. The following example demonstrates how to use variables:

```
#$SiteCollection = Get-SPSite "http://portal.companyabc.com"
#$SiteCollection.Url
#$SiteCollection.Owner
```

The preceding given command saves site collection (from http://portal.companyabc.com) to a variable $SiteCollection; the variable can then be used to retrieve properties. The preceding example shows how to retrieve Url and Owner properties and display them in the shell.

The value stored to $SiteCollection is a SharePoint-specific .NET Framework object: SPSite and exposes all available properties as in any other .NET language.

To learn more about SharePoint 2010 SDK, see the following URL:

http://msdn.microsoft.com/en-us/library/ee557253(office.14).aspx

PowerShell Command Piping

In real life, people use pipes to transfer goods (for example, oil) from one end to another. PowerShell pipes are similar because they enable you to easily transform, modify, or pass the result of one cmdlet to another.

Let's say we want to list all site collections in a SharePoint farm. Get-SPSite cmdlet displays all the site collections, but in large farms it might returns hundreds or thousands of results. If Get-SPSite is combined with a filter command (over pipe), it will return only specific site collections that require attention.

```
Get-SPSite ¦ Where {$_.Url -eq "http://portal.companyabc.com"}
```

By using the pipe "¦", we see results (all site collections) of the Get-SPSite cmdlet that are passed to the Where pipe, which dictates that only site collections whose URL equals to http://portal.companyabc.com will be released to the next cmdlet in pipeline.

The preceding example has only one pipe, but additional pipes could be used:

```
Get-SPSite ¦ Where {$_.Url –like "*portal*"} ¦ Sort RootWeb ¦ Select RootWeb, Url
```

The preceding command lists all the sites collections that contain the word portal in their URL and then sorts them by RootWeb property and displays the results in table format with two columns RootWeb and Url.

Figure 7.5 shows the results of running the preceding code in the SharePoint 2010 Management Shell.

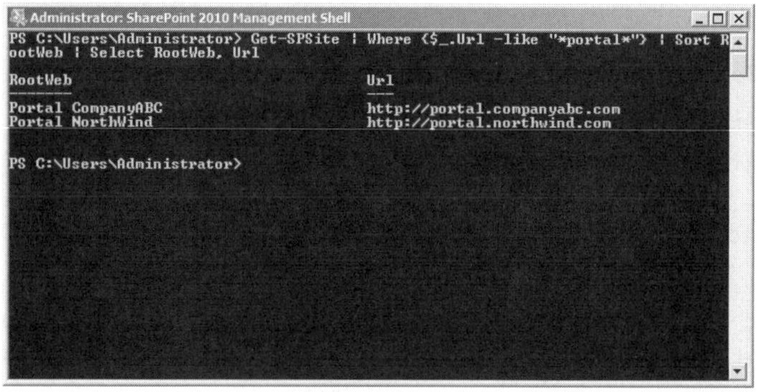

FIGURE 7.5   PowerShell returns a list of site collections with a word **portal** in the URL.

Formatting Results

Results retrieved from PowerShell cmdlets are usually displayed in a tabular form but can be further customized by adding the `format` command. Typical `format` commands are `Format-List`, `Format-Table`, and `Format-Wide`.

```
Get-SPSite ¦ Select RootWeb, Url, Owner ¦ Format-Table
```

The preceding command will list all the site collections and display results in table format. (We selected `RootWeb`, `Url`, and `Owner` properties of site collection to be displayed in the table.)

In addition to formatting results, you can choose a different output destination than a default one (shell screen). One of the useful output destinations is `GridView`:

```
Get-SPSolution ¦ Select * ¦ Out-GridView
```

The preceding command displays all installed SharePoint solutions in a `GridView` format, as shown in Figure 7.6. If you do not have installed solutions, you could combine `Out-GridView` with other cmdlets, such as `Get-SPSite`.

PowerShell—The New STSADM

With the release of SharePoint 2010, PowerShell becomes the most important tool for SharePoint administration automation. Every administration operation is first delivered for PowerShell, and some operations (for example, advanced customization during installation, multitenancy administration, and so on) are available via PowerShell only. The built-in cmdlets have much more options than Central Administration UI and STSADM commands.

FIGURE 7.6   Displaying results of PowerShell cmdlet in a **GridView** format.

Administrators can still combine all three interfaces; an administrator that only periodically needs to create a single site collection should probably still use Central Administration, but PowerShell should be the first choice when it comes to administration and automation.

SharePoint Administration with PowerShell

In this section, we discuss some of the common usage scenarios when you should use PowerShell.

The Naming of PowerShell Cmdlets

As previously mentioned, the naming of PowerShell cmdlets differs from the ones you got used to in the SharePoint Central Administration interface and is much similar to STSADM and API naming. Here are the most commonly used cmdlets in this chapter:

▶ `Get-WebApplication`—Returns all SharePoint web applications

▶ `Get-SPSite`—Returns all site collections

▶ `Get-SPWeb`—Returns all SharePoint sites in a given site collection

Retrieving Site Collections and Sites with PowerShell

One of the most common scenarios when you use PowerShell is retrieving sites collections and sites. To retrieve the list of site collections, simply type **Get-SPSite** in the Shell.

To retrieve the list of all SharePoint sites in a site collection, `Get-SPSite` needs to be combined with `Get-SPWeb`. For example, type the following:

Get-SPSite ¦ Get-SPWeb

This command lists all site collections in a SharePoint farm and then lists all the websites in each site collection.

In case you need to list format or all object properties, type

Get-SPSite ¦ Select *

Your PowerShell shell lists all the site collections with all the associated properties.

Modifying Site Collection Properties with PowerShell

Administrators can use PowerShell to easily modify all the properties of any PowerShell object.

Let's consider the following scenario. An administrator needs to add user CompanyABC.com\John as a secondary administrator for all site collections. This is an ideal example of how PowerShell can help to automate SharePoint administration. To achieve the goal, type the following command:

`Get-SPSite ¦ Set-SPSite –SecondaryOwnerAlias "CompanyABC.com\John"`

In the preceding example, we use `Get-SPSite` to get the list of all the site collections and then combine that with the `Set-SPSite` cmdlet that sets a `Secondary Owner` value to "CompanyABC.com\John".

To verify that the cmdlet completed successfully, run the following command that will display the owner and secondary owner for each site collection:

`Get-SPSite ¦ Select RootWeb, Url, Owner, SecondaryContact`

Working with Solutions and Features

One of the most frequent tasks that administrators perform on SharePoint farms is solution and feature management. Previously, in SharePoint 2007, administrators couldn't install solutions without calling STSADM commands. In SharePoint 2010, this has not changed much; you still can use STSADM to install custom solution, but there are dedicated PowerShell cmdlets that can help you further automate this procedure.

Deploying a Custom Solution with Features

Let's consider the following scenario: A custom solution needs to be deployed to CompanyABC SharePoint Portal. The solution has two features: a content type and custom web part, as shown in Figure 7.7.

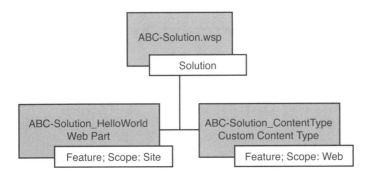

FIGURE 7.7   The structure of custom ABC-Solution. It contains two features: a web part **HelloWorld** and a custom **ContentType**.

Here is the series of steps you need to do to install the ABC feature to a SharePoint environment.

The first step of this procedure is to install the solution from the file system to central solution farm store. Use this command (use the path where you have a .wsp file):

```
Add-SPSolution "C:\My-Solutions\ABC-Solution.wsp"
```

When the command installs the solution, it will be visible in the Central Administration, Solution Management. You need to deploy the solution via the central administration user interface or with the following PowerShell code:

```
Install-SPSolution "CompanyABC_Solution.wsp" -AllWebApplications -GACDeployment -
➡Force
```

The preceding command deploys solutions to all web applications (-AllWebApplications parameter) and also enables custom code to be deployed to Global Assembly Cache (GAC) via the –GACDeployment parameter. If the solution already exists, it will be overwritten (-Force).

To activate features on individual site collection, use the following code. The ABC solution has two features, and each needs to be enabled individually:

```
Enable-SPFeature "ABC-Solution_HelloWorld" -Url "http://portal.companyABC.com"
Enable-SPFeature "ABC-Solution_ContentType" -Url "http://portal.companyABC.com"
```

In the custom `ABC-Solution`, the `HelloWorld` web part is scoped as a site collection (Site) feature, and the `ContentType` is scoped as a site-level (web) feature. To activate it on every site in your site collection, run the following command:

```
Get-SPSite "http://portal.companyABC.com" ¦ Get-SPWeb ¦ ForEach-Object {Enable-
➥SPFeature "ABC-Solution_ContentType" -Url $_.Url}
```

To remove these features and solution, you must call commands in reverse order: First deactivate the feature, uninstall the solution, and then remove it. To perform these operations, type the following:

```
Disable-SPFeature "ABC-Solution_HelloWorld" -Url "http://portal.companyABC.com" -
➥confirm:$false
Disable-SPFeature "CompanyABC-Solution_ContentType" -Url "http://portal.compa
➥nyABC.com" -confirm:$false

Uninstall-SPSolution "ABC-Solution.wsp" -confirm:$false -AllWebApplications:$true
Remove-SPSolution "ABC-Solution.wsp" -confirm:$false
```

PowerShell Backup and Restore Options

Backups can now be completely controlled via a series of cmdlets that perform backups of the SharePoint farm, site collection, and configuration database.

Every cmdlet comes with a `restore` command. SharePoint 2010 also introduced commandlets that provide the ability to export and import site collections, web applications, sites, or lists.

Automating Site Collection Backup and Restore

To perform a backup of an individual site collection, type the following:

```
Backup-SPSite "http://portal.companyABC.com" -path "C:\Backups\portal.dat" -force
```

The command in the preceding example backs up a site collection at the given url to the designated path. Before running this cmdlet, make sure this path (for example, `C:\Backup`) exists. In case there is a previous backup file at this location, use the `–force` parameter to overwrite an existing backup file.

To restore the site collection, type the following:

```
Restore-SPSite "http://portal.companyABC.com" -path "C:\Backups\portal.dat" -force
➥-confirm:$false
```

There are two parameters that must be used for silent site collection restore. `-force` ensures any existing site collection at http://portal.comapanyabc.com will be overwritten and `-confirm:$false` suppresses the overwrite confirmation dialog. By suppressing the confirmation, you can easily automate a restore operation.

Exporting SharePoint Sites and Content

In SharePoint 2010, Microsoft introduced a new ability to export and import SharePoint objects. These new operations enable administrators to more easily move content between different site collections. During import and export operations, administrators can control which content will be transferred and how versions will be affected by the move.

Here is a sample for exporting a site:

```
Export-SPWeb "http://portal.companyABC.com/Team-Site" –path "C:\Exports\Team-
➥Site.dat"
```

The syntax to export a list is similar, but the list path, relative to site path, must be passed as -ItemUrl parameter:

```
Export-SPWeb "http://portal.companyABC.com/Team-Site" –path "C:\Exports\Doc-
➥Lib.dat" -ItemUrl "/Doc-Lib"
```

When exporting lists and libraries, associated workflows and alerts will not be exported along with the content. In addition, item-level permissions will not be maintained.

Sometimes a business might ask for a snapshot of SharePoint for archiving or compliance purposes, and now PowerShell comes to the rescue. The cmdlet `Export-SPWeb` enables administrators to control versions that will be exported to an export file.

To export content of a document library, use the same code as previously given. By using optional parameter –IncludeVersions, you can choose to export: `LastMajor`, `CurrentVersion`, `LastMajorAndMinor`, or `All`.

Importing Exported Content

Export operations can be performed via central administration but import is only available via PowerShell. Before importing, you need to create an empty site in your site collection. A new site can be created via UI or PowerShell, but make sure you use the same site template as the site that was exported.

The following command lists all installed site templates:

```
Get-SPWebTemplate
```

To create a site with a desired template, use the following cmdlet (in this case, a site based on a blank site template will be created):

```
New-SPWeb -url "http://portal.companyABC.com/New-Site" -Template "STS#1"
```

To import a document library, type the following:

```
Get-SPSite "http://portal.companyABC.com/New-Site" ¦ Import-SPWeb –path
➥"C:\Exports\Doc-Lib.dat" –force –UpdateVersions Overwrite
```

The preceding example imports a document library that was previously exported to a file. –Force parameter ensures that existing data will be overwritten, and –UpdateVersions instructs command to overwrite all existing versions. There is also an append switch (versions will be appended to existing versions).

Monitoring SharePoint Databases and Site Collection Usage

To monitor SharePoint databases, first use the following commandlet to retrieve the list of databases:

```
Get-SPWebApplication ¦ Get-SPContentDatabase ¦ Select WebApplication, Name, Server,
➡¦ Format-Table
```

The preceding command displays all SharePoint web applications available in this farm, along with their respective database names and SQL server name.

To check the current size (in bytes) of each site collection, use the following cmdlet:

```
Get-SPSite ¦ Select RootWeb, Url,
@{Name="Size"; Expression={"{0:N2} GB" -f ($_.Usage.Storage/1E9)}},
@{Name="Storage Warning"; Expression={"{0:N2} GB" -f
➡($_.Quota.StorageWarningLevel/1E9)}},
@{Name ="Storage Max"; Expression={"{0:N2} GB" -f
➡($_.Quota.StorageMaximumLevel/1E9)}} ¦ ConvertTo-HTML ¦ Out-File
➡"C:\Temp\SiteUsage.html"
```

The sample might look complicated but actually gets all the site collections and formats the output to make it easy to read. Here are a few notes:

▶ SPSite.Usage property is a complex object, and to retrieve storage usage we had to construct an expression.

▶ A similar expression was used to retrieve quota properties.

▶ An expression also demonstrates PowerShell's capability to convert results to HTML and save it to a file (ConvertTo-HTML ¦ Out – File).

▶ Figure 7.8 shows sample results that could be retrieved by running such a command in CompanyABC's farm.

Set-SPSite also gives you the ability to change quotas for a site collection via PowerShell. To change a quota for a site collection, type this ("My Quota Template" uses the name of an existing quota template available in your farm. A new template can be created via central administration):

```
Set-SPSite "http://portal.companyABC.com" –QuotaTemplate "My Quota Template"
```

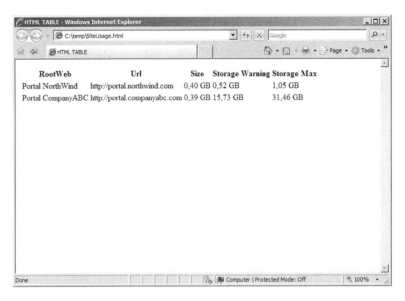

FIGURE 7.8   Displaying results of PowerShell cmdlet in a **GridView** format.

Managing Content Databases and Site Collections

The built-in cmdlets enable you to manage content databases. If a SharePoint farm is not adequately planned, one of your content databases might grow too large. In such scenarios, you can rely on PowerShell to fix the problem. Type the following command to create a new database:

```
#$webApplication = Get-SPWebApplication "http://portal.companyABC.com"
#New-SPContentDatabase -Name "WSS_Portal_Content_New" -WebApplication $webApplication
```

The preceding command will create a new content database for the portal web application. All the other database settings (for example, database server, warning site count, and maximum site count) can be changed at a later stage with the Set-SPContentDatabase cmdlet.

The following example demonstrates how warning and maximum site levels can be changed via PowerShell. Type the following to change the warning and maximum site count to 1000 and 2000, respectively:

```
Set-SPContentDatabases "WSS_Portal_Content_New" –WarningSiteCount 1000 –MaxSite
➥Count 2000
```

With multiple databases per web application, you can now easily move site collections between databases. Use the following code (make sure you already have "WSS_Portal_Content_New" in place):

```
Move-SPSite "http://portal.companyABC.com/sites/sub-site-collection" –
DestinationDatabase "WSS_Portal_Content_New" –confirm:$false
```

The preceding command moves the site collection at the given URL ("http://portal.companyABC.com/sites/sub-site-collection") to the new database. If you omit the `-confirm` parameter, you will be prompted to confirm this operation. As noted in the warning, IIS must be restarted to complete the move. This can be accomplished by using the `iisreset` command.

Analyzing Events in the Event Log

SharePoint 2010 introduced a number of improvements for easier logging and monitoring for SharePoint farms. One of the crucial improvements is the correlation ID displayed to end users in the browser when an error occurs.

PowerShell comes to the rescue when troubleshooting problems with SharePoint. The most important cmdlet for reviewing events is `Get-SPLogEvent`. Running this cmdlet without additional parameters might take a while, so it is advisable to add some additional parameters before running this cmdlet. Here are some examples:

```
# Displays all events that occurred between January 1st and 2nd 2010.
Get-SPLogEvent -StartTime "01/01/2010 00:00" -EndTime "01/02/2010 23:59:59"
# Finds event that occurred between January 1st and 2nd 2010 with the CorrelationID
➡"20ce1e39-5027-4db3-87c2-e0fa17154365"
Get-SPLogEvent -StartTime "01/01/2010 00:00" -EndTime "01/02/2010 23:59:59" ¦ Where
➡{$_.Correlation -eq "20ce1e39-5027-4db3-87c2-e0fa17154365"}
```

Beside the `Get` cmdlet, there are also `Clear`, `Merge`, and `New` cmdlets that enable additional operations over logs.

With PowerShell, administrators can change logging level for different event categories:

```
# Displays logging level for each logging category
Get-SPLogLevel
# Displays logging level for each Access Services categories in a GridView
Get-SPLogLevel ¦ Where {$_.Area –like "*Access Service*"} ¦ Out-GridView
# Changes the least error logging level for "Access Services" to "Error" level
Set-SPLogLevel -Identity "Access Services:*" -EventSeverity Error
```

Cataloging the Best Scripts to Automate SharePoint Administration

In this section, we examine some of the most useful scripts you could use to automate a SharePoint farm. These scripts automate common SharePoint tasks, and in many cases greatly improve the control administrators have over their SharePoint farm.

Automating Creation of Web Applications and Site Collections

Administrators benefit from PowerShell when they need to create a number of site collections. This can often happen when administrating large SharePoint farms or providing hosting services.

Site collection creation operations consist of three steps:

1. Create an IIS web application and application pool.
2. Create a site collection.
3. Choose a template for the site collection.

These operations can be performed via central administration or easily automated via PowerShell. The following example combines all three steps as a single cmdlet:

```
Function New-SPSiteSet
{
    param(
        [Parameter(Mandatory=$true)]
        [string]$SiteName,
        [int]$Port = 80,
        [string]$HostHeader = "",
        [string]$URL = "",
        [Parameter(Mandatory=$true)]
        [string]$ApplicationPool,
        [Parameter(Mandatory=$true)]
        [string]$ApplicationPoolAccount,
        [string]$SiteCollectionOwner = $ApplicationPoolAccount,
        [string]$TemplateName = "Blank Site"
    )

    if($URL -ne "")
    {
        New-SPWebApplication -Name $SiteName -Port $Port -HostHeader $HostHeader -
        ➥URL $Url -ApplicationPool $ApplicationPool -ApplicationPoolAccount (Get-
        ➥SPManagedAccount $ApplicationPoolAccount)
    }
    else
    {
        New-SPWebApplication -Name $SiteName -Port $Port -HostHeader $HostHeader -
        ➥ApplicationPool $ApplicationPool -ApplicationPoolAccount (Get-SPManagedAccount
        ➥$ApplicationPoolAccount)
    }
```

7

```
$webApplication = Get-SPWebApplication $SiteName
$currentUserAlias = "{0}\{1}" -f $Env:USERDOMAIN, $Env:USERNAME
    $templates = Get-SPWebTemplate ¦ Where {$_.Name -eq $TemplateName -or
    ➥$_.Title -eq $TemplateName}
if($templates.Length -eq $null)
{
    $template = $templates.Name
}
else
{
    $template = $templates[0].Name
}


if($template -eq $null)
{
    $templates = Get-SPWebTemplate ¦ where {$_.IsHidden -eq $false -and
    ➥$_.IsRootWebOnly -eq $false}
    $template = $templates[0].Name
}


New-SPSite -Name "SiteName" -Url $webApplication.Url -OwnerAlias
➥$SiteCollectionOwner -SecondaryOwnerAlias $currentUserAlias
Get-SPWeb $webApplication.Url ¦ Set-SPWeb -Template $template


}
```

To execute this function, type the following into the PowerShell shell:

```
New-SPSiteSet -SiteName "NewSiteCollection" -Port 8080 -ApplicationPool
➥"ApplicationPool-NewSiteCollection" -ApplicationPoolAccount
➥"companyABC.com\SPServiceAccount"
```

The script calls all necessary cmdlets and enables you to create a new site collection with a single call. In the previous example, a site collection with the associated pool will be created, and it will be available at port 8080 with the default template (Blank site).

The function can be further customized with additional site collection parameters as needed. Default parameters include

▶ SiteName—Name for your site collection and web application.

▶ Port—Port that will be used for your site collection URL; default port is 80.

▶ HostHeader—Optional host header, for example, portal.companyABC.com. If the host header is not provided, site collection will be available as http://SP_Server_Name:Port.

▶ URL—Custom URL for your site collection.

▶ ApplicationPool—Name of application pool that will be used.

▶ ApplicationPoolAccount—Account that will be used as application pool account (must be managed account).

▶ SiteCollectionOwner—Account that will be primary site collection administrator. If value is not provided, ApplicationPoolAccount will be used instead.

▶ TemplateName—Template that will be applied to newly created site collection. If value is not provided, "Blank Site" will be used.

Creating Site Structures On-the-Fly

SharePoint comes with many built-in templates that you can customize to match your needs. With PowerShell, you can streamline site creation for any purpose you need. You can leverage the built-in cmdlets to create and tear up site structures.

The following sample shows how PowerShell can be used to help you automate creation of a site structure. It combines the ability to list templates and create a new site. The script first lists all available site templates. (Hidden and templates designed for root sites only are not listed.) For each site in that collection, a site will be created.

Here is the sample:

```
Function Create-SPMockupSites($Path)
{
$webTemplates = Get-SPWebTemplate | where {$_.IsHidden -eq $false -and
➥$_.IsRootWebOnly -eq $false -and $_.Name -ne "BICenterSite#0"}$
    New-SPWeb -url ($Path + "/templates") -Template "STS#1" -Name "Templates"
    $rootWeb = Get-SPWeb ($Path + "/templates")

    ForEach($webTemplate in $webTemplates)
    {
        $webTemplate.Title
        New-SPWeb -url ($rootWeb.Url + "/" + $webTemplate.Title) -Template
        ➥$webTemplate.Name -Name $webTemplate.Title -Description
        ➥$webTemplate.Description
    }
}
```

To use the preceding code, type the following:

```
Create-SPMockupSites("http://portal.companyABC.com")
```

The script creates a blank site at http://portal.companyABC.com/Templates, and then a subsite below it for each template available.

In out-of-the-box SharePoint installation, this command creates approximately 20 new sites. Use this script when you are preparing presentations, building demo sites, or preparing educational sites for end users.

Administrators can create a similar sample when you need to create a number of sandbox sites for an upcoming educational course. All these sites could use the same template but have a different site owner.

Automating Site Collection Backups with PowerShell

A script for automating site collection backups via STSADM commands was included in the previous version of this book. This script was one of the most asked-for scripts from the book because it enabled administrators to back up individual site collections to flat files on a nightly basis. Although useful, this script was a four-page Visual Basic script and had some complex logic in it that would enumerate site collections and back them up individually.

SharePoint 2010 now allows for the same functionality, from a simplified interface. You can completely automate the backup procedure with built-in SharePoint PowerShell cmdlets. The following sample script demonstrates some additional things than can be done with a combination of a couple of built-in scripts.

The script enables you to do the following:

▶ Back up all site collections in your server farm.

▶ The backup filename will be a combination of the site collection name and date when the backup was created.

▶ The user running this script can specify the number of previous backups they want to retain.

▶ When the backup finishes, a notification will be sent to a specified email address.

Here is the script listing:

```
Function Backup-SPSiteCollections ()
{
    param(
        [Parameter(
            Position=0,
            Mandatory=$true
        )]
        [Guid]$SPSiteID,
        [Parameter(
            Position=0,
            Mandatory=$true
        )]
        [string]$BackupFolder,
        [Parameter(
```

```
            Position=0,
            Mandatory=$true
    )]
    [string]$RootWeb,
    [Parameter(
            Position=0,
            Mandatory=$true
    )]
    [int]$BackupFilesLimit,
    [Parameter(
            Position=0,
            Mandatory=$false
    )]
    [string]$Email = "",
    [Parameter(
            Position=0,
            Mandatory=$false
    )]
    [string]$SmtpServer = ""
)


# Test if backup folder exists
if (Test-Path $BackupFolder)
{
    # Retrieve previous backup files , sorted by last write time (last modified)
    $files = Get-Childitem $BackupFolder ¦ where {$_.Name -like ("*" + $RootWeb
    ➥+ "*.dat")} ¦ Sort $_.LastWriteTime
    $filesCount = @($files).Count

    # If there are more files in directory than backupFilesLimit
    if($filesCount -ge $BackupFilesLimit)
    {
        # Delete all older files
        for ( $i=0; $i -lt $filesCount-$BackupFilesLimit+1; $i++)
        {
            Remove-Item ($BackupFolder + $files[$i].Name)
        }
    }
}
# If backup folder does not exist it will be created
else
{
    New-Item $BackupFolder -type directory
}
```

```
$backupFileName = ("" + $RootWeb + "_" + (Get-Date -Format yyyy-MM-ddThh-mm-
➥ss) + ".dat")
$backupFilePath = $BackupFolder + $backupFileName
$startTime = Get-Date
Backup-SPSite -identity $_.ID -path ($backupFilePath) -force
$endTime = Get-Date


# Checking if Email and SmtpServer values have been defined
if($Email -ne "" -and $SmtpServer -ne "")
{
    $subject = "SharePoint Site Collection Backup Completed!"
    $body = "The following site collection was backed up: " + $RootWeb + "`n"
    $body += "Site collection was backed up to: " + $backupFileName + "`n"
    $body += "Backup started on: " + $startTime + ", and ended on: " +
    ➥$endTime + "`n`n"
    # Retrieving Site Collection size
    $SiteCollectionSize = Get-SPSite ¦ Where {$_.ID -eq $SPSiteID} ¦ Select
    ➥@{Expression={$_.Usage.Storage/1MB}}
    # Retrieving backup file size
    $backupFileSize = Get-ChildItem $backupFilePath ¦ Select {$_.Length/1MB}
    $body += "Site collection size on SharePoint system is: " +
    ➥$SiteCollectionSize + " MB`n"
    $body += "Backup file size: " + $backupFileSize + " MB"
    $smtp = new-object Net.Mail.SmtpClient($SmtpServer)
    # Sending email
    $smtp.Send($Email, $Email, $subject, $body)
}
}
```

You can execute this script by using the following code snippets:

```
# Backup all site collections in your farm
Get-SPSite ¦ ForEach-Object {Backup-SPSiteCollections -SPSiteID $_.ID -BackupFolder
"C:\Backup-Location\" -RootWeb $_.RootWeb -BackupFilesLimit 5 -Email
"administrator@companyABC.com" -SmtpServer "mail.companyABC.com"}
#Backup a site collection whose URL equals http://portal.companyABC.com
Get-SPSite ¦ Where {$_.ID -eq "http://portal.companyABC.com"} ¦ ForEach-Object
{Backup-SPSiteCollections -SPSiteID $_.ID -BackupFolder "C:\Backup-Location\"
-RootWeb $_.RootWeb -BackupFilesLimit 5 -Email "administrator@companyABC.com" -
SmtpServer "mail.companyABC.com"}
#Backup all site collections whose URL is not equal to http://no-
backup.companyABC.com, no emails will be sent
Get-SPSite ¦ where {$_.ID -ne "http://no-backup.companyABC.com"} ¦ ForEach-Object
{Backup-SPSiteCollections -SPSiteID $_.ID -BackupFolder "C:\Backup-Location\" -
RootWeb $_.RootWeb -BackupFilesLimit 5}
```

The preceding three samples show you how you can execute your script in various scenarios. A backup script has six parameters:

- SPSiteID—GUID that uniquely identifies a site collection. In the previous samples, we pass the ID value from the ForEach-Object loop.

- BackupFolder—Backup folder on a local drive. Leave the trailing backslash \. In case this folder does not exist, it will be automatically created.

- RootWeb—Value of site collection RootWeb property. The value being used forms the backup filename—for example, RootWeb-BackupTime.dat.

- BackupFilesLimit—The number of previous backup files to retain at BackupFolder location. In case this number is five, only five last backups will be left in the backup folder, and all previous files will be deleted.

- Email—The email value used as a To and From email address. This value is optional. If value is not provided, a notification email will not be sent.

- SmtpServer—The address of the SMTP server to send the notification email to. If this value is not provided, an email will not be sent.

Automatic Solution Installation

Sometime when administrators need to prepare a new SharePoint environment, a number of features need to be installed and deployed. New solutions cannot be added from the user interface, only with STSADM or PowerShell. Third-party solutions usually have a built-in installer, but most free solutions or in-house solutions do not come with one. To install and deploy these features, you need to run a few cmdlets. The following script is going to ease that procedure for you.

The following sample "connects" a number or built-in cmdlets and creates a single function that streamlines the installation process. The script is listed here:

```
Function Install-SPFeatures ($Path)
{
    $files = get-childitem $Path | where {$_.Name -like "*.wsp"}

    ForEach($file in $files)
    {
        $existingSolution = Get-SPSolution | Where{$_.Name -eq $file.Name}
        # check if this soltion already exists
        if($existingSolution -eq $null)
        {
            Add-SPSolution -LiteralPath ($Path + "\" + $file.Name)
        }
```

```
    # upgrade existing solution
    else
    {
        # if solution is deployed we will update it with new version
        if($existingSolution.Deployed -eq $true)
        {
            Update-SPSolution -identity $existingSolution.SolutionId -
            ➥LiteralPath ($Path + "\" + $file.Name) -GACDeployment
        }
        # non-deployed solution need to be removed and installed
        else
        {
            Remove-SPSolution -identity $existingSolution.SolutionId
            ➥-confirm:$false
            Add-SPSolution -LiteralPath ($Path + "\" + $file.Name)
        }
    }

    $existingSolution = Get-SPSolution ¦ Where {$_.Name -eq $file.Name}
    if($existingSolution -ne $null)
    {
        Install-SPSolution -identity $existingSolution.SolutionId
        ➥-GACDeployment -force
    }

    }


}
```

To execute this script, call it with

```
Install-SPFeatures "C:\Installation-Store\"
```

`Installation-Store` in the preceding example is the folder on your local drive (or network drive) that contains a number of WSPs. The script will iterate trough WSP files in this folder and try to add and deploy each solution.

There are some limitations in the script. If there is a solution with the same name, it will be upgraded. During deployment, GAC deployments are allowed so use these scripts only with trusted solutions. Solutions will be deployed to all sites.

Understanding Advanced PowerShell Topics

All administrators will eventually reach the point when their PowerShell skills are robust enough to do basic administration of SharePoint. At that point, it becomes valuable to understand how to take your PowerShell skills to the next level.

Remote SharePoint Administration with PowerShell

PowerShell 2.0 introduced an interesting feature, the ability to execute PowerShell cmdlets remotely from a client machine without having to be at the console of a server or use a server control tool such as the Remote Desktop Protocol (RDP). To run a cmdlet from a remote location, make sure every server has the identical PowerShell version (2.0 or later), and run the following script before running cmdlets. Run the following code on every server in a SharePoint farm. (Be sure to start the PowerShell shell as an administrator by right-clicking on the PowerShell icon and choosing Run as administrator):

```
# Enables PowerShell Remoting
Enable-PSRemoting -force
# Enables credential delegation
Enable-WSManCredSSP -role Server -force
# Increases memory buffer size
Set-Item WSMan:\localhost\Shell\MaxMemoryPerShellMB 1000
```

Use the following code to enable remoting on a client machine (replace SPServer1, SPServer2 with the actual names of the SharePoint servers in the farm):

```
Enable-PSRemoting -force
Enable-WSManCredSSP -role Client -DelegateComputer SPServer1, SPServer2 -force
```

The following code sample demonstrates how to execute Get-SPSite on a remote computer. During execution, users will be prompted for the SharePoint administration credentials. Replace SPServer with the actual SharePoint server name:

```
$administrator = Get-Credential
Invoke-Command -Computername SPServer -Credential $administrator -Authentication
credssp {Add-PSSnapin Microsoft.SharePoint.PowerShell; Get-SPSite ¦ Select Url}
```

Beyond Built-In SharePoint PowerShell Cmdlets

The set of 500+ PowerShell cmdlets that come with SharePoint enable you to perform a wide range of SharePoint administration tasks. But for complete automation of SharePoint administration, some areas are not covered via built-in cmdlets. In this section, we explore how we can extend PowerShell beyond its original programming.

Creating Custom Functions with PowerShell

Custom functions in PowerShell enable developers to easily group sections of code together for easier and repeated usage.

Here is a simple HelloWorld function:

```
Function HelloWorld()
{
    Write-Host "Hello World!"
}
```

To execute this function, type the following:

```
HelloWorld
```

The easiest way to get started with functions is with PowerShell ISE and execute the code directly from the ISE. In case the ISE is not available, save the code to a ps1 file with any text editor, such as Notepad. Execute it from a PowerShell shell by typing

```
\HelloWorld.ps1
```

Functions and Parameters

When creating a PowerShell function, you can define a number of parameters that need to be passed when a function is called from the code; the simplest version of a PowerShell function with parameters is the following:

```
Function HelloWorld($YourName)
```

For more flexibility with parameter properties, use the param syntax:

```
Function HelloWorld
{
    Param (
        [Parameter(Mandatory=$true)]
        [string]$YourName ="John Smith",
        [int]$YourAge = 0
    )
    Write-Host "$YourName ($YourAge)"
}
```

With the preceding syntax function, an author can define which parameters are required, variable types for each variable, and default values. Functions with parameters can be called as shown next. When passed, parameters are separated with spaces only; commas are not used:

```
HelloWorld "John Smith" 47
HelloWorld –YourAge 47 -YourName "John Smith"
```

Using the SharePoint .NET API to Extend PowerShell

The set of built-in SharePoint PowerShell cmdlets enable you to manage your SharePoint farm, all the features, site collections, and sites. These cmdlets do not give you access to SharePoint lists, pages, workflows, and so on. This limitation can be easily overcome by using the existing SharePoint .NET API.

To use the additional API (SharePoint, in this example) functions, API must be referenced before using its objects and functions:

```
[System.Reflection.Assembly]::LoadWithPartialName("Microsoft.SharePoint")
```

Retrieving SharePoint Lists with PowerShell

The following example shows how to get a list of SharePoint lists and libraries on a SharePoint site. To display such a list, a custom function is needed:

```
function Get-SPList
{
    param(
        [Parameter(
            Position=0,
            Mandatory=$true,
            ValueFromPipeline=$true
        )]
        [Microsoft.SharePoint.SPWeb]$CurrentWeb,
        [Parameter(
            Position=1,
            Mandatory=$false
        )]
        [string]$Title = $null

    )

    foreach($list in $CurrentWeb.Lists)
    {
        if($list.Hidden -eq $false -and ($Title -eq $null -or $Title -eq ""))
        {
            Write-Output $list
        }
        elseif($list.Title -eq $Title)
        {
            Write-Output $list
        }
    }
}
```

The preceding function receives SPWeb as the object and then invokes the appropriate functions from SharePoint API to retrieve lists (only those available on the Quick Launch menu).

To call this function, type the following:

```
Get-SPSite ¦ Get-SPWeb -Limit ALL ¦ ForEach-Object {Get-SPList -CurrentWeb $_} ¦
➥Select ParentWeb, ParentWebUrl, Title, DefaultViewUrl
```

The Get-SPSite cmdlet lists all site collections (SPSite), pipes the results to Get-SPWeb that lists every site (SPWeb) within the site collection. Finally Get-SPList lists every list (only visible lists; system lists are usually hidden) in each of the sites found. The "-Limit ALL" parameter is optional and should not be switched on for large farms. To display only lists within a single site, use the following code:

```
Get-SPWeb "http://portal.companyABC.com/A-Project-Site" | ForEach-Object {Get-
➥SPList $_} | Select ParentWeb, ParentWebUrl, Title, DefaultViewUrl
```

Creating New Lists and Document Libraries

Administrators can combine the built-in PowerShell cmdlets with the SharePoint .NET APIs to create lists and document libraries on-the-fly. Use the following code sample:

```
function New-SPList()
{
    param(
        [Parameter(
            Position=0,
            Mandatory=$true,
            ValueFromPipeline=$true
        )]
        [Microsoft.SharePoint.SPWeb]$SPWeb,
        [Parameter(
            Position=1,
            Mandatory=$true
        )]
        [string]$Title,
        [Parameter(
            Position=2,
            Mandatory=$false
        )]
        [string]$Description = "",
        [Parameter(
            Position=3,
            Mandatory=$false
        )]
        [string]$ListTemplateType = "DocumentLibrary"
        )


        $SPWeb.Lists.Add($Title, $Description, $ListTemplateType)
}
To call the above given function type the following:
Get-SPWeb "http://portal.companyABC.com/A-Project-Site" | New-SPList -Title "Sample
➥Doc. Lib" -Description "Doc. Lib. Sample"
```

```
Get-SPWeb " http://portal.companyABC.com/A-Project-Site " ¦ New-SPList -Title
➥"Sample Custom List" -Description "Custom List Sample" -ListTemplateType
➥"GenericList"
Get-SPWeb " http://portal.companyABC.com/A-Project-Site " ¦ New-SPList -Title
➥"Sample Calendar" -Description "Calendar Sample" -ListTemplateType "Events"
```

The preceding sample creates three lists on a SharePoint site
("http://portal.companyABC.com/A-Project-Site"). The function New-SPList takes three
parameters: Title, Description, and ListTemplateType. You must supply a unique title
for a list within one site; to pass an appropriate template value, take a look at
SPListTemplateType. For more information, refer to the following URL:

http://msdn.microsoft.com/en-us/library/
microsoft.sharepoint.splisttemplatetype(office.14).aspx

Modify List Properties

Let's consider the following scenario: a site owner wants to uniform versioning settings for
all lists and libraries in the site farm. A combination of PowerShell and API comes to the
rescue in such a scenario. To achieve that, we can combine existing Get-SPSite and Get-
SPWeb cmdlets with a custom function:

```
function Set-SPList()
{
    param(
        [Parameter(
            Position=0,
            Mandatory=$true,
            ValueFromPipeline=$true
        )]
        [Microsoft.SharePoint.SPList]$SPList,
        [Parameter(Mandatory=$false)]
        [bool]$EnableVersioning = $null,
        [Parameter(Mandatory=$false)]
        [bool]$EnableMinorVersions = $null,
        [Parameter(Mandatory=$false)]
        [int]$MajorVersionLimit = -1,
        [Parameter(Mandatory=$false)]
        [int]$MajorWithMinorVersionsLimit = -1
    )


    if($SPList -ne $null)
    {
        if($EnableVersioning -ne $null)
        {
            $SPList.EnableVersioning = $EnableVersioning
```

```
        }
        if($MajorVersionLimit -gt -1)
        {
            $SPList.MajorVersionLimit = $MajorVersionLimit
        }

        if($SPList.BaseType -eq "DocumentLibrary")
        {
            if($EnableMinorVersions -ne $null)
            {
                $SPList.EnableMinorVersions = $EnableMinorVersions
            }

            if($MajorWithMinorVersionsLimit -gt -1)
            {
                $SPList.MajorWithMinorVersionsLimit = $MajorWithMinorVersionsLimit
            }
        }
        $SPList.Update()
    }
}
```

If an administrator needs to enable five major versions, and keep minor versions for three last major versions, the function needs to be called like this:

```
Get-SPSite | Get-SPWeb -Limit All | ForEach-Object {Get-SPList $_ | ForEach-Object
{Set-SPList $_ -EnableMinorVersions $true -EnableVersioning $true -MajorVersionLimit
5 -MajorWithMinorVersionsLimit 3}}
```

Creating List Items On-the-Fly

When building demonstration and presentation sites, a function that might come in handy is the PowerShell function for creating items in a list. The following sample shows how you could build such a function. It creates a list item in a custom list and assigns only a title for the list item, but it could be extended to create more complex items:

```
Function New-SPListItem()
{
    param(
        [Parameter(
            Position=0,
            Mandatory=$true,
            ValueFromPipeline=$true
        )]
        [Microsoft.SharePoint.SPList]$SPList,
        [Parameter(
```

```
        Position=1,
        Mandatory=$true
    )]
    [string]$Title
    )

    [Microsoft.SharePoint.SPListItem] $listItem = $SPList.Items.Add();

    $listItem["Title"] = $Title
    $listItem.Update()
}
```

You can use the preceding function by typing the following:

```
Get-SPWeb "http://portal.companyABC.com/A-Project-Site" ¦ Get-SPList -Title "The
➥Team" ¦ New-SPListItem -Title "John White"
Get-SPWeb "http://portal.companyABC.com/A-Project-Site" ¦ Get-SPList -Title "The
➥Team" ¦ New-SPListItem -Title "Ann Green"
Get-SPWeb "http://portal.companyABC.com/A-Project-Site" ¦ Get-SPList -Title "The
➥Team" ¦ New-SPListItem -Title "Zoey Gray"
```

The preceding code creates three new items (John White, Ann Green, Zoey Gray) in the list
"The Team" located on the site "http://portal.companyABC.com/A-Project-Site".

Managing Backend Systems with PowerShell

PowerShell can also manage backend systems in the SharePoint environment. Microsoft
and third-party vendors released numerous packs to manage various systems, and the
most important ones for SharePoint environment are management packs for IIS, Windows
servers, and Active Directory.

Windows PowerShell Snap-In for IIS 7.5

Microsoft released a PowerShell snap-in for IIS that can help administrators automate most
common operations with IIS sites and pools. SharePoint administrators in complex environments can benefit from the ability to automatically reset individual websites, recycle
application pools, backup IIS configuration, and so on.

The IIS snap-in can be downloaded from the following URL:

http://www.iis.net/expand/PowerShell

After downloading, follow the onscreen instructions to install the snap-in.

To use the snap-ins from this pack, it must be added; type the following:

Add-PsSnapin WebAdministration

This snap-in is no different from the SharePoint one; use `Get-Command` and `Get-Help` to learn more about cmdlets. Use the following code to list all web applications and pools:

```
# Lists all web applications (sites and pools) on IIS
➥Get-WebApplication
# Lists names of all web sites that are stopped
➥Get-WebSite ¦ Where {$_.State -eq "Stopped"} ¦ Select Name
```

Commands with `Start`, `Stop`, and `Restart` verbs enable administrators to perform those actions against websites and pools. To reset a SharePoint central administration pool, type the following:

```
# Restarts the Central Administration application pool
Restart-WebAppPool "SharePoint Central Administration v4"
```

Windows PowerShell Server Management Cmdlets

PowerShell cmdlets for managing Windows servers are built in to the PowerShell core and do not need to be loaded separately. In SharePoint environments, you can use them to control, for example, SharePoint Windows services, file systems, and so on.

The following command lists all SharePoint and ForeFront services currently stopped (ForeFront services are used to sync user accounts):

```
Get-Service ¦ Where {($_.DisplayName -like "*SharePoint*" -or $_.DisplayName -like
➥"*ForeFront*") -and $_.Status -eq "Stopped"}
```

To start a service, type

```
Start-Service ("SharePoint 2010 Timer")
```

Automate User Provisioning with PowerShell

The built-in SharePoint PowerShell cmdlets enable you to easily manage users across site collections, but the real power of PowerShell is revealed when you combine these with Active Directory management cmdlets.

The most common usage scenario for user provisioning occurs when a new user exists in CompanyABC.com. In this scenario, each new employee must be given an AD account and contributor rights to the SharePoint site at http://portal.companyABC.com.

Here is how a new employee procedure could be automated with PowerShell. Use the following sample code to create a new AD account:

```
New-ADUser -Name "JohnS" -GivenName "John" -Surname "Smith" -DisplayName "John
➥Smith" -AccountPassword (ConvertTo-SecureString "pass@word1" -AsPlainText -force) -
➥Enabled $true
```

To completely automate importing from PowerShell, use the `Import-CVS` cmdlet that enables automatic imports to be done from a CSV file. `New-ADUser` has more parameters that you can specify on account creation, but these are beyond the scope of this book.

When you have a new user created in Active Directory, you can use existing SharePoint cmdlets to assign proper user privileges:

```
New-SPUser -UserAlias "companyABC.com\JohnS" -Web "http://portal.comapanyABC.com"
```

PowerShell also gives you the ability to implement a similar procedure for disabling employee access to a particular site and removing it from Active Directory, The following example shows how to disable and remove a user:

```
# Removes a User from a SharePoint Site
Remove-SPUser –Web "http://portal.companyABC.com" -UserAlias "companyABC.com\JohnS"
# Disables AD User
Set-ADUser "JohnS" –Enabled $false
# Removes AD User
Remove-ADUser "JohnS" –confirm $false
```

If you have multiple site collections, you can combine `Remove-SPUser` with results from `Get-SPSite ¦ Get-SPWeb` cmdlets.

Summary

The introduction of Windows PowerShell as a SharePoint management and administration tool gives SharePoint administrators unprecedented control over their farms. When familiar with the concepts of PowerShell, administrators can automate processes that previously took large amounts of time or required clunky tools and procedures.

SharePoint 2010 administrators need to have at least a basic knowledge of PowerShell to properly maintain and administrate SharePoint 2010, so it is subsequently critical that they learn how to leverage the tool. This chapter provides a good first step for understanding PowerShell and includes sample PowerShell scripts that can be used to immediately administrate a SharePoint 2010 environment.

Best Practices

▶ Become familiar with Windows PowerShell for SharePoint 2010 administration.

▶ Understand the concept of piping commands from one commandlet to another to automate processes.

▶ Download the IIS 7.5 Windows PowerShell snap-in to automate IIS configuration.

▶ Use PowerShell for remote administration of SharePoint farm servers and for automation of tasks.

CHAPTER 8

Leveraging and Optimizing Search in SharePoint 2010

One of the core strengths with SharePoint 2010 is its Enterprise search capabilities. A considerable investment has been made by Microsoft into the native search capabilities within the tool, and new features and functionalities have positioned SharePoint's Search as a robust and comprehensive search application for organizations of all sizes.

To further cement Microsoft's credentials in the field of search technologies, Microsoft has added a new search engine known as FAST Search for SharePoint 2010. This search tool is completely independent of SharePoint 2010's native search and provides for advanced search capabilities, such as thumbnail previews and automatic metadata tagging. Organizations now have two search engines to choose from when designing and deploying SharePoint 2010.

This chapter covers all the main deployment and configuration topics related to both native SharePoint 2010 Search and FAST Server for SharePoint 2010. Discussed are the various options in each search component, and how to configure and set up both native and FAST Search for those organizations getting started with SharePoint 2010. In addition, advanced customization and configuration scenarios are discussed as well.

Outlining the Capabilities of SharePoint 2010 Search

SharePoint has always been strong in its search capabilities, and SharePoint 2010's search features improve the situation even more, both from an end user perspective and for administrators. The new end user capabilities of SharePoint 2010 Search include the following:

- ▶ New, rich user interface with Refinement Panel
- ▶ Boolean query syntax
- ▶ Suggestion while typing the query
- ▶ Did You Mean suggestions
- ▶ Enhanced relevance
- ▶ Federated results
- ▶ Related searches
- ▶ View in Browser for Office documents
- ▶ Improved people search
- ▶ Phonetic and nickname matching
- ▶ Search relevance by social behavior of people
- ▶ Windows 7 using a SharePoint 2010 search engine as a federated search location

For administrators, SharePoint 2010 provides the following improvements:

- ▶ Search can be deployed as a service application.
- ▶ The architecture can be scaled out up to hundreds of millions documents.
- ▶ Advanced search dashboard.
- ▶ Full search reporting.
- ▶ Many out-of-the-box search connectors (for example, for Lotus Notes).
- ▶ PowerShell support.

To improve more and more of these capabilities, Microsoft made an acquisition of an enterprise search company, FAST Search&Transfer. Although the original FAST ESP Server product acquired by Microsoft could be installed as a separated server product and integrated into Microsoft Office SharePoint Server 2007, this integration was only via web parts and not at an architectural level.

The first real integrated version that resulted from this acquisition is known as FAST Search Server for SharePoint 2010. It still can be installed independently from SharePoint 2010, but the integration is on the architecture level so that both maintainability and the end user experience are much better.

FAST Search Server for SharePoint 2010 contains all the features of native SharePoint 2010 Search, plus additional capabilities. The end user abilities added include the following:

- ▶ Thumbnails and previews for documents
- ▶ View in Browser link for the document results

- ▶ Visual best bets

- ▶ Deep refiners with item counts in each

- ▶ User context

- ▶ Sorting by any property

- ▶ Similar search

- ▶ Broader, better language support and richer query language

Administrators can use the following benefits of FAST Search Server 2010 for SharePoint:

- ▶ The architecture can be scaled out up to more than 500 million items.

- ▶ Content processing pipeline.

- ▶ Entity extraction.

- ▶ Tunable relevance ranking.

- ▶ Easy to configure (for example, User Context, Visual Best Bets, Documents Promotion/Demotion, Sorting and Refinement)

Part of the process of designing for SharePoint 2010 is to determine whether the native SharePoint 2010 Search will be used or whether FAST Search Server is used instead. Because FAST Search Server is technically a separate product, there may be additional licensing costs associated with it. It is important to first determine whether the enhanced functionality is required before deciding.

Deploying a Native SharePoint 2010 Search Service Application

In SharePoint 2010, Search is deployed as a service application, similar to the Managed Metadata Search, User Profile, or Business Data Connectivity Services. When installing SharePoint 2010, if you choose to use the automated wizard to deploy farm components, it will automatically configure native SharePoint 2010 Search. Although this can be convenient, it doesn't allow for control of the process, so it is recommended to deploy Search manually. To do this, you need to create a new Search Service Application, using the following steps. These steps assume that native SharePoint 2010 Search is deployed. For FAST Search, reference the later sections of this chapter:

1. Go to the SharePoint 2010 central administration site, and choose Application Management, Service Applications, Manage service applications.

2. At the next dialog box, as shown in Figure 8.1, you can find the list of deployed service applications, modify their settings, or add a new one.

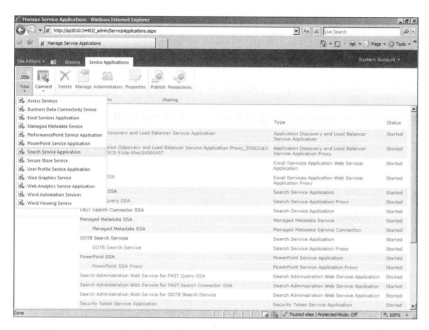

FIGURE 8.1   Service Application Management

3. If you want to add a new Search Service Application, choose the menu New, Search Service Application. You get a pop-up with the required settings for your search service.

4. Give a name to your service—in this example, SharePoint Search Service.

5. To deploy a SharePoint Search Service, choose None for FAST Service Application (this is the default value), as shown in Figure 8.2. To see how to deploy FAST Service Applications, see later sections of this chapter.

6. Select the Search Service Account, a managed account for running the search service on your farm. It is highly recommended to use a dedicated user instead of the default one with high farm administration privileges.

NOTE

The Search Service Account should have the following rights:

▶ Member of the WSS_WPG local group on the SharePoint 2010 server hosting the Search Service Application.

▶ On the SQL Server, it has to be granted as db_owner and public on the Search Crawl Database, Search Service Application Database, and Search PropertyStore Database.

▶ On the SQL Server, it has to be granted as WSS_Content_Application_Pools and public on the SharePoint_AdminContent Database and SharePoint_Config Database.

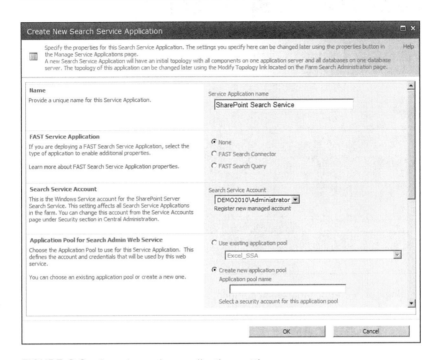

FIGURE 8.2   Search service application settings.

7. Select or create a new Application Pool for the Search Admin Web Service.

8. Select or create a new Application Pool for the Search Query and Site Settings Web Service.

After performing these steps, your Search Service Application is ready to be used in your web applications. But before starting to use that, you need to associate the proper Search Service Application to each web application. To do so, perform the following steps:

1. Go to the SharePoint 2010 Central Administration site. Open the Application, Service Applications, Configure Service Application Associations.

2. On this page, you can find the web applications with the associated service applications. Click the name of the web application, and you see the list of all associated and disassociated services. If you'd like to change the associations, change the group default to custom.

3. Select the service applications you want to associate with the web application, as shown in Figure 8.3. Choose the one created earlier—in this example, the one named SharePoint Search Service.

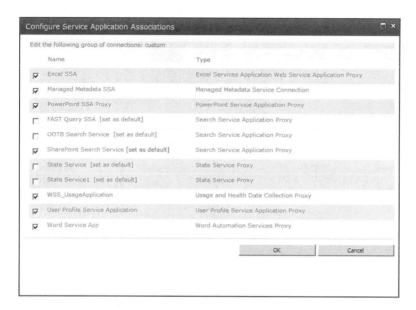

FIGURE 8.3   Configuring service application associations.

Define Content Sources

The SharePoint 2010 search engine can crawl and index various types of contents. The crawled content sources can include the following types of sources:

- ▶ SharePoint sites
- ▶ Websites
- ▶ File shares
- ▶ Exchange public folders
- ▶ Line of business data
- ▶ Custom repository

One of the first steps is to get SharePoint Search to index the local SharePoint sites. To do so, perform the following steps:

1. Go to the administration page of your search service application, and choose Content Sources from the Crawling group of the Quick Launch navigation bar.

2. Click New Content Source.

3. Enter a name for the new content source and choose SharePoint Sites as the type of the content source.

4. Type the start addresses for the SharePoint sites. By default, you have to type the following URLs (in this example, the URL of the main SharePoint site is https://home.companyabc.com and the My Site web application is https://mysite.companyabc.com):

   ▶ https://home.companyabc.com: for crawling the content

   ▶ sps3://mysite.companyabc.com: for crawling people content

5. Choose one of the following options: Crawl Everything Under the Hostname for Each Start Address or Only Crawl the Site Collection of Each Start Address.

6. Define full and incremental scheduling for the content source crawling. During the full crawling, all items of content source will be crawled from scratch. Incremental crawling means that only the differences to the last crawling will be crawled.

   Schedules can be daily, weekly, or monthly; each of them can be configured granularly. For example, Figure 8.4 shows the settings for a weekly schedule.

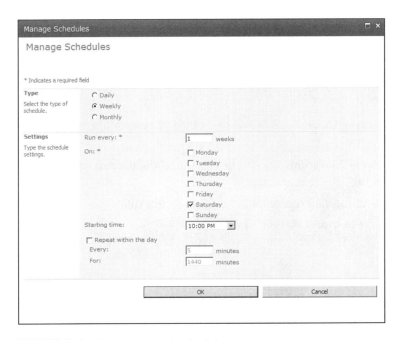

FIGURE 8.4   Managing crawl schedules.

7. Select the priority of this content source. Content sources with high priority will be processed over the content sources with normal priority during the crawling.

8. Select Start Full Crawl of This Content Source if you want to start the crawling process immediately.

The settings of content sources can be modified later. Just click on the name of the content source, select Edit operation from its context menu, and you get the same configuration page.

Search Scopes

After defining content sources, they have to be organized to search scopes to make available the search results to the users and to refine them. Search scopes also can be configured on the admin page of the search service application, by the following steps:

1. Go to the administration page of your Search Service Application, and choose Scopes from the Queries and Results group of the Quick Launch navigation bar.

2. Click New Scope.

3. Add a name and an optional description to the scope (for example, SharePoint Documents).

4. If you've already defined a search center (see later), you can specify a target result page for this scope as well; for example, /search/Pages/results.aspx. Otherwise, you can select the default Use the Default Search Results Page option.

5. Save the scope.

6. Define the rules for the content source. You can add one or more rules to each scope and connect them with various behaviors. The types of rules that can be configured are the following:

   ▶ **Web address**—This type of rule can be created to create search scopes that include content in the search index that has a URL.

   ▶ **Property Query**—This kind of rule can be defined to make property restrictions in the scopes.

   ▶ **Content Source**—You can include all the content of the defined content sources by this rule.

   ▶ **All Content**—All indexed content will be added to this rule.

   These rules can behave in three different ways:

   ▶ Include

   ▶ Require

   ▶ Exclude

   For example, in the scope SharePoint Documents, the content source Local SharePoint Sites has to be included, and the property IsDocument has to be required.

7. By default, there are only a few properties available in the Property Query of scopes, but this list can be extended with other properties. Just go to the Metadata Properties from the group Queries and Results in the Quick Launch navigation bar. Here you can find all the defined properties.

   When editing the IsDocument (or any other) property, you can find a check box Allow This Property to Be Used in Scopes. Check this and save the changes.

   Go back to the scope definition, and the IsDocument property is already available for filtering.

8. After creating each of the rules you need for the scope, the scope has to be updated. This can be done both automatically and manually: SharePoint 2010 runs a timer job in every 15 minutes to update the scopes, but there is an option to do it before the next updating manually: Go to the administration page of the Search Service Application, and click Start Update Now in the System Status section. Here you can see how many scopes are needed to update.

After following these steps, the scope is ready to use: It can be assigned to the Search box at the top of your SharePoint pages, Search Center pages, or search controls on each SharePoint pages.

Federating Search

Sometimes you cannot or do not want to use the SharePoint 2010 search engine for some content sources but still want to return search results from that content. For this scenario, you can consume search results from a federated source.

Federation can be configured from locations that are OpenSearch 1.0/1.1-compatible and can return with RSS or Atom of the result set.

The following is a list of circumstances when federation needs to be used:

▶ The content source is huge, and you don't want to build your own index of it (for example, MSDN, or Wikipedia sites).

▶ The content in the source changes often, and you need immediate crawling instead of SharePoint's scheduled crawling.

▶ The queries have to be processed under a different security context.

▶ You need only the results with specific keywords or keyword patterns in the query.

▶ The content is queried infrequently.

▶ You have more than 500 content sources.

The following list contains the cases when federation should be not used:

▶ There is not enough bandwidth between the SharePoint farm and the federated location.

▶ Content changes often, but immediately crawling is not needed.

▶ The content is not or cannot be crawled by the remote search engine.

▶ The remote server does not return with RSS or Atom.

In most cases, the federated location is some external search engine. However, if SharePoint can crawl the content, but you have other specific requirements (for example, keyword restrictions or different security context), SharePoint can be its own federated location as well.

8

Federated locations can be defined on the admin page of the search service application, by performing the following steps:

1. Go to the administration page of the search service application.

2. Click on Federated Locations in the group Queries and Results of the left navigation bar.

3. Click New Location.

4. Fill in the basic properties: Location Name, Display Name, and Description. Author and Version are optional.

5. Trigger is the field where you can configure when this federated location has to be searched. The trigger types are the following:

   ▶ **Always**—Query should always match.

   ▶ **Prefix**—Query must begin with a specified prefix. For example, if you use the prefix SharePoint, and the query is SharePoint ECM, the federated location will be queried with the term ECM. If the query is ECM, the federated location will not be queried because the prefix SharePoint is missing.

   ▶ **Pattern**—Query must match a specific pattern or a .NET regular expression capture group. For example, use the pattern (^([\w-\.]+)@([\w-]+\.)+([a-zA-Z]{2,4})$) for matching email addresses.

6. Select the Location Type. Use SharePoint Index on This Server if you want to use the local SharePoint index. FAST Index also can be selected for the results of a FAST Search Server. Select OpenSearch 1.0/1.1 to use remote federated location.

7. Configure the Query template. In this expression, the federated location's query URL TEMPLATE can be configured. {searchTerms} means the query term that is passed to the remote search engine. For example, in case of using Bing as a remote search engine, the Query Template looks like this: http://www.bing.com/search?q={searchTerms}&format=rss

8. The More Results link template links to the URL that will be opened when the users click on the More Results link of the federated result set. It can be the same as the Query Template, but it's not necessary.

9. The display formatting can be configured as XSL transformations. The result sets are in XML format so that these XSLs can define how to display them. Feel free to change it or use the default one.

10. Define usage restrictions, if you want to define what site domains can use this location.

11. Federated locations can be accessed with specific credentials different from the default one. Various types of credentials can be configured as follows:

   ▶ Anonymous

▸ Common authentication should be used when all queries have to be run with the same credentials. The types of common authentication are the following:

- ▸ Basic Authentication

- ▸ Digest Authentication

- ▸ NTLM—Application Pool Identity

- ▸ NTML—Username and password

- ▸ Form Authentication

- ▸ Cookie Authentication

▸ User authentication also can be used if you don't have common credentials for the whole company but would like to authenticate each user with a unique account. The types of user authentication are the following; in each case, the user has to be authenticated before using the federated location:

- ▸ Kerberos

- ▸ Basic Authentication

- ▸ Digest Authentication

- ▸ NTLM—Username and password

- ▸ Form authentication

- ▸ Cookie authentication

Table 8.1 describes the advantages and disadvantages of search federation.

TABLE 8.1   The Advantages and Disadvantages of Search Federation in SharePoint 2010

Advantages	Disadvantages
Federation conserves resources of crawling and indexing.	There is no ability to configure ranking in federated result sets.
Federated locations can include content that cannot be crawled by SharePoint Search Engine.	There is no ability to control which results appear in the federated result set.
Federation can provide the latest information from different content sources.	The results cannot be scoped.
	The results of various federated locations cannot be combined into a single result set.
	The more result set web part is on the same page, which increases the time to load.

Federated locations also can be exported and imported. The steps of exporting a location follow:

1. Go to the admin page of your Search Service Location, and choose Federated Locations from the display group Queries and Results in the left navigation bar.
2. Here you can find the configured federated locations. Choose the one you want to export, and open its context menu.
3. Click Export Location.
4. The location definition will be generated in .OSDX format. Choose a place to save it.

The steps for importing an .OSDX definition file are as follows:

1. Go to the admin page of your Search Service Location, and choose Federated Locations from the display group Queries and Results in the left navigation bar.
2. Click Import Location.
3. Enter or browse the full path to the .OSDX file, and click OK.
4. After a successful import, you can edit the newly created location by choosing the option Edit Location, or finish the importing by clicking on Done.

> **NOTE**
>
> The exported federated locations are not only able to be imported as a SharePoint 2010 federated location, but they can be also used in Windows 7. If you save the .OSDX file to your local computer and click it, Windows 7 offers to add this search connector to your client machine. This is the easiest way to use the SharePoint search engine or any other federated location on the client side.

Keywords and Best Bets

Keywords are special words or expressions to be marked as more relevant and displayed more prominently in the search results. The properties of keywords in SharePoint 2010 are as follows:

- ▶ Keyword Phrase
- ▶ Synonyms
- ▶ Best Bets
- ▶ Keyword Definition
- ▶ Contact
- ▶ Publishing Date

FAST Search Server 2010 for SharePoint also gives the capability of Visual Best Bets, Document Promotions, and Demotions to Keywords. Moreover, user contexts can be assigned to the keywords, as shown later in this chapter.

Keywords and all their properties can be customized at the site collection level, by following these steps:

1. Go to the Site Settings of your site, and choose the action Search Keywords from the group Site Collection Administration.

2. Here you can find the list of the existing keywords and can edit them or create a new one. Click the link Add Keyword.

3. Provide the Keyword Phrase; for example, SharePoint.

4. Enter the synonyms separated by semicolons; for example, SPS; SPF; MOSS; WSS.

5. Add Best Bets by clicking Add Best Bet, as shown in Figure 8.5.

FIGURE 8.5   Defining Best Bets for keywords.

6. Providing a keyword definition is optional but can be useful for further reference.

7. The contact person will be informed when the keyword is past its review date.

8. As Publishing Date, there can be three values provided: Start and End dates to set the availability of the keyword (for example, because of a marketing campaign). The Review date defines the deadline of the keyword's review by the contact person.

9. Click OK and save your changes. Your keyword is ready to be used and presented in the search results, such as what is shown in Figure 8.6.

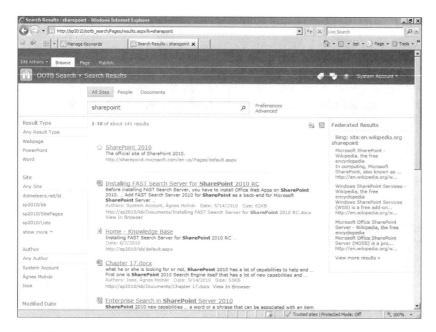

FIGURE 8.6   Viewing Best Bets in the search results.

Customizing the Search User Interface

At a certain point, many organizations will want to consider customizing the default search experience to make it better match their specific needs. This can involve the creation of custom search centers or customizing search scopes, among other things.

Creating Search Centers

Search centers are the web pages that provide for the search user interface most often used in SharePoint. They can be created in an easy way, and they provide a full query and result displaying capabilities.

There are three types of search centers in SharePoint 2010:

▶ A Basic Search Center is a simple site for delivering search functionality. It includes pages for search results and advanced search.

▶ An Enterprise Search Center is a more complex site with more pages and a better user experience. Its pages are organized into tabs that can be easily accessed by the users. By default, there are two tabs on the welcome page: one for the general search results and one for the people results. Site administrators can add more pages and tabs, regarding to the current search requirements. There is also a way to create different pages and tabs for the different scopes so that they can be defined as a Target URL for the searches of each scope.

▶ A FAST Search Center is the search site providing the rich FAST Search experience. The site's content is similar to the Enterprise Search Center but with richer capabilities that take advantage of FAST Search Server for SharePoint 2010.

If you want to create a site for any type of search center, perform the following steps:

1. Go to the site where you want to create the search center. Open the Site Actions menu, and select New Site.

2. Filter the site templates for search on the left navigation bar.

3. Select the type of the search center you want to deploy: Basic, Enterprise, or FAST Search Center.

4. Type the Title and URL of the search center on the right side.

5. Click More Options if you want to set the Description of the new search center, or configure the permissions or navigation inheritance.

6. After selecting the necessary settings, click Create, and the new search center will be ready to use immediately.

Assign Search Pages to the Scopes

Whatever type of search center you deploy, you can create more than one search results page. If you have Enterprise or FAST Search Centers, these pages can be displayed on tabs on the top of all result pages so that the navigation can be easy as well.

The steps for creating a new page and displaying it as a tab are as follows:

1. Open the Site Actions menu and choose the New Page action.

2. Type the name of your page; for example, **Documents.**

3. Click Create, and the page will be created immediately in the Pages library.

4. The page can be edited as any other page in SharePoint 2010. To learn how to create a new search results page, see the subsequent section of this chapter titled, "Creating Custom Search Pages."

5. On the top of any result page of this search center, there are multiple tabs. In Edit mode, there are also two options for managing the tabs: Add New Tab and Edit Tabs.

6. Click Add New Tab, and type a tab name and the page name just created (for example, **documents.aspx**). Typing a tooltip is optional but can be useful to provide detailed information about the results page to the end users.

7. To display the same tab on the Welcome Page of the search center, repeat steps 5 and 6 on the Welcome Page as well.

8. Click Save, and the tab is ready to be used.

8

Of course, these search results pages also can be customized. For example, you can filter the results for a specified scope:

1. Open the Site Actions menu on your search results page, and choose Edit Page.

2. Locate the Search Core Results web part on the page, and edit it.

3. Expand the group Location Properties of the web part settings. Here you can find the field Location, where you can select the list of Federated Locations if you want to use one of them.

   You can also find here the Scope field, where you can type the name of your scope to be used on this search results page (for example, **Documents**), as shown in Figure 8.7.

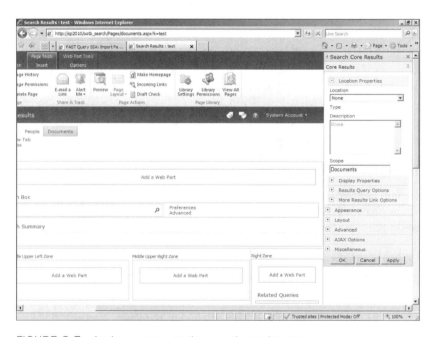

FIGURE 8.7   Assign a scope to the search results page.

4. Save the web part settings; then save and close the page. Now, your page is filtered by the selected scope.

To assign this page (documents.aspx) to a specified scope (Documents), go to central administration and open the admin page of your search service application. Then follow these steps to finish the configuration of scopes and pages:

1. Open the Scopes list from the group Queries and Results on the left navigation bar.

2. Select the scope you want to modify, open its context menu, and choose Edit Properties and Rules action.

3. On the next page, select Change Scope Settings.

4. Here you can find the field Target Results Page. Select the radio button Specify a Different Page for Searching This Scope and type the URL of the page you've configured for this scope (for example, https://home.companyabc.com/ootb_search/Pages/documents.aspx).

5. Click OK and your changes will be saved.

Creating Custom Search Pages

In SharePoint 2010, there is also the possibility to create custom search pages anywhere around the SharePoint farm. These pages can be the part of each search center or any other site type.

Basically, the Search function includes two user interactions: the Search Box for typing queries in and the results that are displayed. Both of them can be placed either on the same page or on different ones, depending on the requirements. In this way, you can build your own interfaces for the search functions. For example, you can insert a Search Box and a Core Results web part to a document center for searching the items in the Documents Scope; or insert a People Search Box to your HR site.

To create a new search page, perform the following steps:

1. Create a new web part page on your site.

2. Edit the page, and insert a Search Box web part.

3. If you want to display the results on the same page, insert a Core Results web part as well; otherwise, open the page that will display the results, and insert the Core Results web part to that.

4. Edit the Search Box properties:

   ▶ Scopes drop-down you can configure if the Scopes drop-down should be displayed and where to default it.

   ▶ Query Text Box format and additional query terms.

   ▶ Query Suggestions are only shown if the check box Show Query Suggestions is checked. Configure the minimum length of the query prefix, the suggestion delay, and the number of suggestions to display.

   ▶ In the Miscellaneous group, there are the options to change the button images, and set the Advanced Search Page URL and the Target Search Results Page URL. Type the page URL you want to use that contains the Search Core Results Web Part.

∞

▶ Scope Display Groups can be defined at the site collection level. By default, there are two groups: one for the Search drop-down and one for the Advanced Search. Feel free to create your own group and associate the proper scopes to it, as shown in Figure 8.8.

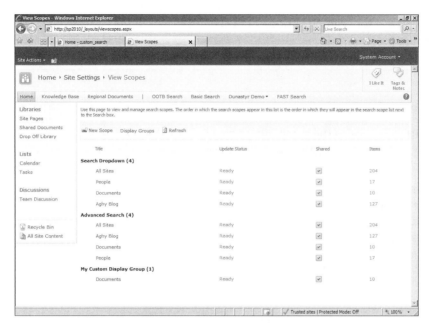

FIGURE 8.8   Creating new Scope Display Groups.

▶ In the settings of the Search Box web part, type the name of the Scope Display Group that you want to use instead of the default one.

▶ Set the general properties of the Search Box web part.

▶ Save your changes.

5. Insert the Search Core Results web part to the page you want to use for displaying the results.

6. Edit the properties of the Search Core Results web part:

▶ Location Properties contain the settings for using Federated Location or to specify a scope available from this site.

▶ Display Properties define the default sorting criteria, number of results per page, characters in summary and URL, and so on.

▶ Results Query Options, such as Query Language, Fixed Keyword Query, and Append Text to Query.

▶ You also can configure the More Results link appearance and URL.

7. Save your page.

Customize the Refinement Panel

The Refinement Panel, shown in Figure 8.9, is part of the search results page of search centers by default, but because it is a web part, it can be added to any results page in your SharePoint 2010 site. Moreover, a Refinement Panel can also be customized to your needs; it is a useful and powerful tool for filtering the result set.

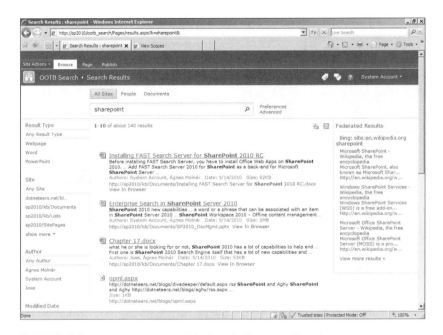

FIGURE 8.9   Viewing the out-of-the-box Refinement Panel.

To customize the Refinement Panel, perform the following steps:

1. Open the search results page for editing.
2. Open the context menu of the Refinement Panel, and choose the action Edit Web Part.
3. Expand the setting group Refinement, and open the Filter Category Definition field, as shown in Figure 8.10, by clicking on the small button labeled '...'.
4. To edit this XML description, it is useful to open an XML editor and copy the XML code there directly.
5. You can find the filter field descriptions in the CustomFilters tag. For example, you can find CustomFilter tags for Email, Excel, Image, PowerPoint, Visio, Webpage, Word, and so on.
6. To add new values to a custom filter, you have to add new OriginalValue tags for each value. For example, the custom filter "PowerPoint" does not contain the extensions pps and ppsx. To add them, insert new OriginalValue tags, as shown in the following code snippet:

```
<CustomFilter CustomValue="PowerPoint">
        <OriginalValue>odp</OriginalValue>
```

```
<OriginalValue>ppt</OriginalValue>
<OriginalValue>pps</OriginalValue>
<OriginalValue>pptm</OriginalValue>
<OriginalValue>pptx</OriginalValue>
<OriginalValue>ppsx</OriginalValue>

</CustomFilter>
```

FIGURE 8.10   Viewing a Filter Category Definition of the Refinement Panel.

7. You can also add new filter fields, by adding new CustomFilter tags to the CustomFilters in the Result Type category.

8. In addition, it is possible to remove any of the filters by deleting its CustomFilter tag from the XML Description.

9. After finishing all modifications desired, copy the XML back to the Refinement Panel web part's editor, click OK, and save the changes.

Installing FAST Search Server 2010 for SharePoint

FAST Search Server 2010 for SharePoint can be added as an additional component of the SharePoint 2010 farm. It can contain one or more FAST admin servers, responsible for running administrative services of FAST Search Server or one or more nonadmin servers. The nonadmin servers connect to the admin server in multiserver deployments, and run nonadmin services such as query matching, indexing, and document processing.

The installation steps of the FAST Search Server for SharePoint 2010 are as follows:

1. Create a domain user for FAST administration tasks (for example, companyabc\fastuser). This user has to be a domain user, a member of the FASTSearchAdministrators on the admin server, and has to have sysadmin privileges on the SQL server.

2. Turn off daylight saving time on the FAST servers to avoid scheduling issues.

3. Office Web Applications should be installed on the farm before installing FAST Search Server 2010 for SharePoint.

4. Install software prerequisites using the FAST Search Server Installation Wizard. FAST Search Server 2010 for SharePoint requires the following components, as shown in Figure 8.11, to be installed and configured:

   ▶ Application Server Role, Web Server (IIS) Role

   ▶ Distributed Transaction Support

   ▶ Windows Communication Foundation Activation Components

   ▶ XPS Viewer

   ▶ Microsoft .NET Framework 3.5 SP1

   ▶ Hotfix for Microsoft Windows (KB976394)

   ▶ Windows PowerShell 2.0

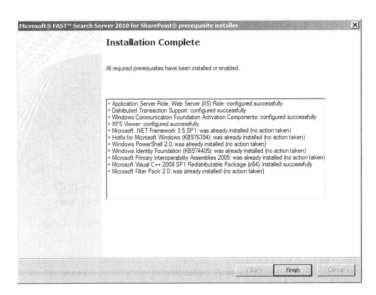

FIGURE 8.11   Installing prerequisites for FAST Search Server 2010 for SharePoint.

▸ Windows Identity Foundation (KB974405)

▸ Microsoft Primary Interoperability Assemblies 2005

▸ Microsoft Visual C++ 2008 SP1 Redistributable Package (x64)

▸ Microsoft Filter Pack 2.0

5. In the Install Wizard, choose Install FAST Search Server 2010 for SharePoint.

6. Select the folder in which FAST Search Server should be installed. Click Next and then Install. The installation will begin, as shown in Figure 8.12.

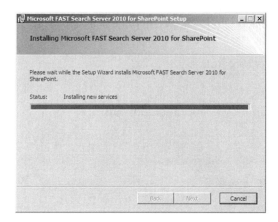

FIGURE 8.12   Installing FAST Search Server 2010 for SharePoint.

7. After the binaries have been installed, run the FAST Search Server 2010 for SharePoint Configuration Wizard, from Start Menu, Microsoft FAST Search Server 2010 for SharePoint.

8. Select the deployment type:

▸ Single Server (stand-alone)

▸ Admin Server

▸ Nonadmin Server

9. Enter the username and password of the FAST user created and granted with the proper permissions before the installation (for example, companyabc\fastuser).

10. Enter a certificate password used for moving certificates required for secure communication between servers.

11. Provide the server settings: the FQDN of the FAST Server (for example, fastsearch.companyabc.com), and the base port (by default, 13000).

12. The Database Connection String has to be the full name of the SQL instance where FAST Search databases will be created. Provide the database name of the FAST Admin database (for example, CompanyABC_Farm1_FASTSearchAdminDatabase).

13. Provide the click-through relevancy settings by select the type of the SharePoint Server installation type: Standalone, Server Farm, or Do Not Enable Click-Through Relevancy. Click-through relevancy is responsible for enabling automatic relevancy tuning based on how search users click on results.

14. Restart the server.

15. After the successful configuration process and restart, check the following:

  ▶ Update the FASTSearchAdministrators group if the FAST admin user is not a member of that.

  ▶ Open the Microsoft FAST Search Server for SharePoint PowerShell command, and run the following command: nctrl status. Make sure that all services' status is Running.

In a multiserver environment, the deployment.xml file describes the topology of the FAST Search architecture. Before running FAST Search Server 2010 for SharePoint Configuration Wizard on each server, you have to prepare the deployment.xml file containing all servers with the proper role. A template for the deployment.xml file can be found in the TechNet article listed here:

http://technet.microsoft.com/en-us/library/ff381243.aspx#BKMK_Install_FAST

After creating the deployment.xml file, you have to run the FAST Search Server 2010 for SharePoint Configuration Wizard on the FAST Admin server first and then on each nonadmin server with the proper settings.

Deploying FAST Search Service Applications

FAST Search Server 2010 for SharePoint requires two service applications to function properly:

  ▶ The FAST Content SSA is responsible for crawling and feeding content for the FAST backend. Its configuration contains all the content sources except People.

  ▶ The FAST Query SSA is responsible for serving the queries and crawling the People content source. This service routes the People Search to the SharePoint 2010 Search engine, and all of other queries to the FAST Search Engine.

Because of that, the deployment of these services is more complex than in the case of SharePoint 2010 Search. To build your FAST Search configuration, first you have to create the FAST Content SSA, and then create the FAST Query SSA. For getting the detailed information of your FAST Server configuration, open the file install_info.txt file, as shown in Figure 8.13, in the FASTSearch folder; you will need it during the configuration.

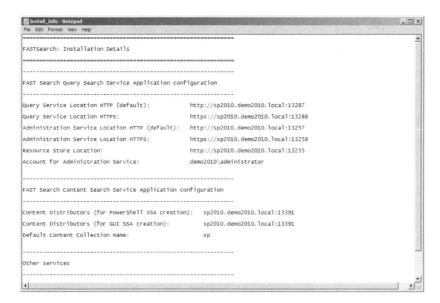

FIGURE 8.13   The install_info.txt file located in the FASTSearch folder.

Follow these steps to create a FAST Content SSA:

1. Go to the SharePoint 2010 Central Administration site, choose Application Management, Service Applications, Manage service applications.

2. Click New and choose the action Search Service Application.

3. Type the name of your Search Service Application (for example, FAST Content SSA).

4. Choose the type of the Search Service Application for FAST Search Connector.

5. Select the Application Pool for the Search Service Application, or create a new one.

6. Provide the location of the Content Distributor(s). The location can be found in the install_info.txt file (for example, fastsearch.companyabc.com:13391) but be careful because this port number (13391) is for HTTPS communication. If you would like to communicate by HTTP, the correct port number is 13390 (port number provided in the install_info.txt minus 1).

7. Set the name of the content collection that will hold the content of this connector. By default, the name of the collection is sp.

8. Click OK, and save your changes.

After performing these steps, your FAST Content SSA is ready to be used and connected to the content sources. Content Sources can be configured immediately by the preceding steps.

The next FAST Query Service Application can be deployed by performing the following steps:

1. Go to the SharePoint 2010 Central Administration site, choose Application Management, Service Applications, Manage Service Applications.

2. Click New and choose the action Search Service Application.

3. Type the name of your Search Service Application (for example, FAST Query SSA).

4. Choose the type of the Search Service Application for FAST Search Query.

5. Set the Application Pool for the Search Admin Web Service or create a new one.

6. Set the Application Pool for the Search Query and Site Settings Web Service or create a new one.

7. Provide the Query Service Location. The requested value can be found in the install_info.txt (for example, http://fastsearch.companyabc.com:13287 or https://fastsearch.companyabc.com:13286).

8. Provide the Administration Service Location, found in the install_info.txt (for example, http://fastsearch.companyabc.com:13257 or https://fastsearch.companyabc.com:13258).

9. Set the resource store location, also found in the install_info.txt (for example, http://fastsearch.companyabc.com:13255).

10. Finally, enter the account for administration service (for example, companyabc\fastuser).

11. Click OK and save your changes.

With these steps, your FAST Search Server is ready to be used in SharePoint 2010. The only thing you have to do is associate the FAST Query Service with your web applications; then create the FAST Search Centers as previously described.

Customizing the FAST Search User Interface

The FAST Search Center, as shown in Figure 8.14, provides a rich user interface for accessing FAST Search Server capabilities from SharePoint 2010. The main parts of the FAST search results page are as follows:

▶ Search Box, with capability of suggestions while typing.

▶ Results set, with document thumbnails, PowerPoint previews, View in Browser links for all documents, and Similar Results link for all result.

▶ A Refinement Panel with deep refiners.

▶ Related Searches, People Matches, and Federated Results.

Sorting Search Results

FAST Search Server 2010 for SharePoint provides the capabilities of sorting search results by property type, as shown in Figure 8.15. To change the default property that results are sorting by, or add/remove properties to the Sorting drop-down, open the results page in edit mode, and follow these steps:

1. Locate the Search Action Links web part, and choose the action Edit Web Part.

2. Expand the settings group Display Properties. Here you can find the properties available to sort by—for example, Site, Document Rank, Created Date, and so on. Select

the check boxes for each property you want to add to the Sorting drop-down, and select the radio button of the property for default sorting, as shown in Figure 8.16.

3. Click OK and save the changes of the web part; then save and close your page.

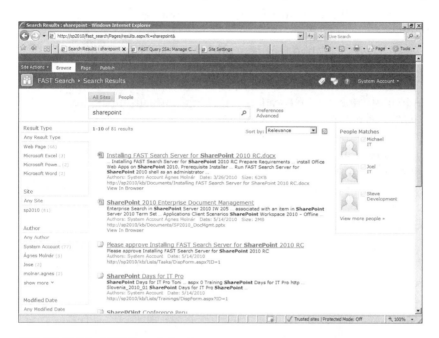

FIGURE 8.14   FAST Search Center.

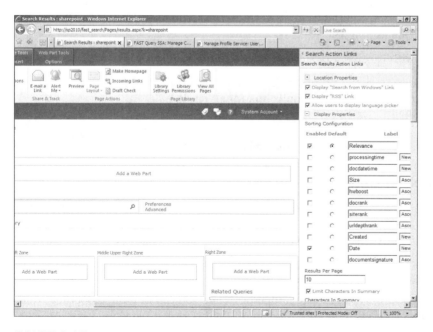

FIGURE 8.15   Sorting FAST Search results.

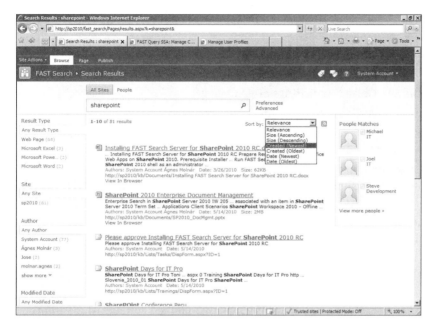

FIGURE 8.16   Change the sorting settings of FAST Search results.

User Contexts

In SharePoint 2010, people can have multiple properties stored in their profiles. These profile differences can be used to further refine search queries.

FAST Search Server 2010 for SharePoint enables us to give different result set to the different users, based on their profile properties. For example, the Sales Manager and the Software Developer gets different set of results to the query of ECM because the Ask Me About properties are different.

Of course, these differentiations are not configured by default; they have to be created by the administrators. The steps to configure different user contexts are the following:

1. Go to the Site Collection Settings of your site.
2. Choose the action FAST Search User Context.

3. Here you can find the list of the user contexts defined before and can add a new one. Click Add User Context.

4. Enter the name of the new user context (for example, Sales Managers or Developers).

5. Provide the filter values Office Location and Ask Me About (for example, sales).

6. Go back to the Site Collection Settings of your site.

7. Choose the action FAST Search Keywords.

8. Here you can define the keywords used by the FAST Search Server in your site. Create a new one with the name **ECM.**

9. Set the new keyword's properties. For example, Best Bets can be configured by user contexts. You can add URLs to display as a Best Bet for each user context. Do the same with Visual Best Bets, Document Promotions, and Demotions as well.

10. Site Promotions and Demotions also can be set by user context. Go back to the Site Collection Settings of your site, and choose FAST Search Site Promotion and Demotion.

11. Add new sites to be promoted or demoted, and set the user contexts to each of them (for example, Sales Managers or Developers).

12. Go to your FAST Search Center, and try the new user context settings with various users and with different user contexts.

Uninstalling FAST Search Server 2010 for SharePoint

If required, FAST Search can be removed from the farm, but it is not a simple process. To remove a FAST Server, first you have to make a deployment reconfiguration, by following these steps:

1. Locate and open to edit the deployment.xml file in the FASTSearch\etc\ config_data\deployment folder on the FAST admin server.

2. Remove the host tag for the server you want to remove from the farm.

3. Stop the services FAST Search for SharePoint and FAST Search for SharePoint Monitoring.

4. Open Microsoft FAST Search Server 2010 for SharePoint shell as administrator, and run the following command to Set-FASTSearchConfiguration to reconfigure the FAST deployment.

5. Start the services FAST Search for SharePoint and FAST Search for SharePoint Monitoring.

If you made this modification in the deployment.xml file, or you have a single server environment, you can uninstall the FAST Server from the server by performing the following tasks:

1. In Control Panel, choose Uninstall a Program from the Programs and Features list.

2. Select Microsoft FAST Search Server 2010 for SharePoint and uninstall it, as shown in Figure 8.17.

3. When the uninstall process finishes, reboot your server.

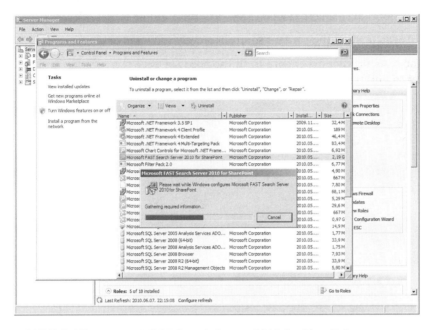

FIGURE 8.17   Uninstall FAST Search Server 2010 for SharePoint.

By following these steps, the FAST Search Server for SharePoint 2010 will be uninstalled from your server, with files and registry keys. Note that you will have to manually remove the FAST Search Server databases, logs, prerequisites, and generated files.

Also, you have to delete the FAST Content SSA and FAST Query SSA from the SharePoint 2010 farm if the full FAST Search environment is uninstalled.

Summary

SharePoint 2010 provides for significant enterprise search functionality out-of-the-box, either with the native SharePoint 2010 Search or via the FAST Search for SharePoint engine. In addition, SharePoint 2010 enables administrators to customize the search experience significantly, allowing for Search functionality that matches the individual needs of organizations of multiple sizes and types. You need to have a good understanding of how to customize and work with Search in SharePoint 2010 to design and deploy a search environment tailored to your individual needs.

Best Practices

▶ Consider a FAST Search Server for SharePoint 2010 if you need advanced search features, such as thumbnail views, visual best bets, or tunable relevance ranking.

▶ Understand the tools available that enable for customization of search relevance.

▶ Use Federated Search when the content source is simply too large or changes often.

▶ Customize the search center experience to fit the needs of your organization and to make it easier to find the type of data commonly requested.

## CHAPTER 9

Managing and Maintaining SQL Server in a SharePoint Environment

SharePoint 2010 introduces multiple new SQL Server databases as part of the Services Application architecture and, subsequently, more SQL Server resources are needed. SQL Server databases are the heart of every SharePoint farm; it is the backend repository for all SharePoint data and provides for critical architectural elements. To achieve maximum stability of a SharePoint farm, administrators must monitor and maintain SQL Server's storage and performance on a regular basis because heavy stress on a SQL Server can ultimately degrade the end-user experience.

This chapter covers the most important SQL Server administration concepts and techniques useful for administrators. It focuses on specifics for monitoring, maintaining, and managing SharePoint databases; discusses the essential monitoring and maintenance tools; and presents guidelines for improving the performance and storage of SharePoint Server solutions running on Microsoft SQL Server.

In addition, at the end of this chapter, administrators learn how to solve the storage, performance, and manageability issues associated with huge SharePoint content databases by making use of the powerful storage externalization capabilities of SQL Server 2008 R2 with the Remote BLOB Storage (RBS) feature.

Monitoring SQL Server in a SharePoint Environment

SharePoint administrators need to know how to proficiently monitor SQL Server performance and storage in SharePoint environments. Understanding monitoring strategies and tools enables administrators to shift from reactively dealing with issues to proactively troubleshooting and fixing problems before the server gets to the point where end users are impacted. This section walks administrators though a range of monitoring tools they should be aware of to efficiently and powerfully monitor, maintain, and troubleshoot SQL Server in SharePoint environments. Topics include WMI, Event Logs, Dynamic Management Views, Reliability and Performance Monitor, Activity Monitor, and Management Data Warehouse. With a vast range of monitoring tools available, choosing the right tool for the job is an important skill.

Windows Management Instrumentation

Windows Management Instrumentation (WMI) is a Microsoft implementation of Web-Based Enterprise Management (WBEM), an industry initiative that establishes management infrastructure standards. WMI supplies administrators with the tools to explore, understand, and use various system devices, resources, and applications of Microsoft operating systems and servers. WMI includes a rich infrastructure that enables efficient and scalable monitoring, data collection, and problem recognition. Think of WMI as a set of functionalities embedded into Microsoft operating systems and servers, including SQL Server, that enables local and remote monitoring and management.

WMI is a huge initiative and certainly deserves an entire book of its own. However, what administrators need to know is that the architecture of WMI enables extensibility through the use of *providers*, which are Dynamic Link Library files that interface between WMI and software or hardware components.

Each provider contains a set of WMI classes. Each WMI class represents a manageable entity, exposes information through properties, and enables the execution of some actions via methods. Because a provider is designed to access some specific management information, the WMI repository is logically divided into several areas called *namespaces*. Each namespace contains a set of providers with their related classes specific to a management area.

Administrators should also know that SQL Server, as part of its installation process, adds two providers to the WMI repository (WMI Provider for Configuration Management and WMI Provider for Server Events):

▶ The WMI Provider for Configuration Management enables administrators to use WMI to manage SQL Server services, SQL Server client and server network settings, and server aliases. For example, after a connection is established with the WMI provider on a remote computer, not only is it possible to retrieve information about SQL Server instances, but it's also possible to perform actions on them such as starting and stopping the instances.

▶ The WMI Provider for Server Events enables administrators to use WMI to monitor events in SQL Server. Included are Data Definition Language (DDL) events that occur when databases are created, altered, or dropped and when tables are created, altered, or dropped, for example. In addition, software developers can write code that responds to these events, and they can even author their own set of monitoring tools. Administrators can also create a SQL Server Agent alert that is raised when a specific SQL Server event occurs that is monitored by the WMI Provider for Server Events.

It's worth mentioning that WMI enables scripting languages such as VBScript or Windows PowerShell or even the WMI command-line utility (Wmic.exe) to manage local and remote servers. This enables administrators to query this huge amount of management information through a SQL-like language called the WMI Query Language (WQL).

To explore the available namespaces, classes, and events, administrators can use a tool such as the WMI Explorer shown in Figure 9.1.

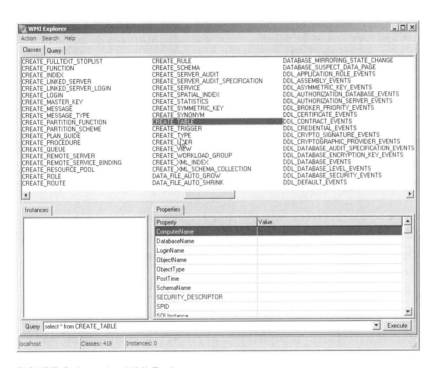

FIGURE 9.1   Using WMI Explorer.

Event Logs

An additional aspect of monitoring often disregarded by some administrators is monitoring the various log files available. SQL Server logs certain system events and user-defined events to the SQL Server error log and the Microsoft Windows application log.

Administrators can use information in the SQL Server error log to troubleshoot problems related to SQL Server. Browsing the SQL Server logs for irregular entries is an essential administration task; preferably, it should be carried out on a daily basis to help administrators spot any current or potential problem areas. An application-aware solution such as Microsoft's System Center Operations Manager (SCOM) can help to automate the process of monitoring SQL (and SharePoint) logs.

SQL Server error log files are simple text files stored on disk, but it is good practice to examine them by using SQL Server Management Studio or by executing the xp_readerrorlog extended stored procedure to prevent any SQL operations from being blocked by opening one of these files in a text editor.

A new error log file is created each time an instance of SQL Server is started; however, the sp_cycle_errorlog system stored procedure can be used to cycle the error log files without having to restart the instance of SQL Server.

The Windows application log describes events that occur on the Windows operating system and other events related to SQL Server and SQL Server Agent. Administrators can use the Windows Event Viewer to view the Windows application log and to filter the information. These event logs should be another place that administrators go to look for information about any issues that take place with SQL Server.

In the past, administrators had to view the SQL Server and Windows event logs independently; however, the SQL Server Management Studio Log File viewer makes it possible for administrators to combine both sets of logs into a united view.

Using the SQL Server Log File Viewer
The following steps show how to view the log files using SQL Server Management Studio:

1. Click Start, All Programs, Microsoft SQL Server 2008 R2, SQL Server Management Studio.
2. Connect to the desired SQL Server database engine instance and expand that instance.
3. In Object Explorer, expand Management.
4. Right-click SQL Server Logs, click View, and then select either SQL Server Log or SQL Server and Windows Log.
5. Double-click any log file, such as the one shown in Figure 9.2.

Log File Cycling
One thing administrators should keep in mind is that in production environments, log files can get quite large and take a long time to open. To avoid huge log files, it is a good idea to cycle them on a regular basis. Restarting the SQL Server service is not good practice. Alternatively, the log file can be automatically cycled using the sp_cycle_errorlog system stored procedure. The more writes to the error log, the more often it should be cycled. To automate the log cycling process, administrators can utilize the SQL Server Agent to create a new agent job with a single T-SQL task to execute the stored procedure, or they can include it in a regular daily or weekly maintenance plan. Maintenance plans will be covered in depth later in this chapter.

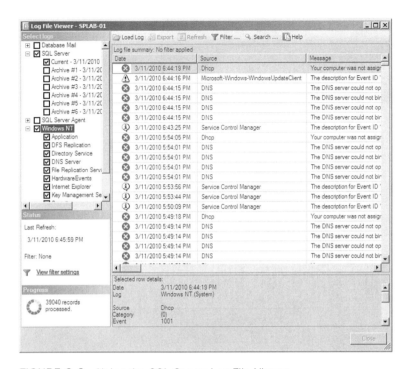

FIGURE 9.2   Using the SQL Server Log File Viewer.

Number of Log Files to Maintain

To keep as much historical information as possible, it is recommended that administrators configure the number of log files to be retained; this number depends on the amount of disk space available and the amount of activity on the server.

The following steps show how to configure the number of log files to be retained:

1. Click Start, All Programs, Microsoft SQL Server 2008 R2, SQL Server Management Studio.

2. Connect to the desired SQL Server database engine instance and expand that instance.

3. In Object Explorer, expand Management.

4. Right-click SQL Server Logs, and click Configure.

5. As shown in Figure 9.3, check the box to limit the number of error logs created before they are recycled. SQL Server retains backups of the previous six logs, unless you check this option and specify a different maximum number of error log files.

6. Specify a different maximum number of error log files, and click OK.

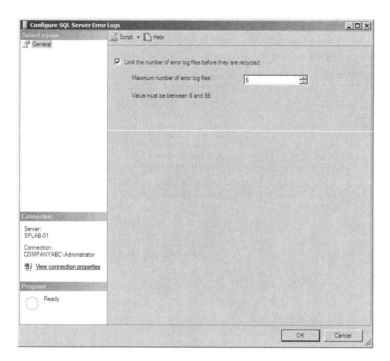

FIGURE 9.3   Configuring the number of log files to be retained.

Dynamic Management Views

Another area to retrieve monitoring information is the Master database; this is where SQL Server stores most of its configuration information. It is not a good idea to directly query the master database, because Microsoft could change the structure of the master database from version to version or even in service pack releases. Rather than developers building solutions that rely on the Master database schema and risking any changes in a service pack messing up the solution, Microsoft instead has created a set of dynamic management views and functions.

Dynamic management views and functions return valuable information that can be used to monitor the health of a server instance, diagnose problems, and tune performance. They give administrators an easy way to monitor what SQL Servers are doing and how they are performing by providing a snapshot of the exact state of the SQL Servers at the point they are queried. They replace the need to query the system tables or to use other inconvenient methods of retrieving system information in use prior to SQL Server 2005. SQL Server 2005 introduced DMVs, and the latest release, SQL Server 2008 (and SQL Server 2008 R2), includes additional useful DMVs.

Whenever an instance is started, SQL Server starts saving state and diagnostic data into DMVs. When an instance is restarted, the information is flushed from the views, and new data begins to be loaded.

DMVs and functions are part of the sys schema in the master database. Administrators can find a list of dynamic views in SQL Server Management Studio under Master/Views/System Views, and the dynamic functions are located under Master/Programmability/Functions/System Functions/Table-valued Functions. Each dynamic object's name has a dm_ prefix.

For example, later in this chapter, the sys.dm_db_index_physical_stats dynamic management function will be used to determine the fragmentation percentage of the indexes for efficient database maintenance.

Reliability and Performance Monitor

One of the Windows tools administrators should be skilled at using is the Reliability and Performance Monitor. Administrators who used perfmon in Windows Server 2003 may find the Reliability and Performance Monitor in Windows Server 2008 (the tool is called just Performance Monitor in Windows Server 2008 R2) a bit confusing when they first explore it. However, in addition to all the features included in previous versions, it now presents some new functionality that can make performance troubleshooting much easier and powerful because it provides a more detailed view of Windows server performance and per-instance SQL Server-specific counters.

The Reliability and Performance Monitor can monitor resource usage for the server and provide information specific to SQL Server either locally or for a remote server. It provides a massive set of counters that can be used to capture a baseline of server resource usage, and it can monitor over longer periods to help discover trends. It can also detect abnormal values at a glance for key performance counters on critical SQL Server instances. Additionally, administrators can configure it to produce alerts when preset thresholds are surpassed.

After opening the Reliability and Performance Monitor, as shown in Figure 9.4, the % Processor Time counter from the Processor object is automatically monitored in real time with a 1-second refresh interval. Additional counters can be appended to the graph by clicking the green plus icon on the toolbar and navigating through objects, which classify the counters into groups. When a SQL Server instance is installed on a server, it adds more than 1,000 new performance counters to the Performance Monitor section of the Reliability and Performance Monitor. Of the many performance counters that can be selected when troubleshooting a SQL Server instance, choosing the appropriate key indicators can significantly help administrators quickly isolate bottlenecks and direct their investigation to the appropriate resources for corrective actions.

Additionally, administrators can capture performance counters to log files for long-term analysis by creating Data Collector Sets. Creating Data Collector Sets is beyond the scope of this chapter.

Activity Monitor

Undoubtedly, the Reliability and Performance Monitor is a great tool for administrators to monitor resource usage; however, an administrator should first leverage the SQL Server Activity Monitor, as shown in Figure 9.5, when needing to gain some quick insight into a

SQL Server system's performance. In SQL Server 2008, the Activity Monitor introduced a new performance dashboard with intuitive graphs and performance gauges with drill-down and filtering capabilities. The new tool's look and feel is similar to the Reliability and Performance Monitor, but the information captured is broken down into five main sections dedicated to SQL Server performance monitoring.

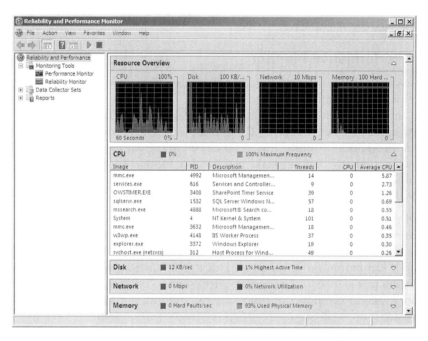

FIGURE 9.4   Reliability and Performance Monitor.

The sections are Overview, Processes, Resource Waits, Data File I/O, and Recent Expensive Queries. In SQL Server 2008 R2, right-clicking a SQL Server instance within Object Explorer and specifying the Activity Monitor will launch the tool, as shown in Figure 9.5.

▶ **Overview**—Shows the graphical display of Processor Time (%), Number of Waiting Tasks, Database I/O (MB/Sec), and the Number of Batch Requests/second.

▶ **Processes**—Lists all the active users who are connected to the SQL Server database engine. This is beneficial for administrators, because they can click any of the session IDs, run a SQL Server Profiler trace to capture all its activities, or even kill a specific process.

▶ **Resource Waits**—Displays resource waits vertically based on the following wait categories: CPU, SQLCLR, Network I/O Latch, Lock, Logging, Memory, Buffer I/O, Buffer Latch, and Compilation. From a horizontal perspective, the Wait Time, Recent Wait Time, Average Waiter Counter, and Cumulative Wait Time metrics are published for each Wait Category. Analogous to the Processes section, data can be filtered based on items within a column.

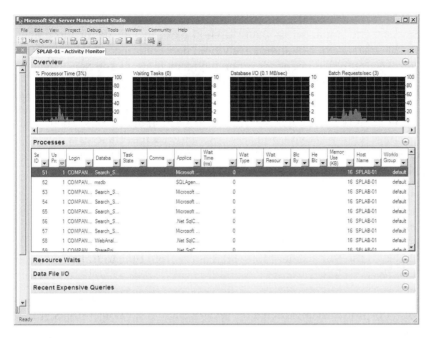

FIGURE 9.5   Activity Monitor in SQL Server 2008 R2.

▶ **Data File I/O**—Displays disk-level I/O information related to all the data and log files of user and system databases. Administrators can use this to rapidly recognize databases that are performing badly because of disk bottlenecks.

▶ **Recent Expensive Queries**—The last section in Activity Monitor is Recent Expensive Queries. This section gives administrators the opportunity to capture the queries that are performing the worst and negatively influencing a SQL Server instance. Approximately 10 to 15 of the worst and most expensive queries are displayed in the performance dashboard. The actual query is displayed with augmenting metrics such as Execution in Minutes, CPU ms/sec, Physical Reads/sec, Logical Write/sec, Logical Reads/sec, Average Duration in ms, and Plan Count. It is also possible to right-click the most expensive query and show the execution plan.

Data Collectors

The Management Data Warehouse provides administrators with a simple mechanism to track statistics over time. By implementing the Management Data Warehouse, administrators can monitor performance and do trend analysis for the SQL Server 2008 R2 instances they manage.

The Management Data Warehouse is a relational database inside the SQL Server 2008 R2 instance that holds a variety of performance-related statistics. The performance statistics in the Management Data Warehouse are gathered via special data-gathering routines, known as *data collections*. The Management Data Warehouse can include data collection information from a sole instance or can alternatively hold data collected from multiple instances. The data collection process depends on prebuilt SSIS routines and SQL Server Agent jobs, which diminishes the number of things administrators need to do to build and maintain a database that contains performance statistics.

SQL Server 2008 R2 provides three different system data collection definitions. These data collections are Disk Usage, Query Activity, and Server Activity. Each of these data collection definitions identifies the data to be collected, how often it should be collected, and how long it should be kept in the Management Data Warehouse.

Data collections can be run manually, can be run on a schedule, or can be run continually. Manual and scheduled data collections collect and upload data into the Management Data Warehouse on the same schedule. These types of data collections are known as *noncached* collections. When a data collection runs continually, data is cached in a directory and then uploaded to the Management Data Warehouse from time to time. These are known as *cached collections*.

It is also worth mentioning that Microsoft has also provided standard reports to enable administrators to drill down into data gathered for each of these collections using SQL Server Management Studio.

Maintaining SQL Server in a SharePoint Environment

To keep SharePoint operating smoothly and with optimal performance, it is highly recommended that SharePoint administrators conduct regular maintenance on each SQL Server database. Such maintenance tasks include rebuilding indexes, checking database integrity, updating index statistics, and performing internal consistency checks and backups. Administrators can perform database maintenance tasks either by executing Transact-SQL commands or by running the Database Maintenance Wizard. This section provides information and recommendations for maintaining the databases that host SharePoint data and configurations. Later in this section, administrators will learn how to automate and schedule the major maintenance tasks by creating database maintenance plans via SQL Server Database Maintenance Wizard.

Checking and Repairing Database Integrity

DBCC CHECKDB is the most frequently used validation command for checking the logical and physical integrity of the whole database. Essentially, DBCC CHECKDB is a superset command that actually runs CHECKALLOC, CHECKTABLE, and CHECKCATALOG.

Here are some recommendations for using DBCC CHECKDB:

> ▶ Administrators should run DBCC CHECKDB rather than the individual operations because it identifies most of the errors and is generally safe to run in a production environment.

▸ After running DBCC CHECKDB, administrators should run it again with the REPAIR argument to repair any reported errors.

▸ DBCC CHECKDB can be time-consuming, and it acquires schema locks that prevent metadata changes; therefore, it is highly recommended that administrators run it during nonproduction hours.

▸ The command should be run on a table-by-table basis if it is used to perform consistency checks on large databases.

Monitoring and Reducing Fragmentation

Although indexes can speed up the execution of queries, some overhead is associated with them. Indexes consume extra disk space and involve additional time to update themselves any time data is updated, deleted, or inserted in a table.

When indexes are first built, little or no fragmentation should be present. Over time, as data is inserted, updated, and deleted, fragmentation levels on the underlying indexes may begin increase.

When a page of data is completely full and further data must be added to it, a page split occurs. To make room for the new arriving data, SQL Server creates another data page somewhere else in the database (not necessarily in a contiguous location) and moves some of the data from the full page to the newly created one. The effect of this is that the blocks of data are logically linear but physically nonlinear. Therefore, when searching for data, SQL Server has to jump from one page to somewhere else in the database looking for the next page it needs instead of going right from one page to the next. This results in performance degradation and inefficient space utilization.

Monitoring Fragmentation

The fragmentation level of an index is the percentage of blocks that are logically linear and physically nonlinear. In SQL Server 2008 R2, SQL Server 2008, or SQL Server 2005, administrators can use the sys.dm_db_index_physical_stats dynamic management function and keep an eye on the avg_fragmentation_in_percent column to monitor and measure the fragmentation level. The value for avg_fragmentation_in_percent should be as close to zero as possible for maximum performance. However, values from 0 percent through 10 percent may be acceptable.

Reducing Fragmentation

In the previous version of SharePoint, it was recommended to track and reduce the fragmentation level by running the database statistics timer job, which in turn updates the query optimization statistics and rebuilds all indexes in the content databases every time it runs. Another option was reorganizing or rebuilding the indexes on a regular basis using the SQL Server 2008 or SQL Server 2005 Maintenance Wizard.

In SharePoint 2010, administrators no longer need to worry about fragmentation because SharePoint can do that on their behalf via the health analyzer. The health analyzer performs "health checks" based on timer jobs and self-heals the database index fragmentation automatically.

Shrinking Data Files

In SQL Server 2005 and SQL Server 2008/R2, administrators can reclaim free space from the end of data files to remove unused pages and recover disk space.

However, shrinking data files is not recommended unless the content database has lost at least half of its content. This typically happens after some activities that create white space in the content database, such as moving a site collection from a content database to another one or deleting a massive amount of data. Shrinking SharePoint databases other than content databases is not recommended, because they do not generally experience as many necessary deletions to contain considerable free space.

Shrinking a Database by Using SQL Server 2008 R2 Management Studio

The following steps show how to shrink a database by using SQL Server 2008 R2 Management Studio:

1. Click Start, All Programs, Microsoft SQL Server 2008 R2, SQL Server Management Studio.

2. Connect to the desired SQL Server database engine instance and expand that instance.

3. Expand Databases, right-click the database to be shrunk, click Tasks, click Shrink, and click Files.

4. Select the file type and filename from the dialog box shown in Figure 9.6.

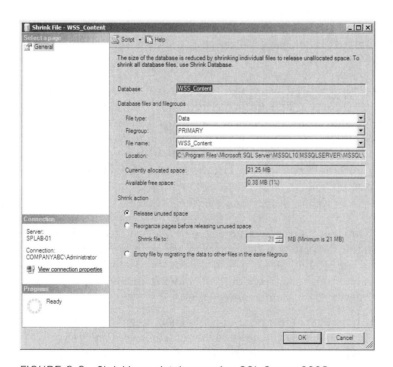

FIGURE 9.6   Shrinking a database using SQL Server 2008.

5. Optionally, select Release Unused Space. Selecting this option causes any unused space in the file to be released to the operating system and shrinks the file to the last allocated extent. This reduces the file size without moving any data.

6. Optionally, select Reorganize Files Before Releasing Unused Space. If this option is selected, the Shrink File option must be set to value. Selecting this option causes any unused space in the file to be released to the operating system and tries to relocate rows to unallocated pages.

7. Optionally, select Empty File by Migrating the Data to Other Files in the Same Filegroup. Selecting this option moves all data from the specified file to other files in the filegroup. The empty file can then be deleted. This option is the same as executing DBCC SHRINKFILE with the EMPTYFILE option.

8. Click OK.

Creating SQL Server Maintenance Plans

Maintaining SharePoint backend databases can significantly improve the health and performance of SharePoint servers. Unfortunately, administrators often do not perform regular database maintenance because maintaining SharePoint 2010 environments involves a huge set of maintenance tasks.

Fortunately, Microsoft has provided *maintenance plans* as a way to automate these tasks. A maintenance plan performs a comprehensive set of SQL Server jobs that run at scheduled intervals. Specifically, the maintenance plan conducts scheduled SQL Server maintenance tasks to ensure that databases are performing optimally, are regularly backed up, and are checked for anomalies. Administrators can use the Maintenance Plan Wizard (included with SQL Server) to create and schedule these daily tasks. In addition, the wizard can configure database and transaction log backups.

It is also worth mentioning that administrators should set any maintenance operations or maintenance plans to run during off-hours to minimize the performance impact on users.

Configuring a SQL Server 2008 R2 Database Maintenance Plan

The following steps show how to configure a SQL Server 2008 R2 database maintenance plan:

1. Click Start, All Programs, Microsoft SQL Server 2008 R2, SQL Server Management Studio.

2. Connect to the desired SQL Server database engine instance.

3. Click Management, right-click Maintenance Plans, and click Maintenance Plan Wizard.

4. On the Welcome to the Database Maintenance Plan Wizard screen, click Next to continue.

5. On the Select Plan Properties screen, as shown in Figure 9.7, enter a name and description for the maintenance plan.

FIGURE 9.7   Creating a database maintenance plan.

6. Decide whether to configure one or more maintenance plans.

   To configure a single maintenance plan, select Single Schedule for the Entire Plan or No Schedule. This option is chosen in the sample here.

   To configure multiple maintenance plans with specific tasks, select Separate Schedules for Each Task.

7. Click Change to set a schedule for the plan. The Job Schedule Properties dialog box appears, as shown in Figure 9.8.

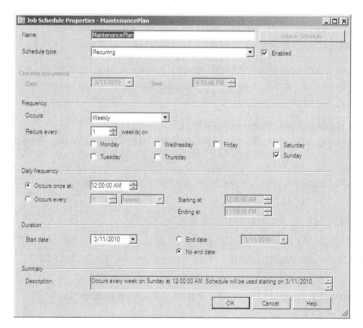

FIGURE 9.8   Scheduling a database maintenance plan.

8. Complete the schedule, click OK, and then click Next to continue.

9. On the Select Maintenance Tasks screen (see Figure 9.9), select the maintenance tasks to include in the plan, and then click Next to continue.

FIGURE 9.9   Selecting database maintenance tasks.

10. In the Select Maintenance Task Order page, change or review the order that the tasks will be executed, select a task, and then click Move Up or Move Down. When tasks are in the desired order, click Next. The wizard guides you through setting the details for each task. For example, Figure 9.10 shows the configuration of the Database Check Integrity Task.

11. On the Select Report Options page, select Write a Report to a Text File, select a location for the files, as shown in Figure 9.11, and then click Next until the wizard is completed.

NOTE

It is highly recommended that administrators include the Check Database Integrity maintenance task for all SharePoint databases and the Maintenance Cleanup Task maintenance task in their plans. It is also recommended not to select the option to shrink the database, primarily because automatically shrinking databases on a periodic basis leads to excessive fragmentation and produces I/O activity, which can negatively influence the performance of SharePoint.

Managing SharePoint Content Databases

As previously explained in the "Monitoring SQL Server in a SharePoint Environment" section, administrators should always keep an eye on the performance and storage of SharePoint backend databases. In response to the data they gather from the vast range of monitoring tools, administrators should also know how to manage SharePoint content databases, how to manually add a content database to a web application, and how to move a site collection between content databases. Some of these tasks can be completed directly from central administration; others can be done only via PowerShell or the deprecated STSADM command-line utility. These different tasks and techniques will be explained in detail in this section.

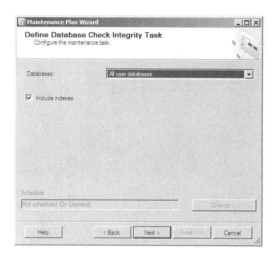

FIGURE 9.10   Configuring database maintenance tasks.

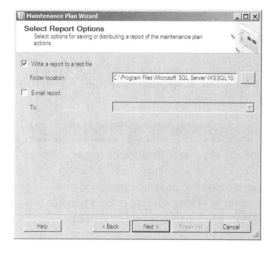

FIGURE 9.11   Saving and emailing maintenance plan reports.

Adding a Content Database

Creating a new content database does not mean that any new content will be stored in it because a site collection cannot span content databases. However, by creating a new content database and following some extra steps, administrators can instruct SharePoint where to create new site collections.

Adding a Content Database Using Central Administration

Administrators can use the following procedure to create a new content database and attach it to the specified web application:

1. Click Start, All Programs, Microsoft SharePoint 2010 Products, SharePoint 2010 Central Administration.

2. On the SharePoint central administration website, click Application Management.

3. In the Databases section, click Manage Content Databases.

4. On the Manage Content Databases page, as shown in Figure 9.12, click Add a Content Database.

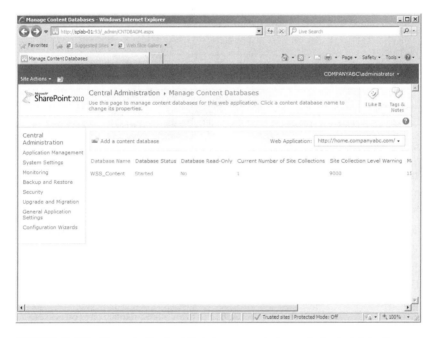

FIGURE 9.12   Manage Content Databases page in central administration.

5. On the Add Content Database page, as shown in Figure 9.13, do the following:

   A. Select a web application for the new database.

   B. Select a database server to host the new database.

   C. Specify the authentication method that the new database will use, and supply an account name and password, if they are necessary.

   D. Specify both the total number of top-level sites that can be created in the database and the number at which a warning will be issued.

6. Click OK.

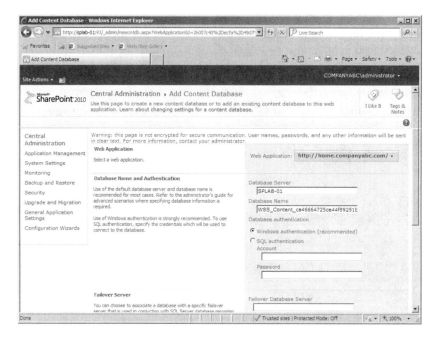

FIGURE 9.13   Add Content Database page in central administration.

Adding a Content Database Using Windows PowerShell

Administrators can use the following procedure to create a new content database and attach it to the specified web application using Windows PowerShell:

1. Click Start, All Programs, Microsoft SharePoint 2010 Products, SharePoint 2010 Management Shell.

2. At the Windows PowerShell command prompt (PS C:\>), type the following command, and then press Enter:

```
New-SPContentDatabase -Name <String> -WebApplication <SPWebApplication-
➥PipeBind>
```

The `-Name` parameter specifies the name of the content database to be created. The `-WebApplication` parameter specifies the web application to which the new database is to be attached.

Creating a Site Collection in a Specific Content Database

To force SharePoint to create new site collections in a specific content database, the target database should be the only one with the Ready status; all the other databases associated with the web application should be set Offline.

Taking a database offline means that from this point on, no new site collection will be created in that database. However, the database is still usable; users can still upload and download content, view web pages, and process workflows, and new subsites under an existing site collection can still be created in it. If a one-to-one site collection to content database association is needed, taking the hosting database offline is a method to accomplish this.

Administrators should not leave the content databases in Offline mode for a long time; they should set the databases back to Ready after creating the new site collection because some timer jobs do not function properly when the database is in Offline mode.

Another approach to creating a site collection in a specific content database is to set the maximum number of sites in the target database to a large number. SharePoint will then choose this content database.

Setting a Content Database Offline Using Central Administration

Administrators can use the following procedure to set a content database offline using central administration:

1. Click Start, All Programs, Microsoft SharePoint 2010 Products, SharePoint 2010 Central Administration.

2. On the SharePoint central administration website, click Application Management.

3. In the Databases section, click Manage Content Databases.

4. On the Manage Content Databases page, select a web application by clicking the Web Applications drop-down list and choosing a web application.

5. Click the database name in the list of the available database names.

6. On the Manage Content Databases Settings page, as shown in Figure 9.14, change the database status to offline.

Creating a Site Collection in a Specific Content Database Using Windows PowerShell

To directly use the content database for a new collection using PowerShell, administrators can use the following procedure:

1. Click Start, All Programs, Microsoft SharePoint 2010 Products, SharePoint 2010 Management Shell.

2. At the Windows PowerShell command prompt (PS C:\>), type the following command, and then press Enter:

```
New-SPSite -Url <String> -OwnerAlias <String> [-ContentDatabase
    <SPContentDatabasePipeBind>]
```

As explained, administrators need to first add a content database and then force the creation of new site collections into it. This makes it a bit confusing afterward for administrators to determine where each site collection lives. Fortunately, SharePoint provides an easy way to figure out which site collection goes with what content database by selecting a site collection from the Site Collection List in central administration rather than relying on naming conventions when creating content databases.

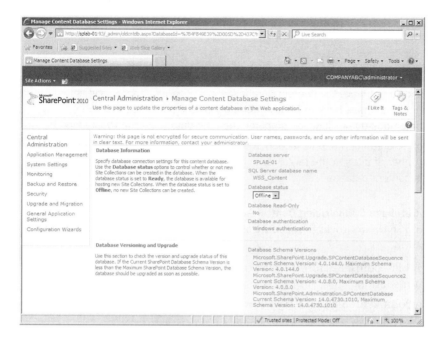

FIGURE 9.14   Manage Content Databases Settings page in central administration.

Moving Site Collections Between Content Databases

There might be some situations when a site collection hosted within a content database is unexpectedly growing, and the database is approaching the 100GB limit recommended by Microsoft. At such times, administrators should manually move the growing site collections from the larger content database to another smaller one.

Determining the Size of the Source Site Collection Using Windows PowerShell

Administrators should always double-check that the destination hard disk can comfortably store the site collection data by determining the size of the site collection that is to be moved. The following procedure can be used to determine the size of a site collection:

1. Click Start, All Programs, Microsoft SharePoint 2010 Products, SharePoint 2010 Management Shell.

2. At the Windows PowerShell command prompt (PS C:\>), type the following command, and then press Enter:

```
Get-SPSiteAdministration –Identity http://ServerName/Sites/SiteName| ft
Url,DiskUsed
```

Replace *http://ServerName/Sites/SiteName* with the name of the site collection.

Moving Site Collections Between Content Databases Using Windows PowerShell

Administrators can use the Windows PowerShell command Move-SPSite to move site collections between content databases:

1. Click Start, All Programs, Microsoft SharePoint 2010 Products, SharePoint 2010 Management Shell.

2. At the Windows PowerShell command prompt (PS C:\>), type the following command, and then press Enter:

```
Move-SPSite <http://ServerName/Sites/SiteName> -DestinationDatabase
   <DestinationContentDb>
```

Replace http://ServerName/Sites/SiteName with the name of the site collection, and replace <DestinationContentDb> with the name of the destination content database.

Externalizing BLOB Storage in SharePoint 2010

By default, SharePoint stores all the uploaded documents and files in its content databases. This has always led to storage, performance, and manageability issues, especially for large SharePoint deployments in SharePoint 2003 and the early days of SharePoint 2007. In SharePoint 2007 SP1, Microsoft made its first attempt to store documents and files out of SQL Server; however, the implementation was difficult and came with many limitations. In SharePoint 2010, Microsoft took this to a completely new level by making use of the powerful storage externalization capabilities of SQL Server 2008 R2. This section explains what BLOBs are, how they are stored in SharePoint, and how Microsoft made use of the Remote BLOB Storage technology in SharePoint 2010 to move the storage of large documents and files from SQL Server to remote stores. At the end of this section, administrators learn how to install and configure RBS in SharePoint 2010 environments and how to migrate and move data between different stores.

Understanding BLOBs

Most of the values stored in SQL Server consist of ASCII (American Standard Code for Information Interchange) characters. A basic explanation of ASCII characters is that they are the letters, numbers, and symbols found on the keyboard. A text editor such as Notepad can alter a file holding only ASCII characters without any consequences. However, data is not limited to strings and numbers; it is always a common requirement to store a large amount of binary data in a SQL Server table along with other ASCII data; Word documents, XML documents, and images are some examples. Binary files contain ASCII characters, special control characters, and byte combinations not found on the keyboard. Opening a Microsoft Word document inside Notepad and modifying it would result in the file being corrupted and not readable, because Notepad cannot correctly interpret or create binary bits. BLOBs, then, are binary files that are large, or Binary Large Objects (BLOB).

SQL Server provides special data types for dealing with such large volumes of binary data. These various data types have changed over time.

In SQL 2000, there were two different families of data type options for this type of data: binary and image. The binary family included two different data types: the binary data type and the VARBINARY data type. The VAR in VARBINARY means that the size is variable rather than fixed, as in the case of the standard binary data type. However, it still has a maximum length of 8,000 bytes.

The image data type family was used to store binary large objects that are greater than 8,000 bytes. This data type is still present in newer versions, but it is deprecated. Microsoft recommends avoiding using these data types in new development work and recommends modifying applications that currently use them.

Starting in SQL Server 2005, Microsoft included the VARBINARY(MAX) data type to the binary data type family. This variation extends the usual limit of around 8,000 bytes and allows storage up to 2GB of data.

Later, in SQL Server 2008, Microsoft introduced the FILESTREAM option for a VARBINARY(MAX) fields. This enables storage, efficient streaming, and integrated management of large BLOBs in a SQL database by using the underlying NTFS file system for BLOB storage/streaming, while managing and accessing it directly within the context of the database.

Instead of being a completely new data type, FILESTREAM is a storage attribute of the existing VARBINARY(MAX) data type. FILESTREAM alters how the BLOB data is stored—in the file system rather than in the SQL Server data files. Because FILESTREAM is implemented as a VARBINARY(MAX) column and integrated directly into the database engine, most SQL Server management tools and functions work without modification for FILESTREAM data.

It is also worth mentioning that the behavior of the regular VARBINARY(MAX) data type remains entirely unchanged in SQL Server 2008, including the 2GB size limit. The addition of the FILESTREAM attribute means a VARBINARY(MAX) column can essentially be unlimited in size. (In reality, the size is limited to that of the underlying NTFS volume.)

BLOB Storage in SharePoint

In SharePoint 2003 and the early days of SharePoint 2007, Microsoft SQL Server stored BLOB data in its databases as a rule, as illustrated in Figure 9.15. As a database's usage increased, the total size of its BLOB data could quickly grow larger than the total size of the document metadata and the other structured data stored in the database. There were no exceptions for this; content metadata and BLOBs had to go into content databases. This was not efficient because Microsoft estimates that as much as 80 percent of the data stored in SharePoint content databases is nonrelational BLOB data, such as Microsoft Office Word documents, Microsoft Office Excel spreadsheets, and Microsoft Office

PowerPoint presentations. Only 20 percent is relational metadata, and this caused storage, performance, and manageability issues, especially for large SharePoint deployments.

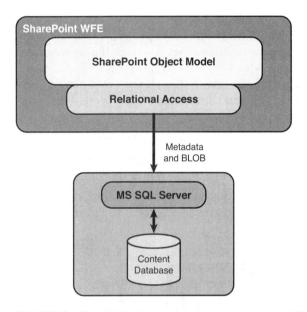

FIGURE 9.15   BLOB storage in previous versions of SharePoint.

In May 2007, Microsoft released a hotfix for Windows SharePoint Services 3.0 and Microsoft Office SharePoint Server 2007 that was later rolled into Service Pack 1. The hotfix exposed an External BLOB Storage API (EBS), which enabled the storage of BLOBs outside content databases by implementing a set of interfaces. This seemed revolutionary, but EBS was difficult to implement because it exposed an unmanaged interface. Accordingly, this part had to be handled by third parties, or independent software vendors (ISVs). In addition, EBS had some limitations; for example, it could be enabled only on the farm level and not on the content database level.

Microsoft heard its customers' feedback loud and clear and decided to fix the BLOB storage pain points. In SharePoint 2010, it is now possible to move the storage of BLOBs from database servers to commodity storage solutions by using Remote Blob Storage technology, which was introduced in SQL Server 2008.

Introducing Remote BLOB Storage

Remote BLOB Storage (RBS) is a library API set designed to move storage of large binary data (BLOBs) from Microsoft SQL Server to external storage solutions. RBS is incorporated as an add-on feature pack for Microsoft SQL Server 2008 and Microsoft SQL Server 2008 Express, and later SQL Server 2008 R2 and SQL Server 2008 R2 Express.

Using RBS, applications can store large amounts of unstructured data (such as Office documents, PDF files, or videos) and enjoy both the relational capabilities of SQL Server and the scalability of a dedicated blob store. Best of all, developers do not have to write the code to handle the job of tying together the SQL metadata and the blob data. RBS handles the transactional consistency completely.

An application stores and accesses blob data by calling into the RBS client library. ISVs and storage solution vendors can create their own RBS Provider Library to enable the use of custom stores with applications written against the RBS API set. Microsoft has even created a provider named FILESTREAM RBS provider, which comes with RBS 2008 R2 and can be used for storing BLOBs on the underlying NTFS file system. The FILESTREAM RBS provider ties the RBS technology with the FILESTREAM feature introduced in SQL Server 2008.

SharePoint 2007 did not take advantage of the recent SQL Server features that Microsoft introduced for unstructured data in SQL Server 2008, such as the FILESTREAM attribute or RBS technology; instead, SharePoint 2007 provided its own options to enhance the storage efficiency and manageability of huge data though External BLOB Storage (EBS).

SharePoint 2010 supports RBS and can leverage the SQL Server FILESTREAM RBS provider, thus providing cheaper storage and much better performance. Figure 9.16 illustrates how RBS works with SharePoint 2010.

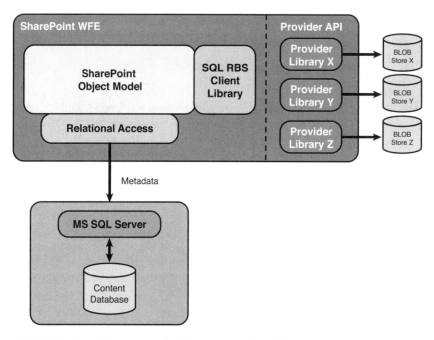

FIGURE 9.16   Externalizing BLOB storage using RBS.

In SharePoint 2010, the FILESTREAM RBS provider can also be used to work around the 4GB database limitation in SQL Server Express. Unlike Windows SharePoint Services 3.0, SharePoint Foundation 2010 does not use the Windows Internal Database, which had no database size limit. Therefore, when Windows SharePoint Services 3.0 users are trying to upgrade their farms, they might fall into a scenario where they have an internal database larger than 4GB, which would exceed the limitation of SQL Server Express. At this point, they will be prompted to download the FILESTREAM RBS provider to use the underlying file system to externalize their BLOBs.

RBS Versus EBS

As mentioned, EBS was an earlier attempt by Microsoft in SharePoint 2007 SP1 to help customers externalize their BLOBs. However, EBS was hard to implement and had some limitations. Microsoft introduced EBS as an immediate help, and it was designed in a way that it is an evolutionary approach in that administrators can move to RBS later. EBS will continue to be supported for SharePoint 2010, but it is on the deprecation list, which means its support will end in a future release of SharePoint. Microsoft recommends using RBS in SharePoint 2010 not only because EBS is on the deprecation list but also because RBS is more powerful and maintainable. Table 9.1 illustrates some of the advantages of RBS over EBS.

TABLE 9.1   Comparison of Legacy Versus RBS

Feature	RBS	EBS
BLOB store scope	Can be configured on the content database level. (Each content database can have its own BLOB store.)	Can be configured only on the farm level
Number of providers	Multiple.	Only one
Interface	Managed.	Unmanaged
Migrating BLOBs from SQL Server stores to BLOB stores and vice versa	Windows PowerShell.	Custom
SharePoint interface	SharePoint 2010 ships with many Windows PowerShell commandlets that can be used to manage RBS installation and configuration.	None

Installing and Configuring RBS

Administrators can use the following procedure to install and configure the BLOB externalization in SharePoint 2010 using RBS and the RBS FILESTREAM provider. Each step in the following procedure is explained in detail:

1. Enable FILESTREAM on SQL Server.
2. Prepare the database, and create a BLOB store.
3. Install the RBS client.
4. Enable RBS using Windows PowerShell.

Enable FILESTREAM on SQL Server

Administrators must enable and configure FILESTREAM on the computer running SQL Server 2008 (RTM/R2) that hosts the SharePoint Server 2010 databases:

1. Click Start, All Programs, Microsoft SQL Server 2008 R2, Configuration Tools, SQL Server Configuration Manager.

2. In the left panel of SQL Server Configuration Manger, click SQL Server Services, which will list all the SQL Server 2008-related services on the right-side panel.

3. Locate the instance of SQL Server on which you want to enable FILESTREAM, right-click the instance, and then click Properties.

4. In the SQL Server Properties dialog box, click the FILESTREAM tab and select the Enable FILESTREAM for Transact-SQL Access check box, which will enable the rest of the options.

5. Select all the check boxes, and then click Apply.

6. Click Start, All Programs, Microsoft SQL Server 2008 R2, SQL Server Management Studio.

7. Connect to the desired SQL Server database engine instance.

8. In SQL Server Management Studio, click New Query to display the Query Editor.

9. In Query Editor, enter the following Transact-SQL code:

```
EXEC sp_configure filestream_access_level, 2; RECONFIGURE
```

10. Click Execute.

Prepare the Database and Create a BLOB Store

The following steps show how to prepare the database and create a BLOB store:

1. Click Start, All Programs, Microsoft SQL Server 2008 R2, SQL Server Management Studio.

2. Connect to the desired SQL Server database engine instance and expand that instance.

3. Expand the databases, select the content database for which a BLOB store will be created, click New Query, and then execute the following commands:

```
use [ContentDatabaseName]
if not exists (select * from sys.symmetric_keys where name =
➥N'##MS_DatabaseMasterKey##')create master key encryption by password = N'Admin
➥Key Password !2#4'

use [ContentDatabaseName]
if not exists (select groupname from sysfilegroups where
➥groupname=N'RBSFilestreamProvider')alter database [ContentDatabaseName] add
➥filegroup RBSFilestreamProvider contains filestream

use [ContentDatabaseName]
alter database [ContentDatabaseName] add file (name = RBSFilestreamFile,
➥filename = 'c:\RemoteBlobStore') to filegroup RBSFilestreamProvider
```

Install RBS

The following steps show how to install RBS:

1. Download RBS 2008 R2 with the FILESTREAM provider (RBS_X64.msi) from
   http://go.microsoft.com/fwlink/?LinkID=165839&clcid=0x409 on the database
   server, all the web frontends, and all the application servers.

2. On the database server, run the following commands from the location of the
   RBS_X64.msi file using the command prompt:

```
msiexec /qn /lvx* rbs_install_log.txt /i RBS_X64.msi
➥TRUSTSERVERCERTIFICATE=true FILEGROUP=PRIMARY DBNAME="ContentDatabaseName"
➥DBINSTANCE="DatabaseInstanceName" FILESTREAMFILEGROUP=RBSFilestreamProvider
➥FILESTREAMSTORENAME=FilestreamProvider_1

msiexec /qn /lvx* rbs_install_log.txt /i RBS_X64.msi DBNAME="
➥ContentDatabaseName " DBINSTANCE=" DatabaseInstanceName "
➥ADDLOCAL="Client,Docs,Maintainer,ServerScript,FilestreamClient,
➥FilestreamServer"
```

This should be run against each content database that should support RBS.

3. On all the web frontends and all the application servers, run the following
   command from the location of the RBS_X64.msi file using the command prompt:

```
msiexec /qn /lvx* rbs_install_log.txt /i RBS_X64.msi DBNAME="
➥ContentDatabaseName " DBINSTANCE=" DatabaseInstanceName "
➥ADDLOCAL="Client,Docs,Maintainer,ServerScript,FilestreamClient,
➥FilestreamServer"
```

These commands kick off an msiexec service that run in a silent mode, not providing any feedback about their success or failure. Administrators can monitor the
service in the Task Manager to ensure that they are finished.

4. Administrators can confirm the RBS installation by looking for the text Product: SQL
   Remote Blob Storage—Configuration Completed Successfully in the RBS log file. The
   previous installation commands create a log file named rbs_install_log.txt in the
   same location as the RBS_X64.msi file. The installation also creates several tables in
   the specified content database with names that are preceded by mssqlrbs.
   Administrators can also look for these tables to confirm the installation.

NOTE

SQL Server 2008 released RBS 2008, which was the first version of RBS API. This version is not supported with SharePoint 2010. The version referred to here as RBS 2008
R2 was enhanced to work with SharePoint 2010, ships with the FILESTREAM provider,
and can be installed on both SQL Server 2008 and SQL Server 2008 R2.

Enable RBS Using Windows PowerShell

The following steps show how to enable RBS using Windows PowerShell:

1. Click Start, All Programs, Microsoft SharePoint 2010 Products, SharePoint 2010 Management Shell.

2. At the Windows PowerShell command prompt (PS C:\>), type each of the following commands and press Enter after each one:

```
$cdb = Get-SPContentDatabase ContentDatabaseName
$blobstoragesettings = $cdb.RemoteBlobStorageSettings
$blobstoragesettings.Enable()
$blobstoragesettings.SetActiveProviderName($blobstoragesettings.GetProviderName
➥s()[0])
```

The `Enable` commandlet enables the usage of RSB for a certain content database. When RBS is enabled, BLOBs get stored in the active BLOB store. When the active BLOB store is disabled through the `Disable` commandlet, the BLOBs get stored back in the content database.

The `GetProviderNames` commandlet can be used to list all the registered providers in the farm, and the names are retrieved from the configuration database.

The `SetActiveProviderName` commandlet is used to activate a certain provider for a certain content database. A farm can have multiple RBS providers, but only one of them can be active at a time for a given content database.

Another useful commandlet that was not used previously is the `MinimumBlobStorageSize` commandlet. This commandlet can be used to set a size threshold. For example, an administrator can decide to store files smaller than 1MB in the content database and larger ones in the BLOB store.

3. Now, all the uploaded documents should go to the BLOB store (c:\RemoteBlobStore) rather than being saved in the specified content database. Figure 9.17 illustrates the upload operation workflow in SharePoint 2010 after enabling RBS.

Migrating and Moving BLOBs Between BLOB Stores

SharePoint 2010 ships with a powerful PowerShell commandlet named `Migrate` that can be used by administrators to move BLOBs from their current locations to the current active RBS provider store. This implies that administrators can use the commandlet to move data from SQL Server to another remote BLOB store, and vice versa. Moving BLOBs from a content database is a typical requirement after installing and configuring RBS on already running SharePoint systems.

It is also worth mentioning that the `Migrate` commandlet performs a deep copy of the BLOBs one BLOB at a time, and there is no downtime required for moving all the BLOBs. The migration process also can be paused and resumed at any time, which means that at a point, part of the BLOBs can be in SQL Server, and the other part can reside in another BLOB store.

This commandlet can even be used to move BLOBs from one BLOB store to another one by moving them back to SQL Server and then migrating them to another store.

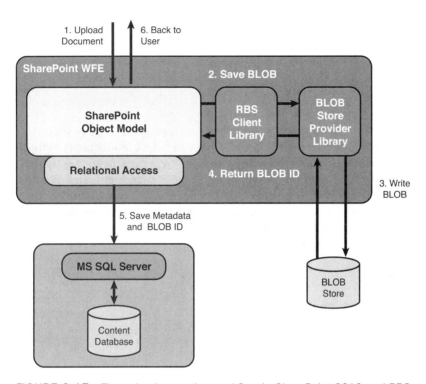

FIGURE 9.17   The upload operation workflow in SharePoint 2010 and RBS.

Migrating BLOBs from a Content Database to the Current Active Provider Store
The following steps show how to migrate BLOBs from a content database to the current
active provider store:

1. Click Start, All Programs, Microsoft SharePoint 2010 Products, SharePoint 2010
   Management Shell.

2. At the Windows PowerShell command prompt (PS C:\>), type each of the following
   commands and press Enter after each one:

```
$cdb = Get-SPContentDatabase ContentDatabaseName
$blobstoragesettings = $cdb.RemoteBlobStorageSettings
$blobstoragesettings.Migrate()
```

Migrating BLOBs from the Current Active Provider Store Back to the Content Database
The following steps show how to migrate the current active provider store back to a
content database:

1. Click Start, All Programs, Microsoft SharePoint 2010 Products, SharePoint 2010
   Management Shell.

2. At the Windows PowerShell command prompt (PS C:\>), type each of the following
   commands and press Enter after each one:

```
$cdb = Get-SPContentDatabase ContentDatabaseName
```

```
$blobstoragesettings = $cdb.RemoteBlobStorageSettings
$blobstoragesettings.Disable()
$blobstoragesettings.Migrate()
```

Summary

The proficient and regular monitoring of SQL Server performance and storage is vital to keeping a SharePoint farm running optimally. Monitoring can help administrators manage and maintain their environments as they grow and can help them proactively deal with catastrophic issues. It is crucial to plan SQL Server monitoring, management, and maintenance to help avoid redundant effort. Following a management and maintenance regimen reduces administration, maintenance, and business expenses while at the same time increases reliability, stability, and performance.

Best Practices

The following are best practices from this chapter:

▶ Keep an eye on SQL Server performance and storage using the vast range of available monitoring tools.

▶ Use the SQL Server Management Studio Log File Viewer to monitor both SQL Server and Windows event logs. It is highly recommended to look through the logs on a daily basis to detect any existing or possible issues.

▶ Use the SQL Server Maintenance Plan Wizard to set up SQL maintenance plans.

▶ Do not to include the option to shrink the database when creating SQL Server maintenance plans; this should be run manually only if the content database has lost at least half of its content.

▶ Set the maintenance plans in production environments to run during off hours.

▶ Ensure that the health analyzer is configured to automatically self-heal the database's index fragmentation.

▶ To enhance the performance of SharePoint implementations, try not to let content databases grow larger than 100GB.

▶ Create new site collections in new content databases; this enhances the performance, simplifies the manageability, and provides flexibility for disaster recovery strategies.

▶ Move the storage of BLOBs from content databases to commodity storage solutions by using the RBS technology introduced in SQL Server 2008 to avoid storage and performance issues.

▶ Use RBS rather than EBS. EBS is on the deprecation list, so its support will end in a future release of SharePoint.

## CHAPTER 10

Backing Up and Restoring a SharePoint Environment

A SharePoint document management and collaboration environment is a critical component, on par with mail in terms of criticality for many organizations. The ability to perform comprehensive backup and restore of a SharePoint 2010 environment is subsequently a critical requirement as part of an enterprise disaster recovery strategy.

SharePoint 2010 includes a wide variety of tools that provide for backup and restore, which can sometimes be confusing. These tools are powerful, but in many cases overlap, and it is not immediately obvious how to use them.

This chapter focuses on the built-in tools provided for Backup and Restore of a SharePoint 2010 environment. Specific guidance around usage of these tools is given, and recommended backup routines are provided.

Backing Up and Recovering SharePoint Components

Backup options in SharePoint 2010 have been scoped across wider areas in comparison to its predecessors. SharePoint 2010 administrators have an array of options to choose from and combine, per best practices outlined in this chapter, to back up and restore SharePoint 2010 content.

In comparison to earlier versions, SharePoint 2010 administrators, can now back up the farm configuration, complete farm, and site collection only or even do a granular level of backup and restore. In addition to this, SharePoint 2010 administrators can now connect to an unattached content database and restore content from it.

The tools covered in this chapter for backup and restore are the following:

▶ **Recycle Bin**—Introduced in SharePoint 2007, this has been a popular tool widely used by the end users and by the SharePoint administrators. Because the data can be restored by the end user within 30 days of deletion and thereafter by the site collection administrators, it has led to reduced IT overheads in data restoration.

▶ **Central Administration**—Central Administration GUI is one of the tools that can be used to back up and restore the SharePoint environment. However, not all backup and restore options are available when using the Central Administration site.

▶ **SharePoint 2010 Management Shell**—SharePoint 2010 introduces Administration Management Shell, which is built on top of Windows PowerShell. Windows PowerShell is a command-line tool that SharePoint Administrators can use to administer the SharePoint environment. Windows PowerShell provides additional options for the SharePoint administrators, which are not available to execute using the Central Administration GUI.

▶ **STSADM**—Although STSADM is available with SharePoint 2010, it has been deprecated and is provided only to support backward compatibility. Windows PowerShell is the preferred option for managing SharePoint 2010 environment. In certain situations, Windows PowerShell is the only option to administer SharePoint 2010 environment.

▶ **IIS backup**—II7 configuration on Windows Server 2008 can now be backed up using the appcmd executable file. The IIS 7 configuration file is composed of web.config files and applicationHost.config files. In a situation in which a system failure occurs, systems administrators can restore the IIS7 configuration from the backup file.

▶ **SQL backup**—SharePoint configuration and content databases stored in SQL Server can be backed up using built-in backup functionality, either by the DBA's initiating this as a once-off task or can schedule tasks to do a full backup. SQL database backup can be combined with other SharePoint backup options, such as Central Administration or SharePoint 2010 Management Shell. Unlike SharePoint restore procedures, SQL restore procedures cannot restore item level objects, only complete database restores.

▶ **Microsoft System Center Data Protection Manager (DPM) 2010**—DPM 2010 is Microsoft's enterprise backup tool. DPM does snapshot-level backup and restore of SharePoint content, providing for full farm or individual item level recovery. DPM is a separate component and is not included with SharePoint 2010.

▶ **Third-party backup tools**—Vendors such as Idera and AvePoint already have backup tools for SharePoint 2007 that facilitates item-level restores. These vendors are currently working on releasing backup tools for SharePoint 2010.

Using the Recycle Bin for Recovery

Recycle Bin functionality was built-in originally with SharePoint 2007 and is available in SharePoint 2010 as well. This functionality is the first line of defense for restores, enabling end users and administrators to restore deleted items easily and reduce overheads associated with restore operations and loss of productivity.

Understanding the Two Stages of the Recycle Bin

As in SharePoint 2007, the Recycle Bin functionality in SharePoint 2010 remains the same: two staged. When an item is deleted, it goes through both Recycle Bins before being deleted completely from the database.

The first Recycle Bin, as shown in Figure 10.1, is at the site level. This Recycle Bin is available and managed by the end users of the site. To restore deleted items from the Recycle Bin, the end user can navigate to the Recycle Bin from the Quick Launch (left navigation in SharePoint), select the deleted items to restore, and click Restore Selection. This action restores the deleted items in their original locations.

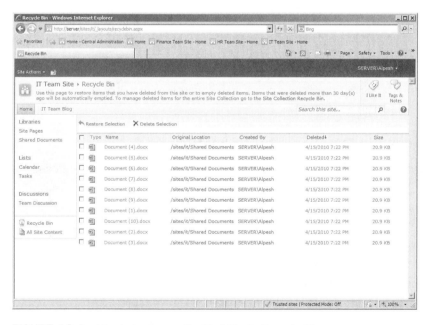

FIGURE 10.1   Viewing a team site First Stage Recycle Bin.

NOTE

End users see only the items that have been deleted by them. They do not see items that have been deleted by other users.

10

If the end users have not restored the deleted items from the site Recycle Bin within the retention period (default is 30 days), or have deleted the items from the Recycle Bin, the items are moved to the secondary Recycle Bin. This Recycle Bin is at the site collection level, and only site collection administrators have access to this Recycle Bin to restore items for the end users, as shown in Figure 10.2.

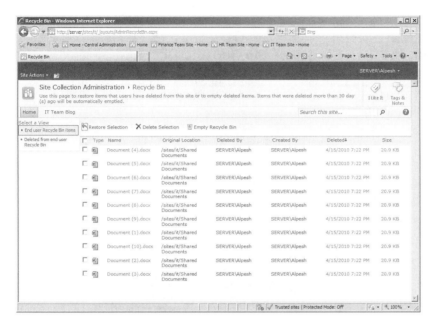

FIGURE 10.2   Viewing a site collection Second Stage Recycle Bin.

Enabling Recycle Bin Functionality in SharePoint

To access the Recycle Bin settings for a particular web application, perform the following steps:

1. Open the SharePoint Central Administration site on SharePoint 2010 Central Administration.

2. Select Application Management in Quick Launch.

3. Under Web Applications, click the link for Manage Web Applications.

4. Highlight the web application that you want to manage.

5. The Ribbon will be highlighted.

6. Click General Settings and select General Settings from the drop-down menu.

7. Scroll down to the Recycle Bin options, modify the settings, and click OK to save these changes.

The Recycle Bin settings listed, shown in Figure 10.3, allow for the following options:

▶ **Recycle Bin Status**—This setting enables the entire web application Recycle Bin, including both stages, to be toggled on or off.

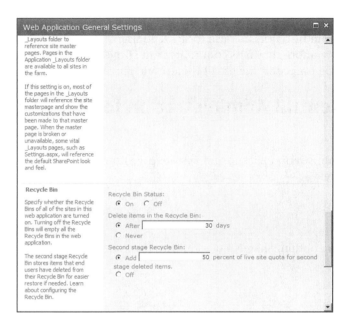

FIGURE 10.3   Understanding Recycle Bin settings for a web application.

▶ **Delete Items in the Recycle Bin**—This sets the number of days before items are removed from the end user Recycle Bin. The default value is 30 days. This setting can be altered with a number of days of your choice, or it can be toggled to never delete items from the Recycle Bin.

▶ **Second Stage Recycle Bin**—The Site Collection Recycle Bin, also known as the Second Stage Recycle Bin, can be either turned off or configured to be emptied after it reaches the specified percentage of the web application's quota. For example, if the web application has a quota of 500MB, a setting of 50 percent enables up to 250MB of data to be stored in the Second Stage Recycle Bin, increasing the effective quota of the web application to 750MB. This setting can be changed to a different number up to 100 percent or can be toggled off.

CAUTION

These settings should be altered only after analyzing the usage pattern of the Recycle Bin at the site level, number of requests received for Second Stage Recycle Bin restore, and the type of restore requests received by the SharePoint administrators. Items retained in the Site Recycle Bin count toward the quota of a site collection, so this setting has to strike a balance between the number of days and the site collection quota. Similarly settings of 100 percent for the Second Stage Recycle Bin would mean that the size of site collection would be twice as much in the content databases.

The Recycle Bin had been introduced in SharePoint 2007 and has proved to be a value add, not only for the SharePoint administrators but also for the end users. The Recycle Bin helps reduce SharePoint restore operations, business continuity, and IT overheads. It is recommended that the end users be trained in the use of the Recycle Bin.

Using SharePoint Central Administration for Backup and Restore

The SharePoint 2010 Central Administration Backup and Restore page now comes with two options for backup and restore:

▶ Farm Backup and Restore

▶ Granular Backup and Restore

Using the Farm Backup and Restore option, SharePoint administrators can back up the following:

▶ Complete Farm

▶ Farm Configuration Only

▶ Individual Components in a Farm

Granular backup and restore is a new addition in SharePoint 2010 Central Administration tool that enables SharePoint administrators to do the following:

▶ Back up site collection

▶ Export document library or list

Ideally the SharePoint Central Administration tool would be used to do a once-off backup or restore operation. As with previous versions, scheduling backups via the SharePoint 2010 Central Administration tool is not an option from within the GUI.

Back Up Using Central Administration

Before backing up using the SharePoint Central Administration tool, the backup location needs to be configured. The backup location can be a local drive on the server or a network share.

Farm Configuration Backup

To back up farm configuration using the SharePoint Central Administration tool, perform the following steps:

1. Open the SharePoint Central Administration site on a SharePoint Server (Start, All Programs, Microsoft SharePoint 2010 Products, SharePoint 2010 Central Administration).

2. Select Backup and Restore in Quick Launch.

3. Under the Farm Backup and Restore section, select Perform a Backup.

4. From the Select Component to Backup page, select the Farm component, as shown in Figure 10.4.

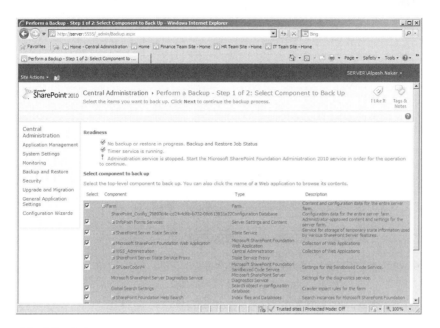

FIGURE 10.4   Backing up a farm from the Central Administration tool.

5. Click Next at the bottom of the page.

6. In the Select Backup Options page, select the full backup, as shown in Figure 10.5. (When performing a backup of the component for the first time, differential backup should not be selected because the backup operation will fail.)

7. In the next section, on the same page, select Back Up Only Configuration Settings and click Next.

8. In the next section, on the same page, enter a backup location and click Start Backup.

After starting the backup, SharePoint 2010 displays the Backup and Restore Job Status page. It might take several minutes for the backup process to appear on the page, depending on the backup type and the data to back up. On this page, the backup and restore progress can be monitored by clicking the View History link, View the Backup, and Restore History.

Backup files can viewed in the Backup location selected earlier and appear as an XML manifest file, as shown in Figure 10.6, and as a folder full of BAK files, as shown in Figure 10.7. It is recommended not to delete the XML manifest file in the root because it will be required to restore your backup components.

10

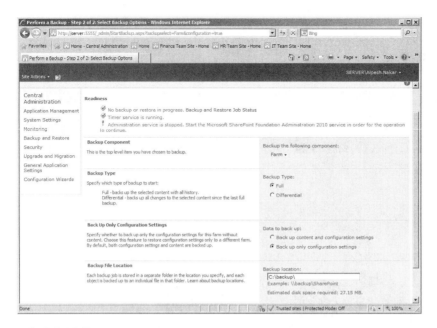

FIGURE 10.5   Choosing backup options in the Central Administration tool.

FIGURE 10.6   Examining a SharePoint backup manifest file.

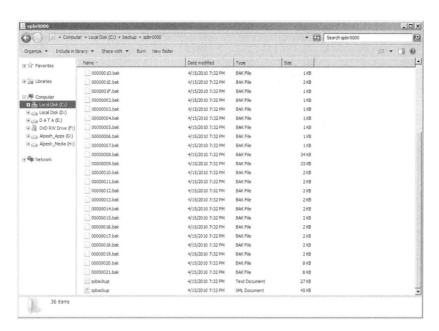

FIGURE 10.7   Viewing a site backup file location.

When doing configuration backup, service application settings, including service proxies, are not included in the backup.

Performing Granular Backup Using the SharePoint Central Administration

Granular backup of SharePoint 2010, previously available only from the STSADM command-line tool, is now available from within the GUI.

Backing Up a Site Collection

To back up a site collection using the SharePoint Central Administration tool, perform the following steps:

1. Open the SharePoint Central Administration site on a SharePoint Server (Start, All Programs, Microsoft SharePoint 2010 Products, SharePoint 2010 Central Administration).

2. Select Backup and Restore in Quick Launch.

3. Select Perform a Site Collection Backup, under the Granular Backup section.

10

4. On the Site Collection Backup page, select a site collection to backup from the drop-down menu, as shown in Figure 10.8.

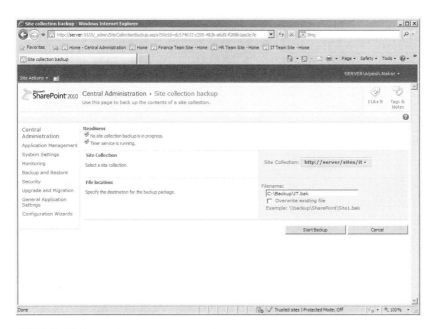

FIGURE 10.8   Performing a granular SharePoint site backup.

5. Enter the backup location and the filename ending with extension .bak in the Filename box. Select Overwrite Existing File if you want to overwrite, and then click Start Backup.

After starting the backup, SharePoint 2010 displays the Granular Backup Job Status page. On this page, the granular backup progress can be monitored and displays site collection backup status and content export status (discussed later in this chapter).

NOTE

Site collection backups don't include workflows.

Unlike the Farm Backup and Restore operation, a detailed history of the granular backup operations cannot be viewed. Second, a backup of the site collection done using SharePoint Central Administration cannot be restored via the SharePoint Central Administration GUI. This backup can be restored only using Windows PowerShell cmdlet Restore-SPSite, which will be covered later in this chapter.

This method is recommended in situations in which a once-off backup of a site collection is required, either in a scenario in which the site collection content needs to be archived or in a scenario in which the site collection needs to move under a different web application.

NOTE

Granular backup and export is a processor-intensive function in comparison to farm backup operation.

Export a Site or List Using the Central Admin Console

To export a site or a list using the SharePoint Central Administration, perform the following steps:

1. Open the SharePoint Central Administration site on a SharePoint Server (Start, All Programs, Microsoft SharePoint 2010 Products, SharePoint 2010 Central Administration).

2. Select Backup and Restore in Quick Launch.

3. Select Export a Site or List, under Granular Backup section.

4. On the Site or List Export page, select a site collection, select the site, and then select the list to export from the drop-down menu, as shown in Figure 10.9.

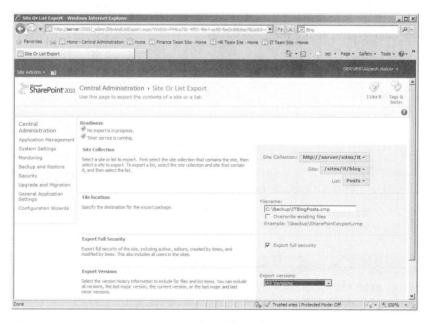

FIGURE 10.9   Exporting a list using Central Admin backup.

5. Enter a backup location and the filename ending with extension .cmp in the Filename box. Select Overwrite Existing File if you want to overwrite.

6. The next toggle gives an option to export full security, including author, editors, created by times, and modified times. If the selection is not at the list level, but at

the site level (that is, exporting a site), then Full Security Export will include all users in the site. Select this option if required.

7. The next drop-down menu gives options to export the version history for files and list items. The options are All Versions, Last Major, Current Version, Last Major, and Minor Versions. Select the desired choice from the drop-down menu, as shown in Figure 10.9, and then click Start Export.

After starting the export, SharePoint 2010 displays the Granular Backup Job Status page. On this page, the granular backup progress can be monitored and displays the content export and site collection backup status (discussed in the earlier section of this chapter).

Unlike the Farm Backup and Restore operation, a detailed history of the granular backup operations cannot be viewed. Secondly, content export done using SharePoint Central Administration cannot be imported via the SharePoint Central Administration GUI. The import operation can be done only using Windows PowerShell cmdlet Import-SPWeb, which will be covered later in this chapter.

This method is recommended in situations in which a site needs to be moved to a different site collection or more commonly moving a SharePoint list to a different site. Earlier this level of export and import was made available in SharePoint Designer 2007 and FrontPage 2003. This feature is not available in SharePoint Designer 2010 and is now made available from SharePoint Central Administration.

Restoring SharePoint Using SharePoint Central Administration

Backups done using the Central Administration tool generate the XML Manifest and files with .BAK extensions. In case of a restore situation, both XML Manifest and files with .BAK extensions will be required. SharePoint administrators can restore these backups onto the same environment or on entirely new environment; for example, User Acceptance Test (UAT) environment or Development environment.

Similarly, in case of a catastrophic failure, hardware, or the entire farm, SharePoint administrators can rebuild the environment and then restore the SharePoint 2010 farm.

> **NOTE**
> Only site collections can be recovered from a site collection backup.

Restore Farm Configuration Using Central Administration

Perform the following steps to restore farm configuration and other components using SharePoint Central Administration:

1. Open the SharePoint Central Administration site on a SharePoint Server (Start, All Programs, Microsoft SharePoint 2010 Products, SharePoint 2010 Central Administration).

2. Select Backup and Restore in Quick Launch.

3. Under the Farm Backup and Restore section, select Restore from a Backup.

4. On the Backup and Restore History page, enter the Backup Directory Location.

5. Select the Farm Component that you want to restore, as shown in Figure 10.10, and click Next.

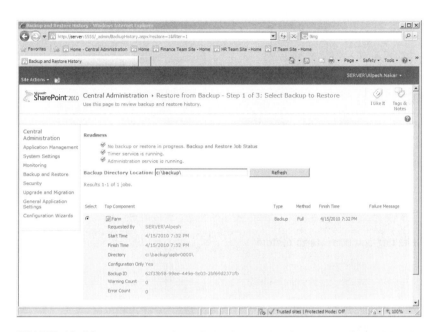

FIGURE 10.10   Restoring a SharePoint farm using SharePoint Central Administration.

6. It takes few minutes before the Select Component to Restore page displays. On this page, select the SharePoint component to restore, as shown in Figure 10.11, and then click Next.

7. On the Select Restore Options page, select New Configuration to restore a farm with different computer names, web application names, or database servers, or select Same Configuration to restore a farm with the same computer names, web application names, and database servers, as shown in Figure 10.12. Click Start Restore to begin the restore process.

Recovering Data from an Unattached Content Database

SharePoint 2010 has the capability to restore content from an unattached content database. The content database does not need to be "attached" to a SharePoint farm but does need to be attached to a SQL. To recover data from an unattached content database, perform the following steps:

1. Open the SharePoint Central Administration site on a SharePoint Server (Start, All Programs, Microsoft SharePoint 2010 Products, SharePoint 2010 Central Administration).

FIGURE 10.11   Selecting components to restore.

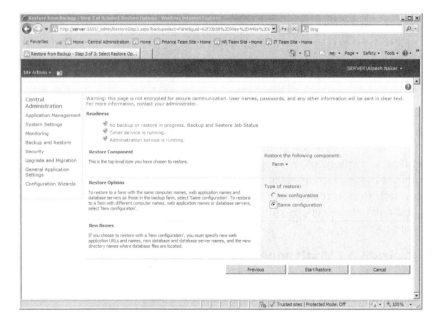

FIGURE 10.12   Finalizing settings for a farm restore.

2. Select Backup and Restore in Quick Launch.

3. Under the Granular Backup section, select Recover Data from an unattached content database.

4. On the Unattached Content Database Data Recovery page, enter the name of the database server, and then enter the database name to connect to. If you use SQL authentication, provide credentials and select the operation to perform, either Browse Content, Backup Site Collection, or Export a Site or List to select a site collection, as shown in Figure 10.13.

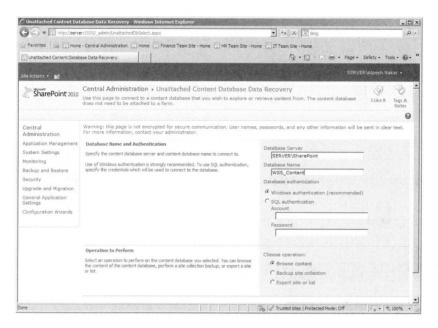

FIGURE 10.13   Recovering data from an Unattached Content Database.

5. On the Browse content page, select the site collection from the drop-down menu. On the site collection dialog page, check the name of the content database and then select the site collection to backup from the unattached content database. Click OK to return to the Browse Content page

6. The Browse Content page looks like Figure 10.14. Select Backup Site Collection Operation and click next.

7. On the Site Collection Backup page, enter backup location and the filename ending with extension .bak in the Filename box. Select Overwrite Existing File if you want to overwrite and then click Start Backup, as shown in Figure 10.15.

After starting the backup, SharePoint 2010 displays the Granular Backup Job Status page. On this page, the granular backup progress can be monitored and displays site collection backup status.

10

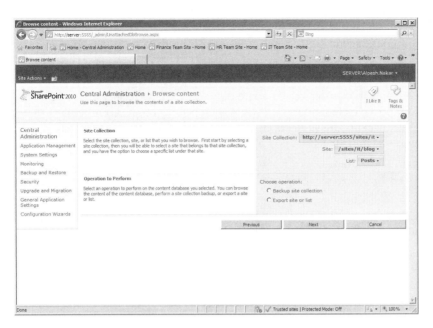

FIGURE 10.14   Browsing for content to restore in an Unattached Content Database.

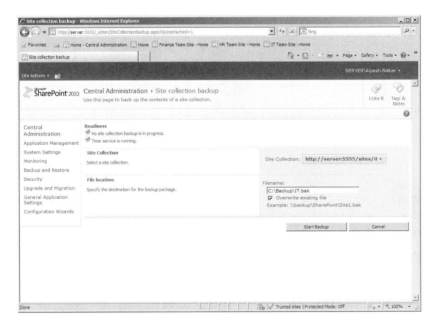

FIGURE 10.15   Extracting content from an Unattached Content Database by backing it up.

This method is recommended in situations in which a site collection or a list needs to be retrieved from a content database not attached to a SharePoint web application but to a SQL Server instance.

> **NOTE**
>
> Unattached databases include read-only content databases and SQL Server database snapshots of content databases.

Site collections, Sites, Lists, and Libraries can be restored from an unattached database.

Using SharePoint 2010 Management PowerShell for Backup and Restore

SharePoint 2010 Management Shell built on Windows PowerShell is installed with SharePoint Foundation and SharePoint Server 2010. Although the STSADM command is available with SharePoint 2010, it has been deprecated to provide backward compatibility with previous versions. SharePoint 2010 administrators have now been armed with a powerful management shell to administer SharePoint 2010 environments. SharePoint 2010 Management Shell is far more powerful than SharePoint Central Administration and STSADM combined. SharePoint Central Administration is limited in functionality to what is represented in GUI, whereas SharePoint 2010 Management Shell is highly extensible with more than 600 prebuilt cmdlets available at the time of writing, in addition to support for creating custom cmdlet.

> **NOTE**
>
> Sample backup and restore scripts are included in Chapter 7, "Leveraging PowerShell for Command-Line SharePoint Administration and Automation."

Backing Up the Farm Configuration Using PowerShell

To back up farm configuration using the SharePoint 2010 Management Shell, execute the following command from within the PowerShell Shell, as shown in Figure 10.16:

```
backup-spfarm –BackupMethod Full –Directory C:\Backup\ -ConfigurationOnly
```

Backing Up an Entire Web Application

To back up a single web application using the SharePoint 2010 Management Shell, execute the following command, as shown in Figure 10.17:

```
backup-spfarm –BackupMethod Full –Directory C:\Backup\ -Item http://server
```

FIGURE 10.16   Backing up the farm using PowerShell.

FIGURE 10.17   Backing up a web application using PowerShell.

> **NOTE**
>
> http://server is the name of the web application to be backed up using the Full
> method. If the web application is being backed up for the first time, it has to be full
> backup, or else the backup will fail in case of first-time differential backup.

The advantage of using Windows PowerShell is in executing multiple instances of
Windows PowerShell scripts to back up site collections using the BackUpThreads parameter in backup-spfarm. The recommended value for SharePoint Foundation is 3 threads.

Restoring a Site Collection

To restore a single site collection using the SharePoint 2010 Management Shell, execute
the following command, as shown in Figure 10.18:

```
Restore-SPSite –identity http://server/sites/it -path c:\backup\it\itbackup.bak –
force
```

> **NOTE**
>
> We have used force to overwrite the site collection in the web application.

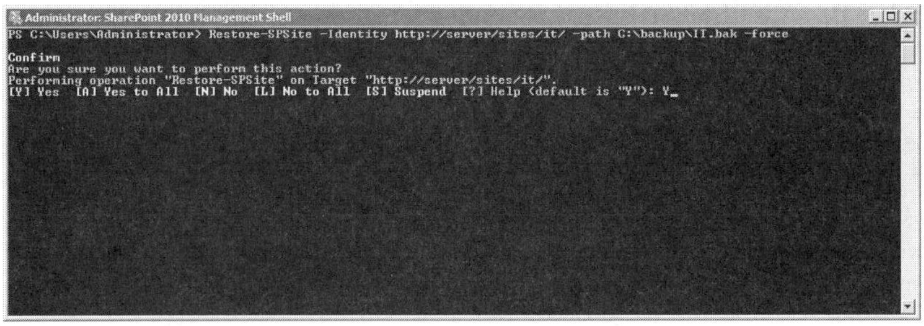

FIGURE 10.18   Restoring a site collection using PowerShell.

Import Site or List

To import a list within a site using the SharePoint 2010 Management Shell, execute the following command from within the PowerShell Shell:

```
Import-SPWeb –Identity http://servers/sites/IT/Announcements/ -Path
➥C:\Backup\IT\Announcements.cmp –IncludeUserSecurity
```

The syntax for the Import-SPWeb command is shown in Figure 10.19.

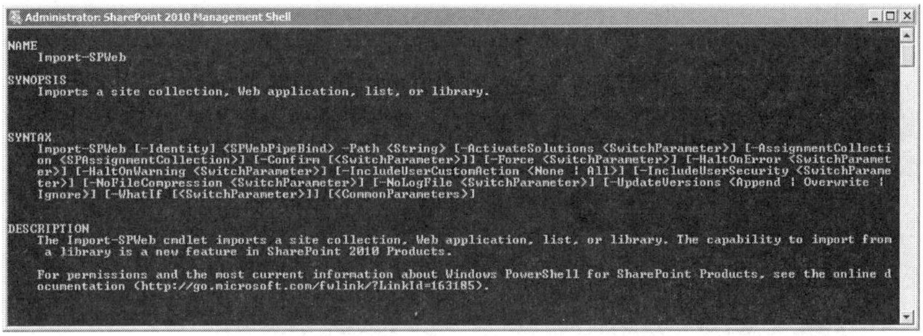

FIGURE 10.19   Examining the syntax for the Import-SPWeb commandlet.

Importing a Site

Before you can import your web, you need to create the site. To create a site using the SharePoint 2010 Management Shell, perform the following steps:

Execute the following command from within the PowerShell Shell:

```
New-SPWeb –URL http://server/sites/IT/Blog/  -Verbose
```

10

Verbose parameter has been used to see how this cmdlet executes and creates a new site, as shown in Figure 10.20. After the site has been created, it can be overwritten with the backup using the following steps:

To import a site using the SharePoint 2010 Management Shell, execute the following command, as shown in Figure 10.21:

```
Import-SPWeb –Identity http://server/sites/IT/Blog/ -Path C:\Backup\IT\Blog.cmp –
➥IncludeUserSecurity –UpdateVersions Overwrite
```

With SharePoint 2010, backup and restore of site collections, sites, or lists can now be easily done with the Central Administration tool or SharePoint 2010 Management Shell. This functionality has been removed from SharePoint Designer 2010.

Backing Up Internet Information Services v7 Configuration

Internet Information Services (IIS) configuration in Windows 2008 can be backed up using the appcmd.exe executable, because the configuration is not backed up by any of the methods previously discussed.

The IIS 7 configuration is split between the web.config files and the applicationHost.config files. The applicationHost.config files include configuration information for the sites, applications, virtual directories, application pool definitions, and the default configuration settings for all sites on the web server.

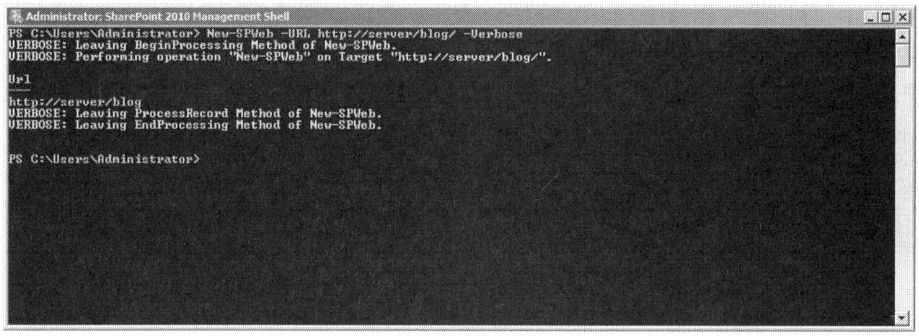

FIGURE 10.20   Creating a new site using New-SPWeb commandlet.

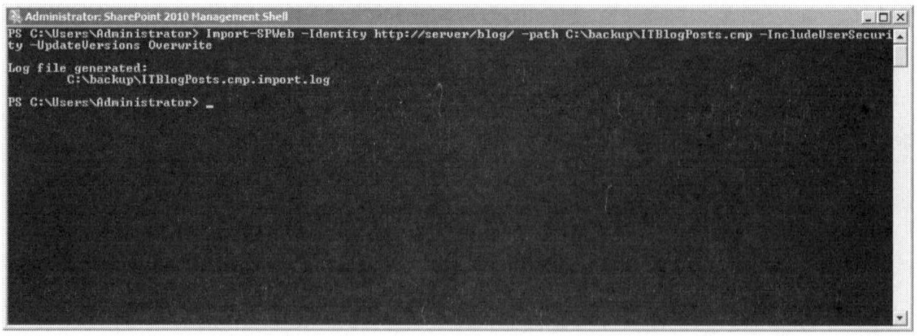

FIGURE 10.21   Importing a site using PowerShell.

To back up the IIS 7 configuration from a command prompt, follow these steps:

1. Log on to the Windows Server 2008 computer with an account that has administrator rights.

2. Open a command prompt by using the Run as Administrator option and change the directory to %windir%\system32\inetsrv.

3. At the command prompt, type **appcmd add backup** *<backupname>*. If you do not include the name of the backup, the system will name it for you by using a date, time format.

SQL Backup Tools

SharePoint 2010, fully loaded and deployed with Office Web Application, all Service applications, Logging database, FAST Search, Content Databases, and Configuration Databases will have approximately 25 databases stored in SQL Server 2008. That is a huge number of databases to maintain and certainly a lot of content in these databases! To minimize the loss of content, it is crucial to incorporate a solid SQL database backup plan to back up all these databases.

Many options are available to back up SharePoint databases in SQL Server. In addition to Central Administration and SharePoint 2010 Management Shell, SQL Server facilitates the backup and restore of SharePoint 2010 databases with the SQL Server Management Studio, SQL Server Maintenance Plans, or Transact-SQL scripts that can be executed from within SQL Server. Further, a third-party SQL backup engine can also be used to back up these SharePoint 2010 databases.

Although the backup options out-of-the-box in SharePoint give an array of tools to back up the configuration and the content databases; critical SQL Server databases such as Master, MSDB, and TempDB cannot be backed up by these tools from within SharePoint. If a catastrophic event or hardware failure occurs, restoring the full SQL Server installation to the point of failure is not possible unless there is a strategic plan to do a backup and recovery of SQL Server databases.

In addition to the standard backup features in SQL Server 2008, Backup Compression has been introduced.

SQL Server Backup Methods

SQL Server offers a wide range of options to back up databases. These include the following:

▶ **Full**—Complete database backup that includes transaction logs.

▶ **Differential**—All data changes since the last full backup is backed up.

▶ **Transaction log backup**—All transactions performed against the database since the last full backup or transaction log back up is backed up.

▶ **File and file group backup**—A portion of the database is backed up.

▶ **Partial backup**—All data in the primary group, every read-write file group, and any specified files are backed up. File groups marked read-only are skipped.

▶ **Differential partial backup**—Although similar to partial backup, this backup records only changes to the data in the file groups since the previous partial backup.

▶ **Copy-only backup**—This backup enables a backup of any type to be taken without affecting any other backups. Normally a database backup is recorded in the database and is identified as part of a chain that can be used for restoration.

To do a full backup of an individual database via the SQL Server Management Studio, perform the following steps:

1. Open the SQL Server Management Studio (Start, All Programs, Microsoft SQL Server 2008, SQL Server Management Studio).

2. In the Connect to Server dialog box, select the database server name to connect to, and click Connect.

3. In the left pane of the Object Explorer, expand the server and the database folder.

4. Select the desired SharePoint Database to back up.

5. Right-click the database, select Tasks, and then click Backup.

6. On the General settings page in the Back Up Database window, review the name of the database(s) to be backed up and confirm that the Backup Type option is set to Full.

7. For the Backup component option, select a Database option.

8. In the Backup set, enter the name and the description for the database backup.

9. In the next Destination section, the Tape option is grayed out if no tape devices are attached to the database server. In such a scenario, the only option available is to back up to disk. Click Add to add up to 64 disk devices that will contain the backup information. The same limit applies to tape media. If multiple devices are specified, the backup information will be spread across those devices. All the devices must be present to restore the database.

10. In the Select Backup Destination dialog box, enter the path and the backup file name in the destinations on the disk where the database is to be backed up. Click OK if the backup is to be initiated, or select Options in the Select a Page pane to configure advanced backup options.

In the Overwrite Media section, you have an array of options to choose from: Append to the Existing Backup Set or Overwrite All Existing Backup Sets. Backup sets can be added to an existing media, in which case you select Append to the Existing Backup Set. If you want to overwrite the backup sets with the latest backup on the media, you should select the Overwrite All Existing Backup Sets option.

NOTE

SQL Server 2008 Enterprise Edition supports compression. It must be noted that compressed and uncompressed database backups cannot co-exist on the same media set. It is to be noted that the Overwriting Backup Sets feature will be removed from the next version of Microsoft SQL Server; therefore, using this feature should be avoided in any new development instances, and any existing applications that use this feature should be modified.

In the Reliability section, you can choose to

▶ **Verify Backup When Finished**—Recommended to select because it verifies the database backup, but it does extend the time it takes to compete the database backup.

▶ **Perform Checksum Before Writing to Media**—Ensures that the database backup is completed without any errors. However, selecting this option adds to the time it takes to complete the database backup.

▶ **Continue on Error**—Database backup continues even if an error has been encountered. Selecting this option has an impact on the performance of the server, because it increases the CPU overheads.

The next Transaction Log section is available only if Backup type selected on the General page is of the type Transaction Log. The Truncate the Transaction Log option removes any inactive portion of the transaction log after the database backup is complete. This is the default option and helps keep the size of your transaction log manageable. The Backup the Tail of the Log option is related to point-in-time restores and is discussed in more detail later in this chapter.

The set of options in the Tape Drive section is enabled only when Tape has been selected for the destination media. The Unload the Tape After Backup option ejects the media tape after the backup completes. This can help identify the end of the backup and prevents the tape from being overwritten the next time the backup runs. The Rewind the Tape Before Unloading option causes the tape to be released and rewound prior to unloading the tape.

New in SQL Server 2008 is the backup compression feature. This is the last option in the backup database option section. This feature is a Microsoft proprietary formula that may shrink the size of the database backup down to 20 percent of the original size. This is dependent on the value specified in the backup-compression default server configuration option.

10

CAUTION

Using the compression option can increase the load on the CPU and affect the processing power.

Continue with the process as follows:

1. In the Options page and Overwrite Media section, maintain the default settings Back Up to the Existing Media Set and Append to the Existing Backup Set.

2. In the Reliability section, choose Verify Backup When Finished, Perform Checksum Before Writing Media, and Continue On Error Options. Click OK to execute the backup.

3. Review the success or failure error messages and click OK to finalize.

4. Repeat for additional SharePoint databases.

Understanding the SQL Server Recover Models

There are three recovery models to choose from: Simple, Full, and Bulk-Logged. The choice of the model depends on various factors that need to be considered, such as the extent to which data loss is acceptable, performance of the SQL Server, and database recovery to the point of failure.

The simple recovery model recovers the database only to the point of the last successful full or differential backup. Content added to the database after the backup cannot be recovered with this model.

The full recovery model recovers the entire database to any point in time, because transaction logs are maintained. It must be noted that because all transactions to the database are logged, SQL Server database performance tends to degrade. It is recommended that transaction logs and the database files are stored on separate hard disks for performance enhancement and recovery.

The bulk logged recovery model is similar to the full recovery model because it maintains a transaction log; however, this model should be used only in situations where large amounts of data are written to the database. To improve performance of the database server in such situations of bulk insertion or indexing, the recovery model should be switched to the bulk logged model temporarily.

Business requirements define the disaster recovery strategies and drive the database administrator's decision on choosing the appropriate recovery model for the database. By default, the SharePoint configuration, AdminContent, and site content databases' recovery model is set to Full. As a result, these databases can be restored to the point of failure.

To set the recovery model on a SharePoint content database, perform the following steps:

1. Open the SQL Server Management Studio (Start, All Programs, Microsoft SQL Server 2008, SQL Server Management Studio).

2. On the screen, select the database server to connect to the SQL database.

3. In the left pane of the Object Explorer, expand the server and then the database folder.

4. Select the desired SharePoint Database to back up. Right-click on the database, and select Properties.

5. In the Database properties dialog box, select the Options node.

6. In the Recovery Mode dialog box, select Full, Bulk-Logged, or Simple from the drop-down list. Full is typically selected in most cases. Click OK to save the changes.

Summary

For SharePoint 2010 administrators, the wide array of options to back up content and configuration can be quite daunting. However, with the correct mix of these options based on the business requirements, SharePoint configuration and content can be backed up and restored effectively without any loss to the business. Although backup and restore functionality has been removed from SharePoint Designer 2010, granular backup and restore via central administration or SharePoint 2010 Management Shell is a more effective and efficient mechanism in situations that require recovery of content.

Best Practices

▶ Implement external vendors SharePoint backup and restore solutions or Microsoft's System Center Data Protection Manager (DPM) 2010 to enable enterprisewide automation of backup and restore capabilities.

▶ For one-off backup and restore, SharePoint 2010 administrators have a choice of either using central administration tool or SharePoint 2010 Management PowerShell.

▶ Consider regular scripted backups using SharePoint 2010 Management Shell and SQL Server 2008 built-in tools.

▶ Perform regular scripted backups of IIS7 configuration.

▶ Confirm that the SQL recovery model is set to Full on SharePoint databases to allow for full restores of SQL data.

▶ SharePoint 2010 Management Shell can be used to back up the entire farm or only business-critical site collections or sites either via one-off backups or via scheduled scripts. However, if the content is business critical, SQL Server tools can be used to back up the content database or, using SQL snapshots options, back up against the SQL snapshot.

▶ Simulation of recovery on regular intervals is highly recommended. This can help in plugging any shortcomings in the backup strategies and plans.

10

Monitoring a SharePoint 2010 Environment

A SharePoint farm is complex, with many moving parts contributing to the functionality of the entire platform. Subsequently, the farm components need to be well maintained and monitored on a regular basis to ensure the smooth functioning of the environment. Of particular emphasis are the SQL databases that SharePoint runs on, which are often neglected but that specifically require regular maintenance and monitoring.

Fortunately for the SharePoint administrator, Microsoft has revamped SharePoint 2010 to include robust monitoring capabilities and features, including a new Health Monitor that automatically determines if there are issues that affect SharePoint health. The SharePoint team has also built-in advanced reporting capabilities natively in SharePoint and improved timer jobs.

In addition to the internal tools, outside of SharePoint, applications such as Microsoft's System Center Operations Manager (SCOM) 2007 R2 provide for SharePoint-aware management capabilities that exceed those of the internal tools.

This chapter focuses on the specifics for monitoring and maintaining SharePoint, including an analysis of the native tools including the SharePoint Health Analyzer and a discussion of System Center Operations Manager 2007 R2 monitoring for a SharePoint 2010 environment. In addition, practical guidance for daily, weekly, monthly, quarterly, and yearly maintenance is provided.

Using the SharePoint Health Analyzer

Previous versions of SharePoint did not include many integrated tools to help with monitoring the health of the SharePoint environment. SharePoint 2010 was built with a native SharePoint Health Analyzer, as shown in Figure 11.1, which greatly improves the ability of SharePoint administrators to quickly detect issues within the farm.

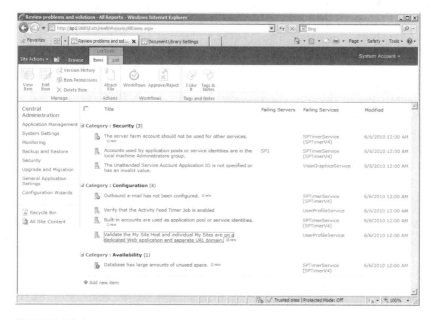

FIGURE 11.1   Viewing the SharePoint Health Analyzer.

Reviewing SharePoint Health Analyzer Settings

The SharePoint Health Analyzer is essentially a SharePoint list, shown in Figure 11.2, that is driven by timer jobs that run on a regular basis. The list settings are XML-driven and can be configured to automatically resolve SharePoint Health issues in certain cases.

In a default installation, there are more than 60 preconfigured rule definitions, in four different categories: Availability, Configuration, Performance, and Security. Each list item is configured to be checked on a regular basis. The following are a list of the default rules created in SharePoint 2010:

- ▶ Accounts used by application pools or service identities are in the local machine Administrators group.

- ▶ Web applications using Claims authentication require an update.

- ▶ The server farm account should not be used for other services.

- ▶ The Unattended Service Account Application ID is not specified or has an invalid value.

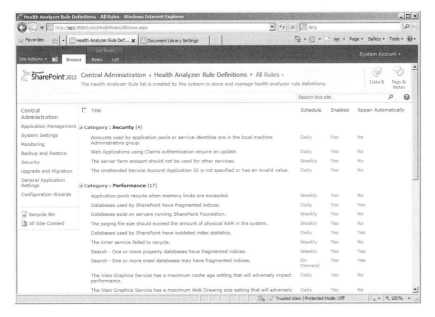

FIGURE 11.2   Examining Health Analyzer Rule Definitions.

▶ Application pools recycle when memory limits are exceeded.

▶ Databases used by SharePoint have fragmented indices.

▶ Databases exist on servers running SharePoint Foundation.

▶ The paging file size should exceed the amount of physical RAM in the system.

▶ Databases used by SharePoint have outdated index statistics.

▶ The timer service failed to recycle.

▶ Search—One or more property databases have fragmented indices.

▶ Search—One or more crawl databases may have fragmented indices.

▶ The Visio Graphics Service has a maximum cache age setting that will adversely impact performance.

▶ The Visio Graphics Service has a maximum Web Drawing size setting that will adversely impact performance.

▶ The Visio Graphics Service has a maximum recalc duration setting that will adversely impact user-perceived performance.

▶ The Visio Graphics Service has a minimum cache age setting that will adversely impact performance.

▶ The Visio Graphics Service has a minimum cache age setting that may cause a security issue.

- ▶ Web Analytics: Monitors the health of the Report Consolidator component.

- ▶ Web Analytics: Monitors the health of the Logging Extractor component.

- ▶ Web Analytics: Monitors the health of the Data Analyzer Light component.

- ▶ Web Analytics: Monitors the health of the User Behavior Analyzer component.

- ▶ Alternate access URLs have not been configured.

- ▶ The Application Discovery and Load Balancer Service is not running in this farm.

- ▶ Automatic Update setting inconsistent across farm servers.

- ▶ Built-in accounts are used as application pool or service identities.

- ▶ Missing server-side dependencies.

- ▶ Databases require upgrade or not supported.

- ▶ Databases running in compatibility range; upgrade recommended.

- ▶ One or more categories are configured with Verbose trace logging.

- ▶ Outbound email has not been configured.

- ▶ Product/patch installation or server upgrade required.

- ▶ Databases within this farm are set to read only and will fail to upgrade unless it is set to a read-write state.

- ▶ Web.config file has incorrect settings for the `requestFiltering` element.

- ▶ Web.config files are not identical on all machines in the farm.

- ▶ The InfoPath Forms Services Maintenance timer job is not enabled.

- ▶ InfoPath form library forms cannot be filled out in a web browser.

- ▶ InfoPath Forms Services forms cannot be filled out in a web browser because no State Service connection is configured.

- ▶ Trial period for this product is about to expire.

- ▶ Expired sessions are not being deleted from the ASP.NET Session State database.

- ▶ The State Service Delete Expired Sessions timer job is not enabled.

- ▶ Verify each User Profile Service Application has an associated Managed Metadata Service Connection.

- ▶ Verify each User Profile Service Application has an associated Search Service Connection.

- ▶ Verify each User Profile Service Application has a My Site Host configured.

- ▶ Verify that the critical User Profile Application and User Profile Proxy Application timer jobs are available and have not been mistakenly deleted.

- ▶ Validate the My Site Host and individual My Sites are on a dedicated web application and separate URL domain.

- ▶ Verify that the Activity Feed Timer Job is enabled.

- ▶ Web Analytics: Verifies that when the Web Analytics is installed and running, usage logging is enabled in the farm.

- ▶ Web Analytics: Verifies that a web application is serviced by at most one Web Analytics service application proxy.

- ▶ Web Analytics: Verifies that the SQL Server Service Broker is enabled for the Web Analytics staging databases.

- ▶ Web Analytics: Verify that there is a data processing service started when there is a web service started.

- ▶ Web Analytics: Verify that the Site Inventory Usage Collection timer job is enabled for all the web applications serviced by the Web Analytics service application.

- ▶ Drives are running out of free space.

- ▶ Drives are at risk of running out of free space.

- ▶ Content databases contain orphaned items. Monthly Yes No

- ▶ Some content databases are growing too large.

- ▶ Database has large amounts of unused space.

- ▶ The Security Token Service is not available.

- ▶ One or more servers is not responding.

- ▶ One or more services have started or stopped unexpectedly.

- ▶ Drives used for SQL databases are running out of free space.

- ▶ All State Service databases are paused for a State Service Application.

- ▶ A State Service Application has no database defined.

- ▶ The settings for Word Automation Services are not within the recommended limits.

- ▶ Critical state of this rule indicates that the Word Automation Services is not running when it should be running.

Modifying Health Analyzer Job Definitions

The default SharePoint Health Analyzer rules can be modified directly from within Central Admin or from PowerShell. In addition, the rules can be easily extended by third-party tools or add-ons to SharePoint. Developers or administrators can also write their own custom rules to look for specific criteria.

Custom rules can be created through creation of code that uses either the `SPHealthAnalysisRule` or `SPRepairableHealthAnalysisRule` classes. Rules are compiled and registered with the Health Analyzer and, when created, are allocated an associated timer job created to run the rule.

For SharePoint administrators, the default content rules can be modified to change how often they run and whether the rule will attempt to automatically fix the problem associated with the rule. Clicking the rule and then clicking Edit Item pulls up a dialog box similar to the one shown in Figure 11.3, which enables for customization of the rule.

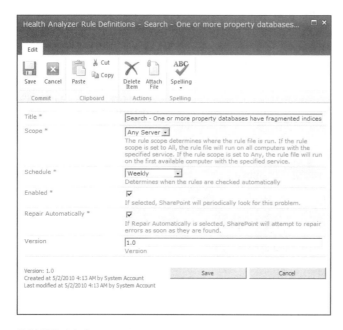

FIGURE 11.3   Modifying SharePoint Health Analyzer rule definitions.

Using SharePoint's Native Reporting Capabilities

Out-of-the-box, SharePoint 2010 gives administrators access to a default set of reports, some of which are shown in Figure 11.4, that can analyze traffic patterns or perform diagnostics on an environment.

The default set of reports can also be extended by third-party utilities or with custom created reports. In addition, SharePoint administrators can customize individual reports to fit their own specific needs.

NOTE

SharePoint reporting can be further extended using SQL Server Reporting Services running in SharePoint Integration Mode.

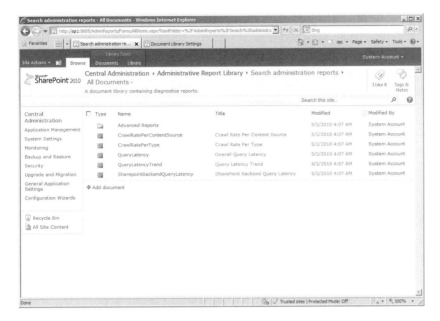

FIGURE 11.4   Examining SharePoint 2010 reports.

Reviewing and Creating Reports

You can view and modify individual reports from the Reporting area of the Monitoring page in the SharePoint Central Admin tool, as shown in Figure 11.5. From this launching point, a SharePoint administrator can view and modify the settings for administrative reports, diagnostic logs, information management policy usage reports, health reports, usage and health data collection, and web analytics reports.

Reports such as the one shown in Figure 11.6 can give useful information about a site and its usage and can be instrumental in troubleshooting and monitoring a SharePoint farm.

Optimizing Usage Data Collection Log Settings

By default, usage data collection logs, which are used to analyze traffic patterns on SharePoint sites, are stored on the default system volume with the rest of the SharePoint data. Because these files can grow quite large, it is recommended to move them to their own volume or limit their growth. To modify these settings for the farm, click the Configure Usage and Health Data Collection link under the Monitoring section of SharePoint Central Admin, and modify the settings, as shown in Figure 11.7.

NOTE

The location for the usage collection logs must exist on all SharePoint servers in the farm. This note applies to any other log location setting defined, because these settings apply to every server within the farm.

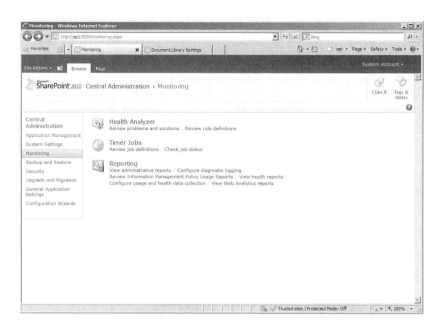

FIGURE 11.5   Viewing the Monitoring page in the SharePoint Central Admin tool.

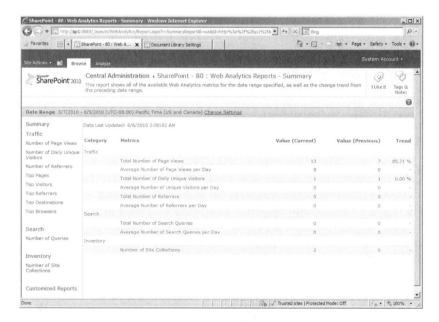

FIGURE 11.6   Viewing a SharePoint 2010 report.

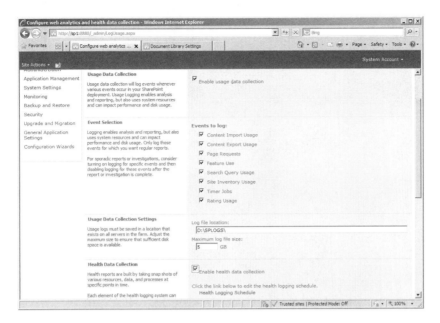

FIGURE 11.7   Modifying the usage data collection log location.

Modifying Diagnostic Log Settings

Diagnostic logs can be used to determine if there are issues with individual services in SharePoint 2010. Logging for individual services can be turned on or off in the Diagnostic Logging dialog box, as shown in Figure 11.8.

Other settings for diagnostic logs, including which drive the trace files are stored on and how large they can grow, can be modified from this same page, as shown in Figure 11.9. It is highly recommended to control the growth of trace files, because they can grow large very quickly. In general, enable only those diagnostic files that you need to avoid growing out of control, and it is good practice to change the location that they are written to something other than the system drive where SharePoint is installed.

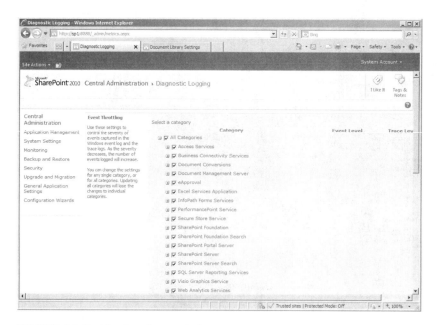

FIGURE 11.8 Viewing diagnostic log settings.

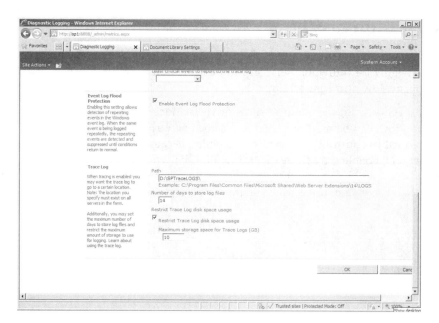

FIGURE 11.9 Modifying the Trace Log default location.

Understanding Timer Jobs for SharePoint 2010

Timer jobs, as shown in Figure 11.10, are critical components in SharePoint jobs. They are used to fire off tasks on a schedule basis and are critical to the smooth operation of a farm. It is critical to understand which timer jobs are configured and how to modify them to understand how to administer a SharePoint environment.

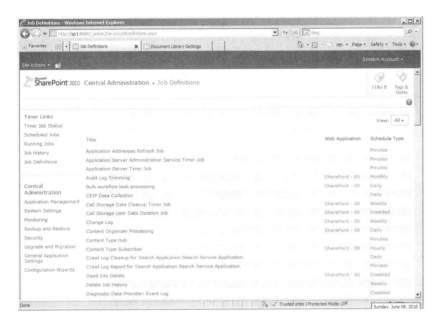

FIGURE 11.10   Viewing timer jobs.

Modifying Timer Jobs

The schedule for individual timer jobs can be modified by clicking on the name of the timer job from within the Timer Job page, located within the Monitoring area of the SharePoint Central Admin Tool. Jobs can be modified to occur as often as every minute or as seldom as monthly. In addition, individual timer jobs can be kicked off by clicking the Run Now button, as shown in Figure 11.11.

Monitoring Timer Jobs

The status for any one timer job can also be easily monitored, this time by clicking the Check Job Status link within the Monitoring page of SharePoint Central Admin. The job schedule is shown at the top of the page, and job status is shown as the bottom, as shown in Figure 11.12.

In addition to the SharePoint Central Admin tool, the PowerShell scripting interface can be used to administer timer jobs. Type **Get-Command *SPTimerJob** from PowerShell to get a list of commands that can be used to administer timer jobs from the command line.

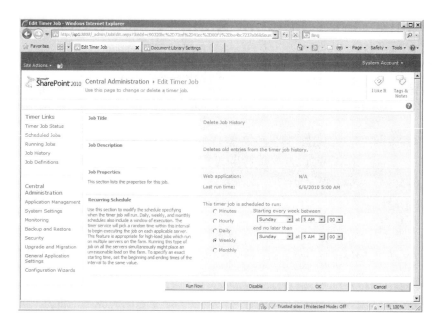

FIGURE 11.11   Modifying the schedule for individual timer jobs.

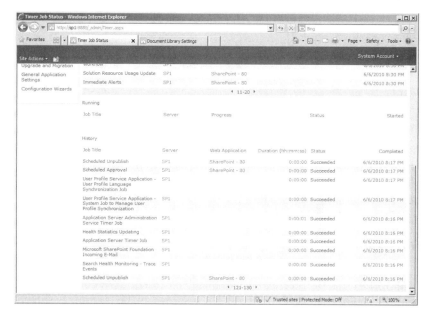

FIGURE 11.12   Monitoring timer job status.

Using System Center Operations Manager to Simplify Management of SharePoint 2010

System Center Operations Manager (SCOM) is an enterprise-class monitoring and management solution for Windows environments. It is designed to simplify SharePoint server management by consolidating events, performance data, alerts, and more into a centralized repository. Reports on this information can then be tailored depending on the environment and the level of detail needed and extrapolated. This information can assist administrators and decision makers in proactively addressing SharePoint server operation and any problems that exist or may occur.

The latest version of SCOM, System Center Operations Manager 2007 R2, can be further extended through the addition of Management Packs for SharePoint Foundation and SharePoint Server, which contain built-in event and performance analysis tools specifically written to ensure smooth functionality of a SharePoint environment. Deployment of a SCOM solution in a SharePoint environment would not be complete without installation of this tool.

Many other intrinsic benefits are gained by using SCOM, including, but not limited to, the following:

▶ Event log monitoring and consolidation

▶ Monitoring of various applications, including those provided by third parties

▶ Enhanced alerting capabilities

▶ Assistance with capacity-planning efforts

▶ A customizable knowledge base of Microsoft product knowledge and best practices

▶ Web-based interface for reporting and monitoring

Taking a Closer Look at System Center Operations Manager

System Center Operations Manager (SCOM) 2007 R2 is the latest version of Microsoft's enterprise monitoring product. Previously owned by NetIQ and then sold to Microsoft, the product has evolved from the a product known as Microsoft Operations Manager (MOM) to the latest generation.

SCOM provides for several major pieces of functionality, as follows:

▶ **Event log consolidation**—SCOM Agents, deployed on managed systems, forward all event log information to a central SCOM SQL Server database, which is managed and groomed by SCOM. This data is used for reporting, auditing, and monitoring of the specific events.

► **Advanced alerting capabilities**—SCOM provides advanced alerting functionality by enabling email alerts, paging, and functional alerting roles to be defined.

► **Performance monitoring**—SCOM collects performance statistics that can let an administrator know whether a server is being overloaded or is close to running out of disk space, among other things.

► **Built-in application-specific intelligence**—SCOM Management Packs are packages of information about a particular application or service, such as DNS, DHCP, Exchange Server, or SharePoint Server. The Microsoft management packs are written by the design teams for each individual product and are loaded with the intelligence and information necessary to properly troubleshoot and identify problems. For example, the SharePoint Management pack will automatically know which event IDs indicate configuration errors in the software and will specifically direct an administrator to the proper location on the web where Microsoft Knowledge Base articles can be used for troubleshooting.

SCOM architecture can be complex but often is as simple as a SQL database running on a server, with another server providing the management server functions of SCOM. This type of server is also known as an SCOM management server.

Installing SCOM Management Packs for SharePoint 2010

As previously mentioned, Management Packs contain intelligence about specific applications and services and include troubleshooting information specific to those services. Microsoft has released three management packs for SharePoint 2010. The first is the management pack for SharePoint Foundation 2010, the second is for the full SharePoint 2010 suite, and the third is specific to FAST Search Server, which may or may not be used, depending on whether FAST Search server is deployed. It is recommended to deploy those management packs that are used within your environment. A full SharePoint Server 2010 environment that isn't using FAST Search Server would deploy the two core Management Packs, for example.

To download these management packs, go to http://pinpoint.microsoft.com and search for SharePoint 2010 Management Pack. Within the Search results, you should see the following available for download:

► Microsoft SharePoint 2010 Products Management Pack for System Center Operations Manager 2007

► Microsoft SharePoint Foundation 2010 Management Pack for System Center Operations Manager 2007

► Microsoft FAST Search Server 2010 for SharePoint Management Pack for Operations Manager 2007

Install and import each management pack individually into SCOM 2007 R2 via the import/export management packs link to enable them in the environment. When installed, they will intelligently sense which servers are SharePoint servers and will deploy scripts and event viewer monitors to those systems.

Installing Additional Management Packs for SharePoint Farms

In addition to the SharePoint 2010 specific management packs, a SharePoint environment should leverage additional management packs installed on SCOM to monitor the other non-SharePoint components:

▶ Microsoft SQL Server Management Pack for Operations Manager 2007

▶ Windows Server Internet Information Services (IIS) for System Center Operations Manager 2007

▶ Windows Server Operating System Management Pack for Operations Manager 2007

▶ Active Directory Management Pack for System Center Operations Manager 2007 (for the domain controllers)

▶ Microsoft Forefront Server Security for SharePoint 10.x Management Pack for Operations Manager 2007 (if Forefront is utilized)

Review the list of components used within the SharePoint environment and compare that list with the list of Management Packs provided. This may mean that additional Management Packs are needed. For example, if Forefront Threat Management Gateway or ForeFront Unified Access Gateway are used to secure inbound HTTPS access to SharePoint, those Management Packs may be required.

Monitoring SharePoint Functionality and Performance with SCOM

After the Management Pack is installed for SharePoint and the agent has been installed and is communicating, SCOM consolidates and reacts to every event and performance counter sent to it from the SharePoint Server. This information is reflected in the SCOM Operations Console.

Performance data for SharePoint can also be displayed in SCOM. This enables reports and performance metrics to be obtained from the farm. For more information on SCOM 2007 R2, see the Microsoft website at the following URL: http://www.microsoft.com/SCOM.

Establishing Maintenance Schedules for SharePoint

Maintaining a SharePoint farm is not an easy task for administrators. They must find time in their fire-fighting efforts to focus and plan for maintenance on the server systems. When maintenance tasks are commonplace in an environment, they can alleviate many of the common fire-fighting tasks.

The processes and procedures for maintaining Windows Server systems can be separated based on the appropriate time to maintain a particular aspect of SharePoint. Some maintenance procedures require daily attention, whereas others may require only yearly check-ups. The maintenance processes and procedures that an organization follows depend strictly on the organization; however, the categories described in the following sections and their corresponding procedures are best practices for organizations of all sizes and varying IT infrastructures.

Outlining Daily Maintenance Tasks

Certain maintenance procedures require more attention than others. The procedures that require the most attention are categorized as daily procedures. It is recommended that a SharePoint administrator take on these procedures each day to ensure system reliability, availability, performance, and security. These procedures are examined in the following three sections.

Checking Overall SharePoint Server Functionality

Although checking the overall server health and functionality may seem redundant or elementary, this procedure is critical to keeping the system environment and users working productively.

Some questions that should be addressed during the checking and verification process are the following:

▶ Can users access data in SharePoint document libraries?

▶ Can remote users access SharePoint via SSL if configured?

▶ Is there an exceptionally long wait to access the portal (that is, longer than normal)?

▶ Do SMTP alerts function properly?

▶ Are searches properly locating newly created or modified content?

Verifying That Backups Are Successful

To provide a secure and fault-tolerant organization, it is imperative that a successful backup be performed every night. If a server failure occurs, the administrator may be required to perform a restore from tape. Without a backup each night, the IT organization is forced to rely on rebuilding the SharePoint server without the data. Therefore, the administrator should always back up servers so that the IT organization can restore them with minimum downtime if a disaster occurs. Because of the importance of the tape backups, the first priority of the administrator each day needs to be verifying and maintaining the backup sets.

If disaster ever strikes, the administrators want to be confident that a system or entire farm can be recovered as quickly as possible. Successful backup mechanisms are imperative to the recovery operation; recoveries are only as good as the most recent backups.

Although Windows Server's or SharePoint's backup programs do not offer alerting mechanisms for bringing attention to unsuccessful backups, many third-party programs do. In addition, many of these third-party backup programs can send emails or pages if backups are successful or unsuccessful. For more information on backing up and restoring SharePoint, reference Chapter 10, "Backing Up and Restoring a SharePoint Environment."

Monitoring the Event Viewer

The Windows Event Viewer is used to check the system, security, application, and other logs on a local or remote system. These logs are an invaluable source of information regarding the system. The following event logs are present for SharePoint servers running on Windows Server:

- ▶ **Security**—Captures all security-related events being audited on a system. Auditing is turned on by default to record success and failure of security events.

- ▶ **Application**—Stores specific application information. This information includes services and any applications running on the server.

- ▶ **System**—Stores Windows Server–specific information.

All Event Viewer events are categorized either as informational, warning, or error.

NOTE

Checking these logs often helps to understand them. Some events constantly appear but aren't significant. Events will begin to look familiar, so it will be noticeable when something is new or amiss in event logs. It is for this reason that an intelligent log filter such as SCOM 2007 R2 is a welcome addition to a SharePoint environment.

Some best practices for monitoring event logs include

- ▶ Understanding the events being reported

- ▶ Setting up a database for archived event logs

- ▶ Archiving event logs frequently

- ▶ Using an automatic log parsing and alerting tool, such as System Center Operations Manager

To simplify monitoring hundreds or thousands of generated events each day, the administrator should use the filtering mechanism provided in the Event Viewer. Although warnings and errors should take priority, the informational events should be reviewed to track what was happening before the problem occurred. After the administrator reviews the informational events, she can filter out the informational events and view only the warnings and errors.

To filter events, do the following:

1. Start the Event Viewer by choosing Start, All Programs, Administrative Tools, Event Viewer.

2. Select the log from which you want to filter events.

3. Right-click the log and select Filter Current Log.

4. In the Filter Current Log window, select the types of events to filter.

5. Optionally, select the time frame in which the events occurred, event source, category, event ID, or other options that will narrow down the search. Click OK when finished.

Some warnings and errors are normal because of bandwidth constraints or other environmental issues. The more logs are monitored, the more familiar an administrator should be with the messages and therefore will spot a problem before it affects the user community.

NOTE

You might need to increase the size of the log files in the Event Viewer to accommodate an increase in logging activity.

Performing Weekly SharePoint Maintenance

Maintenance procedures that require slightly less attention than daily checking are categorized in a weekly routine and are examined in the following sections.

Checking Disk Space

Disk space is a precious commodity. Although the disk capacity of a Windows Server system can seem virtually endless, the amount of free space on all drives should be checked daily. Serious problems can occur if there isn't enough disk space.

One of the most common disk space problems occurs on database drives where all SQL SharePoint data is held. Other volumes such as the system drive and partitions with logging data can also quickly fill up.

As mentioned earlier, lack of free disk space can cause a multitude of problems including, but not limited to, the following:

- ▶ SharePoint application failures

- ▶ System crashes

- ▶ Unsuccessful backup jobs

- ▶ Service failures

- ▶ Inability to audit

- ▶ Degradation of performance

To prevent these problems from occurring, administrators should keep the amount of free space to at least 25 percent.

CAUTION

If needing to free disk space, files and folders should be moved or deleted with caution. System files are automatically protected by Windows Server, but data files are not.

Verifying SharePoint Hardware Components

Hardware components supported by Windows Server are reliable, but this doesn't mean that they'll always run continuously without failure. Hardware availability is measured in terms of mean time between failures (MTBF) and mean time to repair (MTTR). This includes downtime for both planned and unplanned events. These measurements provided by the manufacturer are good guidelines to follow; however, mechanical parts are bound to fail at one time or another. As a result, hardware should be monitored weekly to ensure efficient operation.

Hardware can be monitored in many different ways. For example, server systems may have internal checks and logging functionality to warn against possible failure, Windows Server's System Monitor may bring light to a hardware failure, and a physical hardware check can help to determine whether the system is about to experience a problem with the hardware.

If a failure occurs or is about to occur on a SharePoint server, having an inventory of spare hardware can significantly improve the chances and timing of recoverability. Checking system hardware on a weekly basis provides the opportunity to correct the issue before it becomes a problem.

Archiving Event Logs

The three event logs on all servers can be archived manually, or a script can be written to automate the task. You should archive the event logs to a central location for ease of management and retrieval.

The specific amount of time to keep archived log files varies on a per-organization basis. For example, banks or other high-security organizations may be required to keep event logs up to a few years. As a best practice, organizations should keep event logs for at least three months.

> **TIP**
>
> Organizations who deploy System Center Operations Manager with SharePoint can take advantage of SCOM's capability to automatically archive event log information, providing for a significant improvement to monitoring and reporting of SharePoint.

Performing Monthly Maintenance Tasks

When an understanding of the maintenance required for SharePoint is obtained, it is vital to formalize the procedures into documented steps. A maintenance plan can contain information on what tasks to perform at different intervals. It is recommended to perform the tasks examined in the following sections on a monthly basis.

Maintaining File System Integrity

CHKDSK scans for file system integrity and can check for lost clusters, cross-linked files, and more. If Windows Server senses a problem, it runs CHKDSK automatically at startup.

Administrators can maintain FAT, FAT32, and NTFS file system integrity by running CHKDSK once a month. To run CHKDSK, do the following:

1. At the command prompt, change to the partition that you want to check.
2. Type **CHKDSK** without any parameters to check only for file system errors.
3. If any errors are found, run the CHKDSK utility with the /f parameter to attempt to correct the errors found.

Testing the UPS Battery

An uninterruptible power supply (UPS) can be used to protect the system or group of systems from power failures (such as spikes and surges) and keep the system running long enough after a power outage so that an administrator can gracefully shut down the system. It is recommended that a SharePoint administrator follow the UPS guidelines provided by the manufacturer at least once a month. Also, monthly scheduled battery tests should be performed.

Validating Backups

Once a month, an administrator should validate backups by restoring the backups to a server located in a lab environment. This is in addition to verifying that backups were successful from log files or the backup program's management interface. A restore gives the administrator the opportunity to verify the backups and to practice the restore procedures that would be used when recovering the server during a disaster. In addition, this procedure tests the state of the backup media to ensure that they are in working order and builds administrator confidence for recovering from a true disaster.

Updating Documentation

An integral part of managing and maintaining any IT environment is to document the network infrastructure and procedures. The following are just a few of the documents you should consider having on hand:

- ▶ SharePoint Server build guides

- ▶ Disaster recovery guides and procedures

- ▶ Maintenance checklists

- ▶ Configuration settings

- ▶ Change control logs

- ▶ Historical performance data

- ▶ Special user rights assignments

- ▶ SharePoint site configuration settings

- ▶ Special application settings

As systems and services are built and procedures are ascertained, document these facts to reduce learning curves, administration, and maintenance.

It is not only important to adequately document the IT environment, but it's also often even more important to keep those documents up-to-date. Otherwise, documents can quickly become outdated as the environment, processes, and procedures change as the business changes.

Performing Quarterly Maintenance Tasks

As the name implies, quarterly maintenance is performed four times a year. Areas to maintain and manage on a quarterly basis are typically self-sufficient and self-sustaining. Infrequent maintenance is required to keep the system healthy. This doesn't mean, however, that the tasks are simple or that they aren't as critical as those tasks that require more frequent maintenance.

Checking Storage Limits

Storage capacity on all volumes should be checked to ensure that all volumes have ample free space. Keep approximately 25 percent free space on all volumes.

Running low or completely out of disk space creates unnecessary risk for any system. Services can fail, applications can stop responding, and systems can even crash if there isn't plenty of disk space.

Keeping SQL Database disk space consumption to a minimum can be accomplished through a combination of limiting document library versioning or implementing site quotas.

Changing Administrator Passwords

Administrator passwords should, at a minimum, be changed every quarter (90 days). Changing these passwords strengthens security measures so that systems can't easily be compromised. In addition to changing passwords, other password requirements such as password age, history, length, and strength should be reviewed.

Summary of Maintenance Tasks and Recommendations

Table 11.1 summarizes some of the maintenance tasks and recommendations examined in this chapter.

TABLE 11.1   Maintenance Tasks for SharePoint Servers

Daily	Weekly	Monthly	Quarterly	Task
X				Check overall server functionality, including the SharePoint Health Analyzer.
X				Verify backups.
X				Monitor Event Viewer.
X	X			Check disk space.
X	X			Verify hardware.
	X			Archive event logs.
	X			Check SharePoint logs.
	X			Test the UPS.
		X		Check SQL maintenance plans.
		X		Run CHKDSK.
			X	Update documentation.
			X	Change administrator passwords.
			X	Test farm restores.

Summary

Although SharePoint administrators can easily get caught up in daily administration and firefighting, it's important to structure system management and maintenance to help prevent unnecessary amounts of effort. Following a management and maintenance regimen reduces administration, maintenance, and business expenses, while at the same time increasing reliability, stability, and security.

SharePoint 2010 includes built-in monitoring capabilities using tools such as the SharePoint Health Analyzer, enhanced timer job capabilities, and enhanced logging that can help SharePoint administrators have better control over their SharePoint environment. Combined with an enterprise tool, such as System Center Operations Manager, and together with a comprehensive maintenance schedule composed of daily, weekly, monthly, and quarterly tasks, a SharePoint 2010 farm can be properly monitored and controlled.

Best Practices

- ▶ Use the SharePoint Health Analyzer to proactively identify health issues in a SharePoint 2010 farm.

- ▶ Understand how to modify timer job schedules and to run timer jobs manually.

- ▶ Move the trace and usage logs to a dedicated drive that exists on all SharePoint farm members.

- ▶ Use System Center Operations Manager (SCOM) 2007 R2 to proactively manage SharePoint Server 2007 systems.

- ▶ Download all relevant SCOM Management Packs, including SQL, IIS, and Windows OS Management Packs in addition to the three SharePoint 2010-specific ones.

- ▶ Identify tasks important to the system's overall health and security.

- ▶ Thoroughly test and evaluate service packs and updates in a lab environment before installing them on production servers and client machines.

- ▶ Install the appropriate service packs and updates on each production SharePoint server and client machine to keep all systems consistent.

- ▶ Categorize and document daily, weekly, monthly, and quarterly tasks required to monitor SharePoint farm servers.

## CHAPTER 12

Virtualizing SharePoint Components

Server virtualization technologies have become so commonplace that they are the de facto standard for server deployment in many organizations. It's becoming more and more common to run into data center environments that operate with the assumption that all new servers will be deployed as virtual machines (VMs), unless there's some specific reason not to virtualize. This is a significant change from even just a few years ago when the situation was reversed and servers were deployed on physical equipment unless there was a specific reason to virtualize.

So, what about Microsoft SharePoint? Should you virtualize some or all of a SharePoint environment and take advantage of the consolidation, optimization, and flexibility options that virtualization infrastructure provides? The reality is that SharePoint environments, particularly those running SharePoint Server 2010, can be robustly deployed on virtual servers as long as sufficient resources are allocated to virtual guests and the virtual hosts are scaled correctly. Deploying SharePoint improperly in a virtual environment can lead to slowness and other performance problems, and can decrease management confidence in virtualization as a whole, so it's vital to review virtualization design criteria for SharePoint in advance.

Microsoft's Virtualization Support Story

The support story for Microsoft products running on virtualization hardware is long and complicated. Until several years ago, Microsoft offered limited support for its flagship server products, such as SQL Server, Exchange Server, and SharePoint. Microsoft even left open the option that a support problem might need to be duplicated on physical hardware if support technicians couldn't determine the nature of the problem in a virtual environment. Adding to Microsoft's weak support story was the fact that Virtual Server 2005 R2 was its virtualization product during the early days of Microsoft Office SharePoint Server (MOSS) 2007. Virtual Server 2005 R2 wasn't a hypervisor-based product and couldn't virtualize 64-bit guests, which limited supported environments to those running the 32-bit versions of MOSS 2007. This greatly curtailed the performance that could be achieved, particularly for the database role, which was the most resource intensive and could take advantage of the 64-bit architecture the most. In addition, web front ends typically required significantly more memory than a 32-bit platform.

Two significant developments changed this story. The first was Microsoft's release of a 64-bit-capable hypervisor named Hyper-V. The second was the development of a program called the Server Virtualization Validation Program (SVVP), which outlined Microsoft's official support stance on running its products on third-party hypervisor virtualization platforms. This program, outlined in the Microsoft article "Support Policy for Microsoft Software Running in Non-Microsoft Hardware Virtualization Software" (http://support.microsoft.com/kb/897615), allowed for support of Microsoft products on third-party virtualization products that were validated by Microsoft and complied with certain criteria, namely the ability to have guest sessions have direct access to hardware resources via a virtualization hypervisor. These two developments opened the doors for Microsoft servers running on VMs and gave peace of mind to organizations that needed to deploy supported virtualized solutions.

SharePoint Virtualization Support

The 2007 wave of SharePoint products—which includes Windows SharePoint Services 3.0 (WSS 3.0) and MOSS 2007—was the first to gain broad virtualization support from Microsoft. However, in production, most clients opt to virtualize only the web role and sometimes the query role. Other roles weren't typically implemented, for various reasons. For example, the index role was often implemented only on physical hardware because of heavy processor and memory constraints and the limitation in SharePoint 2007 of one index server per shared services provider.

Microsoft's official SharePoint 2010 support stance is that any SharePoint role or service is supported for hardware virtualization. SharePoint 2010 is positioned as an excellent virtualization candidate because of virtualization technology advances and a reduction of the disk input/output (I/O) requirements for the indexing and search components. In addition, advances in hardware virtualization make it easier to virtualize I/O-intensive applications such as SQL Server, allowing the SharePoint database role to be more easily virtualized. As a result, many organizations are looking at virtualizing their new SharePoint 2010 farms.

Virtualization Infrastructure Requirements and Recommendations

The key to a stable and high-performance virtualized SharePoint environment is using the proper architecture in the virtualization hosts. Out-of-the-box settings and slow disks might work for a test environment, but specific requirements need to be met when building the host system for proper performance to be achieved. Therefore, be sure to follow these minimum requirements when you design the virtualization host infrastructure:

▶ The processors must support hardware-assisted virtualization, which is available in processors that include a virtualization option. Specifically, this means processors with Intel Virtualization Technology (Intel VT) or AMD Virtualization (AMD-V) technology.

▶ Hardware-enforced data execution prevention (DEP) must be available and enabled.

▶ SharePoint guests must be deployed on a Hyper-V hypervisor or a third-party hypervisor that is part of the SVVP.

▶ Sufficient memory must be allocated for the host operating system (OS). If you're using Hyper-V, you need to reserve at least 1GB of random access memory (RAM) for use by the Hyper-V host. If you're using a third-party hypervisor, check with the individual provider to determine the minimum amount of memory required.

▶ A dedicated network interface card (NIC) must be allocated for host management. This NIC must be separate from the NICs used by the VMs.

▶ Use multiple independent drive arrays of disk spindles. Best practice is to allocate a dedicated set of disk spindles or storage array for the host OS, another for the guest OS virtual disks, and at least two more (logs and database volumes) for virtualized SQL Server sessions.

▶ Fixed-size or pass-through Virtual Hard Disks (VHDs) should be used for best guest disk performance. All VHDs used by SharePoint servers should be either fixed-size or pass-through (raw device mapping) disks that are directly connected to a volume on the host storage. Pass-through disks give you the fastest performance, which is highly recommended for SharePoint servers. Fixed-size disks are faster than dynamically expanding disks, which can suffer performance hits when they're resizing.

▶ Consider pass-through (Raw Device Mapping) NICs for the best network performance or, at minimum, configure virtual NICs to use a single virtual switch for SharePoint servers.

▶ A 2:1 ratio for the number of virtual processors to physical cores is the maximum that should be used in a production environment. A virtual host that has too many allocated virtual central processor units (CPUs) can be overloaded and perform poorly. Therefore, you need to have a 2:1 ratio (or less) for the virtual processor–to–physical core ratio. For example, if your host is a two-processor quad-core system (eight cores total), the maximum number of virtual processors that can be allocated and running at any one time is 16. If each VM is allocated four virtual processors, the

12

number of running VMs is capped at four on that host. Highest performance environments will limit the ration to 1:1.

In addition to these technical requirements for the virtualization host, keep in mind these recommendations when you set up your virtual environment:

▶ You should allocate a dedicated NIC for failover, such as in the scenario when you use virtual host failover software such as Hyper-V Live Migration.

▶ You should give as much memory and as many processor cores to your virtual hosts as your budget allows. Virtual hosts with multiple multicore processors and large amounts of RAM (64GB or more) are becoming commonplace because of the virtual host software's ability to take advantage of the additional resources and because host failover solutions require additional resources. When it comes to sizing virtualization hosts, there's a sweet spot that balances the cost of the additional components against the need to have fewer hosts. Generally, the virtualization overhead required to run virtual servers is only 5 percent, so the cost of adding memory and processor cores is more than made up by the advantages of having those additional resources.

▶ You should run only the virtualization software and the virtualization role on the virtual hosts. (The two exceptions are antivirus and backup software.) Overloading a virtual host with other software or other server roles can significantly degrade guest performance. In addition, from a Windows Server licensing perspective, running any roles other than the virtualization role on a Windows Server requires one additional license. However, if the host runs only virtualization host software, the host OS isn't counted when determining the number of Windows licenses used as part of Microsoft's virtualization licensing program.

▶ For performance reasons, you shouldn't install all the SharePoint roles and the SQL Server role on the same VM. Even small environments should use at least two VMs—one for the SQL Server database role, and the other for the SharePoint front-end and application roles.

Software Recommendations and Licensing Notes

It's highly recommended that you use the latest virtualization host software from your particular vendor. For example, the latest version of Hyper-V is included with Windows Server 2008 R2. Hyper-V 2.0 has significant performance improvements over Hyper-V 1.0, such as I/O improvements for fixed-size VHDs. Hyper-V 2.0 also has new features such as Core Parking, Live Migration, TCP Offload, the Jumbo Frames feature, and support for Second-Level Address Translation (SLAT)-enabled processors. If you're virtualizing SharePoint on Hyper-V, also consider deploying the virtual host on Server Core to minimize its security footprint, OS disk overhead (2GB versus 10GB), and memory use.

Microsoft provides cost-effective virtualization licensing options for Windows Server, which lets organizations save significantly on Windows Server licenses when virtualizing servers. The three types of virtualization server licensing are as follows:

▶ Windows Server Standard Edition, which allows a single physical OS environment (POSE) or a single virtual OS environment (VOSE) with each Standard Edition license. Note that a virtualization host that's dedicated to virtualization tasks doesn't consume a license, regardless if it's running Windows Server (such as in the case of Hyper-V).

▶ Windows Server Enterprise Edition, which allows for up to four VOSEs to be run at any one time on the host. Note that only running VMs are counted. So, if a VM is shut down, it doesn't count against the four concurrent VOSEs permitted by the Enterprise Edition license.

▶ Windows Server Datacenter Edition, which is a per-processor (not per core) license for the virtual host (for example, a dual quad-core server would require two licenses) that grants you the right to run an unlimited number of VMs on the host.

These licensing options apply not only to Hyper-V but also to any hypervisor that is part of the SVVP. For organizations with a significant investment in virtualization infrastructure, buying the appropriate number of Datacenter Edition licenses to cover all your virtual hosts is the most cost-effective.

Virtualization of SharePoint Roles

Virtualization requirements vary by server role. It is subsequently important when designing that you understand the individual requirements of each role.

Virtualization of the Web Role

The best candidate for virtualization is the SharePoint server that has the web role, which means it runs Microsoft IIS and handles all web requests sent to SharePoint. Table 12.1 shows resource guidelines for virtualized SharePoint servers that have the web and other roles.

TABLE 12.1   SharePoint Server Role Resource Guidelines

Roles	Virtual Processors	Minimum RAM	Recommended RAM
Web role only	2	6GB	8GB+
Service application role only	2	6GB	8GB+
Search role only	4	8GB	10GB+
Combined web, service application, and search roles	4	10GB	12GB+
Database role	4	8GB	12GB+

As you can see in Table 12.1, a SharePoint server that holds only the web role (otherwise known as the web server) should be allocated at least two virtual processors and a minimum of 6GB of RAM (preferably at least 8GB of RAM), along with a single VHD for the OS. If a web server needs to handle more web traffic, you can simply allocate additional web servers that have the same specifications. The size of the host OS disk should be at least 12GB plus three times the total amount of memory allocated to the VM, but it's good practice to size this volume larger (typically around 50GB to 100GB) to allow the host OS to grow in size.

Virtualization of the Application Roles

The next likely candidates for virtualization include the SharePoint server with one or more service application roles (otherwise known as the application server). Application servers can include various service applications, such as Access Services, PerformancePoint Services, and the Managed Metadata Service. For purposes of design, this excludes the search services, which are technically service applications, but for architectural purposes are usually classified as part of a different server role.

As Table 12.1 shows, the typical virtualized application server consists of a VM with two virtual processors and a minimum of 6GB of RAM allocated to it. It needs a single VHD that's presized in the 50GB to 100GB range for the guest OS. Note that these numbers can vary, depending on how many service applications are installed on a single machine and how many people use the applications.

In smaller organizations, the application role and the web role are often combined onto a single SharePoint server. Combining the roles will increase the memory and processor requirements of the guest session.

Virtualization of the Search Role

Third in line for virtualization is the SharePoint server or servers that hold the search role (otherwise known as the search server), which provides SharePoint's indexing and querying functionality. SharePoint 2010 doesn't have the same single-index restrictions that SharePoint 2007 did, which makes this role more scalable and allows for more distributed deployment models.

The typical virtualized search server consists of a VM with four virtual processors and 8GB of RAM allocated to it (see Table 12.1), assuming that SharePoint 2010's out-of-box search functionality is being used. If FAST Search Server 2010 is used, the RAM requirements will be in the 12GB to 16GB range. Like the application server numbers, the search server numbers can vary, depending on how many items are being indexed and how heavy the search requirements are.

The search server needs a single VHD that's presized in the 50GB to 100GB range for the guest OS and another VHD for the index and query corpus. The size of this VHD will vary, depending on how much full text is indexed from various sources.

The crawler component is used by SharePoint to crawl documents for search purposes. Multiple crawl components can be created on different servers for redundancy.

In smaller organizations, the search role is often combined with the web role. Combining these roles can increase the memory and processor requirements of the guest session.

Virtualization of a Server with All Three Roles

Many organizations combine the web, application, and search roles on a single virtualized SharePoint server. This is often the case in smaller organizations that want to deploy SharePoint across two guest sessions to be highly available but have a smaller number of guests.

Although combining the three roles results in additional load on an individual server session, many of the same processor and memory guidelines that apply to a dedicated web role server apply to a combined server, as Table 12.1 shows.

The typical virtual web/query/search server role system consists of a VM with four virtual processors and 10GB to 16GB of RAM allocated to it, depending on how many users the system will support. It has a single VHD presized in the 50GB to 100GB range for the guest OS and another VHD for the index and query corpus.

SharePoint administrators familiar with SharePoint 2007 might be dismayed at the memory requirements of SharePoint 2010, but the fact is that SharePoint 2010 requires much more memory than earlier versions. RAM requirements can be lessened, however, by turning off nonessential service applications. In general, to reduce the overall requirements of the SharePoint servers, it is recommended to turn on only those service applications required by the business.

Virtualization of the Database Role

The SQL Server database role is the last but most challenging server role to virtualize. The server with the database role (otherwise known as the database server) needs the lion's share of RAM and processor allocation. A minimum of four virtual processors and 8GB of RAM should be allocated to the database server. For best performance, though, at least 12GB of RAM should be allocated.

Like SharePoint VMs, SQL Server VMs require either fixed-sized or pass-through VHDs. The same disk considerations that apply to physical SQL Server machines apply to virtual SQL Server machines. So, be sure to allocate enough disk spindles for the database and logs volumes. In addition, be sure to follow standard best practices for SharePoint–SQL Server optimization, such as presizing the tempdb and moving it to fast disk volumes.

Keep in mind that these guidelines are simply guidelines. Actual performance will be dictated by the type of disk, hardware architecture, and other factors. Some organizations calculate their hardware requirements and then just add RAM or reduce the number of databases on a single SQL Server session.

Microsoft supports both SQL mirroring and clustering as high-availability options in a virtualized SQL Server environment. In addition, host failover options such as Hyper-V Live Migration are supported for SQL Server VMs. One fact to note, however, is that all SQL Server databases within a SharePoint farm need to be restored from the same point in time as the other databases. This applies to virtualization snapshot technology or storage area network (SAN)-based snapshots of SQL Server databases.

Exploring Sample Virtualized SharePoint 2010 Architecture

There are many ways to deploy SharePoint 2010 in a virtualized environment. However, some designs are more widespread than others and reflect common needs across many organizations. For example, high availability is becoming a must for the critical document management and collaboration functionality in SharePoint. All the new high-availability options in SharePoint 2010 are available for virtual environments and can actually be easier to deploy because of the flexibility that virtualization provides.

Figure 12.1 illustrates a small virtualized SharePoint 2010 environment with all components running on a single virtual host. This type of deployment doesn't have any built-in high availability or disaster recovery, but it's the simplest environment to set up, and it can still take advantage of virtualization benefits and scalability. Table 12.2 shows sample server specifications for an environment of this size. These specifications assume 500 active users in the environment.

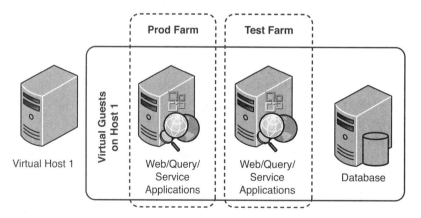

FIGURE 12.1   Conceptualizing a small virtualized SharePoint farm.

TABLE 12.2   Small Virtual SharePoint Environment Deployment Specifications

Server	Memory	Processors	Disk
Virtual host	24GB RAM	2 quad-core (8 cores)	C: drive—OS, Windows Server 2008 R2 with Hyper-V, 50GB dedicated volume D: drive—Dedicated volume for OS VHDs E: drive—500GB dedicated volume for SQL Server database VHDs F: drive—100GB dedicated volume for SQL Server log VHDs
SQL Server server	12GB RAM	4 virtual processors	C: drive—OS, fixed-size VHD (100GB) D: drive—Fixed-size VHD (100GB) for the SQL Server logs E: drive—Fixed-size VHD (500GB) for the SQL Server data
SharePoint web/query/app	10GB RAM	4 virtual processors	C: drive—OS and transport queue logs, fixed-size VHD (100GB) E: drive—Fixed-size VHD (100GB) for indexing and querying

The next design, illustrated in Figure 12.2, provides a virtualization architecture that provides a high level of availability, disaster tolerance, and scalability for an environment with 2,000 active users. The entire SharePoint environment is deployed across two virtual hosts, which provides for high availability of the environment. SQL Server databases are mirrored from one virtual guest to another, and a third SQL witness server monitors the SQL principal server, providing for automatic failover in the event the virtual host or virtual guest fails. For more information about using SQL database mirroring for high availability, see Chapter 17, "Safeguarding Confidential Data in SharePoint 2010."

These high-availability and disaster-recovery options are possible without the need for shared storage, a SAN, or host availability solutions. Table 12.3 lists the sample virtual host and guest architecture guidelines for the solution in Figure 12.2.

TABLE 12.3   Medium-Sized Virtual SharePoint Environment Deployment Specifications

Server	Memory	Processor	Disk
Virtual hosts	48GB RAM	2 quad-core (8 cores)	C: drive—OS, Windows Server 2008 R2 with Hyper-V, 50GB dedicated logical unit number (LUN) D: drive—Dedicated LUN for VHDs Raw volume—100GB dedicated LUN for SQL Server logs Raw volume—2TB dedicated LUN for SQL Server databases

continues

TABLE 12.3   Continued

Server	Memory	Processor	Disk
SQL Server servers	16GB RAM	4 virtual processors	C: drive—OS, fixed-size VHD (50GB) D: drive—Pass-through dedicated LUN (100GB) for SQL Server logs E: drive—Pass-through dedicated LUN (2TB) for SQL Server data
SharePoint web and service application servers	12GB RAM	2 virtual processors	C: drive—OS, fixed-size VHD (100GB)
SharePoint search/query servers	12GB RAM	2 virtual processors	C: drive—OS, fixed-size VHD (100GB) D: drive—Fixed-size VHD (200GB) for indexing and querying
SQL witness server	2GB RAM	1 virtual processor	C: drive—OS, fixed-size VHD (50GB)

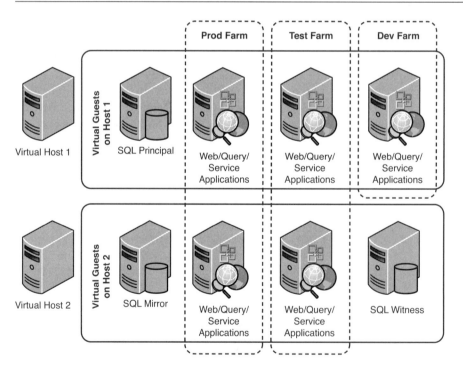

FIGURE 12.2   Conceptualizing a medium-sized SharePoint farm.

Virtualization technologies allow for a high degree of scalability and aren't limited to small and mid-sized organizations. For example, the architecture that Figure 12.3 shows allows for tens of thousands of SharePoint users, full disaster tolerance, and high availability, all with the high performance expected from SharePoint. In this particular model, multiple SQL Server machines are used for the various SharePoint databases, with one used for content databases, one for service application databases, and one for the search databases. Server groups are created for different SharePoint server roles, and the web tier is broken into two components: one for users and another for crawl and administration. In this example, host-based failover solutions such as Hyper-V Live Migration could also conceivably provide for failover of individual guest sessions between failed hosts.

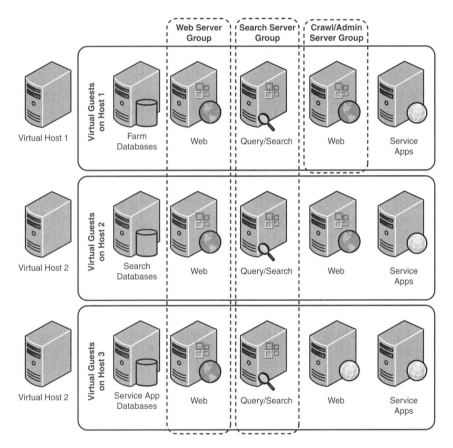

FIGURE 12.3   Conceptualizing a large virtualized SharePoint 2010 environment.

These three samples illustrate some of the potential design options available for a virtual SharePoint environment. Every environment is unique, and specifics will vary based on business and technology needs. However, you can use these sample architectures as a starting point for developing a high-performance virtualized SharePoint 2010 environment.

Virtual Machine Management with System Center Virtual Machine Manager

If managing multiple virtual host machines, centralized management software is also highly recommended. Microsoft has released its own product for VM management and is positioning it as an enterprise utility that allows for centralized control over a broader virtualization environment. This tool, part of the System Center line of products, is known as System Center Virtual Machine Manager (VMM). The latest version of VMM, the 2008 R2 edition, has the following tools and capabilities:

▶ **P2V and V2V**—VMM allows for physical-to-virtual (P2V) or virtual-to-virtual (V2V) migration capabilities, allowing existing physical systems or VMware guests to be migrated to an equivalent Hyper-V guest session.

▶ **Hyper-V and VMware management support**—VMM provides for the ability to manage both Microsoft Hyper-V and VMware guests, through management of a VMware VirtualCenter server. Both VMware and Hyper-V guests and hosts can be managed through the interface.

▶ **Creation of template servers**—VMM supports the creation of server templates, which can be used to automate the creation of virtual guests, including SharePoint role servers, a concept explored in subsequent sections of this chapter.

▶ **Self-service portal**—VMM contains a self-service web portal that can be used by nonadministrators to provision their own systems and remote into them using a web browser.

Exploring the VMM Console

VMM 2008 R2's management console, shown in Figure 12.4, provides a wide degree of functionality that can be used to manage virtual SharePoint guests. This console allows a distributed virtualized SharePoint farm to be more tightly managed, and gives administrators a tool they can use to easily move guest sessions between one or more hosts (and to perform other virtualization tasks).

Exploring the Self-Service Portal

In addition to the default Microsoft Management Console (MMC), VMM includes a web-based self-service portal, shown in Figure 12.5, that enables administrators to delegate the rights to create new guest sessions. This portal can be used by to allow developers, for example, to provision their own test SharePoint server sessions or allow quality assurance (QA) testers to provision guest Windows and Office client sessions for testing.

The permissions allocated to the self-service portal are unique, and users logged in to the portal see only those systems that they created or have rights to manage. In addition, administrators can create "quotas" that define how many guest sessions an individual user may provision at a time.

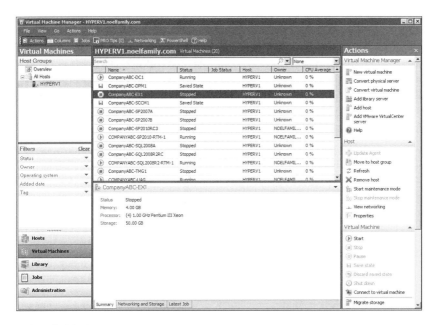

FIGURE 12.4   Using the VMM console.

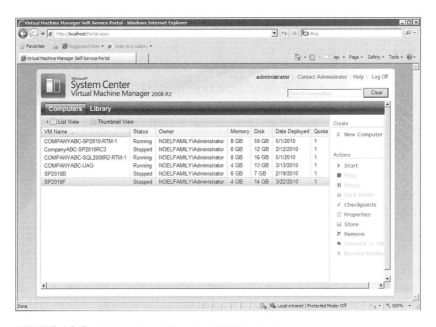

FIGURE 12.5   Using the self-service VMM portal.

Provisioning Farm Members from Virtual Server Templates

VMM allows SharePoint administrators to define a library of templates and VMs that can be used to provision new SharePoint sessions. For example, a Windows Server 2008 R2 server template could be created with the right amount of memory and virtual processors, plus a pair of virtual hard drives for the OS and index files. With SharePoint 2010 binaries installed on that system, it can then be turned into a template that can be used to provision new SharePoint farm members or even entirely new farms.

VMM Template Options, shown in Figure 12.6, allow administrators to have the server created from the template automatically added to a domain, be automatically validated with a valid server key, and also to have a script run after first login. For example, a custom PowerShell script could be run automatically after login that joins the SharePoint template server to an existing farm or creates a new farm from scratch.

FIGURE 12.6   Creating a VM template.

Using this concept, an organization could easily set up a scenario where developers are given the rights, through the self-service portal, to provision a new SharePoint guest session. After provisioning the server, they could then log in to that session and have it automatically run a PowerShell script that would create a new farm. With the proper hardware, developers could provision an entirely new SharePoint environment within 10 to 15 minutes and have that farm completely independent from other farms.

For this scenario to work, the SQL server used must be on a different system, because SQL doesn't lend well to name changes after it has been installed. In this scenario, a single SQL instance can hold the databases from multiple farms. Commonly, a single SQL guest session would be used for all development farms created in this manner.

A sample farm provisioning script (ProvisionFarm.ps1) is provided here as an example of the type of script that can be configured to run automatically upon login to the virtual session provisioned:

```
PROVISIONFARM.PS1
$configType = read-host "Do you wish to join an existing Farm? (Y/N)"
if ($ConfigType -eq "Y") {
    $DatabaseServer = read-host "Sounds good. Please specify the name of your SQL
    ➥Server";
    $ConfigDB = read-host "Next, specify the name of your Farm Configuration
    ➥Database";
    $Passphrase = read-host "Finally, please enter your Farm passphrase" -
    ➥assecurestring
} else {
    $DatabaseServer = read-host "In that case, let's create a new Farm. Please
    ➥specify the name of your SQL Server";
    $FarmName = read-host "Please specify a name for your Farm (ex. SP2010Dev)";
    $ConfigDB = $FarmName+"_ConfigDB";
    $AdminContentDB = $FarmName+"_Admin_ContentDB";
    Write-Host "Please enter the credentials for your Farm Account (ex.
    ➥CONTOSO\SP_Farm)";
    $FarmAcct = Get-Credential;
    $Passphrase = read-host "Enter a secure Farm passphrase" -assecurestring;
    $Port = read-host "Enter a port number for the Central Administration Web App";
    $Authentication = read-host "Finally, specify your authentication provider
    ➥(NTLM/Kerberos)";
}
if ($ConfigType -eq "Y") {
    Add-PSSnapin Microsoft.SharePoint.PowerShell;
    Connect-SPConfigurationDatabase -DatabaseName $ConfigDB -DatabaseServer
    $DatabaseServer -Passphrase $Passphrase
} else {
    Add-PSSnapin Microsoft.SharePoint.PowerShell;
    Write-Host "Your SharePoint Farm is being configured..."
    New-SPConfigurationDatabase -DatabaseName $ConfigDB -DatabaseServer
    ➥$DatabaseServer -AdministrationContentDatabaseName $AdminContentDB -Passphrase
    ➥$Passphrase -FarmCredentials $FarmAcct
}
Initialize-SPResourceSecurity
Install-SPService
Install-SPFeature -AllExistingFeatures
New-SPCentralAdministration -Port $Port -WindowsAuthProvider $Authentication
Install-SPHelpCollection -All
```

```
Install-SPApplicationContent
Write-Host "Your SharePoint 2010 Farm has been created!"
if ($ConfigType -eq "N") {
    $WebAppCreation = read-host "Would you like to provision a Web Application using
    ➥the default Team Site Template? (Y/N)";
    if ($WebAppCreation -eq "Y") {
        $HostHeaderQ = read-host "Would you like to specify a host header? (Y/N)";
        if ($HostHeaderQ -eq "Y") {
            $HostHeader = read-host "Please specify a host header for your Web
            ➥Application (ex. intranet.companyabc.com)";
            $URL = "http://"+$HostHeader;
            Write-Host "Creating your Web Application...";
            New-SPWebApplication -Name "SharePoint 2010 Team Site" -Port 80 -
            ➥HostHeader $FQDN -Url $URL -ApplicationPool "Content_AppPool" -
            ➥ApplicationPoolAccount (Get-SPManagedAccount $FarmAcct.UserName)
            ➥-DatabaseServer
            $DatabaseServer -DatabaseName $FarmName + "_TeamSite_ContentDB_01";
            New-SPSite $URL -OwnerAlias $FarmAcct.UserName -Language 1033 -Template
            ➥"STS#0" -Name "Team Site";
            Write-Host "Configuration completed.";
        }
        else {
        Write-Host "Creating a Web Application using the default Team Site
        ➥Template..."
        }
    }
    else {
        Write-Host "Configuration completed.";
    }
}
Write-Host "Press any key to continue..."
$x = $host.UI.RawUI.ReadKey("NoEcho,IncludeKeyDown")
```

The high-level steps involved in running this scenario are as follows:

1. Create a new Windows Server 2008 R2 guest session in VMM with at least 10GB of RAM and four virtual CPUs allocated to it. (Remember that SharePoint 2010 has large resource requirements.) Give the session two virtual hard drives: one for the OS and another for the index.

2. Install the SharePoint 2010 binaries on the guest session but don't run the Config Wizard. Copy the Provisioning Farm PowerShell script into a directory on the server, such as C:\Scripts. See step 3 for the syntax of the script name.

3. Using VMM, turn the guest session into a server template. Specify within the server template to automatically add the machine into a domain and to run powershell.exe –noexit C:\scripts\ProvisionFarm.ps1, as shown in Figure 12.6.

4. Use the self-service portal to provision a new server based off of the template. After the session has been created and added to the domain, log in to the system and walk

through the farm provisioning script. Because the SharePoint 2010 binaries will already be installed, the script will be able to provision a new farm or to add the server into an existing farm.

Within approximately 15 minutes, a new SharePoint farm can be provisioned with running web applications and services. Using this approach, modifications can also be made to the PowerShell script to expand the functionality of the script, such as by adding the ability to provision service applications. In addition, it can be made to run completely without user input, providing for a 100-percent automated farm provisioning solution.

This same process can be used with other virtualization management software, such as the third-party VMware VirtualCenter. The concepts still apply: Just install the SharePoint 2010 binaries, and then create a server template. Using a provisioning script, you can then automatically create a new virtual farm or add additional members to it.

Summary

Server virtualization can provide significant advantages and can let SharePoint architects design highly available and disaster-tolerant environments more easily than could be done solely on physical hardware. In addition, virtualized environments have consolidation, optimization, and cost-saving benefits that make them ideal for many organizations. With proper thought into host and guest virtualization architecture, you can deploy a fault-tolerant and high-performance SharePoint environment that lets you fully capture the benefits of virtualization for your organization.

Use of a virtualization management tool such as System Center VMM can be particularly advantageous because it allows for scenarios such as the one described in this chapter, where a virtualized SharePoint 2010 farm can be automatically provisioned from templates in a matter of minutes, thus enabling developers and farm architects to provision quality-controlled SharePoint farms on an as-needed basis.

Best Practices

▶ Do not overallocate memory or processor resources; maintain a maximum of a 2:1 ratio between the number of allocated virtual CPUs on guests and the number of cores on the host.

▶ Use an approved hypervisor for virtualization, such as Microsoft's Hyper-V R2 or a third-party hypervisor that is part of the SVVP.

▶ Allocate up to 1GB of the memory of the virtual host to running the virtualization host software.

▶ Highly consider pass-through (Raw Device Mapping) NICs and pass-through disks rather than virtual NICs or virtual hard drives, because the best performance can be achieved with them. This is particularly true for virtual SQL database servers.

▶ If using Microsoft's Hyper-V hypervisor, use the latest version included with Windows Server 2008 R2; it has significant performance improvements over the initial version of Hyper-V.

▶ Do not install anything other than virtualization software on the host sessions. Exceptions to this rule may include backup or antivirus software, although you should avoid these if possible.

▶ Consider the use of Server Core for the host OS session if using Microsoft's Hyper-V hypervisor for virtualization. This will cut down on the overall system requirements and provide a more streamlined host.

▶ Consider the use of a tool such as Microsoft's System Center VMM for virtualization guest and host management and for scenarios such as those where farm members need to be provisioned quickly and reliably.

## CHAPTER 13

Deploying SharePoint for Extranets and Alternative Authentication Scenarios

Many organizations have implemented extranets using SharePoint 2007 to collaborate with partners, vendors, and customers. These organizations have learned to work with many of the issues that are associated with deploying SharePoint 2007 as an extranet solution, such as alert emails sending out the wrong URLs, poor Office client integration, and confusion among teams collaborating via a extranet site.

Microsoft has made a significant investment in many areas of SharePoint 2010, including significant changes to extranet functionality. These improvements include better integration with the Office suite, improvements in the authentication process, flexible deployment scenarios, improved identity management within the application programming interface (API), and many more.

This chapter covers common reasons for using extranet solutions and illustrates the various audiences that extranets are targeted to. It continues by discussing the new security authentication model in SharePoint 2010, and it demonstrates specifics on real-world implementations of extranet solutions. In addition, this chapter discusses how to upgrade an Existing SharePoint 2007 extranet. Finally, it wraps up by discussing security considerations and challenges and best practices around extranet solutions.

Understanding Extranets for Collaborating with Partners, Vendors, and Clients

An extranet is a private network securely extended to share part of an organization's information, resources, or processes with partners, vendors, and clients. In SharePoint specifically, an extranet is a web application that is shared with external users. Extranets are used to collaborate with external users where they have to authenticate to gain access to list and libraries. Extranets are used to solve various challenges, such as sharing medical information with patients and abiding health-care privacy regulations such as HIPAA, which dictates that sensitive documents be uploaded to a secure site instead of emailing the large documents or using an FTP client for uploading. In addition, extranets offer alternatives for employees to work from remote locations.

Outlining Common Extranet Scenarios and Topologies

An important aspect of deploying extranet solutions and sites is to choose the proper network topology for the extranet environment. Different requirements may impact existing infrastructure and topologies, and may require additional hardware and configuration. Implementing different topologies can provide additional benefits, but may require more maintenance and increase the complexity of the enterprise infrastructure.

Outlining Business Requirements and Extranet Considerations

The business should understand the requirements and goals clearly in the early planning stages before deploying an extranet solutions and environment. The business requirements will help identify the different design considerations for their extranet. These are some of the most common design considerations for extranets:

▶ **Network topology and accessibility**—Different topologies serve different needs and requirements and can greatly affect the infrastructure used to provide access. The different topologies can also affect the different types of access requirements used to access shared network resources.

▶ **Identity management (IDM) systems**—Used to identify a specific user and to store additional information related to that user. Different identity management systems impact how accounts will be managed and how other systems can interface with the platform.

▶ **Content security and isolation**—Often content has to be isolated from other external users in common extranets scenario.

▶ **Antivirus solutions**—Ensuring that external users can access secure and virus-free content and data.

▶ **Rich client experience (Office client integration)**—SharePoint offers a rich client experience through Office client integration, where users can edit Microsoft Word documents directly from a SharePoint site using different authentication providers while avoiding multiple authentication prompts.

Understanding Common Partner, Vendor, and Client Extranet Scenarios

When designing an extranet solution, understanding the types of users, the collaboration requirements and the security requirements is important for choosing the type of topology to implement for the extranet solution. It can also change the complexity for implementing and maintaining the extranet solution. Table 13.1 describes several of the benefits for each type of external users.

TABLE 13.1   Types of Extranet Users and Scenarios

Type of User	Description
Remote employees	Access corporate information, line-of-business applications, collaboration sites, and other shared resources remotely from any location. The types of remote employees include employees working from home or customer sites, sales teams, and other geographically dispersed virtual teams. Remote employees are generally managed as part of the primary identity management system of the organization.
Partners	Participate in business processes and collaborate via the extranet with employees of the organization. The types of partners include organizations working together in joint ventures, shared projects, and other collaborative scenarios. Partners are usually managed via a separate identity management system from the organization's identity management system. Some of the challenges in working with partners include managing security and isolating partner data from the internal data, and isolating partner data from other partners.
Vendors and clients	Access branded and targeted information and content based on product lines or by customer profiles. Generally, content is segmented by implementing separate site collections within a farm. Audiences are used to limit content access and reduce the corpus of search results. Generally, vendors and clients accessing branded and targeted information only requires an identity management system for the external users as internal resources aren't shared directly.

Examining Common Deployment Topologies

Before choosing a specific topology, it is beneficial to understand several deployment topologies commonly used for extranet solutions. A topology provides a detailed view of all the servers, devices, links, and ports in your network, both physical and logical. Understanding and planning an appropriate deployment topology will help you avoid inconsistencies or misconfigurations in your physical and logical network and extranet solution.

Edge Firewall Topology

This topology, illustrated in Figure 13.1, uses an edge firewall solution such as Microsoft Forefront UAG or Forefront TMG or third-party firewall as a gateway between intranet and Internet. This configuration uses the firewall as a reverse proxy server that intercepts requests from the Internet and forwards the request to the appropriate web server located and intranet. Using a set of configurable rules, the proxy server verifies that requested URL and translates it into the internal URL. This topology has the following advantages and disadvantages:

Advantages

▶ Most economical and simplest solution that requires the least amount of hardware and configuration.

▶ The entire SharePoint farm resides within the corporate network.

▶ Simplified server management.

Disadvantages

▶ A single firewall separates the corporate network from the Internet.

▶ The corporate network is vulnerable if an external user is compromised.

Back-to-Back Firewall Topology

The back-to-back extranet topology, represented in Figure 13.2, is the recommended network topology for most organizations. In this topology, all the hardware and data resides in the perimeter network. Optionally, the server farm roles and network infrastructure servers such as Active Directory and Exchange Server can be separated across multiple layers with additional routers or firewalls. This is a flexible topology that allows for additional network layers for greater security. External users access the perimeter network through the external proxy server or firewall, and internal users access the perimeter network through an internal proxy server or firewall. This topology has the following advantages and disadvantages:

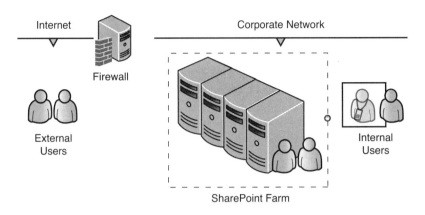

FIGURE 13.1   Edge firewall topology.

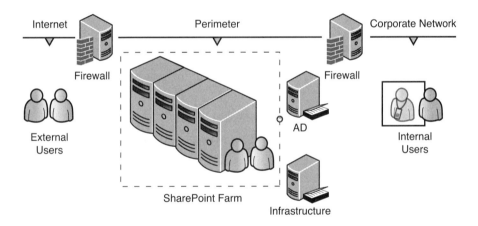

FIGURE 13.2   Back-to-back firewall topology.

Advantages

▶ The corporate network is more secure. If an external user is compromised, only the perimeter network is vulnerable.

▶ The entire SharePoint farm resides within the perimeter network.

▶ External user access is isolated to the perimeter network.

▶ Management of external user accounts is simplified and isolated from the internal identity management system.

Disadvantages

▶ Additional hardware and resources are required for this configuration.

▶ The content databases are vulnerable if the perimeter network is compromised.

▶ Additional overhead is required for managing additional identity management systems.

Split Back-to-Back Firewall Topology

The split back-to-back network topology, shown in Figure 13.3, is similar to the back-to-back topology and further splits the SharePoint farm between the perimeter and corporate networks. The SharePoint web front ends, some application servers, and some infrastructure servers, such as the external identity management system and other resources, reside within the perimeter network. The remaining SharePoint servers and resources, such as the SQL Server databases and other infrastructure servers, reside within the corporate network. This topology has the following advantages and disadvantages:

Advantages

▶ The corporate network is even more secure. If an external user is compromised, only to perimeter network is vulnerable and fewer resources are vulnerable.

▶ The content databases are protected even if the perimeter network is compromised.

▶ External user access is isolated to the perimeter network.

▶ Management of external user accounts is simplified and isolated from the internal identity management system.

Disadvantages

▶ The complexity of the solution is greatly increased.

▶ Additional hardware and resources are required for this configuration.

▶ The form is vulnerable if the perimeter network is compromised and the intruders gain access to the farm accounts.

▶ SharePoint interfarm communication is split between two domains.

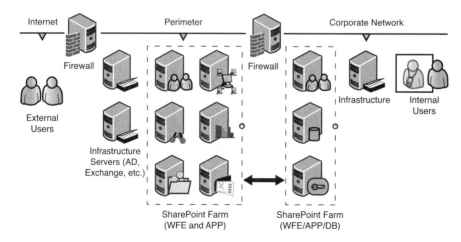

FIGURE 13.3   Split back-to-back firewall topology.

Understanding SharePoint 2010 Extranet Security

Understanding the SharePoint security model requires understanding the difference between the authentication process and authorization process. Authentication is the mechanism whereby systems securely identify the user attempting to access a resource. Authorization is the mechanism by which a system determines the level of access the authenticated user or identity has to a secured resource. The authorization process requires that the authentication process succeeds and establishes an identity. SharePoint itself does not perform any authentication; the authentication process is handled by an underlying authentication system. For example, Windows authentication is handled by Windows server and Internet Information Services (IIS). SharePoint performs the authorization to secured resources contained in sites, lists, libraries, and other such containers. SharePoint 2010 offers two different authentication modes natively: classic authentication mode and claims-based authentication mode.

Understanding Classic-Mode Authentication

Classic-mode authentication in SharePoint 2010 uses the Integrated Windows authentication model supported in legacy versions of SharePoint. In the classic authentication mode, only mixed-mode authentication is available. In mixed-mode authentication, a single SharePoint web application has to be extended to additional IIS applications with different URLs and authentication providers. The same content is used for the different URLs, but the different authentication providers can change the access users have and the permissions.

Understanding Claims-Based Authentication

Claims-based authentication for SharePoint 2010 is built by using the Windows Identity Foundation (WIF) framework. WIF is a set of .NET Framework classes that are used to implement a claims-based identity. Claim-based authentication was developed to provide better fine-grained security for a role-based security model. Most systems, including SharePoint 2007 and its predecessors, use role (or group)-based security. Complex systems can use claims-based security to assign permissions on other attributes (claims) associated with users, such as city or membership in a distribution list.

Claims-based authentication in SharePoint 2010 provides a flexible and extensible authentication system that supports authentication for any identity management system that supports claims authentication. Claims-based authentication offers several benefits, including the following:

▶ Further decoupling SharePoint 2010 from the authentication providers.

▶ Allows SharePoint 2010 to support multiple authentication providers for a single URL.

▶ Allows identities to be passed (and impersonated) between systems without Kerberos delegation.

▶ Enables organizations to use Federation to collaborate.

▶ Allows ACLs to be configured using other membership objects and containers, such as distribution lists, audiences, and organizational units.

▶ Organizations can connect to non-Windows-based identity management systems that support claims.

▶ Provides a common model for performing identity operations for web browsers, web services, and other browser-based applications, including the Office suite.

NOTE

Claims-based authentication is based on open standards such as WS-Federation 1.1, WS-Trust 1.4, and SAML Token 1.1. To learn more about these open standards, go to http://www.oasis-open.org/specs/.

The Claims Authentication Process

Claims authentication provides the benefit of being simple for authentication purposes, but under the covers the process has several components that work together. Claims authentication model has three main components: the identity provider, the relying party, and the user who was authenticated. Each of the three components interacts in the authentication process by exchanging information and claims.

The goal of any authentication process is to establish an identity. An identity is a security principal of an authorized user. The primary component in the claims-based authentication process is a security token that uses the Security Assertion Markup Language (SAML). The security token is used to securely identify and describe an identity by containing of a set of claims (identity assertions) for the identity. A claim is an attribute that is specific to the identity, such as an employee ID, employee title, or username. The claims are used to determine the level of access the identity has to specific SharePoint 2010 resources.

Both the identity provider and the relying party are implemented as Security Token Services where each performs a particular role in the authentication process. The Security Token Service (STS) illustrated in Figure 13.4 handles the exchange of claims, and it builds, signs, and issues the security tokens that can be used to authenticate and authorize an identity. The STS uses a policy to determine the contents of a security token. The policy is a collection of claims and claim rules that has been agreed upon between one or more STSs and the SharePoint web application, as illustrated in Figure 13.5. Policies are available in a policy store and are accessed by an STS, based on the requirements of the calling web application. The attribute stores are made of the various identity systems and providers containing the user account information, such as Active Directory Domain Services (AD DS,) ASP.NET authentication providers, and other SAML token-compliant authentication providers. The STS can perform two roles in the authentication process: the identity provider STS and the relying party STS.

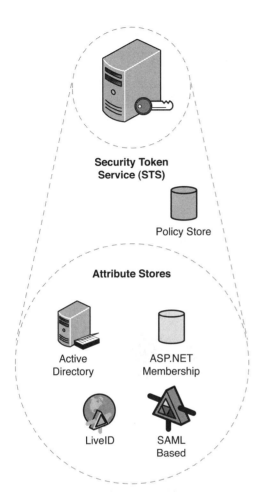

FIGURE 13.4   Secure Token Service.

Identity Provider Security Token Service (IP-STS)

The IP-STS is the identity provider that provides the claim based on the information the user has provided. In SharePoint, the IP-STS is the local identity provider for the requesting web application. The IP-STS receives the authentication request and processes the request. The IP-STS finds the policy for the requesting web application or relying party STS, and creates a security token using the identity claims in the appropriate attribute store.

Relying Party Security Token Service (RP-STS)

The RP-STS is the identity provider that has an established trust relationship with the IP-STS. The RP-STS is used to validate the claims of external users whose credentials are not stored in the local attribute stores. The RP-STS creates security token for the authenticating user and the local SharePoint STS validates the claims for the authenticating user. The requesting web application authorizes the authenticated external user after the local SharePoint STS has validated the claims.

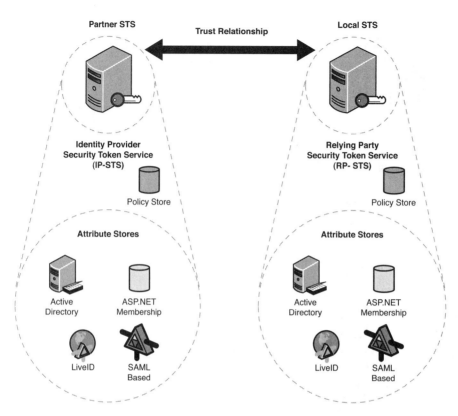

FIGURE 13.5   Claims authentication roles.

Claims Authentication in SharePoint

In SharePoint 2010, claims-based authentication is a SharePoint service. SharePoint contains a local STS as part of the SharePoint farm. A trust relationship exists between the local SharePoint STS and the SharePoint farm web applications.

Figure 13.6 illustrates a sequence of events when a user authenticates in SharePoint using claims-based authentication:

▶ The user attempts to connect to a SharePoint web application using a client (a web browser or office client). The client sends a web request to the web application for a particular resource.

▶ The SharePoint web application using claims-based authentication responds with a 302 response that includes a URL to redirect and authenticate.

▶ The client redirects and submits an authentication request to the URL for a security token. The authentication request is processed by the local STS. The local STS performs the role of the identity provider STS, authenticates the identity of the user, and creates a security token (SAML token) for the authenticated identity.

▶ The client receives a security token from the local STS.

▶ The client sends a web request to the web application for a particular resource with the security token included. The web application validates the user identity and retrieves the resources.

▶ The client receives access the resources it requested, such as a cookie, the HTML page, and its resources.

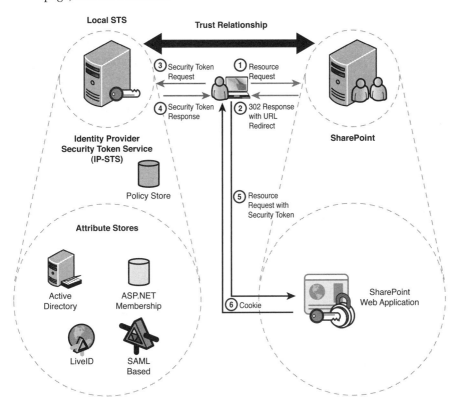

FIGURE 13.6   SharePoint claims authentication process.

Claims Authentication in SharePoint Using Federation

A common scenario for collaborating with partners is to create a trust between the partner STS and the local STS. When external users attempt to authenticate in SharePoint, the request will be made against the partner STS and validated by the local STS in the SharePoint farm. The external user will be able to access the web application with their external credentials.

Figure 13.7 shows the sequence of events when an external user authenticates in SharePoint using claims-based authentication:

▶ The user attempts to connect to a SharePoint web application using a web browser or Office client. The client makes a web request to the web application.

▶ The SharePoint web application that uses claims-based authentication responds with
a 302 response that includes a URL to redirect to the appropriate partner STS and
authenticate.

▶ The client redirects and submits an authentication request to the partner STS for a
security token. The authentication request is processed by the partner STS, authenticates the identity of the user, and creates an identity provider security token (IP-STS
token). The IP-STS token is sent to the local STS for validation.

▶ The local STS receives the IP-STS token and validates the claims for the identity. The
local STS creates a new RP-STS token and sends it to the client. The RP-STS token
includes additional claims from SharePoint to identify the user within SharePoint.

▶ The client receives the RP-STS token from the local STS.

▶ The client sends a web request to the web application for a particular resource with
the RP-STS token included. The web application validates the user identity and
retrieves the resources.

▶ The client receives access the resources it requested, such as a cookie, the HTML
page, and its resources.

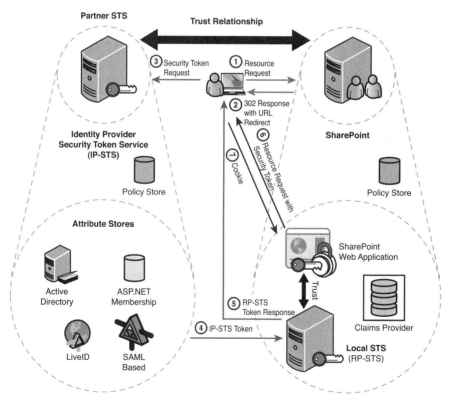

FIGURE 13.7   SharePoint claims authentication process using federation.

NOTE

It is important to note that the IP-STS token is different from the RP-STS token. The RP-STS token contains information and claims specific to the SharePoint identity. The token is used to create the SPUser object within the SharePoint farm.

Implementing Authentication Scenarios

SharePoint can support various authentication scenarios. SharePoint has been used successfully for Internet, intranet, and extranet scenarios. And with the new features in SharePoint 2010, Microsoft has made substantial improvements to better support the different authentication scenarios including multi-authentication scenarios, mixed-mode authentication scenarios, alternate access mappings, and improvements for mobile access.

Configuring Mixed-Mode Authentication Scenarios

Mixed-mode authentication, illustrated in Figure 13.8, uses the same approach used in SharePoint 2007 for authenticating different types of users with different authentication providers. In mixed-mode authentication, the primary web application uses the default security zone with Windows authentication. To use more than one authentication provider, the primary web application must be extended to another IIS application. Each IIS application requires a unique URL. A different authentication provider can be configured for each IIS application. SharePoint recognizes the new IIS applications as part of the primary web application. As a result, the specific IIS applications share the same content (content databases) in SharePoint.

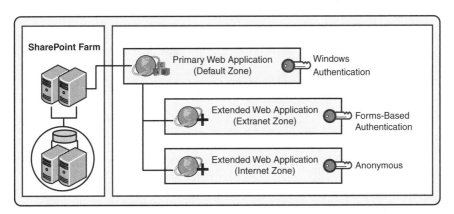

FIGURE 13.8   Mixed-mode authentication.

NOTE

An IIS application supports only a single scheme or protocol. Therefore, two IIS applications are required to support HTTP and HTTPS individually.

Configuring Multiple Authentication Scenarios

Multi-authentication mode, illustrated in Figure 13.9, differs in that it allows for multiple authentication types to be specified on a single web application and does not require a web application to be extended. This allows users to choose the type of login they want to use on the web application.

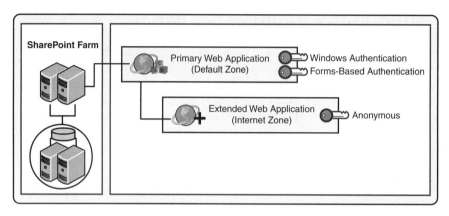

FIGURE 13.9   Multi-authentication mode.

Multiple Authentication Versus Mixed Authentication

Table 13.2 shows a comparison between multimode authentication and mixed-mode authentication, and some of the common usage scenarios for each.

TABLE 13.2   Multimode Versus Mixed-Mode Authentication

	Multi-Authentication Mode	**Mixed-Mode Authentication**
Advantages	Single URL with multiple authentication providers	Automated authentication
	Open standard (more support for third-party authentication systems)	
	Support for complex	
Disadvantages	Single prompt for authentication type	Single URL per authentication provider
Common use scenarios	Single experience for different types of users	Different protocols on different channels:
	Single URL experience	Intranet (HTTP)
	Partner/collaboration sites	Extranet (HTTPS)
	Federation between two organizations	Isolation of authentication providers:
		Internet sites
		Publishing portal authored by employees and consumed by customers

Using Alternate Access Mappings in Extranet Deployments

Alternate access mappings (AAM) are rules used by SharePoint that describe how to map web requests to the proper web application and site. It tells SharePoint what URLs to return in the content so that users can properly navigate the SharePoint site. Most commonly, AAMs are used with reverse proxy-publishing and load-balancing scenarios. A reverse proxy is a device that sits between the end user and the SharePoint server. Requests made to the SharePoint server are first received by the reverse proxy firewall, such as an Internet request via HTTPS. The reverse proxy will then forward the request to the SharePoint server as an HTTP request. This process is referred to as off-box Secure Sockets Layer (SSL) termination. The AAMs are used to translate the internal URL back to the correct public URL. This ensures that the end user navigates the SharePoint site seamlessly when accessing resources from an external URL. Additional AAM scenarios include forwarding the web requests to different port numbers.

Understanding Host-Named Site Collections

In SharePoint, host-named site collections provide a scalable hosting solution with distinct host names or URLs for accessing specific site collections. This allows a user to access a specific root-level site collection using a unique URL, a concept commonly referred to as a "vanity" URL. A single web application can support up to 100,000 host-named site collections. Host-named site collections are only available through the default security zone. Also, users authenticated through other zones cannot access host-named site collections.

In SharePoint 2010, host-named site collections support off-box SSL termination. With host-named site collections, the reverse proxy server cannot modify the host name or the port number (except to 80 and 443 for SSL). Administration of host-named site collections is available through Windows PowerShell commands.

Examining Mobile Administration for SharePoint Extranets

Mobile administration has been very limited in previous versions of SharePoint. In SharePoint 2010, mobile administration has been improved by supporting common mobile interfaces, making improvements to leverage mobile technologies such as SMS, and improving the support for accessing SharePoint websites across firewalls using SSL. Mobile views are enabled by default for most lists and libraries. Custom lists and libraries, and libraries that were created in a previous version of SharePoint (via upgrade), are not enabled by default. Some lists and libraries will contain views where a mobile view is not available, such as the datasheet view and the Gantt view.

In SharePoint 2010, users can enable email and SMS alerts on changes made in SharePoint lists, libraries, or items. For extranet SharePoint websites that are published across the firewall using SSL, administrators must specify a cross-firewall access zone. A cross-firewall access zone is used for generating proper external client and mobile URLs for mobile alert messages. This enables users to send an externally accessible URL from SharePoint by clicking the E-Mail a Link button on the Library Tools or List Tools on the Ribbon.

13

> **NOTE**
>
> To enable SMS alerts in the SharePoint farm, a mobile account for an SMS service must be configured. The mobile account to be configured via central administration or PowerShell. In Central Administration, to enable SMS with the same mobile account, click System Settings, and then under E-Mail and Text Messages (SMS), click Configure Mobile Account. In Central Administration, to enable SMS with the specific mobile accounts per web application, under the Application Management section, click Manage Web Applications. On the Web Applications page, choose the web application to configure. In General Settings on the Ribbon, click Mobile Account.

Implementing a Partner Extranet Solution

This section demonstrates the process for implementing an extranet solution for collaborating with partners. This particular partner extranet solution sample has the following business requirements:

- ▶ Use Windows Authentication for the internal users.

- ▶ Use SQL Server Authentication via forms-based authentication (FBA).

- ▶ The external URL must be http://partner.companyabc.com for all users accessing the site.

- ▶ The Partner team from CompanyXYZ must be able collaborate with the CompanyABC team. Some of the partners must be able to administer and contribute directly to the site.

The partner extranet solution will require the following five major steps:

1. Create the web application using claims-based authentication for the partner extranet site.
2. Create the site collection using the appropriate site template.
3. Configure the authentication providers. Modify the web.config to use FBA. Ensure that SharePoint will have access to the SQL Server database.
4. Assign permissions to the external users.
5. Validate that all user types can access the partner extranet site, http://partner.companyabc.com.

Creating the Extranet Web Application

To create the web application that will be used for the extranet, do the following:

1. Open SharePoint Central Administration from a browser.
2. Click Manage Web Applications under Application Management.
3. Click the New button in the Ribbon.

4. In the Create New Web Application page, as shown in Figure 13.10, choose Claims-Based Authentication.

5. Choose Create a New IIS Website.

6. Enter Port 80 or an appropriate port.

7. Enter Host Header: partner.companyabc.com.

8. Select the identity providers for the web application: Windows Authentication. It is recommended that the web application and site collection be tested before adding or modifying any type of authentication. This helps narrow the scope of issues when diagnosing authentication provider issues.

9. Choose the appropriate application pool configuration for the extranet web application. It is recommended that unique application pool are created with unique application pool accounts for all extranet web applications to ensure proper security isolation.

10. Enter a database name that is appropriate and consistent with the nomenclature established with the organization.

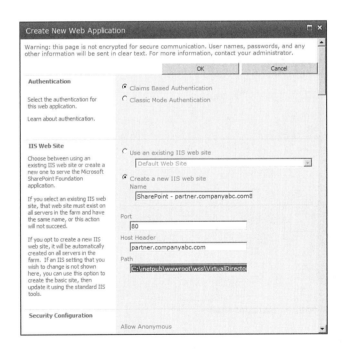

FIGURE 13.10   Create New Web Application page.

Do not use the default group for service application when creating an extranet web application. It is recommended that a custom service application proxy group be created for the extranet web applications, to ensure that only specific service applications are enabled for use in the extranet web applications.

Creating an Extranet Site Collection

To create the site collection used for the extranet, perform the following steps:

1. Open the browser to the Central Administration site.

2. Click Create Site Collections under Application Management.

3. Select the web application for which the new site collection will be created. Choose http://partner.companyabc.com.

4. Enter the title and description for the site collection, as shown in Figure 13.11 (for example, ABC Partner Dash).

5. Select the appropriate site template for the site collection (for example, Group Work Site).

6. Enter the primary and secondary site collection administrators.

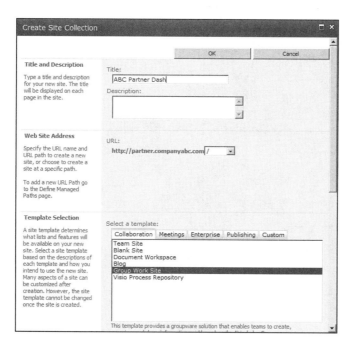

FIGURE 13.11   Create Site Collection page.

Configuring Authentication Providers

This section demonstrates the configuration of forms-based authentication (FBA) using an ASP.NET SQL Server authentication provider. Additional information about configuration and examples for authentication providers can be found on MSDN and TechNet.

The configuration for FBA requires the following major steps:

1. Modify the web.config file in the extranet web application to include the membership provider and role manager for the authentication provider. This step enables the proper behavior of the people picker in the web application.

2. Modify the web.config file in the Central Administration web application to include the membership provider and role manager for the authentication provider. This step enables the proper behavior of the people picker in the Central Administration web application.

3. Modify the web.config file for the STS web services to include the Membership provider and role manager for the authentication provider. This step enables the claims authentication against the SQL authentication provider.

4. Configured the extranet web application to use FBA, and specify the membership provider and role manager.

5. Add the roles and users to the extranet site collection and grant the appropriate permissions and access.

Modify the web.config for the Extranet Web Application

Modify the web.config for each of the web front ends (WFEs) hosting the extranet web applications. Add the following connection string between the `</SharePoint>` and `<system.web>` nodes:

```
<connectionStrings>
<add name="SQLAuthConnectionString" connectionString="Data Source=abc2010sql;User
➡ID=PartnerCredential;Password=********;Persist Security Info=True;Initial
➡Catalog=PartnerIdentitySystem" />
</connectionStrings>
```

Find the `<roleManager>` and `<membershipProvider>` nodes in the `<system.web>` parent node. Add the nodes to include the following entries:

```
<system.web>
...
<roleManager defaultProvider="c" enabled="true" cacheRolesInCookie="false">
<providers>
<add name="c"
```

```
type="Microsoft.SharePoint.Administration.Claims.SPClaimsAuthRoleProvider,
➥Microsoft.SharePoint, Version=14.0.0.0, Culture=neutral, PublicKeyTo-
➥ken=71e9bce111e9429c" />


<add connectionStringName="SQLAuthConnectionString" applicationName="/" descrip-
➥tion="Stores and retrieves roles from SQL Server" name="SQLRoleManager"
➥type="System.Web.Security.SqlRoleProvider, System.Web, Version=2.0.3600.0, Cul-
➥ture=neutral, PublicKeyToken=b03f5f7f11d50a3a" />
</providers>
</roleManager>
<membership defaultProvider="i">
<providers>
<add name="i"
➥type="Microsoft.SharePoint.Administration.Claims.SPClaimsAuthMembershipProvider,
➥Microsoft.SharePoint, Version=14.0.0.0, Culture=neutral, PublicKeyTo-
➥ken=71e9bce111e9429c" />


<add connectionStringName="SQLAuthConnectionString" passwordAttemptWindow="5"
➥enablePasswordRetrieval="false" enablePasswordReset="false" requiresQuestionAn-
➥dAnswer="true" applicationName="/" requiresUniqueEmail="true"
➥passwordFormat="Hashed" description="Stores and Retrieves membership data from SQL
➥Server" name="SQLMembershipProvider"
➥type="System.Web.Security.SqlMembershipProvider, System.Web, Version=2.0.3600.0,
➥Culture=neutral, PublicKeyToken=b03f5f7f11d50a3a" />
</providers>
</membership>
</system.web>
```

Find the `<PeoplePickerWildcards >` nodes in the `<SharePoint>` parent node. Modify the node to "add" the membership provider name to the people picker:

```
<PeoplePickerWildcards>
<clear />
<add key="SQLMembershipProvider" value="%" />
</PeoplePickerWildcards>
```

Modify the web.config for the Central Administration Web Application

Modify the web.config for the Central Administrator web application. Add the following connection string between the `</SharePoint>` and `<system.web>` nodes:

```
<connectionStrings>
<add name="SQLAuthConnectionString" connectionString="Data Source=abc2010sql;User
➥ID=PartnerCredential;Password=********;Persist Security Info=True;Initial
➥Catalog=PartnerIdentitySystem" />
</connectionStrings>
```

Find the `<roleManager>` and `<membershipProvider>` nodes in the `<system.web>` parent node. Add the nodes to include the following entries:

```
<system.web>
...
<roleManager defaultProvider="AspNetWindowsTokenRoleProvider" enabled="true"
➡cacheRolesInCookie="false">
<providers>
<add connectionStringName="SQLAuthConnectionString" applicationName="/" descrip-
➡tion="Stores and retrieves roles from SQL Server" name="SQLRoleManager"
➡type="System.Web.Security.SqlRoleProvider, System.Web, Version=2.0.3600.0, Cul-
➡ture=neutral, PublicKeyToken=b03f5f7f11d50a3a" />
</providers>
</roleManager>
<membership defaultProvider="SQLMembershipProvider">
<providers>
<add connectionStringName="SQLAuthConnectionString" passwordAttemptWindow="5"
➡enablePasswordRetrieval="false" enablePasswordReset="false" requiresQuestion-
➡AndAnswer="true" applicationName="/" requiresUniqueEmail="true"
➡passwordFormat="Hashed" description="Stores and Retrieves membership data from SQL
➡Server" name="SQLMembershipProvider"
➡type="System.Web.Security.SqlMembershipProvider, System.Web, Version=2.0.3600.0,
➡Culture=neutral, PublicKeyToken=b03f5f7f11d50a3a" />
</providers>
</membership>
</system.web>
```

Find the `<PeoplePickerWildcards>` nodes in the `<SharePoint>` parent node. Modify the node to "add" the membership provider name to the people picker:

```
<PeoplePickerWildcards>
<clear />
<add key="SQLMembershipProvider" value="%" />
</PeoplePickerWildcards>
```

Modify the web.config for the STS Web Services

Edit the web.config of the STS web services. The web.config is located at C:\Program Files\Common Files\Microsoft Shared\web server extensions\14\WebServices\SecurityToken:

```
<connectionStrings>
<add name="SQLAuthConnectionString" connectionString="Data Source=abc2010sql;User
➡ID=PartnerCredential;Password=********;Persist Security Info=True;Initial Cata-
➡log=PartnerIdentitySystem" />
```

```
</connectionStrings>
<system.web>
<roleManager defaultProvider="c" enabled="true" cacheRolesInCookie="false">
<providers>
<add name="c"
➥type="Microsoft.SharePoint.Administration.Claims.SPClaimsAuthRoleProvider,
➥Microsoft.SharePoint, Version=14.0.0.0, Culture=neutral, PublicKeyTo-
➥ken=71e9bce111e9429c" />

<add connectionStringName="SQLAuthConnectionString" applicationName="/" descrip-
➥tion="Stores and retrieves roles from SQL Server" name="SQLRoleManager"
➥type="System.Web.Security.SqlRoleProvider, System.Web, Version=2.0.3600.0, Cul-
➥ture=neutral, PublicKeyToken=b03f5f7f11d50a3a" />
</providers>
</roleManager>
<membership defaultProvider="i">
<providers>
<add name="i"
➥type="Microsoft.SharePoint.Administration.Claims.SPClaimsAuthMembershipProvider,
➥Microsoft.SharePoint, Version=14.0.0.0, Culture=neutral, PublicKeyTo-
➥ken=71e9bce111e9429c" />

<add connectionStringName="SQLAuthConnectionString" passwordAttemptWindow="5"
➥enablePasswordRetrieval="false" enablePasswordReset="false" requiresQuestion-
➥AndAnswer="true" applicationName="/" requiresUniqueEmail="true"
➥passwordFormat="Hashed" description="Stores and Retrieves membership data from SQL
➥Server" name="SQLMembershipProvider"
➥type="System.Web.Security.SqlMembershipProvider, System.Web, Version=2.0.3600.0,
Culture=neutral, PublicKeyToken=b03f5f7f11d50a3a" />
</providers>
</membership>
</system.web>
```

Configure the Membership Provider and Role Manager for the Extranet Web Application

To configure the membership provider and role manager for the extranet web application, perform the following steps:

1. Open the browser to the Central Administration site.
2. Click Manage Web Application under Application Management.

3. Select the web application and click the Authentication Providers button in the Ribbon.

4. Click the zone for the authentication provider to configure for FBA.

5. In the Edit Authentication page, check Enable Forms-Based Authentication (FBA), as shown in Figure 13.12.

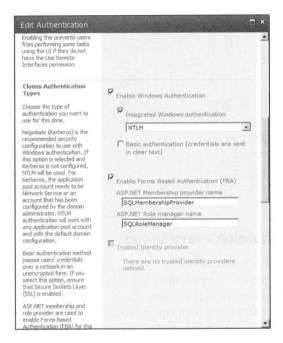

FIGURE 13.12   Edit Authentication page.

6. Enter the membership provider name: **SQLMembershipProvider.**

7. Enter the role manager name: **SQLRoleManagerProvider.**

8. Select the web application and click the User Policy button on the Ribbon.

9. Click Add Users and choose the default zone (or the zone configured with FBA).

10. Add the users, as shown in Figure 13.13, with the appropriate permissions as needed for the FBA website. Then, click Finish.

FIGURE 13.13   Add Users page.

Creating an Extranet Service Application Proxy Group

SharePoint 2010 offers a distributed model for shared services or service applications. Web applications themselves subscribe to use the various service applications. Application proxy groups can be created to define a set of service applications. It is recommended that extranet web applications, one or more application proxy groups be created to ensure only minimum required service applications are enabled for use in the extranet web applications. The following PowerShell commands show how to create a new application proxy group:

1. Open a SharePoint 2010 Management PowerShell console and navigate to Start, All Programs, Microsoft SharePoint 2010, SharePoint 2010 Management Shell.

2. Use the following command to create the new service application proxy group and add a member to it:

```
New-SPServiceApplicationProxyGroup [-Identity <the service application proxy
➥group>]
Add-SPServiceApplicationProxyGroupMember [-Identity <the service application
➥proxy group>] [-Member <members to add to the service application proxy
➥group>]
```

For example:

```
New-SPServiceApplicationProxyGroup -Identity PartnerExtranet
Add-SPServiceApplicationProxyGroupMember -Identity PartnerExtranet -Member
➥bfea704a-e2a1-429f-8c4d-1372e5524bdc
```

Validating the Partner Extranet Solution

To validate whether the solution works properly, do the following:

1. Open the browser to the extranet partner site: http://partner.companyabc.com.
2. Choose the authentication provider from the drop-down, as shown in Figure 13.14, and enter the proper credentials.
3. At this point, you will be logged in to the site using claims-based authentication, as shown in Figure 13.15. Test all the configured authentication providers.

FIGURE 13.14   Login page.

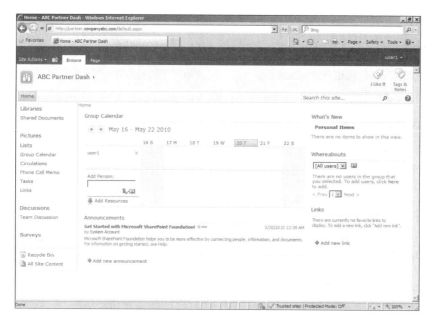

FIGURE 13.15   Successful login to extranet partner site.

Upgrading an Existing Extranet Solution from SharePoint 2007

When an existing SharePoint 2007 extranet web application is upgraded, it will initially use classic mode authentication. To upgrade it to claims-based authentication, perform the following steps:

1. Verify that the upgraded web application works as is in classic mode authentication.

2. Open a SharePoint 2010 Management PowerShell console.

3. Use the following command to convert the web application to use claims-based authentication:

```
$App=Get-SPWebApplication [-Identity <the URL of the Web application>]
$App.UseClaimsAuthentication = "True"
$App.Update()
```

For example:

```
$App=Get-SPWebApplication "http://fba.companyabc.com"
$App.UseClaimsAuthentication = "True"
$App.Update()
```

NOTE

Converting the web application to claims-based authentication cannot be reversed. Make sure that the web application is ready to be converted.

4. After converting the web application, follow the steps listed in the "Configuring Authentication Providers" section, earlier in this chapter. Some of the steps include updating and verifying all the web.config files. Verify the web application configuration and test the site directly.

Security Consideration for SharePoint Extranet Solutions

Security is a complex topic that must be balanced with business requirements and goals. Any system that must be accessed externally will always be more vulnerable than the system within an intranet environment. Security also has its trade-offs, such as usability, supportability, security, and complexity. Each of these affect the others, and has to be weighed by the business and its requirements and goals to establish the proper security model for their specific scenario. The following list should be considered when building extranet solutions in SharePoint:

▶ Use the "least privilege" accounts and security approach. This approach reduces the security risk when any account is compromised and isolates problems and issues to their specific areas. For example, if search is using specific content access accounts, errors while crawling the content sources will be easily identified by the source and also the account. In SharePoint 2010, managed accounts simplify the process of changing passwords by centralizing the management of the accounts in Central Administration.

▶ Include a SharePoint-specific antivirus solution such as Microsoft's Forefront Protection for SharePoint as part of the extranet deployment. This ensures that the antivirus solution can be configured to scan only uploaded files and documents, as opposed to scanning both uploads and downloads. All data contained within the content databases can be considered clean.

▶ Plan the security model for the SharePoint farm according to the business names while minimizing the complexity. Choose a network topology that protects the intranet and any shared resources adequately. Reduce the access points to the shared resources and establish a common nomenclature that is intuitive and descriptive.

▶ Document decisions, configuration, and modifications made as part of the security model. Establish a governance approach around security changes to ensure all documentation is maintained and recorded appropriately.

▶ Consider placing application servers on a private, nonroutable subnet for secure SharePoint interfarm communication. Also, consider securing communication between SharePoint servers (interserver communication) through IPsec or SSL.

▶ Use web applications for isolation, security, and confidentiality.

> **NOTE**
>
> Security is a complex topic. Make sure to understand the authentication providers and the required access to any shared resources. Always minimize the access any user or application has to only the minimum information that is required.

Resources

▶ Logical Architecture Components (http://technet.microsoft.com/en-us/library/cc263121.aspx#section10)

▶ Plan Authentication (http://technet.microsoft.com/en-us/library/ee794879.aspx)

▶ Mobile Administration (http://technet.microsoft.com/en-us/library/ff393820.aspx)

Summary

SharePoint 2010 offers many new features and enhancements that improve extranet scenarios for collaboration with partners, vendors, and customers. Many of the enhancements and features overcome issues and limitations found in SharePoint 2007 extranet solutions. In addition, improved Office client integration with forms-based authentication and other authentication providers make SharePoint 2010 a better extranet solution platform.

This chapter discussed the common reasons and audiences for using extranet solutions, common topologies used to implement extranet solutions, the security authentication models in SharePoint 2010, and how to upgrade an existing SharePoint 2007 extranet. It demonstrates how to configure a SharePoint web applications as an extranet solution using FBA and Windows authentication with a single URL.

Best Practices

▶ Secure your extranet with SSL encryption and always use port 443 inbound only. Using nonstandard ports does not improve security and only complicates the farm configuration. Some services will not work on nonstandard ports.

▶ Choose your authentication mode based on your requirements. Multi-authentication offers a seamless collaboration experience with a single URL, but users always have to choose the authentication method when entering the site. Mixed-mode authentication requires extending the web application; therefore, users may experience confusion due to multiple URLs.

▶ When using additional zones and extending web applications, name the web applications and URLs intelligently and intuitively.

▶ Don't store confidential and secure data in an extranet.

▶ Use web applications for isolation, security, and confidentiality.

▶ Use SharePoint-specific antivirus products such as Microsoft's Forefront Protection for SharePoint (FPSP), as opposed to traditional file-based antivirus products. Traditional antivirus products can cause problems while scanning content and don't work properly with the SharePoint antivirus API.

▶ WFE servers should always be in a secured network. Seek opportunities to reduce the vulnerability surface area.

▶ Consider placing application servers on a private, nonroutable subnet for secure SharePoint inter-farm communication. Also, consider securing communication between SharePoint servers (interserver communication) through IPsec.

▶ Create one or more service application connection groups for the extranet web applications. This will ensure that only specific service applications are enabled for use by the extranet web applications.

▶ Use unique application pools with unique application pool accounts for all extranet web applications to ensure proper isolation.

CHAPTER 14

Protecting SharePoint with Advanced Antivirus and Edge Security Solutions

In today's risk-fraught computing environment, any exposed service is subject to frequent attack from the Internet. This is particularly true for web services, including those offered by SharePoint 2010. Exploits using the Hypertext Transport Protocol (HTTP) that these services use are becoming very common, and it is not considered best practice to make a SharePoint server directly accessible via the Internet.

Fortunately, the productivity gains in SharePoint 2010 can still be utilized and made more accessible by securing them behind a reverse-proxy server such as Microsoft's Forefront Threat Management Gateway (Forefront TMG) 2010 or Forefront Unified Access Gateway (Forefront UAG) 2010. These tools, part of the Forefront Edge line, allow for advanced application layer filtering of network traffic, greatly securing the overall SharePoint environment.

This chapter details the ways that SharePoint 2010 sites can be secured using the Forefront TMG 2010 and Forefront UAG 2010 products. Deployment scenarios for securing SharePoint-related services with Forefront TMG/UAG are outlined, and specific step-by-step guides are illustrated.

In addition to information on the Forefront Edge line, this chapter covers advanced antivirus capabilities using Forefront Protection for SharePoint, Microsoft's SharePoint-aware antivirus utility.

Understanding the Forefront Edge Line of Products

The rise in the prevalence of computer viruses, threats, and exploits on the Internet has made it necessary for organizations of all shapes and sizes to reevaluate their protection strategies for edge services such as SharePoint Server. No longer is it possible to ignore or minimize these threats as the damage they can cause can cripple a company's business functions. A solution to the increased sophistication and pervasiveness of these viruses and exploits is becoming increasingly necessary.

Corresponding with the growth of these threats has been the development of Microsoft's Forefront Edge line of products, including Forefront TMG and Forefront UAG products from Microsoft. These products are fast becoming a business-critical component of many organizations, who are finding that many of the traditional packet-filtering firewalls and technologies don't necessarily stand up to the modern threats of today. The Forefront Edge product provides for that higher level of application security required, particularly for tools such as SharePoint sites and other web services.

> **NOTE**
>
> Although it is possible to secure a SharePoint site with the older version of Forefront TMG, Microsoft's Internet Security and Acceleration (ISA) Server 2006, it is highly recommended to use either Forefront TMG or Forefront UAG because they provide for advanced functionality and features and are "SharePoint aware."

Understanding the Difference Between Forefront UAG and Forefront TMG

The first important distinction that needs to be made is the difference between the two products in the Forefront Edge line. Forefront TMG is the direct replacement for the ISA Server 2006 product, and is positioned by Microsoft as the preferred product for outbound security filtering of web and other traffic. Forefront UAG, on the other hand, is a full-function Secure Sockets Layer/virtual private network (SSL/VPN), and is positioned by Microsoft as the preferred solution for inbound security filtering of traffic destined for SharePoint and other internal published resources.

So, in a perfect world, SharePoint administrators would use the full Forefront UAG product for securing access to a SharePoint site. Indeed, Forefront UAG has a Forefront TMG engine within it, so there is no loss of functionality using the Forefront UAG line. Forefront TMG, however, has fewer overall features and is not a true SSL/VPN, and is primarily positioned as a forward proxy solution rather than a reverse-proxy one, which is what is needed for securing SharePoint.

That said, Forefront TMG does not lose any of its reverse proxy capabilities that it inherited from the older ISA 2006 product, so it can still be used for reverse-proxy securing of inbound SharePoint traffic. Either solution can be used for properly securing critical SharePoint traffic, and both solutions are outlined in this book. This chapter points out instances when there are differences between the two tools, but also assumes that either tool may be used.

At a minimum, it is highly recommended to use an application layer-aware security solution for inbound traffic to SharePoint sites, whether that is the Forefront Edge line or whether it is another third-party solution. Exposing a SharePoint site to direct uninspected access from the Internet is highly discouraged.

Outlining the Need for the Forefront Edge Line for SharePoint Environments

A great deal of confusion exists about the role that the Forefront Edge line can play in a SharePoint environment. Much of that confusion stems from the misconception that Forefront TMG or Forefront UAG are only proxy server products. Both Forefront Edge products are, on the contrary, fully functional firewalls, VPN servers, web caching proxies, and application reverse-proxy solutions. In addition, the Forefront Edge line addresses specific business needs to provide a secured infrastructure and improve productivity through the proper application of its built-in functionality. Determining how these features can help to improve the security and productivity of a SharePoint environment is subsequently of key importance.

In addition to the built-in functionality available within the Forefront Edge line, a whole host of third-party integration solutions provide additional levels of security and functionality. Enhanced intrusion detection support, content filtering, web surfing restriction tools, and customized application filters all extend the capabilities of the Forefront Edge line and position it as a solution to a wide variety of security needs within organizations or many sizes.

Outlining the High Cost of Security Breaches

It is rare when a week goes by without a high-profile security breach, denial-of-service (DoS) attack, exploit, virus, or worm appearing in the news. The risks inherent in modern computing have been increasing exponentially, and effective countermeasures are required in any organization that expects to do business across the Internet.

It has become impossible to turn a blind eye toward these security threats. On the contrary, even organizations that would normally not be obvious candidates for attack from the Internet must secure their services, as the vast majority of modern attacks do not focus on any one particular target, but sweep the Internet for any destination host, looking for vulnerabilities to exploit. Infection or exploitation of critical business infrastructure can be extremely costly for an organization. Many of the productivity gains in business recently have been attributed to advances in information technology functionality, including SharePoint-related gains, and the loss of this functionality can severely impact the bottom line.

In addition to productivity losses, the legal environment for businesses has changed significantly in recent years. Regulations such as Sarbanes-Oxley (SOX), HIPAA, and Gramm Leach Bliley have changed the playing field by requiring a certain level of security and validation of private customer data. Organizations can now be sued or fined for substantial sums if proper security precautions are not taken to protect client data. The

atmosphere surrounding these concerns provides the backdrop for the evolution and
acceptance of the Forefront Edge line of products.

Outlining the Critical Role of Firewall Technology in a Modern Connected Infrastructure

It is widely understood today that valuable corporate assets such as SharePoint sites
cannot be exposed to direct access to the world's users on the Internet. In the beginning,
however, the Internet was built on the concept that all connected networks could be
trusted. It was not originally designed to provide robust security between networks, so
security concepts needed to be developed to secure access between entities on the
Internet. Special devices known as firewalls were created to block access to internal
network resources for specific companies.

Originally, many organizations were not directly connected to the Internet. Often, even
when a connection was created, there was no type of firewall put into place because the
perception was that only government or high-security organizations required protection.

With the explosion of viruses, hacking attempts, and worms that began to proliferate,
organizations soon began to understand that some type of firewall solution was required
to block access to specific "dangerous" TCP or UDP ports that were used by the
Internet's TCP/IP Protocol. This type of firewall technology would inspect each arriving
packet and accept or reject it based on the TCP or UDP port specified in the packet of
information received.

Some of these firewalls were ASIC-based firewalls, which employed the use of solid-state
microchips, with built-in packet-filtering technology. These firewalls, many of which are
still used and deployed today, provided organizations with a quick-and-dirty way to filter
Internet traffic, but did not allow for a high degree of customization because of their
static nature.

The development of software-based firewalls coincided with the need for simpler management interfaces and the ability to make software changes to firewalls quickly and easily.
The most popular firewall brand in organizations today, CheckPoint, falls into this category, as do other popular firewalls such as SonicWall and Cisco PIX. The Forefront Edge
line was built and developed as a software-based firewall, and provides the same degree of
packet-filtering technology that has become a virtual necessity on the Internet today.

More recently, holes in the capabilities of simple packet-based filtering technology has
made a more sophisticated approach to filtering traffic for malicious or spurious content a
necessity. The Forefront Edge line responds to these needs with the capabilities to perform
application-layer filtering on Internet traffic.

Understanding the Growing Need for Application Layer Filtering

Nearly all organizations with a presence on the Internet have put some type of packet-
filtering firewall technology into place to protect the internal network resources from
attack. These types of packet-filter firewall technologies were useful in blocking specific
types of network traffic, such as vulnerabilities that utilize the RPC protocol, by simply

blocking TCP and UDP ports that the RPC protocol would use. Other ports, on the other hand, were often left wide open to support certain functionality, such as the TCP 80 or 443 ports, utilized for HTTP and HTTPS web browsing and for access to SharePoint. As previously mentioned, a packet-filter firewall is only able to inspect the header of a packet, simply understanding which port the data is meant to utilize, but unable to actually read the content. A good analogy to this would be if a border guard were instructed to only allow citizens with specific passports to enter the country, but had no way of inspecting their luggage for contraband or illegal substances.

The problems that are becoming more evident, however, is that the viruses, exploits, and attacks have adjusted to conform to this new landscape, and have started to realize that they can conceal the true malicious nature of their payload within the identity of an allowed port. For example, they can "piggy-back" their destructive payload over a known "good" port that is open on a packet-filter firewall. Many modern exploits, viruses, and "scumware," such as illegal file-sharing applications, piggy-back off of the TCP 80 or 443 ports, for example. Using the border guard analogy to illustrate, the smugglers realized that if they put their contraband in the luggage of a citizen from a country on the border guard's allowed list, they could smuggle it into the country without worrying that the guard will inspect the package. These types of exploits and attacks are not uncommon, and the list of known application-level attacks continues to grow.

In the past, when an organization realized that they had been compromised through their traditional packet-filter firewall, the knee-jerk reaction common was to lock down access from the Internet in response to threats. For example, an exploit that would arrive over HTTP ports 80 or 443 might prompt an organization to completely close access to that port for a temporary or semi-permanent basis. This approach can greatly impact productivity as SharePoint access would be affected. This is especially true in a modern connected infrastructure that relies heavily on communications and collaboration with outside vendors and customers. Traditional security techniques would involve a trade-off between security and productivity. The tighter a firewall was locked down, for example, the less functional and productive an end user could be.

In direct response to the need to maintain and increase levels of productivity without compromising security, application layer "stateful inspection" capabilities were built in to the Forefront Edge line that could intelligently determine whether particular web traffic is legitimate. To illustrate, the Forefront Edge line inspects a packet using TCP Port 80 to determine if it is a properly formatted HTTP request. Looking back to the analogy we have been using, the Forefront Edge line is like a border guard who not only checks the passports, but is also given an x-ray machine to check the luggage of each person crossing the border.

The more sophisticated application layer attacks become, the greater the need becomes for a security solution that can allow for a greater degree of productivity while reducing the type of risks which can exist in an environment that relies on simple packet-based filtering techniques.

Outlining the Inherent Threat in SharePoint Web Traffic

The Internet provides somewhat of a catch-22 when it comes to its goal and purpose. On one hand, the Internet is designed to allow anywhere, anytime access to information, linking systems around the world together and providing for that information to be freely exchanged. On the other hand, this type of transparency comes with a great deal of risk, because it effectively means that any one system can be exposed to every connected computer, either friendly or malicious, in the world.

Often, this inherent risk of compromising systems or information through their exposure to the Internet has led to locking down access to that information with firewalls. Of course, this limits the capabilities and usefulness of a free-information exchange system such as what web traffic provides. Many of the web servers need to be made available to anonymous access by the general public, which causes the dilemma, as organizations need to place that information online without putting the servers it is placed on at undue risk.

Fortunately, the Forefront Edge line provides for robust and capable tools to secure web traffic, making it available for remote access but also securing it against attack and exploit. To understand how it does this, it is first necessary to examine how web traffic can be exploited.

Understanding Web (HTTP) Exploits

It is an understatement to say that the computing world was not adequately prepared for the release of the Code Red virus. The Microsoft Internet Information Services (IIS) exploit that Code Red took advantage of was already known, and a patch was made available from Microsoft for several weeks before the release of the virus. In those days, however, less emphasis was placed on patching and updating systems on a regular basis, because it was generally believed that it was best to wait for the bugs to get worked out of the patches first.

So, what happened is that a large number of websites were completely unprepared for the huge onslaught of exploits that occurred with the Code Red virus, which sent specially formatted HTTP requests to a web server to attempt to take control of a system. For example, the following URL lists the type of exploits that were performed:

http://sharepoint.companyabc.com/scripts/..%5c../winnt/system32/ cmd.exe?/c+dir+c:\

This one in particular attempts to launch the command prompt on a web server. Through the proper manipulation, viruses such as Code Red found the method for taking over web servers and using them as drones to attack other web servers.

These types of web-based attacks were a wakeup call to the broader security community. It became apparent that packet-layer filter firewalls that could simply open or close a port were worthless against the threat of an exploit that packages its traffic over a legitimately allowed port such as HTTP or HTTPS.

Web-based filtering and securing, fortunately, is something that the Forefront Edge line does extremely well, and offers a large number of customization options that enable administrators to have control over the traffic and security of the web server.

Securing Encrypted (SSL) Web Traffic

As the World Wide Web was maturing, organizations realized that if they encrypted the HTTP packets that were transmitted between a website and a client, it would make it virtually unreadable to anyone who would potentially intercept those packets. This led to the adoption of SSL encryption for HTTP traffic.

Of course, encrypted packets also create somewhat of a dilemma from an intrusion detection and analysis perspective, because it is impossible to read the content of the packet to determine what it is trying to do. Indeed, many HTTP exploits in the wild today can be transmitted over secure SSL-encrypted channels. This poses a dangerous situation for organizations that must secure the traffic against interception but must also proactively monitor and secure their web servers against attack.

The Forefront Edge line is uniquely positioned to solve this problem, fortunately, because it includes the ability to perform end-to-end SSL bridging. By installing the SSL Certificate from the SharePoint web front-end server on either the Forefront UAG or Forefront TMG servers, along with a copy of the private key, the server is able to decrypt the traffic, scan it for exploits, and then re-encrypt it before sending it to the SharePoint server. Very few products on the market do this type of end-to-end encryption of the packets for this level of security other than the two Forefront Edge line products. Before Forefront UAG or Forefront TMG can secure SharePoint SSL traffic, however, an SSL Certificate must be placed on the SharePoint server.

Securing SharePoint Traffic with SSL Encryption

By default, SharePoint is configured to use Integrated Windows authentication. This form of authentication works fine if access to the server is over a trusted internal network, but is not feasible for access over the Internet.

Because of this limitation, a form of authentication that can be sent across the Internet must be used. This effectively limits the SharePoint server to using Basic Authentication, which is supported by most web browsers and devices. The problem with Basic Authentication, however, is that the username and password that the user sends is effectively sent in clear text and can be intercepted and stolen in transit. In addition, documents and other confidential information are transmitted in clear text, a huge security issue.

The solution to this problem is to use what is known as Secure Sockets Layer (SSL) encryption on the traffic. SSL encryption is performed using Public Key Infrastructure (PKI) certificates, which work through the principle of shared-key encryption. PKI SSL certificates are widely used on the Internet today; any website starting with a https:// uses them, and the entire online merchant community is dependent upon the security of the system.

For SharePoint, the key is to install a certificate on the server so that the traffic between the device and the server is protected from prying eyes. There are effectively two options to this approach, as follows:

▶ **Use a third-party certificate authority**—A common option for many organizations is to purchase a certificate for SharePoint from a third-party trusted certificate authority (CA), such as Verisign, Thawte, or others. These CAs are already trusted by a vast number of devices, so no additional configuration is required. The downside to this option is that the certificates must be purchased and the organization doesn't have as much flexibility to change certificate options.

▶ **Install and use your own CA**—Another common approach is to install and configure Windows Server 2008 R2 Active Directory Certificate Services (AD CS) to create your own CA within an organization. This gives you the flexibility to create new certificates, revoke existing ones, and not have to pay immediate costs. The downside to this approach is that no browsers will trust the certificate by default, and error messages to that effect will be encountered on the devices unless the certificates are manually trusted or forced out to client domain members via Active Directory Group Policy Objects.

Securing SharePoint Sites with Forefront TMG 2010

SharePoint sites comprise one of the more common types of content that are secured by the Forefront Edge line. This stems from the critical need to provide remote document management while at the same time securing that access. Although Forefront UAG is the preferred solution for reverse proxy of a SharePoint environment, the Forefront TMG product is also a highly capable product that allows for reverse proxy functionality. Both products are covered in this chapter, but this section illustrates the creation of a Forefront TMG publishing rule for a SharePoint site for clients with an investment in Forefront TMG but without a Forefront UAG environment.

> **NOTE**
>
> Organizations with legacy ISA Server 2006 can still use it to secure inbound traffic to SharePoint 2010 because it is still a supported product. The steps to secure a SharePoint site with ISA 2006 are nearly identical to the steps used with Forefront TMG. Just follow the same instructions listed here or refer to *SharePoint 2007 Unleashed*, which describes the process of ISA Server 2006.

Forefront TMG can be used to secure a SharePoint implementation can be deployed in multiple scenarios, such as an edge firewall, an inline firewall, or a dedicated reverse-proxy server. In all these scenarios, Forefront TMG secures SharePoint traffic by "pretending" to be the SharePoint server itself, scanning the traffic that is destined for the SharePoint server for exploits, and then repackaging that traffic and sending it on, such as what is illustrated in Figure 14.1.

Forefront TMG performs this type of securing through a SharePoint site publishing rule, which automatically sets up and configures a listener on the Forefront TMG server. A listener is a Forefront TMG component that listens to specifically defined IP traffic and processes that traffic for the requesting client as if it were the actual server itself. For example, a SharePoint listener on Forefront TMG would respond to SharePoint

HTTP/HTTPS requests made to it by scanning them for exploits and then repackaging them and forwarding them on to the SharePoint server itself. Using listeners, the client cannot tell the difference between the Forefront TMG server and the SharePoint server itself.

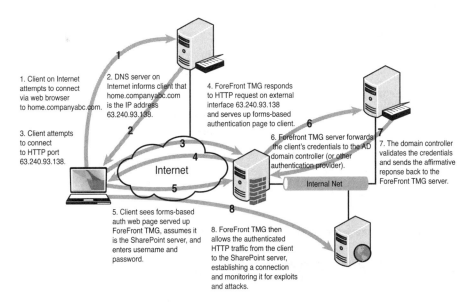

FIGURE 14.1   Conceptualizing the process of securing a SharePoint site using Forefront TMG.

Forefront TMG is also one of the few products, along with Forefront UAG, that has the capability to secure web traffic with SSL encryption from end to end. It does this by using the SharePoint server's own certificate to re-encrypt the traffic before sending it on its way. This also allows for the "black box" of SSL traffic to be examined for exploits and viruses at the application layer, and then re-encrypted to reduce the chance of unauthorized viewing of the traffic. Without the capability to scan this SSL traffic, exploits bound for a SharePoint server could simply hide themselves in the encrypted traffic and pass right through traditional firewalls.

This chapter covers one common scenario that Forefront TMG server is used for: securing a SharePoint site collection (in this example, home.companyabc.com) using Forefront TMG. The steps outlined here describe this particular scenario, although Forefront TMG can also be used for multiple other securing scenarios as necessary.

Configuring the Alternate Access Mapping Setting for the External URL

Before external access can be granted to a site, an alternate access mapping (AAM) must be established for the particular web application. An AAM is a host header value (such as https://portal.companyabc.com, http://server4, https://home.companyabc.com, and so on) that must be consistently applied to the site across all links. If it is not put into place, external clients will not be able to access internal links.

To configure the AAM in this scenario, home.companyabc.com, on a web application, perform the following steps:

1. Open the SharePoint Central Admin Tool.

2. Click the System Settings link in the links provided on the left of the screen.

3. Under Farm Management, click the Configure Alternate Access Mappings link.

4. Click Edit Public URLs.

5. Under Alternate Access Mapping Collection, select the AAM Collection that corresponds to the web application for home.companyabc.com.

6. Enter the https:// AAM needed under the Internet box, as shown in Figure 14.2. In this example, we enter https://home.companyabc.com. If the web application will be addressed by other names, enter all possible names here. Click Save.

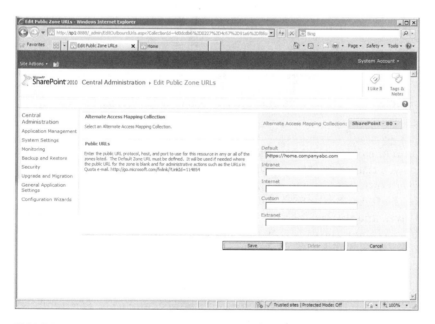

FIGURE 14.2   Creating an alternate access mapping for external published use.

7. Review the AAMs listed on the page for accuracy, and then close the SharePoint Central Admin tool.

Creating a SharePoint Publishing Rule Using Forefront TMG

After an SSL Certificate from the SharePoint server has been installed onto the Forefront TMG server, the actual Forefront TMG SharePoint publishing rule can be generated to secure SharePoint via the following procedure:

> **NOTE**
>
> The procedure outlined here illustrates the Forefront Edge line SharePoint publishing rule that uses forms-based authentication (FBA) for the site, which allows for a landing page to be generated on the Forefront Edge line to pre-authenticate user connections to SharePoint.

1. From the Forefront TMG console, click once on the Firewall Policy node from the console tree.
2. Click the link in the Tasks tab of the Tasks pane labeled Publish SharePoint Sites.
3. Enter a descriptive name for the publishing rule, such as SharePoint Publishing Rule.
4. Select whether to publish a single website, multiple websites, or a farm of load-balanced servers, as illustrated in Figure 14.3. In this example, we choose to publish a simple single website. Click Next to continue.

FIGURE 14.3   Creating a Forefront TMG publishing rule for SharePoint sites.

5. Choose whether to require SSL from the Forefront Edge line server to the SharePoint server, as shown in Figure 14.4. It is recommended to provide end-to-end SSL

support for the Forefront Edge line, although it will require a copy of the SSL certificate with the private key exported to the TMG server for this to be set up properly.
Click Next to continue.

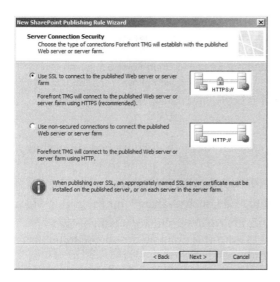

FIGURE 14.4   Configuring SSL for publishing rule.

6. In the Internal Publishing Details dialog box, enter the site name that internal users
   use to access the SharePoint server. Examine the options to connect to an IP address
   or computer name; this gives additional flexibility to the rule. Click Next to continue.

7. Under the subsequent dialog box, enter to accept requests for This Domain Name
   (type below): and enter the FQDN of the server, such as home.companyabc.com.
   This will restrict the rule to requests that are destined for the proper FQDN. Click
   Next to continue.

8. Under Web Listener, click New.

9. At the start of the Web Listener Wizard, enter a descriptive name for the listener,
   such as SharePoint HTTP/HTTPS Listener, and click Next to continue.

10. Again, a prompt is given to choose between SSL and non-SSL. This prompt refers to
    the traffic between client and SharePoint, which should always be SSL whenever
    possible. Click Next to continue.

11. Under Web Listener IP addresses, select the External network and leave it at All IP
    Addresses. Click Next to continue.

12. Under Listener SSL Certificates (if creating an SSL-based rule; if not, you will not be
    prompted for this), click Select Certificate.

13. Select the previously installed certificate (if using SSL) and click the Select button.

14. Click Next to continue.

15. For the type of authentication, choose HTML Form Authentication, as shown in Figure 14.5. Leave Windows (Active Directory) selected and click Next.

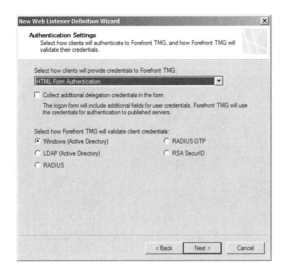

FIGURE 14.5   Selecting to use forms-based authentication for a Forefront TMG publishing rule.

16. The Single Sign On Settings dialog box is powerful; it allows all authentication traffic through a single listener to be processed only once. After the user has authenticated, he can access any other service, be it an Exchange OWA server, web server, or other web-based service that uses the same domain name for credentials. In this example, we enter **.companyabc.com** into the SSO domain name. Click Next to continue.

17. Click Finish to end the Web Listener Wizard.

18. Click Next after the new listener is displayed in the Web Listener dialog box.

19. Under Authentication Delegation, choose Basic from the drop-down box. Basic is used if SSL is the transport mechanism chosen. If using HTTP only, it is recommended to use NTLM authentication to avoid the passwords being sent in clear text. Click Next to continue.

20. At the Alternate Access Mapping Configuration dialog box, shown in Figure 14.6, select that SharePoint AAM is already configured, as we configured the Alternate Access Mapping on the SharePoint server in previous steps.

21. Under User Sets, leave All Authenticated Users selected. In stricter scenarios, only specific AD groups can be granted rights to SharePoint using this dialog box. In this example, the default setting is sufficient. Click Next to continue.

22. Click Finish to end the wizard.

23. Click Apply in the details pane, and then complete the change management options and click Apply again.

24. Click OK when finished to commit the changes.

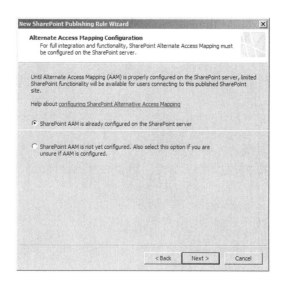

FIGURE 14.6   Creating a Forefront TMG publishing rule for a SharePoint site with AAM already
configured.

The rule will now appear in the details pane of the Forefront TMG server. Double-clicking
the rule brings up the settings. Tabs can be used to navigate around the different rule
settings. The rule itself can be configured with additional settings based on the configuration desired. For example, the following rule information is used to configure our basic
FBA web publishing rule for SharePoint:

▶ **General tab**—Name—SharePoint; Enabled = checked.

▶ **Action tab**—Action to take = Allow; Log requests matching this rule = checked.

▶ **From tab**—This rule applies to traffic from these sources = Anywhere.

▶ **To tab**—This rule applies to this published site = home.companyabc.com; Computer
name or IP address = 10.10.10.105 (internal IP address of SharePoint server). Forward
the original host header instead of the actual one (specified in the Internal Site
Name field) = checked; Specify how the firewall proxies requests to the published
server = Requests appear to come from the Forefront TMG computer.

▶ **Traffic tab**—This rule applies to traffic of the following protocols = HTTPS.

▶ **Listener tab, Properties button**—Networks tab = External, All IP addresses;
Connections tab – Enabled HTTP connections on port 80, Enable SSL connections
on port 443; HTTP to HTTPS Redirection = Redirect authenticated traffic from HTTP
to HTTPS; Forms tab = Allow users to change their passwords, Remind users that
their password will expire in this number of days = 15; SSO tab = Enable Single Sign
On, SSO Domains = .companyabc.com.

▶ **Public Name tab**—This rule applies to requests for the following websites =
home.companyabc.com.

▶ **Paths tab**—External paths = All are set to <same as internal.; Internal paths = /*, /_vti_inf.html*, /_vti_bin/*, /_upresources/*, /_layouts/*, /* (as illustrated in Figure 14.7).

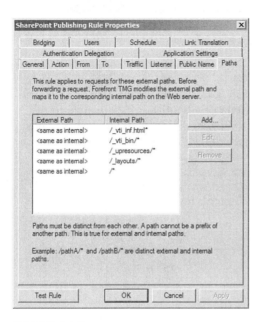

FIGURE 14.7   Viewing the tabs on a newly created SharePoint site publishing rule.

▶ **Authentication Delegation tab**—Method used by the Forefront Edge line to authenticate to the published web server = Basic authentication.

▶ **Application Settings tab**—Use customized HTML forms instead of the default = unchecked.

▶ **Bridging tab**—Redirect requests to SSL port = 443.

▶ **Users tab**—This rule applies to requests from the following user sets = All Authenticated Users.

▶ **Schedule tab**—Schedule = Always.

▶ **Link Translation tab**—Apply link translation to this rule = checked.

Different rules require different settings, but the settings outlined in this example are some of the more common and secure ones used to set up this scenario.

Monitoring Forefront TMG Using the Logging Feature

One of the most powerful troubleshooting tools at the disposal of SharePoint and Forefront TMG administrators is the logging mechanism, which gives live or archived views of the logs on a Forefront TMG computer and allows for quick and easy searching

and indexing of Forefront TMG log information, including every packet of data that hits
the Forefront TMG computer.

> **NOTE**
>
> Many of the advanced features of the Forefront Edge line logging are available only
> when using MSDE or SQL databases for the storage of the logs.

The Forefront TMG logs are accessible via the Logging tab in the details pane of the Logs
and Reports node, as shown in Figure 14.8. They enable administrators to watch, in real
time, what is happening to the Forefront TMG server, whether it is denying connections,
for example, and what rule is being applied for each allow or deny statement.

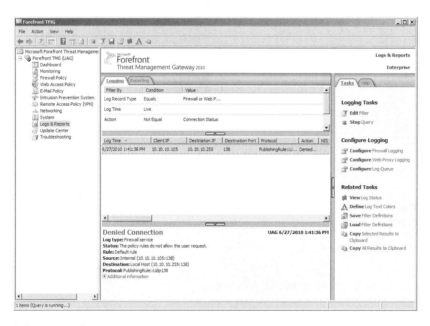

FIGURE 14.8   Examining Forefront TMG logging.

The logs include pertinent information on each packet of data, including the following
key characteristics:

▶ **Log Time**—The exact time the packet was processed.

▶ **Destination IP**—The destination IP address of the packet.

▶ **Destination Port**—The destination TCP/IP port, such as port 80 for HTTP traffic.

▶ **Protocol**—The specific protocol that the packet utilized, such as HTTP, LDAP, RPC,
or others.

▶ **Action**—What type of action the Forefront Edge line took on the traffic, such as initiating the connection or denying it.

▶ **Rule**—Which particular firewall policy rule applied to the traffic.

▶ **Client IP**—The IP address of the client that sent the packet.

▶ **Client Username**—The username of the requesting client. Note that this is populated only if using the firewall client.

▶ **Source Network**—The source network that the packet came from.

▶ **Destination Network**—The network where the destination of the packet is located.

▶ **HTTP Method**—This column displays the type of HTTP method used, such as GET or POST.

▶ **URL**—If HTTP is used, this column will display the exact URL that was requested.

By searching through the logs for specific criteria in these columns, such as all packets sent by a specific IP address, or all URLs that match http://home.companyabc.com, advanced troubleshooting and monitoring is simplified.

> **NOTE**
>
> It cannot be stressed enough that this logging mechanism is quite literally the best tool for troubleshooting Forefront TMG access. For example, it can be used to tell whether traffic from clients is even hitting the Forefront TMG server, and if it is, what is happening to it (denied, accepted, and so forth).

Securing SharePoint Sites Using Forefront UAG

Microsoft's Forefront UAG tool is a full-service SSL/VPN tool that can be used to publish access to multiple services, web based or otherwise. It can be used to strictly control what users have access to, and can be very granular for granting access rights, which makes it an ideal publishing solution for SharePoint 2010, because administrators can define exactly which farms a user needs to have access to.

Architecting Forefront UAG

Forefront UAG is similar to Forefront TMG; in fact, it uses a Forefront TMG engine for the creation of all of its rules. You can even access the Forefront TMG console directly from a Forefront UAG server. Subsequently, the same design criteria that applied to Forefront TMG and that are listed earlier apply to Forefront UAG.

The main difference between Forefront TMG and Forefront UAG is that Forefront UAG allows for the creation of a "trunk," which is essentially a web page that the users hit first that forces them to authenticate and, once authenticated, allows them to have access to various applications through different links on that page. One user will see different applications on that page than another user, depending on their rights.

Creating a SharePoint Application Within a UAG Trunk

An HTTP or (preferably) HTTPS trunk needs to be created before an application such as SharePoint can be defined. Creation of this trunk is outside the scope of this book, but more information can be found at Microsoft.com/forefront on the configuration of HTTPS trunks for Forefront UAG.

From within the trunk, shown later in Figure 14.10, multiple "applications" can be created, such as one for SharePoint. To add SharePoint as an application to a trunk, perform the following steps:

1. From within the trunk, such as the one shown in Figure 14.9, click Add to add a new application.

2. Click Next at the welcome screen.

3. From the Select Application dialog box, select Microsoft SharePoint Server 2010 under the type Web. Click Next to continue.

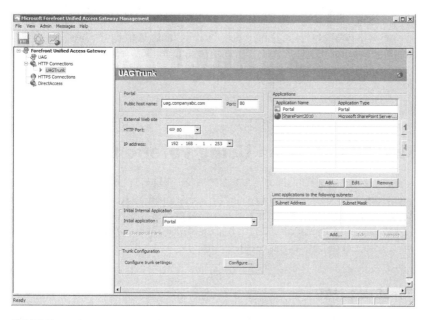

FIGURE 14.9   Viewing a Forefront UAG trunk for a SharePoint site.

4. Give the application a name, such as SharePoint Extranet Farm, and click Next to continue.

5. From the EndPoint Policies screen, select what type of policies will be enabled for the application. Custom policies can be created from within Forefront UAG that allow for restriction of what types of activities are allowed on the site. Microsoft creates default policies that can be used, as well, such as Microsoft SharePoint 2010 Download. Either use the default policies or custom policies, depending on the situation, and then click Next to continue.

6. Under step 4, select to configure either one published server, or multiple servers, depending on how big the SharePoint farm is. For this example, we are configuring a single SharePoint server. Click Next to continue.

7. Enter the IP address of the server, plus the public hostname that the SharePoint environment is known by. (Be sure to configure AAMs for SharePoint, such as what is illustrated earlier in this chapter under the Forefront TMG publishing scenarios.) Click Next to continue.

8. Under step 6, typically leave the SSO settings at the default, unless you have a specific need to customize them. You will need to either add an authentication server or choose one that is already established (such as an AD domain controller). After adding an authentication server, click Next to continue.

9. Select what type of link to include on the SSL/VPN page for the SharePoint application, such as what is shown in Figure 14.10. Click Next to continue.

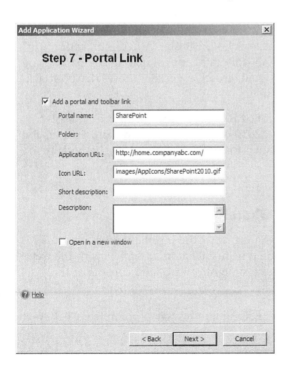

FIGURE 14.10   Creating a SharePoint application within a Forefront UAG trunk.

10. Specify which set of users will be authorized to use the specific application. This gives you the opportunity to restrict who has rights to which application. After making any necessary changes, click Next to continue.

11. Click Finish when completed.

Different SharePoint applications can be created for multiple farms, and then directed at different types of users. Forefront UAG can also be set to authenticate users from multiple directory sources, allowing it to act as a metadirectory gateway for multiple platforms and environments.

Protecting SharePoint 2010 from Viruses Using Forefront Protection 2010 for SharePoint

Built in to SharePoint 2010 is a programming application programming interface (API) known as the Antivirus API. This API can be used by any third-party or Microsoft solution to scan all documents that are injected into SharePoint for viruses. Numerous capable third-party solutions on the market today take advantage of this API to protect SharePoint from viruses and threats. In addition to these third-party products, Microsoft has their own offering that provides for antivirus capabilities in SharePoint. This products is known as Forefront Protection for SharePoint (FPSP).

FPSP's main distinguishing point from its competitors is that it runs as a multiengine antivirus application, allowing for all documents to be scanned by multiple independent antivirus engines from such companies as Kaspersky, VirusBuster, Athentium, and Norman. By scanning with multiple engines all from different competing companies, you have a much better chance of catching individual viruses, especially those "day 0" attack viruses that spread quickly upon initial release.

Although it is not a requirement to install FPSP, it is highly recommended to at least install a third-party antivirus tool. SharePoint 2010 does not have native antivirus capabilities, and client antivirus might not always be up-to-date or can be missing, especially in extranet scenarios.

Installing Forefront Protection for SharePoint

To install Forefront Protection 2010 for SharePoint, copy the installation binaries to a web role server in the farm. The binaries should be installed on all servers with the web role in that particular farm. Installation is quite straightforward, and consists of the following steps:

1. Start the Setup Wizard, and agree to the licensing terms when prompted. Click Next to continue.

2. Click Next when prompted to restart services.

3. Select the appropriate installation folders for program files and data, and then click Next to continue.

4. If using a proxy server, enter the proxy settings; otherwise, click Next to continue.

5. Enter the credentials of the SharePoint installation account, as shown in Figure 14.11. Note the required rights this account will need to have. Click Next to continue.

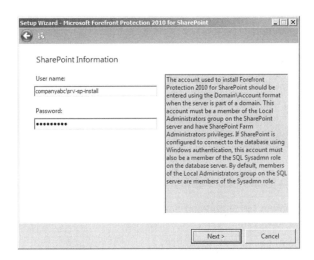

FIGURE 14.11   Installing Forefront Protection for SharePoint.

6. Select whether to use Microsoft Update (recommended), click Next to continue.

7. Select whether to join the Customer Experience Improvement Program, and then click Next to continue.

8. Review and confirm settings, and then click Next to begin the installation.

9. Wait for the Installation Wizard to finish, and then click the Finish button.

10. Repeat the installation process on all web role servers within the farm.

Using Forefront Protection 2010 for SharePoint 2010

Once installed, the FPSP console can be opened directly from the Start menu. When opening for the first time, you will be prompted to Activate, which is highly recommended as soon as possible. Note that you do have 120 days to activate, but after that time period, the software will no longer update the antivirus engines, and it will not clean additional viruses.

The Forefront Protection 2010 console, shown in Figure 14.12, is comprehensive and enables administrators to review quarantine, handle incidents, set up configuration notifications, and monitor the environment.

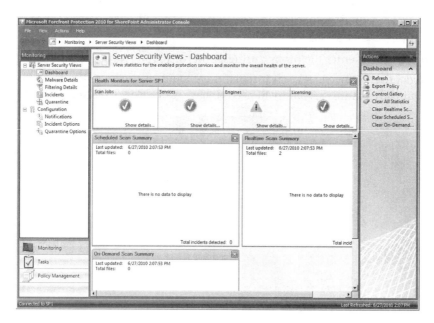

FIGURE 14.12   Viewing the Forefront Protection for SharePoint console.

Two key administrative tasks using Forefront Protection 2010 for SharePoint are key to
understanding the product. The first is that the actual antivirus API settings are controlled
from within SharePoint Central Admin itself, and those settings are grayed out in the FPSP
console, as shown in Figure 14.13. If you think of FPSP as a bolt-on to the SharePoint
Antivirus API, this makes more sense.

The second concept to understand is how to modify the "Intelligent Engine Management"
engine, or to be able to manually control which antivirus engines run on the individual
server. By default, these settings are automatically controlled from the Advanced Options
node under Policy Management – Global Settings, as shown in Figure 14.14. Modifying
these settings enables administrators to be able to change which antivirus engines are
running at any one time.

After installing FPSP, it is a good idea to familiarize yourself with the options and functionality that is immediately available in the console. Navigating the console and finding
settings is straightforward, and Microsoft has a good help file included in the product. For
more information about FPSP and the other Forefront products from Microsoft, refer to
http://microsoft.com/forefront.

FIGURE 14.13   Viewing SharePoint Antivirus API settings from within the FPSP console.

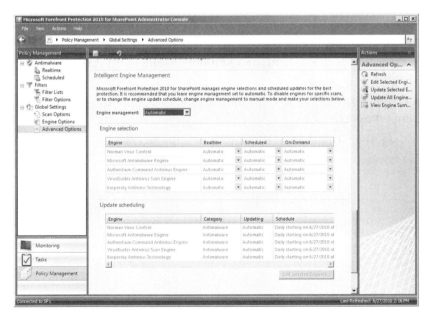

FIGURE 14.14   Modifying engine settings from within the FPSP console.

Summary

The capabilities of the Forefront Edge line to secure and protect SharePoint Products and Technologies gives it capabilities not present in other firewall solutions. In addition, the Forefront Edge line's ability to be easily deployed in the DMZ of existing firewalls as a dedicated security appliance further extends its capabilities and allows it to be deployed in environments of all shapes and sizes. Together with advanced antivirus functionality included in tools such as Forefront Protection for SharePoint, these tools allow for a higher degree of security and data integrity than would normally be possible with SharePoint 2010.

Best Practices

▶ Use SSL encryption to secure the traffic to and from a SharePoint server, particularly if that traffic will cross an unsecured network, such as the Internet.

▶ Monitor Forefront TMG using the MSDE or SQL logging approaches to allow for the greatest level of monitoring functionality.

▶ Secure any edge-facing service such as SharePoint with a reverse-proxy system such as Forefront TMG or Forefront UAG.

▶ It is recommended to use Forefront UAG for inbound securing scenarios, but not necessarily required, as Forefront TMG also has significant reverse-proxy functionality.

▶ Environments with legacy ISA 2006 can still use it to publish SharePoint 2010 sites, but performance will be limited due to the 32-bit-only nature of ISA 2006.

▶ Use either Forefront Protection for SharePoint or another third-party antivirus product that is compatible with the SharePoint 2010 Antivirus API to protect SharePoint content from viruses.

▶ Deploy the Forefront Edge line of products in the existing DMZ of a firewall if it is not feasible to replace existing firewall technologies.

## CHAPTER 15

Implementing and Validating SharePoint 2010 Security

Microsoft SharePoint Server 2010 was built to be a robust, capable, and scalable environment. Along with SharePoint's capabilities comes the responsibility to secure its vital components, protecting them from attacks and data loss. Fortunately, SharePoint allows for a wide range of security functionality, features, and tools to properly secure a SharePoint farm. Knowledge of these capabilities is a must for a SharePoint administrator.

This chapter focuses on the aspects of information security that an organization can implement to protect information stored in a SharePoint environment. This includes server-level security from a network operating system and web services perspective, Active Directory integration, firewall and access to intranet and extranet information, file-level security for information stored and indexed on non-SharePoint-managed data stores, file-level security for information stored within a SharePoint-managed data store, user-level security for access to SharePoint data, and administrative controls to monitor and manage user and access security.

In addition, tools and services useful for securing SharePoint such as the Microsoft Baseline Security Analyzer, IPsec, Public Key Infrastructure (PKI), and others are covered to provide for enhanced security.

Identifying Isolation Approaches to SharePoint Security

Various organizations have varying security needs. Some organizations, for example, require strong security and cannot tolerate even the slightest risk to their business. Other organizations have a much higher tolerance for security risks and often choose to make a system more functional at the expense of security. SharePoint scales its security well to the needs of these different organizations and provides a wide spectrum of security options that can be suited to the needs of many different organizations.

Arising from these ideas is the concept of security through isolation. SharePoint servers running on an isolated network segment, for example, are highly secure compared to those directly located on the Internet. The following section deals with approaches to isolate users via security boundaries in SharePoint. Each option further isolates users and increases the security offered. With the increased security comes decreased functionality, however. The functional needs of an organization must be weighed against the security needs.

Isolating SharePoint Data with Separate SharePoint Lists

The simplest, most straightforward approach to security through user isolation comes through the application of security on the list level in SharePoint. This model involves the entire pool of users having access to the site but then being disallowed or allowed access to SharePoint content through security set at the list level.

This model, although the most functional, also is weakest in security. Administrators in parent sites can seize access, and users are subject to potential cross-site script attacks in this design, which limits its security.

Isolating SharePoint Through Deployment of Separate Sites or Site Collections

Granting various groups of users access to SharePoint content by organizing them into sites is a more secure approach to SharePoint design. Users are limited in the types of access they receive to other sites, and searching can be limited to specific information. Administrative overhead is increased in this example, however, as separate groups of users and permissions need to be maintained. It is also more difficult to manage because all sites must use the same content database, reducing the scalability of the system.

Deploying users into separate site collections goes even further down the path of security and scalability. Separate site collections can be more easily scaled out than separate sites because each host can theoretically host millions of sites, if required. Both of these models are still vulnerable to cross-site scripting attacks, however. If a site is vulnerable to this type of activity, a more secure model may be needed.

Isolating SharePoint with Separate Web Applications

The problem of cross-site scripting attacks can be addressed through the creation of multiple host headers or virtual servers in SharePoint. Host headers allow for multiple domain names to correspond to different site collections in SharePoint. As a result, you can have a single SharePoint farm correspond to http://sharepoint.companyabc.com and http://sharepoint.cco.com and have them point to separate sets of data. This allows for an increased level of security between the sites because users cannot see the data from the other site collections. This, of course, reduces the amount of collaboration that can take place between the sites and is limited in scope.

By doing this, each site collection can be associated with a separate application pool. Each application pool is logically separate from the others and is theoretically not subject to failure if another one goes down or becomes corrupt. This also helps to further secure the SharePoint data because users are on separate physical processes from each other.

Isolating SharePoint with Separate Physical Farms

The last, most secure, and also most expensive option for SharePoint security through isolation is by deploying each site collection on separate servers or in separate networks. By deploying on separate servers, a great deal of independence is achieved as attacks and snoops from one site are physically removed from the resources of another. This can prove to be expensive, however, because individual servers need to be purchased, configured, and maintained.

The ultimate security boundary for interconnected networks is to simply disconnect them from each other. It goes without saying that the most secure SharePoint farm is the one connected to an isolated network. There are some major disadvantages to this, however, because access from any other location becomes impossible.

Physically Securing SharePoint Servers

One of the most overlooked but perhaps most critical components of server security is the actual physical security of the server itself. The most secure, unbreakable web server is powerless if a malicious user can simply unplug it. Worse yet, someone logging in to a SharePoint SQL database role server could potentially copy critical data or sabotage the machine directly.

Physical security is a must for any organization because it is the most common cause of security breaches. Despite this fact, many organizations have loose levels, or no levels, of physical security for their mission-critical servers. An understanding of what is required to secure the physical and login access to a server is a must.

Restricting Physical Access to Servers

Servers should be physically secured behind locked doors, in a controlled-access environment. Soft-felt cubicles do not provide much in the realm of physical security, so it is therefore unwise to place mission-critical servers at the feet of administrators or in similar, unsecure locations. Rather, a dedicated server room or server closet that is locked at all times is the most ideal environment for the purposes of server security.

Most hardware manufacturers also include mechanisms for locking out some or all the components of a server. Depending on the other layers of security deployed, it may be wise to use these mechanisms to secure a server environment.

Restricting Login Access

All servers should be configured to allow only administrators to physically log in to the console. By default, such use is restricted on systems such as Active Directory domain controllers, but other servers such as SharePoint servers and SQL servers must specifically forbid these types of logins. To restrict login access, follow these steps:

1. Choose Start, All Programs, Administrative Tools, Local Security Policy.
2. In the left pane, navigate to Security Settings, Local Policies, User Rights Assignment.
3. Double-click Allow Log On Locally.
4. Remove any users or groups that do not need access to the server, as shown in Figure 15.1. Click OK when finished.

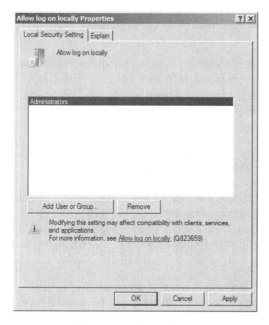

FIGURE 15.1   Restricting login access to a SharePoint server.

NOTE

A group policy set on an OU level can be applied to all SharePoint servers, simplifying the application of policies and negating the need to perform it manually on every server.

Physically Securing SharePoint Access by Using Smartcards

The ultimate in secured infrastructures utilizes so-called smartcards for login access; these smartcards are fully supported in Windows Server. A smartcard is a credit card-sized piece of plastic with an encrypted microchip embedded within. Each user is assigned a unique smartcard and an associated PIN. Logging in to a workstation is as straightforward as inserting the smartcard into a smartcard reader and entering the PIN, which can be a combination of numbers and letters, similar to a password.

Security can be raised even higher by stipulating that each smartcard be removed after logging in to a console. In this scenario, users insert into the smartcard reader a smartcard physically attached to their person via a string. After entering their PIN, they log in and perform all necessary functions. Upon leaving, they simply remove the smartcard from the reader, which automatically logs them off the workstation. In this scenario, it is nearly impossible for users to forget to log off because they must physically detach themselves from the computer to leave.

Securing SharePoint's SQL Server Installation

SQL Server has a strong relationship with SharePoint Server 2010 as it is the back-end database repository for SharePoint data. All of SharePoint configuration and content databases are stored within SQL Server, which makes it highly important and recommended to follow security best practices on SQL Server, just as one would when securing SharePoint to minimize vulnerabilities.

The enforcement of SQL Server security should be one of the most important tasks SQL Server database administrators commit themselves to. Furthermore, to properly ensure that vulnerabilities are minimized, SQL Server security should be a part of both the test and production SQL Server systems.

Equally important, as a result of continuous advancements made by Microsoft, SQL Server 2005/2008 has significant enhancements to the security model of the database platform, which now provides more precise and flexible control resulting in tighter security. Some of the features that have been enhanced include the advanced security of surface area reduction, data encryption, native encryption, authentication, granular permissions, and user and schema separations. These advancements contribute to Microsoft's Trustworthy Computing initiative that defines the steps necessary to help support secure computing.

At present, numerous SQL Server security best practices are applicable when deploying SharePoint. The following sections discuss some of these best practices.

Windows Versus SQL Server Authentication

Authentication is a security measure designed to establish the validity of a user or application based on criteria such as an account, password, security token, or certificate. Typically, once the validity has been verified, the user or application is granted authorization to the desired object.

SQL Server continues to support two modes for validating connections and authenticating access to database resources: Windows authentication and SQL Server authentication. Both authentication methods provide the SharePoint application access to SQL Server and its resources, such as the SharePoint config, site, and content databases.

Windows Authentication Mode

Windows Authentication mode leverages Active Directory user accounts or groups when granting access to SQL Server. This is the default and recommended authentication mode, and it allows IT professionals to grant domain users access to the database server without creating and managing a separate SQL Server account. In addition, when using Windows Authentication mode, user accounts are subject to enterprise-wide policies enforced in the Active Directory domain such as complex passwords, password history, account lockouts, minimum password length, and maximum password length.

SQL Server Authentication Mode

SQL Server authentication also referred to as mixed-mode authentication utilizes either Active Directory user accounts or SQL Server accounts when validating access to SQL Server. Unless some reason exists for using mixed-mode authentication, it is highly recommended not to use this with SharePoint and to instead use Windows Authentication mode.

Determining Which Authentication Mode to Utilize

Windows Authentication works best if the SQL Server will be accessed from within the organization and all user accounts needing access reside in Active Directory. For example, Windows Authentication can be used when deploying SharePoint if both the SharePoint and SQL Server reside in the same domain or in separate domains that are trusted. On the other hand, SQL Server mixed-mode authentication works best if users or applications require access to SQL Server and are not associated with the domain that SQL Server resides in. For example, SQL Server authentication should be leveraged if the SharePoint server is not in the same domain as the SQL Server and a trust does not exist between the two environments.

Even though SQL Server now has the ability to enforce policies such as SQL Server account password complexity, password expiration, and account lockouts, Windows Authentication mode is still the recommended alternative for controlling access to SQL Server. The added advantage of Windows Authentication is that Active Directory provides an additional level of protection with the Kerberos protocol and administration is reduced by leveraging Active Directory groups when providing access to SQL Server.

Minimize SQL Server Attack Surface

Once SQL Server for SharePoint has been installed the SQL, Server Surface Area Configuration tool should be run to reduce the system's attackable surface area by disabling unused services, components, features, and remote connections.

To reduce surface attack and secure the SQL Server installation for SharePoint, it is recommended that an IT professional launch the SQL Server Surface Area Configuration tool and disable all unnecessary services, components, and connections that will not be used.

Typically, only the Database Engine, SQL Server Agent, and SQL Server Browser services are required for a base SharePoint installation. If, however, SharePoint Reporting or

PowerPivot capabilities are required, more advanced SQL installations involving Analysis Services and Reporting Services may be needed.

Using SQL Server Security Logs

Enabling security auditing on SQL Server will monitor and track activity to log files that can be viewed through Windows application logs or SQL Server Management Studio. SQL Server offers four security levels with regards to security auditing, as follows:

▶ **None**—Disables auditing so no events are logged.

▶ **Successful Logins Only**—Audits all successful login attempts.

▶ **Failed Logins Only**—Audits all failed login attempts.

▶ **Both Failed and Successful Logins**—Audits all login attempts.

Security auditing is set to Failed Logins Only by default. It is a best practice to configure security auditing to capture both failed and successful logins. At the very least, security auditing should be set to Failed Logins Only. As a result, failed logins can be saved, viewed, and acted upon.

Utilizing Security Templates to Secure a SharePoint Server

Windows Server contains built-in support for security templates, which can help to standardize security settings across servers and aid in their deployment. A *security template* is simply a text file formatted in such a way that specific security settings are applied uniformly. For example, the security template could force a server to lockdown Windows Firewall ports, or not attempt to use down-level (and less secure) methods of authentication across the network.

Application of a security template is straightforward and can be accomplished by applying a template directly to an OU, site, or domain via a Group Policy Object (GPO). Security templates can be enormously useful in making sure that all servers have the proper security applied, but they come with a large caveat. Often, the settings defined in a template can be made too strict, and security templates that are too strong for a server can break application or network functionality. It is therefore critical to test all security template settings before deploying them to production.

Shutting Off Unnecessary Services

Each service that runs, especially those that use elevated system privileges, poses a particular security risk to a server. Although the security emphasis in Windows Server reduces the overall threat, there is still a chance that one of these services will provide entry for a specialized virus or determined hacker. A great deal of effort has been put into the science of determining which services are necessary and which can be disabled. Windows Server simplifies this guessing game with an enhanced Services MMC snap-in.

As shown in Figure 15.2, the Services console not only shows which services are installed and running but also gives a reasonably thorough description of what each service does and the effect of turning it off. It is wise to audit the Services list on each deployed server and determine which services are necessary and which can be disabled. Many services such as the Print Spooler, Telephony, and others are unnecessary on a SharePoint server and simply create more potential security holes. Finding the happy medium is the goal because too many running services could potentially provide security holes, whereas shutting off too many services could cripple the functionality of a server.

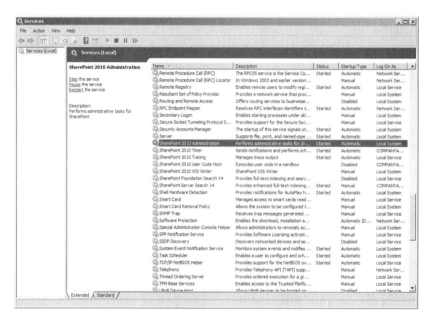

FIGURE 15.2   Using the Services console to administer the server.

File-Level Security for SharePoint Servers

SharePoint controls access to files stored within its database through user authentication, site groups, and similar SharePoint-specific security mechanisms. In addition to these considerations, care must be taken to secure actual file-level access to SharePoint itself. A secured database is useless if an unauthorized user can simply delete it or copy it off. A full understanding of the file-level security inherent in Windows Server is a must for a complete understanding of SharePoint security itself.

Exploring NT File System Security

The latest revision of the NT File System (NTFS) is used in Windows Server to provide for file-level security in the operating system. Each object referenced in NTFS, which includes files and folders, is marked by an access control list (ACL) that physically limits who can and cannot access a resource. NTFS permissions utilize this concept to strictly control read, write, and other types of access on files.

Although SharePoint servers are not often file servers, they can still grant or deny file access in the same way and should have the file-level permissions audited to determine whether there are any holes in the NTFS permission set.

> **NOTE**
>
> Take care when applying security settings. Propagating incorrect security settings can lock out all subfolders on a server. When modifying security, a full understanding of the directory structure is required.

Auditing File Access to SharePoint Servers

A good practice for file-level security is to set up auditing on a particular server, directory, or file. Auditing on NTFS volumes allows administrators to be notified of who is accessing, or attempting to access, a particular directory. For example, it may be wise to audit access to SharePoint servers, to determine whether anyone is attempting to access restricted information, such as the location of database files.

Verifying Security Using the Microsoft Baseline Security Analyzer

Like Microsoft SharePoint Server, Windows Server and Microsoft SQL Server also require the latest service packs and updates to reduce known security vulnerabilities. Microsoft offers an intuitive free downloadable tool, the Microsoft Baseline Security Analyzer (MBSA), to streamline this procedure. This tool identifies common security vulnerabilities on SharePoint servers by identifying incorrect configurations and missing security patches for Windows Server, Internet Information Services (IIS), and Microsoft SQL Server.

MBSA not only has the potential to scan a single SharePoint server, but it can also scan multiple instances of SQL Server if multiple instances are installed. The MBSA SQL Server scan detects and displays SQL Server vulnerabilities such as the following: members of the sysadmin role, weak or blank SQL Server local accounts and SA passwords, SQL Server authentication mode, SQL Server on a domain controller, and missing service packs and updates.

Scanning for Security Vulnerabilities with MBSA

MBSA can scan a single computer or a range of computers based on an IP address, range of IP addresses, computer name, or all computers in a domain. The security scanner can identify known security vulnerabilities on several Microsoft technologies such as Windows, IIS, or SQL Server. In addition, MBSA can identify weak passwords and missing service packs and updates.

To scan a SharePoint server for known SQL or Windows vulnerabilities, weak passwords, and security updates, follow these steps:

1. Choose Start, All Programs, Microsoft Baseline Security Analyzer 2.1.

2. Click Scan a Computer to pick the system to scan. An administrator also has the opportunity to scan more than one computer by either entering a valid IP address range or a domain name.

3. On the next screen, enter the computer name or IP address of the desired SharePoint server. Select all options desired and click Start Scan, as shown in Figure 15.3.

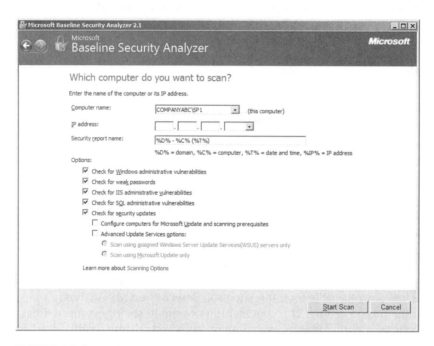

FIGURE 15.3   Using the MBSA Scan tool to scan a SharePoint server.

Viewing MBSA Security Reports

A separate security report is generated for the desired SQL server when the computer scan is completed. A report is generated regardless of a local or remote scan. Scan reports also are stored for future viewing on the same computer on which the MBSA tool was installed.

The MBSA security reports are intuitive and address each vulnerability detected. If MBSA detects a missing SQL Server service pack, Windows patch, or hot fix, it displays the vulnerability in the Security Update Scan section and provides the location that will focus on the fix.

Review the security report generated from the scan conducted in the example, as shown in Figure 15.4. Each section scanned has a score associated with it. An end user or an administrator can easily browse each section identifying known security vulnerabilities, verifying what was scanned, checking the results, and analyzing how to correct any anomalies that MBSA detected.

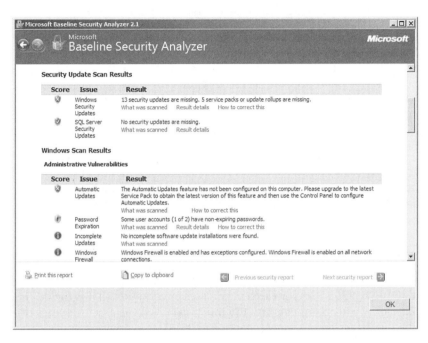

FIGURE 15.4   Analyzing an MBSA scan report.

Deploying Transport-Level Security for SharePoint

The very nature of interconnected networks requires that all information be sent in a format that can easily be intercepted by any client on a physical network segment. The data must be organized in a structured, common way so that the destination server can translate it into the proper information. This is especially the case for SharePoint environments. This simplicity also gives rise to security problems, however, because intercepted data can easily be misused if it falls into the wrong hands.

The need to make information unusable if intercepted is the basis for all transport-level encryption. Considerable effort goes into both sides of this equation: Security specialists develop schemes to encrypt and disguise data, and hackers and other security specialists develop ways to forcefully decrypt and intercept data. The good news is that encryption technology has developed to the point that properly configured environments can secure their data with a great deal of success, as long as the proper tools are used. SharePoint's operating system, Windows Server, offers much in the realm of transport-level security, and deploying some or many of the technologies available is highly recommended to properly secure important data. This is particularly true for SharePoint content, because without transport-level security, the data sent between critical SharePoint systems, such as the communications between SharePoint web role servers and SQL database role servers, is unencrypted and can be intercepted.

Realizing Security by Deploying Multiple Layers of Defense

Because even the most secure infrastructures are subject to vulnerabilities, deploying multiple layers of security on critical network data is recommended. If a single layer of security is compromised, the intruder has to bypass the second or even third level of security to gain access to the vital data. For example, relying on a complex 128-bit "unbreakable" encryption scheme is worthless if an intruder simply uses social engineering to acquire the password or PIN from a validated user. Putting in a second or third layer of security, in addition to the first one, makes it that much more difficult for intruders to break through all layers.

Transport-level security in Windows Server uses multiple levels of authentication, encryption, and authorization to provide an enhanced degree of security on a network. The configuration capabilities supplied with Windows Server allow for the establishment of several layers of transport-level security.

Understanding Encryption Basics

Encryption, simply defined, is the process of taking intelligible information and scrambling it so as to make it unintelligible for anyone except the user or computer that is the destination of this information. Without going into too much detail on the exact methods of encrypting data, the important point to understand is that proper encryption allows this data to travel across unsecured networks, such as the Internet, and be translated only by the designated destination. If packets of properly encrypted information are intercepted, they are worthless because the information is garbled. All mechanisms described in this chapter use some form of encryption to secure the contents of the data sent.

Using Virtual Private Networks to Secure Access to SharePoint

A common method of securing access to SharePoint farms from across unsecured networks is to create a virtual private network (VPN), which is effectively a connection between two private nodes or networks that is secured and encrypted to prevent unauthorized snooping of the traffic between the two connections. From the client perspective, a VPN looks and feels just like a normal network connection to SharePoint (hence the term *virtual private network*).

Data sent across a VPN is encapsulated, or wrapped, in a header that indicates its destination. The information in the packet is then encrypted to secure its contents. The encrypted packets are then sent across the network to the destination server, using a VPN tunnel.

Examining VPN Tunnels

The connection made by VPN clients across an unsecured network is known as a *VPN tunnel*. It is named as such because of the way it "tunnels" underneath the regular traffic of the unsecured network.

VPN tunnels are logically established on a point-to-point basis but can be used to connect two private networks into a common network infrastructure. In many cases, for example, a VPN tunnel serves as a virtual WAN link between two physical locations in an organization, all while sending the private information across the Internet. VPN tunnels are also widely used by remote users who log in to the Internet from multiple locations and establish VPN tunnels to a centralized VPN server in the organization's home office. These reasons make VPN solutions a valuable asset for organizations, and one that can be easily established with the technologies available in Windows Server.

> **NOTE**
>
> VPN tunnels can either be voluntary or compulsory. In short, voluntary VPN tunnels are created when a client, usually out somewhere on the Internet, asks for a VPN tunnel to be established. Compulsory VPN tunnels are automatically created for clients from specific locations on the unsecured network and are less common in real-life situations than are voluntary tunnels.

Reviewing Tunneling Protocols

The tunneling protocol is the specific technology that defines how data is encapsulated, transmitted, and unencapsulated across a VPN connection. Varying implementations of tunneling protocols exist and correspond with different layers of the Open System Interconnection (OSI) standards-based reference model. The OSI model is composed of seven layers, and VPN tunneling protocols use either Layer 2 or Layer 3 as their unit of exchange. Layer 2, a more fundamental network layer, uses a frame as the unit of exchange, and Layer 3 protocols use a packet as a unit of exchange.

The most common Layer 2 VPN protocols are the Point-to-Point Tunneling Protocol (PPTP) and the Layer 2 Tunneling Protocol (L2TP), both of which are fully supported protocols in Windows Server and are also natively available in Microsoft's Forefront Threat Management Gateway (TMG) and Unified Access Gateway (UAG) products.

Outlining the PPTP and L2TP Protocols

Both PPTP and L2TP are based on the well-defined Point-to-Point Protocol (PPP) and are accepted and widely used in various VPN implementations. L2TP is the preferred protocol for use with VPNs in Windows Server because it incorporates the best of PPTP, with a technology known as Layer 2 Forwarding. L2TP allows for the encapsulation of data over multiple network protocols, including IP, and can be used to tunnel over the Internet. The payload, or data to be transmitted, of each L2TP frame can be compressed, as well as encrypted, to save network bandwidth.

Both PPTP and L2TP build on a suite of useful functionality introduced in PPP, such as user authentication, data compression and encryption, and token card support. These features, which have all been ported over to the newer implementations, provide for a rich set of VPN functionality.

Detailing the L2TP/IPsec Secure Protocol

Windows Server offers an additional layer of encryption and security by utilizing IP Security (IPsec), a Layer 3 encryption protocol, in concert with L2TP in what is known, not surprisingly, as L2TP/IPsec. IPsec allows for the encryption of the L2TP header and trailer information, which is normally sent in clear text. This also has the added advantage of dual-encrypting the payload, adding an additional level of security into the mix. IPsec is particularly useful in communications between SharePoint servers because information sent between members of a farm is unencrypted by default, making it more vulnerable to snooping.

L2TP/IPsec has some distinct advantages over standard L2TP, namely the following:

▶ L2TP/IPsec allows for data authentication on a packet level, allowing for verification that the payload was not modified in transit, as well as the data confidentiality provided by L2TP.

▶ Dual-authentication mechanisms stipulate that both computer-level and user-level authentication must take place with L2TP/IPsec.

▶ L2TP packets intercepted during the initial user-level authentication cannot be copied for use in offline dictionary attacks to determine the L2TP key because IPsec encrypts this procedure.

An L2TP/IPsec packet contains multiple, encrypted header information, and the payload itself is deeply nested within the structure. This allows for a great deal of transport-level security on the packet itself.

Examining Integration Points Between SharePoint and Public Key Infrastructure

The term *Public Key Infrastructure (PKI)* is often loosely thrown around, but is not often thoroughly explained. PKI, in a nutshell, is the collection of digital certificates, registration authorities, and certificate authorities that verify the validity of each participant in an encrypted network. Effectively, a PKI itself is simply a concept that defines the mechanisms that ensure that the user who is communicating with another user or computer on a network is who he says he is. PKI implementations are widespread and are becoming a critical component of modern network implementations.

PKI is a useful and often critical component of a SharePoint design. The PKI concepts can be used to create certificates to encrypt traffic to and from SharePoint virtual servers to the Internet. Using Secure Sockets Layer (SSL), encryption is a vital method of securing access to a SharePoint site and should be considered as part of any SharePoint farm that enables access from the Internet.

Understanding Private Key Versus Public Key Encryption

Encryption techniques can primarily be classified as either symmetrical or asymmetrical. Symmetrical encryption requires that each party in an encryption scheme hold a copy of a private key, which is used to encrypt and decrypt information sent between the two parties. The problem with private key encryption is that the private key must somehow be transmitted to the other party without it being intercepted and used to decrypt the information.

Public key, or asymmetrical, encryption uses a combination of two keys mathematically related to each other. The first key, the public key, is widely available and can be used to encrypt the information. The second key, the private key, is kept closely guarded and is used to decrypt the information. The integrity of the public key is ensured through certificates. The asymmetric approach to encryption ensures that the private key does not fall into the wrong hands and only the intended recipient will be able to decrypt the data.

Using SSL Certificates for SharePoint 2010

A certificate is essentially a digital document issued by a trusted central authority and used by the authority to validate a user's identity. Central, trusted authorities such as VeriSign are widely used on the Internet to ensure that software from Microsoft, for example, is really from Microsoft, and not from a rogue source.

Certificates are used for multiple functions, such as the following:

- Secured SharePoint site access
- Secured email
- Web-based authentication
- IP Security (IPsec)
- Code signing
- Certification hierarchies

Certificates are signed using information from the subject's public key, along with identifier information such as name, email address, and so on, and a digital signature of the certificate issuer, known as the certificate authority (CA).

Utilizing Active Directory Certificate Services for SharePoint Servers

Windows Server 2008 and 2008 R2 include a role that incorporates a PKI hierarchy. This role is known as Active Directory Certificate Services or AD CS. AD CS can be used to create and manage certificates; it is responsible for ensuring their validity. AD CS is often used to generate SSL Certificates for SharePoint virtual servers if there is no particular need to have a third-party verify an organization's certificates. It is common practice to set up a standalone CA for network encryption that issues certificates only for internal parties. Third-party CAs such as VeriSign are also extensively used but require an investment in individual certificates.

Certificate services for Windows Server can be installed as one of the following CA types:

- ▶ **Enterprise root CA**—The root of a certificate chain that is also incorporated into an Active Directory domain and can be used to automatically enroll clients and systems with certificates.

- ▶ **Enterprise subordinate CA**—Must get a CA certificate from an enterprise root CA but can then issue certificates to all users and computers in the enterprise.

- ▶ **Standalone root CA**—The root of a hierarchy that is not related to the enterprise domain information. Multiple standalone CAs can be established for particular purposes. An enterprise subordinate CA can be created from a standalone root CA, which is often the case in security situations where the root needs to be on a workgroup system, not a domain member.

- ▶ **Standalone subordinate CA**—A standalone subordinate CA receives its certificate from a standalone root CA and can then be used to distribute certificates to users and computers associated with that standalone CA.

Examining Smartcards PKI Authentication for SharePoint

A robust solution using a PKI network can be found in the introduction of smartcard authentication for users. Smartcards are plastic cards that have a microchip embedded in them; this chip allows them to store unique information in each card. User login information, as well as certificates installed from a CA server, can be placed on a smartcard. When a user needs to log in to a system, she places the smartcard in a smartcard reader or simply swipes it across the reader itself. The certificate is read, and the user is prompted only for a PIN, which is uniquely assigned to each user. After the PIN and the certificate are verified, the user can log in to the domain and access resources such as SharePoint.

Smartcards have obvious advantages over standard forms of authentication. It is no longer possible to simply steal or guess someone's username and password in this scenario because the username that allows access to SharePoint can be entered only via the unique smartcard. If stolen or lost, the smartcard can be immediately deactivated and the certificate revoked. Even if a functioning smartcard were to fall into the wrong hands, the PIN would still need to be used to properly access the system. Layering security in this fashion is one reason why smartcards are fast becoming a more accepted way to integrate the security of certificates and PKI into organizations.

Using IPsec for Internal SharePoint Encryption

IPsec, mentioned briefly in previous sections, is essentially a mechanism for establishing end-to-end encryption of all data packets sent between computers. IPsec operates at Layer 3 of the OSI model and uses encrypted packets for all traffic between members.

IPsec is often considered to be one of the best ways to secure the traffic generated in an environment and is useful for securing all SharePoint farm servers in high-risk Internet access scenarios and also in private network configurations for an enhanced layer of security. Without a technology such as IPsec, communications between farm members can be intercepted and their contents easily defined.

Reviewing the IPsec Principle

The basic principle of IPsec is this: All traffic between clients, whether initiated by applications, the operating system, services, and so on, is entirely encrypted by IPsec, which then puts its own header on each packet and sends the packets to the destination server to be decrypted. Because every piece of data is encrypted, this prevents electronic eavesdropping, or listening in on a network in an attempt to gain unauthorized access to data.

Several functional IPsec deployments are available, and some of the more promising ones are actually built in to the network interface cards (NICs) of each computer, performing encryption and decryption without the operating system knowing what is going on. Aside from these alternatives, Windows Server includes a robust IPsec implementation by default, which can be configured to use a PKI certificate network or the built-in Kerberos authentication provided by Active Directory on Windows Server.

Detailing Key IPsec Functionality

IPsec in Windows Server provides for the following key functionality that, when combined, provides for one of the most secure solutions available for client/server encryption:

- **Data privacy**—All information sent from one SharePoint machine to another is thoroughly encrypted by such algorithms as 3DES, which effectively prevent the unauthorized viewing of sensitive data.

- **Data integrity**—The integrity of IPsec packets is enforced through ESP headers, which verify that the information contained within an IPsec packet has not been tampered with.

- **Antireplay capability**—IPsec prevents streams of captured packets from being re-sent, known as a "replay" attack, blocking such methods of obtaining unauthorized access to a system by mimicking a valid user's response to server requests.

- **Per-packet authenticity**—IPsec utilizes certificates or Kerberos authentication to ensure that the sender of an IPsec packet is actually an authorized user.

▶ **NAT transversal**—The Windows Server implementation of IPsec now allows for IPsec to be routed through current Network Address Translation (NAT) implementations, a concept defined more thoroughly in the following sections.

▶ **Diffie-Hellman 2048-bit key support**—Nearly unbreakable Diffie-Hellman 2048-bit key lengths are supported in the Windows Server IPsec implementation, essentially ensuring that the IPsec key cannot be cracked.

Setting Up the Monitoring Environment for IPsec Communications

IPsec is built in to all Windows Server machines and is also available for client systems. It is a straightforward process to install and configure IPsec between SharePoint servers and should be considered as a way to further implement additional security in a SharePoint environment.

NOTE

IPsec is highly recommended, although there is a performance penalty. Assume an approximately 10 percent overhead to use IPsec on network communications. That said, it is extremely easy to configure and highly useful for providing for transport-level security of data between SharePoint farm servers. Transport-level security from clients to web servers should always take the form of Secure Sockets Layer (SSL) certificate encryption.

The procedure outlined in the following sections illustrates the setup of a simple IPsec policy between a SharePoint web role server and a SQL database server holding SharePoint databases. In this example, the SharePoint server is SP1, and the SQL DB server is SQL1. The OS on both servers is Windows Server 2008 R2.

To view the current status of any IPsec policies, including the ones that will be created in this procedure, the IPsec Security Monitor MMC snap-in on SP1 needs to be opened. The MMC snap-in can be installed and configured by following these steps:

1. Choose Start, Run and type `mmc` into the Run dialog box. Click OK when complete.
2. In MMC, choose File, Add/Remove Snap-in.
3. Scroll down and select IP Security Policy Management and click Add.
4. Select Local Computer and click OK.
5. Scroll down and select IP Security Monitor; then click the Add button, followed by the OK button.
6. Both the IP Security Policies and the IP Security Monitor MMC snap-in should now be visible, as shown in Figure 15.5. Click OK.

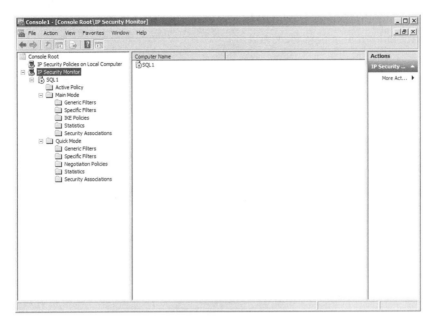

FIGURE 15.5   Configuring monitoring of IPsec transport-layer security between SharePoint servers.

7. In MMC, expand to Console Root\IP Security Monitor\SP1.

8. Right-click SP1 and choose Properties.

9. Change the autorefresh setting from 45 seconds to 5 seconds or less. Click OK when finished. You can then use the MMC IP Security Monitor console to view IPsec data.

Establishing an IPsec Policy on the SharePoint Server

Default IPsec policies must be enabled on any server in the SharePoint farm that will need to communicate over IPsec. To enable a simple IPsec policy that uses Active Directory Kerberos (as opposed to certificates-based IPsec), do the following on each server:

1. From the MMC Console setup in the previous step, right-click IP Security Policies, and then click Create IP Security Policy.

2. Click Next at the Welcome Wizard.

3. Give a name to the IP security policy, such as SharePoint IP Security Policy, and click Next to continue.

4. Do *not* check the box to activate the default response rule, but do click Next to continue. The default response rule is only used for down-level systems.

5. Leave the Edit Properties check box marked and click the Finish button.

6. In the Security Rules dialog box, click Add.

7. Click Next to continue.

8. At the Tunnel Endpoint dialog box, shown in Figure 15.6, choose that the rule does not specify a tunnel, and click Next to continue.

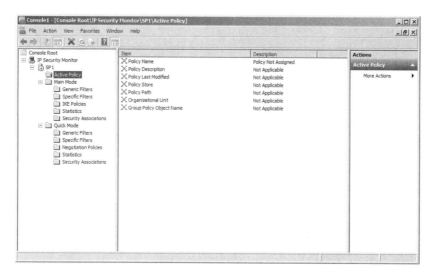

FIGURE 15.6 Creating an IP security policy.

9. From the Network Type dialog box, choose All Network Connections and click Next to continue.

10. In the IP Filter List dialog box, click Add to add an IP filter.

11. Give a name to the IP filter, and then click Add.

12. Click Next at the Welcome Wizard.

13. Leave the Mirrored check box intact and click Next to continue.

14. For Source Address, leave the default at Any IP Address and click Next.

15. For Destination Address, leave the default at Any IP Address and click Next.

16. For Protocol, leave the default at Any, shown in Figure 15.7, and click Next.

17. Click Finish at the Completion Wizard for the IP filter.

18. Tick the circle for the filter list just created, and then click Next to continue.

19. Under Filter Action, click Add to create a filter action.

20. At the Welcome Wizard, click Next to continue.

21. Enter a name and description for the filter action and click Next.

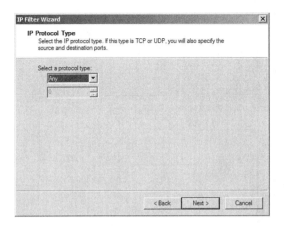

FIGURE 15.7   Creating an IP filter list.

22. Choose Negotiate Security, shown in Figure 15.8, and click Next to continue.

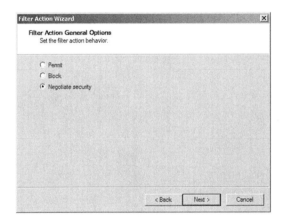

FIGURE 15.8   Selecting authentication type.

23. Select Do Not Allow Unsecured Communication and click Next to continue. Note that if you have servers that do not support IPsec, you may have to choose the less-secure option to allow unsecured communications in some cases.

24. In the IP Traffic Security dialog box, choose the security method of Integrity and Encryption and click Next to continue.

25. Click Finish.

26. Tick the circle for the filter action just created, as shown in Figure 15.9, and click Next to continue.

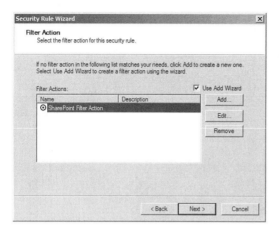

FIGURE 15.9 Selecting a filter action.

27. Select Kerberos v5 authentication and click Next to continue.

28. Click Finish to complete the wizard.

29. The Security Policy Settings should look similar to what is shown in Figure 15.10. Click OK to close the dialog box.

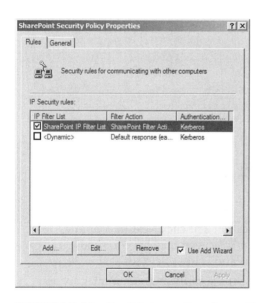

FIGURE 15.10 Finalizing security policy settings.

30. From within the IP Security Policies MMC Snap-in, choose the SharePoint security policy just created, right-click it, and choose Assign.

31. Repeat on additional SharePoint servers.

Verifying IPsec Functionality in Event Viewer

After the local IPsec policies are enabled on both SQL1 and SP1, IPsec communications can take place. To test this, either ping the server from the client desktop or perform other network tests, such as accessing SP1's SharePoint site.

A quick look at the IP Security Monitor that was established in MMC on SP1 shows that IPsec traffic has been initialized and is logging itself. Traffic statistics, such as those shown in Figure 15.11, should subsequently be shown. All communications between the SharePoint farm members are now highly encrypted and secured.

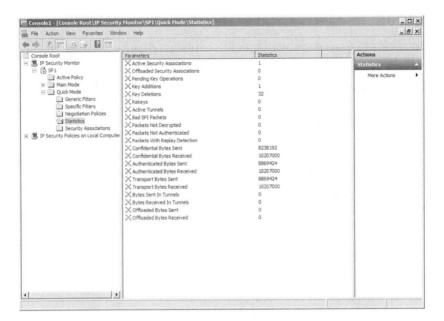

FIGURE 15.11   Viewing IPsec statistics.

These default IPsec policies are useful in establishing ad hoc IPsec between SharePoint clients on a network but are limited in their scope. Enterprise-wide IPsec policies can be accomplished through the use of group policies, but proper planning of an enterprise IPsec implementation is necessary to effectively secure an entire environment using custom IPsec policies.

Summary

SharePoint comes fully loaded with a wide variety of security mechanisms, tools, and techniques to help protect and secure data within the environment. Without a full understanding of these tools, however, it can be difficult if not impossible to properly secure a SharePoint 2010 environment.

Using a layered approach to security with SharePoint, it becomes possible to deploy multiple lines of defense against hackers, scripts, or snoops. SharePoint combines its integrated security with the security capabilities of the Windows Server operating system and the lockdown capabilities of the Baseline Security Analyzer, allowing for robust file security and physical security. All these options make SharePoint a formidable product, ready-for-enterprise deployment.

In addition, transport-level security in the form of IPsec can greatly secure interserver communications between SharePoint farm members, reducing the risk of data being intercepted and exposed.

Best Practices

▶ Use a layered approach to security, with more than one mechanism in place to deter attackers.

▶ After validating in a prototype environment, use the latest patches and updates on SharePoint servers to further protect the server against attack.

▶ Use the Microsoft Baseline Security Analyzer (MBSA) tool to verify the security of SharePoint servers.

▶ Use Secure Sockets Layer (SSL) certificates on any SharePoint traffic that traverses a public network such as the Internet.

▶ Use an internal Public Key Infrastructure (PKI) deployment with Active Directory Certificate Services to generate SSL certificates for SharePoint if third-party certificates are not being used.

▶ Physically secure SharePoint servers behind locked doors and in secure locations.

▶ Highly consider the use of IPsec to encrypt traffic between SharePoint servers.

▶ Use the MSBA to audit the security of SharePoint servers.

▶ Turn on SQL auditing so that failure attempts or potentially all access is audited.

▶ Design SharePoint with isolation approaches to security in mind.

▶ Utilize Server Security templates to secure the Windows Server operating system that SharePoint runs on, but ensure that the security settings are tested in advance.

▶ Restrict login access to SharePoint servers.

▶ Consider the use of PKI smartcards for user authentication to SharePoint.

▶ Consider the use of VPNs to secure remote access to internal SharePoint sites from the Internet.

▶ Limit anonymous access to SharePoint farms that do not contain any proprietary information.

▶ Limit console logins on SharePoint servers to select administrators.

▶ Enable password and account lockout policies on SharePoint servers.

## CHAPTER 16

Configuring Email-Enabled Content, Presence, and Exchange Server Integration

One of the most impressive improvements to SharePoint 2010 is the ability of the platform to directly accept email messages and place their contents into SharePoint content, such as document libraries, discussions groups, and lists. This type of functionality has been highly sought by those looking for an alternative to Exchange public folders and those who want to use SharePoint as a messaging records platform.

In addition to serving as an ideal replacement for Exchange public folders, SharePoint 2010 was built with integration with Exchange in mind, particularly with the latest version of Exchange, Exchange Server 2010. This chapter focuses on a discussion of the integration points between SharePoint 2010 and Exchange 2010, discussing in step-by-step fashion how to take advantage of email-enabled content within SharePoint and how to use Exchange as an outbound relay for SharePoint alerts.

A broad overview of Exchange 2010 is also outlined in this chapter, discussing the components that make up Exchange infrastructure and giving a high-level view of Exchange 2010 design.

In addition, this chapter focuses on how to integrate SharePoint with a Microsoft Communications Server environment to provide for presence information for users in the platform.

Enabling Incoming Email Functionality in SharePoint

As previously mentioned, SharePoint 2010 can process inbound email messages and accept them and their attachments as content for SharePoint document libraries, lists, and discussion groups. Indeed, SharePoint technically does not require the use of Exchange for this component, as it utilizes its own SMTP virtual server that it can use to accept email from any SMTP server, including non-Exchange boxes.

Integration with Exchange, however, has significant advantages for SharePoint. Most notably, new email-enabled content within SharePoint can be configured to have contacts within Exchange automatically created within a specific organizational unit (OU) in Active Directory. This makes it so that email administrators don't need to maintain the email addresses associated with each SharePoint list or document library in the farm.

Installing the SMTP Server Service on the SharePoint Server

The first step to setting up a SharePoint server as an inbound email platform is to install the SMTP Server service on the SharePoint server. Typically, this service is installed on the server or servers running the web role. To install the SMTP Server Service on the server, perform the following steps (these steps assume Windows Server 2008 R2):

1. Open Server Manager (Start, All Programs, Administrative Tools, Server Manager).
2. Under the Features node, click Add Features.
3. Click the check box for SMTP Server.
4. From the dialog box shown in Figure 16.1, choose to add the required role services.
5. Click Next to continue.
6. Click Next at the Web Server intro dialog box.
7. Leave the Role Services set at the defaults and click Next to continue.
8. From the Confirm Installation dialog box, shown in Figure 16.2, click Install to install the SMTP Server feature on the server.
9. Click Close when complete. Repeat for any remaining web front ends where the incoming email feature will be supported.

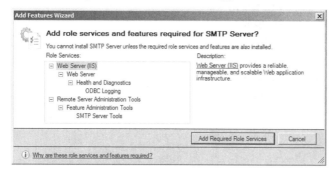

FIGURE 16.1   Adding the SMTP Server feature to a SharePoint server.

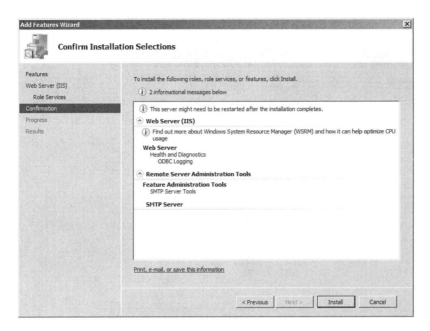

FIGURE 16.2   Finalizing the installation of the SMTP Server feature on a SharePoint server.

Configuring the Incoming Email Server Role on the SharePoint Server

After the SMTP Service has been installed on the server, inbound email can be enabled through the SharePoint Central Admin tool. Incoming email functionality can be configured in two ways: automatic mode or advanced mode. Automatic mode sets up inbound mail access using default settings, whereas advanced mode allows for more complex configuration to take place, but should only be used if the SMTP service is not used to receive incoming email, but rather the server is configured to point to a different SMTP server. To enable incoming email functionality in a SharePoint farm, and configure it with the most ideal options, do the following:

1. Open the SharePoint Central Administration Tool from the server console (Start, All Programs, Microsoft SharePoint 2010 Products, SharePoint 2010 Central Administration).

2. Click the System Settings link in the navigation bar.

3. Under E-Mail and Text Messages (SMS), click the link Configure Incoming E-Mail Settings.

4. From the Configure Incoming E-Mail Settings dialog box, shown in Figure 16.3, click Yes to enable sites on the server to receive email.

5. Set the Settings mode to Automatic.

6. Select Yes to use the SharePoint Directory Management Service.

FIGURE 16.3   Enabling incoming email for a farm.

7. Enter an Active Directory OU where the new distribution groups and contact objects for SharePoint will be created. This OU must be created in AD in advance, and the SharePoint service account must have rights to create and modify objects in this OU. The OU must be listed in LDAP format (for example, OU= SharePoint,OU= Contacts, OU= Resources,DC= companyabc,DC= com).

8. Enter the SMTP mail server for incoming mail, which will be the SharePoint server name in this example. If load balancing multiple incoming email servers, enter an alias that can be used to connect to a load-balanced VIP.

9. Under the setting for accepting messages from authenticated users only, click Yes, so that only authenticated domain users can send email to the server. This setting can be changed to No if you want to accept anonymous email from the Internet into the site content.

10. Scroll down in the page, and examine the settings listed in Figure 16.4. Check to allow the creation of distribution groups from SharePoint sites.

11. Enter a display address for the incoming email server; it should match the domain alias of the organization. An SMTP address policy must also be created in Exchange to match this domain name if it doesn't already exist.

12. Finally, configure which email servers SharePoint will accept email from. Enter the IP address of any Exchange hub transport servers that will be relaying mail to SharePoint. In this example, 10.10.10.103 is the IP address of the Exchange hub transport server.

13. Click OK to save the changes.

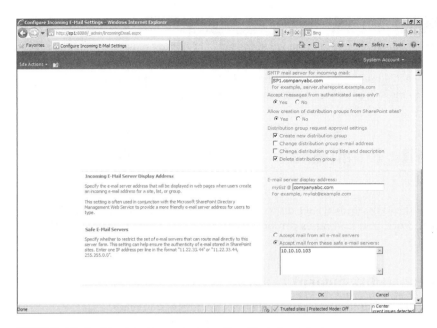

FIGURE 16.4   Finalizing incoming email settings for a farm.

Using the Directory Management Service

The Directory Management Service in SharePoint 2010 uses a timer job within SharePoint to automate the creation of contact objects. These contacts are automatically created to allow inbound mail to document libraries or lists within SharePoint to be automatically enabled.

For example, when a document library called Companyabc-doclib is created and selected to be email-enabled, the SharePoint Directory Management Service automatically creates a contact object in Active Directory that has a primary SMTP address of companyabc-doclib@sp1.companyabc.com, in this example. This contact then inherits a secondary SMTP address of companyabc-doclib@companyabc.com through Exchange recipient policies. These policies need to be set up if they are not already in place.

After the contact is automatically created, users can send email to this address and have it flow through the Exchange server, which then forwards it to the SharePoint server (the primary SMTP address). It is then accepted into the SMTP virtual server on the SharePoint server, and then imported into SharePoint via a timer job that runs on the server. In this way, all emails sent to that address appear in the companyabc-doclib document library.

NOTE

For the Directory Management Service to work, the account that runs as the SharePoint
Central Admin application pool identity account needs to have add and modify rights to
the OU that is specified under the Incoming Email Settings page. If this account does
not have rights to the OU, automation of these contacts will fail.

Working with Email-Enabled Content in SharePoint 2010

After the SharePoint server has been set up to allow inbound SMTP messages, specific
SharePoint lists and document libraries can be configured to store the contents of the
email messages, the attachments in the messages, or both.

Using Email-Enabled Document Libraries

To email-enable a document library in a SharePoint site, do the following:

1. From the document library, click the Library tab; then select the Library Settings
   button from the Ribbon.

2. Under the Communications category, click the link for Incoming E-Mail Settings.

3. From the Incoming E-Mail Settings for the document library, check to allow the doc
   library to receive email, as shown in Figure 16.5.

4. Enter an email address. This email address will be added to the contact object that
   will be created in AD.

5. Select how to handle attachments, whether to save the original .eml file, and what
   type of security policy you will set on the document library. If messages can be
   received from any sender, this may open up the document library to spam.

6. Click OK. After the contact object is created, usually within a few minutes, the document library will be ready to accept messages.

This same process can be followed for any document library or list within the
SharePoint farm.

Understanding Microsoft Exchange Server 2010

Exchange Server 2010 is the evolution of a product that has been continuously improved
well over a decade of development. It provides for robust messaging capabilities, in addition to a dizzying array of new functionality. The one area of development that has always
been missing in Exchange, however, has been the collaboration and document management capabilities. Attempts to build this functionality in Exchange public folders were
short-lived, and Microsoft shifted development of this aspect of Exchange to the
SharePoint Products and Technologies line, the subject of this book.

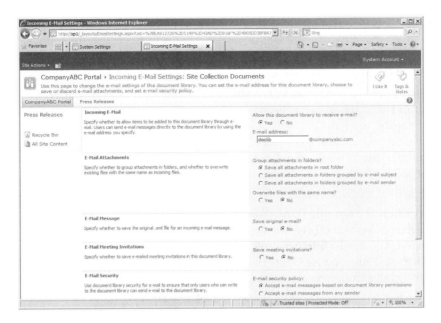

FIGURE 16.5   Enabling incoming email on a document library.

Taking the history of development with Exchange into account, SharePoint 2010 is the collaboration piece of Exchange that has always been missing in the platform. Because of this codependence between the platforms, many Exchange environments are considering deploying SharePoint 2010, and vice versa. Subsequently, an in-depth knowledge of Exchange 2010 is highly useful for SharePoint administrators. This section of this chapter focuses on a high-level overview of what Exchange 2010 is and how it fits in within a SharePoint 2010 environment.

Outlining the Significant Changes in Exchange Server 2010

The major areas of improvement in Exchange Server 2010 have focuses on several key areas. The first is in the realm of user access and connectivity. The needs of many organizations have changed, and they are no longer content with slow remote access to email and limited functionality when on the road. Consequently, many of the improvements in Exchange focus on various approaches to email access and connectivity. The improvements in this group focus on the following areas:

- ▶ **"Access anywhere" improvements**—Microsoft has focused a great deal of Exchange Server 2010 development time on new access methods for Exchange, including an enhanced OWA that works with a variety of Microsoft and third-party browsers, Outlook Mobile improvements, new Outlook Voice Access (OVA), Unified Messaging support, and Outlook Anywhere (formerly known as RPC over HTTP). Having these multiple access methods greatly increases the design flexibility of Exchange because end users can access email via multiple methods.

▶ **Protection and compliance enhancements**—Exchange Server 2010 now includes a variety of antispam, antivirus, and compliance mechanisms to protect the integrity of messaging data. These mechanisms are useful to protect SharePoint email-enabled content from viruses and spam, as well.

▶ **Admin tools improvements and PowerShell scripting**—The administrative environment in Exchange 2010 has been completely revamped and improved, and the scripting capabilities have been overhauled. It is now possible to script any administrative command from a command-line MONAD script. Indeed, the GUI itself sits on top of the PowerShell scripting engine and simply fires scripts based on the task that an administrator chooses in the GUI. This allows for an unprecedented level of control.

▶ **Database Availability Groups (DAGs)**—One of the most anticipated improvements to Exchange Server has been the inclusion of the concept of database availability groups. These technologies allow for "log shipping" functionality for Exchange databases, allowing for up to 16 replica copies of an Exchange database to be constantly built from new logs generated from the server. This enables administrators to replicate in real time the data from a server to another server in a remote site or locally on the same server.

Outlining Exchange Server 2010 Server Roles

Exchange Server 2010 continued the concept of server roles for Exchange servers that were introduced with Exchange Server 2007. In the past, server functionality was loosely termed, such as referring to an Exchange Server as an OWA or front-end server, bridgehead server, or a mailbox or back-end server. In reality, there was no "set" terminology that was used for Exchange server roles. Exchange Server 2010, on the other hand, distinctly defines specific roles that a server can hold. Multiple roles can reside on a single server, or there can be multiple servers with the same role. By standardizing on these roles, it becomes easier to design an Exchange environment by designating specific roles for servers in specific locations.

The concept of server roles is not unique to Exchange, but is also included as a concept for SharePoint servers, as well, with roles such as search and index, web, database, Excel Services, and the like driving design decisions for SharePoint.

The server roles included in Exchange Server 2010 include the following:

▶ **Client Access Server**—The Client Access Server (CAS) in Exchange 2010 is used for all client traffic, including standard MAPI traffic. In this version of Exchange, all client communications is routed through the CAS tier, and the CAS servers communicate directly with the Exchange mailbox servers. The CAS servers also handle Outlook Web Access (OWA), Exchange ActiveSync, POP3, and IMAP traffic. CAS servers are the replacement for Exchange 2000/2003 front-end servers and can be load balanced for redundancy purposes. As with the other server roles, the CAS role can coexist with other roles for smaller organizations with a single server, for example.

▶ **Edge transport server**—The edge transport server role is unique to Exchange 2007/2010, and consists of a standalone server that typically resides in the DMZ of a firewall. This server filters inbound SMTP mail traffic from the Internet for viruses and spam, and then forwards it to internal hub transport servers. Edge transport servers keep a local Active Directory Lightweight Directory Services (AD LDS) instance that is synchronized with the internal AD structure via a mechanism called EdgeSync. This helps to reduce the surface attack area of Exchange.

▶ **Hub transport server**—The hub transport server role acts as a mail relay for all messages sent and received in Exchange, including messages sent between recipients on the same server. The hub transport role is also used for policy enforcement via hub transport policies. There can also be multiple hub transport servers to provide for redundancy and load balancing.

▶ **Mailbox server**—The mailbox server role is intuitive; it acts as the storehouse for mail data in user's mailboxes and down-level public folders if required. The mailbox servers can be configured with DAG replicas to provide for both high availability and disaster recovery of the mail data.

▶ **Unified messaging server**—The unified messaging server role is new in Exchange 2007/2010 and allows a user's inbox to be used for voice messaging and fax capabilities.

Any or all of these roles can be installed on a single server or on multiple servers. For smaller organizations, a single server holding all Exchange roles is sufficient. For larger organizations, a more complex configuration may be required.

Planning for an Exchange Server 2010 Environment

It is important for a SharePoint administrator to understand the deployment options for Exchange if considering integrating SharePoint with an Exchange environment. This is of particular emphasis, as both applications can make heavy use of the Active Directory domain service. An in-depth look at Exchange 2010 itself is subsequently ideal.

Planning for Exchange Active Directory Design

Because Exchange Server 2010 uses Active Directory for its underlying directory structure, it is necessary to link Exchange with a unique Active Directory forest.

In many cases, an existing Active Directory forest and domain structure is already in place in organizations considering Exchange 2010 deployment. In these cases, Exchange can be installed on top of the existing AD environment, and no additional AD design decisions need to be made. It is important to note that Exchange 2010 can be installed only in a Windows Server 2003 functional level (or greater) Active Directory forest, and Windows 2000 functional level forests are not supported. Windows Server 2008 R2 or the latest AD functional level is recommended.

In some cases, there may not be an existing AD infrastructure in place, and one needs to be deployed to support Exchange. In these scenarios, design decisions need to be made for the AD structure in which Exchange will be installed. In some specific cases, Exchange may be deployed as part of a separate forest by itself. This model is known as the Exchange Resource Forest model. This is often the case in an organization with multiple existing AD forests.

In any case, AD should be designed with simplicity in mind. A single-forest, single-domain model, for example, will solve the needs of many organizations. If Exchange itself is all that is required of AD, this type of deployment is the best practice to consider.

> **NOTE**
>
> The addition of Exchange 2010 into an Active Directory forest requires an extension of the AD forest's Active Directory schema. Considerations for this factor must be taken into account when deploying Exchange onto an existing AD forest.

Microsoft has gotten serious recently about support for Exchange Server across multiple forests. This was previously an onerous task to set up, but the ability to synchronize between separate Exchange organizations has been simplified through the use of a product called Forefront Identity Manager (FIM). FIM now comes with a series of precon-figured scripts to replicate between Exchange forests, enabling organizations that, for one reason or another, cannot use a common forest to unite the email structure through object replication.

Planning for the Mailbox Server Role

The mailbox server role is the central role in an Exchange topology, as it is the server that stores the actual mailboxes of the user. Subsequently, mailbox servers are often the most critical for an organization, and are given the most attention.

With the Enterprise version of Exchange, a mailbox server can hold anywhere from 1 to 100 databases on it. Each of the databases are theoretically unlimited in size, although it is wise to keep an individual database limited to 100GB or less for performance and recovery scenarios.

> **NOTE**
>
> In large organizations, a single server or a set of servers is often dedicated to individual server roles. That said, a single server can also be assigned other roles, such as the CAS role, in the interest of consolidating the number of servers deployed. The only limitation to this is the edge server role, which must exist by itself and cannot be installed on a server that holds other roles.

Planning for the Client Access Server Role

The CAS role in Exchange is the role that controls access to mailboxes from all clients. It is the component that controls access to mailboxes via the following mechanisms:

- ▶ MAPI on the Middle Tier (MoMT)
- ▶ Outlook Web Access (OWA)
- ▶ Exchange ActiveSync
- ▶ Outlook Anywhere (formerly RPC over HTTP)
- ▶ Post Office Protocol (POP3)
- ▶ Interactive Mail Access Protocol (IMAP4)

In addition, CAS servers also handle the following two special services in an Exchange topology:

- ▶ **Autodiscover Service**—The Autodiscover Service allows clients to determine their synchronization settings (such as mailbox server and so on) by entering in their SMTP address and their credentials. It is supported across standard HTTPS connections.
- ▶ **Availability Service**—The Availability Service is the replacement for Free/Busy functionality in Exchange 2000/2003. It is responsible for making a user's calendar availability visible to other users making meeting requests.

Client access servers in Exchange 2010 are the replacement for Exchange 2000/2003 front-end servers, but include additional functionality above and beyond what front-end servers performed. In addition, one major difference between the two types of servers is that client access servers in Exchange 2010 communicate via fast RPC between themselves and mailbox servers. Exchange 2000/2003 servers used unencrypted HTTP to communicate between the systems.

16

> **NOTE**
>
> In addition to providing for HTTP access to Exchange data, CAS servers fulfill an important role with regard to SharePoint. They provide for a direct link to SharePoint sites via the OWA interface.

Planning for the Edge Transport Role

The edge transport role is new in Exchange 2007/2010 and is a completely new concept. Edge transport servers are standalone, workgroup members that are meant to reside in the DMZ of a firewall. They do not require access to any internal resources, save for a one-way synchronization of specific configuration information from Active Directory via a process called EdgeSync.

Edge transport servers hold a small instance of AD LDS, which is used to store specific configuration information, such as the location of hub transport servers within the topology. AD LDS is a service that is often known as "Active Directory Light," and can be thought of as a scaled-down version of a separate Active Directory forest that runs as a service on a machine.

The edge transport role is the role that provides for spam and virus filtering, as Microsoft has moved the emphasis on this type of protection to incoming and outgoing messages. Essentially, this role is a method in which Microsoft intends to capture some of the market taken by SMTP relay systems and virus scanners, which have traditionally been taken by third-party products provided by virus-scanning companies and UNIX sendmail hosts.

In large organizations, redundancy can be built in to edge transport services through simple DNS round-robin or with the use of a third-party load-balancing service between requests sent to the servers.

Planning for the Hub Transport Role

The hub transport role is a server role responsible for the distribution of mail messages and policy enforcement within an Exchange organization. There must be at least one hub transport role defined for each Active Directory site that contains a mailbox server.

> **NOTE**
>
> The hub transport role can be added to a server running any other role, with only one exceptions. It cannot be added to a server that is an edge transport server. If software-based network load balancing is used, it also can't be installed on a mailbox server running a DAG replica.

Several special considerations exist for hub transport servers, as follows:

▶ Multiple hub transport servers can be established in a site to provide for redundancy and load balancing.

▶ Exchange 2010 built-in protection features (antivirus and antispam) are not enabled by default on hub transport servers. Instead, they are enabled on edge transport servers. If needed, they can be turned on a hub transport server by running a Management Shell script.

▶ Messaging policy and compliance features are enabled on hub transport servers and can be used to add disclaimers, control attachment sizes, encrypt messages, and block specific content.

Planning for the Unified Messaging Role

The unified messaging role in Exchange 2010 allows fax, voicemail, and email to all be integrated into a user's mailbox. The unified messaging role can be installed on multiple servers, although it is recommended that it only be installed when the infrastructure to support it exists in the organization. The unified messaging role requires integration with a third-party PBX system. As Exchange 2010 progresses, this role will become more important.

Integrating Exchange 2010 with SharePoint 2010

In addition to allowing for inbound mail access from Exchange directly into SharePoint libraries and lists, SharePoint 2010 and Exchange 2010 contain several other integration points, such as the ability to relay outgoing alert messages through the Exchange server and the ability for personal sites to link directly to Exchange inboxes, calendars, and other information directly from a SharePoint site.

Using an Exchange Server as an Outgoing Email Server for SharePoint

SharePoint needs an external SMTP server to provide for relaying of alerts and reports to farm users. This server needs to be configured to allow access and relaying from the SharePoint server. To set up an outgoing email source within a SharePoint farm, perform the following steps:

1. Open the SharePoint Central Administration tool from the server console.
2. Click the System Settings link in the navigation bar.
3. Under E-Mail and Text Messages (SMS), click the Configure Outgoing E-Mail Settings link.
4. From the page shown in Figure 16.6, enter the FQDN of the outbound SMTP server (the Exchange server). Enter a from address and a reply-to address, and leave the Character Set left at the defaults. Click OK to save the settings.

Linking to Calendars, Contacts, and Inbox Items in Exchange 2010 from SharePoint Sites

SharePoint 2010 web parts allow for smooth integration with Exchange OWA, allowing for inboxes, calendars, and other mail data to be accessed directly from a SharePoint site. SharePoint 2010 contains built-in web parts to link to Exchange OWA content, and integrates best with Exchange 2010 OWA. Older versions of Exchange, such as Exchange 2003 OWA, are supported, but the integration is not as tight.

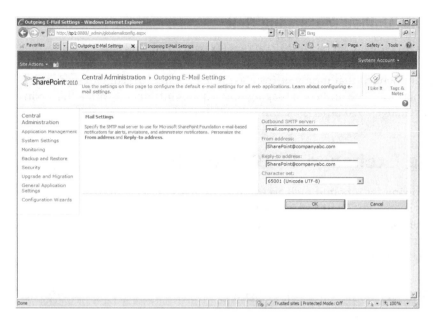

FIGURE 16.6   Enabling outbound email functionality.

Using SharePoint 2010 to Replace Exchange Public Folders

As previously mentioned, SharePoint 2010 is listed as the successor to public folder technology in Exchange 2010. SharePoint functionality has slowly been replacing all of
Exchange's public folder functionality, and is close to providing all the functionality that
was previously provided by public folders. With the concept of email-enabled content,
where emails are automatically added to content libraries and lists, SharePoint moves even
closer to this goal.

Enabling Presence Information in SharePoint with Microsoft Communications Server 2010

SharePoint 2010 Products and Technologies give organizations unprecedented document
management capabilities, allowing knowledge workers to collaborate more efficiently and
share ideas more freely. In addition to its robust document management capabilities,
SharePoint 2010 allows organizations to integrate with a presence management platform
to help users of the platform to easily tell whether the author of a document is online and
available, allowing for instant collaboration with that individual.

SharePoint integrates with this type of online presence information if used in collaboration
with Microsoft's presence platform, Communications Server 2010 and its predecessors,
Office Communications Server 2007 R2 and Live Communications Server 2005. Using one

of these platforms, SharePoint users can more easily collaborate with knowledge workers real-time, using an instant messaging client such as the Communicator 2010 product.

Configuring Presence Within SharePoint

Microsoft SharePoint Server 2010 allows for the ability to readily determine the online status of fellow co-workers and other members of a SharePoint site through the concept of online presence information, displayed to the user through a construct known as a smart tag next to the user's name.

The color of the smart tag enables a user to quickly identify if the user is available (green), busy (yellow), or not available (blank). Right-clicking these smart tags allows for a sequence of options to be displayed, such as sending an email to the user or instant messaging with them directly. This makes it easier for users to collaborate with the owners of documents, allowing for quick and easy communications.

Enabling and using presence information within a SharePoint environment requires presence to be enabled on the web application within SharePoint, and also requires the correct version of instant messaging software on the client. In addition, for enterprise instant messaging functionality, an enterprise IM solution such as Communications Server 2010 is recommended.

Enabling Presence Information on a Web Application

Online presence information is enabled by default on a SharePoint web application. In certain circumstances, however, it may be necessary to disable online presence information for troubleshooting. It is subsequently important to understand where in the SharePoint administrative hierarchy the presence information is stored and how it can be turned on and off.

To toggle online presence on or off an individual web application, do the following:

1. From the SharePoint Central Administration tool on a SharePoint server, navigate to the Application Management link in the navigation bar.
2. Under Web Applications, click the Manage Web Applications link.
3. Choose the web application to toggle the settings on, and then choose General Settings, General Settings.
4. From the General Settings page, shown in Figure 16.7, select either Yes or No under the Enable Additional Actions and Online Status for members, depending on whether you want to turn presence on or off.
5. Click OK to save the changes.

NOTE

Online presence info can only be turned either on or off for the entire web application. It is not possible to toggle the setting for any subcomponent of a web application.

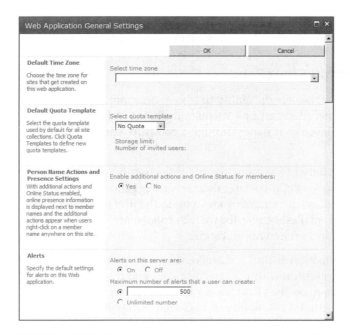

FIGURE 16.7   Toggling presence settings on a web application.

Examining Presence Functionality within a SharePoint Site Collection

By default, any time a user's name appears within an Office 2010 application such as SharePoint, Exchange, Word, Excel, and so on, online presence information appears next to that user via the user's smart tag. The status information must be fed to the application from an instant messaging client, however, or else the smart tag will not be able to display the status of the individual and will appear blank.

The following instant messaging clients are supported for viewing presence information in a SharePoint 2010 site:

▶ Office Communicator 2007/2010

▶ MSN Messenger/Windows Live Messenger version 4.6 or later

▶ Microsoft Windows Messenger version 4.6 or later

By default, SharePoint 2010 will only show presence for users who are a member of the user's contacts within the IM client. If a user is a contributor to a SharePoint site, but is not in contact list of another user, that user's presence information will not be displayed by default. To display a user's presence when he or she is not in the contact list of the other user, a centralized enterprise instant messaging platform must be used in conjunction with SharePoint 2010.

SharePoint 2010 supports both the Live Communications Server (LCS) 2005 server software, Office Communications Server (OCS) 2007, Office Communications Server (OCS)

2007 R2, and Communications Server 2010 software to provide for this additional layer of presence information within a SharePoint site.

Summary

SharePoint 2010 is the missing collaboration side of the Exchange 2010 platform, providing Exchange users with advanced document management and portal capabilities. With the ability to provide for email-enabled content, SharePoint allows administrators to receive inbound emails directly into document libraries and lists, further extending the capabilities of the platform.

In addition to email-enabled content capabilities, SharePoint 2010 has other strong integration points with Exchange 2010, including outbound alert forwarding and OWA inbox and calendar web parts. It is subsequently no small surprise why Exchange 2010 and SharePoint 2010 are often installed together in many environments.

Best Practices

▶ Use the Directory Management Service to automate the creation of AD contacts that correspond to email-enabled content on the SharePoint server, but be cautious about allowing users to auto create groups because this can lead to a major proliferation of Distribution Groups in Active Directory.

▶ Enabling recipient policies in Exchange to stamp the SharePoint-created contacts with secondary email addresses for the domain in which they will be accepted. If using Exchange 2007 or Exchange 2010, also configure an MX record for the SharePoint server.

▶ Load balance the SMTP incoming email role on multiple SharePoint servers to provide for failover and high availability of this function. Use software network load balancing if a hardware load balancer is not available. Configure a VIP name for the contacts in this scenario, such as spsmtpin.companyabc.com, so that the emails will be sent to the load-balanced SMTP servers.

▶ Restrict email messages to be received from only the IP addresses of Exchange servers to avoid having your SharePoint server used as a relay for spam.

▶ Replace public folders with SharePoint technologies wherever possible, because Microsoft will likely deprecate support for public folders in the near future.

▶ Consider deploying an enterprise corporate instant messaging application, such as Communications Server 2010, to provide for rich presence functionality in SharePoint sites.

▶ Incorporate SharePoint 2010 design concepts with Exchange 2010, so that both components can fit into an overall messaging and collaboration strategy.

CHAPTER 17

Safeguarding Confidential Data in SharePoint 2010

Protecting SharePoint data goes beyond simple backup and restore. Protection involves managing what happens to data in the event of a site outage, in the event of a major disaster, or simply what happens if someone gains unauthorized access to that data.

In today's complex data management world, administrators are increasingly being tasked with the management of the entire lifecycle of their data, from content creation to content expiration, and the penalties for inadvertently leaking confidential data to unauthorized personnel can be substantial.

SharePoint 2010 and related database technologies using Microsoft SQL Server enable administrators to better control what happens to their data throughout its entire lifecycle. Disaster recovery and high availability of the data can be achieved through SQL database mirroring, and encryption of content in databases can be handled with SQL Transparent Data Encryption (TDE). In addition, rights protection of the content can be enabled by integration with Active Directory Rights Management Services (AD RMS).

This chapter covers these various data protection technologies related to SharePoint. With a fundamental grasp of these technologies, administrators can dramatically improve the security of their critical SharePoint data.

Understanding the Threats to SharePoint Data

A SharePoint document management and collaboration environment is a mission-critical service for many organizations. In many cases, a SharePoint environment contains the physical representation of the intellectual property of an organization, and it is subsequently critical that the data in a SharePoint environment is secure and reliable.

Modern threats to SharePoint data integrity take many forms, but organizations can't afford to ignore them. Some common issues are as follows:

▶ **Data redundancy**—The ability to have an up-to-date copy of data in more than location is a critical requirement because it provides a data redundancy solution for hardware and site disaster scenarios or outages. This type of requirement is provided for SharePoint 2010 with SQL database mirroring.

▶ **Data high availability**—The ability to eliminate single points of failure in an environment that houses mission-critical data is key. High availability in SharePoint can take multiple forms, but often includes network load balancing used together with either SQL clustering or SQL database mirroring.

▶ **Data integrity**—The ability to control the integrity and security of data, in transit, at rest, and when backed up, is critical. Technologies such as SQL TDE can help to secure data in storage and when backed up, providing better overall data integrity.

▶ **Data leakage**—The ability to control what happens to sensitive data after it has been accessed is becoming more and more critical. Technologies such as AD RMS can be used to provide for this much-needed functionality, as they restrict the ability of users to print, copy/paste, or send data outside of a company.

Each of these technologies is covered in more detail in this chapter, and are all highly recommended components of a SharePoint 2010 environment.

SQL Server Database Mirroring for SharePoint Farms

Introduced in SQL Server 2005 Service Pack 1, database mirroring is a software solution that delivers high availability/database redundancy of SQL databases, including SharePoint databases. SQL mirroring is highly valuable for SharePoint environments because it provides the promise of having an always-available constant replica of SharePoint databases on a different server and being able to fail over to that server, either automatically or manually, as needed.

There are two primary partners in a database mirroring session: the principal server and the mirror server. Essentially, database mirroring works by maintaining a copy of the same database or databases on both partners. This is accomplished by streaming the active transactional log records from the principal server to the mirror server, which in turn applies the log records to the mirror database. In comparison to failover clustering, database mirroring works on a per-database basis, and provides high availability and data protection for both storage and hardware failures. In addition to the two partners involved in a database mirroring session, a third server instance, known as the witness server, can be added to provide automatic failover by verifying whether the principal server is up and functioning.

Utilizing SQL database mirroring for a SharePoint environment can have the advantage of having a second, fully complete copy of all SharePoint content automatically replicated to a secondary location. This is the equivalent of running a constant backup of SharePoint data, and has the added advantage of allowing for instant failover to a secondary SQL server in the event of a failure. Indeed, this version of SharePoint has been written to be "mirror-aware," and all databases can be configured with a secondary SQL server instance chosen to allow for mirroring failover scenarios.

Understanding Operating Modes

There are essentially three operating modes for database mirroring, as follows:

> **High-safety mode (synchronous)**—After a database mirroring session is initiated under high-safety mode, the mirror server database synchronizes with the principal server database and then writes the logs to disk. After the logs have been written to disk, all transactions are committed on both servers. Although this mode guarantees no data loss between the two servers, it does come with the expense of increased transaction latency.

> **High-availability mode (synchronous)**—Also referred to as high-safety mode with automatic failover, this operating mode is made available only with the presence of a witness server. This mode is the recommended operating mode for database mirroring within a SharePoint farm because of its ability to provide increased high availability through automatic failover. Similar to high-safety mode, the mirror server synchronizes the mirror database with the principal database and proceeds by committing transaction logs on both servers after the mirror server has written the logs to disk.

> **High-performance mode (asynchronous)**—Running under asynchronous operation, this operating mode provides an increased level of performance by sending logs from the principal server to the mirror server and then immediately committing the transactions on the principal server without waiting on the mirror server to write the logs to disk. By minimizing the latency of committed transactions, this mode increases the overall performance of the principal server. However, it also increases the risk of data loss between the two partners. Asynchronous mirroring is available only with the Enterprise edition of SQL Server, whereas the other two modes are available in either the Standard or Enterprise editions.

Although it is possible to switch between operating modes once a database mirroring session is configured, it is essential that administrators understand each operating mode and their respective advantages and disadvantages to successfully meet the availability requirements of their organization.

17

Understanding Transaction Safety Levels

Transaction safety levels work hand in hand with operating modes. Based on the configured operating mode, the transaction safety level will either be set to FULL or OFF. In turn, if the database mirroring session is configured using Transact-SQL statements instead of SQL Server Management Studio, the transaction safety level determines the operating mode. Essentially, if the operating mode is running under synchronous transfer mode, the transaction safety level will be FULL, whereas if the transfer mode is running asynchronously, the transaction safety level will be OFF.

When using SQL Server Management Studio to configure a database mirroring session, the transaction safety level will automatically be set to FULL if the partner and mirror servers operate in either high-safety or high-availability mode. If the two partners are configured for high-performance mode, the transaction safety level will automatically be set to OFF. If Transact-SQL statements are used to configure a database mirroring session, the SAFETY property in the ALTER DATABASE statement should be set to either FULL or OFF, depending on the desired operating mode. The following statement is an example of setting the transaction level safety to FULL:

```
ALTER DATABASE WSS_Content SET SAFETY FULL;
```

Table 17.1 lists the different operating modes and their respective transaction safety levels.

TABLE 17.1   Operating Modes

Operating Mode	Transaction Safety Level	Transfer Mode
High Safety	FULL	Synchronous
High Performance	OFF	Asynchronous
High Availability	FULL	Synchronous

Examining Supported Topologies

A drastic improvement for SharePoint in terms of high availability is the full support of database mirroring. Content databases, configuration databases, and the majority of the service application databases can now be mirrored to provide for automatic data redundancy, provided that synchronous mirroring is used, because the config database and other noncontent databases need to be in exact alignment with each other.

If using asynchronous mirroring, however, only content databases can be supported for mirroring.

Using these concepts, there are effectively three types of mirroring topologies supported for SharePoint content, as discussed in the following sections.

Single Data Center High-Availability Model

In this model, shown in Figure 17.1, SQL mirroring is used solely to create a backup copy of the SharePoint databases so that they can be used to failover the environment in the event of a problem on the principal SQL server. Because synchronous DB mirroring is used, all SharePoint databases (excluding a few services databases that cannot be mirrored; more on this later) can be mirrored from the principal server to another.

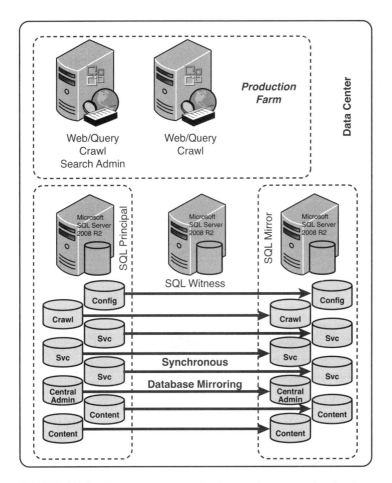

FIGURE 17.1   Examining the single-site synchronous mirroring farm example.

This model requires two distinct SQL instances, and uses a SQL witness server to fail over from the principal to the mirror databases in the event of a failure. Because all SharePoint servers are in the same data center, there are only two SharePoint Web/Query/Service App servers in the farm.

Cross-Site High-Availability Model

In the next model, illustrated in Figure 17.2, the same concepts apply, except that the SQL mirror, witness, and additional SharePoint farm members are physically housed in a separate site. This is an ideal model, but it requires a backup data center that is physically close by because the network latency must be less than 1ms and the bandwidth between sites must be verifiably above 1Gb at all times.

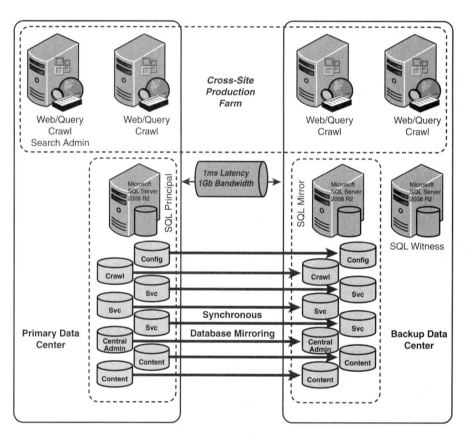

FIGURE 17.2   Examining the cross-site high-availability SQL mirroring model.

In this model, if the primary data center were to completely fail, the SharePoint environment would continue to run on the synchronously mirrored databases in the backup data center.

As a side note, Microsoft has supported enviroments with latency levels up to 10ms, but it is critical that there not be spikes in the WAN traffic and that there is guaranteed bandwidth and low latency because these spikes can cause transactions to timeout on the production side of the SQL mirror. That said, the official Microsoft stance at the time of this writing is that 1ms of latency is required.

Multiple-Farm Cross-Site Model

In the next supported SQL mirroring model, shown in Figure 17.3, only the SharePoint content databases are mirrored to a remote location, using SQL Enterprise edition's asynchronous mirroring. Failover to the remote site is manual, and involves attaching the content databases to a new farm that is identically configured to the main production farm.

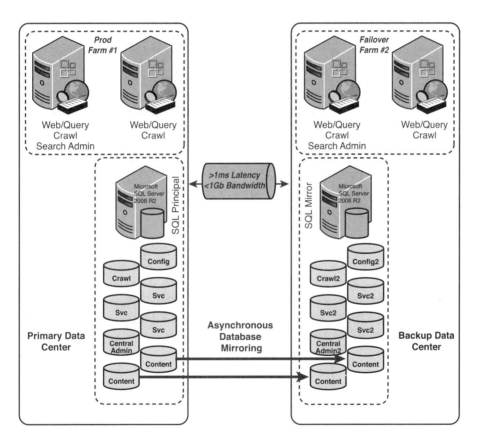

FIGURE 17.3   Examining the multifarm cross-site SQL mirroring model.

This model is ideal for environments that are separated by greater distances or that don't have the necessary bandwidth to support synchronous mirroring. A suboption to this model is one where the failover farm itself is only provisioned in the event of a site outage, rather than built as a "warm" farm.

> **NOTE**
>
> These three models are supported using native Microsoft technologies. A broad third-party space exists that provides tools that allow for full two way replication of data between multiple SharePoint farms that can provide for similar or greater DR and HA functionality.

Outlining Database Mirroring Requirements

The following requirements apply to a SQL Database mirroring environment.

Examining Supported SQL Server Editions

SharePoint 2010 supports SQL Server 2005, SQL Server 2008, and SQL Server 2008 R2. However, if planning for database mirroring, it is strongly recommended to deploy a version of SQL Server 2008 or SQL Server 2008 R2 to take advantage of the core performance enhancements for database mirroring. One of these major enhancements includes the ability to compress the stream of log records from the principal server to the mirror server, resulting in a sizable performance increase.

Table 17.2 lists the available database mirroring features within the supported versions of SQL Server 2005 and SQL Server 2008.

TABLE 17.2   Available Database Mirroring Features in SQL Server 2005 and SQL Server 2008

Database Mirroring Feature	Enterprise Edition	Standard Edition	Workgroup Edition	Express Edition
Partner	Yes	Yes	No	No
Mirror	Yes	Yes	No	No
Witness	Yes	Yes	Yes	Yes
Synchronous mode	Yes	Yes	No	No
Asynchronous mode	Yes	No	No	No

> **CAUTION**
>
> Although the witness server can run Workgroup or Express edition of SQL Server, both the principal and mirror servers must be running the same version of SQL Server. To ensure proper business continuity, it is also recommended to have both the principal and mirror servers running on similar hardware, if not identical.

Considering Security Requirements

There are two types of authentication for a database mirroring session: Windows Authentication (NTLM or Kerberos) or certificates. After a database mirroring session is initialized, the principal server sends a load of transaction logs to the mirror server using TCP. In addition to transporting log files between the two partners in a database mirroring session, TCP is used by the witness server to monitor the state of the two partners and determine when an automatic failover is necessary. In fact, all communication between the principal server, the mirror server, and the witness server (if available) is done through TCP over a specified port on each server.

Examining Supported Databases

Listed here are the services that do not support database mirroring, simply because the data associated with these services do not reside in a database. In other words, they are not needed for a restore: No information is stored or needed for these services because they are stateless and can simply start up and restart anytime without the need to store any data.

- ▶ Visio Graphics Service

- ▶ Access Services

- ▶ Excel Services

- ▶ Word Viewing Service

- ▶ PowerPoint Service

- ▶ State Service

Considering Performance and Scalability

With the increased number of configuration and service databases in SharePoint 2010, it is recommended that administrators thoroughly test the hardware capabilities of their SQL servers for performance and scalability issues when creating database mirroring sessions. Although Microsoft has stated that the practical maximum number of mirrored databases should not exceed 50, this number will vary depending on the following factors:

- ▶ **Network latency**—It is recommended that network latency between the principal server and mirror server not exceed 1ms. This applies to synchronous mirroring only.

- ▶ **Network bandwidth**—It is recommended that the network bandwidth between the principal server and mirror server be at 1Gb per second and less than 1ms of latency for synchronous mirroring. Asynchronous mirroring does not have these same requirements, but does require sufficient bandwidth to handle the flow of data from principal to mirror.

▶ **Memory**—The amount of memory on both the principal server and mirror server should follow the hardware recommendations for deploying a SharePoint 2010 farm.

▶ **Processing power**—Two threads are created for each database mirroring session; therefore, sufficient processing power is necessary on both the principal and mirror server to handle each database mirroring session without severely effecting performance.

▶ **Disk I/O**—Because database mirroring involves writing potentially large amounts of logs to disk, it is recommended that disk I/O is optimized for faster disk access.

Enabling SQL Database Mirroring

To enable SQL Database mirroring for a SharePoint environment, follow the steps outlined in this section.

Exploring the High-Level Steps Involved with Setting Up a Database Mirror

The steps to set up a simple mirror relationship between principal and mirror instance are relatively straightforward. In essence, you just need to back up and restore the databases to the mirror server and configure the server:

1. Set the transaction level to FULL for all databases that will be mirrored (if not already set).
2. Perform a full backup of the databases.
3. Perform a logs backup of the databases.
4. Restore the full backup onto the mirror server with the NO RECOVERY option.
5. Restore the logs backup onto the mirror server with NO RECOVERY option.
6. Configure security between principal and mirror using the wizard. If necessary, configure the witness server.
7. Enable mirroring between databases.

Each step is explored in more detail in subsequent sections.

Backing Up the Databases to Be Mirrored

SQL mirroring works by creating an exact copy of a database on a separate server and then keeping that copy in sync with the original copy. To set up mirroring, the secondary, mirror server subsequently requires a restore of the original database to set up the initial mirror copy. That restore does not have to be an exact copy of the database as it is today, but it should be a relatively recent restore. After the mirror has been set up, the database will automatically replicate any changes made to the database since it has been backed up.

Both a full backup and a logs backup will need to be performed. These can be performed directly from the GUI, such as what is shown in Figure 17.4, or a TSQL script can be created, such as the example shown here:

```
BACKUP DATABASE WSS_CONTENT
        TO DISK = 'C:\Backup\WSS_Content.bak'
      WITH INIT
GO
BACKUP LOG WSS_CONTENT
        TO DISK = 'C:\Backup\WSS_Content_Log.bak'
      WITH INIT
GO
```

Replace WSS_Content with the database to be backed up. Repeat for additional databases. After being backed up, the databases will need to be moved, either across the network or physically using tape or other medium.

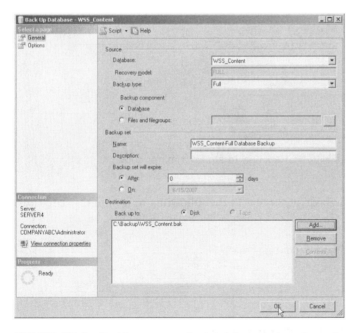

FIGURE 17.4   Backing up a content database to be mirrored.

Restoring the Databases onto the Mirror Server

After the database backups have been transferred to the mirror server, they should be
restored onto that SQL instance. What is critical is that both the full backup and the logs
backup must be restored with the NORECOVERY option chosen. If this is not chosen
during the restore process, the mirror won't be able to be created. If restoring using the
GUI, choose the Restore with NoRecovery radio button in the Options tab, and be sure to
do it for both database and logs restores, as shown in Figure 17.5.

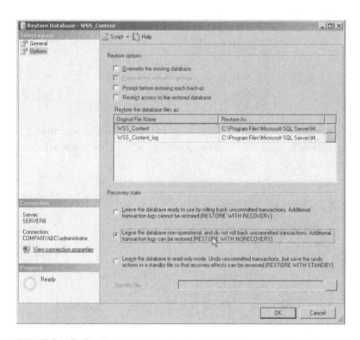

FIGURE 17.5   Restoring the logs with No Recovery to set up a mirror copy.

You can also choose to use a TSQL script, similar to the following, to restore the databases:

```
RESTORE DATABASE WSS_CONTENT
        FROM DISK = 'C:\Restore\WSS_Content.bak'
        WITH NORECOVERY,
                REPLACE
GO
BACKUP LOG WSS_CONTENT
        FROM DISK = 'C:\Restore\WSS_Content_Log.bak'
        WITH NORECOVERY
GO
```

Replace the file location and the database name to match your environment and repeat for additional databases. After both the full backup and the logs backups have been restored with NORECOVERY, you can configure the mirroring.

Configuring Security and Enabling Mirroring

There are two steps to the mirroring process. The first is to set up a security relationship between the principal server and the mirror server. The second step is to actually configure the mirror itself.

By right-clicking the source database (on the principal SQL instance) and choosing properties, and then selecting the Mirroring node in the navigation pane, you get the dialog box shown in Figure 17.6. Note that the mirroring options are grayed out. Click Configure Security to set up the relationship between the principal instance and the mirrored instance. This wizard also allows you to choose whether there will be a witness server.

FIGURE 17.6   Beginning the process to configure security for the mirror.

During the wizard, accept the default port of 5022 (be sure this is open in the Windows Firewall) and the default endpoint name of Mirroring. Ensure that service accounts are the same on both sides, or specify the various service accounts. After running the wizard, it should show a successful endpoint configuration on both principal and mirror, as shown in Figure 17.7.

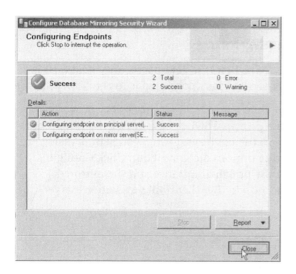

FIGURE 17.7   Configuring security between principal and mirror.

After the wizard runs, you will have the option of immediately configuring mirroring or waiting and turning on mirroring later. Once enabled, the dialog box should look similar to what is shown in Figure 17.8 and the database should show up in the SQL Management Console with a (Mirror, Synchronized) tag after the name of the database. Repeat this process for each remaining databases.

Using SQL Transparent Data Encryption (TDE)

SQL Transparent Data Encryption (TDE) is a simple yet extremely effective solution that can be used to protect your SharePoint content databases. Consider the following information when implementing SQL TDE.

Understanding the Problem

By default, SharePoint data is secured by access control lists (ACLs), but the data in the database itself is not encrypted in any form. If a rogue agent were to gain access to either the SQL server or the SQL database backups, they would be able to overwrite SharePoint security ACLs and gain access to the data in the database quite easily.

For security and for compliance reasons, it may become necessary to enforce data encryption of the SQL databases. Within SQL Server 2008 and SQL Server 2008 R2 Enterprise edition, Microsoft includes a new feature known as Transparent Data Encryption (TDE) that allows for this type of functionality.

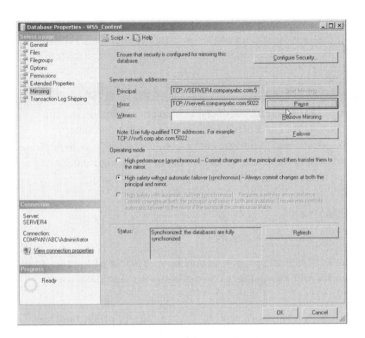

FIGURE 17.8   Enabling SQL database mirroring.

Encryption Solutions

TDE is actually only one of several SQL Server encryption solutions available. Each encryption solution works in different ways, however, so it is important to understand first what the available encryption solutions are and how they can be utilized.

> ▶ **Cell-level encryption**—Cell-level encryption encrypts individual database cells, rather than the entire database. This type of encryption is not supported for SharePoint databases.

> ▶ **File-level encryption**—File-level encryption includes technologies such as BitLocker and the Encrypting File System (EFS). These technologies encrypt the entire hard drive and can be used with SQL. They do not, however, encrypt backups of the SQL databases that are stored on other volumes.

> ▶ **Active Directory Rights Management Services (AD RMS)**—AD RMS is an encryption solution that uses encryption techniques to enforce rights protection on data, restricting what a user can and can't do with the data (for example, can't print, copy/paste content). AD RMS, covered in later sections of this chapter, does not encrypt the data "at rest." It is encrypted only when it is viewed by the client.

> ▶ **Transparent Data Encryption**—TDE is the ideal solution for SharePoint content database encryption because it encrypts the entire database while in storage, while

being used in tempdb, and when backed up. In addition, the encryption is completely handled by SQL, and SharePoint does not even know that the encryption is taking place.

NOTE

The solutions listed in this chapter are storage-level encryption solutions. To encrypt SharePoint content at the transport layer, use Secure Sockets Layer (SSL) Certificate encryption from the client to the server, and use IPsec encryption for the traffic between the farm members. You can find more information about setting up and using transport layer encryption in Chapter 15, "Implementing and Validating SharePoint Security."

Understanding How TDE Works

There are several key things to note about TDE, as follows:

▶ When enabled on a database, TDE encrypts the database, its associated log file, snapshots, backups, and mirrored database instances associated with that database, if applicable.

▶ The tempdb for the SQL instance is also encrypted. This can affect other databases on the same instance. It is subsequently recommended to create a dedicated instance for encrypted databases so that they can have their own dedicated tempdb.

▶ Backup cannot be restored to other servers if those servers do not have a copy of the private key used to encrypt. Stolen database files are subsequently worthless to the thief.

▶ The overhead associated with enabling TDE is only a 3 percent to 5 percent performance penalty on the box, so minimal server resources are required to enable.

Understanding the TDE Key Hierarchy

TDE works by establishing a hierarchy of keys. It is critical to understand what these keys are and how they are used to encrypt each other. Figure 17.9 illustrates the key hierarchy used by TDE.

At the root, the Windows Data Protection API (DPAPI) is used to create and protect the service master key (SMK). The SMK is unique to each server and does not need to be backed up or recovered on any other systems. The SMK is then used to create and protect the database master key (DMK). The DMK is then subsequently used to create and protect the TDE Certificate, which in turn is used to create a Database Encryption Key (DEK), which encrypts the content DB itself.

Understanding TDE Requirements and Limitations

There are a few requirements and limitations to TDE that should be known in advance of its deployment, as follows:

▶ The Enterprise edition of SQL Server is required for TDE. This version of SQL Server is considerably more expensive than the Standard edition.

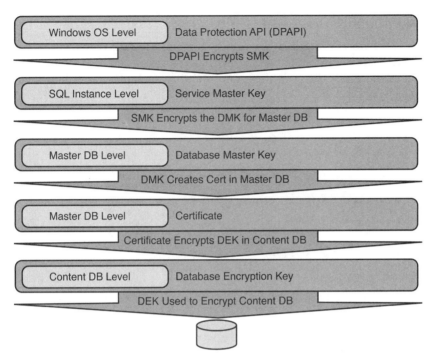

FIGURE 17.9   Understanding the TDE key hierarchy.

▶ TDE does not encrypt the communication channel. IPsec is the solution for this.

▶ TDE cannot take advantage of SQL 2008 RTM/R2 backup compression.

▶ Replication or FILESTREAM data is not encrypted when TDE is enabled.

▶ The tempdb is encrypted for the entire instance, even if only one database is enabled for TDE.

Enabling TDE for SharePoint Content Databases

The steps for enabling TDE on an existing SharePoint content database are straightforward and involve the following high-level tasks:

1. Create the DMK.
2. Create the TDE Certificate.
3. Back up the TDE Certificate.
4. Create the DEK.
5. Encrypt the database.
6. Monitor the progress.

Creating the Database Master Key (DMK)

The first step in the TDE process is to create the DMK. None of the TDE steps can be done from the SQL GUI; they must all be run as TSQL scripts. It is recommended to create the scripts in advance and then run them one at a time, such as what is illustrated in Figure 17.10.

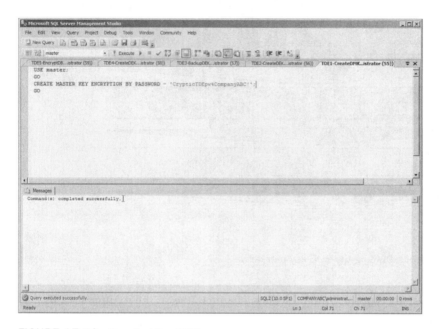

FIGURE 17.10   Creating the DMK.

The TSQL script for creating the DMK is as follows. Change the password value to one specific to your organization and store the password in a safe place:

```
USE master;
GO
CREATE MASTER KEY ENCRYPTION BY PASSWORD = 'CrypticTDEpw4CompanyABC';
GO
```

After the DMK is created, it can then be used to create the TDE Certificate.

Creating the TDE Certificate

Using TSQL commands again, the TDE Certificate can be generated from the DMK on the server. Replace the certificate name and subject with one relevant to your organization:

```
USE master;
GO
```

```
CREATE CERTIFICATE CompanyABCtdeCert WITH SUBJECT = 'CompanyABC TDE Certificate';
GO
```

Back Up the TDE Cert

Upon creation of the certificate, you will want to immediately back it up and store it in a safe place, away from the SQL backups for SharePoint. If this key backup is lost, the SQL backups will be worthless. To back up the certificate, use TSQL syntax similar to the following:

```
USE master;
GO
BACKUP CERTIFICATE CompanyABCtdeCert TO FILE = 'C:\Backup\CompanyABCtdeCERT.cer'
WITH PRIVATE KEY (
FILE = 'C:\Backup\CompanyABCtdeCert.pvk',
ENCRYPTION BY PASSWORD = 'CrypticTDEpw4CompanyABC!');
GO
```

> **CAUTION**
>
> It is extremely critical that this key is backed up and stored in a safe, fault-tolerant place. If it is lost, all SharePoint content in encrypted databases could be lost forever.

Note that the TSQL script also specifies that the private key is backed up (CompanyABCtdeCert.pvk). This private key must be stored together with the certificate backup and restored with the TDE Certificate if you want to recover TDE-encrypted databases to another server. Also note that we are encrypting the certificate with a manual password; this will need to be used to restore the private key and certificate, so be sure to write it down and store it in a safe place.

Creating the DEK

The TDE Certificate can then be used to create a DEK that will be used for the individual SharePoint content database that will be encrypted. Use syntax similar to the following, but substitute SharePointContentDB for the name of your SharePoint Content DB. A unique DEK will need to be created for each Content DB encrypted:

```
USE SharePointContentDB;
GO
CREATE DATABASE ENCRYPTION KEY
WITH ALGORITHM = AES_256
ENCRYPTION BY SERVER CERTIFICATE CompanyABCtdeCert
GO
```

Encrypt the DB

Finally, use the DEK to encrypt the specific SharePoint content database. Replace the name of the DB here with your own DB. Repeat the previous step and this step for any remaining SharePoint Content DBs:

```
USE SharePointContentDB
GO
ALTER DATABASE SharePointContentDB
SET ENCRYPTION ON
GO
```

Monitoring Progress

TDE will immediately begin to encrypt the content DB. It can do this on the fly as the database is being used. Depending on the size of the database, this might take a while. Progress of the encryption can be monitored with another script shown here, which returns all database with encryption state 3. An encryption state of 1 = no encryption, whereas a state of 2 indicates that encryption has begun. A state of 3 means that encryption is complete. Run this command until the results show the database as having a state of 3, as shown in Figure 7.11. The TDE encryption process will then be complete:

```
USE SharePointContentDB
GO
SELECT *
FROM sys.dm_database_encryption_keys
WHERE encryption_state = 3;
GO
```

Repeat for any remaining databases.

Restoring the TDE Encrypted DB to Another Server

If a restore attempt of a TDE encrypted backup file is attempted, a failure such as the one shown in Figure 17.12 will occur. To be able to restore the backup file, the target server will need to have the TDE Certificate restored to it.

The high-level steps for restoring a TDE-encrypted database to another server are as follows:

1. Create new DMK on target server. (Each DMK is unique, so simply create a new one using the TSQL listed in previous steps. This DMK does not need to match the one from the source server.)

2. Back up the certificate and private key from the source using the TSQL script shown previously.

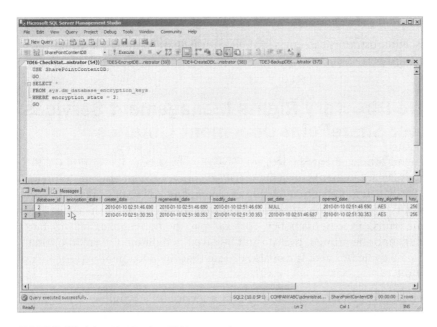

FIGURE 17.11   Monitoring TDE encryption status.

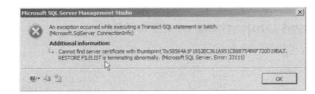

FIGURE 17.12   Viewing an error generated when attempting to restore a TDE-encrypted database from backup.

3. Restore the TDE Certificate and the private key onto the target (no need to export the DEK, as it is part of the backup file). Use similar syntax to what is shown here:

```
USE master;
GO
CREATE CERTIFICATE CompanyABCtdeCert
FROM FILE = 'C:\Restore\CompanyABCtdeCert.cer'
WITH PRIVATE KEY (
FILE = 'C:\Restore\CompanyABCtdeCert.pvk'
, DECRYPTION BY PASSWORD = 'CrypticTDEpw4CompanyABC!'
    )
```

4. Restore the database file from backup.

Note that the decryption password needs to match the one chosen in the previous steps.

Using this process, administrators can encrypt their critical SharePoint data without the need for complex third-party solutions.

Using Active Directory Rights Management Services (AD RMS) for SharePoint Document Libraries

Active Directory Rights Management Services (AD RMS) is a Data Leak Prevention (DLP) technology that uses Digital Rights Management (DRM) concepts in an attempt to prevent critical data from easily being transferred outside of a company. AD RMS works by encrypting documents, and then only allowing them to be unencrypted if the client application agrees to the terms of the rights policy. For example, the rights policy may dictate that the document cannot be printed, that it can't be saved in a different format, or that data from it cannot be copied/pasted. It can also dictate that the document expires after a certain period of time.

AD RMS is independent from SharePoint, and runs as a service on a Windows Server 2008 or Windows Server 2008 R2 server. Clients can encrypt files directly from their Office clients, or via Outlook, with or without SharePoint. Where the SharePoint integration comes into place, however, is in SharePoint's ability to define a rights policy on all documents within a document library and have those rights policies enforced by an AD RMS server in the domain.

Understanding Prerequisites and Limitations of AD RMS

It is important to understand first what AD RMS can and can't do in a SharePoint environment. The following key facts are important:

▶ AD RMS does not encrypt files in storage. Instead, the AD RMS rights policies are enforced only when the document is pulled out of the document library. This allows SharePoint indexing to be able to index the documents. If storage-level encryption is required, a technology such as SQL TDE, covered earlier in this chapter, is required.

▶ You can only establish one rights policy per document library and, once established, those policies apply to all documents, both existing and new documents in the library.

▶ The rights policies in SharePoint document libraries only define whether a user can print or programmatically access data or not. Other rights restrictions on documents actually depend on the SharePoint rights that a user has to the document library. If they have full contributor rights, they can do more with the content. If they simply have reader rights, they are fully restricted in what they can do.

▶ The AD RMS fully qualified domain name (FQDN) cannot be changed for existing content. Give considerable thought to what the FQDN will be and enable SSL encryption immediately on RMS. If you choose a flat name such as http://rmsserver for your URL, you will never be able to turn on external access to RMS. Instead, consider choosing something like https://rms.companyabc.com from the beginning, even if you don't intend on turning on external access.

▶ Users using rights-protected documents or document libraries must have web-based access to the AD RMS FQDN to be able to open documents. If SharePoint is published on the outside, for example, the users will need to be able to access the FQDN of the AD RMS site. In the previous example, this means being able to get to rms.companyabc.com. This means that this must be published as a site if this type of functionality is required.

▶ After a service connection point (SCP) is published in AD, all users will immediately be able to use it. Consider waiting to publish the SCP until the environment has been fully tested. You can test out AD RMS by modifying the client registry to point to the AD RMS server instead of using an SCP initially.

Add multiple AD RMS servers for redundancy, and load balance them. This makes it even more critical to use an FQDN that can point to multiple servers or a load balanced VIP, such as rms.companyabc.com. You won't be able to add a second AD RMS server into a cluster until the SCP has been published.

Installing AD RMS

For environments that don't already have an AD RMS server in place (legacy Windows Server 2003 RMS will work as well), a new Windows Server 2008 R2 AD RMS environment is required. Note that the RMS server requires a separate server from the SharePoint farm servers, and will also require a database for the AD RMS database. In many cases, the AD RMS database server will be the same server as the SharePoint database server.

To install and configure AD RMS on a server, first install Windows Server 2008 R2, (Standard, Enterprise, or Datacenter will work) with the default installation options and then add it to the domain. Log in as an account with local admin access to the box and perform the following steps to install AD RMS:

1. On the RMS server, run the Add Roles Wizard from Server Manager.
2. Click Next to start the wizard.
3. Check the box for Active Directory Rights Management Services
4. Choose to add the required role services when prompted.
5. Ensure that AD RMS and Web Server are checked in the summary dialog box, shown in Figure 17.13, and choose Next to continue.

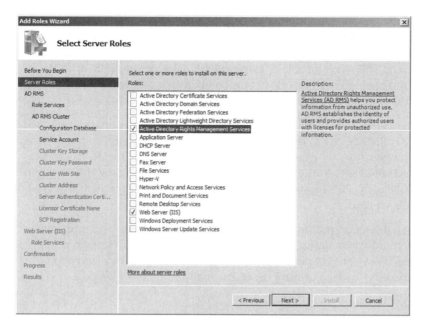

FIGURE 17.13   Installing the AD RMS role.

6. Click Next at the AD RMS Welcome dialog box.

7. Under Role Services, leave the default in place and click Next.

8. From the RMS Cluster dialog box, choose to create a new RMS cluster and click Next to continue.

9. From the Database dialog box, shown in Figure 17.14, choose to either use a local Windows Internal DB on the server or use a centralized SQL Server instance on another server. It is highly recommended to choose a separate SQL server, such as the SharePoint database server, for this.

10. Specify a domain user account in the subsequent dialog box that will be used for AD RMS. This account should not have any special rights other than domain user rights in the domain. You will need to create this account in advance before proceeding. Click Next to continue.

11. Under the Cluster Key Storage dialog box, choose the default AD managed key storage and click next to continue.

12. Enter a password for the cluster. Be sure to save this password; you'll need it to add additional RMS servers into the cluster in the future. Click Next to continue.

13. Use the default website and click Next to continue.

14. Select whether to use an SSL-encrypted connection to RMS or an HTTP connection, such as what is shown in Figure 17.15. It is highly recommended to use SSL now, because content will display this name at all times. In addition, do not use a server name for the FQDN. Use a name that can be transferred to a VIP or another server in

the future, such as rms.companyabc.com. Ideally, your RMS address will then always be https://rms.companyabc.com. Click Next to continue.

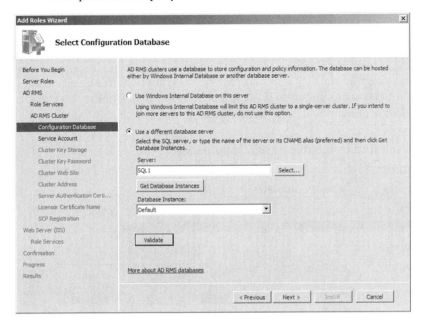

FIGURE 17.14   Selecting the database for AD RMS.

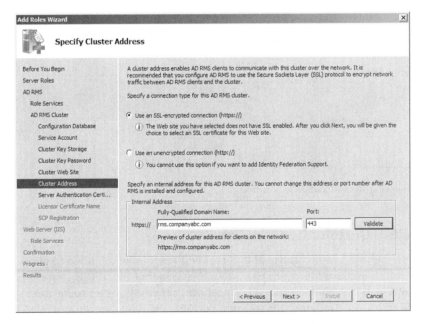

FIGURE 17.15   Specifying the FQDN for AD RMS.

15. At the subsequent dialog box, choose the SSL certificate that matches the FQDN chosen (that is, rms.companyabc.com). If it is not created yet, choose to install it later. This certificate must be installed for RMS to work properly. It is not recommended to use a self-signed certificate. Click Next to continue.

16. Choose the name of the server licensor certificate (accept the default in most cases) and click Next to continue.

17. Select whether to register the SCP now or later. Typically, the SCP will be registered immediately, but be sure to understand the implications of this. Once registered, all Office clients in the domain will "see" the RMS server and will be able to start encrypting content.

18. Accept the default for the web role wizard, and then click Next.

19. Review the settings, such as those shown in Figure 17.16, and choose Install.

20. Choose Close when the wizard completes.

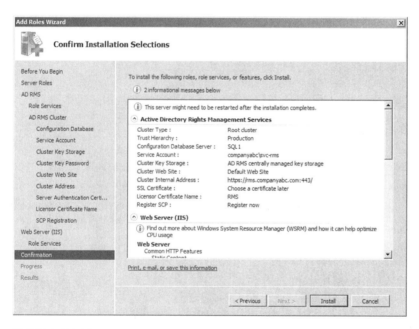

FIGURE 17.16   Reviewing AD RMS installation settings.

Modifying the RMS Certification Pipeline

After an RMS server is installed, a file on the RMS server will need to be modified to allow the SharePoint server and a local RMS group to be able to access that file. If this step is not performed, SharePoint won't be able to make a connection to the RMS server to be able protect document libraries. To configure this security, perform the following steps while logged in as a local administrator on the RMS server:

1. On the RMS server, navigate to C:\Inetpub\wwwroot_wmcs\Certification.

2. Right-click the ServerCertification.asmx file and choose Properties, and then click the Security tab.

3. Click Edit and then Add.

4. Click Object Types, select Computers, and then click OK.

5. Enter the name of all SharePoint web roles servers into the box and then click OK.

6. Click Add.

7. Select Object Types of Groups, and then click OK.

8. Type **RMSServer\AD RMS Service Group** (where *RMSServer* is the name of your RMSServer), and then click OK.

9. Review the security settings, which should be similar to what is shown in Figure 17.17.

10. Click OK to close the security dialog box.

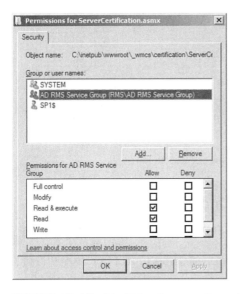

FIGURE 17.17   Modifying the security on the ServerCertification.asmx file on the RMS server.

Enabling IRM Support in SharePoint Central Admin

After the ServerCertification.asmx file has been modified on the RMS server, switch to the SharePoint server to be able to turn on Information Rights Management (IRM) support and integrate the SharePoint servers with the AD RMS environment. To turn on this functionality, perform the following tasks:

1. From SharePoint Central Admin, navigate to the Security link in the navigation pane.

2. Under Information Policy, click Configure Information Rights Management.

3. If the SCP is published in AD, choose Use the Default RMS Server Specified in Active Directory, as shown in Figure 17.18, and then click OK.

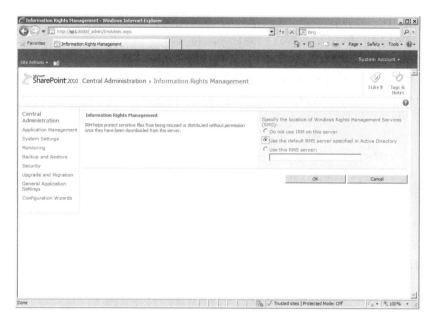

FIGURE 17.18   Enabling AD RMS support in SharePoint Central Admin.

Enabling IRM Support on an Individual Document Library

After enabled in SharePoint Central Admin, IRM protection can be enabled on individual document libraries within the farm by any site administrator who has full rights to the document library. To enable IRM protection on an individual document library, perform the following steps:

1. Within a SharePoint site, select a document library.

2. From the Ribbon, choose Library Tools, Library, and then click the button for Library Settings.

3. Under Permissions and Management, choose Information Rights Management.

4. Check the Restrict Permission to Documents in This Library on Download box, as shown in Figure 17.19. Enter the remaining fields depending on how the policy will be applied, whether there is expiration of policy, whether readers to the site can print or access content programmatically, and so on. Click OK.

Once enabled, all current documents and future documents in that document library will have the rights protection policy chosen added to them as they are viewed or modified from within the SharePoint Site. To turn off rights protection, just go back into the document library settings and uncheck the box for IRM. This will remove IRM protection for all documents within the library.

FIGURE 17.19   Enabling IRM support on a SharePoint document library.

Summary

Protecting critical SharePoint data goes well beyond making sure to change backup tapes on the weekend. It involves making data redundant, protecting the integrity of the data, and preventing it from leaking out of an organization. By using tools discussed in this chapter such as SQL Server database mirroring, SQL TDE, and AD RMS, administrators can provide for drastically improved control over the lifecycle of their data.

Best Practices

- ▶ Highly consider SQL database mirroring for high availability and disaster recovery.

- ▶ Ensure that network links are at least 1Gb and ideally have less than 1ms of latency (possibly up to 10ms in some scenarios) if using synchronous database mirroring. In addition, make sure there are no spikes in WAN traffic and ensure that there are guaranteed levels of service on the network links.

- ▶ Be sure that the hardware of the SQL principal and mirror servers are equivalent and ideally identical.

▶ For the best overall data security for a SharePoint environment, use SSL Certificates for client traffic to SharePoint, use IPsec for communications between farm servers, and use SQL TDE for encryption in storage.

▶ Use a separate SQL instance for TDE-encrypted databases so that the encrypted tempdb from that instance won't affect the performance of other databases.

▶ Back up and store the TDE Certificate and private key in a safe, fault-tolerant place, but ensure that that place is separate from the database backups themselves.

▶ Publish the AD RMS SCP in AD only after it has been fully tested, because it will be made immediately available within Office clients for client use once published.

## CHAPTER 18

SharePoint Foundation Versus SharePoint Server 2010

A common question when discussing SharePoint products is this: What is the difference between SharePoint Foundation 2010 and SharePoint Server 2010? As this chapter will show, this is not an easy question to answer, and there are differences across the board not only between SharePoint Foundation 2010 and SharePoint Server 2010 but also between the Standard and Enterprise editions of SharePoint Server 2010.

This chapter gives guidelines from the author's experience with hundreds of different clients with a wide range of business needs and software requirements, and delves more deeply into the specific tools and features offered by the three different products.

A primary goal for this chapter is to help business decision makers and SharePoint designers and architects make the decision about which product is right for the organization. Therefore, a number of tables are provided that specify which tools and features are provided in each product, to aid in the decision-making process.

Clarifying the Different SharePoint Products from a High Level

Nomenclature has been a challenge all the way back to the beginning of the SharePoint product line. Without recounting the various different names the different SharePoint products have carried, there have always been two different "flavors" of the SharePoint products. There has been the "free" version, which organizations can install without having to purchase SharePoint server licenses or CALs (client access licenses) from Microsoft. The "not free" version of the product required that the organization purchase both SharePoint server licenses and end-user CALs.

The following sections will clarify the differences between the products to help you understand the pros and cons of choosing SharePoint Foundation 2010 or SharePoint Server 2010 for use in the organization.

An Overview of Licensing

In the SharePoint 2007 product line, the "free" version is officially known as WSS 3.0, or Windows SharePoint Services 3.0, which is rebranded in the 2010 product line as SharePoint Foundation 2010. This version (in both the 2007 and 2010 product lines) offers a core set of collaboration and document management tools. Microsoft also provides a more feature-rich version that, in the SharePoint 2007 product line, is titled SharePoint Server 2007; this is now called SharePoint Server 2010 in the current version and, like the 2007 product, comes in Standard and Enterprise editions. The higher-end products contain all the features offered in the entry-level products, plus many additional tools and capabilities, which are reviewed in depth later in this chapter.

One of the first points to clarify is that the "free" version of SharePoint still requires that the organization pay for the server operating system that is in use (Windows Server 200x), the CALs required for users to access the server, and the SQL Server software (unless an Express version is being used) and SQL Server CALs. So, the only component that is free with the current version of SharePoint is SharePoint Foundation 2010, not the supporting software. This is important to remember if the organization wants to use SharePoint Foundation 2010 on the Internet or as an extranet. If SharePoint Foundation 2010 is going to be used to host a public site on the Internet that is open to anonymous access, there could be hundreds, thousands, or even millions of users visiting the site; the organization is responsible for valid Windows Server licenses and, if the full version of SQL Server is being used, for those licenses as well. Prices vary based on the level of agreement the organization has with Microsoft.

If the organization has an extranet based on SharePoint Foundation 2010, and is creating accounts for users not a part of the organization, it is responsible for tracking the number of users and purchasing the appropriate number of user licenses. For example, an engineering firm uses SharePoint Foundation 2010 for a project management extranet, and adds 50 accounts to an Active Directory organizational unit (OU) called Extranet Users. This company is using SQL Server 2008 Enterprise to store the SharePoint data, and Windows Server 2008 as the operating system to house SharePoint Foundation 2010. This company will need to be able to show an auditor that it does in fact have sufficient Windows Server 2008 and SQL Server 2008 CALs for these 50 users if an audit occurs.

With regard to the "full" SharePoint product, SharePoint Server 2010, Microsoft does offer SharePoint Server 2010 for Internet sites, Standard and SharePoint Server 2010 for Internet sites, and Enterprise. These licenses are costlier, but cover unlimited access to the licensed servers; as mentioned earlier, the organization also needs to purchase licenses for the server operating system and the version of SQL Server in use, if other than the Express version.

To make matters even more complicated, the SharePoint Server 2010 product can be installed with either the Standard features enabled or the Enterprise features enabled. If the Standard features are enabled, the organization must have a standard CAL for each user, whereas if the Enterprise features are enabled, the organization must have both the Standard CAL and the Enterprise CAL for each user. As with all licensing from Microsoft, check with your software provider to see whether these conditions have changed at time of purchase.

Database Requirements of SharePoint Foundation 2010 and SharePoint Server 2010

Another variable in the architecture and installation of the SharePoint 2010 products is the choice of database. This topic is covered in depth in Chapter 2, "Architecting a SharePoint 2010 Deployment," but is worth addressing to a limited extent in the context of licensing costs and limitations with the Express database products.

SharePoint Foundation 2010 and SharePoint Server 2010 products store data in the Express versions of SQL products when installed using the "standalone" option. It is important to note that with the 2010 products, the SQL 2008 Express maximum database size is 4GB, as shown in Table 18.1. So for organizations anticipating content database size exceeding 4GB, the full SQL Server products should be used; in other words, the "standalone" installation option is not recommended.

TABLE 18.1   SharePoint 2010 Content DB Limitations

Product	SQL 2008 Express Content DB Size Limit	SQL Server 2008 Content DB Size Limit
SharePoint Foundation 2010	4GB	"None" (generally recommended to limit size to <100GB)
SharePoint Server 2010	4GB	"None" (generally recommended to limit size to <100GB)

Experienced SharePoint administrators will quickly point out that SharePoint configurations can consist of multiple content databases, so it is possible to avoid the 4GB limit in standalone configurations where SQL 2008 Express is used by creating multiple content databases and managing growth so that no content database hits the 4GB limit. However, this is a management challenge and could potentially backfire, so is not generally recommended.

Microsoft SQL Server Express 2008 R2 supports databases up to 10GB. If your installation includes databases that are larger than 4GB but smaller than 10GB, you can upgrade to Microsoft SQL Server Express 2008 R2 for your content database storage solution.

Business Applications for Different Versions of SharePoint 2010

Before moving on with a detailed comparison of the features that can be found in the different products, it is helpful to provide some high-level business examples where clients made decisions between the SharePoint Foundation 2010 and SharePoint Server 2010 products. Because SharePoint 2010 is still a new product, examples given in this section draw from decisions that clients made not only with the 2010 product but also with the 2007 products, which are quite similar to 2010 in terms of feature placement and distribution between the "free" version of the product and the "not free" versions.

The following options represent a sampling of different configuration options based on features and cost combined with function. This is not an all-inclusive list, but is intended to help designers and decision makers categorize their requirements, and decide between the different options of SharePoint 2010 (Foundation versus Server) and between the different databases (SQL Express versus SQL Server). Specific costs can't be provided due to variables in numbers of servers, virtual versus physical servers, specifications of servers, numbers of users accessing the environment, and many types of licensing agreements offered by Microsoft.

Sample SharePoint Foundation 2010-Based Solutions

1. **Basic Features/Low Cost Team Collaboration Solution/Intranet:** SharePoint Foundation 2010 installed in standalone mode makes an excellent starter environment for simple collaboration needs in small to medium-sized organizations. It is a good choice when budget has not been allocated for a SharePoint Server 2010 implementation. As mentioned in the previous section, SQL 2008 Express has a 4GB maximum database size, so this should be taken into account. Because this is for internal use only, it is assumed that CALs have already been purchased for each user's access to Windows Server, which will house the solution.

2. **Basic Features/Low Cost Internet Site/Extranet Site:** Similar to option 1, SharePoint Foundation 2010 installed in standalone mode can make an effective platform on which to create an Internet-facing site. The organization is still responsible for purchasing the Internet license for the server operating system, but does not need to purchase CALs for SharePoint Foundation 2010. If the site is a read-only Internet site, a wide range of web parts are available to present information and documents to visitors. If the site is designed to offer extranet functionality, external users would be able to log in to the site and interact with content.

3. **Basic Features/Medium Cost Team Collaboration Solution/Intranet:** SharePoint Foundation 2010 connecting to SQL Server 2008 (or earlier) database server still saves cost when compared to using SharePoint Server 2010 with SQL Server 2008 databases, because CALs do not need to be purchased with SharePoint Foundation 2010. The organization does need to purchase SQL Server CALs or the processor-based licenses. The per-database limit does not apply, so the collaborative environment does not need to be as closely monitored or tightly controlled.

4. **Basic Features/Medium Cost Internet Site/Extranet Site:** As with option 3, SharePoint Foundation 2010 connecting to SQL Server 2008 (or earlier) database server controls the cost of the solution, while removing the content database size limitations, so is better suited to medium and large corporations, or even for smaller organizations who predict that the databases will quickly grow beyond the 4GB size limit. Note that the processor-based license is generally needed in this scenario for Internet sites, or extranet sites supporting large numbers, or potentially unlimited numbers of users.

Sample SharePoint Server 2010-Based Solutions

5. **Medium Features/Medium-High Cost Team Collaboration Solution/Intranet:** This solution includes SharePoint Server 2010 Standard edition installed in stand-alone mode using SQL Express, but is typically considered only for very limited use due to the limited database sizes. The organization is responsible for the CALs for the operating system and for SharePoint Server 2010, but not for SQL Server. Therefore, the costs are more than options 1 and 2, and most likely higher than options 3 and 4. Some organizations will use this configuration for a proof of concept or temporary configuration assuming the databases will be migrated to SQL Server 2008 in the near future.

6. **Medium Features/Medium-High Cost Internet Site/Extranet Site:** Similar to option 5, this includes SharePoint Server 2010 Standard edition installed in stand-alone mode using SQL Express and includes similar costs, and the organization is responsible for unlimited user licenses for the Windows operating system and SharePoint Server 2010. Once again the database size limit applies, making this a less-popular solution.

7. **Medium-High Features/High Cost Team Collaboration Solution/Intranet:** This option includes SharePoint Server 2010 Standard or Enterprise edition connecting to SQL Server 2008 databases. The organization is responsible for CALs for the Windows OS, SharePoint Standard or Enterprise, and SQL Server, so the licensing costs accumulate. That said, this is the most popular option for organizations that are committed to the SharePoint platform and want the most scalability and want to leverage the full range of SharePoint features. A key design decision for this option is whether to implement SharePoint Server 2010 Standard or Enterprise, because Enterprise adds cost for each CAL.

8. **Medium-High Features/High Cost Internet Site/Extranet Site:** As with option 7, this option includes SharePoint Server 2010 Standard or Enterprise edition connecting to SQL Server 2008 databases. The organization is responsible for the same costs as in option 7, but needs the unlimited user license for the server operating system, SharePoint and the processor-based licensing for SQL Server.

18

Feature Comparison Between SharePoint Foundation 2010 and SharePoint Server 2010 for Farm Administrators

An excellent way to gain insight into the differences between the SharePoint Foundation 2010 and SharePoint Server 2010 Standard and Enterprise products is to install all three and then walk through what features are provided with each version. This exercise is strongly recommended for organizations that want to validate which version best meets their needs and are new to the SharePoint product line, or want to perform more in-depth evaluations. Of course, not everyone has time for this level of testing, so the following information provides a top-down review of the features provided by each product by starting with the service applications provided in SharePoint Foundation 2010 and SharePoint Server 2010 Standard and Enterprise, and then reviewing the management tools provided in the Central Administration site, and finally reviewing the site settings tools for a site collection in SharePoint Foundation 2010 and SharePoint Server 2010.

Service Applications Available in the Different Versions of SharePoint 2010

In SharePoint 2007, most services were housed in the SSP (shared services provider), which is no longer available in SharePoint 2010. Instead, in SharePoint 2010 products the "services" are now known as "service applications" and are available in the Central Administrator Application Management page. A service application provides a set of functionalities that can be shared across sites within a farm or across multiple farms and can be enabled or disabled on a web application level.

Table 18.2 lists the service applications of interest available in SharePoint Foundation 2010 and SharePoint Server 2010 Standard and Enterprise, and helps to clarify "what" service applications are. Several subsequent sections provide more information about these service applications, so it will become more clear if and how these may be of interest to the collaboration and management needs of the organization as a whole. Figure 18.1 shows the Service Applications page for SharePoint Foundation 2010, and Figure 18.2 shows a portion of this page for SharePoint Server 2010 Enterprise version. The blue links on these pages lead to additional pages where the details of the application services can be configured.

TABLE 18.2   Service Applications Available in SharePoint Foundation 2010 Compared to SharePoint Server 2010

Service Application	SharePoint Foundation 2010	SharePoint Server 2010 Standard	SharePoint Server 2010 Enterprise
Access Services	No	No	Yes
Application Discovery and Load Balancer Service	Yes	Yes	Yes

TABLE 18.2   Continued

Service Application	SharePoint Foundation 2010	SharePoint Server 2010 Standard	SharePoint Server 2010 Enterprise
Business Data Connectivity Service	Yes	Yes	Yes
Excel Services	No	No	Yes
Managed Metadata Service	No	Yes	Yes
PerformancePoint Service	No	No	Yes
Search Service	No	Yes	Yes
Secure Store Service	No	Yes	Yes
Security Token Service	Yes	Yes	Yes
State Service	No	Yes	Yes
Usage and Health Data Collection	Yes	Yes	Yes
User Profile Service Application (including My Site)	No	Yes	Yes
Visio Graphics Service	No	No	Yes
Web Analytics Service	No	Yes	Yes
Word Automation Services	No	Yes	Yes

NOTE

The User Profile service application contains an important set of tools, including My Site, so it is important to note that My Site is not provided in SharePoint Foundation 2010. A number of other related tools and resources are not provided in SharePoint Foundation 2010 including the Manage User Profiles, Manage Audiences, Manage Organization Properties, and Manage Social Tags and Notes tools.

18

By quickly reviewing this table, it is clear that SharePoint Foundation 2010 includes only a small subset of these service applications, including: Business Data Connectivity, Usage and Health Data Collection, and Microsoft SharePoint Foundation Subscription Settings Service. SharePoint Server 2010 Standard adds several additional service applications, including Managed Metadata Service, Search, Secure Store Service, State Service, User Profile, and Word Automation Services. On the high end of the scale, Microsoft requires the purchase of the Enterprise edition of SharePoint Server 2010 for a number of features to be available, including Access Services, Excel Services, Performance Point, PowerPoint, and Visio Graphics Service.

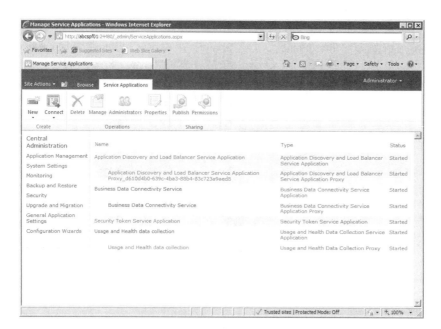

FIGURE 18.1 Service Applications page in SharePoint Foundation 2010.

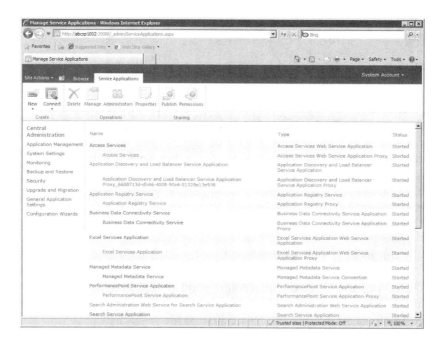

FIGURE 18.2 Service Applications page in SharePoint Server 2010 Enterprise.

Search in SharePoint Foundation 2010 and SharePoint Server 2010

It might be alarming that the SharePoint Foundation 2010 does not include the Search
Service application, but rest assured that the SharePoint Foundation 2010 does in fact
provide a functional and powerful set of search tools, similar to the search tools offered in
WSS 3.0 in the earlier version of the product. The search tools provided in SharePoint
Foundation 2010 are somewhat limited when compared to the full range of search services
available in SharePoint Server 2010.

Both SharePoint Foundation 2010 and SharePoint Server 2010 provide "basic" search
features, which include indexing of the content held within standard Microsoft applications. These "basic" search features allow users to search on one or more words, use
Boolean symbols and terms such as * and to use AND, OR, NOT in search strings. Figure
18.3 shows a sample of a search string in SharePoint Foundation 2010, and Figure 18.4
shows the result of the same string in SharePoint Server 2010. In both of these cases, an
asterisk was used after the word root Share, returning any words starting with these characters, and the Boolean NOT was used, so the results exclude the following term (SQL, in
this case). More sophisticated strings can of course be used by users, but with a little training, users can create precise search strings.

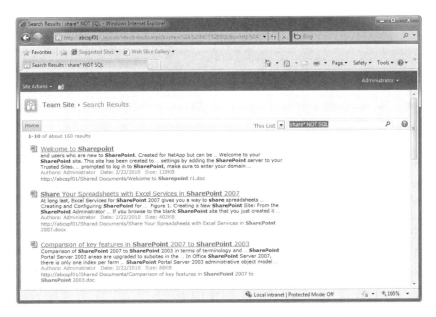

FIGURE 18.3   Search Results page in SharePoint Foundation 2010.

Note in Figure 18.4, which shows the results from SharePoint Server 2010 Enterprise, there
are refinements available along the left side, including result types (Word, Webpage,
PowerPoint), Site (Any Site, abcsp1002), and Author (Any Author, System Account, Colin

Spence, Colin), and hidden from sight on the page is also the option for Modified Date. These refinements are just one of the features in SharePoint Server 2010 that make search more powerful for end users.

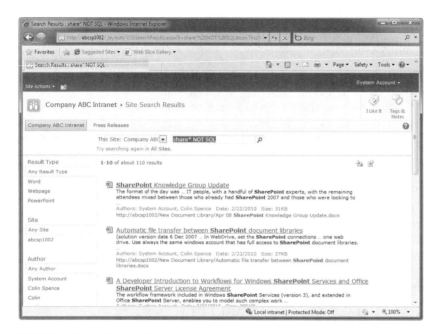

FIGURE 18.4   Search Results page in SharePoint Server 2010.

Another important point to clarify is that SharePoint Foundation 2010 provides a single search scope of This Site when performing a search, whereas SharePoint Server 2010 offers three scopes by default: This Site, All Sites, and People (and more can be added by a farm administrator). So, SharePoint Server 2010 lets users be more specific about what content is being searched than SharePoint Foundation 2010, and SharePoint Server 2010 allows searching of data related to "people," which is contained in the profile database that pulls data from Active Directory.

The Search Service application accessible via the Central Administration website is available only in SharePoint Server 2010 Standard or Enterprise and offers a wealth of features for tuning the search engine. The set of tools offered here allow the administrator to define additional sources of data to index, such as non-SharePoint websites, file shares, Exchange public folders, and other sources. Ranking of search results can be affected by defining most authoritative pages, second- and third-level authoritative pages, and even sites to demote or URLs to remove. Figure 18.5 shows the Search Administration tools for the Search Service application.

Additional products are available from Microsoft to enhance search capabilities, and these are Search Server 2010 Express, Search Server 2010, and FAST Search Server 2010 for SharePoint. Search Server 2010 Express could be used by companies that implement

SharePoint Foundation 2010 due to budget constraints but still want to provide more than the basic search features that SharePoint Foundation 2010 offers.

FIGURE 18.5   Search Administration for the Search Service application in SharePoint Server 2010.

For a more detailed look at the capabilities of SharePoint Server 2010, see Chapter 8, "Leveraging and Optimizing Search in SharePoint 2010."

Access Services, Excel Services, Visio Graphics, and Word Automation Services

As noted in Table 18.2, a variety of other service applications refer to other Microsoft Office software applications: Access Services, Excel Services, Visio Graphics Service, and Word Automation Services. These service applications can be extremely useful for organizations looking for deeper integration with the Microsoft Office applications in use such as Excel, Visio, and Access. Brief descriptions can be found in the following bullets, and other chapters, including Chapter 25, "Using Office 2010 Applications with SharePoint 2010," and Chapter 26, "Extending SharePoint 2010 with Excel Services, Access Services, and Visio Graphics Services," delve into more detail and provide business-related examples of how these can be of benefit:

▶ Access Services allows users to create an Access 2010 database, along with tables, forms, and reports, and then publish them to a SharePoint Server 2010 Enterprise site collection that has Enterprise features enabled, creating a new site for that database. Users of the site can then access data stored in the tables, add new data, and view and modify the tables, forms, and reports.

▶ Excel Services allows Excel 2010 users to publish worksheets or named objects in a worksheet to SharePoint Server 2010 Enterprise site collection libraries where Enterprise features are enabled. Unlike with Access Services, interaction is limited, but options are provided to users to open the workbook in Excel, download a snapshot, or download a copy, as shown in Figure 18.6. Cells can be enabled for user input but input won't be saved to the workbook. A new feature in Excel Services for SharePoint 2010 is the Slicer, which is a new type of data filter that enables Excel 2010 users to write OLAP data models and build interactive reports around them. The reports can then be published via Excel Services and can be interacted with in the same way as in the Excel client.

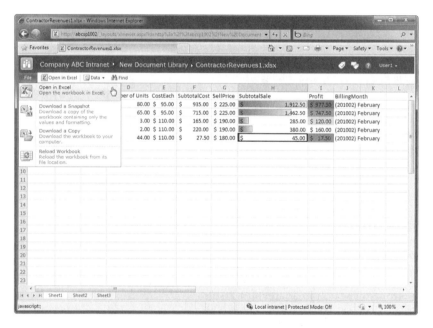

FIGURE 18.6   View of Excel worksheet published via Excel Services.

▶ Visio Graphics Service allows users to share and view Microsoft Visio diagrams, and supports a variety of data connections, such as to SQL Server, Excel workbooks published to the same farm, SharePoint server lists, OLEDB or ODBC connections. This extends Visio from "just a pretty picture" to a data-driven visual resource that is of value to the organization.

▶ Word Automation Services provides server-side automated conversion of file types that Word can open to PDF or XPS file types. The file types that can be converted include the related .docx, .doc, .rtf, .mht, and .xml file types.

Business Data Connectivity Service
Microsoft SharePoint Server 2010 builds upon the Business Data Catalog (BDC) introduced in SharePoint 2007 with Business Connectivity Services (BCS), which are a set of services

and features that provide a way to connect SharePoint solutions to sources of external data (such as SQL Server databases, web services, custom applications, and SharePoint sites) and to define external content types. A common challenge with SharePoint 2007 BDC was creating the solutions the enabled the connectivity to the data sources. With SharePoint 2010, SharePoint Designer 2010 and Visual Studio 2010 are the recommended tools for creating these solutions and have been enhanced for ease of use and functionality.

An organization can use BCS to build solutions that enhance SharePoint collaboration capabilities by including external business data and even modify that external data. For example, a SQL database that contains customer information can be made accessible in a SharePoint list that displays the desired fields, and salespeople can interact directly with the data from SharePoint. This enhances SharePoint's Server 2010's ability to act as a full-service portal, so users don't have to use a different tool for interacting with each different business application, but instead just need to visit the appropriate site in the SharePoint environment and use the standard document library or list tools that they are used to.

Developing these solutions is not trivial, and requires experienced developers and power users to minimize the impact on the IT support staff and to minimize potentially negative impact to the environment or the data being connected to.

Managed Metadata Service

Metadata is one of the key advantages of using SharePoint as a document management and collaboration tool, and is, simply put, data about data. One of the challenges of effectively implementing SharePoint in a complex business environment is creating a taxonomy of metadata that will be intuitive to users and also make the system more effective at managing files, because otherwise, SharePoint can simply be a more expensive and complex file share. A frustrating limitation of defining metadata using site columns and content types in SharePoint 2007 was that they didn't cross over the logical boundaries between site collections, and many SharePoint implementations consist of multiple site collections. This meant that larger enterprises needed to either re-create the content types and site columns for each site collection or find a third-party application to perform this task for them, which could be costly.

With Managed Metadata Services, the "metadata manager" creates a managed metadata service application, which can then be made available for use in site columns, and terms can be added to the term set from the site column gallery. Administrators can be defined for the managed metadata service, and group managers and contributors defined for the groups of terms under the managed metadata service, and stakeholders identified who should be informed of changes.

Site columns are an important building block of content types, so a content type (for example, Proposal Content Type) could include several managed metadata site columns, such as Project Name, Region, and Industry. If this content type is then made available in a document library, when a salesperson adds a new proposal, she could easily choose the metadata from managed metadata for each of the three fields. Figure 18.7 shows a sample of this process where the user has selected a project name from the options provided by managed metadata service and is viewing the description attached to the Project X project name. Chapter 22, "Managing Metadata and Content Types in SharePoint 2010," discusses external content types in more detail.

FIGURE 18.7   Accessing a managed metadata term set in a document library.

PerformancePoint Service Application

PerformancePoint is Microsoft's high-level offering for more advanced business intelligence requirements. It was offered as a separate "for purchase" product with SharePoint 2007 until Microsoft started including Performance Point with SharePoint 2007 Enterprise licensing. Now that PerformancePoint is a service application, it is fully integrated with SharePoint, providing better security, management, and scalability, along with ease of configuration. This integration should also speed adoption among corporate clients, because the tools are easily available for experimenting with, and the installation is relatively easy when compared to the installation process for the PerformancePoint 2007 products.

PerformancePoint allows power users and financial analysts to create dashboards with scorecards, analytic reports, and filters to pull data from a variety of sources, such as SharePoint lists, Excel Services, SQL Server databases, SQL Server Analysis Services, and other sources. New features include a Visual Decomposition Tree report, Key Performance Indicator (KPI) Details report, an improved Dashboard Designer tool, and support for SQL Server 2008 and Analysis Services 2008.

Figure 18.8 shows a visual representation of the BI products from Microsoft that clarifies the basic vision for the product line. This diagram includes Visio and Visio Services, an Excel and PowerPivot add-in, Excel Services, PerformancePoint Services, and Report Builder and Reporting Services, and suggests that the more complex tools (to the right) build on the simpler tools (in terms of learning curve for the average user) on the left.

Chapter 30, "Business Intelligence in SharePoint 2010 with PerformancePoint Services," delves more deeply into the capabilities of the PerformancePoint application.

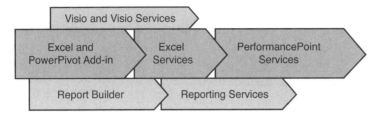

FIGURE 18.8   Diagram of business intelligence products from Microsoft.

Reviewing the Central Administration Tools on the Home Page in SharePoint Foundation 2010 and SharePoint Server 2010

Whereas the previous section calls out the service applications that come with SharePoint Foundation 2010 and the Standard and Enterprise editions of SharePoint Server 2010, which directly impact the tool sets that the user community will have, this section covers the administration tools that the farm administrators will have access to from the home page of the Central Administration site. A simple overview is that SharePoint Server 2010 provides a larger number of management tools, and therefore more time and training is needed to ensure that farm administrators are comfortable with the full range of tools. This is not an insignificant point because many IT resources are overburdened and may not be able to take time off to attend training and so might very well have to educate themselves on these tools.

SharePoint Foundation 2010 and SharePoint Server 2010 Enterprise Administration Tools Compared

Table 18.3 compares the tools that are available from the home page for the Central Administration site for SharePoint Foundation 2010 and SharePoint Server 2010 Enterprise. A quick glance at the table will show that the toolsets are fairly similar, suggesting that farm administrators have roughly the same suite of tools to access when managing their farms.

One difference is a lack of several reporting tools in SharePoint Foundation 2010, as shown in the table, because SharePoint Foundation 2010 doesn't include the View Web Analytics Reports. Also SharePoint Foundation 2010 doesn't provide the ability to configure content deployment paths and jobs or to manage form templates.

TABLE 18.3   Comparison of Tools Available from the Home Page of the Central Administration Site

Tool	Included in SharePoint Foundation 2010?	Included in SharePoint Server 2010 Standard?	Included in SharePoint Server 2010 Enterprise?
Manage Web Applications	Yes	Yes	Yes
Create Site Collections	Yes	Yes	Yes
Manage Service Applications	Yes	Yes	Yes

continues

TABLE 18.3   Continued

Tool	Included in SharePoint Foundation 2010?	Included in SharePoint Server 2010 Standard?	Included in SharePoint Server 2010 Enterprise?
Manage Content Databases	Yes	Yes	Yes
Review Problems and Solutions	Yes	Yes	Yes
Check Job Status	Yes	Yes	Yes
View Web Analytics Reports	No	Yes	Yes
Manage the Farm Administrators Group	Yes	Yes	Yes
Configure Service Accounts	Yes	Yes	Yes
Configure Send to Connections	Yes	Yes	Yes
Configure Content Deployment Paths and Jobs	No	Yes	Yes
Manage Form Templates	No	No	Yes
Manage Servers in this Farm	Yes	Yes	Yes
Manage Services on Server	Yes	Yes	Yes
Manage Farm Features	Yes	Yes	Yes
Configure Alternate Access Mappings	Yes	Yes	Yes
Perform a Backup	Yes	Yes	Yes
Restore from a Backup	Yes	Yes	Yes
Perform a Site Collection Backup	Yes	Yes	Yes
Convert Farm License Type	No	Yes	Yes

TABLE 18.3   Continued

Tool	Included in SharePoint Foundation 2010?	Included in SharePoint Server 2010 Standard?	Included in SharePoint Server 2010 Enterprise?
Check Product and Patch Installation Status	Yes	Yes	Yes
Check Upgrade Status	Yes	Yes	Yes

Comparing the Monitoring Tools in SharePoint Foundation 2010 and SharePoint Server 2010 Enterprise

If the Monitoring link is clicked from the Central Administration home page, and the tools further compared, it can be seen that SharePoint Foundation 2010 provides a subset of the monitoring tools that SharePoint Server 2010 Enterprise provides.

SharePoint Foundation 2010 provides the following tools that overlap with SharePoint Server 2010:

▶ Configure Diagnostic Logging

▶ View Health Reports

▶ Configure Usage and Health Data Collection

SharePoint Foundation 2010 does provide several reports out of the box that will be of interest to the farm administrator. The Health Reports, by default, list only the slowest pages and top active users. The Configure Usage and Health Data Collection capabilities are the same for SharePoint Foundation 2010 and SharePoint Server 2010 enterprise, and allow the farm administrator to log the following events: Content Import Usage, Content Export Usage, Page Requests, Feature Use, Search Query Usage, Site Inventory Usage, Timer Jobs, and Rating Usage.

SharePoint Foundation 2010 does not provide the following reporting tools that both SharePoint Server 2010 Standard and Enterprise offer:

▶ View Administrative Reports

▶ Review Information Management Policy Usage Reports

▶ View Web Analytics Reports

The default Administrative reports include CrawlRatePerContentSource, CrawlRatePerType, QueryLatency, QueryLatencyTrend, and SharePointBackendQueryLatency. The Web Analytics reports provide metrics on items such as Total Number of Page Views, Average Number of Page View per Day, Total Number of Daily Unique Visitors per Day, and other metrics, as shown in Figure 18.9. Note that when the Analyze tab is selected, the farm

18

administrator has the option to filter by criteria such as Preceding Day, Preceding 7 Days, Preceding 30 Days, and under the More drop-down menu, 90, 180, 365, or Custom Dates. This allows the farm administrator to get an "instant" overview of high-level activities transpiring on the farm, and she can also export these to a spreadsheet it desired.

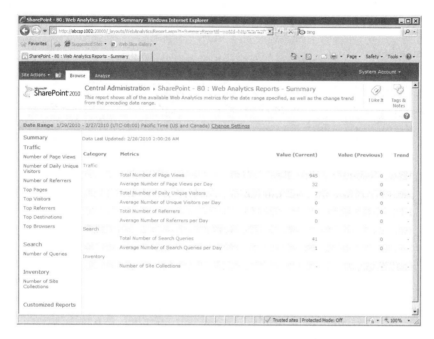

FIGURE 18.9   Web Analytics report for a SharePoint site collection.

Comparing General Application Settings in SharePoint Foundation 2010 and SharePoint Server 2010 Enterprise

Although the home page of the Central Administration site shows similar features and tools available between SharePoint Foundation 2010 and SharePoint Server 2010 Enterprise, there are some revealing differences in the General Application Settings page, as shown in Table 18.4. The only tools provided in SharePoint Foundation 2010 are the External Service Connections tools and the SharePoint Designer settings tool.

TABLE 18.4   Comparing General Application Settings in SharePoint Foundation 2010 to SharePoint Server 2010 Enterprise

Tool	Included in SharePoint Foundation 2010?	Included in SharePoint Server 2010 Standard?	Included in SharePoint Server 2010 Enterprise?
External Service Connections	Yes	Yes	Yes

TABLE 18.4   Continued

Tool	Included in SharePoint Foundation 2010?	Included in SharePoint Server 2010 Standard?	Included in SharePoint Server 2010 Enterprise?
InfoPath Forms Services	No	No	Yes
Site Directory	No	Yes	Yes
SharePoint Designer	Yes	Yes	Yes
Search	No	Yes	Yes
Content Deployment	No	Yes	Yes

SharePoint Server 2010 Standard and Enterprise provide numerous other tools such as InfoPath Forms Services (Enterprise edition only), Site Directory, Search, and Content Deployment tools. InfoPath Forms Services allows farm administrators to make InfoPath forms available via the web browser to SharePoint users, and these users do not need to have InfoPath available on their desktops. The Site Directory tool allows the farm administrator to define a site directory, which is a site that captures new site collections, which is helpful in larger organizations where there may be hundreds or thousands of sites created, and grouping them in logical subgroups can make navigation much easier for end users.

As mentioned in the "Search in SharePoint Foundation 2010 and SharePoint Server 2010" section, earlier in this chapter, both SharePoint Foundation 2010 and SharePoint Server 2010 provide basic search tools, but SharePoint Server 2010 provides a number of additional management tools that may be of interest during the architecture and design process. The General Application Settings page provides access to a selection of farm-level search settings, such as proxy server, timeout, and the option to ignore Secure Sockets Layer (SSL) warnings. In addition, crawler impact rules can be set here, which allow the farm administrator to fine-tune how many documents are requested at a time from sites being crawled by SharePoint Server 2010.

NOTE

Search is a bit confusing from a design and management standpoint because there are different tools available for SharePoint Foundation 2010 search and more advanced configuration and management tools for SharePoint Server 2010 Standard and Enterprise Search. In addition, there is the Search Server Express 2010 product that can be added to SharePoint Foundation 2010 and the FAST Search product that can be added to the SharePoint Server 2010 products, making the overall design process somewhat complex for organizations new to the SharePoint 2010 product line.

Finally, content deployment is also only included in SharePoint Server 2010 Standard or Enterprise, and is used to deploy content from one site collection to another site collection. This is typically used by organizations who create content in one tier (for example, a staging tier), and then publish it regularly to a production tier, which could house the production intranet portal, or to an external Internet-facing farm that houses an Internet website. Content deployment requires the creation of paths and jobs, which can be full or incremental.

Site Collection Options in SharePoint Foundation 2010 and SharePoint Server 2010

A basic decision that all farm administrators must make at least once is which type of site collection template to use when configuring a new site collection. SharePoint Foundation 2010 provides a number of different templates for creating new site collections that are listed in Table 18.5. Team Site is typically the most widely used, but SharePoint Server 2010 Standard and Enterprise provide a number of other options, including the popular Publishing Portal, Document Center, and Records Center options.

TABLE 18.5   Templates Available in SharePoint Foundation 2010 and SharePoint Server 2010

Template Name	Available in SharePoint Foundation 2010?	Available in SharePoint Server 2010 Standard?	Available in SharePoint Server 2010 Enterprise?
Team Site	Yes	Yes	Yes
Blank Site	Yes	Yes	Yes
Document Workspace	Yes	Yes	Yes
Blog	Yes	Yes	Yes
Group Work Site	Yes	Yes	Yes
Visio Process Repository	No	Yes	Yes
Basic Meeting Workspace	Yes	Yes	Yes
Blank Meeting Workspace	Yes	Yes	Yes
Decision Meeting Workspace	Yes	Yes	Yes
Social Meeting Workspace	Yes	Yes	Yes

TABLE 18.5   Continued

Template Name	Available in SharePoint Foundation 2010?	Available in SharePoint Server 2010 Standard?	Available in SharePoint Server 2010 Enterprise?
Multipage Meeting Workspace	Yes	Yes	Yes
Document Center	No	Yes	Yes
Records Center	No	Yes	Yes
Business Intelligence Center	No	No	Yes
Enterprise Search Center	No	Yes	Yes
My Site Host	No	Yes	Yes
Basic Search Center	No	Yes	Yes
FAST Search Center	No	No	Yes
Publishing Portal	No	Yes	Yes
Enterprise Wiki	No	Yes	Yes
Select Template Later	Yes	Yes	Yes

A detailed review of each of these templates is beyond the scope of this chapter. Chapter 21, "Designing and Managing Pages and Sites for Knowledge Workers," provides additional details on the pros and cons of different site collections and site templates. This chapter also discusses the differences between publishing sites and nonpublishing sites.

It is worth mentioning that site collections can be nested; so, for example, a SharePoint Server 2010 Enterprise farm administrator can create a top-level site collection using the Team Site template, and then create nested site collections using a Records Center, Social Meeting Workspace, and Business Intelligence Center if needed. Some additional configuration is needed to "tell" SharePoint that site collections are nested using the managed path tool.

Site Settings Compared in SharePoint Foundation 2010 and SharePoint Server 2010

After a site collection has been created by the farm administrator, the site administrator will then have a selection of tools at his disposal. Table 18.6 shows the site collection administration tools available to site admins of SharePoint Foundation 2010 and SharePoint Server 2010 Standard and Enterprise site collections.

TABLE 18.6   Site Collection Administration Tools in SharePoint Foundation 2010 and SharePoint Server 2010 Standard and Enterprise

Tool Name	Available in SharePoint Foundation 2010?	Available in SharePoint Server 2010 Standard?	Available in SharePoint Server 2010 Enterprise?
Search Settings	No	Yes	Yes
Search Scopes	No	Yes	Yes
Search Keywords	No	Yes	Yes
Recycle Bin	Yes	Yes	Yes
Site Collection Features	Yes	Yes	Yes
Site Hierarchy	Yes	Yes	Yes
Site Collection Audit Settings	No	Yes	Yes
Audit Log Reports	No	Yes	Yes
Portal Site Connection	Yes	Yes	Yes
Site Collection Policies	No	Yes	Yes
Content Type Publishing	No	Yes	Yes
SharePoint Designer Settings	Yes	Yes	Yes
Visual Upgrade	Yes	Yes	Yes
Help Settings	Yes	Yes	Yes

From a complexity standpoint, SharePoint Foundation 2010 can be seen as a better choice for organizations that don't have experienced SharePoint administrators on staff, or where staff members are overwhelmed with daily activities and pursuing training is not a viable option. It can also be noted that a number of the tools not available in SharePoint Foundation 2010 could be very valuable for SharePoint administrators, such as Audit Log Reports and Site Collection Policies.

Figure 18.10 shows the AuditSettings.aspx page available to site administrators in SharePoint Server 2010 Standard or Enterprise. The audit log can audit events such as opening or downloading documents, viewing items, editing items, deleting items, searching site content, or editing users and permissions. This is a more complete list of activities that can be audited than the basic tools available in SharePoint Foundation 2010, which provides access to just the very limited Web Analytics tools found on the Site Settings page. Note that a SharePoint Foundation 2010 farm administrator can access more complete reports from the Central Administration site (discussed previously in the "Comparing the Monitoring Tools in SharePoint Foundation 2010 and SharePoint Server 2010 Enterprise" section), but in most organizations, the number of users allowed to access the farm-level management tools is very limited.

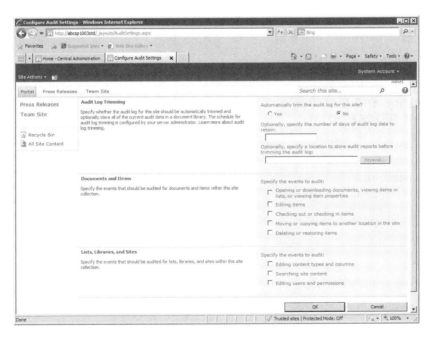

FIGURE 18.10   Configure Audit Settings page in SharePoint Server 2010 Standard.

Site collection policies can be created by a site administrator in SharePoint Server 2010 Standard or Enterprise and can include retention policies, auditing, use of barcodes, and use of labels. These are powerful tools that can be very valuable or even essential to more complex document management solutions. For example, a retention policy created in a site collection policy causes a stage to activate a certain amount of time after the created date, last modified, or declared record date of an item, and allows the site administrator to determine what action is triggered at that stage, with the following options: move to recy-cling bin, permanently delete, transfer to another location, start a workflow, skip to next stage, declare record, delete previous drafts, and delete all previous versions. A site collec-tion policy can be a handy house-cleaning tool, enabling all earlier versions of a document to be deleted after a period of time since the last modification (for example, one year).

Additional tools available within a publishing site in SharePoint Server 2010 Standard or Enterprise include the following:

- ▶ Site Collection Cache Profiles
- ▶ Site Collection Output Cache
- ▶ Site Collection Object Cache
- ▶ Content Type Service Application Error Log (Enterprise only)
- ▶ Variations
- ▶ Variation Labels
- ▶ Translatable Columns
- ▶ Variation Logs
- ▶ Suggested Content Browser Locations

Document Library and List Options in SharePoint Foundation 2010 and SharePoint Server 2010

The next topic to review is the differences in list, library, and page options between the products. It is important to mention that the base functionality in document libraries is similar between SharePoint Foundation 2010 and SharePoint Server 2010 with the same basic tools available in the different versions. These include the following:

- ▶ New Document/Upload Document
- ▶ New Folder
- ▶ Edit Document
- ▶ Check Out/Check In/Discard Check Out
- ▶ View Properties/Edit Properties
- ▶ Version History
- ▶ Document Permissions
- ▶ Delete Document
- ▶ Email a Link
- ▶ Download a Copy/Send To/Manage Copies/Go To Source
- ▶ Workflows
- ▶ Publish/Unpublish/Approve/Reject/Cancel Approval

However, SharePoint Server 2010 Standard and Enterprise add the I Like It and the Tags and Notes options, which can be valuable to collect social information and metadata.

Within the document library settings for SharePoint Foundation 2010, you have a more limited selection of tools to work with, as shown in Table 18.7.

TABLE 18.7   Tools Available in a Document Library in Different Versions of SharePoint 2010

Tool Name	Available in SharePoint Foundation 2010?	Available in SharePoint Server 2010 Standard?	Available in SharePoint Server 2010 Enterprise?
Title, Description, and Navigation	Yes	Yes	Yes
Versioning Settings	Yes	Yes	Yes
Advanced Settings	Yes	Yes	Yes
Validation Settings	Yes	Yes	Yes
Common Default Value Settings	No	Yes	Yes
Rating Settings	No	Yes	Yes
Audience Targeting Settings	No	Yes	Yes
Metadata Navigation Settings	No	Yes	Yes
Per-Location View Settings	No	Yes	Yes
Form Settings	No	No	Yes
Delete This Document Library	Yes	Yes	Yes
Save Document Library as Template	Yes	Yes	Yes
Permissions for This Document Library	Yes	Yes	Yes
Manage Files Which Have No Checked in Version	Yes	Yes	Yes
Workflow Settings	Yes	Yes	Yes
Generate File Plan Report	No	Yes	Yes

18

continues

TABLE 18.7   Continued

Tool Name	Available in SharePoint Foundation 2010?	Available in SharePoint Server 2010 Standard?	Available in SharePoint Server 2010 Enterprise?
Enterprise Metadata and Keywords Settings	No	Yes	Yes
Information Management Policy Settings	No	Yes	Yes
RSS Settings	Yes	Yes	Yes

Chapter 19, "Using Libraries and Lists in SharePoint 2010," covers these tools in more detail, including how they will affect the day-to-day experience of document library users.

Table 18.8 continues the comparison between SharePoint Foundation 2010 and SharePoint Server 2010 capabilities by covering the different library and list options available from the create.aspx page on a site. As expected, some additional lists and libraries can be created if SharePoint Server 2010 Standard or Enterprise are installed, but these are limited and only include the Asset Library, Slide Library, Data Connection Library, Report Library, and Status List, as shown in the table.

TABLE 18.8   Library and List Options in SharePoint Foundation 2010 and SharePoint Server 2010 Standard and Enterprise

Template Name	Available in SharePoint Foundation 2010?	Available in SharePoint Server 2010 Standard?	Available in SharePoint Server 2010 Enterprise?
Document Library	Yes	Yes	Yes
Form Library	Yes	Yes	Yes
Wiki Page Library	Yes	Yes	Yes
Picture Library	Yes	Yes	Yes
Asset Library	No	Yes	Yes
Slide Library	No	Yes	Yes
Data Connection Library	No	No	Yes
Report Library	No	No	Yes
Announcements	Yes	Yes	Yes
Contacts	Yes	Yes	Yes

TABLE 18.8   Continued

Template Name	Available in SharePoint Foundation 2010?	Available in SharePoint Server 2010 Standard?	Available in SharePoint Server 2010 Enterprise?
Discussion Board	Yes	Yes	Yes
Links	Yes	Yes	Yes
Calendar	Yes	Yes	Yes
Tasks	Yes	Yes	Yes
Project Tasks	Yes	Yes	Yes
Issue Tracking	Yes	Yes	Yes
Survey	Yes	Yes	Yes
Custom List	Yes	Yes	Yes
Custom List in Datasheet View	Yes	Yes	Yes
External List	Yes	Yes	Yes
Import Spreadsheet	Yes	Yes	Yes
Status List	No	No	Yes
Page	Yes	Yes	Yes
Web Part Page	Yes	Yes	Yes
Blog	Yes	Yes	Yes

18

Web Parts Available in SharePoint Foundation 2010 and SharePoint Server 2010

The final comparison for this chapter covers web parts available in the different versions of SharePoint 2010 products. Web parts are the modules of code that can be added to a page to provide views of data contained within lists or libraries on the site or to perform other tasks such as filter data or display a video on a page. Essentially, web parts are the units of construction the page designer has at his disposal to present text, data, and graphics to site visitors, so the more web parts available, the more flexibility the designer has in creating pages and sites.

It stands to reason that SharePoint Foundation 2010 would provide a smaller selection of web parts for use by site administrators after a site has been created. Table 18.9 lists the web parts available in SharePoint Foundation 2010 and SharePoint Server 2010 Standard and Enterprise when viewing the Web Part Gallery from a site created using the Team Site

site collection template. Although this is a daunting list, and the average site administrator won't need to know what each and every web part does, the list is helpful from a design standpoint, especially if an organization is trying to decide between SharePoint Foundation 2010 and the SharePoint Server 2010 products and whether SharePoint Server 2010 Enterprise is needed.

TABLE 18.9   Web Parts Available in SharePoint Foundation 2010 and SharePoint Server 2010

Web Part	Available in SharePoint Foundation 2010?	Available in SharePoint Server 2010 Standard?	Available in SharePoint Server 2010 Enterprise?
AdvancedSearchBox.dwp	No	Yes	Yes
AuthoredListFilter.webpart	No	No	Yes
BusinessDataActionsWebPart.dwp	No	No	Yes
BusinessDataAssociationWebPart.webpart	No	No	Yes
BusinessDataDetailsWebPart.webpart	No	No	Yes
BusinessDataFilter.dwp	No	No	Yes
BusinesDatItemBuilder.dwp	No	No	Yes
BusinessDataListWebPart.webpart	No	No	Yes
CategoryResultsWebPart	No	Yes	Yes
CategoryWebPart.webpart	No	Yes	Yes
Contactwp.dwp	No	Yes	Yes
DateFilter.dwp	No	No	Yes
DualChineseSearch.dwp	No	Yes	Yes
FilterAction.dwp	No	No	Yes
IndicatorWebPart.dwp	No	No	Yes
KpiListWebPart.dwp	No	No	Yes
Microsoft.Office.Excel. WebUI.dwp	No	No	Yes
Microsoft.Office.InfoPath. Server.BrowserForm.webpart	No	No	Yes
MossChartWebPart.webpart	No	No	Yes
MSContentEditor.dwp	Yes	Yes	Yes
MSImage.dwp	Yes	Yes	Yes

TABLE 18.9   Continued

Web Part	Available in SharePoint Foundation 2010?	Available in SharePoint Server 2010 Standard?	Available in SharePoint Server 2010 Enterprise?
MSMembers.dwp	Yes	Yes	Yes
MSPageViewer.dwp	Yes	Yes	Yes
MSPictureLibrarySlideshow.webpart	Yes	Yes	Yes
MSSimpleForm.dwp	Yes	Yes	Yes
MSUserDocs.dwp	Yes	Yes	Yes
MSUserTasks.dwp	Yes	Yes	Yes
MSXML.dwp	Yes	Yes	Yes
OlapFilter.dwp	No	No	Yes
Owa.dwp	No	Yes	Yes
Owacalendar.dwp	No	Yes	Yes
Owacontacts.dwp	No	Yes	Yes
Owainbox.dwp	No	Yes	Yes
Owatasks.dwp	No	Yes	Yes
PageContextFilter.webpart	No	No	Yes
PeopleRefinement.webpart	No	Yes	Yes
PeopleSearchBox.dwp	No	Yes	Yes
PeopleSearchCoreResults.webpart	No	Yes	Yes
ProfileBrowser.dwp	No	Yes	Yes
QueryStringFilter.webpart	No	No	Yes
QuerySuggestions.webpart	No	Yes	Yes
Refinement.webpart	No	Yes	Yes
RSSViewer.webpart	No	Yes	Yes
SearchActionLinks.webpart	No	Yes	Yes
SearchBestBets.webpart	No	Yes	Yes
SearchBox.dwp	No	Yes	Yes
SearchCoreResults.webpart	No	Yes	Yes
Searchpaging.dwp	No	No	Yes

continues

18

TABLE 18.9   Continued

Web Part	Available in SharePoint Foundation 2010?	Available in SharePoint Server 2010 Standard?	Available in SharePoint Server 2010 Enterprise?
Searchstats.dwp	No	No	Yes
Searchsummary.dwp	No	No	Yes
Silverlight.webpart	Yes	Yes	Yes
Siteframer.dwp	No	Yes	Yes
SocialComment.dwp	No	Yes	Yes
SpListFilter	No	No	Yes
SummaryResults.webpart	No	Yes	Yes
TagCloud.dwp	No	Yes	Yes
TextFilter.dwp	No	No	Yes
TopAnswer.webpart	No	Yes	Yes
UserContextFilter.webpart	No	No	Yes
VisioWebAccess.dwp	No	No	Yes
VisualBestBet	No	No	Yes
WhatsPopularWebPart.dwp	No	Yes	Yes
WSRPConsumerWebPart.dwp	No	No	Yes

For example, the Business Data web parts can be found only in SharePoint Server 2010 Enterprise, along with the KPI web part, again clarifying that adding that functionality to a web part page or dashboard page requires SharePoint Server 2010 Enterprise. Likewise, the People web parts, Search web parts, and OWA web parts are not included in SharePoint Foundation 2010. So, if that level of functionality is desired, the SharePoint Server 2010 products are needed.

Summary

This chapter addresses differences between SharePoint Foundation 2010 and SharePoint Server 2010. Although not every possible difference between the products can be addressed in a single chapter, comparisons were provided on many different levels to help decision makers, designers, and architects make informed decisions about which product best meets their organization's requirements. For many organizations, this content will be a starting point, and will lead to more in-depth conversations about the pros and cons of different approaches, which might require hands-on testing to come to a final decision.

Best Practices

- ▶ Understanding the basics of service applications and which ones are available in SharePoint Foundation 2010 can help architects and decision makers determine whether SharePoint Foundation 2010 might meet their needs.

- ▶ SharePoint Foundation 2010 offers feature-rich search capabilities, but this is only a subset of the search tools and capabilities of the Search Service application included with SharePoint Server 2010 Standard and Enterprise.

- ▶ Business Connectivity Services (BCS) can be extremely useful for accessing data stored in other databases and services, but generally requires developers who are trained in SharePoint Designer 2010 or Visual Studio 2010.

- ▶ Managed Metadata Services should be strongly considered by any organization interested in leveraging metadata standards via site columns and content types who have multiple site collections.

- ▶ The PerformancePoint tools are now integrated with SharePoint Server 2010 Enterprise edition and provide an extremely powerful set of tools to create dashboards, scorecards, and key performance indicators for analysis of data from a variety of courses. As with BCS, effectively leveraging these tools requires training for power users and most likely developers' time.

- ▶ This chapter provides multiple tables comparing a wide range of features for decision makers, designers, and architects to help them make more informed decisions about which version of the SharePoint 2010 family to choose. It is suggested that the tables be used as starting points for discussions about which tools and features are required for the success of the SharePoint implementation for the organization.

18

Using Libraries and Lists in SharePoint 2010

Lists and libraries are two fundamental building blocks of a SharePoint 2010 environment and offer the tools that dramatically differentiate SharePoint from a file share. They allow users to manage documents by uploading them to libraries or to manage rows of information in a list—similar to a spreadsheet in many ways—manage versions, alert the user if anything changes, and offer a wide range of other powerful features. The goal of this chapter is to present a high-level overview of the standard tools offered in libraries and lists provided by SharePoint Server 2010 and SharePoint Foundation 2010. Examples are provided to illustrate the capabilities of the basic tools that will be most commonly used by end users and library and list administrators.

The next three chapters cover related topics that will be of interest to information workers, architects, and managers alike. Chapter 20, "Customizing and Managing Libraries and List to Meet Business Requirements," builds on the content provided in this chapter to provide additional information about the standard management tasks required to customize and maintain sites and workspaces. Chapter 21, "Designing and Managing Pages and Sites for Knowledge Workers," moves beyond lists and libraries to focus on the design and management of the containers that hold them and that provide views of the data and files contained within. And then Chapter 22, "Managing Metadata and Content Types in SharePoint 2010," focuses on the complex topic of metadata for readers interested in the process of building a vibrant taxonomy for the organization.

NOTE

This chapter assumes that users are using the Windows 7 operating system, with Internet Explorer 8. For users with different environments, be sure to test the appropriate combination of operating system and browser, and be aware that the user experience may vary based on the combination of software products used. For example, the experience of a user with Windows XP, IE 6, and Office 2003 will differ from that of a user with Windows 7, IE 8, and Office 2010. Likewise, a user with a Macintosh using Safari will also have a different experience.

Empowering Users Through SharePoint 2010 Libraries

Many users wonder what the difference is between simply continuing to store their files in a file share on their network, keeping them on their local hard drives to make sure they are close at hand, or using their email in boxes as storage and management tools. They also want to understand the differences in level of effort required to use the SharePoint tools, and get an inkling of the benefits they and their organization will see after investing in the new technologies presented by the SharePoint 2010 product line.

SharePoint 2010 document libraries offer a variety of features that have proven to be useful to a wide range of users and projects and that empower the site administrators to customize the storage and collaborative features of the library and enhance user productivity. Advantages provided by a SharePoint document library include the following:

▶ The administrator of a document library has a great deal of control over who can add, modify, and delete documents, or just read them, which often is not the case if a file share on the network is being used. Therefore, a departmental manager can easily control the set of users who can read or modify documents under her control without filing a help desk ticket or needing special privileges on the network. Permissions can be modified for an individual document or folder within the document library, as well.

▶ Versioning can be turned on for a document library that keeps a complete copy of previous versions of the document for reference or recovery purposes. Both major and minor versions can be tracked, encouraging a more formal process of determining when a document is ready for general use or still in the development cycle.

▶ Alerts can be set on a document within the library, a folder in the library, or for the entire library so that the user receives an email notification if a document is modified, added, or deleted and can set other criteria, such as weekly summaries to minimize in-box clutter.

▶ Documents can be checked out, with the name of the person who has the document checked out listed in the library, so that other users can't modify the document. Checking out can be required before a user can edit a document to further ensure best practices for document editing.

▶ A template can be stored in the document library that can be used to create a new document that is stored in the library by default. So, for example, a document library designed to hold technical specifications documents can provide a Word template document with the latest format, layout, and sections in it.

▶ Metadata can be added to a document library that enables users to better describe what type of document it is based on company standards (for example, Proposal, Project Plan, Report, Procedure), which product it covers, who owns the document (as opposed to who last modified it), or pretty much any other kind of textual or numerical information. SharePoint 2010 adds more control over default settings in a document library and allows ratings to be added. Figure 19.1 shows ratings in the far-right column.

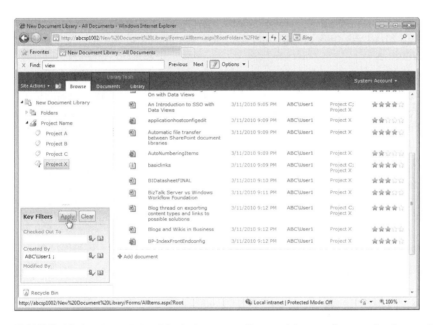

FIGURE 19.1   SharePoint 2010 document library with metadata navigation tools and Ratings column.

▶ Views can be created that group documents by certain criteria, sort them by any of the columns in the library, or only display documents that meet certain criteria. For example, the view from the home page may well be different from the view within the document library to minimize the amount of space taken up on the home page and to only show the last ten documents modified, for example.

▶ The ability to search within the library for text contained within the document, a feature often not available on a corporate network. In addition, the ability to search the metadata associated with a document makes it easier for users to find the desired document more quickly. Entering a search term in the search bar in a SharePoint

19

2010 document library defaults to the This List scope, and the user can then expand and fine tune the search from the search results page.

▶ If the organization decides on certain standards for the customization of a document library, it can create a template that can include the content if desired and can be used in other sites. This helps promote standards for document library design and features supported.

▶ SharePoint 2010 libraries offer additional features such as the I Like It tag, and additional tags and notes can be added to documents by users to encourage comments and input from the users.

▶ Metadata navigation allows users of the library to easily click a few items and filter what appears in the view. Figure 19.1 shows an example of how a user chooses to view only documents with metadata tags of Project X for Project Name, and that were modified by User1. This feature is new to SharePoint 2010 and more intuitive and easy to use than the filters in SharePoint 2007, which had to be accessed at the top of the columns.

▶ Workflows can be created on-the-fly or predesigned for use within the document library to get feedback or approval, or more complex workflows can be designed by developers to start more complex processes that involve more complex actions and business logic. A Quick Step can be defined that appears on the Ribbon to allow one-click actions that are custom designed for the library users.

▶ Incremental changes in the document library such as the Ribbon interface, and the ability to check the document or documents you are working on, make it easier for administrators and end users to quickly come up to speed with the array of tools offered in the document library. Figure 19.2 shows the Ribbon interface, with the Documents tab active, and three documents selected, and the cursor hovering over the Delete button.

▶ The contents of the document library can be downloaded to SharePoint Workspace or the Outlook client so that it can be accessed when the user is offline.

▶ A two-stage recycle bin is available, to rescue users' documents from the inevitable accidental deletions that occur.

NOTE

Mastering all of these features can be complex for the document library administrator as well as for the users. It is important to balance the complexity of the library and the number of features leveraged with the sophistication of the typical users of the library, and the type of content that will be stored in the document library. Better to "start simple" with a few metadata columns, the ratings column, versioning enabled, and standard workflows, than to overcomplicate the document library if users are brand new to SharePoint. On the other hand, if the document library users have been using SharePoint 2007 for several years, it can make sense to enable more complex features, such as complex metadata, document workspaces, and custom workflows.

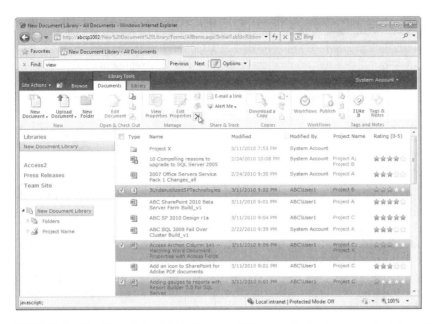

FIGURE 19.2   SharePoint 2010 document library with the Documents tab on the Ribbon visible, and several documents selected.

Although a percentage of users of SharePoint document libraries may complain about learning yet a new software application, after a little training, they will quickly appreciate the features that make their working day more productive. For example, one immediate benefit of having versioning enabled is that only the latest version shows up in the document library. This means that users don't have to spend extra time deciphering complex filenames or looking at modification dates to make sure they are in fact editing the latest version. The ability to check out a document makes it easy for a user to "reserve" a document that he doesn't want anyone else modifying and knows he needs to work on over the weekend. By allowing users to rate documents, the document library takes on an added dimension of social interaction, further differentiating best-of-breed documents from mediocre and worst-of-breed documents.

Administrators will quickly come to appreciate the ability to add new columns of information to a document library that help them manage their documents, and help their users quickly find the exact document they are looking for, to create customized views, and leverage granular search, and metadata navigation. For example, by simply adding a column called Client, a sales manager can make it clear which client a document was created for. In addition, by providing a column titled Value of Opportunity, the total dollar amount of the proposal can easily be seen without opening the document. And if the Ratings column is enabled, an administrator can see over time which documents are the most popular and well received, and learn about the needs of the users, as well as archive the less-useful documents if applicable.

NOTE

The inclusion of the Ribbon interface in SharePoint 2010 is more than just a cosmetic change. It dramatically reduces the learning curve for new and existing users and administrators alike. The large number of tools available to users and admins are now available in a tabbed interface in one place, rather than spread out among different drop-down menus, and the use of visually relevant icons truly makes a difference and reduces the learning process.

Using the View All Site Content Page in SharePoint 2010

SharePoint 2010 offers a number of different libraries, which will be compared later in this chapter, but it is important to understand which type of document library you are working with. This may not be that easy if you are using a SharePoint 2010 environment created by someone else, so a good place to start is by accessing the View All Site Content link from the Site Actions drop-down menu or from the bottom of the Quick Launch area under the Recycle Bin. Figure 19.3 shows the viewlsts.aspx page revealing the document libraries and picture libraries on the site (in this case, a SharePoint Server 2010 Enterprise publishing site).

FIGURE 19.3   View All Site Content page in SharePoint Server 2010 Enterprise for a publishing site.

This is a useful page to visit because it gives the visitor a summary of all the lists and libraries that she has access to. Other information is obvious on this page, such as the names of the libraries and the lists, any notes provided about a specific library or list, and the number of items in each one and the last modified date. This gives a very quick overview of how complex the site is, which lists and libraries have been modified the most recently, and how many items in each one. If none of the lists or libraries have been modified in a number of months, for example, it is a clear indication that no one has added, modified, or deleted content on the site in that amount of time, and it might be time to find out why.

As mentioned previously, the viewlsts.aspx page is for a publishing site, and a subset of the notes visible in Figure 19.3 state the library "was created by the Publishing feature...," which clearly identify the site as a publishing enabled site, a topic that will be covered in more detail in Chapter 21. Note also in Figure 19.3 that a number of lists have no notes in the central column, which simply means that a user or administrator created the list or library and decided not to add any notes during the creation process. In addition, there are different icons next to different types of libraries.

> **NOTE**
>
> It is generally a bad idea to delete or rename document libraries created by SharePoint during a site creation (which will be clarified on the viewlsts.aspx page in the notes provided for the library) because they might store documents important to the functionality of the site.

The different libraries offered in the different SharePoint 2010 products are listed in Chapter 18, "SharePoint Foundation Versus SharePoint Server 2010," in the section titled "Document Library and List Options in SharePoint Foundation 2010 and SharePoint Server 2010."

A Brief Tour of a Document Library

This section summarizes the main features of a document library to provide an overview of the tools and features provided, and then the following section drills down more deeply into more of these tools

Figure 19.4 shows a document library titled New Documents at the root of a Team Site created in SharePoint Foundation 2010. Note that as shown in the URL, the view displayed is the AllItems.aspx page. The basic components include navigation tools in the Quick Launch area on the left, which includes links to libraries and lists the site administrator has chosen to include in the Quick Launch, as well as the Recycle Bin and All Site Content links. The Ribbon tools along the top include the Site Action drop-down menu, Navigate Up icon, and Browse, Documents, and Library tools tabs. Figure19.4 shows the cursor hovering over a drop-down menu under the All Documents item in the breadcrumb, which is the new location for the View drop-down menu that used to be located on the right side of the toolbar in SharePoint 2007 products. On the right side can be found a search field, and a ? button that will access the Help feature.

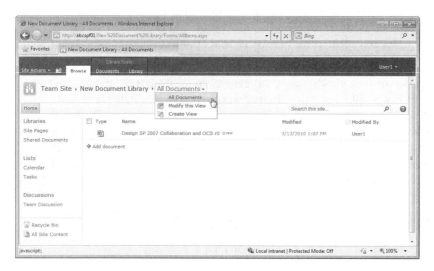

FIGURE 19.4   Document library in a team site.

In the working area, one document is visible with a Word icon in the Type column, name of the document in the Name column, modified date in the Modified column, and modified-by information in the Modified By column. It is worth noting that because SharePoint 2010 is a fourth-generation product, Microsoft has worked diligently and taken end-user input to create an environment that provides a good combination of aesthetics, features, and usability, and SharePoint 2010 has an excellent balance of these components. Be aware that smaller monitors may limit a user's productivity if it can't display at least a 1024×768 resolution.

Adding Documents to a Document Library

The primary means of adding items to a document library is to access the Add Document link, which lives at the bottom of the working area of the document library. Figure 19.5 shows the Upload Document window that opens when this link is clicked, and this window provides the Browse button, which allows the user to browse for and select a single document for uploading, and a check box to Overwrite Existing Files.

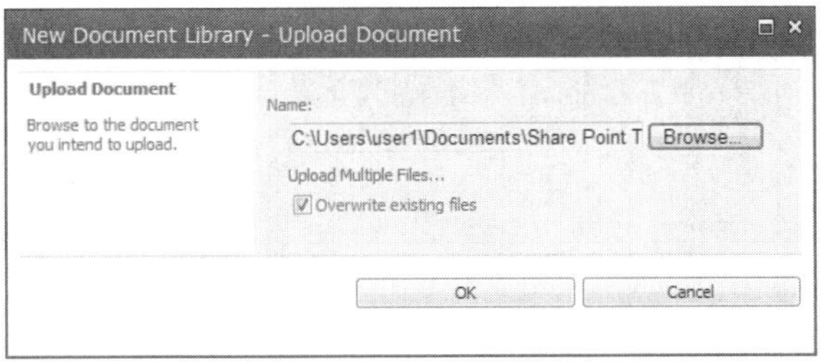

FIGURE 19.5   Upload Document window.

NOTE

The SharePoint 2010 now employ AJAX for the pop-up menus instead of aspx pages for most data input prompts. AJAX stands for Asynchronous JavaScript and XML and arguably offers many advantages over the previous system of having a new aspx page render for data entry. To begin with, the previous page stays in the background and does not need to be re-rendered or downloaded when the AJAX window is gathering input, as shown in Figure 19.5. Less data is being transferred between the server and the client, and with hundreds or thousands of simultaneous connections this can add up to a significant difference. It should be noted also that the AJAX interfaces aren't actual SharePoint pages, so you can't bookmark them or use the back and forward buttons to navigate through them. Finally, the options for resizing the windows are limited for many of the interfaces (standard size or full screen), which might affect user experience.

There is also a link to Upload Multiple Files, which is shown in Figure 19.6, and is dramatically different from the SharePoint 2007 Upload Multiple Documents, which launched an Office component for browsing for and uploading multiple documents. SharePoint 2010 Upload Multiple Documents window enables the user to drag files and folders from a Windows Explorer window to the upload pane, or to click a Browse for Files Instead link. The process of dragging files and folders to the upload pane is more flexible because the user can drag over virtually any combinations of folders and files, as shown in Figure 19.6, where the user has dragged a folder and two documents from the Windows Explorer window. The Upload Multiple Documents window lists upload information; there are four files to upload, for a total of 693KB in the example given in Figure 19.6. After the upload has completed, the user has to then close the window.

Users of previous SharePoint products might wonder what happened to the Explorer view, because it does not appear in the drop-down list of views in Figure 19.4. This tool can now be found on the Library tab in a document library, and is titled Open in Explorer. For users new to the SharePoint world, the Explorer view is a standard view in SharePoint document libraries that allows users to add documents to the library by copying from Windows Explorer and pasting into Explorer View in the document library and clicking Paste. While this is a "bread and butter" tool for many users, it can be a headache for SharePoint administrators because it doesn't work with all desktop configurations.

19

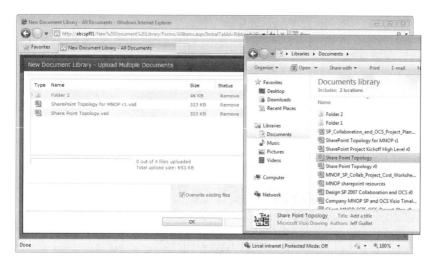

FIGURE 19.6   Upload Multiple Documents window.

Another method that will be of interest to power users is the ability to enter in the address of the document library into the address bar of Windows Explorer in the format \\server-name\site\libraryname (also referred to as WebDAV access). Figure 19.7 shows an example where Windows Explorer was opened in Windows 7, the address was entered as \\abcspf01\new document library, and the contents that were just uploaded using the Upload Multiple Documents method appear. If a user right-clicks an item, the normal range of Explorer tools, such as Open, New, Print, Cut, Copy, Delete, and Rename, are available.

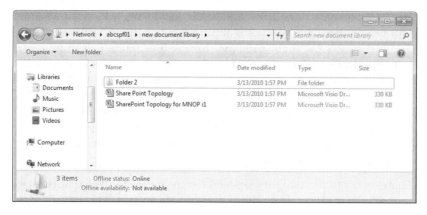

FIGURE 19.7   Accessing a SharePoint document library using Windows Explorer.

NOTE

Explorer view (WebDAV) access is not always available to end users on a corporate network; it might be disabled on purpose, or disabled due to operating system configurations. Microsoft KB Article 841215 (http://support.microsoft.com/kb/841215) provides additional information about the topic, along with ways to remedy this behavior should Explorer view access to SharePoint 2010 content be important to the organization.

An additional method of adding items to a document library is to use the in-bound email feature for the document library. A farm administrator would need to enable inbound email from the Configure Incoming E-Mail Settings page in the Central Administration site, and an email address then assigned to the document library from the Incoming E-Mail Settings link on the Document Library Settings page. After that is enabled, users can send emails with attachments to the document library. The configuration process is covered in Chapter 16, "Configuring Email-Enabled Content, Presence, and Exchange Server Integration."

NOTE

To determine which types of documents are allowed to be uploaded, a farm administrator needs to access Web Applications Management page in Central Administration, where the Blocked File Types icon provides access to all blocked file types. These include .bat, .cmd, .com, .dll, .exe, .vb, and a number of other file types.

NOTE

The default maximum upload size for a SharePoint 2010 document library is inherited from the web application that is managed in the Central Administration site. A farm administrator needs to access the Web Application General Settings for the web application and change the Maximum Upload Size setting, which is 50MB by default. Although this upload size could be theoretically as large as 2GB, most organizations choose to keep this in the range of 100MB to 200MB because "very large" files can take a long time to save and to open when stored in SharePoint. This is an important decision for the organization to make when setting standards for SharePoint governance.

Working with the Other Standard Tools in a Document Library

19

Now that the basic layout of a document library and the process of adding documents to a document library have been covered in the previous section, the additional tools available from the Documents Ribbon and the drop-down menu will be reviewed. A number of tools are available, and the tools differ between SharePoint Foundation 2010 and SharePoint Server 2010 Standard and Enterprise, so the version of SharePoint being used in each case will be clarified. Be aware that the features enabled in the document library and privileges of the user accessing the tools will also affect which tools will and won't display on the Ribbon and the drop-down menu, as well as which will be grayed out or available for use. What you see in your environment may differ from in these examples.

Figure 19.8 shows a SharePoint Foundation 2010 document library with several items in it. For one of these documents, the user has accessed the drop-down menu, which results in a checkmark being added to the left of the document signifying that the document is selected. Note that the Documents tab under Library tools on the Ribbon interface becomes active when the document is selected. The user could also check the box to access the Documents tab and the tools in it rather than accessing the drop-down menu.

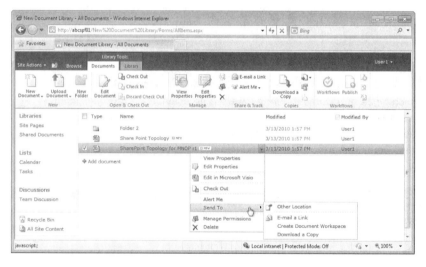

FIGURE 19.8   The Documents tab and drop-down menu for a document in a document library.

The Documents tab is a new feature in SharePoint 2010 that brings the Ribbon interface introduced in Office 2007 products to the SharePoint environment. Note in Figure 19.8 that there is not a direct mirror of tools provided in the Documents tab to what is available in the drop-down menu. The order of the tools in the drop-down menu has stayed similar to the drop-down menu from SharePoint 2007, so users familiar with SharePoint 2007 drop-down menus will immediately be at home with the SharePoint 2010 drop-down menus, even though they might need some time to get familiar with the layout of the tools on the Ribbon.

The tools in the Documents tab are covered in the following sections, from left to right, and will include both the tools from SharePoint Foundation 2010 and SharePoint Server 2010 with comments made on when tools are specific to SharePoint Server 2010.

Working with the New Document and Upload Document Tools

Located to the far left of the Documents tab on the Ribbon, the New Document and Upload Documents tools are frequently used tools that allow a user with sufficient permissions to create a new document using the template assigned to the document library or upload documents. The Upload Document tool was discussed in detail in the "Adding Documents to a Document Library" section and so won't be covered in more detail in this section.

Follow these steps to use the New Document tool:

1. From within a document library, using an account with contributor or greater permissions, click the New Document icon.

2. A warning message may appear when the template.dotx or other template file (if defined by the administrator) loads; click OK.

3. Word 2010 loads and displays the template. Customize the template in whatever fashion desired, and click the Save icon. SharePoint remembers that the template was stored in the document library, so will prompt for a document name to save to the library. Provide a document name and click Save.

4. Click Exit from the File Menu in Word 2010 and Word will close, and the new document will appear in the document library. It will be tagged with a NEW label.

5. Hover over the document in the document library and select View Properties for the new document, and a window will open that shows the properties of the document, including several tools, the Created date and time and user as well as the Last Modified date, time, and user, as shown in Figure 19.9.

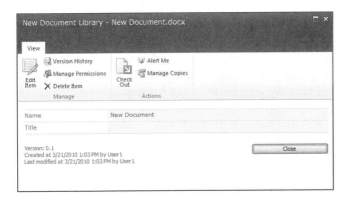

FIGURE 19.9   View Properties for a new document.

The document library administrator can edit the template from the Document Library Settings page, Advanced Settings link. Also, if the document library has been configured to allow management of content types by the library administrator (also available from the Document Library Settings page, Advanced Settings link), the content types available in the document library will appear in this menu.

The Upload Document tool replicates the functionality the Add Document link covered previously in this chapter with the exception that accessing the drop-down menu beneath the icon in the Documents tab of the Ribbon bar gives the option of Uploading Multiple Documents directly. If you click the Add Document link at the bottom of the page, you then have to click a second time to select Upload Multiple Documents. Although not a huge time saver, end users often appreciate tips of this nature.

> **NOTE**
>
> Users will only be able to use tools that their permission levels allow them to use. For example, if a user with reader permissions is visiting a document library, he will not be able to click the Edit Document icon. It will be grayed out because he only has the ability to read documents in the library. However, he can still access some other tools, such as E-mail a Link, Alert Me, and Download a Copy.

Pros and Cons of the New Folder Tool

An icon for the New Folder tool will be available for use to the right of the Upload Document icon, if the library administrator allows the creation of new folders in the document library (accessible from the Document Library Settings page, Advanced Settings link). If the New Folder icon is clicked, the folder can then be named and used to store documents or other folders. Folders can have unique permissions assigned to them, users can create alerts based on the contents of folders, and they can be connected to Outlook, but they are not as manageable as standard items in a document library. For example, metadata columns added to a document library will not be editable for a folder in that document library.

There are various stances about the usefulness of folders in SharePoint that have been argued for years. One point of view is that folders should not be used in SharePoint because they can be seen as keeping alive old and possibly bad habits from file shares. Extending this train of thought, folders in SharePoint are familiar to users, and comforting to less-sophisticated users, and so can have value in their familiarity. Savvy SharePoint document library administrators know that views can be created in document libraries that completely ignore folders and display all contents in a flat hierarchy. Savvy administrators also know that folders can have unique permissions applied to them but also have lived through the difficulties involved in managing document libraries with folder-based and item-based permissions.

Another "minus" of using folders in SharePoint document libraries in SharePoint 2007 was that they made navigation difficult, and it was difficult to see "where you are" in the folder hierarchy. However, SharePoint 2010 now provides an elegant navigation tool, as shown in Figure 19.10, available from the Navigate Up tab to the left of the Browse tab, which clearly shows the folder structure and makes it easy to navigate up the chain to a higher-level folder.

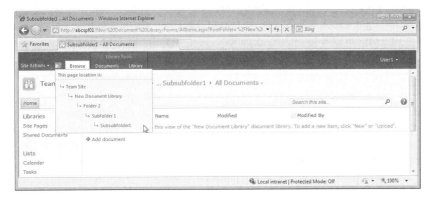

FIGURE 19.10   The Navigate Up tool in a SharePoint document library.

A plus of using folders in SharePoint 2010 becomes apparent if a user accesses the drop-down menu of a folder and then clicks the Connect to Outlook icon. By following the prompts that then appear, assuming the user has a current version of Outlook client installed, he can link the folder or subfolder to Outlook and have the contents of this folder available when offline. This is a handy way to synchronize a portion of the contents of a document library with the Outlook client, rather than synchronizing the entire document library, which could be many megabytes or gigabytes in size.

Finally, the use of folders in SharePoint document libraries that contain many thousands of documents can speed up the performance of the library. For example, a document library with 20,000 documents that doesn't use folders may perform more slowly when a user is using filters to try and find the document she wants, whereas if these documents were split up among 20 folders of roughly 1,000 documents each, the performance within each folder should be faster.

Using the Edit Document Tool, Check Out, Check In, and Discard Check Out Tools

The Edit Document, Check Out, Check In, and Discard Check Out tools are typically the most often-used tools in a collaborative document library, and so time and effort should be dedicated to providing training to end users and administrator on these tools, even if they seem intuitive and "everyone" should know how to use them instinctively.

19

> **NOTE**
>
> It is important to note that desktop configurations can affect the end-user experience with these tools. For example, a user with Office 2003 will have a different experience interacting with documents stored in a SharePoint 2010 document library than a user with Office 2010. The organization should make support materials, FAQs, and training available to users with differing desktop configurations. And don't forget Mac users!

Clicking the Edit Document icon when a document is selected will open the Microsoft Office application and allow the user to edit the document, assuming she has permissions to modify the document in that library. The user may be shown the Open Document window with a warning that "some files can harm your computer" but then can open the file in the appropriate application. Chapter 25, "Using Office 2010 Applications with SharePoint 2010," goes into more detail on best practices of using Office applications with SharePoint 2010.

This is widely considered one of the more important features of a document management system and differentiates SharePoint from a file share and puts it on par with other ECM (enterprise content management) products or document management products.

> **NOTE**
>
> If non-Microsoft file types are going to be stored in document libraries (for example, Adobe Photoshop, Autodesk AutoCAD files), IT should carefully test the behaviors of these files in SharePoint 2010 document libraries. In many cases, users may need to copy the file to their desktop, and then open the file for editing and then save to the desktop, and finally upload back to the SharePoint 2010 document library.

The recommended best practice is for every user to check out a document before he or she is going to work on it. The user will then be asked whether to use the local drafts folder. After the user clicks OK, the document will be checked out, and the Type icon for the document changes to include a small green arrow, as shown in Figure 19.11. If the user elected to use her local drafts folder, a copy of the document will be placed in the SharePoint Drafts folder in the user's Documents folder (which will be created if it doesn't already exist). The options in the drop-down menu now include the tools Check In and Discard Check Out, as shown in Figure 19.11.

> **NOTE**
>
> Checking out a document can be made mandatory by a document library administrator from the Document Library Settings page, Versioning Settings link, and in the Require Check Out section, click Yes under Require Documents to be Checked Out Before They Can Be Edited.

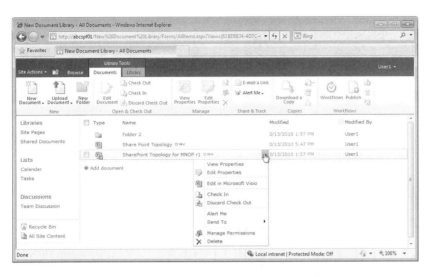

FIGURE 19.11   A checked-out document in a document library.

Now that the user has the document checked out, she can elect to then edit the document or wait until later. Other users will see that the document is checked out by the changed icon, and if the library administrator has elected to include the Checked Out To column in the view of the documents, it will be even more clear not only that the document is checked out, but to whom.

Reviewing the View Properties and Edit Properties Tools

All documents have properties, whether they are saved in SharePoint document libraries or not. Documents have filenames, created date and time, modified date and time, author, and other tags attached to the document. SharePoint allows document library administrators to define additional properties, which are metadata fields, that will be stored in that document library. Unlike some basic file properties, properties defined by metadata fields may get stripped from the document if it is moved to a different document library that doesn't contain the same metadata columns. The View Properties and Edit Properties tools allow users of the library to see what information is available within the document library about the document.

Figure 19.12 shows the Edit Properties window for a document stored in a document library that has been customized with the addition of a Project Name column, Ratings column, Document Owner column, and Type of Document column. A SharePoint Server 2010 Enterprise document library has been used for this example. The version number of the document is visible at the bottom of the window and indicates that versioning is on for the document library, and the Created and Last Modified date, time, and user account information is also provided.

19

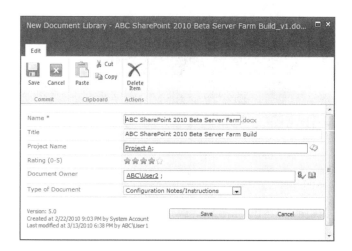

FIGURE 19.12   Edit Properties windows for a document.

The document library administrator chose to add several columns to better categorize documents using metadata and to encourage user participation by asking for users to rate the document. By adding a column titled Document Owner that requires the entry of a domain user account name, it is clearly defined who the ultimate authority is for that specific document. Otherwise, the document library tracks who created the document (or uploaded it) and who last modified it, but neither of these people may actually be responsible for the document. By adding the Type of Document column, a list of options is given to the user to choose from, saving time and encouraging users to better define the type of document because document names can be confusing and may actually give little insight into the type of document it is.

Chapter 22, "Managing Metadata and Content Types in SharePoint 2010," provides more information about this essential topic.

Using the Version History Tool

The next row of buttons on the toolbar includes the Version History, Document Permissions, and Delete Document buttons, each of which is reviewed in this section. Note that Version History will not be available unless versioning is enabled for the document library (accessible through Document Library Settings, Versioning Settings, and then choosing either Create Major Versioning or Create Major and Minor (draft) Versions).

Version history shows the different versions of a document in the library if versioning was enabled in the library, and provides information about changes that were made to the metadata of the document. Figure 19.13 shows a sample version history for a document with several major versions. The topmost version is indicated as being the current published major version, and the date and time modifications that took place are clearly indicated, along with the logged-in user who made the changes, the size of the document, and any comments added.

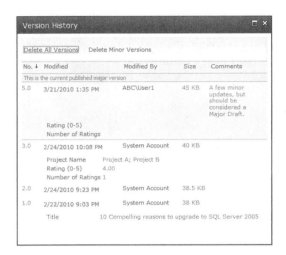

FIGURE 19.13   Version history for a document.

Each version has a drop-down menu that provides the options to View, Restore, and either Unpublish or Delete. The Restore tool will "promote" that version to be the latest version by making a copy of the older version and incrementing the number. Note that there are also tools to Delete All Versions and Delete Minor Versions above the version listing. Chapter 20, "Customizing and Managing Libraries and Lists to Meet Business Requirements," provides more information about the options for versioning and pros and cons of these options.

> **NOTE**
>
> Versioning is such an important feature in SharePoint 2010 that it is critical that administrators and end users feel comfortable with working with major and minor versions. They also must understand the importance of following best practices of always checking out documents before working on them, then checking them back in when complete, and deciding whether the new version should be a minor or draft version (0.1, 0.2 version) or a major or published version (1.0, 2.0 version). Comments should always be added when checking a file back in to facilitate later review of previous versions, if necessary.

Versioning is discussed in more detail in the "How to Use the Publish, Unpublish, and Cancel Approval Tools" section, later in this chapter, and discussed in the context of the Publish and Approve/Reject tools.

Using the Document Permissions Tool

Document permissions allow a user with sufficient permissions (members of the Owners group by default) to modify the permissions applied to a specific document. Figure 19.14 shows the Permission Tools page for a document in a document library in SharePoint Foundation 2010. Note that underneath the Ribbon, a note reads "This document inherits permissions from its parent," which is the default behavior. On the Ribbon itself are icons to Manage Parent, Stop Inheriting Permissions, and Check Permissions.

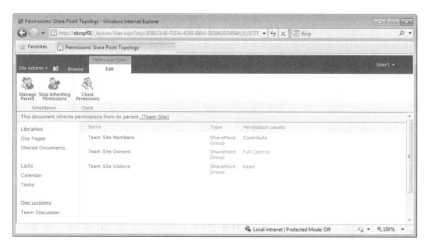

FIGURE 19.14   Permission tools for a document.

If needed, the document library administrator can grant unique permissions to this specific document, but this should only be used when absolutely necessary due to the added overhead and complexity of managing overly customized document libraries. That said, a new addition to permissions management is provided: the Check Permissions tool. Figure 19.15 shows the results of using the Check Permissions tool on a document with customized permissions for the AD group Consultants. After the Check Now button is clicked, the tool validates that ABC\Consultants have no permissions to the document. This is especially useful if AD groups are used to define permissions on a site level, because a document library administrator might not know absolutely which users are in which AD groups.

Using the Delete Button and Recycle Bins

The Delete button on the Documents tab sends one or more documents to the Recycle Bin for the document library. The ability in SharePoint 2010 document libraries to check one or more items as being selected allows a user who has contributor permissions or an administrator to easily delete a number of items. Note that the Delete key on the keyboard can also be used.

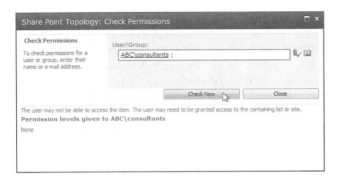

FIGURE 19.15   Check Permissions window for a document with unique permissions.

After the items are sent to the Recycle Bin, a member with full control permissions can restore anyone's items, or a member with contributor permissions can restore items he has deleted. A member with read permissions won't have access to the Recycle Bin. An administrator with site collection administrator privileges can access the Site Collection Recycle Bin (otherwise known as the second-level Recycle Bin) that contains items deleted from the End User Recycle Bin, or to see and restore items still in the End User Recycle Bin.

Note that a farm administrator needs to determine the base settings for the Recycle Bin for the site collection in question. A farm administrator can access the Web Application General Settings interface from the Central Administration site to determine the following settings:

- ▶ Recycle Bin Status On or Off.

- ▶ The amount of time after which to recycle items in the Recycle Bin. The default is 30 days, and the number of days can be changed, or Never can be checked.

- ▶ The percentage of live site quota allocated for the second stage deleted items, with 50 percent being the default, or the Second Stage Recycle Bin (otherwise known as the Site Collection Recycle Bin) can be turned off.

This combination of tools has come a long way since SharePoint 2003, where there wasn't a Recycle Bin at all!

Reviewing the E-mail a Link and Alert Me Tools

The next two tools on the Documents tab are E-mail a Link and Alert Me. The E-mail a Link opens an email and pastes the link to the document that has been checked. Only a single document can be selected. This is a great time saver when a user wants to share a document with another user because it requires just one click to open the email and paste in the link. This also helps IT reduce the number of files attached to emails that end up bloating inboxes.

19

The Alert Me tool allows the user to create an alert on a specific document, if one is checked, or to Manage My Alerts, which opens the My Alerts on this Site page. Then the user can create an alert for a list or library. Alerts are another powerful tool that sets SharePoint document libraries apart from traditional file storage solutions, because they allow SharePoint to communicate directly to end users via email alerts when existing documents change or new documents are added to a specific document library. The following example shows show additional benefits of the toolset.

The following steps can be taken to create an alert for a document library, which is a common task that a user or a site or document library administrator will perform:

1. From within a document library, access the Documents tab from the Ribbon and then click the drop-down arrow next to the Alert Me icon.

2. Click Manage My Alerts.

3. Click Add Alert.

4. Select a document library or list that you want to keep track of. Click the Next button.

5. Provide a title for the alert. It is a best practice to include the name of the list or library in the title, and then an abbreviation for the type of alert, such as New Document Library All Changes.

6. Add the users/groups the alerts will be sent to, separated by semicolons. Note that you can add whomever you like in this field, which is a power that shouldn't be abused! Typically, you will be creating the alert for your own use, but administrators and managers may put in a group name.

7. Leave the delivery method set to E-mail, unless the farm is configured to send text messages (SMS).

8. Select the Change Type to trigger the alert. This can be All Changes, New Items Are Added, Existing Items Are Modified, or Items Are Deleted.

9. Select additional criteria in the Send Alerts for These Changes section. These options are Anything Changes, Someone Else Changes a Document, Someone Else Changes a Document Created by Me, and Someone Else Changes a Document Last Modified by Me.

10. Select an option for the When to Send Alerts section. The options are Send Notification Immediately, Send a Daily Summary, or Send a Weekly Summary. For the daily summary and weekly summary options, a time or day and time need to be selected. Figure 19.16 shows the Change Type, Send Alerts for These Changes, and When to Send Alerts settings for a sample alert.

11. Click OK to complete the alert.

12. If the SharePoint 2010 environment is configured properly, the people listed in the Send Alerts To field will receive emails letting them know the alert was successfully created.

FIGURE 19.16   Creating an alert for a document library.

Understanding the Download a Copy, Send To, Manage Copies, and Go To Source Tools

Next on the Documents Ribbon are the grouping of tools that include Download a Copy, with a large icon, and then to the right, the tools Send To, Manage Copies and Go To Source.

> **NOTE**
>
> The tools in this section (Download a Copy, Send To, Manage Copies, and Go To Source) should be considered advanced tools, and end users should be educated about the complexities and limitations of these tools. A criticism of these tools is that they go against one of the purposes of SharePoint, which is to centralize and consolidate documents rather than have multiple copies in different places, which these tools make possible. That said, sometimes these tools can be very useful, or even essential, but should still be used with caution.

The Download a Copy is self-explanatory and, if clicked, allows the user to save a copy of the document to another location. Ideally, this option rarely needs to be used, since there are a variety of ways to take content offline, including syncing a folder with Outlook or using SharePoint Workspace or third-party tools, but there are occasions where downloading a copy is useful. The primary situation is when a user has the document checked out

19

and another user really needs to use the document for reference or possibly to edit it as well. Although a primary purpose for the check-out process is exactly so other people don't edit the document, people sometimes forget they have the document checked out, and the user who needs it is in a rush and doesn't want to bother an administrator or file a help desk ticket. It is important to note that downloading a copy, editing it, and then saving back to the library once the version stored by the library has been checked in is a bad practice because the changes made in the previous version will be "buried" in the previous versions.

For example, User 1 checks out a Visio, and makes changes, such as adding a server icon, and then forgets to check it in. User 2 downloads a copy because he needs to make an edit and adds a printer icon to the Visio. User 2 now can't save back to the document library as the same name, so saves to the document library with a slightly different name (rev1). User 1 later checks in his version. Now there are two different primary documents, which is a classic problem from a file share, and this is confusing to users. A better practice is for User 2 to email User 1 and request he check the document back in, and if that fails after a reasonable amount of time, have the administrator force a check in. This way, the versioning system will keep all the versions together, and there won't be multiple primary documents in the library.

The Send To tool provides two options: Other Location and Create Document Workspace. The Other Location can be defined on-the-fly by the user and must be a SharePoint 2010 document library that the currently logged-in user has contribute privileges in, or it can be defined by the farm administrator in the Central Administration site, via the Configure Send to Connections tool under General Application Settings, or by the document library administrator in document library settings, Advanced Settings page. Figure 19.17 shows the Copy window that opens when a user chooses the Send to Other Location option. The user then types in the name of the destination document library and can edit the name of the document if desired. The user has the option to ask that the author send out updates when the document is checked in and to create an alert on the source document. Although not perfect, these are both good methods of helping to ensure that the person who made the copy is aware if the source document has changed. When the process completes, a copy of the document will be created in the destination library.

An interesting feature of the Send To tool and process is that SharePoint is aware that there is another copy of the document, or even that there are multiple copies of the document. Figure 19.18 shows the Manage Copies window for the document that was just copied using the Send To command. This window allows the user to create a new copy if needed, or to update copies of the document. The user can remove links to documents if desired by clicking the Edit button next to the destination URL. Note, however (and this relates to the note on the topic of document workspaces), that the document library is not aware of the copy of the document placed in the document workspace, which can cause administrative challenges.

Document workspaces won't be discussed in detail here because they are covered in Chapter 21. A document workspace is actually a site that can be created by a user with sufficient privileges that will contain a copy of the document as well as other lists designed for collaboration purposes. Note, however, that unlike when the Send To command is used, a document workspace copy of a document does not maintain a connection to the original, which can lead to confusion on the part of users about which is the latest and greatest version of the document (the one in the document library on the parent site, or the one in the document library in the workspace). The document workspace does provide the tool Publish to Source Location, under the drop-down menu for the document in the Send To section, which the administrator of the document workspace needs to remember to use once the usefulness of the workspace is fulfilled and the document is complete.

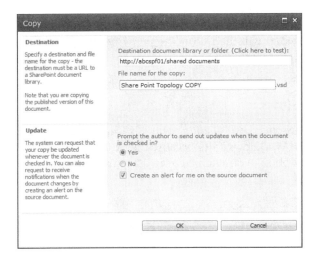

FIGURE 19.17   Copy window resulting from the using the Send To tool in a document library.

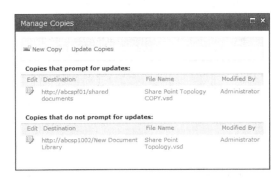

FIGURE 19.18   Manage Copies window for a document.

19

NOTE

Although a good idea, and a tool that has been around for years and several versions of SharePoint, creating document workspaces can be overly complex to administer, so many organizations decide to discourage their use and lock down which users have the permissions to create workspaces. For example, when a new workspace is created, the creator needs to perform the role of a site administrator and give permissions to users, to allow them to access the workspace, and then make sure the right version of the document is being edited, and finally publish the document back to the source document library when the collaboration is complete.

The final tool in this section, Go to Source, will be active if the document selected is connected to a source document. If clicked, it will then show the property information of the source document.

A High-Level Overview of Workflows

Workflows are a complex topic and justify their own chapter, which is Chapter 28, "Out-of-the-Box Workflows and Designer 2010 Workflows," but because the Workflow tool is provided in the Documents tab on the Ribbon, it should be covered at this time from a high level.

NOTE

The three-state workflow is the only workflow template provided in SharePoint Foundation 2010, while others are available in SharePoint Server 2010. SharePoint Server 2010 Standard and Enterprise provides the following workflow templates: Disposition Approval, Publishing Approval, Collection Signatures, Approval, and Collection Feedback.

A workflow must have been created by a document library administrator for it to be available to users of the document library. The document library administrator decides whether the workflow starts automatically or if it can be started manually by users with Edit Item permissions or if users must have manage list permissions to start the workflow. Once started, the workflow communicates to participants via email, which gives instructions of what they need to do. At the same time, tasks are created in a SharePoint tasks list, which the participants interact with and update as they perform their tasks.

If more complex workflows are required, developers and administrators can use tools such as SharePoint Designer 2010, Visio 2010, Visual Studio 2010, and other tools to create more complex workflows. InfoPath 2010 could be used to create advanced forms that are used within the workflow, emails can be customized, and complex business logic can be created if needed.

Procedurally, to start a workflow, a user with sufficient rights follows these steps:

1. The user either selects Workflows from the drop-down menu or clicks the Workflow button in the Documents Ribbon after selecting the document.

2. The Workflow.aspx opens, and shows the user any workflows associated with the document library. The user clicks the desired workflow. If no workflows are available, the document library administrator will need to be contacted to create one.

3. The user then modifies the settings for the workflow entered by the document library or site administrator, which can include who is involved in the workflow, a text message, due dates for all tasks, duration per task, and other fields depending on the workflow. Figure 19.19 shows a sample workflow based on the out-of-the-box Collect Feedback workflow.

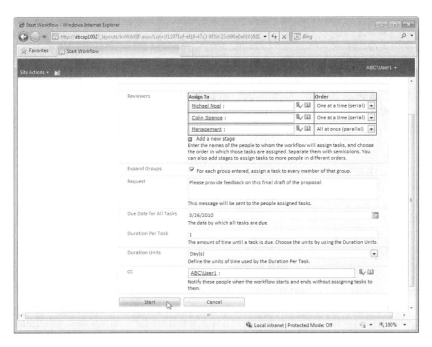

FIGURE 19.19   A sample Collect Feedback workflow.

4. The user then clicks Start to kick off the workflow, and emails will be sent to the participants with instructions on the steps to take.

The next section provides an example of a Page Approval workflow, to provide a context for how an out-of-the-box workflow can be useful in an approval process.

How to Use the Publish, Unpublish, and Cancel Approval Tools

To begin with, the Publish, Unpublish, and Cancel Approval tools are active only when a document library has versioning enabled and configured to allow the creation of major and minor (draft) versions. A major version is considered the published version.

Versioning is a key component of SharePoint 2010 and other document management applications because it not only keeps track of previous versions of a document but also hides them from end users in the standard views, to make errors less likely when working with the document.

With versioning enabled, there is no question which version is the latest version because the version that appears in the document library is the latest and greatest. The only case where a previous version will show up as the current version in the document library is if a user purposefully looks for an older version of the document, by accessing the Version History tool (covered previously in this chapter) and selects an older version and clicks Restore. This will make that older version the "latest" version, with the highest version number, that will appear in the document library. But it is a safe assumption that a user would only do this if he realizes that this older version contains the most valid version of content for one reason or another.

> **NOTE**
>
> Be aware that when versioning is enabled, each version of the document adds the full document size to the SQL content database. Versioning in SharePoint 2010 does not just track differences between the documents, but keeps a full copy. Administrators should keep this in mind when determining the policy for enabling versioning for lists and libraries.

The process of turning a draft version (for example, 0.1) into a major (for example, 1.0) version is called publishing in SharePoint parlance, and the Publish button is used to either start a workflow or instantly publish the document. It is up to the document library administrator whether to use a workflow for this process, which is more complex and time-consuming, or to enable instant publishing. The following example walks through the process of uploading a document to a document library with major and minor versioning enabled, scheduling enabled, and workflows enabled.

The scheduling feature can be turned off or on for a document library by the library administrator. Scheduling determines when a document will be published and available for general viewing by users of the site. Before the scheduled start date is reached, the item will remain in draft status, and once that date is reached, but before the end date is reached, the document will be promoted to major version published status. After the end date is reached, if there is one set, the document will return to draft status.

The Draft Item Security settings, which are set by the document library administrator and accessible from the Document Library Settings page via the Versioning Settings page, determine who can see draft (unpublished) versions of documents. The options are Any User Who Can Read Items, Only Users Who Can Edit Items, and Only User Who Can Approve Items (and the author of the item). So it is important for a document library administrator to determine the most appropriate combination of settings. This topic will be revisited in Chapter 20.

Some document libraries that are created during the creation of a publishing site or site collection will have major and minor versioning enabled, and will also have Content

Approval turned on, which means that a user with approver privileges needs to approve a document before it is published as a major version. And scheduling may also be enabled for the library, which determines when the item, once approved, will be available for the general public. The following example will help clarify the process, as outlined in the following steps:

1. A user of a site collection documents library in a publishing site in SharePoint Server 2010 Enterprise uploads a document to the library. This library has major and minor versioning enabled, requires content approval for submitted items, has a Page Approval workflow configured, as well as scheduling enabled, and so requires a number of steps to take place before an uploaded document is available to the general public.

2. As shown in Figure 19.20, the user is prompted to verify the name and title of the document, and decide whether the scheduling start date should be immediately or a fixed date, and whether the end date should be never or a fixed date. In this example, the user wants the document to not be published to a major version until a given date, and wants it to stay published for only a few weeks. After he likes the setting, he clicks Save.

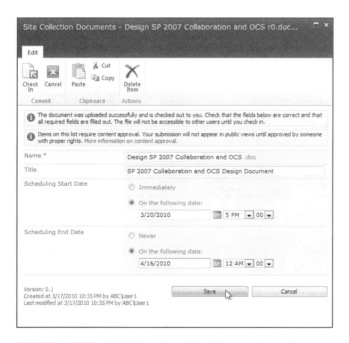

FIGURE 19.20   Finishing the upload process for a document library with Scheduling enabled.

3. The document is now saved in the document library, but is in draft status, with a version number of 0.1. Based on the settings of the document library, only users who can edit items in this document library can now see the document, which includes the user himself.

4. The user, having decided that the document is ready to be published, then accesses the drop-down menu for the item in the All Items view, and clicks the Publish button on the Documents tab of the Ribbon.

5. Because the Page Approval workflow was automatically configured as active on this document library, the Workflow.aspx page opens, and provides the Page Approval workflow as the only option in the Start a New Workflow section. The user clicks the Page Approval icon to start the workflow.

6. As shown in Figure 19.21, the user enters additional information to complete the workflow—including request text, a due date, duration for the task—and clicks Start.

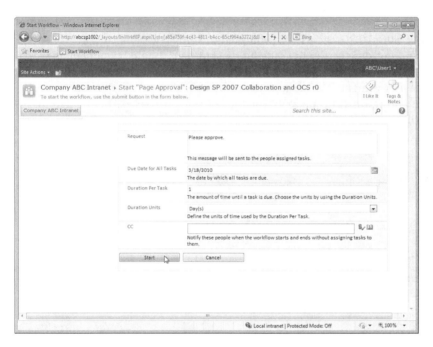

FIGURE 19.21   Starting a Page Approval workflow in a publishing library.

7. The approval status of the document is now set to pending, and will remain that way until an approver approves the document.

8. At this point, members of the approvers group on the site will receive emails that a document needs approval, as shown in Figure 19.22. The approver clicks the Open This Task button in the Outlook 2010 Ribbon for the email, and a form opens up with the options to Approve, Reject, Cancel, Request Change, or Reassign Task. The approver clicks Approve.

9. Now the document is approved to be published on the scheduled start date. As shown in Figure 19.23, the Approval Status in set to Scheduled with the start and end dates shown in the two columns to the right. Note also in Figure 19.23 that the Cancel Approval icon is active, so a user can choose to cancel the approval if needed and start the process once again.

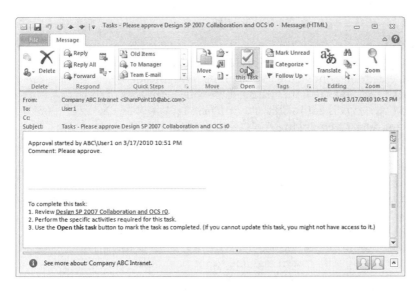

FIGURE 19.22   Email requesting approval for a document submitted for publishing.

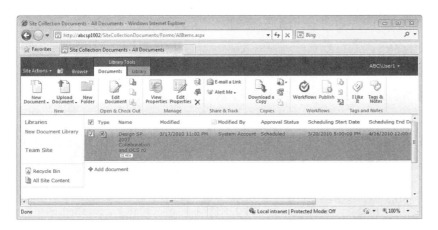

FIGURE 19.23   Document that has been approved and is scheduled to be published.

This example shows the management possibilities of enabling major and minor versioning in a document library, requiring content approval for documents, using a Page Approval workflow, as well as using Scheduling Start and End dates. Enabling the full combination of features does add overhead and complexity to the process, but helps ensure that content is reviewed by one or more members of the approvers group for that site before the "general public" can see the document in a major, published version. This complexity does require testing and training for administrators, approvers, and end users to avoid frustration during the process.

Using the I Like It and Tags & Notes Tools

The I Like It icon and the Tabs & Notes icon are not available from SharePoint Foundation 2010, but are available in both SharePoint Server 2010 Standard and Enterprise, and are shown on the Documents toolbar in Figure 19.23 on the far-right side. These features are also referred to as social tags and the note board and provide a great set of tools to promote users' adding tags to content in SharePoint. These tools will be discussed more in Chapter 23, "Leveraging Social Networking Tools in SharePoint 2010."

These tools are easy to use, and engaging enough to end users that they will soon find themselves experimenting with them to understand the full breadth of their potential. For example, if the Tags & Notes icon is surrounded by a colored band, this indicates that there are tags or notes on the page. For a specific item, such as shown in Figure 19.24, if Tags & Notes is clicked, the window for Tags and Note Board will open. In this example, several tags were added by the user to this document, and other recent activities are listed at the bottom of the window, which show tagging activities by other users. This allows users to quickly create and apply their own tags and to see how others are tagging this item. Users can also set tags as Private if they don't want other users to see how they are tagging items. Users can also visit their My Site to see histories of tags they have applied. Figure 19.25 shows a sample My Site for a user (User1) who has been creating tags and posts recently, and they are displayed on the right side of the page. A tag cloud on the left side of the screen shows the frequency that tags have been used, as indicated by the size of the fonts.

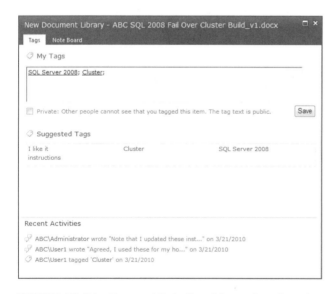

FIGURE 19.24   Tags and Note Board for an item in a document library.

As with any other tool that makes it easy to post comments, there is the possibility for abuse, but the user community should be informed of any policies surrounding inappropriate use of the tools and the repercussions of inappropriate language or use.

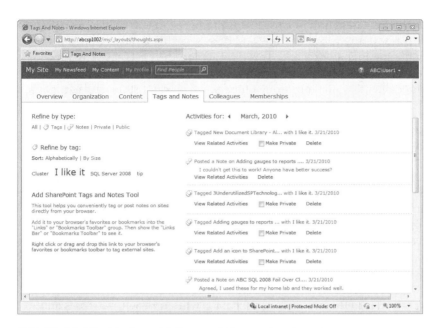

FIGURE 19.25   My Site with Tags and Notes tab selected.

NOTE

The social tags and note board Ribbon controls can be disabled by a farm administrator from the Central Administration site by accessing the System Settings page, and then clicking Manage Farm Features. Scroll down to the Social Tags and Note Board Ribbon Controls and click Deactivate.

Empowering Users Through SharePoint 2010 Lists

As the previous section showed, there are many very powerful features and tools provided by SharePoint libraries, and SharePoint lists provide a similar set of tools and features. Because a number of these tools and features overlap with libraries, this section concentrates on the differences between lists and libraries and gives examples that will help users and administrators grasp the differences and how to best utilize lists. Examples will also be given of how list administrators and site administrators can customize lists to make them better suited to the needs of the users.

Differentiating Lists from Libraries

Although libraries are one of the most frequently used building blocks for SharePoint-based collaboration and information management systems, lists are the other. Libraries store files, while lists are designed to store rows of information, in much the same way as a spreadsheet stores rows of data defined by columns that are configured to support certain types of data, such as text, numbers, date and times, choices, and others.

When a user clicks the New Item link in a list, she is prompted to enter different types of information, such as text, currency value, time and date, selecting an item from a list of items, or perhaps entering in a user's name. This information then gets saved as a row in the list and is given a unique ID number. No document needs to be uploaded at this point, which is a fundamental difference from a library, which can't store data without a document to attach it to.

Another revealing exercise for an administrator is to anticipate ways in which end users, especially power users, might get themselves into trouble. Figure 19.7 showed, earlier in the chapter, how a user can navigate to a SharePoint folder by using Windows Explorer (WebDAV) and entering the SharePoint server name, site name, and document library in the following format (for example: \\servername\libraryname). In this previous example, there is no specific site name needed because the document library exists as part of the root site and the user could see the contents of the document library clearly shown as documents and even a folder. Navigating to a list in a similar fashion isn't quite as friendly a process, as shown in Figure 19.26, where there is a folder titled Announcement, one titled Attachments, and then several documents that can be seen to be ASP.NET Server Pages are also apparent. Double-clicking the Announcement folder does not actually show the data that was entered into the list because the data is written to SQL databases and stored in tables. And data cannot be added from the Explorer interface, so there is arguably no benefit to end users of accessing a list in this fashion.

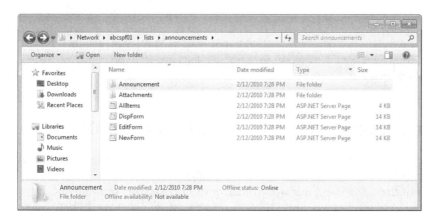

FIGURE 19.26   Explorer view of an announcement list in SharePoint 2010.

The organization should decide whether to allow Explorer view (WebDAV) access to SharePoint 2010 content, because the results end users see when visiting lists, in terms of the folders and ASP.Net pages end users find, may confuse them. Furthermore, an overzealous power user who deletes the folders or forms can impact the functionality of the list.

A fact that can be confusing to new users and administrators is that a SharePoint list can also store attachments to a list item, so be prepared for discussions along the lines of pros and cons of using lists and libraries to store items. These attachments are stored in the Attachments folder seen via the Explorer view in Figure 19.26. Another difference between list and library functionality pertains to versioning. Even if versioning is turned on for a list, one or more attachments will not have their versions tracked if they are changed. This can lead to potential confusion or even lost productivity if users are expecting attachments in a list to be versioned. Along these lines, a user could delete an attachment to a list item, and it will not be recoverable by just recovering an older version of the item because the attachments aren't tracked with the versioning tool. Note that attachments that are deleted will end up in the Recycle Bin for recovery if needed. An additional point on versioning is that lists offer only major versions and do not allow the saving of minor versions, making them less well suited for more intricate document review and approval processes. Possibly for these reasons, lists can be configured so that attachments to list items are disabled.

Reviewing Several Common Lists Found in a Team Site Template

By reviewing several of the basic lists that are provided with a SharePoint Team Site, the flexibility of lists can easily be seen. A Team Site template includes an Announcements list, Calendar list, Links list, and Tasks list. Each of these is comprised of several columns, different views, and in some cases some special functionality that has been added by Microsoft. An overview of the columns included in each list and a brief description of enhancements are as follows:

▶ The Announcements list stores announcements that consist of a Title, a Body section, and an Expiration Date. This makes it well suited as a starting point to input data that will make up an announcement on the site, which will "expire" and no longer display after a certain date.

▶ The Calendar list stores rows of data that include a number of columns of data, including: Title, Location, Start Time (and date), End Time (and date), Description, Category, whether it's an All Day Event, whether there is Recurrence, and whether a Workspace is needed. Collected together, each row of data serves to represent an event taking place and can be displayed on a special calendar-like view, and provides different display options and navigation tools.

▶ The Links list is quite simple, and just provides a URL field, with description field, and a Notes field. This list is designed to track URL information while displaying a friendly description instead of the whole URL.

▶ The Tasks list is also quite complex, and stores data including Title, Predecessors, Priority, Status, % Complete, Assigned To, Description, Start Date, and Due Date. This list has specially configured views to display only items that meet certain filters, such as My Tasks, Due Today, Active Tasks, By Assigned To, and By My Groups.

Chapter 18 provides additional details comparing the different lists and libraries that are available in the different versions of the SharePoint 2010 products, but this initial handful of lists gives some insight into each list.

19

Examining the Tools in an Announcements List

Figure 19.27 shows an Announcements list in SharePoint Foundation 2010 with an item selected in it, and the Items tab on the List Tools Ribbon visible. These tools should all look familiar, and were covered in the earlier walk through for a library. Because this is housed in a SharePoint Foundation 2010 site collection, the I Like It and Tags & Notes tools are not included, but would be if the list were housed in SharePoint Server 2010 Standard or Enterprise.

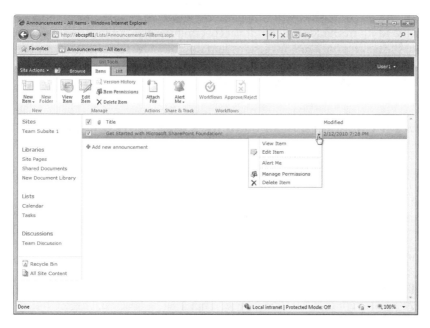

FIGURE 19.27   Items tab for an Announcements list.

One new tool offered in the list is the Attach File tool, which allows the user to browse for a single file and then save it as an attachment. Attachments are saved in the Attachments folder within the list, and although there is no published limit to the number of attachments that can be added to a list item, there are few benefits to storing documents in this manner, as discussed earlier in this section.

The process of creating a new item in the list is simpler than in a library, and the user just needs to click the New Item icon, and then add content to the fields, as shown in Figure 19.28. For this example, an image was also included, which was uploaded from the user's Pictures folder, and SharePoint allows the user to simultaneously choose the picture to use and also to upload it to a desired library on the site. Although this might not sound groundbreaking, in SharePoint 2007, the process for including images in rich text required that the image first be uploaded, the URL for the image copied, and then the picture placeholder used in the content (a much more laborious process). The text formatting tools can be seen, which have also improved since SharePoint 2007, and the graphic image can be resized from within the AJAX editing window. These tools make it very simple and quick for users to create quite intricate postings. After the Save button is clicked, the content is saved to the list.

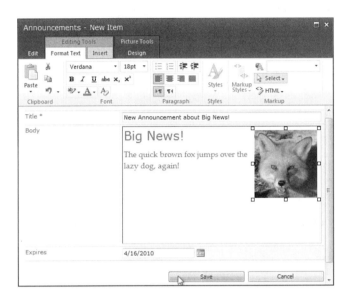

FIGURE 19.28   Creating a new announcement in a list.

As with a library, an item in a list can be checked as active, and then the relevant tools become active. Figure 19.29 shows the List tab of the List Tools Ribbon, as a list administrator will need to become familiar with these tools to fully realize the potential of lists. A valuable set of tools is revealed in the next section, which covers the Datasheet view from a high level, and to round out this chapter, the Create View and Add a Column tools are demonstrated and discussed.

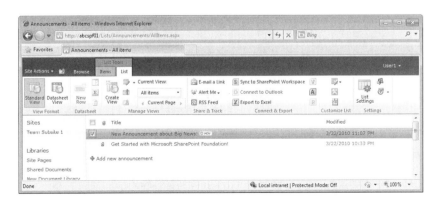

FIGURE 19.29   The List tab for an Announcements list.

Adding a Column in a List and Updating a List Item

Although libraries store documents, and can be extremely useful even if additional meta-data columns aren't added, lists derive their value from the columns that make up the list, so adding columns to lists is a frequently performed task. Figure 19.30 shows the Create Column window that opens when a user with the manage lists list permission clicks the Create Column button. Similar to in a spreadsheet, a number of different column options are provided. In SharePoint Foundation 2010, these are as follows:

- ▶ Single line of text
- ▶ Multiple lines of text
- ▶ Choice (menu to choose from)
- ▶ Number
- ▶ Currency
- ▶ Date and Time
- ▶ Lookup (information already on this site)
- ▶ Yes/No (check box)
- ▶ Person or Group
- ▶ Hyperlink or Picture

FIGURE 19.30   Create Column window in a list.

▶ Calculated (calculation based on other columns)

▶ External Data

SharePoint Server 2010 Standard or Enterprise also give the option of creating Managed Metadata columns in lists. Chapter 22 provides additional information about the column choices.

In this example, the Choice column is chosen, and several items that will appear in the drop-down menu are provided. Radio buttons or check boxes can also be selected, and fill-in choices can be allowed, as well as a default value provided. After OK is clicked, the column is added, and if the check box is left checked to Add to Default View, the new column will be added to the default view. In the example given immediately above, the new column named Topic can be seen on the right side of the Announcements list in Figure 19.31, since the Add to Default View check box was selected when then new column was added. The arrow next to the column header Topic is shown selected in Figure 19.31, and sorting options are provided; once there is content in this column, the different distinct values will be available for selection for the filter. To populate this new column with data, several different sets of steps can be followed, as described in the following three sections.

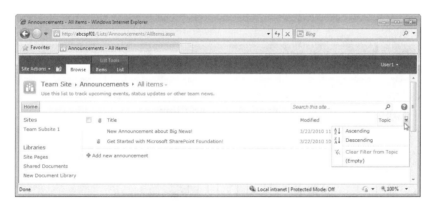

FIGURE 19.31   New column added to a list.

Clicking the Item Title to Edit Content

This first section describes the process of editing content by clicking the title of an item in a list:

1. The easiest option, and most intuitive is to simply click the title of the item (for example, New Announcement About Big News! shown in Figure 19.31) and the AJAX window for the item in View mode will open.

2. Then click Edit Item from the View tab, and the item changes to Edit mode, as shown in Figure 19.32. Now make a change, such as clicking the drop-down arrow next to the Topic field, and select from the provided choices.

3. Then click Save to save the modification and return to the previous view of the list.

19

FIGURE 19.32   Edit window for a list item.

Accessing the Drop-Down Menu to Edit an Item

This section describes the process of editing content by accessing the drop-down menu:

1. As shown in Figure 19.33, hover over the Title for the list item in the list, and then access the drop-down menu to the right and click Edit Item.

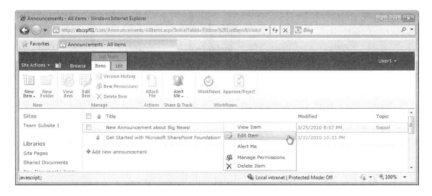

FIGURE 19.33   Drop-down menu for a list item.

2. The list item then opens in Edit mode. Update one or more fields and click Save.

Selecting the Item and Choosing Edit Item

This section describes the process of editing an item by first selecting it and then choosing Edit Item from the Ribbon:

1. Hover over the list item until the box appears to the left of the title, and then check the box.

2. The Items tab under List Tools is then active. Click Edit Item, and the list item opens in Edit mode. Update one or more fields and click Save.

> **NOTE**
>
> The check box might not always be enabled in a list or library.

Interacting with Lists Using the Datasheet View

The Datasheet view is extremely useful for quickly entering data into a list, or also for rapidly entering metadata for items in a library. As shown in the preceding three processes, editing a single item can involve several hovers, clicks, more mouse-work, entering the information, and then another click to save the data. Datasheet view appeals to the efficiency conscious part of many users, and should be introduced to new users. Follow these steps to use the Datasheet view in an Announcements list, and most other lists:

1. Click the List tab under List Tools.

2. Click the Datasheet View icon in the List tab Ribbon. Figure 19.34 shows an Announcements list in Datasheet view. The user clicked in an empty cell under the bottom announcement, entered a new announcement title, tabbed past the Modified cell (because this cell will be populated by SharePoint automatically), and then selected Social from the drop-down menu in the Topic column. If the user tried to enter any data in the Modified column, he'll get a message that says, "The selected cells are read-only."

3. Click Enter, and the selected cell drops to the next row down, triggering a save of the data entered.

Note that the Body column is not visible in this view, so the user can't actually enter in the body of the announcement.

In Figure 19.34, the task pane has been extended on the right side of the Datasheet view, and it provides easy access to tools such as Cut, Copy, Paste, Undo, Custom Sort, Remove Filter, and a number of tools under the Office links section. These tools allow export of content to Access and Excel, and will be reviewed in more detail in Chapter 25 and Chapter 26, "Extending SharePoint 2010 with Excel Services, Access Services, and Visio Graphics Services."

With a little experimentation, it can be seen that the Datasheet view allows a user to quickly enter in data in lists (or libraries), cut, and paste into other cells if needed, which dramatically cuts down on the time it takes when compared to selecting items one at a time, accessing the drop-down menu, or selecting the item and then accessing the Edit Item tool on the Ribbon.

19

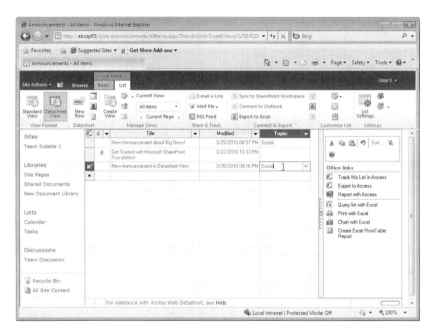

FIGURE 19.34   Datasheet view in a tasks list.

At the time of this writing, per TechNet (http://technet.microsoft.com/en-us/library/ ee681792(office.14).aspx) the Edit in Datasheet view technology is not supported by the 64-bit version of Office 2010. This can be a big surprise if an organization plans on heavily using the Datasheet view, which is an extremely helpful interface and considered essential in some orgs.

Not every type of field can be edited in Datasheet view. Some columns are read-only, which means that SharePoint will populate them automatically, or SharePoint blocks them from being edited in Datasheet view. For example, a Multiple Lines of Text column that is configured to allow enhanced rich text (Rich text with pictures, tables, and hyperlinks) cannot be edited in Datasheet view. However, multiple lines of text configured to allow plain text or rich text (bold, italics, text alignment, and hyperlinks) does allow editing in Datasheet view. For this reason, if Datasheet view will be used extensively, lists should be configured to allow editing of all the different fields that a typical user would need to edit.

Creating a View in a List

Another important concept to understand when using SharePoint 2010 lists is that of views. When someone visits a list, the default view will display. Every list is created with a default view, and then the list administrator can either modify that view or create new views, one of which could be set to be the default. The tools required are accessed in the List tab of the Ribbon toolbar and include the Create View tool, Modify view, and List Settings tools. The List Settings tool is the "long way" of getting to the link to modify a view.

In the following example, a user decides a new view is needed in the Announcements list that was modified in the previous example by having a new column titled Topic added. Follow these steps to create a new view in the list:

1. Click the List tab, and then click the Create View tool.

2. Several view formats are offered: Standard View, Calendar View, Access View, Datasheet View, Gantt View, and Custom View in SharePoint Designer. For this example, click Standard View.

3. The ViewNew.aspx page opens, as shown in Figure 19.35. Enter in a name for the view, such as New View, and check the box next to Make This the Default View, if desired.

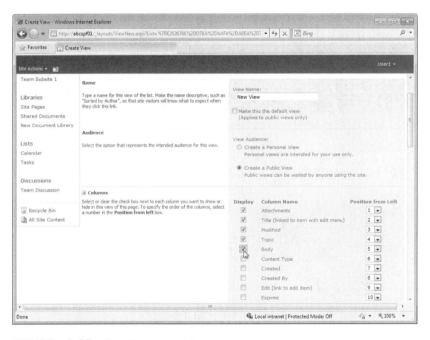

FIGURE 19.35   Creating a new view.

19

4. In the next section, leave Create a Public View checked, or select Create a Personal View, if you intend to use only this view and you don't want to share it with other users of the list. In this example, leave Public View checked.

5. In the Columns section, check any column names that you want included in the view. Change the number in the Position from Left column if needed; this often takes some trial and error to get just right. In this example, the column titled Body is checked because it was left out of the default view.

6. In the Sort section, determine which column to sort by. In this example, choose Title from the drop-down menu under First Sort by the Column, and check the circle next to Show Items in Ascending Order.

7. In the Filter section, choose whether to filter items and only display items that meet certain criteria. Leave the Show All Items in this View option checked for this example.

NOTE

The Inline Editing option for a view adds an editing icon to the view, which allows the user to edit content for a column that contains multiple lines of text in rich text or enhanced rich text formats. Figure 19.36 shows an example of this. The Save button must be clicked after editing or the changes won't be saved. However, even if Inline editing is enabled, certain cells still can't be edited in Datasheet view, including multiple lines of text in enhanced rich text format. So, the Inline Editing option should be provided to users when enhanced rich text format is being used in lists on a trial basis to see whether it is well received.

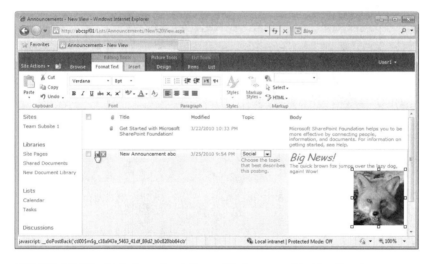

FIGURE 19.36   List view after inline editing was enabled for the view.

8. Feel free to experiment with the various other settings on the ViewNew.aspx page, such as Inline Editing, Tabular View, Group By, Totals, Style, Folders, Items Limit, and Mobile. Figure 19.37 shows a sample of a mobile view for the Announcements list. The URL for the mobile view is provided in the Mobile section of the ViewEdit.aspx page.

9. Click OK to save the changes.

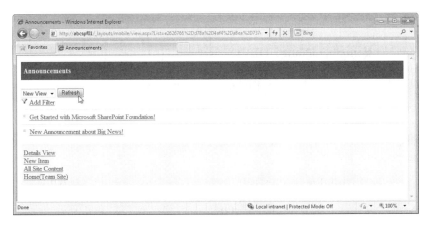

FIGURE 19.37   Mobile view for a list.

The Group By option can be very useful for lists with numerous items as it allows the contents of one or more columns to be used to group items. Groupings can be displayed by default in collapsed mode, so a user can easily browse through different groups by expanding a header, and then reviewing the contents to see whether they are of interest.

In the Folders section for the ViewEdit.aspx page, the option is provided to either Show items inside folders or to Show All Items Without Folders. Although this might seem a fairly innocuous option, realize that the efforts to organize content in folders can be completely ignored by simply checking the circle next to Show All Items Without Folders. Any granular security settings applied to contents of folders will still be honored; the view will simply be flattened. With this simple option, SharePoint allows a list administrator to be freed from the constraints of folders inside of lists, even if users demand folders for peace of mind or comfort level.

Summary

Document libraries and lists are arguably the most important features of SharePoint 2010 since they will contain the documents and data that users will be interacting with every day. Although an in-depth review of every tool and feature available from every document library and list in SharePoint is beyond the scope of this chapter, it highlights the most important and commonly used features and sets the stage for Chapter 20. SharePoint 2010 builds upon and refines the features provided by SharePoint 2007 lists and libraries in many important ways that turn SharePoint into a world-class and (just as important) easy-to-use document and data management tool.

19

Best Practices

▶ The improvements from SharePoint 2007 to SharePoint 2010 make it easier for administrators and end users to interact with the documents and data stored in document libraries and lists and reduce the learning curve as well.

▶ There are a variety of ways to upload documents to SharePoint 2010 document libraries, including using the Open with Explorer button on the Library tab, the Upload Multiple Documents option, and using Windows Explorer to navigate to the SharePoint server, site, and library.

▶ Folders can be created within a document library, and as discussed in this chapter, there are pros and cons to using folders in SharePoint document libraries. A best practice is for the organization to understand the pros and cons of using folders and make informed decisions on where they make sense (for example, document libraries with tens of thousands of documents) and where they don't (for example, smaller document libraries where the organization wants to promote the use of metadata for organization rather than folders).

▶ Although creating unique permissions for documents in a document library creates added overhead for administrators, the new Check Permissions tool allows administrators to check and see what permission levels are given to users or groups, which allows the administrator to quickly check whether specific users or groups have any access to the document.

▶ Alerts can be created for items or lists or libraries and are a very easy way to keep track of activities within a list or library or of any changes made to a document that a user is specifically interested in. Use daily and weekly summary alerts to keep the number of emails sent out to a minimum.

▶ Although document libraries provide tools in the toolbar that can make a copy of a document in another library (the Send To tool) and track that copy and maintain the connectivity to a certain extent by requesting updates, or can create a document workspace that contains a copy of the document, this can be a confusing and complicated process for less-experienced users and administrators. A best-practice recommendation is to recommend against using these tools unless specifically required for a business solution when the user base and administrators are new to SharePoint.

▶ Document library administrators have the ability to enable versioning in a document library, decide whether major and minor versions will be tracked, whether content approval is required, who can see draft versions, whether workflows are used to approve a document, and even whether scheduling is used to determine when the content is published. A best practice is to make sure that the right combination of these features is applied based on the content of the document library and the sophistication of the user base. Enabling too many of these features for a user base that is new to SharePoint 2010 may steepen the learning curve and make employees hesitant to use the document libraries.

▶ Although the Datasheet view is available for use in both lists and libraries, it is most often used in lists for rapid data entry or bulk changes, because many users use SharePoint lists for similar tasks as the normally use spreadsheets for. The Datasheet View is not compatible with 64-bit versions of Office 2010, which is an important point to take into mind when planning integration between Office and SharePoint.

▶ The Datasheet view also provides access to the task pane, which provides additional useful tools, such as Export to Access, Report with Access, Print with Excel, and Chart with Excel.

▶ Lists are another main building block of SharePoint collaborative environments, but are designed primarily for storing rows of information rather than documents. As discussed in this chapter, lists can store documents as attachments, but do not manage documents as well or as thoroughly as libraries. For example, lists do not manage versions of attachments.

▶ For lists to be useful, they must contain the appropriate combination of columns. A variety of lists come with SharePoint 2010 out-of-the-box, but an administrator should get familiar with the wide variety of columns that can be created, and the usefulness of the list will increase as these are properly leveraged.

▶ Views are also key to the efficacy of lists, and a list administrator should become familiar with the process of creating a new view, setting it as the default, and working with sorting, filtering, and grouping within list views.

▶ Mobile views are created by default with any new view, and the URL is available on the Edit View page (ViewEdit.aspx), in the Mobile section at the bottom of the page.

## CHAPTER 20

Customizing and Managing Libraries and Lists to Meet Business Requirements

The preceding chapter provided an overview of the wide and powerful range of tools available to SharePoint 2010 users in lists and libraries. This chapter now builds on this information to help SharePoint architects and administrators design an environment that will meet the various needs of end users by focusing on the main containers of information in SharePoint 2010: lists and libraries.

This chapter concentrates on the tools available within lists and libraries, primarily from the Library tab on the Ribbon, and settings page, with the goal of exposing administrators to the range of tools they will be using to initially configure lists and libraries and will access to manage them on an ongoing basis.

The chapter also covers two of the site features that can be activated by site administrators that provide toolsets that pertain specifically to the management of files and data within lists and libraries: document sets and the content organizer.

Planning the List and Library Ecosystem

The process of planning the appropriate combination of lists and libraries to meet the needs of different business units and groups can be very simple or very complex, depending on the general philosophies surrounding the SharePoint project and the needs of the organization. Some organizations spend a minimal amount of time planning, build one or more SharePoint site collections with sites defined for business units, departments, or groups, and then allow end users to customize these environments with the lists and libraries that they deem best suited to their needs. Other organizations create sites and site collections using carefully crafted templates that have specific combinations of preconfigured lists and libraries, and carefully weigh the pros and cons of the different types of lists and libraries and related features that can be provided. And then there are other permutations. For the sake of discussion, it is posited here that four primary strategies can be employed:

1. Minimal planning and testing; minimal restrictions on list and library use and configuration

2. Minimal planning and testing; more restrictions on list and library use and configuration

3. More extensive planning and testing; minimal restrictions on list and library use and configuration

4. More extensive planning and testing; more restrictions on list and library use and configuration

By using the minimal planning and testing approach, the organization shortens the time frame of the implementation, which generally controls the costs of the project. In general, the risks of "missing the mark" are higher in the minimal planning and testing approach. This can manifest, from the author's experience, in sluggish adoption of the lists and libraries, unless end users are already experienced with, and even clamoring for, SharePoint technologies, or have training made readily available. Alternatively, assuming end users adopt the technology, this "blank slate" approach encourages end users to modify the tools to meet their specific needs. Combine this minimal planning approach with minimal restriction on the types of lists and libraries that can be used, and empower certain users to configure these lists to meet their needs, and the results can be positive. Tightly control the range of lists and libraries that can be used and restrict end users' ability to change the configuration of lists and libraries, and IT stays integrated in the adoption cycle, learns what the end users are requesting in terms of functionality, and can develop best practices along the way.

On the other hand, more extensive planning and testing requires more time and resource involvement and can add to the overall costs of the project. Pilots, prototypes, and proof of concepts can be executed and managed, with specific decisions made along the way of which lists and libraries will be made available and which tools enabled in the lists and libraries. Following the implementation, end users can be more or less empowered to create new libraries and lists and customize the configurations.

Every organization has its own processes and methodologies for planning and testing, so those topics won't be addressed in detail, but the topics revolving around list and library use and configuration will be looked at in detail to help readers better understand the capabilities of the lists, libraries, and related tools provided by SharePoint 2010, and then decide which are appropriate for the implementations.

Understanding the Range of List and Library Options

Chapter 18, "SharePoint Foundation Versus SharePoint Server 2010," provided some initial information about the lists and libraries provided in the different versions of SharePoint 2010 in Table 18.8. This section delves into more detail on the different options and provides some guidance on how they should be used from a high level. Due to the sheer number of lists and libraries as shown in Table 20.1, a detailed overview of each one is beyond the scope of this chapter. This table clarifies whether the template will create a list or a library, whether the template is available in SharePoint Foundation 2010 or SharePoint Server 2010 Standard or Enterprise, and provides notes on what the list or library is designed by Microsoft to be used for, and key tidbits of information about effectively using the list or library.

Although this list is certainly not enough to make the final decision about which lists and libraries the organization will support and make available to specific sets of users, it can serve as a starting point, and the grid can be expanded for use during the planning process. The design team can simply review the lists and libraries, make decisions about whether to use each one, and determine whether specific lists or libraries meet the needs of a subset of users, groups, or divisions and verify that they are all included in the version of SharePoint that the organization has chosen. If an older version of Office is being used by the organization, such as Office 2003, certain libraries will have limited functionality, such as the Slide Library, which can only have slides published to it from PowerPoint 2007 or 2010. Likewise, InfoPath is required to publish forms to a form library and recommended to create ODC or UDC files in a data connection library.

Leveraging the Team Site Template for Standardized Lists and Libraries

Organizations that want to minimize the design and planning process can of course choose to use the team site template and stick to the default lists and libraries provided in it, rather than spend time discussing the merits of the range of lists and libraries. The team site template contains the following lists and libraries:

- Shared Documents document library

- Site Assets document library

- Site Pages wiki library

- Announcements announcements list

- Calendar calendar list

- Links links list

- Tasks tasks list

- Team Discussion discussion board

20

TABLE 20.1   Library and List Options in SharePoint Foundation 2010 and SharePoint Server
2010 Standard and Enterprise

Template Name	List or Library?	Available in SharePoint Foundation 2010?	Available in SharePoint Server 2010 Standard?	Available in SharePoint Server 2010 Enterprise?	Functionality and Notes
Document Library	Library	Yes	Yes	Yes	Designed for general document storage.
Form Library	Library	Yes	Yes	Yes	Intended for storage of InfoPath Forms. Requires InfoPath 2007 or 2010 on the desktop for end users or SharePoint Server 2010 Enterprise and Enterprise CALs for end users.
Wiki Page Library	Library	Yes	Yes	Yes	Manage wiki pages in one library.
Picture Library	Library	Yes	Yes	Yes	General graphical file managements. Microsoft Picture Manager needs to be installed on the desktop to upload multiple files.
Asset Library	Library	No	Yes	Yes	Designed to store Image, Audio, or Video files. Has Image, Audio, and Video content types enabled by default.
Slide Library	Library	No	Yes	Yes	Store PowerPoint slides. Must be published from PowerPoint 2007 or 2010.

TABLE 20.1   Continued

Template Name	List or Library?	Available in SharePoint Foundation 2010?	Available in SharePoint Server 2010 Standard?	Available in SharePoint Server 2010 Enterprise?	Functionality and Notes
Data Connection Library	Library	No	No	Yes	Store Office Data Connection (ODC) file or a Universal Data Connection (UDC) file. InfoPath 2010 is recommended for use in creating ODC or UDC files.
Report Library	Library	No	No	Yes	Designed to store reports. Has the Report and Web Part Page with Status List content types available.
Announcements	List	Yes	Yes	Yes	Designed to store announcements with title, body, and expiration date information.
Contacts	List	Yes	Yes	Yes	Designed to store contact information. If Connect to Outlook is used, will be recognized as Outlook 2007 or 2010 Contacts list and can be edited.
Discussion Board	List	Yes	Yes	Yes	Designed to store threaded discussions.
Links	List	Yes	Yes	Yes	Designed to store links with URL and Notes.

20

continues

TABLE 20.1   Continued

Template Name	List or Library?	Available in SharePoint Foundation 2010?	Available in SharePoint Server 2010 Standard?	Available in SharePoint Server 2010 Enterprise?	Functionality and Notes
Calendar	List	Yes	Yes	Yes	Designed to store items with start and end date and times. Has the Event content type available. If Connect to Outlook is used, will be recognized as Outlook 2007 or 2010 calendar, and can be edited.
Tasks	List	Yes	Yes	Yes	Designed to store task items assigned to a single person and have start date and due dates assigned to them along with other data. The Task and Summary Task content types are available by default. If Connect to Outlook is used, will be recognized as Outlook 2007 or 2010 task list and can be edited.
Project Tasks	List	Yes	Yes	Yes	An extension of the standard Tasks list, the Project Tasks list includes a Gantt style visualization feature. Can also be connected to Outlook 2007 or 2010.

TABLE 20.1   Continued

Template Name	List or Library?	Available in SharePoint Foundation 2010?	Available in SharePoint Server 2010 Standard?	Available in SharePoint Server 2010 Enterprise?	Functionality and Notes
Issue Tracking	List	Yes	Yes	Yes	Designed to store items assigned to a single person, and includes description, category, and other data. Can have related issues.
Survey	List	Yes	Yes	Yes	Designed for soliciting input from users. Input can have usernames visible or by anonymous. Branching logic can be used. Ratings scale and Likert scale are available.
Custom List	List	Yes	Yes	Yes	Blank list that contains the Title field and can be customized to add additional fields as needed.
Custom List in Datasheet View	List	Yes	Yes	Yes	Same as Custom List, but uses a Datasheet view for the default view. The client configuration must support Datasheet view or user won't be able to use the Datasheet view.
External List	List	Yes	Yes	Yes	This requires that an External content type has been defined by the farm administrator.

20

continues

TABLE 20.1   Continued

Template Name	List or Library?	Available in SharePoint Foundation 2010?	Available in SharePoint Server 2010 Standard?	Available in SharePoint Server 2010 Enterprise?	Functionality and Notes
Import Spreadsheet	List	Yes	Yes	Yes	Creates a list from an Excel spreadsheet and translates Excel columns to SharePoint columns.
Status List	List	No	No	Yes	Allows the creation of Indicators that access a view within a list or library, and then calculate the number or percent-age of items that meet certain criteria. Values can then be defined for Red (warning value reached), Yellow (between warning value and goal value), and Green (goal exceeded) values.

The team site template has evolved over several editions of SharePoint and so represents a great deal of thought and review of which lists and libraries are of the most interest to typical user groups. Use of site templates and the process of customizing site templates is covered in Chapter 21, "Designing and Managing Pages and Sites for Knowledge Workers."

TIP

Add a picture library and a contacts list to departmental or team sites created from the Team Site template. The picture library is better suited to storing images than the Site Assets document library that is provided by default, and the contacts list is a very useful way of listing key internal or external contacts that are pertinent to site users.

Creating Lists and Libraries

After the high-level decisions have been made about which lists and libraries will be used and supported by the organization, the next step is to configure a test site with these lists and libraries and configure them to meet the expected needs of the end users and capabilities of IT to support the environment. The following section gives high-level guidelines for these tasks.

Creating lists and libraries requires that the user have the manage lists permission, which permits the creation and deletion of lists, add or remove columns in a list, and add or remove public views of a list. This is available in the full control permission level and the design permission level.

The following methods can be used to create lists and libraries:

▶ From the Site Actions menu, click New Document Library, enter the required information, and then click OK to create the document library.

▶ From the Site Actions menu, click More Options, click the library or list desired, and enter the required information, and then click OK to create the list or library.

▶ From the Site Actions menu, click View All Site Content, click Create underneath the Ribbon area, and click the library or list desired, enter the required information, and then click OK to create the list or library.

Making Basic Decisions About the List or Library

After the template has been selected, the administrator will need to enter in information such as a name for the library, descriptive text, decide whether to enable versioning, and make other choices based on the type of list or library such as whether to email enable the list or library. A general tendency is to "wing it" and make decisions when the individual lists and libraries are configured, but this should be resisted, because lack of consistency will make the environment harder to manage. For example, lack of standards for a list of library names can make it more confusing for visitors to the site, whereas lack of standards on versioning, or whether libraries are configured to allow in-bound emails, can also cause confusion.

For more managed and controlled environments, it is recommended that the organization make decisions on standards for the following items:

▶ **Name and description for the list or library**—Although this sounds pretty self-evident, coming up with a naming scheme can be helpful. It is generally recommended that the name of the list or library include the type of list or library used that is then customized to the specific site that holds it. For example, a slide library created in the HR site could be titled HR Slide Library or HR Slides. If there are

20

multiple document libraries on a site, names like HR Document Library 1, HR Document Library 2 may not seem as memorable as HR Shared Documents or HR Private Documents but scales to dozens of libraries, whereas the "creative" process in coming up with unique descriptive names for a dozen document library can result in confusion.

> **NOTE**
>
> The name chosen initially for the list or library will remain in the URL even if the administrator changes the name and description by accessing the title, description, and navigation link from the settings page.

▶ **Choose whether to display the document library on the Quick Launch**—The Quick Launch can get cluttered quite quickly in a site that is highly utilized and end users are allowed to create new lists and libraries as they need them. Typically, only the most utilized lists and libraries should be included on the Quick Launch. Users should be reminded to use the All Site Content link to get the full listing of lists and libraries (and subsites).

▶ **Decide whether the list or document library can receive email, and what the email address should be**—Although not all lists and libraries support in-bound email, a number do, and this requires that in-bound email has been configured for the farm and is enabled for the site collection. After the basic decision is made, the administrator will need to follow up with configuring the email options from the list or library settings Incoming E-Mail Settings page. This topic is covered in more detail later in this chapter.

▶ **Decide whether versioning is enabled for the document library**—This is a complex decision, and options are discussed later in the chapter. The organization should ideally set a standard for whether versioning is encouraged and supported.

▶ **Select a document template for the document library**—Typically this will be a Word document, but the organization may choose to have different document libraries for different types of templates and then customize the templates once the library is created.

There are also some unique requirements for certain lists or libraries that need to be defined when creating the list or library. For example:

▶ When creating a tasks, project tasks, or issues list, an option is given to Send Email When Ownership Is Assigned. This is a great feature to enable to convey the power of SharePoint alerts to end users, and project managers will love the fact that the person the task is assigned to (or issue) immediately gets an email, so they can't claim they didn't know about the assignment!

▶ When creating a calendar, the administrator must determine whether the calendar is a standard SharePoint calendar, or a Group Calendar, and can be used to share members' schedules. Figure 20.1 shows a calendar that was created to share member's schedules. It will default to only showing the events for the logged-in user, but other users' calendars can be shown by entering their account name in the Add Person field.

▶ When creating a survey, usernames can be shown in survey results, or hidden, and multiple responses can be allowed, or only single responses. The survey wizard will immediately start, allowing the administrator to create the survey on-the-fly, and of course, to return later to modify or add more questions.

▶ An external list requires an External Content Type to be defined before it can be created. External Content Types will be covered in Chapter 22, "Managing Metadata and Content Types in SharePoint 2010."

▶ Before an import spreadsheet list can be created, an Excel spreadsheet must be selected. The administrator then defines the range of data to be imported from the spreadsheet, and clicks Import. SharePoint then attempts to match the type of data stored in the Excel columns to the columns it creates in the list, but because SharePoint doesn't offer all the same columns that Excel does, there may be some differences in how the data is treated, so the results of the import should be reviewed.

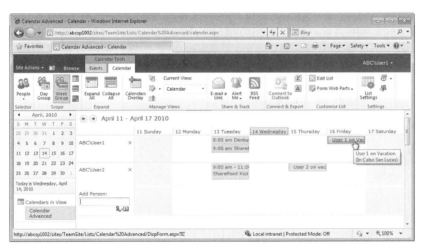

FIGURE 20.1   Group calendar.

20

For organizations that see the value in more extensive planning and testing, it is strongly recommended that each of the lists and libraries available in the version of SharePoint 2010 that will be implemented be created and then tested to determine its relevance to the user community and goals of the project, ease of use, and anticipated support challenges. For example, a form library requires InfoPath 2007 or 2010 to publish forms to it, and then requires trained users to create the forms, and some training for end users to use the forms, and may overcomplicate an implementation that has a limited timeline, and no explicit requirement for SharePoint-based forms. Another example would be the status list, which allows the creation of graphical key performance indicators, which are generally considered essential to dashboards and are visually impressive to end users and managers alike.

Mastering the Library Tab from the Ribbon

Chapter 19, "Using Libraries and Lists in SharePoint 2010," covered the tools available on the Documents tab on the Ribbon inside a document library. This section follows up by reviewing the tools on the Library tab, which are generally of more interest to a document library administrator and power users.

As with the Documents tab, the Library tab allows users to access only the tools that they have permissions to use and that are enabled for the list or library. For example, as shown in Figure 20.2, User2 is logged in and can only use a subset of the tools because she is a member of the Members group for the site, and therefore has contribute-level permissions. The tools that are enabled for a user with contribute-level permissions are as follows:

- ▶ Standard View

- ▶ Datasheet View

- ▶ Show Task Pane (available for use in Datasheet view)

- ▶ Show Totals (available for use in Datasheet view)

- ▶ Refresh Data (available for use in Datasheet view)

- ▶ Create View

- ▶ Navigate Up (available for use if in a subfolder)

- ▶ E-mail a Link

- ▶ Alert Me

- ▶ Sync to SharePoint Workspace (requires that SharePoint Workspace is installed on the PC)

- ▶ Connect to Office with submenu tools of Add to SharePoint Sites, Remove from SharePoint Sites and Manage SharePoint Sites (requires that Office 2010 is installed on the PC)

- ▶ Connect to Outlook (requires that Outlook 2007 or 2010 is installed on the PC)

- ▶ Connect to Excel (requires that Excel 2007 or 2010 is installed on the PC)

- ▶ Open with Explorer

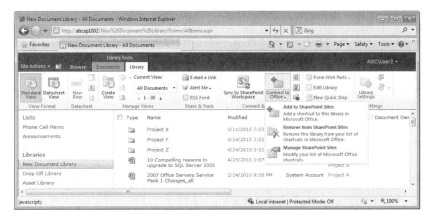

FIGURE 20.2   Library tab in a document library as seen by a user with contribute permissions.

The tools that are not enabled (grayed out) for a user with contribute-level permissions are as follows:

- New Row
- Modify This View
- Create Column
- RSS Feed (because RSS feeds are not enabled for the library)
- Form Web Parts
- Edit Library
- New Quick Step
- Library Settings
- Library Permissions
- Workflow Settings

Chapter 19 covers the Datasheet view in the section titled "Interacting with Lists Using the Datasheet View," and Chapter 25, "Using Office 2010 Applications with SharePoint 2010," provides additional information about the Sync to SharePoint Workspace and Connect to Outlook tools.

This section focuses on those tools that are only available to list and library administrators, with the exception of the Create View tool, which is of critical importance to list and library administrators.

20

Creating and Managing Views

The process of creating views was covered in Chapter 19, in the section titled "Creating a View in a List," and so will be reviewed from the perspective of the list administrator in this section.

One of the main concerns a list or library administrator should have pertains to the columns that are shown in the default view for a list or library (the view that shows by default when a user visits the list) and how it presents the information. It is generally an ongoing process for the list administrator to experiment with the best way to present the data stored in the list or library by manipulating the view by showing or hiding columns, using filtering, using grouping, totals, limiting the number of items shown in each view, and tuning the other options. An example is given in this section of a view that is created using a specific style to leverage the metadata that is available for documents by default (such as created date and time, and created-by information).

TIP

A recommended best practice is to create a view titled Home Page View for each list or library that will have its list view web part added to the home page or other web part page. Generally, the default view can be modified and several columns hidden, which results in the list view web part taking up less space on the page that displays it, which is often the home page to the site.

When the administrator clicks the Create View button from the Library tab on the Ribbon in a document library, several options are provided, which are affected by the software installed on the PC. The basic options are to create Standard View, Datasheet View, Calendar View, or Gantt View. A general recommendation is to experiment with the different views, but in most cases, the Standard view will be used. It is generally recommended that Calendar views be used with a list created from the Calendar template, and the Gantt view be used with a list created from a Project Tasks list.

Options Available When Modifying a View

If the administrator clicks the Modify View button from the Library tab on the Ribbon, he has the option of changing which columns are displayed, and in which order, whether sorting is used, whether filtering is used, and if in-line editing is allowed. Also, the administrator has the option to use Tabular view, which determines whether individual item check boxes are displayed. These allow users to perform bulk operation by checking multiple items at a time. Items in the list or library can be grouped by one or more columns, and the display can default to collapsed or expanded, which can make navigating the list or library much easier. Totals can be displayed for some types of columns, but not all, and the Totals section will show which columns can be totaled, and the options of Count, Average, Maximum, Minimum, Sum, Std Deviation, or Variance will be offered based on the type of data. It is worth noting that calculated columns cannot be totaled.

A variety of styles are offered that change the appearance of the data. For example, the Shaded view style colors each other row a darker shade, making it easier for users to track metadata associated with a document as they scroll to the right. The preview pane is a powerful new view that displays the columns that are selected in the Edit View page. Figure 20.3 shows a document library view that is using the preview pane that was customized to show a subset of columns in the preview pane to provide a data-rich preview of the metadata attached to the document. Note that the documents' filenames are displayed to the right of the Quick Launch, and then when a document name is hovered over, the pane on the right shows the columns that the library administrator has chosen to be shown in the Edit View page. In Figure 20.3, the following columns are displayed:

▶ **ID**—Available in all lists and libraries. Because document names can be long and confusing, showing the ID number of the document that was assigned by SharePoint when the item was uploaded is a quick way to uniquely identify the document.

▶ **Type**—Available in all lists and libraries. The icon associated with the type of document is shown, which is a quick way for the user to tell the type of Office document they are looking at. This is especially useful because the Name column hides the extension of the document.

▶ **Name**—Available in all lists and libraries. This is the name of the file.

▶ **Type of Document**—A column added to this list. The user selects a category for the type of document from a drop-down list.

▶ **Project Name**—A column added to this list. The user selects a project name from a drop-down list.

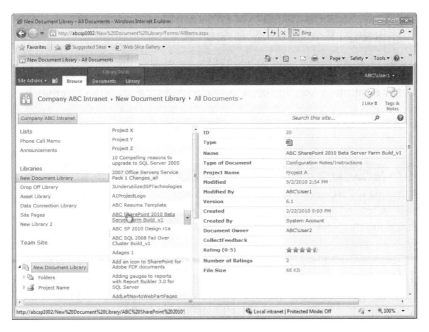

FIGURE 20.3   Example of using the preview pane in a document library.

▶ **Modified**—Available in all lists and libraries. This column displays the date and time the document was last modified.

▶ **Modified By**—Available in all lists and libraries. This column shows the user who modified the document last.

▶ **Version**—Available in all lists and libraries where versioning is enabled. This column shows the version number of the document.

▶ **Created**—Available in all lists and libraries. This column shows the date and time the document was created.

▶ **Created By**—Available in all lists and libraries. This column shows the username who created the document, or who uploaded it originally. It can be helpful to display this column in addition to Modified By because they are often different users, and the user who uploaded it can have significance.

▶ **Document Owner**—A column added to the library, this value needs to be filled in on a per-item basis. Because the Created By value and Modified By values may be different from the person who is responsible for the overall content of the document, a best practice is to add this column for documents that are critical to the operations of the group that uses the site.

▶ **Collect Feedback**—This column was added when the Collect Feedback workflow was added to this list.

▶ **Rating (0-5)**—Ratings were enabled on this library, and this field shows the average rating.

▶ **Number of Ratings**—Shows the number of ratings given for this item. In general, the more ratings given to an item, the more valid the rating.

▶ **File Size**—Available in all lists and libraries. Shows the size of the file in kilobytes. This is a useful value to provide so users have an idea of how long it will take to open the file. For example, a user accessing the SharePoint site over the Internet from a relatively slow connection might decide not to open a document for casual review if it is over 10MB in size.

NOTE

When editing or creating a view, not all columns can be totaled. For example, calculated columns cannot be totaled, which is an annoyance when tracking financial information or other numeric information where calculated columns are used.

In addition, when editing a view, the administrator can choose whether to show folders or show items without folder, and to show the view in all folders, in the top-level folder only, or in folders of a certain content type. Item limits can be set per view, and the administrator enters an integer for the number of items to display, and whether to display in batches of the specified size, or limit the total number of items returned to the specified amount. Finally, the administrator can determine whether the view is enabled for mobile access, and if it is the default view for mobile access, and the number of items to display in web part for the view. This is important to test with any mobile devices supported because the size of the screens will affect the ease of interacting with the view and how many items can be displayed.

Access Views Explained

If the Access View option is chosen from the Create View page, SharePoint will open Access 2007 or 2010 and ask the user to name and save the database that is then created, using the .accdb extension. Right off the bat, there is obviously more to the process than simply creating a "view," but in fact a database is created for which forms, pivot charts, pivot tables, or reports can be created. This database will remain connected to the SharePoint list, so changes in the SharePoint list will be synced with this database.

Figure 20.4 shows the Create Access View window that appears after the Access View option is chosen and the database is named and saved. Figure 20.5 shows the results of choosing the Split Form option. This form can be customized to display exactly the fields that the administrator wants to show, but this is a more advanced and complex process than most administrators will want to engage in to simply modify a view. Content is also displayed in a "nonfriendly" fashion in several fields, such as the Project Name, which includes some characters before the Project Name, and the Rating (0-5) field, where the average rating is displayed to 14 decimal places.

FIGURE 20.4   Creating an Access view from a document library.

20

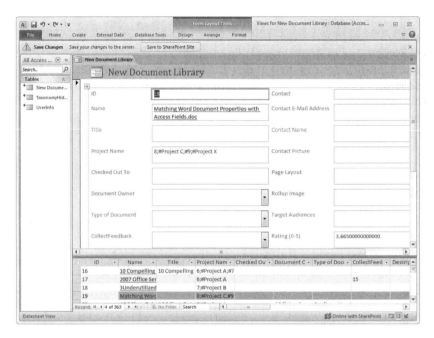

FIGURE 20.5   Split form created in Access.

Synching Content to SharePoint Workspace

If SharePoint Workspace is installed on the computer and the administrator has decided to allow syncing to SharePoint Workspace (by checking Yes for Allow Items from This Document Library to Be Downloaded to Offline Clients from the Advanced Settings page for the document library), this icon will be clickable; otherwise, it will be grayed out. SharePoint Workspace is covered in Chapter 25, "Using Office 2010 Applications with SharePoint 2010."

Connect to Office Options

If the administrator or user clicks the Connect to Office button on the Library tab of the Ribbon, the following options are provided:

▶ **Add to SharePoint Sites**—This adds a shortcut to the list or library in Microsoft Office. If selected, the user will be prompted with a message that states "...your machine must register the user profile service application used by this site...." If Yes is selected, a Library Added message will display, briefly indicating that the process succeeded. Now when the user clicks Save from the Office 2010 application, such as Word 2010, these sites will appear in the Favorites grouping under SharePoint Sites, as shown in Figure 20.6.

▶ **Remove from SharePoint Sites**—Removes the link from SharePoint Sites. A Library Removed message will appear briefly to show that the process completed successfully.

▶ **Manage SharePoint Sites**—Opens the MyQuickLinks.aspx and allows the user to Add Link, Edit Links, Delete, or Create Tag from Link.

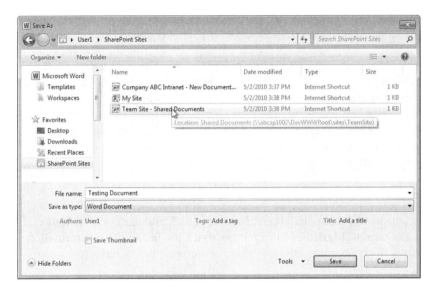

FIGURE 20.6   SharePoint sites links available in the Save As window from Word 2010.

TIP

Using the Add to SharePoint Sites option from the Connect to Office drop-down list in a library is a great way to make it easier for end users to save their documents to a SharePoint library. If they add to SharePoint Sites, the library will then show up in the Save As window underneath Favorites in the SharePoint Sites folder. These links can be easily managed by using the Manage SharePoint Sites tool also available in the Connect to Office drop-down menu.

Connect to Outlook Export to Excel and Open with Explorer Buttons

The Connect to Outlook button is covered in Chapter 25, whereas the Export to Excel button is covered in Chapter 26, "Extending SharePoint 2010 with Excel Services, Access

Services, and Visio Graphics Services." The Open with Explorer button opens the library in a new window using Windows Explorer, and the user can then drag and drop documents into the document library or right-click a document and use the available tools, such as Print, Send to a Compressed (zipped) Folder, Send to the Desktop (create shortcut), Delete the Item, or View Properties of the Item.

Modify Form Web Parts Tools

The Modify Form Web Parts button on the List tab of the Ribbon allows the administrator to open the forms present for the list or library for editing. The editing allowed includes inserting text, image, video and audio, web parts, or the existing list view web part. The properties of the body of the form can be edited, too, such as height, width, chrome state, layout, advanced, and miscellaneous properties. This allows the administrator a great deal of control over how the various forms, such as New, Edit, and Display forms, appear, and over forms associated with content types in use in that list or library. For a simple example, an administrator could add a Video and Audio web part to the New form for a list, which provides instructions on how to fill out the form.

Edit Library Tool

When clicked, this button will open SharePoint Designer 2010, and as shown in Figure 20.7, provides an extensive dashboard of information about the library. This information can be invaluable for a library administrator, as discussed briefly in this section.

From a list administrator's perspective, the dashboard of information provided by SharePoint Designer 2010 provides insight into a variety of areas:

▶ **List Information**—Name and description of the library or list, web address, list ID, last modified, and number of items.

▶ **Customization**—Provides links to the Edit list columns page and Permissions page for this list. Figure 20.8 shows the Columns that exist for the document library New Document Library and show the Column Editor window for the column titled Calculated Column.

▶ **Settings**—Allows the administrator to quickly change settings such as whether to display the list on the Quick Launch, Hide from Browser, Display New Folder Command on the New Menu, Require Content Approval for Submitted Items, Create Versions, Allow Management of Content Types, and provides the Document Template URL.

▶ **Content Types**—Allows the administrator to add new content types, or view and manage settings for existing content types.

▶ **Views**—Create new views or edit existing views.

▶ **Forms**—Create new forms or edit existing forms.

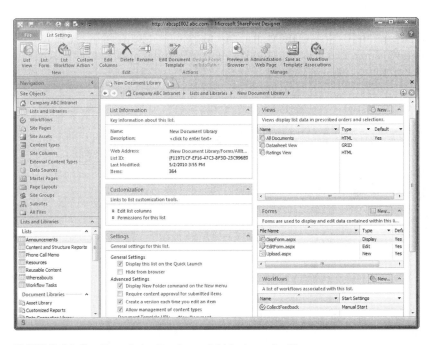

FIGURE 20.7   SharePoint Designer 2010 view of a library.

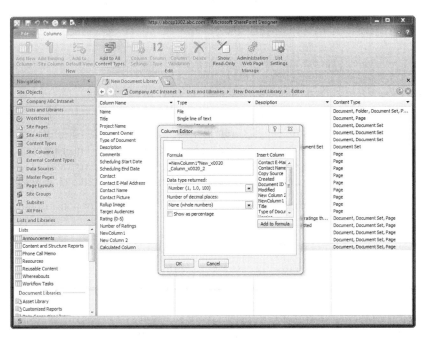

FIGURE 20.8   Column Editor window in SharePoint Designer 2010.

▶ **Workflows**—Create new workflows or edit existing workflows. As shown in Figure 20.9, which shows the result of clicking the Collect Feedback workflow in Figure 20.7, workflow information is provided, customization is allowed, settings and start options can be modified, and forms used are shown.

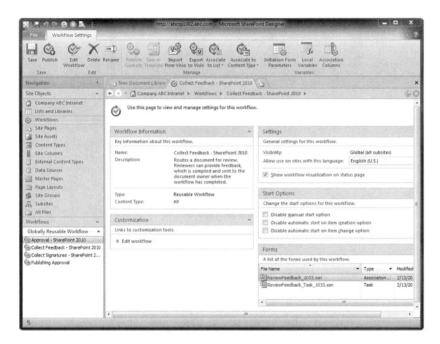

FIGURE 20.9   Workflow Information dashboard in SharePoint Designer 2010.

Just from this quick overview of tools, it appears that SharePoint Designer 2010 offers an alternative to the administrator to the tools provided in the SharePoint 2010 user interface, as reviewed throughout this chapter. It is arguably a faster way for an experienced site administrator to quickly navigate between sites and between lists and make changes.

For example, as visible in the List Settings Ribbon in Figure 20.7, a number of actions can be completed that include:

▶ **List View**—Allows the administrator to create a list view.

▶ **List Form**—Allows the administrator to create a list form.

▶ **List Workflow**—Allows the administrator to create a list workflow.

▶ **Custom Action**—Allows the administrator to create a custom action of the types List Item Menu, Display Form Ribbon, Edit Form Ribbon, New Form Ribbon, and View Ribbon. An example is given later in the chapter on creating a custom action.

▶ **Edit Columns**—Add, edit, or delete column settings.

▶ **Delete**—Delete specific components.

▶ **Rename**—Rename specific components.

▶ **Edit Document Template**—Edit the document template associated with the library.

▶ **Design Forms in InfoPath**—Open InfoPath to create new forms.

▶ **Preview in Browser**—Preview the list or library at different resolutions.

▶ **Administration Web Page**—Opens the Settings page for the list or library.

▶ **Save as Template**—Save the list or library as a template, with the option to include content.

▶ **Workflow Associations**—Opens the Workflow Settings page for the list or library and allows the administrator to decide which items are configured to run the workflow, add or remove workflows, or view workflow reports.

The administrator should work with the tools provided in SharePoint Designer 2010, as well as the user interface provided by SharePoint 2010, and decide which is their preferred method of managing SharePoint lists and libraries.

An Example of Creating a Custom Action

From SharePoint Designer 2010, with a library opened (for example, by clicking the Edit Library link from the Library tab of the Ribbon), follow these steps to add an entry to the drop-down menu in a document library. This is a powerful way for an administrator to provide added functionality within a list or library, but should be considered an advanced and potentially dangerous process:

1. Click the Custom Action drop-down menu and select List Item Menu.

2. Per Figure 20.10, enter a name and description and then specify either Navigate to Form, Initiate Workflow, or Navigate to URL. For this example, a link will be added that simply navigates to a different website. Enter the Name as `Go To Microsoft's Web Site`, set the action as Navigate to URL, and enter http://www.microsoft.com.

3. Scroll down, and in the Rights Mask section, enter `EditListItems`. This will result in this menu item only displaying to users with EditListItems permissions.

> **TIP**
>
> For additional information about the options for rights masks, access the following link: http://msdn.microsoft.com/en-us/library/microsoft.sharepoint.spbasepermissions. aspx. Some examples include ViewListItems, Open, and DeleteListItems. Understanding which default groups have which permissions allows the site administrator to create menu entries that only appear for the appropriate users.

4. Click OK. This will save the new menu item to the document library. No save is needed from Designer 2010.

FIGURE 20.10   Create Custom Action window in Designer 2010.

5. Navigate to the document library that was opened in SharePoint Designer 2010; in this example, it was named New Document Library. Access the drop-down menu for an item, and validate that the new entry appears, as shown in Figure 20.11.

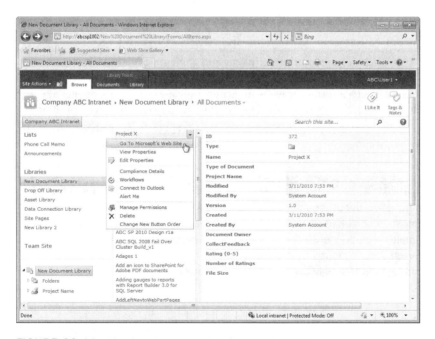

FIGURE 20.11   Viewing the new action for a library item.

6. Next access the Sign in as Different User from the drop-down menu next to the user-name in the upper-right corner, and log in as a user who does not have EditListItems permissions (in this example, User3 is a member of the Visitor's group, and does not have EditListItems permissions) and verify that this new menu item does not appear.

New Quick Step Button

The New Quick Step button opens SharePoint Designer 2010 and a window titled Add a Button, which provides the options to Start a New Workflow or Start an Existing Workflow and to define the Button Label and link to a Button Image. Creating workflows in SharePoint Designer 2010 is covered in Chapter 28, "Out-of-the-Box Workflows and Designer 2010 Workflows."

Document Library Settings Page Tools Reviewed

As one of the most commonly used libraries, the document library is a good starting point for the tools that are available for list and library administrators. The document library settings page is reached by entering the document library, clicking the Library tab on the Ribbon, and then clicking the Library Settings icon on the right-hand side of the toolbar. The resulting array of tools will vary based on whether SharePoint Foundation 2010, SharePoint Server 2010 Standard, or Enterprise is being used. Only users with the Manage Lists permission will be able to click the Library Settings icon, as it will be grayed out for other users.

Figure 20.12 shows the document library settings page for a document library created with the team site template in SharePoint Foundation 2010, and Figure 20.13 shows the document library settings page for a document library created with the team site template in SharePoint Server 2010 Enterprise. It is immediately apparent that the SharePoint Foundation 2010 document library has fewer tools in the General Settings, Permission, and Management and Communications sections of the page. Because of this, the job of the library or list administrator is technically easier with SharePoint Foundation 2010 than with SharePoint Server 2010 Standard or Enterprise, simply due to there being fewer tools and features available.

Table 20.2 provides an overview of the different tools available on the Document Library Settings page for the three different versions of SharePoint 2010, and for sites that are publishing enabled sites. The tools available depend on which version of SharePoint 2010 is being used and which site and site collection features are enabled. So, for example, if SharePoint Server 2010 Enterprise is in use, and the site administrator doesn't see a tool in the document library settings, the culprit is most likely that a feature for the site or site collection has not been enabled. These can be configured from the Site Settings page in Site Actions, by clicking Manage Site Features in the Site Actions section, or by clicking Site Collection Features in the Site Collection Administration section.

20

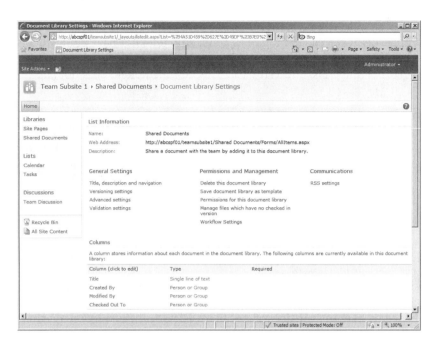

FIGURE 20.12   Document library settings for a SharePoint Foundation 2010 document library.

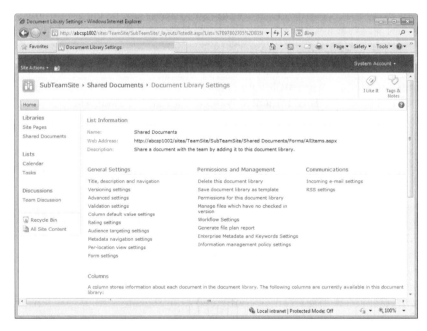

FIGURE 20.13   Document library settings for a SharePoint Server 2010 Enterprise document library.

TABLE 20.2   Document Library Settings Tools for Document Libraries

	SharePoint Foundation 2010 Document Library	SharePoint Server 2010 Standard Document Library (in Nonpublishing Site)	SharePoint Server 2010 Standard Document Library (in Publishing Site)	SharePoint Server 2010 Enterprise Document Library (in Nonpublishing Site)	SharePoint Server 2010 Enterprise Document Library (in Publishing Site)
Title, description and navigation	Yes	Yes	Yes	Yes	Yes
Versioning settings	Yes	Yes	Yes	Yes	Yes
Advanced settings	Yes	Yes	Yes	Yes	Yes
Validation settings	Yes	Yes	Yes	Yes	Yes
Column default value settings	No	Yes	Yes	Yes	Yes
Manage item scheduling	No	No	Yes	No	Yes
Rating settings	No	Yes	Yes	Yes	Yes
Audience targeting settings	No	Yes	Yes	Yes	Yes
Metadata navigation settings	No	Yes	Yes	Yes	Yes
Per-location view settings	No	Yes	Yes	Yes	Yes
Form settings	No	No	No	Yes	Yes
Delete this document library	Yes	Yes	Yes	Yes	Yes

continues

TABLE 20.2   Continued

	SharePoint Foundation 2010 Document Library	SharePoint Server 2010 Standard Document Library (in Nonpublishing Site)	SharePoint Server 2010 Standard Document Library (in Publishing Site)	SharePoint Server 2010 Enterprise Document Library (in Nonpublishing Site)	SharePoint Server 2010 Enterprise Document Library (in Publishing Site)
Save document library as template	Yes	Yes	Yes	Yes	Yes
Permissions for this document library	Yes	Yes	Yes	Yes	Yes
Manage files that have no checked-in version	Yes	Yes	Yes	Yes	Yes
Workflow settings	Yes	Yes	Yes	Yes	Yes
Enterprise metadata and keywords settings	No	Yes	Yes	Yes	Yes
Generate file plan report	No	Yes	Yes	Yes	Yes
Information management policy settings	No	Yes	Yes	Yes	Yes
Record declaration settings	No	Yes	Yes	Yes	Yes
Incoming email settings	No	Yes	Yes	Yes	Yes
RSS settings	Yes	Yes	No	Yes	No

Versioning Settings

Document versioning is often one of the driving goals for a SharePoint or other document management platform implementation project. This is a "basic" functionality not available with a standard file share and allows users to save copies of the document as it evolves without having to change the actual filename of the document. An example is given of a document uploaded as a draft and then approved below to illustrate what an end user would experience when interacting with a document library with major and minor versioning enabled.

Figure 20.14 shows the Versioning Settings page for a document library, which includes the Content Approval, Document Version History, and Draft Item Security sections of the page. Not visible in the figure is the final option to require documents to be checked out before they can be edited.

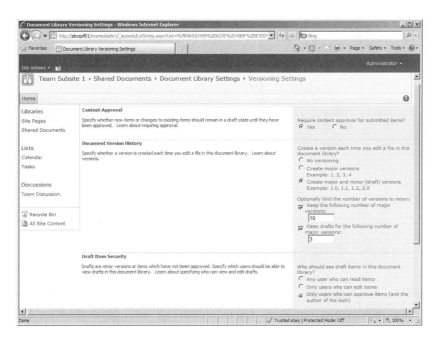

FIGURE 20.14   Versioning Settings page for a document library.

As with many SharePoint 2010 features, this one is complex, and there are many different combinations that can be configured. In this example, the library is configured for maximum control because Require Content Approval for Submitted Items is set to Yes, major and minor versions are enabled, a maximum number of major versions is set, as well as a number of major versions for which minor versions will be kept. Finally, at the bottom of the page, the library is configured so that only users who can approve items and the author of the item can see the item. So, a sample flow of a document submitted to this library is as follows:

1. User2 uploads a document to the library.

2. The document is saved, but in Draft Status (version 0.1), and no one but users of the site with approve items privileges and the author (User2) can see the document.

3. User2 believes the document is ready for others to see it, and decides to "publish" the document, which will create a major version (version 1.0). User2 selects the document and clicks the Publish button in the Documents tab Ribbon. User2 enters comments about this document and clicks OK.

4. User1 checks the document library regularly and in the Approve/Reject items view of the document library, available from the Browse tab, sees that there is one document with approval status Pending. User1 accesses the drop-down menu for the document and selects Approve/Reject. The Approve/Reject window opens, as shown in Figure 20.15, and User1 selects Approved, enters comments, and clicks OK.

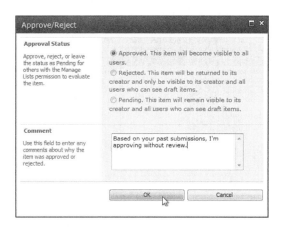

FIGURE 20.15   Approve/Reject window.

5. User2 now can see that the approval status of the document is set to Approved, and after checking version history for the document, sees that there is now only one version, version 1.0, because the version number was incremented at the approval stage.

Chapter 19, in the section titled "How to Use the Publish, Unpublish, and Cancel Approval Tools," covers additional tools related to versioning and publishing, and an even more involved example is provided that includes the use of a workflow that automatically notifies participants in the process that their involvement is needed. Also, the topic of content scheduling is covered in this section.

Returning to the concept of planning lists and libraries, Table 20.3 provides some guidelines for when to use versioning, page approval, content approval, and scheduling features. A recommendation that can be seen in this table is to enable only major versioning in environments where "basic collaboration" is required, and where the users are new to SharePoint. This is a generalization, but after testing the different configuration options, most organizations realize that the process can easily become overly complex and frustrating for users who only need basic collaboration ("some place to store my files other than the file share") and haven't used SharePoint or another document management or enterprise content management system.

TABLE 20.3   Guidelines for Using Versioning, Page Approval Workflows, Content Approval, and Scheduling in Document Libraries

	Basic Collaboration (New SharePoint Users)	Basic Collaboration for (Experienced SharePoint Users)	Managing Content That Should Be Approved Before the "General Public" Can View It (New SharePoint Users)	Managing Content That Should Be Approved Before the "General Public" Can View It (Experienced SharePoint Users)	Date-Sensitive Materials (Negative Effects if Released Too Soon)
Require Content Approval Enabled	No	No	Yes	Yes	Yes
Major Versioning Enabled	Yes	Yes	Yes	Yes	Yes
Minor Versioning Enabled	No	No	Yes	Yes	Yes
Draft Item Security Locked Down?	No	No	Maybe	Yes	Yes
Require Check Out Before a Document Can Be Edited?	No	Maybe	Maybe	Yes	Maybe

continues

TABLE 20.3   Continued

	Basic Collaboration (New SharePoint Users)	Basic Collaboration for (Experienced SharePoint Users)	Managing Content That Should Be Approved Before the "General Public" Can View It (New SharePoint Users)	Managing Content That Should Be Approved Before the "General Public" Can View It (Experienced SharePoint Users)	Date-Sensitive Materials (Negative Effects if Released Too Soon)
Page Approval Workflow Enabled	No	No	No	Yes	Maybe
Scheduling Enabled	No	No	No	No	Yes

Advanced Settings Examined from a Library Design Standpoint

The Advanced Settings link on the Document Library Settings page reveals additional tools of interest to the architect or administrator. In fact, these settings are so fundamental to the overall functionality of the document library that time should be spent reviewing these options and the pros and cons to the organization during the design and testing phases.

For example, the decision of whether to Allow Management of Content Types can have wide-reaching impact on the complexity of the environment and amount of training required for users and administrators of the libraries. The ability to edit the template used by the document library may lead the architects to choose to create document libraries dedicated to the management of a single type of document (for example, resumes) and configure the template accordingly. In addition, the architects may decide that content from certain document libraries should not be able to be synced to Outlook clients or to the SharePoint Workspace product. All of these settings are accessed via the Advanced Settings link. A more detailed summary of these options is as follows:

▶ **Allow Management of Content Types**—The options are Yes or No. Content types can be an extremely powerful tool for more sophisticated document management in organizations that have invested time in creating a taxonomy for managing resources in SharePoint. Content types are discussed more in Chapter 22.

▶ **Provide a Template URL**—This option will be grayed out if Allow Management of Content Types is set to Yes because in that case, the templates are managed with each content type. If content types are not enabled for the library, the administrator can click the Edit Template link to open the document in the appropriate application (such as Word) and then edit the template. This is an easy way for the library administrator to customize the template document for the library and is most useful if the document library has been created for a specific purpose, such as containing a specific type of document (for example, proposals, resumes, diagrams, spreadsheets, or other standard Microsoft document types).

NOTE

Although it appears that the URL of "any" document stored in a SharePoint document library can be entered in the Provide a Template URL field, the template must actually exist in the Forms directory of the document library. This is accessible by using the Edit Template link on the Advanced Settings page below the URL field. If a different URL is provided, an error will be given once the administrator tries to save the configuration.

▶ **Determine Open Behavior for Browser-Enabled Documents**—The options are to Open in the Client Application, Open in the Browser, or Use the Server Default (Open in the Browser).

▶ **Define a Custom Send to Destination**—This location will be visible if a user selects a document and then clicks the Send To icon in the Documents tab of the Ribbon, or accesses the drop-down menu for an item in the document library and clicks the Send To submenu. By inputting a URL of a different document library, the library administrator makes it easy for users to send documents to a specific location. Although this feature isn't commonly used, it can encourage users to make a copy of the document in another document library and can prompt the author to send out updates when the document is checked in and create an alert on the source document.

▶ **Make New Folder Command Available**—The library administrator should decide whether to allow the use of folders within the document library, a topic discussed in detail in Chapter 19, in the section titled "Pros and Cons of the New Folder Tool."

▶ **Allow Items from This Document Library to Appear in Search Results**—Bearing in mind that all SharePoint search results are security trimmed, so only users with permissions to at least view the document will see its contents appear in searches, there are still rare situations where the contents of a document library should not appear in search results. For example, a document library may be created for brainstorming, but the contents of that document library should be moved to another document library (possibly by using a custom send to destination) before being available via the search tool. This helps ensure that the results of searches are as relevant as possible.

▶ **Allow Items from This Document Library to be Downloaded to Offline Clients**—This applies both to using SharePoint Workspace and syncing with the Outlook client. If this option is enabled, users will receive errors if they try and

20

synchronize to Outlook or use SharePoint Workspace to sync content. The error messages are very clear. For example, the error from the Resolve tab in SharePoint Workspace states, "Your administrator has prevented this list from being taken offline." Note that content can still be Exported to Excel.

▶ **Should This Library Be a Site Assets Library**—If Yes is checked, this library will be presented as the default location in the drop-down list for storing images or other files that users upload to their wiki pages. This does not convert the library into an assets library, and does not add any content types to the library.

▶ **Allow Items in This Document Library to Be Edited Using the Datasheet**— The datasheet option was covered in more detail in Chapter 19, in the section titled "Interacting with Lists Using the Datasheet View," and this setting allows the administrator to make the datasheet view available or not. Although the datasheet view can be a time saver, it can also facilitate massive changes to metadata and might not be recommended for new users. Alternatively, the Datasheet view can be enabled initially when documents are uploaded and tagged with metadata, but then turned off once that process is complete.

▶ **Launch Forms in a Dialog**—Setting this to No will cause the whole page to change instead of the AJAX form to load. For example, if this is set to No, when a user clicks Upload Document, the whole page changes to the upload.aspx page, rather than the AJAX form loading and the background dimming. This may be more comfortable to users familiar with previous versions of SharePoint and should be considered for testing.

Validation Settings

If this link is clicked, the library administrator will be taken to the Validation Settings page, as shown in Figure 20.16, where she can specify a formula to validate the data when new items are saved to the list or are edited. User message text can be entered as well, so the end user is informed of the criteria that weren't met successfully. In this example, the formula is as follows:

```
=ProjectNumber>5000
```

This translates to: The value entered in the ProjectNumber column must exceed 5000 to provide a value of True.

If the results of the equation entered do not equal a value of True, the user will get an error, which will be in one of two formats, depending on whether the user is trying to upload a document and enter incorrect/invalid metadata or if the user is trying to edit metadata for an existing document in the library. If the user is uploading a document and enters incorrect metadata, an error screen will display that says "List data validation failed" but will not display the user message text. If the user is editing metadata for a document already in the library, she will see the actual message text entered. In this example, the message is "You must enter a number greater than 5000 to pass validation."

This feature is examined in more detail in Chapter 22.

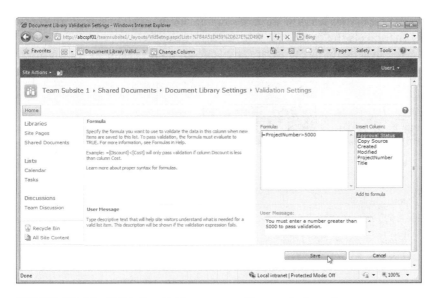

FIGURE 20.16   Validation Settings page with sample formula.

Column Default Value Settings

Not available in SharePoint Foundation 2010, this tool allows the library administrator to set a default value for columns in the library. This feature is covered in more detail in Chapter 22. From a list or library design standpoint, it is important to know that by using the Column Default Value Settings link from the Document Library Settings page, the administrator can set values based on folders, which can be a much more powerful and useful ability than setting default values on a column basis.

Manage Item Scheduling

This feature on the Document Library Settings page will be seen only in document libraries on publishing-enabled sites, and is not available in SharePoint Foundation 2010. The tool will be available only if the list or library has major and minor versioning enabled, as well as content approval enabled. Assuming that the library meets these criteria, the Enable Scheduling of Items in This List option can be enabled from the Manage Item Scheduling page. Once enabled, any items that have content types that include start and end dates can be scheduled for publication.

20

Figure 20.17 shows the Properties window for a document that has just been uploaded to a document library that meets the criteria for scheduling. The content type of Page is selected, which includes a Scheduling Start Date and Scheduling End Date, as shown in Figure 20.17.

FIGURE 20.17   Entering scheduling start and end dates for a document.

Because content approval needs to be enabled, the document would need to be published to a major version and then approved by a user with Approve Items permissions in the library. Then, once the scheduling start date and time is reached, the item will be available for users who didn't have the ability to see the draft version of the document to now see it and interact with it as their permissions allow.

Item scheduling is a fairly specialized tool, and because it has several dependencies that need to be configured for it to be available, as mentioned in this section, it is typically enabled only when there is a specific need to limit the timeframe during which the item is available.

Rating Settings

This page allows the library administrator to decide whether items in the list or library can be rated. If Allow Items in This List to Be Rated? is set to Yes, users with read permission level of higher can provide ratings in a list or library. If ratings are enabled for a list or library, two ratings fields are added to the content types available for the list: average rating and number of ratings. In addition, a column Rating (0-5) is added to the default view.

Ratings are a powerful tool that encourages users to rate documents or list items on a scale of 0 to 5. Although it is impossible to enforce "responsible" use of ratings, users should be informed that SharePoint does in fact track who rates documents how, and in fact, other users can see what ratings a specific user applies from their My Site from the My Newsfeed tab. So if, for example, a user chooses to rate everything as a 1, other users will see this and possibly apply social pressure on the user to be more constructive in his ratings. If enough users apply ratings, the number of ratings will make the frivolous ratings less significant through the power of averages. Figure 20.18 gives an example of a document library where a view was created that sorts the documents by the value in the Rating (0-5) column. This view could be set as a default, so users would immediately see the "most popular" documents in the library as ranked by their co-workers.

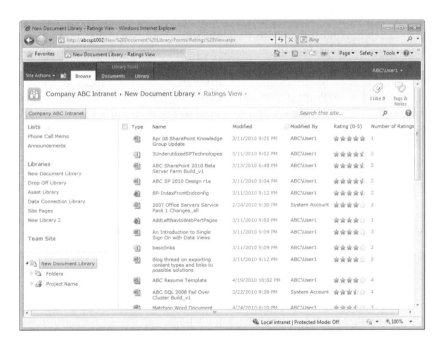

FIGURE 20.18   A document library view sorted by ratings.

The use of ratings from My Site is covered in Chapter 23, "Leveraging Social Networking Tools in SharePoint 2010."

Audience Targeting

Audience targeting can be enabled for lists and libraries, but audiences are compiled based on settings configured from Central Administration. This topic is covered in Chapter 21, because the audience targeting process happens when web parts are configured on a SharePoint page to use audience targeting to filter the content that is displayed.

It is important for a list and library administrator to understand the topic and decide whether it should be enabled for some or all libraries/lists because this will be another

metadata item that end users or list administrators will need to configure to ensure that
members of a specific audience are in fact seeing all the documents that should be
targeted to them.

Metadata Navigation

Metadata navigation is a powerful tool available in SharePoint Server 2010 Standard or
Enterprise, and involves the configuration of hierarchy fields, key filters, and the management of column indices. Essentially, the Navigation Hierarchy fields allow a user to click
in a tree structure to view the content contained in folders, or that meet the field criteria
(such as using a specific content type). The Key Filter fields allow the user to also filter the
results based on specific criteria, such as modified by a certain user.

This fills a functionality "hole" that was present in SharePoint 2007 and earlier versions,
because document libraries could be difficult to navigate within if folders were used and
filters were somewhat difficult to use. Navigating down into folders required only a click
the folder, but navigating up required using the back arrow in the browser, or using the
breadcrumb trail. Filtering in SharePoint 2007 required clicking the column heading and
then choosing the type of filter, but once set, the user couldn't tell what the filter was, so
in complex searches, it was easy to get confused. With these two new tools, it is intuitive
to navigate within document libraries using folders, content types, managed metadata,
and to apply multiple filters to the content.

This topic is covered in more depth in Chapter 22.

Per-Location View Settings

Next on the Document Library Settings page, is the link to Per-Location View settings. As
covered previously in this chapter, views are a fundamental tool for the list or library
administrator to make the end user experience with the list or library a productive one.
SharePoint 2010 allows the list or library administrator to determine which views are
available from within folders in the list or library.

Figure 20.19 shows the Per-Location View page for a document library. The Location to
Configure tree on the left shows the items defined from the Document Library Settings
Metadata Navigation Settings. The topmost entry in each of these has customized Per-
Location Views, and correspondingly slightly modified icons. In other words, these "loca-
tions" do not inherit all the view settings from their parents, and they match the settings
visible but not yet saved in Figure 20.19. This means that an end user who has navigated
to the Project X folder will see only the views that are defined as available at that location.
Likewise, a user who clicks one of the other Metadata Navigation Settings options, such as
Project A, will see only the views defined as available for that location.

Although possibly confusing initially, this is yet another toolset for the list administrator
who has created multiple views and uses folders and metadata to manage files in the
document library to control which views are available to end users who navigate to the
folders or use the Metadata Navigation tool.

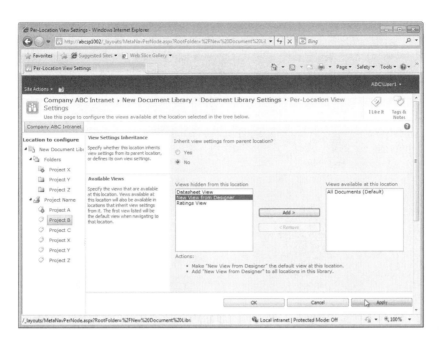

FIGURE 20.19   Per-Location View page.

Form Settings Tool

SharePoint 2010 will not allow the use of this tool for all lists and libraries, and clicking the Form Settings link may simply display a message that states "InfoPath does not support customizing the form used for this list." But if the forms are supported, the administrator can open the form in InfoPath 2010, and then edit the form to her heart's content.

An example is given in this section of creating a rule in InfoPath that should impress readers with the power suddenly placed in their hands by InfoPath via this tool. A good example to use is the ubiquitous Announcements list. Follow these steps to edit the form used in an Announcements list (InfoPath Designer 2010 must be installed on the computer in use):

1. Navigate to an Announcements list, click the List tab on the Ribbon, and click List Settings.
2. Click Form Settings from the General Settings column.
3. Under Content Type, the Announcement content type should be selected and the circle next to Customize the current form using Microsoft InfoPath checked. Click OK.
4. InfoPath Designer 2010 will open and display the form.
5. Click the Expires field, also shown in Figure 20.20, and then click Add Rule from the Home tab.

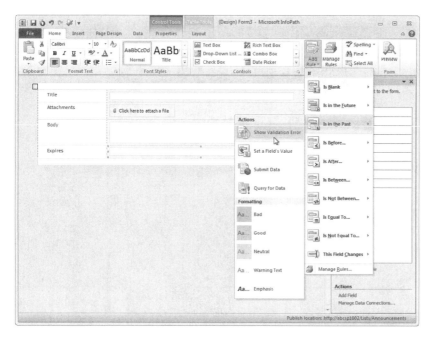

FIGURE 20.20   Editing an Announcements form in InfoPath Designer 2010.

6. Select Is in the Past, and then Show Validation Error from the Actions submenu, as shown in Figure 20.20.

7. Review the results in the Rules menu on the right side of the screen. Notice that a screen tip is autopopulated: "Enter today's date or a date in the future."

8. Click the File tab, and then click the Quick Publish button to publish the updated form to the SharePoint 2010 Announcements list.

9. Navigate to the SharePoint 2010 Announcements list, and click Add New Announcement, and enter a new announcement with a date that is in the past, and once that date is entered, an error message should display, as shown in Figure 20.21. SharePoint will not allow the form to be saved unless the date entered is in the past.

This simple example just scratches the surface of the power of InfoPath in the hands of experienced list and library administrators who can easily customize the form used to add a new list item or edit a list item in a few minutes.

Permissions and Management Tools for Lists and Libraries

The Permissions and Management column on the Document List Settings page provides even more tools that the list or library administrator must be familiar with. This section covers a subset of these tools because a number of them are covered in other chapters, which are referenced as needed.

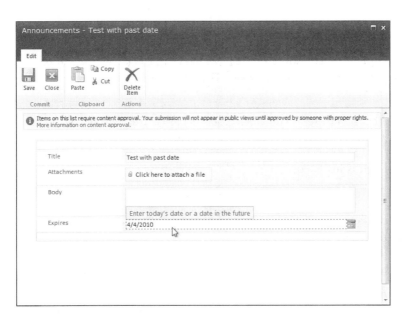

FIGURE 20.21   Validation error when a value doesn't match the InfoPath rule.

Delete This Document Library

Every once and a while, the site administrator may need to delete a document library, and the tool will execute as soon as the Delete This Document Library link is clicked. The administrator will see a message that states "This document library will be removed and all its files will be deleted. Are you sure you want to send this document library to the site Recycle Bin?" If the administrator clicks OK, the document library and all its content will be moved to the site Recycle Bin. The End User Recycle Bin will now list the document library. If deleted from the End User Recycle Bin, it will be listed in the site collection Recycle Bin, so a site collection administrator can still restore it. If deleted from the Site Collection Recycle Bin, it will be permanently deleted and will need to be recovered from other backups of the site collection.

Save Document Library as Template

Most organizations will customize a selection of lists and libraries and then use them as templates. This section gives an example of creating a List template from a document library and some tips pertaining to the use of these templates (as well as some of the limitations). Although these templates can be very useful, a site administrator should test them thoroughly to become familiar with the upsides as well as downsides of using them, and might want to focus instead on using site templates for reasons provided next.

To create a List template, follow these steps:

1. From the Document Library Settings page for the library, click the Save Document Library as Template link.

2. Enter a filename (for example, **DocLib050410**) and a template name (which can be the same as the filename). Leave the Save Content box unchecked. Click OK.

3. The Operation Completed Successfully message will appear. Click the List Template Gallery link visible in the body of the message. The List Template Gallery for the site collection will open.

The templates are stored in the List template gallery, accessible via the Site Settings page for the site, by clicking List Templates from the Galleries section. After a List template has been saved, it will be available from the Create.aspx page for lists and libraries, or the Create window if SilverLight is installed.

The following list provides some tips for effectively using it:

▸ Create a site that contains the template lists and libraries so they can be edited at a later date and then save to the List Template Gallery. Do not use this site for production purposes (for example, storing "live" files or list data) because it will be modified in the future and new templates created from it, possibly Site templates, as well.

▸ Create a logical naming scheme for the List templates that includes an identifier, such as the date it was created. For example, a name such as ProjectDocLib010110 is more useful than DocLibraryV1 because it describes the type of library (a project library) and contains the date when it was created, which will be visible when creating new libraries from it.

▸ Although the option is given to Include Content when creating a template, there is a fairly small size limit of 50MB. Therefore, this is not a very powerful backup and restore tool for document libraries because most document libraries quickly exceed this limit, but could be useful for lists.

▸ List templates are only shared within a site collection. List templates can be saved locally from one List Template Gallery and then uploaded to other List Template Galleries for other site collections.

▸ Changes to the List template will not affect lists previously created with the List template. So, for example, if five lists have been created using AnnouncementsTemplate050410, each one will need to be visited separately to replicate the changes.

▸ When the List template is used to create a list at a later date, consider putting the name of the template used in the description field of the list. This will make it easier to tell which template was used to create which list at a later date.

▸ If too many List templates are created, the Create page or Create window will become very cluttered and confusing. Consider creating Site templates rather than List templates for this reason.

Although it is not a recommended best practice to modify the List template, more advanced administrators may be interested in viewing the contents of the List template.

Follow these steps to view the contents of a List template manifest xml document for a template created for a document library:

1. Visit the List Template Gallery and choose a template. Right-click the name of the template (DocLib050410, for example, as created previously) and click Save Target As. Save the document to your desktop using the same name. Note that the file extension is .stp.

2. Click Open Folder when the download completes.

3. Right click the STP file and click Rename. Change the extension of the file from .stp to .cab. Press Enter.

> **NOTE**
>
> You might need to change the view settings in Control Panel if you can't edit the extension. For Windows 7, navigate to the Control Panel, click Folder Options, click the View tab, unselect Hide Extensions for Known File Types, and then click OK, and you should be able to now change the extension.

4. Click Yes for the Rename warning. The file will now be listed as a .cab file.

5. Right-click the file and click Open. This will show the contents of the .cab file.

6. Right-click the manifest XML file and click Extract. Save to the desktop once again.

7. Locate the manifest file on the desktop, right-click the document, and choose Open With, and select Internet Explorer. You will now be able to see all the contents of the manifest file.

Armed with the preceding information, the site administrator should experiment with using List templates and determine whether they provide value for the organization or whether creating these templates clutters up the list creation options and will be confusing, and whether site templates, each with customized lists, make more sense for the organization.

Permissions for This Document Library

Site administrators should be aware that lists permissions can be customized, and be familiar with the process. However, they should also be aware that lists and libraries with customized or "unique" permissions can be difficult to manage, and records should be kept of the changes that are made. There is no "magic" report that lists all unique permissions used within a site collection or site, so a general best practice is to avoid customizing permissions for lists and libraries unless strictly necessary.

20

TIP

Instead of customizing permissions on a list or library basis, consider creating a sub-site with the revised permissions for that site—for example, if a site (http://intranet/SiteA) is accessible to "everyone" (for example, abc\domain users have read access to it) in the organization. The site administrator wants to have a few libraries and lists that are only accessible to a select group (for example, abc\IT). Instead of modifying the permissions on those lists and libraries, he creates a subsite that houses those lists and libraries (http://intranet/SiteA/SiteAPrivate) and stops inheriting permissions for the site, and then removes abc\domain users from access to that site, and gives abc\IT users contribute permissions. Although this might seem like overkill initially, users can be easily taught that the subsite (SiteAPrivate) is where they upload documents that are for more restricted use, while the parent site (SiteA) is where documents that are available for anyone with a domain account to read. And the administrator now doesn't need to customize permissions for any lists or libraries on either site!

Follow these steps to customize permissions for document library:

1. For the document library, access the Document Library Settings page and click Permissions for this document library.

2. Notice whether a note appears that says "This library inherits permissions from its parent." If this message appears under the Ribbon, any changes to the parent will affect this document library. To change the permissions, click Stop Inheriting Permissions on the Edit tab of the Ribbon.

3. Click OK when the warning appears, stating "You are about to create unique permissions for this document library."

4. Check boxes next to the individual users or groups that are to be removed or modified. Then click Remove User Permissions or Edit User Permissions as appropriate, and repeat until the desired result is achieved.

5. Before exiting, click the Check Permissions icon and enter one or more individuals' names, and then click the Check Now button to see what permissions, if any, the users or groups have after the changes made in step 4.

6. Finally, the Inherit Permissions icon can be clicked to overwrite your changes with the permissions assigned at the parent site level. This is basically a "get out of jail free" tool that can be used to undo undesirable changes.

Manage Files That Have No Checked-In Version

It is a fairly rare occurrence that a file will have no checked-in version, but the Manage Files Which Have No Checked In Version tool on the Document Library Settings page does come in handy is certain situations. This tool is not helpful if a user simply checks out a file and then forgets to check it back in because there will be a checked-in version that exists before the file is checked out.

Where this tool is handy is when documents are uploaded to the document library but required metadata is not entered. This can happen when the Open with Explorer button on the Library tab of the Ribbon is used and multiple documents are pasted into it, or the upload multiple documents tool is used from the Documents tab. Because many end users will want to save time, it can occur that the uploaded files will end up in a checked-out status, and the list administrator will need to access this link and add the required metadata to the items and then check them in.

Workflow Settings

This page allows the administrator to see the number of workflows in progress for the list or library, to set the types of items that the workflows are configured to run on, and to as add and remove workflows and view workflow reports. As noted on this page, selecting a different type will navigate the user to the Workflow Settings page for the content type that is modified.

The Three-State Workflow is the only workflow template provided in SharePoint Foundation 2010, whereas others are available in SharePoint Server 2010. SharePoint Server 2010 Standard and Enterprise provides the following workflow templates: Disposition Approval, Publishing Approval, Collection Signatures, Approval, and Collection Feedback.

The workflow reports available are the Activity Duration Report and Cancellation & Error Report, and are generated on-the-fly, saved to a SharePoint library, and can then be immediately opened after generation without having to go to the library.

Document Sets Compared to Folders as Organizational Tools in Document Libraries

Document sets are a powerful tool that can be enabled for site collections that allow users to keep related documents together as a "set" to facilitate collaboration on the documents. When a user clicks a document set, such as Project X Document Set used in the examples in this section, all the files stored in the document set will be visible, as shown in Figure 20.22. In this way, document sets are similar to folders, but as explained in this section, they have a variety of differences that are important to understand from an administrative standpoint that are reviewed in this section. From a high level, folders are simpler to enable, are more limited in functionality, and so make a better choice for less-advanced users or simpler collaboration requirements. But once the capabilities of document sets are understood, many organizations will benefit from their capabilities.

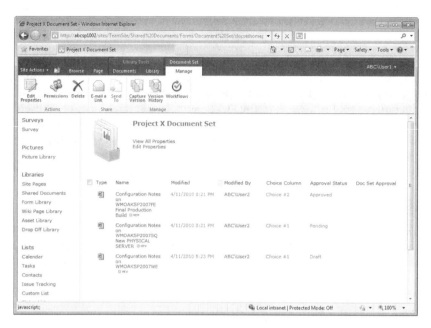

FIGURE 20.22 Sample document set in a document library.

Document sets are designed specifically to help users organize groups of files as a unit and give some special tools to users to facilitate the management of the group of documents as a whole such as the ability to assign metadata to a document set, start a workflow on a document set, and capture a version of the entire set of documents. Following are some key technical details of document sets:

▶ Document sets are not available in SharePoint Foundation 2010.

▶ Document sets are available in SharePoint Server 2010 Standard and Enterprise editions.

▶ A document set is a content type, with Document Collection Folder as the parent, and uses the Name column from the Folder content type and title from the Item content type.

▶ There is no hard limit on the number of documents that can exist in a document set.

▶ Permissions changes to a document set do affect all items within the document set.

▶ An alert set on a document set will apply to contents of the document set.

▶ Deleting a document set sends the document set and all members of the document set to the Recycle Bin.

▶ If the Send To feature is used with a document set, the sum for all documents in a document set cannot be larger than 50MB.

▶ Metadata assigned to the document set is not automatically assigned to members of the document set.

Figure 20.22 shows a sample document set after the document set icon was clicked in a document library. A fairly large icon representing the document set is visible below the Ribbon, which gains a Document Set Manage tab, shown active in Figure 20.22. In this example, a workflow titled Doc Set Approval was started on the document set and the column with the same title is visible on the right. If the Capture Version button in clicked from the Document Set Manage tab, the user is prompted to capture Latest Major Versions Only or Latest Major or Minor Versions. Figure 20.23 shows the Version History window that appears after the capture version is completed for the document set, which clearly displays each document title with the version number appended. This function lets a user capture the exact state of more than one document at a point in time, which is in essence a way of taking a backup of a set of documents and being able to manage these backups by deleting previous backups in the future.

FIGURE 20.23   Version history for a document set.

NOTE

Document sets can have the Capture Version tool run to create a version of the document set, which includes the latest major or major and minor versions of documents contained within the document set. This adds another level of granularity to versioning because not only can individual documents be versioned, but also whole sets of documents can be versioned, to "snapshot" the document set at a point in time.

20

Document sets do require some additional configuration to be available to end users, as they need to be enabled from the Site Collection Features, which is explained later in the chapter. The document set content type then needs to be added to the document library before it can be used. Folders, on the other hand, can easily be configured to either be available or not available for a document library from the list or library settings page, by accessing the Advanced Settings link. Document sets can have metadata associated with the document set itself, which is different from folders, which cannot have metadata manually assigned to them. Several other notable differences should be kept in mind when determining whether the organization should use them:

▶ Document sets are not available in SharePoint Foundation 2010 while folders are available.

▶ Document sets can be created only in document libraries, whereas folders can be created in either libraries or lists.

▶ Folders are not allowed within document sets.

▶ Document sets can't be nested, whereas folders can be nested.

▶ Metadata can be assigned to document sets but not folders.

▶ Workflows can be started on document sets but not folders.

TIP

If a view is configured to Show All Items Without Folders, the items in a document set will be visible, just as items within a folder will be visible. Unique permissions will still be honored in both scenarios, so administrators don't need to worry about users seeing documents they shouldn't see. This should be considered a means of flattening out the contents of a document library that users document sets or folders extensively if users are complaining about having to navigate a complex set of folders, or to encourage users to use SharePoint features such as filters and metadata navigation hierarchies and key filters.

Enabling Document Sets from Site Collection Features

To enable Document Sets feature for a document library, first ensure that the feature is active for the site collection, and then add the content type to the document library by following the steps in this section. First enable the site collection feature by following these steps:

1. Access the Site Settings page for the site collection. Under the Site Collection Administration section, click Site Collection Features.

2. On the Features page, for Document Sets, click Activate. The Document Set content type will now appear in the Content Type Gallery for the site collection.

To add the content type to the document library, follow these steps:

1. Navigate to the document library that will have the Document Set content type added; in this example, the document library is named Shared Documents. Click the Library tab on the Ribbon, and click Library Settings.

2. Click Advanced Settings in the General Settings section.

3. In the Content Types section, under Allow Management of Content Types?, click the circle next to Yes.

4. Scroll to the bottom of the page and click OK to save the change and return to the Document Library Settings page.

5. Scroll down to the Content Types section, which may have not been visible before. Click Add from existing content types.

6. From the Add Content Types page, access the drop-down menu under Select Site Content Types From, and choose Document Set Content Types. Click Document Set in the Available Site Content Types box, and then click the Add button, as shown in Figure 20.24, and then click OK.

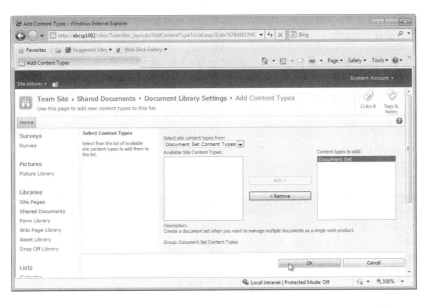

FIGURE 20.24   Adding the Document Set content type to a document library.

7. Click the document library name in the breadcrumb from Document Library Settings to return to the document library.

Now, to create a document set, follow these steps:

1. Click the Documents tab on the Ribbon, and access the drop-down menu for New Document; there should now be an entry for Document Set. Click Document Set.

2. Enter a name for the document set, such as **Project X Document Set**, and click OK. The document set will now display. There are no documents within this document set yet.

3. Click the name of the document library in the Browse tab to return to the document library default view, and the document set will be visible as an "item" in the document library.

Content Organizer as a Document Routing Tool

The Content Organizer is a new feature in SharePoint Server 2010 Standard or Enterprise that allows content uploaded to the Drop Off Library to be routed to other libraries based on the Content Organizer rules that have been created. This is an important tool to be familiar with in the context of list and library design because it can automate the task of moving content to a specific library, which will affect the overall management of content.

To create a Content Organizer rule, follow these steps in SharePoint Server 2010 Standard or Enterprise. This first set of steps walks a site administrator through the process of enabling or verifying that the Content Organizer feature is on, and then the process of configuring the Content Organizer settings:

1. First, verify that the Content Organizer feature is turned on for the site in question. Click Site Actions drop-down menu, select Site Settings.

2. From the Site Settings page, in the Site Actions section, click Manage Site Features.

3. Check the status of the Content Organizer feature. If it is not set to Active, click the Activate button. After it has activated, click Site Settings in the breadcrumb to return to the Site Settings page. Note that a Drop Off Library will be created as part of the feature activation process.

> **NOTE**
>
> Another option on the Manage Site Features page, under Content Organizer, is the E-mail Integration with Content Organizer. This will add another option to the Content Organizer Settings page, in the Submission Points section.

4. Click the Content Organizer Settings link in the Site Administration section of the Site Settings page.

5. The first option on this page in the Redirect Users to the Drop Off Library is Require Users to Use the Organizer When Submitting New Content to Libraries with One or More Organizer Rules Pointing to Them. If this box is checked, users will see a notice in the upload window that states "Documents uploaded here are automatically moved to the correct library and folder after document properties are collected." Generally, this option should be enabled to ensure that the Content Organizer rules are applied to new content uploaded. Otherwise, users can bypass the rules by

uploading to whichever library they choose, and ignoring the Drop Off Library. For this example, check the box next to Require Users to Use the Organizer.

6. In the Sending to Another Site section, the next decision to make is whether to check the box next to Allow Rules to Specify Another Site as a Target Location. This box should be checked if site quotas are in use and IT expects the total amount of data uploaded to exceed this amount. In general, however, this will complicate the management of content and can confuse end users, so leave it unchecked unless there are specific requirements for checking this box. Leave it unchecked in this example.

7. The Folder Partitioning section allows the option to Create subfolders after a target location has too many items as shown in Figure 20.25. The administrator can specify the number of items allowed in a single folder, and the format of the folder names that will be created. Once again, it is up to IT to determine whether this is recommended as a best practice as there are pros and cons to the use of folders in SharePoint lists and libraries, but they can enhance performance when there are large numbers of items in the list or library. For this example, check the box, and leave the defaults, which should be 2500 for the number of items in a single folder, and Submitted after %1 for the format of the folder name.

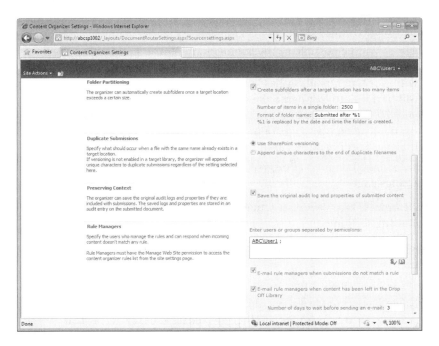

FIGURE 20.25   Content Organizer Settings page.

8. The Duplicate Submissions section gives the choices: Use SharePoint Versioning or Append Unique Characters to the End of Duplicate Filenames. In general, it is recommended to use SharePoint Versioning because users will be familiar with its use. For this example, check the box next to Use SharePoint Versioning.

20

NOTE

If Use SharePoint Versioning is checked but the destination library does not have versioning enabled, the duplicate file or files will be appended with a string of six unique characters.

---

9. In the Preserving Context section, decide whether to Save the Original Audit Log and Properties of Submitted Content. For this example, uncheck this box.

10. In the Rule Managers section, enter users or groups who manage the rules and can respond when incoming content doesn't match any rule. Then choose whether to check the box next to E-mail Rule Managers When Submissions Do Not Match a Rule or E-mail Rule Managers When Content Has Been Left in the Drop Off Library; if this second box is checked, enter in a number of days to wait before sending an email. For this example, enter appropriate users or groups that will have rule manager responsibilities. As noted on this page, rule managers must have the manage web site permission to access the content organizer rules list from the site settings page. It is a good general practice to check both of these options and to set a waiting period of several days. For this example, check both of these options and enter 3 for the number of days to wait.

11. Finally, no actions will be possible in the Submission Points section unless the Site Feature E-mail Integration with Content Organizer is enabled for the site. If E-mail Integration with Content Organizer has been enabled from the Manage Site Features page, there will be a link to Configure the Organizer's Incoming Email Settings, as shown in Figure 20.26. After these settings are reviewed, click OK. Notice that you will end up on the listedit.aspx page for a list titled Submitted E-mail Records, which is a hidden list that does not show up in the All Site Content view.

12. After the settings are configured as desired, click OK to save the settings and return to the Site Settings page.

The next step in the process is to create an actual Content Organizer rule, which is outlined in the following section:

1. From the Site Settings page, in the Site Administration section, click Content Organizer Rules.

2. Click Add New Item to create a new rule.

3. In the Rule Name field, provide a name for the rule that will make sense to other content organizers. For this example, use the title **Audio Routing Rule 1.**

4. In the Rule Status and Priority section, select Active, and set the priority to 5 (Medium). A nice option here is to set the rule to Inactive, as opposed to having the delete the rule.

5. In the Submission's Content Type section, choose from the content types available to the site, which by default are Digital Asset Content Types, Document Content Types, Page Layout Content Types, Publishing Content Types, Special Content Types. An additional group, Content Organizer Content Types, may also appear if E-mail

Integration with Content Organizer is enabled for the site. For this example, choose Digital Asset Content Types, and then select Audio. Uncheck This Content Type Has Alternate Names in Other Sites.

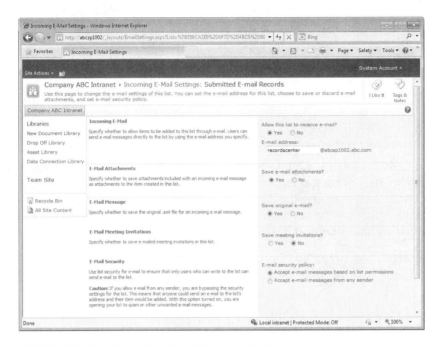

FIGURE 20.26   Submitted E-mail Records Settings page.

6. In the Conditions section, choose from the Property drop-down list and then choose an operator. For this example, select Author as the property and "is equal to" as the operator and enter a value of **User1** (or a value that is valid in your environment, such as your username).

TIP

Many administrators may not find the Property value that they think would be the most efficient for a powerful Content Organizer rule. For instance, in the example, the Audio content type is matched with the condition of Author, equaling a specific value to determining the final location of the file. If in this example the administrator wanted to add a property to the content type (such as Artist), that can be done by accessing the Site Content Types gallery. Then the Audio site content type can have a column added to it. This process is covered in more detail in Chapter 22.

---

7. In the Target Location section, the Browse button can be clicked and the administrator can select the destination library. In this example, the library Asset Library is selected, and it is added to the field in the format of /Asset Library. There is also the

option to Automatically Create a Folder for Each Unique Value of a Property that can be used.

> **NOTE**
>
> Note that the content type associated with the rule must be available at the target location. This means that the destination document library must have Allow Management of Content Types set to Yes, and the content type in question (for example, Audio in this example) added to the Content Types section on the Document Library Settings page.

---

8. Click OK once the rule is completed.

To test that the Content Organizer is working, you can visit the Drop Off Library, upload a document that matches the criteria just set for the rule (for example, content type is Audio, and the author is User1), and then save the document to the Drop Off Library. Assuming the document metadata matches the rule, you will be informed that the item has been moved to the destination library defined in the rule (Asset Library in this example).

Summary

Four possibilities are presented for general philosophies for customizing and managing lists and libraries in a SharePoint 2010 environment, as follows:

1. Minimal planning and testing; minimal restrictions on list and library use and configuration

2. Minimal planning and testing; more restrictions on list and library use and configuration

3. More extensive planning and testing; minimal restrictions on list and library use and configuration

4. More extensive planning and testing; more restrictions on list and library use and configuration

Regardless of which strategy the organization takes, site administrators need to be familiar with a wide range of tools to ensure that the adoption of SharePoint 2010 lists and libraries is successful and that they meet end-user needs. This chapter covered tools on the Library tab of the Ribbon, as well as the tools available from the Document Library Settings page, and examined document sets as well as the Content Organizer tool to round out the coverage of tools that SharePoint 2010 list and library administrators should be familiar with.

Best Practices

▶ Versioning is one of the primary capabilities of a document management system and architects or lists and libraries should agree upon the right combination of content approval, versioning, draft item security, and other related tools should be used based on the requirements of the user community and their experience with document management systems. The basic recommendation is to keep it simple, and just enable major versions for basic collaboration needs, and a table is offered to assist with choosing the right combination of features for the organization.

▶ A table is provided in this chapter that lists the tools available from the Document Library Settings page based on which version of SharePoint is in use. This table clearly shows that SharePoint Foundation 2010 provides a much more limited set of tools, and will therefore require less training for administrators to master, but correspondingly limits the range of tools available for end users. A recommended best practice is to review the features and tools available in different versions of SharePoint and decide which will have value for the organization.

▶ Using SharePoint Designer 2010 to manage lists and libraries should be investigated as an alternative to using the tools provided from within the list or library in SharePoint 2010. SharePoint Designer 2010 is generally considered to be a more advanced toolset, and can be a time saver for experienced administrators, and provides access to tools not available in the SharePoint 2010 user interface, such as creating SharePoint Designer workflows, creating custom actions, and editing document templates.

▶ The Advanced Settings page accessible from the Document Library Settings page provides access to a number of key features that can be enabled, disabled, or configured for the library. A best practice is to review these options as a group during the design phase to see which will be enabled for different document libraries and for different levels of users. For example, content types can be turned on or off here, the document template can be edited, folders can be enabled or disabled, and offline client availability can be enabled or disabled, as can the Datasheet view.

▶ Document sets offer a unique set of features that will be of interest to organizations with high-end collaboration needs and fairly sophisticated users. They differ from folders in a number of ways, as outlined in this chapter, which should be understood to help determine when folders are appropriate and when document sets are appropriate. For example, document sets can have metadata assigned to them, can have workflows run on them, and can have versions of the entire contents of the document set taken, saving a "snapshot" of the entire document set. Folders, however, are available in SharePoint Foundation 2010 (whereas document sets are not), can be created in lists, can be nested, and don't require the training to use that document sets may require.

▶ Enable the Content Organizer feature for a site collection in SharePoint Server 2010
  Standard or Enterprise to allow you to then create rules that define where uploaded
  content is eventually stored when a user uploads a document to the Drop Off
  Library. The Content Organizer Rule Wizard is very sophisticated, allowing the site
  administrator to define with great specificity where documents assigned to different
  content types with attributes matching certain criteria are stored when uploaded to
  the Drop Off Folder.

## CHAPTER 21

Designing and Managing Pages and Sites for Knowledge Workers

This chapter can be considered a "survival guide" and is aimed at the site collection administrator or site administrator who is charged with creating, customizing, or managing a new or existing site collection and making it meet the needs of the organization. Depending on the size of the company, the site collection might have been created for a variety of purposes, such as for the company intranet, for an extranet to handle trusted external partners, for Internet users, or for internal only use, perhaps just by one group such as IT.

This chapter concentrates on the processes involved in creating site collections, sites, and pages, and on the wealth of tools available for managing sites and site collections from the Site Settings page. Due to the sheer number of tools, specific tools are focused on that tend to be the most used by site collection and site administrators, whereas others are just summarized. For example, understanding the Users and Permissions tools is critical, to ensure that the site administrator has a tight grasp on "who can do what" in the site collection.

Site variations are covered in more detail than many other features because of their complexity and also because of their power and capabilities to handle multilingual requirements of larger companies. Audience targeting is also covered because this tool can be leveraged to customize the content that is shown to different site visitors based on rules defined in SharePoint.

Understanding Site Collection Options

It is important for the farm administrator to be conversant with the different site collection templates available and to understand when it is appropriate to create a site collection and when a site will suffice. The range of site collection templates available in the different versions of SharePoint 2010 is provided in Chapter 18, "SharePoint Foundation Versus SharePoint Server 2010," and summarized in Table 18.5 in that chapter.

This section reviews the different categories of site collections, and touches briefly on best practices for mapping out a site collection or group of site collections to meet the organization's requirements. When a farm administrator wants to create a new site collection, the Create Site Collections tool can be found under the Site Collections section on the Application Management page. These tools are broken into Collaboration, Meetings, Enterprise, Publishing, and Custom groupings, as follows:

▶ **Collaboration site collection templates**—These include Team Site, Blank Site, Document Workspace, Blog, Group Work Site, and Visio Process Repository. Many organizations use the Team Site template because it includes a very useful set of lists and libraries. The Group Work site includes Group Calendar, Circulation, Phone-Call Memo, a Document Library, and other basic lists. The Visio Process Repository is designed to store Visio process diagrams, and announcements, tasks, and discussion lists.

▶ **Meetings site collection templates**—These include Basic Meeting Workspace, Blank Meeting Workspace, Decision Meeting Workspace, Social Meeting Workspace, and Multipage Meeting Workspace. It is fairly unusual to create a site collection for meetings, but if an organization knows it will be extensively using Meeting Workspaces, this can be a convenient way to organize them under a root URL.

▶ **Enterprise site collection templates**—These include Document Center, Records Center, Business Intelligence Center, Enterprise Search Center, My Site Host, Basic Search Center, and FAST Search Center. These are fairly specialized templates, all of which (except the Business Intelligence Center) can be created as a subsite beneath a nonpublishing top-level site.

▶ **Publishing site collection templates**—Comprised of Publishing Portal and Enterprise Wiki. Publishing sites are designed for sites that provide content to a large group of readers, and are better suited to that purpose. There are limitations on which sites can be created beneath publishing sites, so there are fewer options from a site collection design standpoint. A Publishing Portal, for example, would be a good choice for an intranet, but not if it will house departmental sites at the second level, unless they are created as site collections.

▶ **Custom site collection templates**—An empty site can be created, and a template assigned at a later time.

Designing the Site and Site Collection Wireframe

A sample wireframe is provided in Figure 21.1, which is a simplified design often used for medium-sized companies (500–5,000 users) and includes a top-level site collection for intranet purposes, separate site collections for departments such as IT and HR, and a site collection for cross-departmental uses (such as projects).

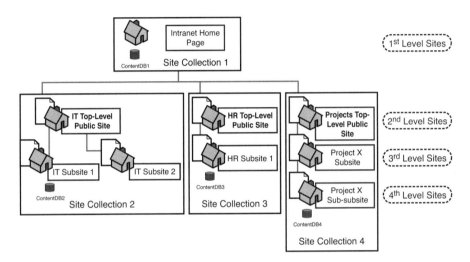

FIGURE 21.1   Sample site collection wireframe.

This simple example shows a ContentDB icon for the top-level site collection, which in this example contains intranet content, and ContentDB icons for three other site collections that are nested beneath the top-level site collection. Each organization will need to work on balancing the depth of the structure with its breadth, because a structure that is too "deep" can be hard to navigate, as can a structure that is too wide. There are management complexities involved in creating too many site collections, whereas on the other hand, too few site collections may result in content databases that grow to "unwieldy" sizes (for example, hundreds of gigabytes, or even a terabyte or more).

A tool such as this makes it easy for design committees to understand the logical design and can be expanded to include the lists and libraries that will be included in each site, and the permissions for each site, and thus become a useful management tool.

Creating a Site Collection

In many environments, the site collection administrator is also a farm administrator, and will need to know how to create site collections. Although some organizations use a single site collection for all of their needs, a best practice is to create separate site collections for groups that will be saving a large amount of data (50GB to 100GB or more) and creating a content database for each of those site collections. Although this is not a universal rule, by creating multiple content databases, SQL Server will be managing more databases that are smaller in size, which can be advantageous when designing disaster recovery strategies and service level agreements.

In addition, as discussed in the following sections, a large number of tools are available for each site collection; these allow customization of one site collection that won't affect other site collections. For example, Site Collection Features can be turned on for features such as Document ID Service, Document Sets, or PerformancePoint Services features that will be available only to sites contained within the site collection.

To create a site collection from the Central Administration site, simply follow these steps:

1. From the Central Administration home page, click Create Site Collection in the Application Management section.

2. From the createsite.aspx page, enter a title for the site (**Dept X Site Collection**, for this example), optionally enter a description, and provide a URL for the site collection (in this example, select /sites/ from the drop-down menu and enter Dept X for the site collection name). Choose the Team Site template. An example is shown in Figure 21.2.

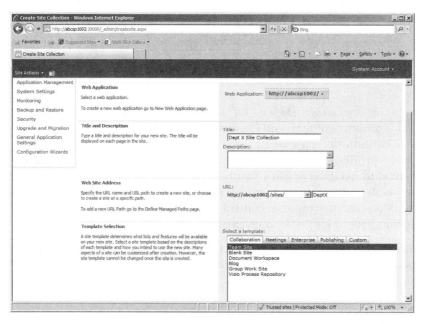

FIGURE 21.2   CreateSite.aspx page from the Central Administrator site.

3. Scroll down on the page, and enter a primary site collection administrator and secondary site administrator (**abc\administrator** and **abc\user1** in this example). Click the Check Names icon next to the fields to make sure the usernames were entered properly. Leave the quota template selection to No Quota. Click OK.

4. After the site has been created, the Top-Level Site Successfully Created Page (sitecreated.aspx) will display, and will include a link to the new site collection. Click the link to view the new site collection. Figure 21.3 shows the site created in this example.

FIGURE 21.3   Home page of a New Team Site site collection.

5. Access the drop-down menu for Site Actions and click Site Settings. Figure 21.4 shows the Site Settings page for the new site collection. A sampling of the different tools will be covered in the following sections.

Reviewing the Scope of an Existing Site Collection

When a site collection administrator starts working with existing site collection, it is important to determine whether additional subsites are under the existing site collection. If the site collection is new, and hasn't been configured, this will most likely be an easy task, but if the administrator is taking over a site collection that has been in use for several months or years, this can be more involved.

Site collection administrators charged with taking over an existing site collection can become familiar with the site collection by visiting the Site Settings page and clicking the Sites and Workspaces link in the Site Administration section, as shown in Figure 21.4. This will show the administrator whether there are any subsites beneath the existing site. However, this might not tell the full story because there may be managed paths for the web application, which may contain additional site collections, each of which may contain additional sites.

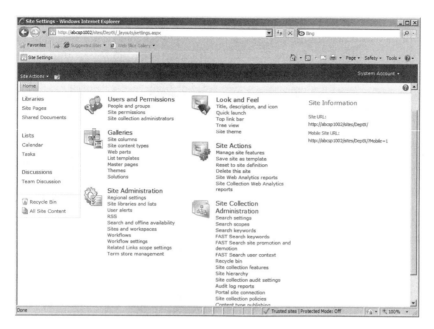

FIGURE 21.4   Site Settings page for a New Team Site site collection.

For example, a new site collection administrator should check with the farm administrator to see whether there are any managed paths such as /sites/ that contain additional subsites. Figure 21.5 shows the Sites and Workspaces page from the Site Settings page on a sample site collection (http://abcsp1002/). It looks like there are only a half dozen sites located beneath the top level, so the administrator may think he has a relatively easy job ahead of him. However, Figure 21.6 shows the Site Collection List page for the web application that houses the root site collection (http://abcsp1002/), and there are managed paths /my and /sites that each contain site collections beneath them. Suddenly, the administrator realizes he needs to review each of the site collections located under /sites to see the number of sites under each. The sites listed under /my are personal site collections that may also pose administrative challenges, but won't be addressed in this chapter.

Note also in Figure 21.6 that the Site Collection List page lists the URL for the site collection, the title, description, primary site collection administrator, his or her email, and the content database name on the right side.

> **NOTE**
>
> The managed paths for a web application can be found under Application Management, in the Web Applications section, by clicking Manage Web Applications, and then the name of the web application that houses the site collection. Click the name of the web application, and then click Managed Paths from the Web Applications tab on the Ribbon. An example is shown in Figure 21.7.

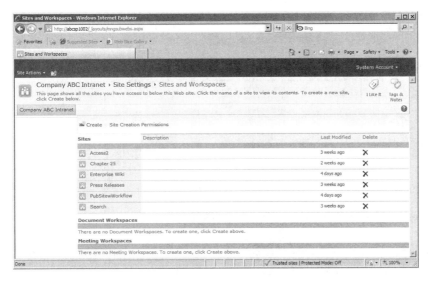

FIGURE 21.5   Sites and Workspaces page for a site collection.

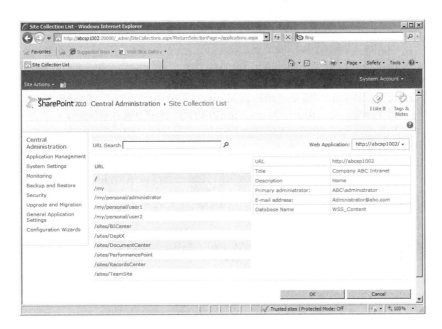

FIGURE 21.6   Site Collection List page.

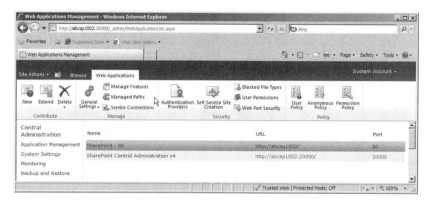

FIGURE 21.7   The Managed Paths tool for a web application.

NOTE

For a site collection administrator to effectively manage the site collection, it is important to fully investigate the contents of the site collection in terms of subsites and nested site collections. Visit the Site Collection List page in the Central Administrator site or request that the information be provided by the farm administrator.

An additional tool is available from the Site Settings page for the top-level site of the site collection: the Site Hierarchy link in the Site Collection Administration section. This will show all websites created under the current site, as shown in Figure 21.8. This page (similar to the Sites and Workspaces page) shows the sites that exist directly below the current site, but also does not include the managed paths. The Site Hierarchy page provides the site URL, title of the site, and a Manage link that, when clicked, takes the administrator to the Site Settings page for that site.

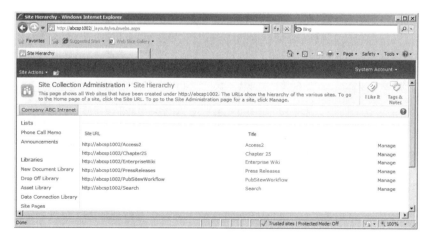

FIGURE 21.8   Site Hierarchy page.

Controlling Who Can Create Sites

Another recommended step to take for site administrators for new or existing site collections is to take a few minutes and review who has the ability to create sites. By default, only users with full control permissions in the site collection have the ability to create subsites (including document workspaces and meeting workspaces), which only include site collection administrators and members of the Owners group for the site collection. However, other permission levels may be able to create sites, which can be a good thing, if the organization wants to encourage the use of document workspaces and meeting workspaces and empower more users to build sites for collaboration purposes. Or it can be a bad thing and lead to an accumulation of sites and workspaces that users may abandon, or that may confuse users.

The Sites and Workspaces page discussed in the previous section provides a link for Site Creation Permissions. By clicking this link, the administrator can provide site and workspace creation permissions to different permission levels, as shown in Figure 21.9. From this page, the administrator can check the boxes next to permission levels such as design or contribute, and by clicking OK will add the Create Subsites site permission for that permission level.

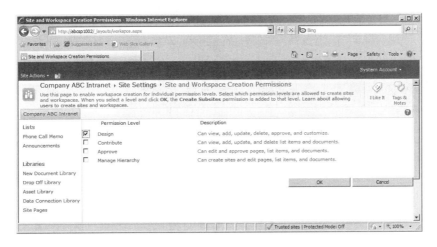

FIGURE 21.9   Site and Workspace Creation Permissions page.

Another important tool to know about is the Self-Service Site Collection Management tool. This tool is accessed from the Central Administration site by clicking the Security link in the Quick Launch area and then clicking Configure Self-Service Site Creation in the General Security section. From this page, shown in Figure 21.10, the farm administrator can enable or disable Self-Service Site Creation, and can require a secondary contact be supplied during the site creation process in case the primary contact leaves the company or is not available in the future. Figure 21.11 shows the announcement created when this is enabled, which provides a link to the _layouts/scssignup.aspx page where users can create new sites.

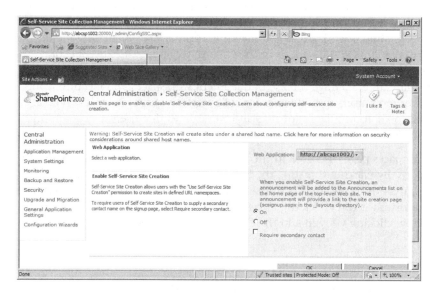

FIGURE 21.10   Self-Service Site Creation page.

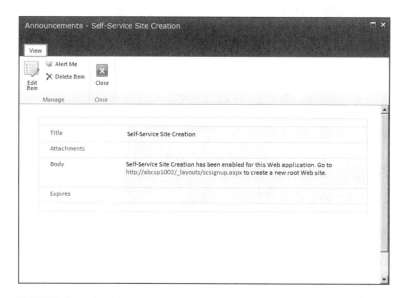

FIGURE 21.11   Self-service site creation announcement with link.

> **TIP**
>
> A general best practice is to control the number of individuals who can create sites and workspaces until users are trained about the pros and cons of site and workspace creation and the management of the sites they create. A common complaint of organizations using SharePoint products is the "sprawl" of sites, subsites, and workspaces that can grow over time if too many users are allowed to create sites and workspaces.

Creating Pages and Sites

This section provides an overview of the processes of creating pages and sites, as well as an overview of the options available for pages and sites. An administrator or power users needs Create Subsites privileges to create sites and Add and Customize Pages privileges to create pages.

The site administrator can create sites from several places. The primary tool to access is the Site Actions drop-down menu, and then click New Site.

The All Site Content page also provides a Create button, which leads to the Create page, where the Sites and Workspaces link is available, which then opens the New SharePoint Site page.

The Manage Content and Structure available from the Site Actions drop-down menu on a Publishing Site also allows the administrator to create sites, lists, or pages, as shown in Figure 21.12.

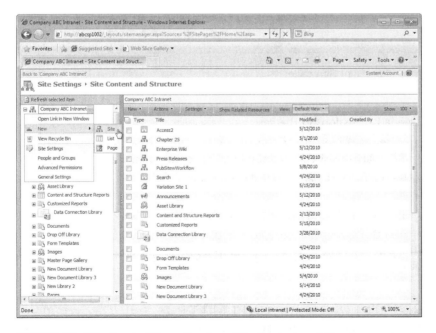

FIGURE 21.12   Create Site option from Site Content and Structure page.

Follow these steps to create a site from the Site Actions menu on a nonpublishing site:

1. From a nonpublishing site, access the Site Actions menu, and click New Site.
2. Enter title, description (optional), and URL information.
3. Select the Team Site template from the Collaboration tab. An example is shown in Figure 21.13.

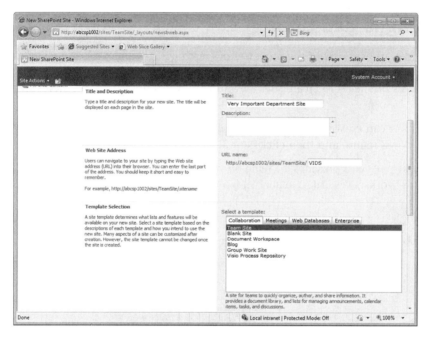

FIGURE 21.13   New SharePoint Site page.

4. Select Use Unique Permissions in the Permissions section.
5. In this example, select Yes to Display this site on the Quick Launch of the parent site, and Yes to Display this site on the top link bar of the parent site.
6. Select Yes to Use the top link bar from the parent site.
7. Click Create.
8. As shown in Figure 21.14, the Set Up Groups for this Site page will display. Leave the defaults, which in this example are to Use an Existing Group for Visitors (the Visitors group from the parent site), Create a New Group for Members, and Create a New Group for Owners. Click OK, and the new site will render.

NOTE

The steps will be slightly different if SilverLight is installed.

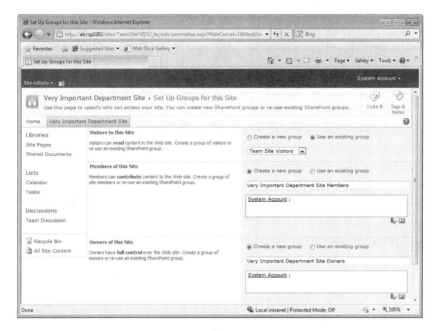

FIGURE 21.14   Set up groups for this site page.

Table 21.1 provides a list of page and site options in the different versions of SharePoint 2010.

TABLE 21.1   Page and Site Options in SharePoint Foundation 2010 and SharePoint Server 2010 Standard and Enterprise

Template Name	Page or Site?	Available in SharePoint Foundation 2010?	Available in SharePoint Server 2010 Standard?	Available in SharePoint Server 2010 Enterprise?	Functionality and Notes
Assets Web Database	Site	No	No	Yes	A site that creates Access databases for a sample web database site. Document libraries include AppImages and Report Definitions; lists include Assets, MSysASO, Tasks1, Users, and USysApplicationLog. Tabs include Current Assets, Retired Assets, Users, Report Center, and Getting Started (which provides videos on how to use the site).

continues

TABLE 21.1   Continued

Template Name	Page or Site?	Available in SharePoint Foundation 2010?	Available in SharePoint Server 2010 Standard?	Available in SharePoint Server 2010 Enterprise?	Functionality and Notes
Basic Meeting Workspace	Site	Yes	Yes	Yes	A site for collaborating on meeting-oriented topics; can be created from a calendar list. Includes document library, agenda, attendees, and objectives lists.
Basic Search Center	Site	No	Yes	Yes	Provides a single page with a search field. Includes Tabs in Search Pages and Tabs in Search Results lists.
Blank Meeting Workspace	Site	Yes	Yes	Yes	A site designed for meeting topics; can be created from a calendar list; contains no lists or libraries.
Blank Site	Site	Yes	Yes	Yes	A site containing an attendees list, but no libraries.
Blog	Site	Yes	Yes	Yes	A blog site containing photos library, categories, comments, links, and posts lists.
Charitable Contributions Web	Site	No	No	Yes	A site that creates Access databases for a sample web database site. Document libraries include AppImages and Report Definitions; lists include Campaigns, Donations, Donors, EventAttendees, Events, MSysASO, Settings, Tasks, and USysApplicationLog lists.

TABLE 21.1   Continued

Template Name	Page or Site?	Available in SharePoint Foundation 2010?	Available in SharePoint Server 2010 Standard?	Available in SharePoint Server 2010 Enterprise?	Functionality and Notes
Contacts Web Database	Site	No	No	Yes	A site that creates Access databases for a sample web database site for managing contacts. Document libraries include AppImages and Report Definitions; lists include Comments, Contacts, MSysASO, Tasks 1, and USysApplicationLog lists.
Decision Meeting Workspace	Site	Yes	Yes	Yes	A site designed for meetings that can be created from a calendar. Contains document library, agenda, attendees, decisions, objectives, and tasks lists.
Document Center	Site	No	Yes	Yes	Site designed for storing and managing documents. Includes document library and tasks list. All documents are assigned a unique document ID.
Document Workspace	Site	Yes	Yes	Yes	A site for collaborating on one or more documents. Can be created from a document library or from the Create page/window. Includes document library, announcements, calendar, links, tasks, team discussion, and lists.
Enterprise Search Center	Site	No	Yes	Yes	This site includes a welcome page with a search box and tabs for general search and people search.

continues

TABLE 21.1   Continued

Template Name	Page or Site?	Available in SharePoint Foundation 2010?	Available in SharePoint Server 2010 Standard?	Available in SharePoint Server 2010 Enterprise?	Functionality and Notes
Enterprise Wiki	Site	No	Yes	Yes	A site with wiki functionality designed for co-authoring content. Includes document images and page libraries as well as workflow tasks list.
FAST Search Center	Site	No	No	Yes	Provides welcome page with search box with tabs for general searches and people searches and provides enhanced FAST search features.
Group Work Site	Site	Yes	Yes	Yes	A site designed for group collaboration; contains document library, announcements, circulations, group calendar, links, phone call memo, resources, tasks, whereabouts, and team discussion lists.
Issues Web Database	Site	No	No	Yes	A site that creates Access databases for a sample web database site for managing issues. Document libraries include AppImages and Report Definitions; lists include Comments, Issues, MSysASO, Tasks 1, Users, and USysApplicationLog lists.

TABLE 21.1   Continued

Template Name	Page or Site?	Available in SharePoint Foundation 2010?	Available in SharePoint Server 2010 Standard?	Available in SharePoint Server 2010 Enterprise?	Functionality and Notes
Multipage Meeting Workspace	Site	Yes	Yes	Yes	Specialized meeting site that allows administrators to create new pages. Includes agenda, attendees, and objectives lists.
Page	Page	Yes	Yes	Yes	An aspx page that can contain rich text, images, links, and web parts.
Personalization Site	Site	No	Yes	Yes	Designed for My Sites; contains no lists or libraries by default but contains Current User Filter and Profile Property Filter, which send the current user's user ID to connected web parts to filter the content shown in other web parts.
Projects Web Database	Site	No	No	Yes	A site that creates Access databases for a sample web database site for managing projects. Document libraries include AppImages and Report Definitions; lists include Customers, MSysASO, ProjectHistory, Projects, Tasks, Tasks 1, Users, and USysApplicationLog lists.
Publishing Page	Page	No	Yes	Yes	Stored in the pages list of a publishing site; can use scheduling workflow, caching, and other publishing features.

continues

TABLE 21.1 Continued

Template Name	Page or Site?	Available in SharePoint Foundation 2010?	Available in SharePoint Server 2010 Standard?	Available in SharePoint Server 2010 Enterprise?	Functionality and Notes
Publishing Site with Workflow	Site	No	Yes	Yes	A site for publishing web pages; includes document, image, and page libraries and workflow tasks list. Only sites using this template can be created under one of these parent sites.
Records Center	Site	No	Yes	Yes	Site designed for storing and managing records that should be stored for long-term archival. Includes Drop Off Document library and Record library. All documents are assigned a unique document ID.
Social Meeting Workspace	Site	Yes	Yes	Yes	A site for social meetings, which can be created from a calendar list. Contains picture library, attendees, directions, things to bring, and discussion board lists.
Team Site	Site	Yes	Yes	Yes	A site for team collaboration, and one of the most commonly used templates. It includes document, site assets, site pages libraries and announcements, calendar, links, tasks, and team discussion lists.

TABLE 21.1   Continued

Template Name	Page or Site?	Available in SharePoint Foundation 2010?	Available in SharePoint Server 2010 Standard?	Available in SharePoint Server 2010 Enterprise?	Functionality and Notes
Visio Process Repository	Site	No	No	Yes	A site designed for sharing Visio diagrams. Includes Documentation and Process Diagrams libraries, as well as announcements, tasks, and team discussion lists.
Web Part Page	Page	Yes	Yes	Yes	Provides Page Content section, Header, Right, Top Left, Top Right, Center Left, Center, Center Right, and Footer web part zones.

Creating Pages

The process of creating pages is similar to that of creating sites, but generally simpler, although once the page is created, it needs to be customized. Pages can be created from the Create page accessible from the All Site Content Page. Figure 21.15 shows a standard page created from the Create page. Two web parts were added to the page by clicking Web Part from the Insert tab. The Edit Web Part tool was accessed for the Content Query web part, which caused the appearance of the tools pane on the right side of the screen.

Accessing the Pages library for a publishing site is a good place to learn more about the range of pages available. From the Pages library, if the New Document drop-down is accessed from the Documents tab on the Ribbon, the options of Page, Article Page, and Welcome Page are provided.

The simplest option, Page, is a system content type that includes the following columns (which can be found by accessing the Site Collection's Site Content Types gallery, scrolling to the Publishing Content Types section, and clicking Page):

▶ **Title**—Single line of text

▶ **Comments**—Multiple lines of text

▶ **Scheduling Start Date**—Publishing schedule start date

▶ **Scheduling End Date**—Publishing schedule end date

▶ **Contact**—Person or group

▶ **Contact Email Address**—Single line of text

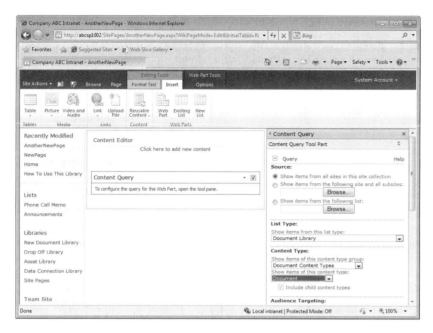

FIGURE 21.15   New page created from the Create page.

▶ **Contact Name**—Single line of text

▶ **Contact Picture**—Hyperlink or Picture

▶ **Rollup Image**—Publishing Image

▶ **Target Audience**—Audience Targeting

The Article Page adds some columns to this base content type:

▶ **Page Image**—Publishing Image

▶ **Page Content**—Publishing HTML

▶ **Summary Links**—Summary Links

▶ **Byline**—Single line of text

▶ **Article Date**—Date and Time

▶ **Image Caption**—Publishing HTML

The Welcome page adds some slightly different column to the base content type:

▶ **Page Image**—Publishing Image

▶ **Page Content**—Publishing HTML

▶ **Summary Links**—Summary Links

▶ **Summary Links 2**—Summary Links

For page layouts, the administrator can choose from a number of templates, including the following:

- ▶ Article Page – Body Only
- ▶ Article Page – Image on Left
- ▶ Article Page – Image on Right
- ▶ Article Page – Summary Links
- ▶ Enterprise Wiki Page – Basic Page
- ▶ Project Page – Basic Project Page
- ▶ Redirect Page – Redirect
- ▶ Welcome Page – Advanced Search
- ▶ Welcome Page – Blank Web Part Page
- ▶ Welcome Page – People Search Results
- ▶ Welcome Page – Search Box
- ▶ Welcome Page – Search Results
- ▶ Welcome Page – Site Directory Home
- ▶ Welcome Page – Splash
- ▶ Welcome Page – Summary Links
- ▶ Welcome Page – Table of Contents

It is highly recommended to experiment with the wide range of different pages that can be created, and the almost limitless combinations of page layouts, web parts, and other items that can be added to pages. Many bloggers post "how to" examples on the Internet for a wide variety of applications.

Reviewing the Users and Permissions Tools

In the Users and Permissions section of the Site Settings page are links to People and Groups, Site Permissions, and Site Collection Administrators. A quick review of the Site Collection Administrators assigned to the site is important, as in some cases the accounts listed here are not correct or appropriate. The site collection administrator should review and modify these as appropriate.

Next, click the Site Permissions link to review the groups that exist for the site collection, as well as any individual users or AD groups that have been granted direct permissions.

Figure 21.16 shows the Permissions page for a new site collection. The Edit tab provides a number of tools:

▶ **Grant Permissions**—Add users or AD groups and grant permissions by adding to an existing SharePoint group or give direct permissions for full control, design, contribute, read, or view only. A welcome email can be sent to the users added.

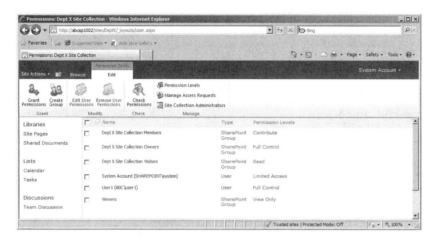

FIGURE 21.16   Permissions page for a new site collection.

▶ **Create Group**—Define a new SharePoint group and description, define the Group Owner, define who can view the membership of the group (Group Members, Everyone) and who can edit the membership of the group (Group Owner, Group Members). Also choose whether to allow requests to join/leave the group, auto-accept requests, and define the email address to which membership requests go. Most important, choose the permission level group members get on the site (full control, design, contribute, read, or view only).

▶ **Edit User Permissions**—If a group or user is selected, allows the permission level to be modified.

▶ **Remove User Permissions**—If a group or user is selected, clicking this button will remove all permissions for the user or group to the site.

▶ **Check Permissions button**—Allows the entry of a user or group name, and when the Check Now button is clicked, provides a summary of the permission levels given to the group or user and whether they were given directly or via a specific group.

▶ **Permission Levels**—Clicking this icon opens the Permission Levels page that allows the addition of a permission level, deletion of a permission level, or modification of a permission level.

▶ **Manage Access Requests**—Either allows or denies requests for access and defines the email address these requests will go to.

> **NOTE**
>
> Double-check the email address that is defined if allowing requests for access is enabled. Often, the email is for an administration account that may not be monitored.

▶ **Site Collection Administrators**—Provides access to the list of users defined as site collection administrators and allows the addition of new site collection administrators or the removal of existing ones.

Clicking the name of the group from the Permissions page will show the users or AD groups that are part of the group. The administrator can also add users to the group from and perform other actions, including the following:

▶ Add users or AD groups to the SharePoint group

▶ Email users in the group

▶ Call/message selected users based on the tools available (such as if Office Communication Server is configured)

▶ Remove users from the group

▶ Access group settings

▶ View group permissions by listing the URLs to sites, lists, or items that inherit permissions from these URLs

▶ Make the group the default group for the site

▶ Provide access to the list settings for the User Information List

Table 21.2 provides an overview of the permissions that Approvers, Owners, Members, Visitors, and Designers groups receive by default in a SharePoint Server 2010 Enterprise site and summarizes the privileges for each group. Table 21.3 continues to provide an overview of the privileges of Hierarchy Managers, Records Center Web Service Submitters, Restricted Readers, Style Resource Readers, and Viewers.

TABLE 21.2   Default Permissions for Approvers, Members, Owners, Visitors, and Designers Groups in SharePoint Server 2010 Enterprise

	Approvers (Approve Permission Level)	Owners (Full Control Permission Level)	Members (Contribute Permission Level)	Visitors (Read Permission Level)	Designers (Design, Limited Access Permission Levels)
List Permissions					
Manage Lists	No	Yes	No	No	Yes

continues

TABLE 21.2 Continued

	Approvers (Approve Permission Level)	Owners (Full Control Permission Level)	Members (Contribute Permission Level)	Visitors (Read Permission Level)	Designers (Design, Limited Access Permission Levels)
Override Check Out	Yes	Yes	No	No	Yes
Add Items	Yes	Yes	Yes	No	Yes
Edit Items	Yes	Yes	Yes	No	Yes
Delete Items	Yes	Yes	Yes	No	Yes
View Items	Yes	Yes	Yes	Yes	Yes
Approve Items	Yes	Yes	No	No	Yes
Open Items	Yes	Yes	Yes	Yes	Yes
View Versions	Yes	Yes	Yes	Yes	Yes
Delete Versions	Yes	Yes	Yes	No	Yes
Create Alerts	Yes	Yes	Yes	Yes	Yes
View Application Pages	Yes	Yes	Yes	Yes	Yes
Site Permissions					
Manage Permissions	No	Yes	No	No	No
View Web Analytics Data	No	Yes	No	No	No
Create Subsites	No	Yes	No	No	No
Manage Web Site	No	Yes	No	No	No
Add and Customize Pages	No	Yes	No	No	Yes

TABLE 21.2   Continued

	Approvers (Approve Permission Level)	Owners (Full Control Permission Level)	Members (Contribute Permission Level)	Visitors (Read Permission Level)	Designers (Design, Limited Access Permission Levels)
Apply Themes and Borders	No	Yes	No	No	Yes
Apply Style Sheets	No	Yes	No	No	Yes
Create Groups	No	Yes	No	No	No
Browse Directories	Yes	Yes	Yes	No	Yes
Use Self-Service Site Creation	Yes	Yes	Yes	Yes	Yes
View Pages	Yes	Yes	Yes	Yes	Yes
Enumerate Permissions	No	Yes	No	No	No
Browse User Information	Yes	Yes	Yes	Yes	Yes
Manage Alerts	No	Yes	No	No	No
Use Remote Interfaces	Yes	Yes	Yes	Yes	Yes
Use Client Integration Features	Yes	Yes	Yes	Yes	Yes
Open	Yes	Yes	Yes	Yes	Yes
Edit Personal Information	Yes	Yes	Yes	No	Yes
Personal Permissions					
Manage Personal Views	Yes	Yes	Yes	No	Yes

continues

21

TABLE 21.2   Continued

	Approvers (Approve Permission Level)	Owners (Full Control Permission Level)	Members (Contribute Permission Level)	Visitors (Read Permission Level)	Designers (Design, Limited Access Permission Levels)
Add/Remove Personal Web Parts	Yes	Yes	Yes	No	Yes
Update Personal Web Parts	Yes	Yes	Yes	No	Yes

TABLE 21.3   Default Permissions for Hierarchy Managers, Records Center Web Service Submitters, Restricted Readers, Style Resource Readers, and Viewers in SharePoint Server 2010 Enterprise

	Hierarchy Managers (Manage Hierarchy Permission Level)	Records Center Web Service Submitters (Records Center Web Service Submitters Permission Level)	Restricted Readers (Restricted Read Permission Level)	Style Resource Readers (Limited Access Permission Level)	Viewers (View Only Permission Level)
List Permissions					
Manage Lists	Yes	No	No	No	No
Override Check Out	Yes	No	No	No	No
Add Items	Yes	No	No	No	No
Edit Items	Yes	No	No	No	No
Delete Items	Yes	No	No	No	No
View Items	Yes	No	Yes	No	Yes
Approve Items	No	No	No	No	No
Open Items	Yes	No	Yes	No	No

TABLE 21.2 Continued

	Hierarchy Managers (Manage Hierarchy Permission Level)	Records Center Web Service Submitters (Records Center Web Service Submitters Permission Level)	Restricted Readers (Restricted Read Permission Level)	Style Resource Readers (Limited Access Permission Level)	Viewers (View Only Permission Level)
View Versions	Yes	No	No	No	Yes
Delete Versions	Yes	No	No	No	No
Create Alerts	Yes	No	No	No	Yes
View Application Pages	Yes	No	No	No	Yes
Site Permissions					
Manage Permissions	Yes	No	No	No	No
View Web Analytics Data	Yes	No	No	No	No
Create Subsites	Yes	No	No	No	No
Manage Web Site	Yes	No	No	No	No
Add and Customize Pages	Yes	No	No	No	No
Apply Themes and Borders	No	No	No	No	No

continues

TABLE 21.3   Continued

	Hierarchy Managers (Manage Hierarchy Permission Level)	Records Center Web Service Submitters (Records Center Web Service Submitters Permission Level)	Restricted Readers (Restricted Read Permission Level)	Style Resource Readers (Limited Access Permission Level)	Viewers (View Only Permission Level)
Apply Style Sheets	No	No	No	No	No
Create Groups	No	No	No	No	No
Browse Directories	Yes	No	No	No	No
Use Self-Service Site Creation	Yes	No	No	No	Yes
View Pages	Yes	No	Yes	No	Yes
Enumerate Permissions	Yes	No	No	No	No
Browse User Information	Yes	No	No	Yes	Yes
Manage Alerts	Yes	No	No	No	No
Use Remote Interfaces	Yes	Yes	No	No	Yes
Use Client Integration Features	Yes	No	No	Yes	Yes
Open	Yes	Yes	Yes	Yes	Yes
Edit Personal Information	Yes	No	No	No	No

TABLE 21.3   Continued

	Hierarchy Managers (Manage Hierarchy Permission Level)	Records Center Web Service Submitters (Records Center Web Service Submitters Permission Level)	Restricted Readers (Restricted Read Permission Level)	Style Resource Readers (Limited Access Permission Level)	Viewers (View Only Permission Level)
Personal Permissions					
Manage Personal Views	Yes	No	No	No	No
Add/Remove Personal Web Parts	Yes	No	No	No	No
Update Personal Web Parts	Yes	No	No	No	No

NOTE

A best practice recommendation is to not change the settings for these default Owners, Members, and Visitors groups. In fact, the Owners group permissions can't be changed. Although it may seem like a good idea to modify the permissions of the Members or Visitors groups to meet specific requirements (for example, to remove the ability of the Visitors group to View Versions in a list and to Create Alerts), this can lead to confusion from an administrative and end-user standpoint. Other administrators may not know about these customizations, and users may not know either, and may think that, for example, their inability to create alerts is due to a SharePoint error and file a help desk ticket. The best practice is to create one or more new groups, such as Members Customized or Visitors Customized, and use those instead. This will call out clearly that the default settings have been customized. There is a Copy Permission Level button at the bottom of the Edit Permission Level page that makes it easy, for example, to copy the permissions for the standard Members group and then give it a name and add or remove permissions.

For this table, all site and site collection features have been enabled, to ensure that the full list of groups is provided.

Reviewing the Galleries Tools

Beneath the Users and Permissions section on the Site Settings page is the Galleries section, which contains links to all the galleries available for the current site, including the Site Columns, Site Content Types, Web Parts, List Templates, Master Pages and Page Layouts, Themes, and Solutions.

In general, the Site Columns and Site Content Types galleries will be actively used by an organization that is seeking to leverage the metadata capabilities provided by SharePoint 2010, while the other galleries will be used less often and can generally be ignored. Site designers will be interested in the Master Pages and Page Layout gallery and the Themes gallery. The administrator should review the List Templates gallery periodically to make sure that there aren't too many List templates accumulating because they can clutter up the Create page that is accessed when creating new lists and libraries.

Site columns and site content types are covered in Chapter 22, "Managing Metadata and Content Types in SharePoint 2010."

> **NOTE**
>
> Although site galleries allow administrators to delete items from the gallery, this should be done only if the administrator is confident of what the impact will be to base site functionality. A general best practice is to leave the default items in these galleries unless there is a specific business reason to delete items.

High-level descriptions are as follows:

- **Site Columns**—A number of predefined site columns already exist and are useful to peruse and test when creating a taxonomy for the organization. Types of site columns will include some or all of the following, based on the type of site and features enabled: Base Columns, Core Contact and Calendar Columns, Core Document Columns, Core Task and Issue Columns, Custom Columns, Document and Record Management Columns, Email Submission Columns, Enterprise Keywords Group, Extended Columns, Help Columns, Page Layout Columns, PerformancePoint, Publishing Columns, Ratings, Reports, and Status Indicators. New site columns can be created from this gallery as well.

- **Site Content Types**—A number of content types are in this gallery by default, which should be reviewed and tested so the administrator becomes familiar with their use and capabilities. Types of content types will include some or all of the following, based on the type of site and features enabled: Business Intelligence, Content Organizer Content Types, Digital Asset Content Types, Document Content Types, Document Set Content Types, Folder Content Types, Group Work Content Types, Help Content Types, List Content Types, Page Layout Content Types, PerformancePoint, Publishing Content Types, and Special Content Types.

▶ **Web Parts**—This gallery contains the web parts available to administrators and designers on this site. Chapter 18, "SharePoint Foundation Versus SharePoint Server 2010," provides a list in Table 18.9 of the web parts available in different versions of SharePoint 2010, and the selection for a specific website will depend on the type of site created and the features enabled for that site.

▶ **List Templates**—This gallery is empty for new sites and site collections, but will show any List templates created for the site collection. These List templates will be available to use for creating new lists and libraries within the site collection.

▶ **Master Pages and Page Layouts**—This gallery contains a variety of .xml, .aspx, and .master files and pages. SharePoint Designer 2010 is the tool of choice for editing the .aspx page layouts, and the .master pages. As shown in Figure 21.17, Modified Date and Time, Modified By, Checked Out To, Compatible UI, and Approval Status columns are shown by default.

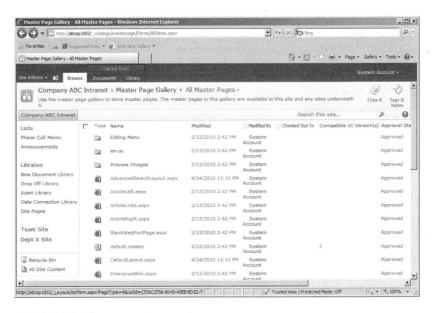

FIGURE 21.17   Master Page gallery.

▶ **Themes**—A number of themes (.thmx file format) are provided that can be applied to the site to change the basic look and feel of the site.

▶ **Solutions**—If any solutions have been deployed to the site collection by third-party providers or developers, they will be shown here. By default, a quota of 300 server resources are allowed for solutions, and this page shows Current Usage and Average Usage.

Reviewing the Site Administration Tools

On the Site Settings page in the Site Administration section are a number of links to additional tools that the site collection administrator should be familiar with. The links that show will vary based on the version of SharePoint 2010 in use and on the features enabled for the site and site collection.

Of particular interest are the Regional Settings tools, which are useful for multinational organizations and customizing information such as the time zone and setting the workdays and standard work hours for the organization. The RSS, Search and Offline Availability, and Workflow Settings links enable the administrator to determine whether specific features are going to be made available in the site collection.

A summary of these tools is as follows:

▶ **Regional Settings**—Allow the administrator to set locale, sort order, time zone, calendar type, alternate calendar, days in the workweek, first day of the week, start time, first week of the year, end time, and time format.

▶ **Site Libraries and Lists**—Shows all lists and libraries in the current site. Allows creation of new lists and libraries, pages, and sites.

▶ **User Alerts**—Shows any existing alerts on the site and allows their deletion. This can be useful to simply see whether users are taking advantage of alerts, but also to delete alerts after a user changes roles or positions, or leaves the company.

▶ **RSS**—Defines whether RSS feeds are allowed in this site collection, and whether they are allowed in the site itself, and if copyright information is attached to RSS feeds, who the managing editor and webmaster are, and defines the time to live in minutes.

▶ **Search and Offline Availability**—Allows the administrator to determine whether the site will appear in search results, the site's aspx page indexing behavior, and whether items can be downloaded to offline clients.

▶ **Sites and Workspaces**—Shows sites, document workspaces, and meeting workspaces that exist below the current site. This was discussed earlier in the chapter in the section titled "Reviewing the Scope of an Existing Site Collection."

▶ **Workflows**—Shows which workflows are active and inactive and the number of associations each has and the number in progress.

▶ **Workflow Settings**—Lists workflows associated with the site and allows the administrator to add a workflow.

▶ **Related Links Scope Settings**—Allows the administrator to add URLs that will be part of "This and Related Sites" search scope.

▶ **Term Store Management**—Allows the administrator to review the keywords available to use for tagging items in the site collection and to add or remove keywords.

▶ **Searchable Columns**—Columns can be selected here that will be excluded from search indexing, so their contents will not appear in search results.

▶ **Content and Structure**—As shown in Figure 21.18, this page (sitemanager.aspx) provides a tree view of all lists, libraries, and sites underneath the current site collection and allows a wide range of interaction with these entities. New sites, lists, or pages can be created beneath the top-level site, new items can be created in lists or libraries, list settings can be modified, and individual items can be edited, copied, deleted, and managed.

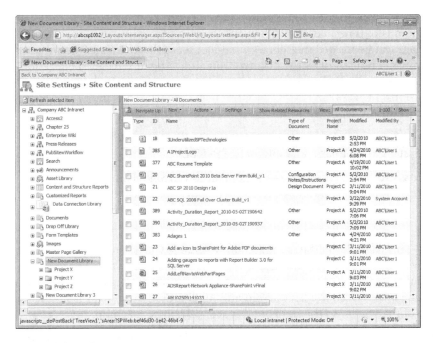

FIGURE 21.18   Site Content and Structure page.

Reviewing the Look and Feel Tools

The tools that appear in this section of the Site Settings page will vary based on the version of SharePoint 2010 in use and the type of site collection created. For example, the Welcome Page link is available only in publishing sites. The site administrator should review these tools because they are all relatively straightforward and allow quick customization of the site and site collection. A custom icon can be referenced that will appear on the home page and other pages that end users interact with. The master page, which defines the look and feel of the SharePoint environment, can be changed from these tools, which when designed by qualified resources can dramatically change the look and feel of the environment and make it less generic and more closely match corporate marketing standards. A number of other choices can be made about what navigation aids to provide and which global and local navigation links to provide.

Following is a summary of the tools provided:

▶ **Welcome Page**—Allows the administrator to select a different page that will be presented when a user navigates to the site. In a publishing site, the default page is Default.aspx located in the Pages library.

▶ **Title, Description, and Icon**—Allows the administrator to quickly change the title of the site that displays in the breadcrumb trail and home tab on the navigation bar. Also if a custom URL is desired, the URL to the location of the icon can be entered. The icon image can be located in a library (that all users will need read access to or else the icon won't render) or in the "14 hive" on all front-end servers. The location of the image is generally C:\Program Files\Common Files\Microsoft Shared\Web Server Extensions\14\TEMPLATE\IMAGES, but may vary. The icon image will need to be placed in this folder on all front-end web servers in the farm.

▶ **Master Page**—This page allows the administrator to select the Site Master page, as well as the System Master page, and alternate CSS URLs.

▶ **Page Layouts and Site Templates**—A great addition to SharePoint 2010, this tool allows administrator to determine which site templates, page layouts, and default page layout for new pages will be used when administrators or users create subsites and pages.

▶ **Tree View**—This page allows the administrator to enable Quick Launch and enable Tree view, or disable either. Note that some organizations feel that the Quick Launch takes up valuable real estate on the screen or is simply distracting and not useful and choose to hide it. However, the Recycle Bin and All Site Content tools will still be on the left side of the screen, so the horizontal space will still be taken up.

▶ **Site Theme**—On this page, the site can be configured to inherit the theme from the parent or to have its own theme. Predesigned themes can be selected and customized by choosing different text/background colors, accent colors, hyperlink colors, and heading and body fonts. The theme can then be previewed and applied to the current site or pushed to subsites, as well.

▶ **Navigation**—Some tools will be grayed out if this link is accessed from a top-level site. The full range of tools available allow the administrator to define how the global navigation works (which is shown near the top of the page under the Ribbon on most pages) and the local navigation works (shown in the Quick Launch on most pages). For global and current navigation, the navigation items on the parent site can be included, or only items below the current site will be shown. And the option to show subsites and pages is provided, along with a field to enter the maximum number of items to show (20 by default). In the Navigation Editing and Sorting section of the screen, shown in Figure 21.19, new headings and links can be added or existing ones edited. In Figure 21.19, a new heading (Links to External Sites) and a new link beneath that heading (Company XYZ Web Site) was added. This link is being edited in the figure, and note that a check box exists to allow opening of the link in a new window. Audience targeting can also be applied to this link.

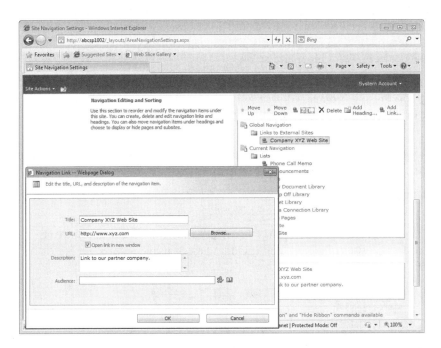

FIGURE 21.19   Editing a navigation link from the Navigation Settings page.

Reviewing the Site Actions Tools

The Site Actions section of the Site Settings page provides a set of tools that allow the administrator to enable site features, reset to a site definition, delete the site, or view reports about activity on the site. If the site is a nonpublishing site, the administrator will be able to save the site as a template and include content, assuming it is less than 50MB of data.

Site features are reviewed in more detail later in this section, but enable the site collection administrator to control which toolsets are available to site collection and site users.

The reports can be very useful for a site collection administrator to see the number of users visiting a specific site and the top pages visited on that site and who the top visitors are, while the site collection reports add information on overall activities for the site collection as well as for search activity. Viewing search activity can be very useful for site collection administrators because if certain terms keep appearing in search terms, they should probably be incorporated into the taxonomy for the organization, if they aren't already.

The Site Actions section contains the following tools:

- ▸ **Manage Site Features**—These are discussed in more detail in the section "Reviewing Site Collection and Site Features" in this chapter.

- ▸ **Save Site as Template**—Not available for publishing sites, this tool is very useful for saving sites that have been customized for specific uses, such as for specific types of groups of users such as US Departments, EMEA Departments, Small Projects, Cross Departmental Projects, Team Blog, and so on.

- ▸ **Reset to Site Definition**—This tool is generally only used in situations where the site or a page on the site is damaged. Using this tool will remove all customizations from a page or all pages on the site, including web part zones, custom controls, and inline text.

- ▸ **Delete This Site**—Permanently deletes the site and all of its contents. A deleted site will not appear in the Recycle Bin of the parent site.

- ▸ **Site Web Analytics Reports**—Provides reports of Traffic and Inventory for the site, an example of which is shown in Figure 21.20.

- ▸ **Site Collection Web Analytics Reports**—Provides the same reports as Site Web Analytics, but for the site collection, and includes Search usage reports.

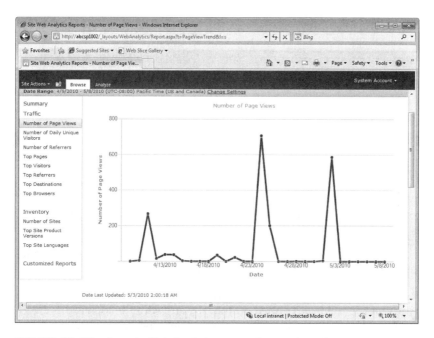

FIGURE 21.20   Sample Web Analytics report for number of page views.

An Overview of Site Collection Administration Tools

These tools are visible only to a site collection administrator and only from the top-level site of the site collection. Lower-level sites will have a link in this section of the page labeled Go to Top Level Site Settings. These tools affect the full range of sites in the site collection and can affect search settings, site collection features, auditing, policies, content types, the use of SharePoint Designer, and numerous other features:

▶ **Search Settings**—Allows custom scopes to be enabled by connecting this site collection with a Search Center, or limits scope to simply This Site. A variety of drop-down modes for search boxes are also available to choose from, and the site collection search results page can be changed. This allows for granular customization of the search tools:

▶ **Search Scopes**—Shows the existing search scopes (such as All Sites and People) as well as the Advance Search scopes. New scopes are created from the Central Administrator site, by accessing the Application Management page, then Manage Service Applications, choosing the Search service application, and then choosing Scopes from the Quick Launch area, and then creating a new scope and rules, or modifying an existing scope.

▶ **Search Keywords**—Keywords can be defined by the administrator to link to Best Bet sites in this interface. For example, a keyword of "benefits" could be linked to a Best Bet for the HR Department site, so the HR Department site would be marked with a star and display at the top of the list if the term "benefits" was searched for.

> **NOTE**
>
> FAST Search keywords, FAST Search site promotion and demotion and FAST Search user context are covered in Chapter 8, "Leveraging and Optimizing Search in SharePoint 2010."

▶ **Recycle Bin**—Displays the End User Recycle Bin and give a link to the Deleted from End User Recycle Bin (otherwise known as the Second Level Recycle Bin). The administrator can restore list or library items as well as lists and libraries that have been deleted.

▶ **Site Collection Features**—These are discussed later in this chapter in the section titled "Reviewing Site Collection and Site Features."

▶ **Site Hierarchy**—Shows all websites that have been created under the current site. This was discussed earlier in the chapter in the section titled "Reviewing the Scope of an Existing Site Collection."

▶ **Site Collection Navigation**—Enabled by default, navigation links can be disabled from this page. If disabled, the navigations bars will be hidden. Security trimming on navigation is also on by default, but can be turned off. If turned off, users will see links even if they don't have permissions to access the URLs the links connect to. Audience targeting, also on by default, can be turned off for navigation links.

▶ **Site Collection Audit Settings**—Provides access to a number of settings pertaining to audit logs, such as automatic trimming of audit logs, specifying the events that will be audited on documents and items, as well as on lists, libraries, and sites.

▶ **Audit Log Reports**—This page provides access to several categories of reports: Content Activity Reports, Custom Reports, Information Management Policy Reports, Security, and Site Settings Reports. The Custom Report link allows the administrator to define the specific events to report on such as deleting or restoring items or searching site content. These reports will be generated when selected, and the administrator simply needs to enter a destination for the report and it will be generated and can be opened immediately.

▶ **Portal Site Connection**—A portal site can be specified. If specified, it will appear in the options accessible from the Folder icon located to the right of the Site Actions drop-down menu. This is most often used when site collections are created beneath an existing site collection and provides a means of navigating from the top-level site of the nested site collection to the higher-level site collection. Without this connection, there is no built-in navigational tool to reach to topmost site.

▶ **Site Collection Policies**—Policies can be created or imported from this page. Figure 21.21 shows some of the options available for enabling retention and retention stages, enabling auditing of opening or downloading documents, editing items, or checking out, moving, or deleting items. Barcodes and labels can also be enabled.

▶ **Record Declaration Settings**—After an item has been declared a record, additional restrictions and retention policies can be applied. This page provides the Record Restrictions, Record Declaration Availability, and Declaration Roles tools. For example, Block Edit and Delete can be selected, which means that items declared to be records can't be edited or deleted. Also, the ability to manually declare a record can be enabled or disabled, and the declaration of records and undeclaration of records can be set to be performed by list contributors and administrators, only list administrators, or only policy administrators.

▶ **Site Collection Cache Profiles**—Cache profiles determine the behavior of the page output cache for the items it is applied to which can be a site collection, and individual site, or a master page. Four cache profiles are provided by default, and additional ones can be added by clicking the Add New Item link. The default cache profiles are Disabled, Public Internet (Purely Anonymous), Extranet (Published Site), and Intranet (Collaboration Site). Figure 21.22 shows the default Intranet cache profile, and if Edit Item is clicked from the View tab on the Ribbon, the administrator can read more about the different settings and their impact on performance and security.

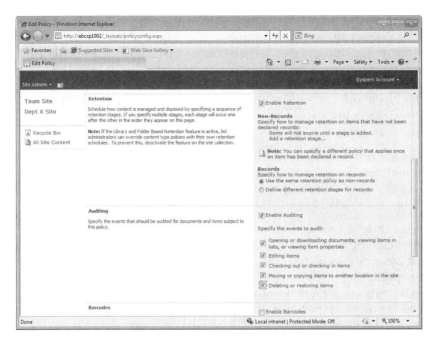

FIGURE 21.21   Creating a new policy.

FIGURE 21.22   Cache Profile for Intranet (Collaboration Site).

▶ **Site Collection Object Cache**—Object cache applies to complete field data for a page, excluding data for any web part controls on the page, and can speed up rendering of navigation data and data accessed through cross-list queries because these items are running queries to compile the data presented to the user. The maximum cache size can be set here (default is a massive 100MB, so this can easily be reduced for smaller site collections), the object cache can be reset for troubleshooting purposes, and cross-list query results (for example, from the Content Query web part) can be cached for a specified amount of time.

▶ **Content Type Service Application Error Log**—This list stores content type publishing error information for all subscriber sites to help the administrator troubleshoot issues related to publishing content types. Basically, if the log is empty, SharePoint is not seeing any obvious errors.

▶ **Site Collection Output Cache**—This page allows the administrator to determine whether output caching is enabled. If enabled, the anonymous cache profile and authenticated cache profiles (configurable from the Site Collection Cache Profiles tool), whether publishing sites can use a different page output cache profile, and whether page layouts can use a different page output cache profile. An option is also provided to enable debug cache information on pages, which shows the date and time the page contents were last rendered.

▶ **Content Type Publishing**—The first entry on the page allows the administrator to refresh all published content types on next update. The Managed Metadata Service hub, if one is defined, will be displayed, as well as any subscribed content types.

> **NOTE**
>
> Variations, Variation Labels, and Translatable columns and Variation logs are discussed in the "Site Variations Demystified" section, later in this chapter.

▶ **Suggested Content Browser Locations**—This list allows the administrator to specify links to SharePoint libraries that contain useful resources to be included in web pages. Page editors are able to see these locations when inserting assets into the web pages.

▶ **Document ID Settings**—Although all documents are assigned an ID number when added to a library, this is not a unique number, and SharePoint 2010 allows the creation of unique document IDs. The Document ID Settings page provides the options to assign document IDs, define the character set the document IDs will begin with, reset all document IDs in this site collection to begin with a set of characters, and define the search scope that can be used to search for these IDs. Figure 21.23 shows this page after the administrator has decided to begin IDs for the site collection with the characters UNLEASHED1 and then clicked the Reset All Document IDs box and clicked OK. A message on the page indicates that a job needs to run before the IDs will be changed. This job is the document ID enable/disable job, which is set to run daily by default.

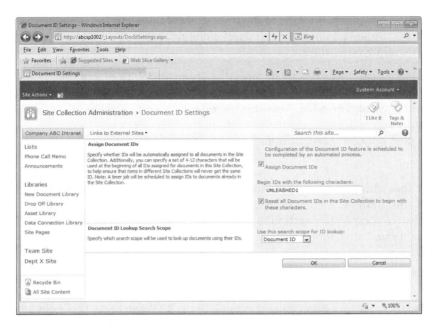

FIGURE 21.23   Document ID Settings page.

▶ **SharePoint Designer Settings**—This link allows the administrator to enable or disable the following settings: Enable SharePoint Designer, Enable Detaching Pages from the Site Definition, Enable Customizing Master Pages and Page Layouts, and Enable Managing of the Web Site URL Structure.

▶ **Visual Upgrade**—If the environment has been upgraded from SharePoint 2007, this page allows the administrator to Hide Visual Upgrade or Update All Sites. By default, the old SharePoint 2007 look and feel is maintained.

▶ **Help settings**—A number of different help features can be enabled here, including FAST search, PerformancePoint, Search Server 2010, and SharePoint Server 2010. The administrator should decide which to enable based on the features enabled and whether the organization is encouraging the use of some of these more advanced features (such as PerformancePoint).

Understanding and Using Site Variations

Site variations are designed for organizations that support users who speak a number of different languages, and expect to see sites in the language they use on their computer. More specifically, once site variations are defined, users will be redirected based on the language their browser is set to, assuming a site is defined and the prerequisites are configured.

SharePoint 2010, unfortunately, does not do any translation, so the organization will be responsible for performing the translations of the content. The Translatable Columns link

610 CHAPTER 21 Designing and Managing Pages and Sites for Knowledge Workers

from the Site Settings page provides access to the full list of columns used in the site collection, and allows the site administrator to select columns that are "translatable" and will be flagged as requiring translation.

Note also that variations can be used only on sites that are created with one of the Publishing site templates, or on sites for where the SharePoint Server Publishing Infrastructure feature has been enabled. Also, it is important to point out that by default, the variations feature copies only publishing pages from the Pages library of the source variation site and does not copy content from lists or document libraries.

To test variations, follow these steps:

1. Create a site that will serve as the variations root site that uses the Publishing Site template. In this example, a site was created and titled Variation1 under the root (full URL is http://abcsp1002/variation1). The hierarchy will be created under this site once the "labels" are defined and the Create Hierarchies process has completed.

2. From the Site Settings page for the site collection that contains the site just created (http://abcsp1002 in this case), click the Variations link in the Site Collection Administration section.

3. From the Variation Settings page, enter the name of the site created (in this example, /**variation1**) in the Variation Home field. Leave the other settings at their defaults, which in this example are the following: Automatically Create Site and Page Variations, Recreate a New Target Page When the Source Page Is Republished, Update Web Part Changes to Target Pages When Variation Source Page Update Is Propagated, Send Email Notification to Site and Page Contacts When a New Site or Page Is Created or a Page Is Updated by the Variation System, and Reference Existing Resources. Click OK.

4. Next click the Variation Labels link from the Site Settings page, and click New Label on the toolbar.

5. Enter **English** as the Label Name, and enter English as the Display Name. From the Locale drop-down menu, select English (United States).

6. In the Source Variation section, click the box next to Set This Variation to Be the Source Variation. A warning will appear that states "After you click 'Create Hierarchies' on the Variations Labels page, you will be unable to change the source variation on this label." Click OK.

7. Select the Publishing Site template from the drop-down menu in the same section. The page should look the same as Figure 21.24. Click OK.

8. From the Variations Label page, click New Label on the toolbar, and this time enter **Francais** as the Label Name, and enter Francais as the Display Name. From the Locale drop-down menu, select French (France).

9. Leave the box next to Set This Variation to Be the Source Variation unchecked and click OK.

10. From the Variation Labels page, click the Create Hierarchies icon.

11. A message will be provided that indicates "A Variation Hierarchy will be created" and provides the name of the job (Variations Create Hierarchies Job Definition, in

this example) and the time the job will run (daily between 00:00:00 and 03:00:00). Click OK to close this message. Figure 21.25 shows the Variations Labels page after the job has been scheduled.

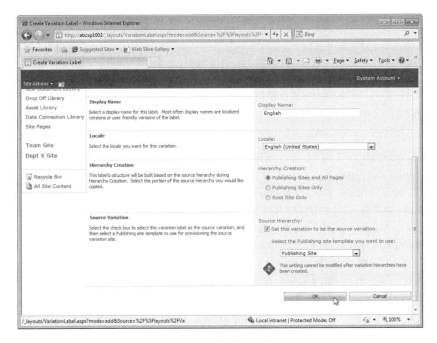

FIGURE 21.24   Creating the Source Variation label.

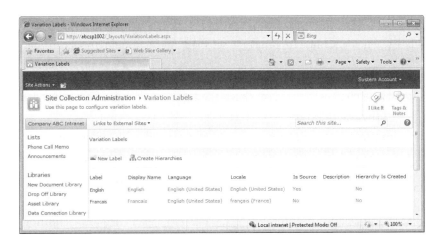

FIGURE 21.25   The Variation Labels page after the Create Hierarchies job has been scheduled.

12. Wait for the Variations Create Hierarchies Job Definition to complete, if you are patient; alternatively, visit the Central Administration site if you are less patient and

want the job to execute immediately. From the Central Administration home page, click Monitoring, and then click Review Job Definitions and find the Variations Create Hierarchies Job Definition and click the link. Click Run Now from that page and the job will run.

13. When the Variation Labels page marks the Hierarchy Is Create with Yes, the variation sites have been created.

14. Visit the top-level site that was created to host these sites (http://abcsp1002/variation1 in this example) and check the View All Site Content page to verify that the sites were created. There should be two sites created: one titled English and one titled Francais.

To test that the variations are working, change IE's settings as follows:

1. Open IE (assume version 7 or 8), access the Tools menu, and click Internet Options.

2. Click the Languages button, and then click the Add button, and find French (France) and click OK. Then choose French (France) from the Language preference and click Move Up to place it as the preferred language. Click OK twice to close the windows.

3. Close all browser sessions, and open a new session and enter the URL for the top-level containing site (http://abcsp1002/variation1) and press Enter. You should end up at the Francais page, which will be a blank page at this point.

4. Reset the browser language to English as the preferred language, and you should end up on the English page, proving the redirect is working.

Next modify the blank page on the English version of the page by following these steps:

1. Visit the English page (http://abcsp1002/variation1/English/Pages/Default.aspx) and click Site Actions, Edit page, and add some content to the page.

2. To add an image, click the Click Here to Insert a Picture from SharePoint in the Page Image field, and then click the Browse button and locate an image stored in a SharePoint library. Click OK once the image is selected, and it should appear in the Page Image field.

3. Size the image by clicking the Design tab on the Ribbon and change the horizontal size which should also change the vertical size if the Lock Aspect Ratio box is checked.

4. Enter some text in the Page Content field. Figure 21.26 shows a sample.

5. Click Publish from the Publish tab, enter comments if desired, and click Continue.

6. The variations process will now replicate these changes to the Francais page once the Variations Propagate Page Job Definition job runs. By default, this is set to run hourly, so you can wait for it to run, or visit the Job Definitions page on Central Administration. To do so, click Monitoring from the Central Administration home page, click Review Job Definitions, find the Variations Propagate Page Job Definition job, and then click Run Now.

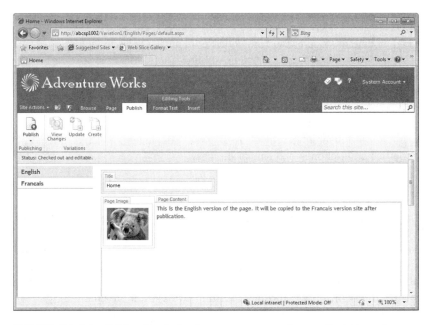

FIGURE 21.26   Editing the Default.aspx page on a Source Variation site.

7. After this job completes, the Francais site will reflect the changes made on the English site, as shown in Figure 21.27.

FIGURE 21.27   A Variations page updated by the Variations Propagate Page Job definition.

> **NOTE**
>
> An organization can modify the code of the Variations Root Landing Logic to look at something other than the language setting of the users' browsers. MSDN provides an overview of the process at http://msdn.microsoft.com/en-us/library/ ms562040(office.14).aspx. In short, the VariationsRootLanding.ascx and one user control that is defined in the VariationsRootLanding.ascx file define the behavior and can be modified. For example, you might have target variation sites with pages designed for display on devices that have different screen sizes or screen resolutions, which could be useful for supporting smartphones and similar devices.

Reviewing Site Features and Site Collection Features

Site features and site collection features allow the site collection administrator to turn on and off a variety of features. These pages are fairly intimidating if SharePoint Server 2010 Enterprise is installed, so the site collection administrator should carefully consider which, if any, of these features to enable above and beyond the features that are enabled by default when the site collection is created. Some site features require that site collection features are enabled, and error messages will indicate when there is a prerequisite that has not been met.

For planning purposes, a list is provided of the standard site features provided by SharePoint Server 2010 Enterprise:

- ▶ **Content Organizer**—Enabling the Content Organizer feature will add the Content Organizer Settings and Content Organizer Rules that were covered in Chapter 20, "Customizing and Managing Libraries and Lists to Meet Business Requirements."

- ▶ **Email Integration with Content Organizer**—Requires that the Content Organizer feature is enabled.

- ▶ **Group Work Lists**—Enables additional functionality for calendars so they can show scheduled events for the logged-in user from Exchange, and other users' calendars can be added for comparison purposes.

- ▶ **Hold and eDiscovery**—Enabling the Hold and eDiscovery site feature is used to track external actions such as litigation, investigations, and audits and will add a Hold and eDiscovery section to the Site Settings page. This topic is covered in Chapter 24, "Governing the SharePoint 2010 Ecosystem."

- ▶ **Metadata Navigation and Filtering**—This allows the use of metadata tree view hierarchies and filter controls to enhance navigation within lists and libraries. This topic is covered in Chapter 22, "Managing Metadata and Content Types in SharePoint 2010."

- ▶ **Offline Synchronization for External Lists**—This enables synchronization with Outlook and SharePoint Workspace.

- ▶ **PerformancePoint Services Site Features**—This site feature has a dependency on the Site Collection feature. If both are active, allows the use of PerformancePoint web parts.

- ▶ **SharePoint Server Enterprise Site Features**—Includes features such as Visio Services, Access Services, and Excel Services applications.

- ▶ **SharePoint Server Publishing**—Has a dependency on a Site Collection feature. When enabled, adds libraries, master pages, and other features to facilitate the use of SharePoint as a publishing platform.

- ▶ **SharePoint Server Standard Features**—Includes features such as user profiles and search.

- ▶ **Team Collaboration Lists**—Makes standard lists such as document libraries and issues available.

- ▶ **Wiki Page Home Page**—When active, creates a wiki page as the site home page.

- ▶ **Report Server File sync**—When active, allows synchronization with SQL Server Reporting Services.

The following list covers the site collection features provided by SharePoint Server 2010 Enterprise:

- ▶ **Advanced Web Analytics**—Includes advanced web analytics reports, data-driven workflows, the Web Analytics web part, and customize report functionality.

- ▶ **Content Type Syndication Hub**—Provisions a site to be an enterprise medadata hub site. This is covered in Chapter 22.

- ▶ **Custom Site Collection Help**—Creates a Help library that can be used to store custom help for the site collection.

- ▶ **Disposition Approval Workflow**—When active, enables the Disposition Approval workflow, which allows participants to decide whether to retain or delete expired documents.

- ▶ **Document ID Service**—When active, assigns IDs to documents in the site collection.

- ▶ **Document Sets**—When active, enables document sets to be used, as covered in Chapter 20, in the section titled "Document Sets Compared to Folders as Organizational Tools in Document Libraries."

- ▶ **In Place Records Management**—When active, enables the definition and declaration of records in place.

- ▶ **Library and Folder Based Retention**—Allows list administrators to override content type retention schedules.

- ▶ **Open Documents in Client Applications by Default**—Configures links to documents so that they open in client applications instead of web applications by default.

▶ **PerformancePoint Services Site Collection Features**—Enables the PerformancePoint site, including content types and site definitions for the site collection.

▶ **Publishing Approval Workflow**—Enables the Publishing Approval workflow that allows Approvers to approve or reject the page.

▶ **Reporting**—When active, creates reports about activities in SharePoint 2010.

▶ **Search Server Web Parts**—When active, uploads all web parts required for the Search Center site template.

▶ **SharePoint 2007 Workflows**—When active, provides the out-of-the-box workflows provided by SharePoint 2007.

▶ **SharePoint Server Enterprise Site Collection Features**—When active, allows the use of features such as InfoPath Forms Services, Visio Services, Access Services, and Excel Services.

▶ **SharePoint Server Publishing Infrastructure**—When active, provides libraries, content types, master pages, and page layouts to facilitate the use of SharePoint as a publishing environment. Adds site collection documents and site collection images, as well, to the top-level site in the site collection.

▶ **SharePoint Server Standard Site Collection Features**—Provides features such as user profiles and search.

▶ **Three-State Workflow**—When active, enables the Three-State workflow.

▶ **Workflows**—When active, allows use of out-of-the-box SharePoint workflows.

▶ **Report Server File sync**—When active, allows synchronization with SQL Server Reporting Services.

Audience Targeting Explained and Demonstrated

The creation of audiences may be outside of the control of the humble site administrator, but she should understand how they are compiled and how they can be used. This section provides an example of creating an audience, compiling it, and then configuring a document library to use audience targeting, and the configuration of a web part on a home page to use audience targeting. This example combines tasks that would be performed by library administrators, site administrators, as well as farm administrators, but is necessary to fully provide an example of the process of using audiences. It is also important to note that audiences do not affect the access permissions of documents, but simply filter content that appears in web parts, and that is also illustrated in this example.

For this reason, in this author's experience, audiences are not used that often, except in sites where there are a variety of different groups accessing the content from the home page, and there is value in filtering the data each person sees in specific web parts based on their membership in one or more audiences.

This example starts with the task of defining and compiling the audience, which needs to be done by a user with Central Administrator site access, typically someone in the farm administrator role. The audience is then defined as follows:

1. From Central Administration, click Application Management, and then click Manage Service Applications.

2. Scroll down to User Profile Service Application and click it.

3. Click Manage Audiences in the People section.

4. From the View Audiences page, click New Audience on the toolbar.

5. Give the audience a name and description and assign an owner, as shown in Figure 21.28. In this example the name **Project X Audience** is used. Decide whether the audience should include users who satisfy all of the rules or any of the rules, and then click OK.

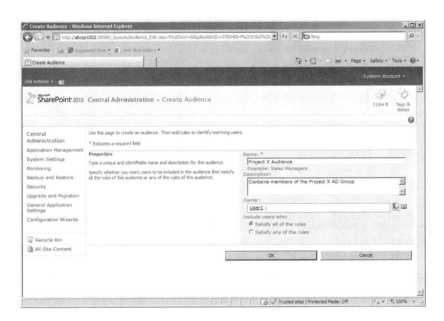

FIGURE 21.28   Creating an Audience screen 1.

6. On the next page, leave User selected in the Operand section, select Member Of in the Operator drop-down menu, and enter the AD group that contains the users for the audience. In this example, the AD group **Project X Group** is entered as shown in Figure 21.29. This group contains User1 and User4. Click OK to complete.

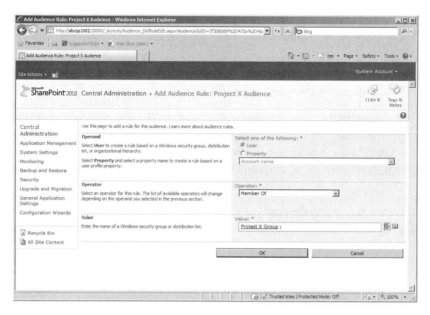

FIGURE 21.29   Creating an Audience screen 2.

7. After this is completed, return to the Manage Profile Service page, and then from the People section, click Compile Audiences. After this completes, the audience will be ready to use.

This next section can be performed by an administrator with full control permissions on a site (for example, a site administrator or other user in the Owners group, or of course, a site collection administrator). To test the audience, follow these steps:

1. From a document library that has audience targeting enabled, upload a new document by clicking the Upload button, and then provide target audience information in the Target Audience field, as shown in Figure 21.30. Click Save. Repeat for additional documents if desired.

2. The item is now tagged with a specific audience (Project X Audience, in this example).

3. Navigate to the home page of the site, click Site Actions drop-down list, and then click Edit Page.

4. Click Add a Web Part from the Left zone, and choose the web part that corresponds to the document library you have enabled audience targeting in and in which you tagged one or more documents in step 1. In this example, the web part is New Document Library, as shown in Figure 21.31. Click Add to add the web part to the page.

5. Next, as shown in Figure 21.32, hover over the title section for the new web part just added (New Document Library in this example) and hover over the down arrow and select Edit Web Part; the Editing Panel will open on the right side of the screen.

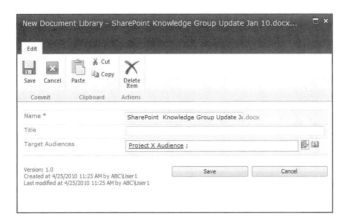

FIGURE 21.30   Defining a target audience for a document.

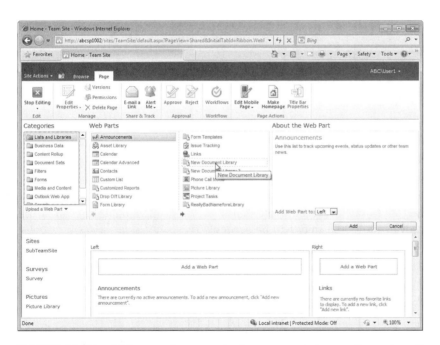

FIGURE 21.31   Adding a web part to the home page to test audience targeting.

6. Expand the Advanced menu in the panel, scroll down to the section titled Target Audience, and enter the name of the audience to use for this web part (in this example, **Project X Audience**). Click OK.

7. Now only the documents that have been tagged for this audience will appear in this web part, if the logged-in user is a member of the audience. For example, assume User2 is logged in to this site. Because she isn't a member of the Project X AD group,

and therefore not included in the Project X Audience, she won't see the documents tagged for the Project X group show up in this web part.

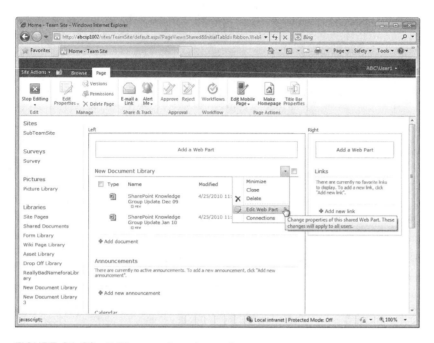

FIGURE 21.32   Editing a web part on a home page.

8. Click Stop Editing to save changes. (Note that if you are using a publishing site with content approval, additional steps will be needed)

9. Test the performance of the audience targeting by logging in as a user who is a member of the group (User1 or User4 in this example) and then as a user who isn't a member (User2 in this example). Note that the document tagged for the audience won't appear in the web part for the user who isn't a member of the group.

NOTE

It is important to realize that assigning an audience or audiences to documents does not change the permissions of the document. So in the previous example, just because one or more documents were tagged as being targeted for the Project X Audience, this doesn't mean that users who aren't part of that group can't still access the document. The security settings of the document library and the folder and the document itself determine who can read, edit, delete, or modify the document, not the audience tags.

Summary

This chapter took on the challenging task of covering the tools that site collection administrators and site administrators will need to be comfortable with if they are to effectively plan, design, build, and support site collections. The process of creating a site collection was reviewed briefly, and recommendations were given on how the administrator can review the scope of the site collection to thoroughly understand the scope of the administrative challenge. One of these challenges involves controlling who can create sites within the site collection. Then the process of creating pages and sites was discussed and demonstrated, and a full list of the page and site template options in the full range of SharePoint 2010 product was provided, which included notes on the functionality and distinguishing features of each item. The wide range of tools available on the Site Settings page was reviewed, but because of the sheer number of items, in many cases only high-level descriptions were given. Site Variations were looked at in more detail and ideas provided on how they can be used and even "hacked" for other business purposes. The range of site features and site collection features were covered, and finally the process of audience targeting was explained and demonstrated to round out the chapter. This final step-by-step example gives the reader a chance to work with configuring a page by adding web parts and then configuring the web part to use audience targeting.

Best Practices

- ▶ The site collection administrator needs to understand the differences between creating a site collection, which is done from the Central Administrator site, and creating sites, which can be done in a variety of ways from within the site collection, and creating pages, which can also be done in a variety of ways from within sites and libraries.

- ▶ The Site Settings page contains myriad tools that the site collection and site administrators should be conversant with. The tools shown will vary based on the site collection features, site features enabled, and the version of SharePoint 2010 installed.

- ▶ A site collection administrator taking over an existing site collection should thoroughly review the subsites that exist in the site collection, as well as any managed paths that contain additional site collections. The Site Settings page offers the Sites and Workspaces link that shows subsites, document workspaces, and meeting workspaces, as well as the Site Hierarchy link that shows all subsites. However, the Site Collection List should be visited from the Central Admin site to see whether managed paths exist, which can contain additional site collections, each of which can have any number of subsites.

- ▶ Administrators should review which permission levels have the ability to create sites and workspaces in the environment. This is done by accessing Site Settings, Sites and Workspaces, and then clicking Site Creation Permissions. Also, Self-Service Site Creation settings should be checked from the Central Administration site, Security page, by clicking Configure Self-Service Site Creation.

▶ Another area a site collection administrator needs to be familiar with is the Users and Permissions section in the Site Settings page, and especially the Site Permissions interface, and the permissions that are granted by default to the standard SharePoint Groups, especially Owners, Members, and Visitors, because these are the most widely used groups.

▶ Variations are a powerful new feature that allow the site administrator to design an environment that automatically routes users to a specific site based on the language setting in IE. They are specifically designed for organizations supporting multiple languages but can be customized for other uses as well.

▶ Audience targeting allows farm administrators to create audiences and then compile them based on the rules created. A list or library then needs to have audience targeting enabled, and items in that list or library need to be assigned to one or more audiences. Then web parts added to a page, such as the home page, can use audiences to filter which files are displayed in that web part. Audiences do not affect the permissions of users to view or modify documents; they are simply filtering mechanisms.

CHAPTER 22

Managing Metadata and Content Types in SharePoint 2010

Metadata has been mentioned many times in this book in previous chapters. This chapter provides a thorough overview of the different ways that metadata can be created and managed, starting with the creation of columns in lists and libraries and then to site columns and content types. Finally, managed metadata is discussed, along with ways in which it facilitates the metadata management process.

Instead of spending a lot of time on the theory of metadata and creating taxonomies that involve metadata, a hands-on approach is taken in this chapter. A number of step-by-step exercises are provided, and going through these steps is a key component in the learning process. The sections in this chapter build upon each other, so it is strongly recommended that the exercises be done in order for the latter exercises to make sense for new SharePoint administrators.

Effectively Using Metadata in Lists and Libraries

Essentially, metadata is "data about data," and even users who don't use SharePoint have experience with it every day. Any file created will have some metadata associated with it. For example, a simple Microsoft Word document needs to have a filename, which is a key piece of metadata. In addition, it will have a creation date and last modified date, and then Microsoft Word allows users to add additional metadata to the document. SharePoint 2010 exposes this basic metadata that is embedded in the document and allows administrators to add new metadata columns in document libraries that store the files.

Lists are essentially nothing but metadata, unless one or more attachments are added to an item in a list. Administrators and power users will very quickly become accustomed to adding metadata columns when working with lists.

This section starts with an investigation into the interaction between metadata stored in a Word 2010 document and the library that ends up housing that document. Following this, a high-level walk-through is provided, covering the column choices included in SharePoint 2010. The chapter then provides tips and notes on certain column types, and then a series of exercises to help administrators and power users gain hands-on experience with metadata.

Working with Metadata in a Word 2010 Document and Document Libraries

The following section and step-by-step exercises provide a thought-provoking introduction to the functionality of metadata in SharePoint 2010 and the interaction of SharePoint with the embedded metadata in a Word 2010 document. By following these steps, an administrator will gain a better understanding of the interaction between SharePoint 2010 document libraries and the documents that will be stored in them, and will probably want to perform additional testing to further master the topic.

This exercise walks an administrator through the process of creating two different document libraries that contain different metadata columns, and the process of accessing the properties for a Word 2010 document, populating metadata within the document, and then uploading the document and adding additional metadata. The document is then moved to the second document library, where some of the metadata appears to be lost, but is in fact still contained within the Word document.

The following steps cover the actions needed to complete the exercise:

1. Create a new document library on a SharePoint 2010 site. Leave the settings at their defaults. Title it **Metadata Test1**. Steps for creating a new document library are provided in Chapter 20, "Customizing and Managing Libraries and Lists to Meet Business Requirements," in the "Creating Lists and Libraries" section.

2. Click the Library tab, and click the Create Column icon.

3. Name the column **Subject**, and choose Single Line of Text, and leave the rest of the settings at their defaults and click OK.

4. Click the Library tab, and click the Create Column icon again.

5. This time, name the column **Project Name**, and choose Choice (menu to choose from) as the column type. In the Type Each Choice on a Separate Line box, delete the default entries and add `Project ABC`, `Project DEF`, and `Project GHI`, as shown in Figure 22.1. Clear the Default Value field, leave the other fields at their defaults, and click OK.

6. Create a second document library, but title it **Metadata Test 2**, and add the column titled Subject to it, as well, but do not add the Project Name column.

7. Next, create a new Word 2010 document and enter some sample text.

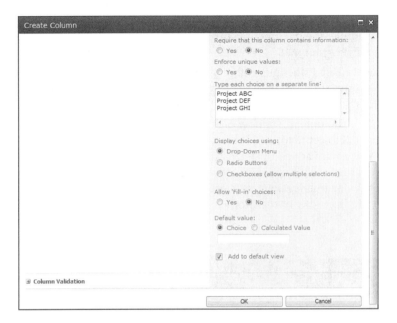

FIGURE 22.1   Creating a choice column.

8. Click the File tab, click the Info link on the left side, and then click the Properties drop-down menu on the right side and select Show Document Panel.

9. The Document Panel will now appear for the document. Enter a value into the Subject field (for example, `Mission Statement`), and the results will look like Figure 22.2.

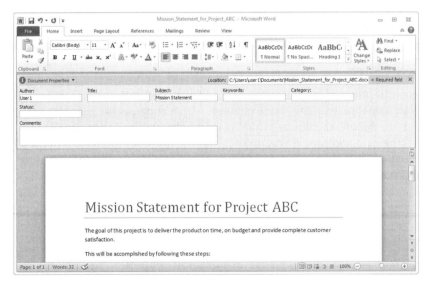

FIGURE 22.2   Entering metadata in Word 2010.

10. Now click the Save icon, save the document locally to My Documents, and close the document. For this example, the document is saved as **Mission_Statement_for_Project_ABC.**

11. Navigate to the Metadata Test 1 document library and upload the document by clicking the Upload button, then the Browse button, and locating the document, clicking Open, and then clicking OK.

12. As shown in Figure 22.3, the upload window prompts for additional metadata, including the Title field, Subject field, and Project Name drop-down list. Recall that Subject and Project Name were added in steps 3 to 5. Note that content is already populated in the Subject field. This is because the Word document has a metadata field defined within the document named Subject in which text was entered from Word in step 9. Select Project ABC in the drop-down menu next to Project Name. Click Save.

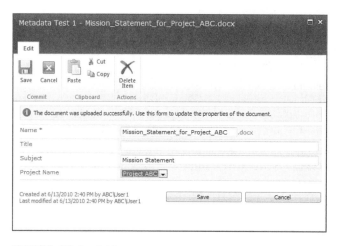

FIGURE 22.3   Adding metadata to the document on upload.

13. The document will now appear in the document library Metadata Test 1 with several metadata columns populated: The Name column, which contains the filename of the document; the Modified column, which contains the date and time the file was last modified (the date and time it was uploaded to the document library) and modified by information; and the Subject and Project Name metadata columns that were added in this exercise.

14. Next, the document will be moved to the second document library that was created. To accomplish this, click the Library tab, click the Open with Explorer button, and a new window will open, showing the contents of Metadata Test 1 document library.

15. Return to SharePoint and navigate to Metadata Test 2 library that was created in step 6, click the Library tab, and click the Open with Explorer button.

16. Click the document in the Explorer window for Metadata Test 1 and drag it to the Explorer window for Metadata Test 2. This will move the document from Metadata Test 1 library to Metadata Test 2.

17. Navigate to the Metadata Test 2 library and the document will appear as shown in Figure 22.4. The Subject column will be populated, but there is no Project Name column. A valid question to ask at this point is this: "What happened to the metadata in the Project Name column?"

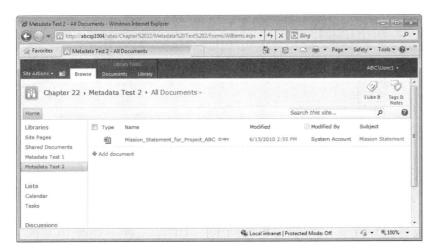

FIGURE 22.4   Document copied to second document library without the Project Name metadata field.

18. To answer this question, from the Metadata Test 2 library, hover over the document and click Edit in Microsoft Word from the drop-down menu, click OK for the warning, and it will open in Word.

19. Click File tab, click the Info link on the left side, and then click the Properties drop-down menu on the right side and select Show Document Panel.

20. This time, the Document Panel will display the Server properties information by default because the document is being opened from a SharePoint document library. Notice that the Subject field is populated, but there is no Project Name field visible because that metadata column does not exist in the document library (Metadata Test 2) it was opened from.

21. To find the Project Name metadata, click the drop-down menu next to Document Properties - Server and choose Advanced Properties from the list. The Advanced Properties window will open.

22. Click the Custom tab, and note that Project Name appears in the Properties window, with the value Project ABC (as shown in Figure 22.5), which was added to the document in step 12.

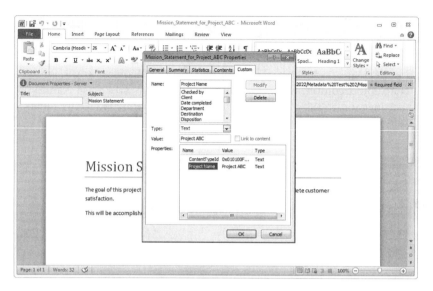

FIGURE 22.5   Advanced Properties, Custom tab showing metadata exists in the Word document.

A natural question at this point is, "How do non-Microsoft Office documents behave in similar tests?" The administrator should experiment with different types of files, such as a PDF file, for example.

Reviewing the Column Choices in SharePoint 2010

A powerful feature of SharePoint 2010 lists and libraries is the ability for an administrator to customize the list or library in many ways, one of which is to add columns, similar to the process of adding a column in Excel. This is accomplished from the Document Library Settings page, which is reached by entering the document library, clicking the Library tab on the Ribbon, and then clicking the Library Settings icon on the right side of the toolbar. Only users with the manage lists permission will be able to click the Library Settings icon; it is grayed out for other users. By default, members of the Owners, Designers, and Hierarchy Managers groups have manage lists permissions.

After on the Document Library Settings page, the Columns section is found midway down the page, and provides the options of Create Column, Add from Existing Site Columns, Column Ordering, and Indexed Columns. If Create Column is clicked, the administrator will have a selection of columns to choose from, which will vary slightly based on the version of SharePoint 2010 in use because SharePoint Foundation 2010 will not offer the Managed Metadata option. Descriptions of these columns are as follows:

▶ **Single line of text**—Has the following options: Description (text), Require That This Column Contains Information (Yes or No), Enforce Unique Values (Yes or No), Maximum Number of Characters, Default Value (Text or Calculated Value), Add to All Content Types, and Add to Default View.

▶ **Multiple lines of text**—Has the following options: Description (text), Require That This Column Contains Information (Yes or No), Allow Unlimited Length in Document Libraries (Yes or No), Number of Lines for Editing (Integer), Add to All Content Types (Yes or No), and Add to Default View (Yes or No).

▶ **Choice (menu to choose from)**—Has the following options: Description (text), Require That This Column Contains Information (Yes or No), Enforce Unique Values (Yes or No), Type Each Choice on a Separate Line, Display Choices Using (Drop-Down Menu, Radio Buttons, Checkboxes [Allow Multiple Selections]), Allow Fill-in Choices (Yes or No), Default Value (Text or Calculated Value), Add to All Content Types (Yes or No), and Add to Default View (Yes or No).

▶ **Number**—Has the following options: Description (text), Require That This Column Contains Information (Yes or No), Enforce Unique Values (Yes or No), Specify a Minimum and Maximum Allowed Value (Two Integers), Number of Decimal Places (Integer), Default Value (Number or Calculated Value), Show as a Percentage (for example, 50%), Add to All Content Types (Yes or No), and Add to Default View (Yes or No).

▶ **Currency**—Has the following options: Description (text), Require That This Column Contains Information (Yes or No), Enforce Unique Values (Yes or No), Specify a Minimum and Maximum Allowed Value (Two Integers), Number of Decimal Places (Integer), Default Value (Currency or Calculated Value), Currency Format (for example, United States), Add to All Content Types (Yes or No), and Add to Default View (Yes or No).

▶ **Date and Time**—Has the following options: Description (text), Require That This Column Contains Information (Yes or No), Enforce Unique Values (Yes or No), Date and Time Format (Date Only, Date & Time), Default Value (None, Today's Date, Date in M/D/YYYY format) or Calculated Value), Add to All Content Types (Yes or No), and Add to Default View (Yes or No).

▶ **Lookup (information already on this site)**—Has the following options: Description (text), Require That This Column Contains Information (Yes or No), Enforce Unique Values (Yes or No), Get Information From (drop-down menu to select list or library), In This Column (drop-down menu to select the column), Allow Multiple Values (Yes, No), Allow Unlimited Length in Document Libraries (Yes, No), Add a Column to Show Each of These Additional Fields (Title, Expires, ID, Modified, Created, Version, Title [linked to item]), Add to All Content Types (Yes or No), Add to Default View (Yes or No), and Enforce Relationship Behavior (Restrict Delete, Cascade Delete).

▶ **Yes/No (check box)**—Has the following options: Description (text), Default Value (Yes or No), Add to All Content Types (Yes or No), and Add to Default View (Yes or No).

▶ **Person or Group**—Has the following options: Description (text), Default Value (Yes or No), Require That This Column Contains Information (Yes or No), Allow Multiple Selections (Yes or No), Allow Selection Of (People Only, People, and Groups), Choose

From (All Users, SharePoint Group), Show Field (ID, Name, Modified, Created, Account, Email, Mobile Number, SIP Address, Department, Job Title, Name [with Presence], Name [with Picture], Name [with Picture and Details], Content Type), Add to All Content Types (Yes or No), and Add to Default View (Yes or No).

▶ **Hyperlink or Picture**—Has the following options: Description (text), Require That This Column Contains Information (Yes or No), Format URL As (Hyperlink, Picture), Add to All Content Types (Yes or No), and Add to Default View (Yes or No).

▶ **Calculated (calculation based on other columns)**—Has the following options: Description (text), Formula, Insert Column (shows valid columns to add to the formula), The Data Returned from This Formula Is (Single Line of Text, Number, Currency, Date and Time, Yes/No), Add to All Content Types (Yes or No), and Add to Default View (Yes or No).

▶ **External Data**—Has the following options: Description (text), Require That This Column Contains Information (Yes or No), External Content Type, Select the Field to Be Shown on This Column, Display the Actions Menu (Yes or No), Link This Column to the Default Action of the External Content Type (Yes or No), Add to All Content Types (Yes or No), and Add to Default View (Yes or No).

> **NOTE**
>
> External data is discussed in Chapter 31, "Business Intelligence in SharePoint 2010 with Business Connectivity Services," and an example is given of creating an External Content type to connect to an AdventureWorks database using SharePoint Designer 2010 as well as using the External Data column type. After the External Content type is created, it can be selected from the External Data column settings. Note that a number of steps are required that are also discussed in Chapter 31, including installing the AdventureWorks database. The main difference between an external list and a regular SharePoint list is that the actual contents of the external list live outside of SharePoint lists or libraries.

▶ **Managed Metadata**—Has the following options: Description (text), Require That This Column Contains Information (Yes or No), Enforce Unique Values (Yes or No), Add to All Content Types (Yes or No), Add to Default View (Yes or No), Allow Multiple Values (Yes or No), Display Value (Display Term Label in the Field or Display the Entire Path to the Term in the Field), Use a Managed Term Set (Find and Reset buttons) or Customize Your Term Set, Allow Fill-in Choices (Yes or No), and Default Value (Browse button). Managed Metadata is covered later in this chapter in more depth.

With this wide range of choices, it should be obvious that an incredible number of combinations can be created to meet business needs. This chapter provides examples of several different column types, but an administrator should become familiar with the capabilities of the different columns through experience and trial and error and by taking the effort to meet specific end-user and business requirements through lists and libraries.

> **CAUTION**
>
> Keep in mind that some restraint should be used when creating more complex lists and libraries that involve dozens or even hundreds of columns. Microsoft offers a white paper titled "DesigningLargeListsMaximizingListPerformance.docx" that provides information about topics such as row wrapping, lookup columns, and indexes that should be reviewed for more complex designs. For example, it is not unusual for an organization to want to move away from a very complex Excel spreadsheet and leverage a SharePoint 2010 list instead. Some spreadsheets have hundreds of columns in one worksheet, and although a SharePoint 2010 list can replicate this design, this can result in the SQL database requiring multiple rows to store the data. For example, if there are more than eight date and time columns in a list, each item will use two SQL Server database table rows. If there are more than 16 date columns, each item uses 3 rows. According to the Microsoft document, the performance impact in larger lists is in the range of 35 percent per additional row. So, this document is recommended reading for SharePoint architects and administrators who are tasked with more daunting list designs involving a large number of columns.

An Introduction and Practical Application of Calculated Columns

Calculated columns are enticing and powerful, but can be frustrating to use without some background. A starting rule of thumb is this: If it works in Excel, it will probably work in SharePoint. SharePoint, unfortunately, has a wide range of restrictions when compared to Excel, so this rule should be understood with a dose of healthy skepticism.

Some important rules and guidelines are as follows:

- ▶ Arithmetic operators supported include + (addition), - (subtraction), * (multiplication), / (division), % (percent), and ^ (exponentiation).

- ▶ Parentheses are supported in equations.

- ▶ Comparison operators supported include = (equal to), > (greater than), < (less than), >= (greater than or equal to), <= (less than or equal to), and <> (not equal to).

- ▶ & (ampersand) connects two values to produce one continuous text value.

- ▶ Lists and libraries do not support the RAND and NOW functions.

- ▶ The TODAY and ME functions are not supported in calculated columns but are supported in the default value setting of a column.

- ▶ You cannot reference a value in a row other than the current row.

- ▶ You cannot reference a value in another list or library.

- ▶ Many Excel functions are supported in SharePoint calculated columns, but testing should be performed to verify functionality.

An example is as follows that adds a calculated column to see whether the profit on an item exceeds the goal of a 10 percent profit. A new list is created and several columns added to it, one of which is a calculated column. Then some sample items are added to the list and the calculated column works its magic to determine whether the Sell Price exceed a 10 percent profit:

1. Create a new list using the Custom List template and name it **CalculatedColumnTest**. Steps for creating a new list are provided in Chapter 20, in the "Creating Lists and Libraries" section.

2. From the CalculatedColumnTest list, click the List tab, and then click List Settings.

3. Scroll down and click the Create Column link.

4. Name the new column **Cost** and check Currency; leave the other settings and click OK.

5. Scroll down and click the Create Column link once more.

6. Name the new column **Sell Price** and check Currency; leave the other settings and click OK.

7. Scroll down and click the Create Column link a third time.

8. Name the new column **Meets Profit Goal** and check Calculated.

9. Scroll down to the Additional Column Settings section, and enter the following formula:

    ```
    =IF(Cost>([Sell Price]-(Cost*(10/100))),"No","Yes")
    ```

    The IF function is described in more detail in Excel 2010 help, and the syntax is the same in a SharePoint 2010 calculated column. A translation of the syntax is "IF(logical_test, [value_if_true], [value_if_false])." In the case of the formula used in this example, this translates to "If the Cost is greater than the Sell Price minus 10 percent of the Cost, display the value No; if not, display the value Yes."

10. Verify that Single Line of Text is checked below the formula; then leave the other settings at their defaults. Click OK.

11. Click CalculatedColumnTest from the breadcrumb to return to the All Items view of the list.

12. Click Add New Item.

13. Enter a title for the entry, such as **Widget**, and enter 20 in the Cost field, and enter 22 in the Sale Price field, and click OK.

14. Click Add New Item a second time.

15. Enter a title for the entry, such as **Gadget**, and enter 40 in the Cost field, and enter 43.99 in the Sale Price field, and click OK.

16. Click Add New Item a third time.

17. Enter a title for the entry, such as **Mousetrap**, and enter 60 in the Cost field, enter 66 in the Sale Price field, and click OK.

18. The results will look like Figure 22.6. This makes it very easy for a manager to glance at the list and see whether items are being sold at an acceptable level of profit.

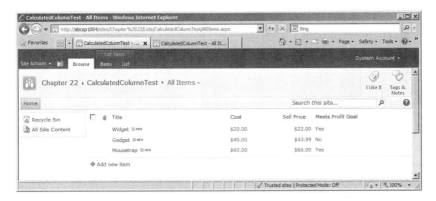

FIGURE 22.6   Example of a list with a calculated column to determine whether a sale price meets a profit goal.

Leveraging Validation Settings

Another means of ensuring that the correct data is entered into columns in a list and library is through the use of validation settings, which can be added to the list or library on the List Settings or Library Settings page, or to an individual column. The equations that can be used are more limited, as the result of the equation must equal the value True or the user won't be able to save the entry.

A simple example is

```
=[ColumnA]>[ColumB]
```

Assuming the value in ColumnA is greater than ColumnB, the formula generates the value True and therefore passes the validation test.

Building on the list created in the previous section, follow these steps to add validation to the CalculatedColumnTest list:

1. Navigate to the CalculatedColumnTest created in the previous section that contains the columns Title, Cost, and Sell Price, as described in the example, as well as sample data, as shown in Figure 22.6.

2. Click the List tab on the Ribbon, and then click Create Column.

3. Enter **Invoice Number** as the column name, and then choose Single Line of Text.

4. Scroll down to the Description field and enter **Enter a valid invoice number starting with "2010-" and then up to 4 digits.**

5. Click Enforce Unique Values.

6. Enter **9** for Maximum Number of Characters.

7. Expand the Column Validation section by clicking the + and enter the following in the Formula field:

   ```
   =FIND("2010-",[Invoice Number], 1)
   ```

   The FIND function is also defined in Excel 2010 Help, and the syntax translates to "FIND(find_text, within_text, [start_num])," or in this example to "Find the string 2010- in the column Invoice Number, starting with the first character in the string and the value is True." This logic is pretty hard for a careless or even malicious user to beat because there is a limit of nine characters that can be entered in the field and it must include the string 2010-. Furthermore, the entry must be unique.

8. Finally, enter the following in the User Message field: **You have entered an invalid invoice number** (see Figure 22.7). Click OK to save.

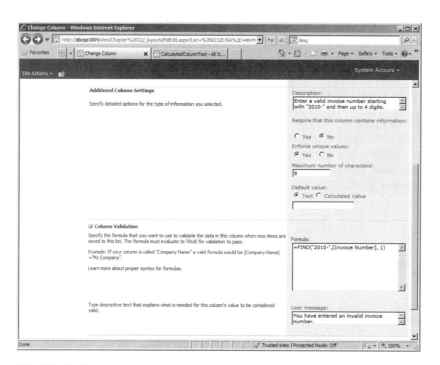

FIGURE 22.7   Column settings for a column using column validation.

9. Click OK to the message stating: "This column must be indexed to enforce unique values. Do you want to index this column?"

10. Click Add New Item and enter the title as **Whoozit**, the Cost as **100**, the Sell Price as **150**, and Invoice Number as **123456789**. Click Save. A red error message will display, stating "The validation formula has evaluated to an error," as shown in Figure 22.8, because this invoice number doesn't meet the validation.

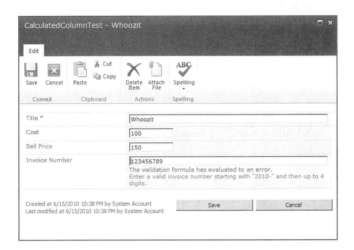

FIGURE 22.8   Validation formula error for a New List item.

11. Reenter the invoice number as **2010-123** and click Save; this time the entry succeeds because it meets the validation requirements.

Enforcing Unique Values in Columns

Certain column types offer the option to Enforce Unique Values for the column. This is a capability that has been requested by many clients over the years, and various workarounds were developed using workflows or leveraging the ID value of the list item. For example, a list that tracks serial numbers, employee IDs, invoices, or many other values will be less valuable if data entry errors can lead to nonunique numbers.

Table 22.1 summarizes what column types can and cannot be used to create unique columns.

TABLE 22.1   Unique Column Options

Supported Unique Column Types	Unsupported Unique Column Types
Single line of text	Multiple lines of text
Choice (single value)	Choice (multivalued)
Number	Calculated

continues

TABLE 22.1   Continued

Supported Unique Column Types	Unsupported Unique Column Types
Currency	Hyperlink or Picture
Date and Time	Custom Columns
Lookup (single value)	Lookup (multivalued)
Managed Metadata	Person or Group
	Yes/No

CAUTION

If Content Approval is enabled for a document library and then unique values are enabled, a warning note displays that "This list or document library has content approval enabled. A column that enforces unique values may let users determine information about a list item or document even if they do not have permission to view it." This is logical because when a user sees an error about the item not being a unique value, she can deduce that there already exists a list item with that value.

Differences in Multiple Lines of Text Columns in Libraries and Lists

An interesting difference exists in the capabilities of the Multiple Lines of Text column when it is used in a library as opposed to when it is used in a list. When a Multiple Lines of Text column is added to a document library, there is an option to Allow Unlimited Length in Document Libraries. If this option is selected, a message will display that states "Columns with long text are not supported by most applications for editing documents and could result in loss of data. Only remove this limit if users will be uploading documents through the website, and not saving directly from the application." Otherwise, the column configuration is straightforward.

A major irritation, if unlimited length is not allowed in a document library, is that the end user doesn't know how many characters have been entered because SharePoint does not provide a character counter. Nor is any warning provided until the user clicks Save. So, a user could type his life's story in the text box and click Save only to be told "This field can have no more than 255 characters." So, a best practice is to add a note about the limitation of 255 characters in the Description field when a Multiple Lines of Text column is added to a document library, and in addition, provide a second Multiple Lines of Text column for document libraries where it is expected that more lengthy descriptions might be needed.

If a Multiple Lines of Text column is created in a list, on the other hand, the options are quite different. As shown in Figure 22.9, a Multiple Lines of Text column in a list offers additional options:

- ▶ Plain Text
- ▶ Rich Text (bold, italics, text alignment, hyperlinks)
- ▶ Enhanced Rich Text (rich text with pictures, tables, and hyperlinks)
- ▶ Append Changes to Existing Text

The options for Multiple Lines of Text columns in lists, which are not available in libraries, clarify a key difference between the two. The metadata attached to documents added to document libraries is meant to be purely informational and textual, whereas the metadata added to lists can be rich text and include pictures, tables, and hyperlinks and so is well suited for providing visually complex information and images on a SharePoint page. It is recommended for administrators and power users to experiment with the differences between these different types of Multiple Lines of Text columns, especially to determine the differences between rich text and enhanced rich text.

With regards to the Append Changes to Existing Text option for a Multiple Lines of Text column, versioning must be turned on for the list before it can be enabled. After it is enabled, the changes to the content will be tracked and visible to users who view the list item. Figure 22.10 shows an example of an item in an Announcements list (which has versioning enabled) that has been edited by several users. Most likely, this is not the best setting to apply to an Announcements list because what should most likely be behind the scenes editing will become visible to readers.

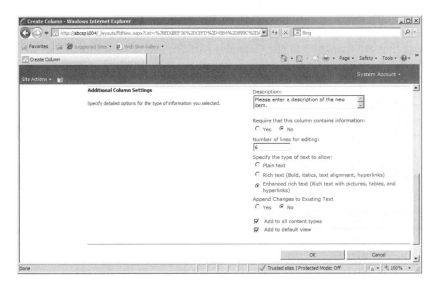

FIGURE 22.9   Additional options for Multiple Lines of Text column in a list.

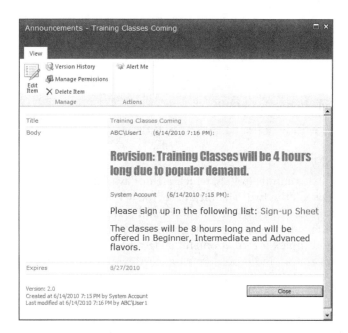

FIGURE 22.10   Example of Append Changes to Existing Text setting for a Multiple Lines of Text column in a list.

Working with Lookup Columns in Document Libraries

This next exercise uses two standard lists in a SharePoint 2010 Team Site: the Calendar list and the Tasks list. The goal of this example is to show the basic capabilities of the lookup column using a business example where a department tracks tasks using a Tasks list, and has weekly meetings that are managed in the Calendar list. The manager wants to use SharePoint to make the meeting more productive and wants to use the lookup column to pull additional information from the Tasks list into the Calendar list.

Consider the possibility that the Tasks list might have different permissions configured than the Calendar list. For example, on this site, the administrator may only allow project managers to edit the Calendar list, whereas all departmental employees can add to the Tasks list.

Before jumping into the example, some information about the functionality and limitations of the lookup column should be provided. To begin with, only certain column types are available to lookup columns. The following list shows the supported column types:

▶ Single Line of Text

- ▶ Number
- ▶ Date and Time
- ▶ Calculated

If other column types exist in the list that is being connected to with the lookup column, they will not be available for selection. This limitation should be kept in mind when planning for the use of lookup columns.

22

CAUTION

Exceeding eight lookup columns per list view consumes a large amount of SQL resources, which can result in performance degradation when the view is rendered. Although there can be more than eight lookup columns in the list, make sure to limit the number that are included in specific views.

Follow these steps to learn more about the lookup column's functionality:

1. Create a new site using the Team Site template. Instructions for creating a site are provided in Chapter 21, "Designing and Managing Pages and Sites for Knowledge Workers," in the section titled "Creating Pages and Sites."

2. Click the link to the Tasks list from the Quick Launch.

3. Click the List tab on the Ribbon, and click the Create Column icon.

4. Title the column **Flags**, and select Single Line of Text as the column type. Leave the other fields on their default values and click OK to save.

5. From the Tasks list, click Add New Item. Enter the following content in the appropriate fields:

   - ▶ **Title**—Enter **Lookup Task 1**
   - ▶ **Status**—Not Started
   - ▶ **% Complete**—Enter **0%**
   - ▶ **Assigned To**—Enter a sample username
   - ▶ **Start Date**—Enter a sample start date in the future
   - ▶ **End Date**—Enter a sample end date that is after the start date
   - ▶ Flags—Enter **Scope of work not clear**

   Leave the other fields with the default values. Click Save when the data has been entered.

6. After again, click Add New Item. Enter the following content in the appropriate fields:

   - ▶ **Title**—Enter **Lookup Task 2**

▶ **Status**—In Progress

▶ **% Complete**—Enter `10%`

▶ **Assigned To**—Enter a sample username

▶ **Start Date**—Enter a sample start date in the past

▶ **End Date**—Enter a sample end date in the future

▶ **Flags**—Enter `Team lead is on vacation`

Leave the other fields with the default values. Click Save when the data has been entered.

7. The task list should look similar to Figure 22.11.

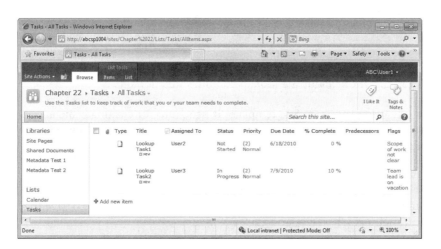

FIGURE 22.11   Tasks list with sample tasks to use in a lookup column.

8. Now click the link to Calendar from the Quick Launch.

9. Click the Calendar tab on the Ribbon, and then click List Settings.

10. Scroll down until the link to Create Column appears, and then click Create Column.

11. Enter `Task Lookup` as the title of the column, and then click Lookup (information already on this site).

12. Scroll down to the Additional Column Settings section, and click the drop-down menu under Get information From, and select Tasks. The page will update to now show the columns that are valid lookup columns.

13. Select Title (linked to item) from the list.

14. Check the box next to Allow Multiple Values.

15. Then check the boxes next to % Complete, Start Date, Due Date, and Flags. Leave the other values at their defaults, as shown in Figure 22.12, and click OK.

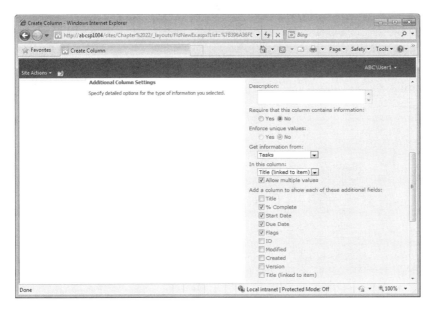

FIGURE 22.12   Settings for the lookup column in the Calendar list.

16. Click Calendar from the breadcrumb trail to return to the Calendar list.

17. Click the Events tab, and then click New Event from the Ribbon.

18. Enter the following values in the new event:

   ▶ **Title**—Status Meeting

   ▶ **Location**—Meeting Room A

   ▶ **Start Time**—Enter a date and time in the next week

   ▶ **End Time**—Enter a date and time one hour after the start time

   ▶ **Task Lookup**—Click Lookup Task 1 and click the Add button; then click Lookup Task 2, and click the Add button.

   Leave the other fields at their defaults and click Save.

19. The event will now appear on the calendar on the date specified. Click the name of the event to see the event details, and it should be similar to Figure 22.13. Note that even though only the tasks names were selected, the list item is populated with additional values from the Tasks list: % Complete, Start Date, Due Date, and Flags

information is populated. The links to Lookup Task1 and Lookup Task2 can be clicked on from this screen to open the tasks to see additional information.

FIGURE 22.13   Calendar event with lookup data values.

20. Close the Calendar item window by clicking Close.

21. From the Calendar, click the Calendar tab, and then click List Settings.

22. Locate the Task Lookup:% Complete column, and click it. Change the column name to **Task % Complete** and click OK. Note that the name of the column is now changed without breaking the functionality of the column. So, the administrator can make these lookup column titles more user friendly than the default names that are assigned.

An additional option provided in a lookup column is to Enforce Relationship Behavior. While experimenting with this functionality, it is not unusual to see a message display that states "This lookup field cannot enforce a relationship behavior because this list contains incompatible fields." The following example provides a case where Enforce Relationship Behavior can be tested.

Testing Enforce Relationship Behavior

To continue the process of understanding lookup columns, the Enforce Relationship Behavior setting needs to be experienced. The example provided in this section leverages an Announcements list and a lookup column to connect to a list of donated items, which makes it easy for an organization to create an announcement when someone offers an item of value to other employees. The Restrict Delete setting will be applied to ensure that once the announcement has gone out, the details of the donated item are still available. Restrict Delete means that the child item cannot be deleted because it is related to an item in the "parent" list. Following that configuration, the Cascade Delete option will be configured, and in that case, the deletion of the child item causes a deletion of the parent item.

This example scratches the surface of what's possible in enforced relationships between lists but provides a real-world example that can be leveraged in numerous ways within the organization. Database developers will immediately see the similarities between this capability and the types of joins and other interactions possible between database tables and will no doubt be able to leverage lookup columns in many creative ways.

Follow these steps to create two lists and leverage the Enforce Relationship Behavior setting:

1. Create a new site using the Team Site template. Instructions for creating a site are provided in Chapter 21, in the section titled "Creating Pages and Sites."

2. Create a new list using the Custom List template and name it **Donations.** Steps for creating a new list are provided in Chapter 20, in the "Creating Lists and Libraries" section.

3. From the Donations list, click the List tab, and then click List Settings.

4. Scroll down and click the Create Column link.

5. Name the new column **Item Description** and check Single Line of Text; leave the other settings and click OK.

6. Return to the list all items view by clicking the list name in the breadcrumb.

7. Click Add New Item.

8. Enter a title for the entry, such as **Kodak Z7590 Camera**, and enter text in the Item Description field such as `5.0 Megapixels, 10x zoom, very portable, works great.`

9. Click All Site Content from the Quick Launch, and click Announcements in the Lists section of the page.

10. In the Announcements list, click the List tab, and then click List Settings.

11. Scroll down and click Create Column.

12. Title the column Donation Lookup and select the Lookup type of column.

13. In the Additional Column Settings section of the screen, click the drop-down menu under Get Information From, and select Donations. Verify that Title appears in the drop-down menu under In This Column. Check the box next to Item Description in the next section down, as shown in Figure 22.14.

14. Check the box next to Enforce Relationship Behavior, and then check the circle next to Restrict Delete, as is also shown in Figure 22.14.

15. Click OK. Click OK for the message "This column must be indexed to enforce a relationship behavior. Do you want to index this column."

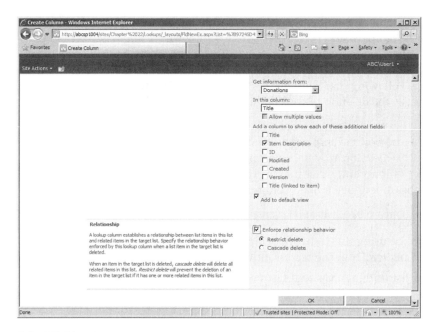

FIGURE 22.14   Selecting the Enforce Relationship Behavior option for a lookup column.

16. Click the Announcements link from the breadcrumb to return to the All Items view of the Announcements list.

17. Click the Add New Announcement link.

18. Enter a title for the announcement (for example, `Generous donation!`). Click the drop-down list in the Donations Lookup field and select Kodak Z7590 Camera. Click OK. The result should look like Figure 22.15.

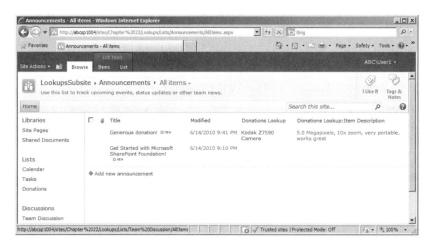

FIGURE 22.15   Announcement with lookup information.

19. Return to the Donation list by clicking its link in the Quick Launch.

20. Access the drop-down menu for the list item entered in steps 7 and 8, and click Delete Item. Click OK to confirm the deletion. An error message will appear, stating "This item cannot be deleted because an item in the 'Announcements' list is related to an item in the 'Donations' list."

TIP

Use lookup columns with the Enforce Relationship Behavior option and Restrict Delete to ensure that the target item of the lookup can't be deleted if it is referenced by an item in the "parent" list.

21. Next, the lookup column will be set to Cascade Delete. Start by clicking All Site Content from the Quick Launch, and click Announcements from the Lists section.

22. Click the List tab, and then click List Settings.

23. Scroll down to the Columns section and click Donations Lookup column.

24. Scroll down to the Relationship section, and this time select Cascade Delete. Click OK.

25. Navigate to the Donations list by clicking its link in the Quick Launch.

26. Access the drop-down menu for the list item (Kodak Z7590 Camera in this example) and click Delete Item. A message will appear, stating "Sending this item to the site Recycle Bin will also send any related items in the following lists to the site Recycle Bin: [Announcements]. Are you sure you want to send the item(s) to the site Recycle Bin?" Click OK.

27. Navigate to the Announcement list to verify that the announcement is also deleted.

TIP

When related items are deleted in a Cascade Delete enforced relationship, restoring the child item from the Recycle Bin also restores the related item.

Setting Metadata Standards with Default Values

For the metadata entered to be useful in searches and filters, it is important that it be accurate. List and library administrators can use a variety of methods to control the entries that users provide.

List or library administrators can set default values for metadata when the column is being created, or can return to the list settings page at a later date to change the default values. Setting a default value may not be advisable in some cases because end users who are in a rush, or feeling lazy, may simply leave the default setting when uploading a document. So, consideration should be given to the pros and cons of using default values.

Figure 22.16 shows a section of the settings available for a choice column in a document library. In the Default Value section, the administrator can choose to set one of the choices in the list above as the default value, or can have a Calculated value. In this figure, the default value will be Choice #1. If the field is cleared of text, the default value will be left empty. If Calculated Value is chosen, the administrator will need to enter an equation in the field provided.

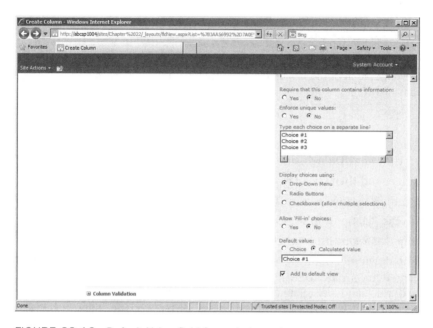

FIGURE 22.16   Default Value field for a choice column.

Note also that there is the option to Allow Fill-in choices for the choice column, which may be a good option if strict control over the metadata entries is not critical for this column and library.

Setting Default Values from the Settings Page

By accessing the Column Default Value Settings link from the Document Library Settings page, the administrator can set values based on folders, which can be a much more powerful and useful ability than setting default values on a column basis. The following section provides an example of using the Column Default Value Settings for folders within a document library:

1. Choose a document library (or create a new one) that has one or more folders in it and one or more columns that have been added to the document library. In this example, the document library contains folders titled Folder 1 and Folder 2, and a column titled Subject and one titled Choice Column.

2. From the document library, click the Library tab on the Ribbon, and then click Library Settings.

3. Click Column Default Value Settings link in the General Settings section.

4. From the Change Default Column Values page, click one of the folders in the left pane. In this example, Folder 2 is selected.

5. Click the column name to change. In this example, the Choice Column link was selected.

6. In the Edit Default Value window, check the circle next to Use This Default Value and enter the desired default value in the field. An error message will display if you enter an invalid choice. In this example, Choice #2 is entered, as shown in Figure 22.17. Click OK.

FIGURE 22.17   Assign default column values for folder contents in a document library.

7. As shown in Figure 22.18, the Change Default Column Values page will now show what the default value is by column and by folder. A folder with a gear icon on it has a default value assigned to it. Other folders without specific default values assigned and documents not stored in a folder will be assigned the document library default.

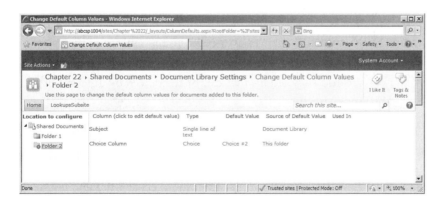

FIGURE 22.18   Change Default Column Values page.

While at first glance this feature seems of limited use, if the document library uses folders or is designed to hold a specific type of documents that will share default settings, the default values can be a great time saver and help ensure that the proper values are set for documents. This is especially true for organizations where end users are "addicted" to folder structures and are reluctant to give them up. The administrator can create a column titled Folder Name and then assign default values to this column on a folder-by-folder basis that mirrors the names of the folders. Then views can be created that ignore the folder structure for more advanced users, but the documents will be tagged with the folder name so that information is still captured. This also solves the problem of users knowing which folder items "live" in when they are using a view that is set to ignore the folder structure.

> **NOTE**
>
> If the default column value is changed, it will not affect documents already uploaded to the document library, only documents that are uploaded after the default value is changed.

Site Columns Practical Applications

Previously in this chapter, a variety of columns have been created for the examples. Each of these columns exists in only one place: inside of the list where it was created. For example, in one example a column was created that was named Project Name and used the Choice variety of column, and had several values added to it: Project ABC, Project DEF, and Project GHI. This is fine if that column needs to be used in only one list or library, but if the administrator suddenly finds that this column needs to be used in multiple lists and libraries by the project managers, for example, several things can be done:

▶ The administrator can manually create the same column in the other lists and libraries that need it. If changes are needed to the settings of the column, the administrator will need to manually make the changes in each list and library.

▶ The administrator can create a template of the entire document library or list and then use that template to create a new list or library and it will contain the Project Name column and choice values. If changes are needed to the settings of the column, the administrator will need to manually make the changes in each list and library.

▶ The administrator can create a site column that can be referenced by different lists and libraries and even different sites within the site collection. Changes can be made to the site column that will be immediately reflected in the locations where this column is used. The column can also be modified from the libraries and lists where it is used.

▶ The administrator can create a site column, and also create a content type that uses the site column. This allows the benefits of the site column capabilities and leverages the content type's capabilities.

Follow these steps to create a site column called Project Name and then add it to a list, and then experiment with making changes to the site column from the list to verify these changes do not go "upstream":

1. Access the Site Settings page for the top-level site of a site collection where the site column will be used using an account that is a member of the Site Collection Owners group.

2. Click Site Columns in the Galleries section.

22

> **NOTE**
>
> To create or manage a site column, the user must have web designer privileges on the site collection. If an administrator does not have the appropriate access rights to a child site, the push-down process to that child site will fail.

3. The Site Columns page will display. Note that there are a large number of site columns already in existence for the site collection, many of which are self-explanatory. Click the Create link on the toolbar.

4. Enter the title **Project Name** and choose the Choice column type. Note that there are several columns types that may be new to the administrator. These include Full HTML Content with Formatting and Constraints for Publishing, Image with Formatting and Constraints for Publishing, and Hyperlink with Formatting and Constraints for Publishing.

5. Scroll down to the Group section and click the circle next to New Group and enter the name **Company ABC Columns.**

6. Scroll down to the Additional Column Settings section and enter in several choices for the project names. In this example, enter **Project ABC**, **Project DEF**, **Project GHI**. Select Yes under Allow Fill-In Choices, and clear the text in the Default Value field.

7. Expand the Column Validation section, and enter the following formula, as shown in Figure 22.19:

```
=FIND("Project",[Project Name], 1)
```

8. Enter text in the User Message section: **Value must include the word "Project".**

9. Click OK to save. The Site Columns page will now show the new site column. If needed, the name of the site column can be clicked and the settings modified.

Now that the site column has been created, it can be used in a list or library. Follow these steps to use the site column in a list and to test the addition of values:

1. Create a Tasks list and title it **Site Column Test**. Steps for creating a new list are provided in Chapter 20, in the "Creating Lists and Libraries" section.

2. Click List Settings from the List tab on the Ribbon.

3. Click Add from Existing Site Columns in the Columns section.

4. On the Add Columns from Site Columns page, access the group Company ABC Columns created in the previous exercise. Click Project Name entry in the Available Site Columns pane and click the Add button, as shown in Figure 22.20. Click OK to save.

5. Click the name of the list in the breadcrumb to return to the list and click the Add New Item link.

6. Create a new task with the title of **Task 1**; leave the default values and scroll down to where the field Project Name is visible. Note that there is a drop-down list with the field values defined in the previous exercise. Verify that Project ABC, Project DEF, and Project GHI appear.

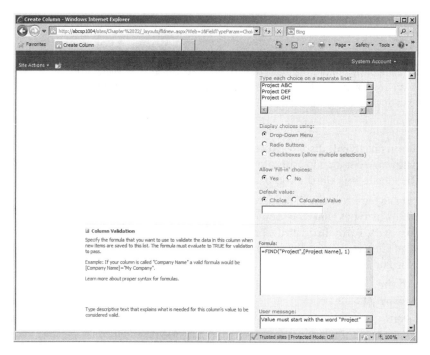

FIGURE 22.19   Creating a site column with choices and column validation settings visible.

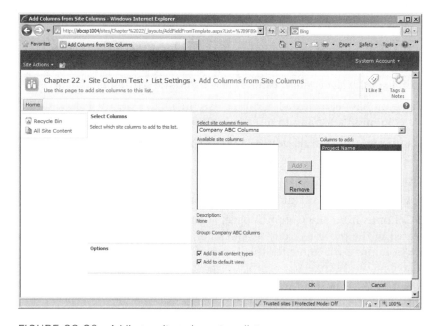

FIGURE 22.20   Adding a site column to a list.

7. Click the circle next to Specify Your Own Value and enter the text **Project JKLMNOP** and click Save.

8. Now see whether the new value added modifies the site column by navigating to the Site Settings page by accessing Site Settings from the Site Actions drop-down menu and clicking Site Columns.

9. Click Project Name in the Company ABC Columns section and verify that the new project name was not added to the site column.

Now that the site column has been created and it is referenced in a list, the administrator can experiment with further modifications to get a better sense for the connectivity between the site column and the list. For example, the following tests will be revealing:

▶ Modify the title of the column in the list where it is used. Note that this doesn't change the site column settings in the Site Column Gallery.

▶ Modify the type of column (for example, change it from Choice to Single Line of Text) and verify this doesn't change the site column settings in the Site Column Gallery.

▶ Add a new value to the site column in the Site Column Gallery and verify that it populates to the instance of the site column in the test list.

▶ Remove a value from the site column choice fields that is actually used in the list, and verify that the value in the list still remains even after the site column has been modified.

NOTE

When pushing down site column changes, the entire list column definition is overwritten with the current site column definition. Therefore, any changes you have made to the list column are overwritten. If errors are encountered, the process will move on to the next use of the site column and report errors.

Content Types Practical Applications

Now that metadata has been reviewed in detail, the initially confusing concept of content types should make more sense. Just as site columns were accessed from the Site Settings page, Site Column link, Content Types are accessed from the Site Content Types link. Each content type can contain the following settings and components:

▶ Name, description, and group.

▶ Advanced settings, including the URL of an existing document template or a new document template that can be uploaded. The option to set the content type as read only is provided, and the option to update all content types inheriting from this content type is provided.

▶ Workflow settings allow the addition of a workflow to the content type. Workflows available in SharePoint Server 2010 will be affected by site collection features enabled, but can include Disposition Approval, Three-State, Approval, Collect Signatures, Publishing Approval, and Collect Feedback.

▶ Document Information panel settings. These setting allow the administrator to use the existing template, point to an existing .xsn template to use (which can be created in InfoPath), or upload a new .xsn template. In addition, the Document Information panel can be set to always show on document open and initial save.

▶ Information management policy settings provide options including the following: policy statement that displays when the item is opened, enabling retention and definition of retention stage, enabling auditing of interactions between end users and the documents, enabling barcodes, and enabling labels.

▶ Columns can be added from existing site columns, or created for the content type.

▶ When creating a new content type, a parent content type can be defined to which additions or changes are made.

As with site columns, there are a large number of content types already in place to include the following groupings:

▶ Business Intelligence

▶ Content Organizer Content Types

▶ Digital Asset Content Types

▶ Document Content Types

▶ Folder Content Types

▶ Group Work Content Types

▶ List Content Types

▶ Page Layout Content Types

▶ Publishing Content Types

▶ Report Server Content Types

▶ Special Content Types

This list may vary based on the version of SharePoint 2010 in place and the site collection features enabled.

These content types can be associated with lists or libraries, and when this has taken place the content type will be available for selection from the New menu. If a content type is added after content already exists in the list or library, it can then be assigned to items.

Follow these steps to add the site column created in the previous section to an existing content type:

1. Navigate to the Site Content Types page by accessing Site Settings for the top-level site of the site collection as a site collection administrator and clicking Site Content Types.

2. Click Create.

3. Enter a name for the content type (in this example, **Company ABC Task**), select List Content Types from the Select Parent Content Type drop-down, and select Task from the Parent Content Type drop-down menu.

4. Select Custom Content Types from the Put This Site Content Type into the Existing Group drop-down menu, as shown in Figure 22.21. Click OK to save.

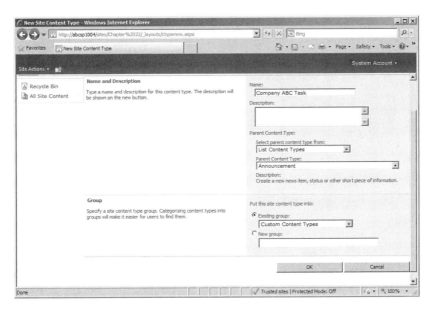

FIGURE 22.21   Creating a new content type based on a parent content type.

5. The ManageContentType.aspx page will then open for the new content type. This page shows the settings inherited from the parent and allows the administrator to make changes that will only affect this new content type and future content types that inherit from it. In this example, the administrator wants to add the site column Project Name created previously.

6. Click Add from Existing Site Columns under the Columns list. The Add Columns to Content Type page opens.

7. In the Select Columns From drop-down, select Company ABC Columns, and then select Project Name from the Available Columns pane, and click the Add button. Click OK to save.

8. As shown in Figure 22.22, the ManageContentType.aspx page will now show the new column in the Columns table, and unlike the other columns, it will have no listing under Source, indicating that it was added to this content type.

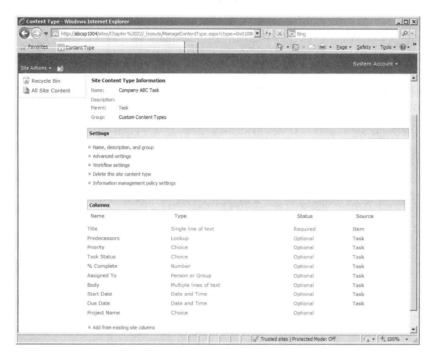

FIGURE 22.22 New Content Type Management page showing added site column.

9. To validate that this content type is functional, create a new Tasks list titled **New Tasks List.**

10. From the new Tasks list, access List Settings for the list and click Add from Existing Site Content Types in the Content Types section.

TIP

If there is no Content Types section, click the Advanced Settings link, and then select Yes in the Content Types section under Allow Management of Content Types, and then click OK to save the changes.

---

11. Select Custom Content Types from the drop-down menu under Select Site Content Types From, and then click Company ABC Task in the Available Site Content Types section and click the Add button. Now the Company ABC Task content type should appear in Content Types list.

12. Return to the list by clicking the list name in the breadcrumb. Click the New Item drop-down list form the Items tab and click Company ABC Task.

13. Give the item a title such as **Task Testing New Content Type** and scroll down to the Project Name field and verify that the expected choices from the site column are shown (in this example, Project ABC, Project DEF, and Project GHI), as shown in Figure 22.23. Select one of these values and click OK.

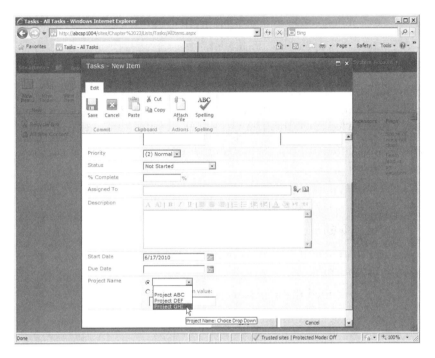

FIGURE 22.23   Adding a new item to a Tasks list that uses the new content type.

14. The Project Name column isn't shown, so click the List tab and then the Modify View button.

15. From the Edit View page, find the Project Name entry in the Columns section, and check the box in the Display column. Click OK, and now the Project Name column should display.

Considering the Dublin Core Content for Taxonomy Inspiration

Neatly tucked away in the Site Content Types gallery, in the Document Content Types section, is an entry titled the Dublin Core Columns. Spending some time with this content type is a great way to gain insight into a full set of columns that can be used to describe the elements of a document to enable it to fit into an overall taxonomy, or structure.

The Dublin Core metadata element set contains descriptors designed to make it easy for users to easily understand the content described by the metadata elements regardless of the type of content managed. This element set has been widely accepted as documented by the National Information Standards Organization (NISO) in their document titled "The Dublin Core Metadata Element Set" (ISSN: 1041-5653).

The elements are as follows and some description of the value of the fields is given where appropriate:

▶ **Name**—This is the standard filename field.

▶ **Contributor**—One or more people or organizations that contributed to the resource.

▶ **Coverage**—The extent or scope of the document.

▶ **Creator**—The primary author who may be different from the individual or account uploading the document.

▶ **Date Created**—This is different from the automatic metadata value tracked by the system. A date and time for when the item was actually created can be entered.

▶ **Date Modified**—Also different from the system tracked modified value; a date and time can be added here.

▶ **Description**—A standard multiple lines of text column where descriptive text can be entered.

▶ **Format**—Media type, file format, or dimensions can be entered as appropriate.

▶ **Resource Identifier**—An identifying string or number, usually conforming to a formal identification system.

▶ **Language**—Language in which the item is recorded or written.

▶ **Publisher**—The person, organization or service that published this resource.

▶ **Relation**—References to related resources.

▶ **Rights Management**—Information about rights held in or over this resource.

▶ **Source**—References to resources from which this resource was derived.

▶ **Keywords**—Standard multiple lines of text to enter in keywords.

▶ **Subject**—Single line of text field for the subject.

▶ **Title**—Single line of text.

▶ **Resource Type**—A set of categories, functions, genres, or aggregation levels.

This may be "overkill" in terms of complexity for most organizations, but there may be items in this content type that can be adopted for the organization. For example, the concept of adding the creator information to an item is a powerful one because the person who created the document may well be different from the person who uploaded it. Tagging the item with format metadata is also helpful in many cases because SharePoint can make it hard to see the file extension, and adding paper sizes for Visio or CADD documents can be useful.

Creating and Using Managed Metadata

Managed metadata was described from a high level in Chapter 18, "SharePoint Foundation Versus SharePoint Server 2010," in the section titled "Service Applications Available in the Different Versions of SharePoint 2010." This section builds on the basic concepts presented in that section and gives an example of creating managed metadata and how it can be used to make centrally managed metadata available to multiple site collections.

Managed Metadata Service is a service application managed and accessed from the Central Administration site. For testing purposes, it is generally a good idea to create a new service application, by completing the following steps. The first step is to set a content type, then create the service application, and then define the term sets.

1. Access a site collection that will be used as the content type syndication hub and access site settings from the top-level site. Click Site Collection Features.

2. Locate the content type syndication hub and click Activate.

3. Next, access the Central Administrator site and click Manage Service Applications under the Application Management section.

4. Click the New drop-down menu on the Ribbon and select Managed Metadata Service.

5. Give a title to the service application (for example, **Test Managed Metadata Service App**).

6. Scroll down and verify that the SQL server name is correct and provide a name for the database that will be created (for example, **TestManagedMetadataServiceApp**).

7. In the Application Pool section, click Use Existing Application Pool, and select SharePoint Web Services Default.

8. In the Content Type Hub field, enter the URL for the site collection that was activated in step 2, as shown in Figure 22.24.

9. Leave the other settings at their defaults and click OK. The service application will be created along with the database, and it will then be shown on the ServiceApplications.aspx page.

10. Click the top line of the new service application so that the line is selected (do not click the active hyperlink), and then click the Properties button on the Ribbon. This page lists the settings that were just entered. Click Cancel to return to the ServiceApplications.aspx page.

11. Now click the actual link to the service application (Test Managed Metadata Service App, in this example); the Term Store Management Tool page will open.

12. Click the top-level node in the left Taxonomy Term Store area and then select New Group from the drop-down menu on the right side of the top-level node.

13. A new node will appear. Click the new node, give it a title such as **Company ABC Terms**, and press Return.

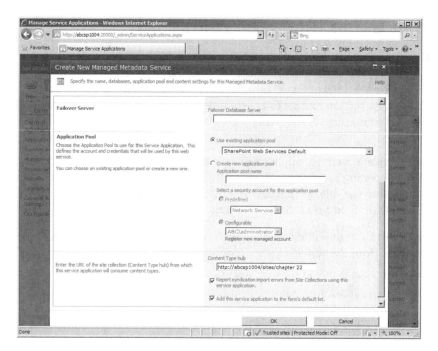

FIGURE 22.24   Creating a new Managed Metadata Service.

> **NOTE**
>
> Enterprise keywords can also be added to the Managed Metadata Service application, as shown in Figure 22.25. After added, these words or phrases that can then be used by tagging tools in SharePoint 2010 site collections. Enterprise keywords are part of a single, nonhierarchical term set called the keyword set.

14. Click New Term Set from the drop-down menu on the new node (Company ABC Terms in this example), as shown in Figure 22.25. Title this node **Client Codes** and press Return.

15. Next access the drop-down menu for Client Codes node and click Create Term.

16. Title the term **Company DEF Codes** and press Return.

17. Click the node for Company DEF, and access the drop-down menu for it and click Create Term.

18. Title the term below as **Company DEF USA**, which would correspond to a division of Company DEF with offices in the United States, and then press Enter.

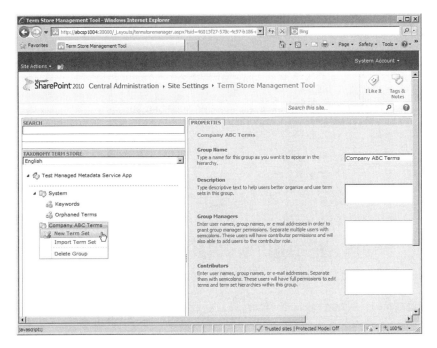

FIGURE 22.25   Creating a new term set.

TIP

When creating a term, the option exists to provide other labels to the term, which are also called synonyms. For example, when the term Company DEF USA is defined, a synonym might be DEFCo New York, which is another way to refer to Company DEF USA branch. Another might be DEFCo LA (if there is also an office in Los Angeles). The farm administrator did not want to create individual terms underneath the Company DEF USA term because that is "too granular," and for the organization's requirements, having end users differentiate between the different international branches of Company DEF is sufficient.

---

19. Repeat step 17 to create additional nodes under Company DEF, as shown in Figure 22.26.

20. Click the node Company DEF Codes, and the right pane should show additional settings for the term. Uncheck the box next to Available for Tagging because this is an organizational term rather than a term the administrator wants end users to use as metadata. Click Save to save the changes to the term.

21. Click the node Client Codes and review the settings in the right pane. Note that there are fields for Description, Owner, Contact, Stakeholders, a choice to leave the

term set Open or Closed, and a check box to allow the term set to be used for tagging or not.

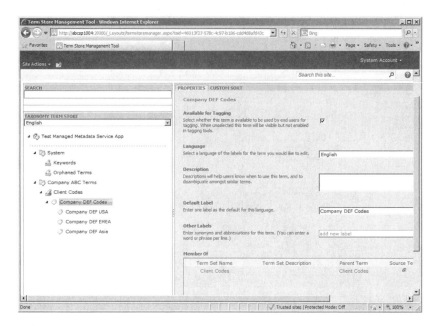

FIGURE 22.26   Adding additional terms to the Company ABC term set.

These terms will now be available to use from SharePoint lists and libraries. As briefly reviewed earlier, a number of configuration options are available for each term. In the following section, this managed metadata will be accessed from a list to show the power of the tool.

> **NOTE**
>
> A *term* is a word or a phrase that can be associated with an item in SharePoint Server 2010. A *term set* is a collection of related terms. Local term sets are created within the context of a site collection. For example, if you add a column to a list in a document library, and create a new term set to bind the column to, the new term set is local to the site collection that contains the document library. Global term sets are created outside the context of a site collection.

Adding Managed Metadata in a List

After the managed metadata term set has been created, as demonstrated in the previous section, it can be used in lists and libraries, as shown in the following steps:

1. Access a site collection and create a new list using the Discussion Board List template. Title the list **ManagedMetadataTestDiscussion** and click Create.

2. From the list, click List Settings from the List tab.

3. Click Create Column in the Columns section.

4. Title the column **Client Codes** and check the circle next to Managed Metadata.

5. Scroll down to the Term Set Settings section and enter the text **DEF** in the field under Find Term Sets that Include the Following Terms and click the binoculars button. As shown in Figure 22.27, the term set created in the previous section should be returned.

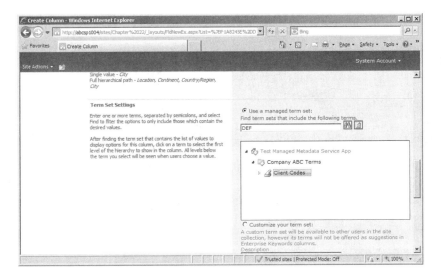

FIGURE 22.27   Adding a managed metadata column to a list.

6. Click the Client Codes node in the results from the search. This will be the "anchor point" for the options that are shown to users of this list. Leave the other settings at their defaults. Click OK to save the settings. Note in the Columns section of the listedit.aspx page that this column is listed as managed metadata in the Type column.

7. Return to the AllItems.aspx view by clicking the list name in the breadcrumb and click Add New Discussion.

8. Provide a title for the discussion item (for example, **Company DEF not paying bills!**), and then scroll down to the Client Codes field and click the Browse for a Valid Choice icon to the right of the field.

9. The Select: Client Codes window will open. Drill down under Company DEF codes and select Company DEF USA, as shown in Figure 22.28. Then click the Select button to select the term. Click OK.

10. Click Save to save the list item and return to the AllItems.aspx page.

Content Type Syndication Hubs

A site collection feature that can be enabled is the Content Type Syndication Hub, and this provisions a site to be an enterprise metadata hub site. When a content type is created in a content type hub, the content type will be available to other site collections that are part of web applications associated with that Managed Metadata Service instance. The Content Type Hub and Content Type Subscriber jobs needs to run for the content type to be synchronized and logs to be update. Note that in Site Settings for the Content Type Syndication Hub site collection, the tool Content Type Publishing provides a check box to Refresh All Published Content Types on Next Update.

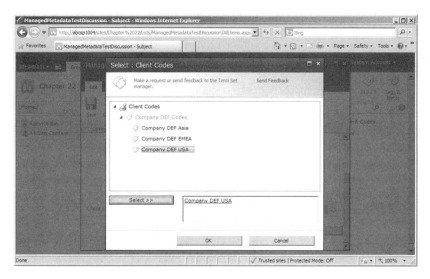

FIGURE 22.28   Choosing a managed metadata term from a list.

Metadata as a Navigation Aid

One of the primary reasons that organizations put time and effort into creating taxonomies and enforcing their use is to help knowledge workers quickly and precisely locate the documents they are looking for.

Metadata navigation is a powerful tool available in SharePoint Server 2010 Standard or Enterprise, and involves the configuration of hierarchy fields, key filters, and the management of column indices to facilitate browsing for specific types of content within a document library and creating filters to limit the results.

The terminology is a bit confusing, so the best way to understand how it works is to experiment with it. The following example walks through the process of creating a new document library, enabling content types, adding a content type to a document library, and then configuring the metadata navigation settings:

1. Create a new document library by accessing the Site Actions drop-down menu and clicking New Document Library. Tile the library **Metadata Navigation Library.**

2. After the document library is created, click Library Settings from the Library tab on the Ribbon.

3. Next click Advanced Settings in the General Settings section. Click Yes under Allow Management of Content Types. Click OK to save this setting and return to the Document Library Settings page.

4. Scroll down to the Content Types section and click Add from Existing Site Content Types.

5. From the Add Content Types page, as shown in Figure 22.29, change the content types to Document Content Types in the Select Site Content Types From drop-down menu. Select Basic Page and click the Add button. Click OK to add this content type and return to the Document Library Settings page.

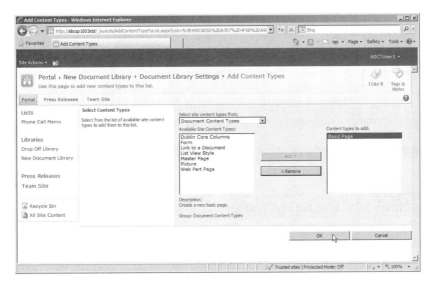

FIGURE 22.29   Adding a content type to a document library.

6. Click the Metadata Navigation Settings link in the General Settings section.

7. Content Type should be highlighted in the Available Hierarchy Fields area, so click the Add button to add it to selected hierarchy fields.

NOTE

Other fields can be selected in the Available Hierarchy Fields section. Besides Content Type, Single-Value Choice Field and Managed Metadata Field can also be selected.

8. In the Configure Key Filters section, in the Available Key Filter fields, click Modified By, and then click the Add button. The screen should now match Figure 22.30.

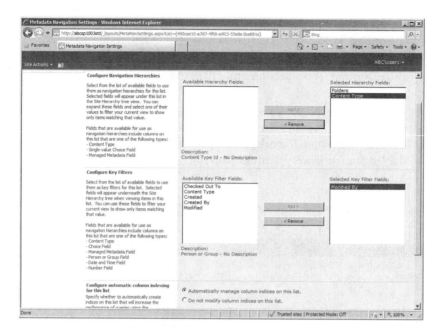

FIGURE 22.30 Selecting hierarchy fields and key filter fields.

NOTE

A variety of fields can be used as key filters. These include Content Type, Choice field, Managed Metadata field, Person or Group field, Date and Time field, and Number field.

9. Leave Automatically Manage Column Indices on This List checked. Click OK to save the changes and return to the Document Library Settings page.

NOTE

Leaving Automatically Manage Column Indices on This List selected will improve the performance of queries when the Navigation Hierarchy and Key Filter tools are used. There are a maximum of 20 columns that can be indexed in a list or library, so on rare occasions, the administrator might need to decide which 20 are indexed.

10. Click the name of the document library in the breadcrumb to return to the library itself. The library should now have the hierarchy fields in the Quick Launch area on the left, and below it the key filter fields. Test these tools by creating several folders and uploading several documents to the library and assigning them to the Document and Basic Page content types during the upload process.

Figure 22.31 shows the navigation hierarchy after several folders have been created, and where the user has clicked the Basic Page content type, as well as the key filter section where the user has entered ABC\User1 and the filtering criteria for the Modified By field of metadata. This very intuitive navigation tool enables users to quickly navigate to folders and subfolders and to see only certain content types or other fields, such as managed metadata fields.

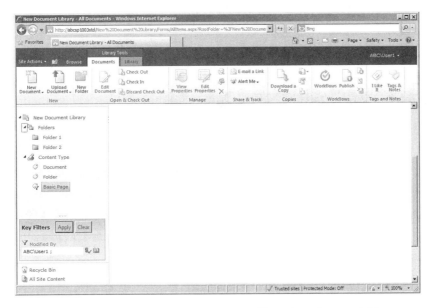

FIGURE 22.31   Navigation hierarchy and key filters in a document library.

Enabling the Developer's Dashboard for Troubleshooting

A final topic for this chapter involves enabling the Developer's Dashboard, which can be of assistance when troubleshooting issues with a complex list or library. The Developer's Dashboard can be enabled via the command prompt using the stsadm tool, or through PowerShell. This tool provides a summary of the web server, database queries, web part events, and other items of interest to developers.

Follow these steps to enable the Developer's Dashboard using the stsadm tool:

1. From the SharePoint 2010 front-end server that houses the Central Administrator site, access the command prompt by clicking the Start button and typing **cmd** into the Search field. The command prompt should open.

2. From the command prompt, navigate to the folder containing the stsadm tool if needed. Typically, this tool is located in the following folder: C:\Program Files\Common Files\Microsoft Shared\Web Server Extensions\14\BIN.

3. Then enter the following command:

```
stsadm -o setproperty -pn developer-dashboard -pv on
```

4. The message "Operation completed successfully" should result. If an error message displays, check the syntax, and replace the dashes in the code one by one, especially if the code was pasted from Word or the Internet.

5. Now the Developer's Dashboard is on for the farm and information should display at the bottom of all SharePoint pages (which will obviously be a nuisance for end users, so bear that in mind). Figure 22.32 shows an example.

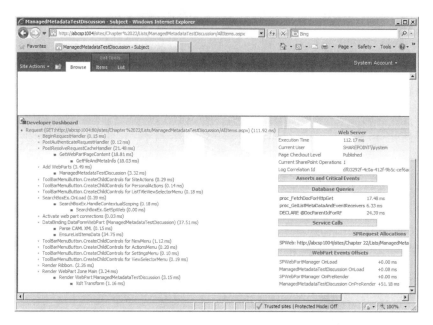

FIGURE 22.32   Sample Designer's Dashboard information on a SharePoint 2010 page.

6. The Developer's Dashboard can be turned off with the following command:

```
stsadm -o setproperty -pn developer-dashboard -pv off
```

7. Alternatively, the Developer's Dashboard can be set to ondemand mode. In this mode, a small icon will appear in the upper-right corner of the page, and when clicked once, it will reveal the Developer's Dashboard information at the bottom of the page; if clicked again, it will hide the data. Use this code to set the dashboard to ondemand:

```
stsadm -o setproperty -pn developer-dashboard -pv ondemand
```

Summary

This chapter provides a thorough overview of the wide range of applications of metadata in SharePoint 2010 by using hands-on exercises as well as feature discussions and examples. Because of the ways that metadata is enmeshed with SharePoint 2010, administrators must "get their hands dirty" to set standards for how metadata will be used and which SharePoint 2010 metadata-related features will be used.

In this chapter, a summary of the different types of columns available from lists and libraries was provided, along with examples of how metadata is populated to documents. Exercises involving the calculated column and lookup column types were provided, and features such as validation settings and enforcing unique values in columns were discussed and practical applications were covered. Default values and the enforce relationship behavior were also discussed. The chapter then moved on to cover site columns and content types once the "basics" of metadata had been covered, because effective use of site columns and content types require a familiarity with the capabilities of metadata columns used in lists and libraries. Finally, managed metadata and using metadata as a navigation aid was discussed and exercises were provided.

Best Practices

▶ A recommended best practice for a farm or site collection administrator is to become familiar with the process of creating metadata columns in lists and libraries and the range and options available for the different column types.

▶ Set standards for document libraries and lists in terms of the standard metadata columns added to ensure consistency across libraries in one site or across multiple sites.

▶ Calculated columns support a wide range of mathematical functions, and Excel users can leverage their skills creating complex formulas in SharePoint 2010. Be sure to test the Excel formulae in SharePoint because not all Excel functions are supported and there are other restrictions, some of which are pointed out in this chapter.

▶ Column validations and validation settings for a list or library help IT ensure that users are entering valid values in lists and libraries, and also leverage Excel equations, which generate the results of true or false.

▶ Lookup columns are very powerful, but also have limitations in terms of which columns can be connected to. Also understanding the capabilities of the Restrict Delete and Cascade Delete options in the Enforce Relationship Behavior section for a lookup column is important and can lead to powerful applications built on relationships between lists.

▶ Site columns allow an administrator to create a column once that can be added to any list or library in the site collection. Changes push down only, so changes to the site column from the list level do not affect the site column itself, which is stored in the Site Column Gallery.

▶ Content types provide additional features and settings that make them effective and powerful tools, and can leverage site columns. They are defined in content type galleries.

▶ Managed metadata is defined at the Central Administrator site level, and multiple Managed Metadata Service applications can be created. The term sets created within the service applications can then be managed centrally and made available to lists and libraries throughout the farm.

▶ Not only does metadata allow for effective management of documents and list items, but it can also be used to facilitate navigation within lists and libraries.

▶ The Developer's Dashboard tool can prove to be extremely helpful if complex lists or libraries are performing poorly. It can be turned on, off, or set to ondemand mode by using the stsadm command.

## CHAPTER 23

Leveraging Social Networking Tools in SharePoint 2010

W hen discussing SharePoint 2010 designs (or earlier versions of SharePoint) with clients, the issue of My Site sites and social networking invariably involves discussions of whether they are "good" or "bad" for the organization, and IT decision makers tend to have strong opinions one way or the other. Those for My Site sites see them as having the potential to get users more involved with SharePoint 2010 implementations, and a way to not only make the project more successful from an adoption standpoint, but to provide social collaboration tools that can enhance the productivity of users. Those against My Site sites tend to see the sites as potential time wasters, are afraid that the users are not sophisticated enough to understand how to use them, or are afraid that users will use them as "dumping grounds" for personal documents.

Both stances are valid, and after all, IT management tends to have good insight into the types of users who will be interacting with the SharePoint environment, and their concerns are most likely justified. That said, the SharePoint 2010 My Site tools and capabilities (available in SharePoint Server 2010 Standard or Enterprise) are dramatically improved and different from My Sites in SharePoint 2007, so much so that they seem to be a whole new product. Therefore, it makes sense for IT to at least test and evaluate My Site capabilities to see its potential before a firm choice is made.

This chapter is designed more for the farm administrator than the end user. It reviews the key configuration settings that need to be in place in the Central Administration site, as well as the processes involved in creating a new My Site infrastructure, including creating the My Site host and User Profile service application as well as a number of other administrator-level configurations related to the overall well-being of the My Site environment. Some time is allocated for reviewing the basics of a My Site configuration, but the full walk-through of all My Site features is left to the end users.

Reviewing the Components of a Healthy My Site Configuration

A My Site environment contains a number of "moving parts," and this section reviews these from a high level. Although in most cases a My Site environment will be "up and running," it is important for the farm administrator to understand the various components that need to be in place for the My Site environment to function. This will be especially useful if users report errors or issues with their personal sites.

The User Profile service application is generally created when the farm is provisioned, unless either something goes wrong in the process or the person configuring the farm decides not to allow the wizard to configure the User Profile service application automatically. It is certainly possible to damage a User Profile service application so that, for example, the synchronization connection simply won't run, or other errors are encountered when trying to create My Site sites.

An initial step to take is to verify that My Site sites can be created and that all basic features are working. Continue through this chapter to get a better sense of the depth and breadth of these services; there are quite a few. Assuming that My Site and the social networking features are in fact working, the farm administrator should still review the components and their configurations in Central Administration and then validate that they meet the overall requirements of the organization. For example, is the same web application hosting the production SharePoint 2010 intranet as well as all My Site sites? And will all users be getting My Site sites? Are all the fields being used in AD being mapped to SharePoint 2010 My Site, or only a subset?

The following sections help a farm administrator understand the steps involved in setting up a new web application to house My Site sites, as well as to create a new User Profile service application. Because of variables in the process, the full complement of steps won't be covered, but the high-level requirements are summarized and references to the lengthy and detailed Microsoft TechNet documents that provide the full steps are provided.

From a high level, the following need to be in place in the Central Administration site:

▶ One or more My Site hosts is required.

▶ One or more User Profile service applications needs to be in place and working.

▶ The User Profile service application must be synchronizing properly with AD.

CAUTION

User Profile synchronization cannot be used in a single-server SharePoint 2010 configuration that uses the built-in database installation.

High-Level Review of Steps Required to Create a New My Site Host

A key component for a functional My Site implementation is the My Site host. As mentioned in the next section, "High-Level Steps Required to Create a New User Profile Service Application," one of the steps involves specifying the My Site host. So, before starting that process, a My Site host needs to be in place.

> **NOTE**
>
> Creating a new My Site host may not be required. These steps are for administrators who know they need to perform these steps because no My Site host was created by the Installation Wizard, or My Site and the User Profile Service aren't operating properly, or for administrators who want the experience of creating a new My Site host.

## 23

Step 1: Create a New Web Application

When testing, it is a recommended best practice to create a new web application and then create the My Site host location. Many organizations choose to do this in their production environments as well as for My Site. This provides separation between the My Site sites and the production site collection that houses the SharePoint sites and resources that will be used every day by the organization. In addition, every time a user creates a My Site site, a site collection is created, so from a management standpoint, having these organized in a separate web application has its advantages.

The full process of creating a new web application is covered in the Microsoft document at http://technet.microsoft.com/en-us/library/cc261875.aspx. This allows the administrator to determine the following:

- ▶ The type of authentication to be used
- ▶ Whether to use an existing or create a new IIS website
- ▶ Set the port number to use
- ▶ Set the path for the virtual directory in IIS
- ▶ Set the URL that will be used to access the web application
- ▶ Whether to use a new or existing application pool
- ▶ Specify the database server, database name, and type of authentication
- ▶ Specify the failover database server, if any

Step 2: Reviewing the Settings from the Manage Web Applications Page

Once the new web application is created, by clicking Application Management from the Quick Launch in Central Administration and then clicking Manage Web Applications, the farm administrator can manage the new (and existing) web applications. It is a best practice to review these setting thoroughly to better understand the settings and what is permitted within the new web application.

An example is shown in Figure 23.1 of the Manage Web Applications page, where a sample web application was created to house the My Site site collection (SharePoint – 8080), along with the other existing web applications (Central Administration web application and the web application that houses the SharePoint site collections [SharePoint – 80]).

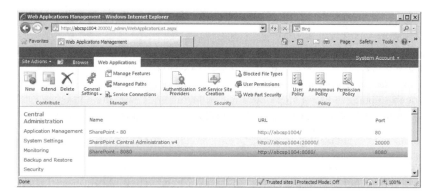

FIGURE 23.1   Manage Web Applications page.

A quick review of the managed paths settings for the web application is accomplished by clicking the Managed Paths button. This shows that for this new web application that the Sites path is a Wildcard Inclusion type, and the Personal path is also a Wildcard Inclusion. This allows for the creation of site collections beneath /sites and /personal in the web application, which is required for users to create their own My Site sites.

Self-Service Site Creation is required for My Site site provisioning and is managed from the Manage Web Applications page, also shown in Figure 23.1. By default, Self-Service Site Creation is enabled in SharePoint Server 2010 for all authenticated users. To verify that this is on, with the User Profile Services web application selected, click the Self-Service Site Creation button and review the settings. If this is set to Off for the My Site web application, when end users click the link to My Site the first time, their My Site site will appear to be created and they will see the My Newsfeed page, but when they click the link for My Content, an error message will display that states the following: "Your personal site cannot be created because Self-Service Site Creation is not enabled. Contact your site administrator for more information."

Step 3: Create a New My Site Host Site Collection

For testing purposes and in many production environments, it is also recommended to then create a new My Site host location. The steps required to create a My Site host are covered in the following Microsoft document: http://technet.microsoft.com/en-us/library/ff729456.aspx. From a high level, this requires creating a new site collection that references the web application created, which involves the following steps:

▶ Providing a title, description, and URL for the site

▶ Selecting My Site Host as the site collection template

▶ Entering the primary and secondary site collection administrators

The site collection will then be created using the My Site Host template, and should then be ready for the User Profile service application to be created. The farm administrator can verify the site collection by visiting the Central Administration site, clicking Application Management on the Quick Launch, and then clicking View All Site Collections in the Site Collections section. Make sure the web application is selected from the Web Application drop-down menu, and all site collections that exist within the web application will be shown. Figure 23.2 shows the contents of a web application created for My Site management and the site collections created within it after several test users have created their own My Site sites.

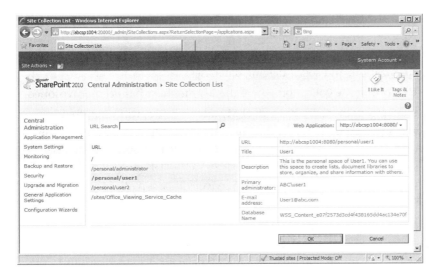

FIGURE 23.2   Site collection list for a My Site web application.

High-Level Review of Steps Required to Create a New User Profile Service Application

Although it is generally not required to create a new User Profile service application, a farm administrator may choose to do so during the testing process, and to better understand the inner workings of My Site and profiles, or to change the default configuration that results when the wizard is used to configure the farm. The previous sections should be reviewed because they cover the steps required to create a new web application and site collection to house the My Site sites, which is a generally recommended configuration.

The steps required to create a new User Profile service application are covered in detail in the following Microsoft site:

http://technet.microsoft.com/en-us/library/ee721052.aspx#createapp

The process to create the service application using PowerShell is also covered. From a high level, the steps are as follows:

1. Create a new User Profile service application from the Manage Service Applications page.
2. Use an existing application pool or create a new one.
3. Choose the database server and provide a name for the profile database that will be created.
4. Choose the database server and provide a name for the synchronization database that will be created.
5. Choose the database server and provide a name for the social tagging database that will be created.
6. Provide failover database server names if database mirroring is being used for the profile, synchronization, and social tagging databases.
7. Provide the URL of the site collection where the My Site host has been provisioned.
8. Provide the managed path where individual My Site web sites will be created.
9. Determine which type of username will be used to create My Site sites: User Name (Do Not Resolve Conflicts), User Name (Resolve Conflicts by Using domain_username), or Domain and User Name (Will Not Have Conflicts).
10. Select whether the proxy of this User Profile Service will be a part of the default proxy group on this farm.

Once the service application is created, it will appear in the list of service applications on the Service Applications page in Central Administration (accessible by clicking Application Management in the Quick Launch and then clicking Manage Service Applications in the Service Applications section). Clicking the User Profile service application that was created will take the administrator to the Manage Profile Service page for the User Profile service application.

Verify the User Profile Service and User Profile Synchronization Service Are Started
After the User Profile service application is created, or for general troubleshooting of User Profile service application, visit the Services on Server page, by clicking System Settings in the Quick Launch from Central Administration site and then clicking Manage Services on Server.

User Profile Service and User Profile Synchronization Service should show as Started. If User Profile Synchronization Service is shown as Stopped, which often happens after the creation of a new User Profile service application, click the Start link and enter the information requested. This involves selecting the User Profile application, which will be the one just created, and providing passwords for the service account used. The process of starting the User Profile Synchronization Service can take 5 to 10 minutes, and an IIS reset command from the command prompt is also required.

Reviewing the User Profile Service Application Settings

The following sections give overviews of the process of re-creating the User Profile service application as well as a web application and site collection to house the My Site sites. The User Profile Service is a service application in SharePoint Server 2010 that provides a central location for configuring and managing the following personalization settings:

▶ **People**—Tools are provided to Manage User Properties as well as to Manage User Profiles, Manage User Sub-Types, Manage Audiences, Schedule Audience Compilation, Manage User Permissions, Compile Audiences, and Manage Policies.

▶ **Synchronization**—Tools provided include Configure Synchronization Connections, Configure Synchronization Timer Job, Configure Synchronization Settings, and Start Profile Synchronization. These are important because they will determine where the user profiles get their data from and the update schedule.

▶ **Organizations**—Tools include Manage Organization Properties, Manage Organization Profiles, and Manage Organization Sub-Types.

▶ **My Site settings**—Setup My Sites, Configure Trusted Host Locations, Configure Personalization Site, Publish Links to Office Client Applications, Manage Social Tags, and Notes.

An example of a healthy User Profile service application is shown in Figure 23.3. Note that on the right side, there are a number of User Profiles that were synchronized from Active Directory.

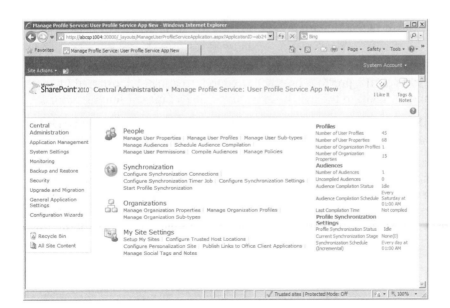

FIGURE 23.3   Manage Profile Service page for a New User Profile service application.

Forefront Identity Manager's Involvement in Synchronization

Although this topic won't be covered in depth, it is important to understand that Microsoft Forefront Identity Manager (FIM), formerly known as Microsoft Identity Integration Server (MIIS), is used to facilitate the synchronization process. FIM is automatically installed when SharePoint 2010 is installed but it won't show up in Programs and Applications.

When troubleshooting synchronization issues, check the services running on the server housing the User Profile services application and verify that the following services are running when the synchronization process is running. These services may show as disabled until a profile synchronization is started:

▶ Forefront Identity Manager Service

▶ Forefront Identity Manager Synchronization Service

Reviewing the Setup My Sites Link in the My Site Settings Section

Available on the Manage Profile Service page for the User Profile service application, as shown in Figure 23.3, the Setup My Sites link in the My Site Settings section provides access to several tools that should be familiar to the farm administrator for effective My Site management. These include the following:

▶ **Preferred Search Center**—The farm administrator should decide whether to use the default search center or to map to a different search center. If the organization has customized the configuration of the Advanced Search page, for example, and wants the My Sites search to be consistent, the administrator would use this tool to insert the desired page. For example, if the path of http://*portalname*/search/advanced.aspx was entered, when users search from their My Site, the advanced search page will display.

▶ **My Site Host**—This can be changed if needed for the service application. However, any existing sites on the previous host will need to be manually transferred (that is, backed up and restored) to the new host, which can be a time-consuming process.

▶ **Personal Site Location**—Typically set to Personal, this can be changed if needed. A managed path matching this setting will need to exist on the web application hosting the My Site.

▶ **Site Naming Format**—The farm administrator can choose between User Name (Do Not Resolve Conflicts), User Name (Resolve Conflicts by Using domain_username), and Domain and User Name (Will Not Have Conflicts). Note that domain and username are displayed as ...personal/domain_user (for example, ...personal/abc_user6).

Changing this setting will affect any future personal sites created, and will not affect existing personal sites.

▶ **Language**—Users can be allowed to set the language of their My Site.

▶ **Read Permission Levels**—These accounts will be given read permissions when new personal sites are created.

▶ **My Site Email Notifications**—An email string should be entered here, and it will be used when SharePoint sends out email notifications.

Reviewing Other Configuration Tools in the My Sites Settings Section

Configure Trusted Host Locations, Configure Personalization Site, and Publish Links to Office Client Applications Settings can be found in the My Sites Settings section on the User Profile service application page. Each of these is relatively straightforward but can add value to the process of managing and customizing My Site. Configuring trusted host locations can be of specific interest to larger organizations with thousands of users who want to leverage My Site sites, because the idea of putting all users in one "basket" (that is, managed by one service application and stored in one My Site host site collection) may be unappealing. And audiences can be leveraged to determine which user is created in which My Site host to ensure automation of the process. Personalization sites and published links to Office client applications allow the organization to customize the user experience based on audiences, too (as described throughout this chapter).

Following are summaries of the capabilities of these tools:

▶ **Configure trusted host locations**—If there are other User Profile service applications, links can be created that specify the URL of the host managed by the service application, and a target audience can be created to determine which users' personal sites are hosted by that host. A large organization (for example, with 10,000 users) may want to create multiple User Profile service applications, each of which has a My Site Host site collection, and then split up where individuals' My Site sites are created based on which branch office they are in. Several audiences would need to be created for this purpose, which look at the value of the Office field in AD, and if it matches a specific value, the user becomes a member of that audience when it is compiled. The audiences would then be used to determine where the users' My Site personal sites are created.

▶ **Configure personalization site**—If a link is added here, it will appear at the top of the My Site page. Audiences can also be applied here, to specify which users see a specific link.

▶ **Published links to Office client applications**—Links can be created here as a means of publishing links to SharePoint sites and lists when opening and saving documents from Office client applications. Audiences can be applied to determine which users receive these links, and the type of link can be specified as well. For example, Document Library, Slide Library, Portal Site, Team Site, and other options are provided.

Managing Social Notes and Tags

This tool will assuage many of the fears of the farm administrator, who may well be concerned about allowing users to post "whatever they want" in a forum that other users can see. The nature of posting a note tends to encourage off-the-cuff comments, and the farm administrator may want to do periodic searches for certain words to make sure they aren't appearing. Or an employee may leave the company, and IT decides that his tags should be removed.

This tool is not self-explanatory and can appear to "not work," so a quick review of how to use it will be beneficial to administrators. In the following example, Contractor1 entered a comment that offended User4, who filed a help desk ticket. User4 didn't give much information, so the farm administrator needs to do a general search and see whether he can locate and remove the comment. Follow these steps to learn more about the process of managing social tags and notes:

1. Click the User Profile service application from the Manage Services Applications page, and then click Manage Social Tags and Notes in the My Site Settings section.

2. From the Type drop-down menu, select Tags or Notes. In this example, the farm administrator was told it was an offensive note.

3. Either click a User Name and click the Check Names button to resolve, or use the Browse tool to find the username required. Multiple names cannot be entered. In this example, Contractor1 is entered in the name field, and Check Names is clicked.

4. A URL can also be entered to narrow down the search. However, the view in which the comment appears must be entered or no results will return. In this example, this field is left blank because the farm administrator doesn't know which list or library the comment was made in.

5. A date range can be entered. The farm administrator believes the note was entered recently, so he enters a time span encompassing the last week.

6. The Tag/Note Contains field can be filled out, but in this example, the farm administrator doesn't have any specific words to search for and so he leaves it blank.

7. The farm administrator clicks Find to see what Contractor1 has been posting over the past week. A number of results appear, as shown in Figure 23.4.

8. The farm administrator checks the box next to the one comment that returns, because he agrees it could be offensive, and clicks the Delete button. He clicks the OK button to confirm the deletion, and the note is deleted immediately.

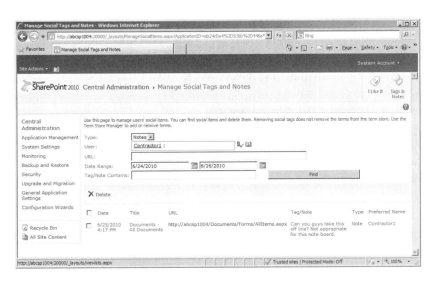

FIGURE 23.4   Using the Manage Social Tags and Notes feature.

> **NOTE**
>
> A site collection administrator can also delete notes directly from the document library or list by clicking Tags & Notes in the list or library and visiting the Note Board and clicking the Delete button. Other users can edit their own comments at a later date if needed.

Restricting User Access to and Creation of My Site Sites

Some administrators want to restrict the use of My Site sites because they may want to pilot the use of these sites with a limited number of users, in the short term, or permanently exclude certain groups of users for a variety of business reasons. As discussed previously in the chapter, Self-Service Site Creation needs to be activated for the site collection that houses the My Site host.

Assuming that is enabled, the most straightforward way to control access is for a user who has site collection privileges to the My Sites Host site collection to access his My Site and then access Site Settings and modify user permissions. Follow these steps to modify the My Site settings and remove NT Authority\Authenticated Users from access to the My Site site collection and then add specific groups who will be able to then create and access their My Site sites:

1. For the farm in question, access the portal home page using an account that has site collection administrator privileges for the site collection that houses My Site for the

portal. If in doubt, access the account's My Site page, and if the account doesn't have access to Site Settings page, this account isn't a site collection admin.

2. Once logged in with the appropriate account, click the link to My Site from the drop-down menu by the username; in this example, the user is User1.

3. Once My Site loads, click Site Actions menu, and select Site Settings, and the familiar management page will load. Click Site Permissions.

4. This page will show the permission levels assigned to different groups, which will vary based on the configuration of the My Site host; in this example, this will include Members, Owners, Visitors, the NT Authority\Authenticated Users group, and other individuals or groups.

5. Check the box next to NT Authority\Authenticated Users and click Remove User Permissions on the Ribbon, and click OK at the confirmation that pops up.

6. Then click the Grant Permissions button on the Ribbon and add individual users or AD groups that should have permissions to create and use My Site accounts. These users and groups can be added to an existing group or given direct permissions. Read permissions are the minimum requirement because Self-Service Site Creation is enabled, allowing the account to create its own site collection to which the creator will have sufficient permissions for normal usage.

7. To restore My Site access, the NT Authority\Authenticated Users group can be added by clicking Grant Permissions and providing the group Read. However, a general best practice is to instead add the *domainname*\domain users group, which is a true AD security group and generally considered to be more secure, and grant it read permissions.

Another method is to create a user policy for the web application. This will affect access to the entire web application, so this should not be used to restrict access to My Site sites if they are housed on the same web application that houses the intranet or portal site collection! So, the assumption here is that a separate web application was created for My Site and the user policy will stop certain users from accessing that web application. Follow these steps to create a policy denying access to a My Site dedicated web application:

1. Access the Central Administrator site, click Application Management, and then click Manage Web Applications.

2. Select the My Site web application and click the User Policy button from the Web Applications tab on the Ribbon.

3. Click Add Users.

4. Keep All Zones selected. Click Next.

5. From the Add Users window, add the username or AD group name to the Choose Users field, as shown in Figure 23.5, and click the Check Names button, or use the Browse button to add the users or groups. In this example, the AD group Contractors will be denied all access to the web application housing My Site to ensure they don't access any personal sites. Click OK.

6. Then log on to SharePoint using the account that is a member of the group that the policy applies to and try to access My Site. In this example, the user Contractor1,

who is a member of the Contractors group, gets an "Access Denied" message when trying to access her My Site.

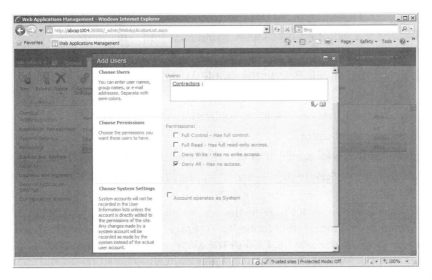

FIGURE 23.5   Creating a policy for a My Site web application to deny an AD group all access.

TIP

Web application policies "win" over site collection policies, and web application deny policies win over web application allow policies. For example, in the previous exercise, a policy was created for the My Site Host web application that denies all access to members of the Contractors group. If a site collection administrator gives direct permissions to the Contractors group to the My Site Host site collection, any member of the group will still get an "Access Denied" error. This is useful to know when troubleshooting these types of errors.

Mapping a SharePoint Profile Field to Active Directory

This section covers the steps necessary to configure a SharePoint profile field to pull content from an AD field, and points out some of the other connectivity options.

Prerequisites for this next configuration exercise are as follows:

▶ Verify that there are one or more AD accounts that have the Mobile field populated. This field is available by opening Active Directory Users and Computers, locating the user's name, right-clicking the user's name and clicking Properties, and then accessing the Telephones tab and verifying that there is an entry in the Mobile field. In a test environment, simply enter in a fictitious mobile number and click OK.

▶ A User Profile service application needs to be configured, and synchronization with AD needs to be functional.

Follow these steps to map the Mobile field in the profile database to the Mobile field in Active Directory:

1. From the Central Administration site, click Application Management.

2. Click Manage Service Applications.

3. Locate the User Profile service application and click the title of the application.

4. When the Manage Profile Service page opens, click the link for Manage User Properties.

5. When the Manage User Properties page opens, scroll down to the section header Contact Information and locate the Mobile Phone entry. Note that it is not mapped to an Active Directory field, since the field in the Mapped Attribute column is empty. Hover over the Mobile Phone item and access the drop-down menu and click Edit.

6. Scroll down to the Add New Mapping section. Click the Attribute drop-down menu and locate and then click the entry titled Mobile. Verify that the Direction field is set to Import; then click the Add button. This attribute will now appear in the section immediately above the Add New Mapping section titled Property Mapping for Synchronization, as shown in Figure 23.6.

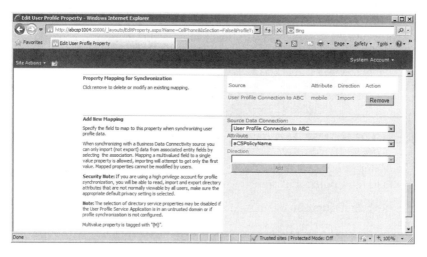

FIGURE 23.6   New property mapped for synchronization.

7. Click OK to save the changes and return to the Manage User Properties page.

8. Return to the User Profile service application by clicking Application Management in the Quick Launch, and then by clicking Manage Service Applications and then clicking the title of the User Profile service application.

9. Click Start Profile Synchronization.

10. Make sure that the Start Incremental option is selected and click OK.

11. Once the synchronization has completed, the information should be added to the user's profile. Validate that the information has been added by clicking Manage User Profiles in the People section of the Manage Profile Service page.

12. Enter a username that had the mobile field populated (per the prerequisites to this exercise) in the Find profiles field and click Find. Click the username when it is found in the Account Name column, access the drop-down menu for the name, and click Edit My Profile.

13. Scroll down to the Mobile Phone field, and it will show the Mobile number from Active Directory, as shown in Figure 23.7.

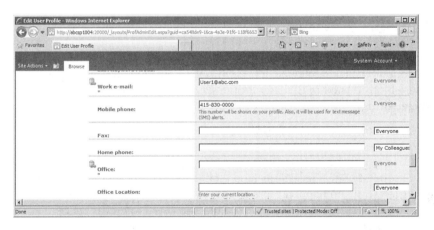

FIGURE 23.7   New property value shown in the user profile record.

14. To validate that the data shows up on the actual My Site page, access the SharePoint 2010 top-level site using one of the users who has the Mobile field populated in AD (as specified in the prerequisites section prior to these steps), click the drop-down menu under the username (User1 in this example), and click My Site.

15. When the user's My Site opens, click My Profile from the links available on the upper-left portion of the screen. Click the More Information link to the right of the placeholder for the photo, and the Mobile Phone information should display, as shown in Figure 23.8.

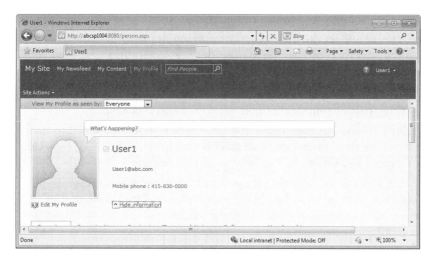

FIGURE 23.8   New property value shown on a user's My Site on the My Profile page.

User Profile Job Review

The farm administrator should also be familiar with the jobs that are involved with My Site. These can be found by clicking Review Job Definitions from the Monitoring page. There are a number of jobs related to the User Profile service application, and IT might want to adjust these settings. Just click the link to read more about the specific job.

Although it is generally not recommended to change the Schedule Type for jobs, IT may decide to modify one or more of these settings. For example, by default the Activity Feed Job is off, which is covered in the next section, and this may not be desirable for the organization. In addition, the My Site Suggestions Email job is set to monthly by default, and IT may want these suggestions to happen more regularly. Similarly, IT may decide to reduce the frequency of some of these jobs; for example, the User Profile Language Synchronization Job, which is described as follows: "Looks for new language pack installations and makes sure that strings related to user profile service are localized properly."

The full list of jobs is as follows:

- User Profile Service App New - Activity Feed Cleanup Job

- User Profile Service App New - Activity Feed Job

- User Profile Service App New - Audience Compilation Job

- User Profile Service App New - My Site Suggestions Email Job

- User Profile Service App New - Social Data Maintenance Job

- User Profile Service App New - Social Rating Synchronization Job

▶ User Profile Service App New - System Job to Manage User Profile Synchronization

▶ User Profile Service App New - User Profile Change Cleanup Job

▶ User Profile Service App New - User Profile Change Job

▶ User Profile Service App New - User Profile Incremental Synchronization

▶ User Profile Service App New - User Profile Language Synchronization Job

▶ User Profile Service App New - User Profile to SharePoint Full Synchronization

▶ User Profile Service App New - User Profile to SharePoint Quick Synchronization

Activity Feed Settings

Activity Feed lets users add feeds of events to their My Site web sites. Feeds might give information about activities of their colleagues, such as updates to profile properties and creation of social tags and notes. Activity Feed does not enable tracking of activities that a user does not have permissions to see.

Activity Feed is off by default in a User Profile service application. To turn on this feature, a farm administrator must configure the User Profile service Activity Feed timer job. Follow these steps to turn on the Profile Service – Activity Feed Job:

1. On the Central Administration site, click Monitoring from the Quick Launch.
2. In the Timer Jobs section, click Review Job Definitions.
3. Click User Profile Service – Activity Feed Job in the list of timer jobs.
4. On the Edit Timer Job page, leave the default settings and click Enable.

Once this job runs, users will see content on their My Newsfeed page of their My Site, as shown in Figure 23.9. This example shows several activities by User5 who has recently added a new colleague, updated his profile in terms of interests, skills, and his Ask Me About information. In addition, User4 recently added several new colleagues. The My Newsfeed and other components of the My Site are discussed in the next section.

Components of My Sites

So far, this chapter has been focused on the "behind-the-scenes" components of My Sites, which are of course important to IT and the farm administrators, but end users will want to get hands-on experience with the tools. As the previous sections have shown, it is not a trivial process to fully configure the My Site environment and make sure that the correct users can create My Site sites while restricting some users, customizing the behavior of search in My Site sites, creating customized links along the top navigation bar, and enabling the My Newsfeed function. So, the preceding sections should be reviewed before setting the end users loose with My Site sites.

That said, once the farm administrators are comfortable that the different moving parts are functioning properly and have customized the My Site to meet their needs, end users should be invited to start testing them and give feedback on what they like, what they don't like or don't understand, and what they can't figure out.

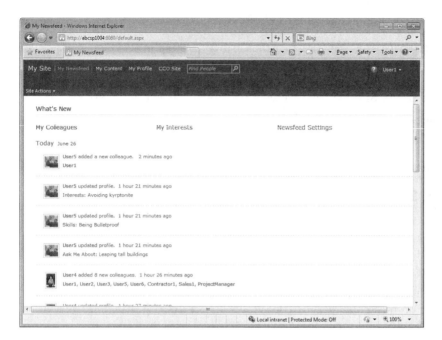

FIGURE 23.9   Example of My Newsfeed.

Creating and Exploring a My Site

Once the environment is ready to support My Site, new users should be instructed to create their personal site and perform some basic configuration steps as follows:

1. From the Portal home page, click the drop-down arrow next to the username in the upper-right corner and click My Site; the My Site home page will open, which is also the My Newsfeed page. The URL shows the location of this page, which is a default.aspx page. Note that the URL does not include the user's name or any personal information, as shown in Figure 23.10.

2. From here, the user (TestUser1 in this example) can click My Colleagues, My Interests, or Newsfeed settings in the body of the page, and start configuring that information, or he can click one of the links along the top: My Content, My Profile, or any other links that the farm administrator has decided to add from Central Administration. Figure 23.10 shows an additional link CCO Site that was added by the farm administrator. Ideally, users will immediately configure their profile, so click My Profile.

3. From the My Profile page (note that the URL is still generic, and the page is Person.aspx), click Edit My Profile under the placeholder for the picture.

4. As shown in Figure 23.11, this page allows the user to enter information in the About Me field, choose a picture, and populate information in a number of other areas, which by default include Ask Me About, Phone Numbers, Office Location, Time Zone, Assistant, Past Projects, Skills, Schools, Birthday, Interests, choose which activities will generate email notifications, and which activities the user wants to see about their colleagues. For this example, upload a photo and enter some information into each of the fields.

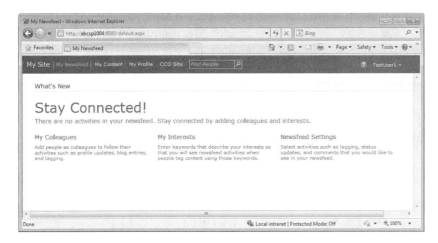

FIGURE 23.10   My Site My Newsfeed home page.

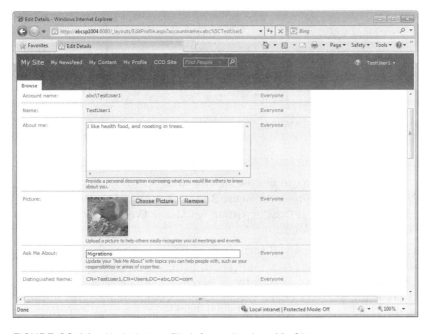

FIGURE 23.11   Updating profile information in a My Site.

5. To upload the photo, just click Choose Picture, browse for a photo, and then click OK.

6. Entering information into the other fields should be simple, and some provide the ability to determine which users will be able to see the information based on the

options Everyone, Only Me, My Manager, My Team, and My Colleagues. Click Save and Close once the desired information is entered. The resulting view will look like Figure 23.12.

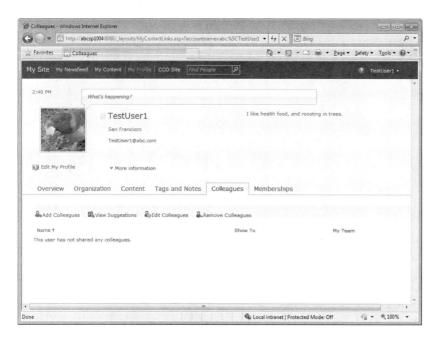

FIGURE 23.12   My Profile page after updating.

7. Click the Colleagues tab, and then click Add Colleagues.

8. Enter in the names of users who can be considered colleagues (in this example, User1, User2, User3, User4), as shown in Figure 23.13. Click Yes under the Add to My Team option, use the General Existing Group, and leave Everyone selected under Show These Colleagues To. Click OK.

9. The Suggested Colleagues window will then open, which will suggest other colleagues based on email and IM communications patterns. Check the box next to one or more of these suggestions, or click the X to remove the suggestion. Click Yes under Add to My Team, use the General Group, and click Add. Figure 23.14 shows the results on the Colleagues tab, where the new users are displayed as colleagues.

10. Next click My Content, and now the My Site site collection for the user will be created and a message to that extent will display while the site is created. A message will then display that states "Microsoft Office can remember your My Site to synchronize documents stored here in Outlook and to show it when opening and saving files. Do you want Office to remember this site...?" Click Yes for this sample user.

11. Note that the URL, as shown in Figure 23.15, now contains the user's name, based on how the settings are configured for the User Profile service application in the Setup My Sites tool, as covered previously in this chapter. The user also now has

access to a site actions drop-down menu, making this a good training ground for tools the user wouldn't normally have access to in a production site collection.

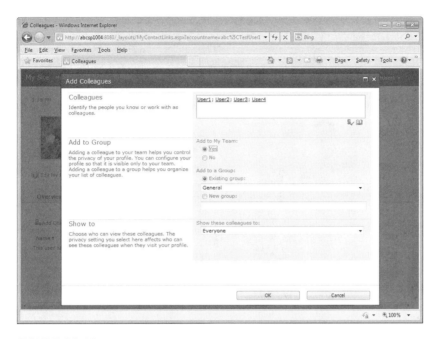

FIGURE 23.13   Adding colleagues.

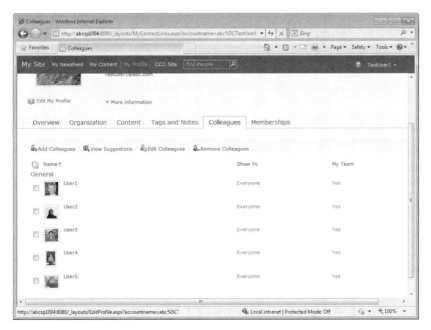

FIGURE 23.14   Colleagues added.

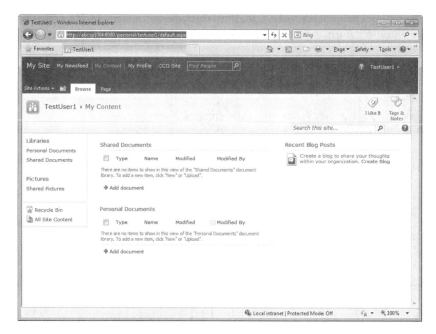

FIGURE 23.15   My Content page for new My Site.

12. Click Site Actions, and then Site Settings, and review the tools available.

The user can delete this site, and all the content contained within it will be deleted. Then, the next time the user clicks My Content, a new site collection will be created.

Using Bookmarklets

Just as users can add tags or notes to SharePoint pages, lists, and libraries, they can add tags to external sites. These are referred to as bookmarklets. A bookmarklet is a JavaScript control that users can save as a bookmark in their browsers and when accessed, allows the user to add tags or notes to external sites. SharePoint users who are at all interested in external research are likely to be excited by this feature because it can easily allow them to tag non-SharePoint websites, such as legacy intranets or non-Microsoft sites in use inside the organization as well as resources available on the Internet.

The following steps illustrate how to use this powerful tool:

1. Access a My Site and click the My Profile link.

2. Click the Tags and Notes tab.

3. Scroll down to the Add SharePoint Tags and Notes tool. As stated in this section, "This tool helps you conveniently tag or post notes on sites directly from your browser. Add it to your browser's favorites or bookmarks into the 'Links' or 'Bookmarks Toolbar' group. Then show the 'Links Bar' or 'Bookmarks Toolbar' to see it." Just right-click the link that reads "Right click or drag and drop this link to your browser's favorites or bookmarks toolbar to tag external sites," and then select Add to Favorites.

4. A message will appear that reads "You are adding a favorite that might not be safe. Do you want to continue." Click Yes.

5. Then give a name to the favorite, or keep the default Tags and Note Board, and click Add.

6. Now access an external website, such as Microsoft.com, and access the Favorites menu. Click the entry Tags and Note Board, as shown in Figure 23.16.

FIGURE 23.16   Adding a bookmarklet to a non-SharePoint site.

7. A Tags and Note Board tab will open, where the user can add Tags from the Tags tab, or click Note Board and enter more involved notes. In this example, the user wants to tag this using managed metadata (covered in Chapter 22, "Managing Metadata and Content Types in SharePoint 2010") and types the word *Project*, and then chooses from the options provided by the managed metadata, as shown in Figure 23.17. When done, click Save.

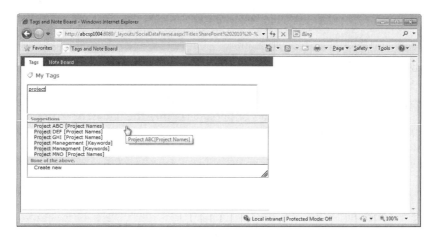

FIGURE 23.17   Tagging an external site with managed metadata.

8. To now access this bookmarklet, return to the My Site and click My Profile. The recent tagging of the external site will be shown in the Recent Activities section under the Overview tab, as well as on the Tags and Notes tab.

For "extra credit" in this exercise, it is recommended for the administrator or tester to visit a number of sites and apply numerous tags and notes to sites and then return to the My Site for the logged-in account and experiment with the different ways of sorting the links, which are functional but come up short in several areas. For example, if a user tags dozens of sites and pages, both external and internal, with a term such as *SharePoint*, it can be an arduous task finding a specific website based on the tag, unless the tags are well thought-out.

Summary

This chapter approaches the My Site component of SharePoint 2010 as a powerful set of tools, but one that needs to be understood from a functionality and management standpoint, before it is made available to end users. In addition, this chapter walks through making sure the supporting components (My Site host and User Profile service application) are in working order, and if not, how to rebuild them from scratch. Tips and recommended best practices are provided to further assist in managing the My Site environment, and the basic steps that end users need to take to set up and customize their personal sites are covered. Much more could certainly be written about the wealth of features available to end users, but due to space limitations, these could not all be covered, so appetites were simply whetted in this area.

Best Practices

▶ Before actively enlisting users to create My Site sites, the farm administrator should verify that all the Central Administration components are properly configured and meet the needs of the organization and that AD synchronization is functional.

▶ For many organizations, a recommended best practice is to create a new web application and My Sites Host site collection and a User Profile service application. Not only is this a great way to better understand how My Site sites work, but it allocates a web application to the My Sites host, which can then be more granularly managed.

▶ Site collection administrators of the My Site host can manage permissions from the My Site host, and if a dedicated web application is used to host My Site, user policies can be created to deny access to My Site sites.

▶ The My Sites link in the My Site Settings section provides access to a number of important configuration tools, such as Preferred Search Center, My Site Host, Personal Site Location, Site Naming Format, and Read Permission Levels, which should be reviewed before determining that SharePoint My Site sites are ready for general usage.

▶ Social notes and tags can be leveraged to allow users to express their opinions and collaborate on pages, lists, and libraries housed in SharePoint 2010 site collections, as well as on non-SharePoint internal or external sites using bookmarklets.

▶ The Activity Feed is off by default in the User Profile service application. To turn on this feature, a farm administrators group must configure the User Profile service Activity Feed timer job.

▶ Mapping additional fields in the User Profile service application to Active Directory fields with the Manage User Properties tool is an easy way to import additional fields into the SharePoint Profile database to be shared in users' My Site sites.

▶ Managed metadata, along with audiences, can be leveraged in many places in the My Site environment and should be considered as vital tools to the success of a well thought-out My Site strategy.

23

Governing the SharePoint 2010 Ecosystem

Managing any software product takes time and energy, but few software products provide the number of tools and allow for the same range of interactivity with end users and their data and ideas as the SharePoint product line. With many software products, the work is mostly done when the servers are built and the software installed and working. But with SharePoint 2010 (and previous versions), it can be said that the work is just beginning when the environment is configured and in use.

Of course, SharePoint 2010 can be locked down so that a very limited number of users can add documents, use My Site sites, or add items to lists, but then the value of what is at heart a set of collaboration tools diminishes. At the other end of the spectrum, allowing complete freedom to all users to create sites, delete sites, and leverage every tool in the SharePoint 2010 arsenal would most likely lead to a state of anarchy where users would have little faith in security and stability of the environment.

The term *governance* in the context of SharePoint 2010 includes concepts of maintenance of the hardware and software that supports the tools, but is more focused on creating and enforcing policies, rules of conduct and the process of understanding "what's going on" in the environment. This chapter discusses governance from a high conceptual and process-oriented level, while giving examples of specific SharePoint 2010 tools and components that should be included in the governance plan, many of which are covered in other chapters of this book in greater detail.

Ultimately, this chapter shares strategies and tools to consider for defining a governance plan for a SharePoint

2010 environment that any sized or shaped company should consider and helps provide impetus to get started on the road to effective governance.

The Importance of Governance

Is governance something that needs to be implemented with SharePoint, or should the SharePoint environment be a place for creativity and freedom? Although cases can be made for lack of structure, most organizations don't need to think for too long before they can come up with examples of IT projects that could have gone better and produced better results, and of technologies that failed to deliver the functionality that was expected. A governance plan must carefully balance user innovation and freedom versus manageability and support.

An almost universal experience is that of data repositories that have not had the proper governance, whether it be paper-based files, file shares, or the email environment, and these generally tend to be inefficient and sources of contention. There are many strong reasons for putting governance in place for any applications, three of which follow:

▶ Although maintenance costs of "unmanaged applications" seem low initially, the impact on the organization can be significant in the long term in less tangible ways. User complaints about "not being able to find anything," or not understanding the purpose of different applications through lack of training, or not being able to get support when issues are encountered, erode the level of confidence in the application and ultimately in IT.

▶ Unmanaged applications over time will either become abandoned or fail to garner user adoption. Consider a poorly managed intranet. It may have cost a considerable amount of time and money to create, and there may be recurring software costs and resources dedicated to keeping it running, but without appropriate governance, it can become disorganized, the content stale, and users unhappy with levels of support provided.

▶ Unmanaged applications are difficult to secure. If policies for entitlement and rights are not well defined from the beginning, securing vital corporate assets can be difficult later on. It is typically harder to take away user privileges and tools than just to control what is provided to begin with.

SharePoint is a powerful tool with tremendous potential. By spending time prior to or during the implementation of SharePoint 2010 on the governance plan, IT can help ensure that the project is initially perceived as a success, that the environment offers a well-defined set of tools to end users, and that it will be managed over time as it evolves.

A final thought for this section is that the governance plan does not need to fall into place all at once. There can certainly be phases to a governance plan, as there are phases to technology implementation projects.

Creating the Governance Plan

Governance is the process of governing, or managing, the SharePoint environment, which consists of hardware, software, data, processes, and people. Determining the right level of governance for the organization requires an understanding of the goals of the SharePoint 2010 infrastructure and related projects. If the SharePoint environment is being built to simply provide My Site sites for employees to get to know each other better, the goals are quite different from an implementation where SharePoint houses the corporate Internet site and allows customers to conduct monetary transactions. Therefore, a key step is defining the governance plan from a high level that takes into account the goals for the SharePoint implementation and sets forth a plan of action for ensuring that those goals will continue to be met after the "go live" of the SharePoint environment.

This section discusses the importance of having vision and scope of work documents in place before diving into the governance plan, and provides recommendations on a starting point for the governance plan creation process through a visualization tool, and then moves into the components of the governance plan.

Reviewing the Vision and Scope Documents

Before beginning the governance plan, the vision and scope of work documents should be dusted off. If they don't exist, these elements need to be defined. Even for the smallest implementation, documenting the vision and the scope of work are critical factors for success, even if each is made up of a few bullets on a Post-It. The vision document should provide high-level goals and objectives for the project, whereas the scope of work document should describe the tasks to take place, timeline, roles and responsibilities, communications plan, training, and support. These two documents provide the foundation for the governance plan.

> **NOTE**
>
> An important variable in the process of creating the governance plan is the current state of the SharePoint 2010 environment. If the environment has not been built yet, the process is different from if there is already a SharePoint 2010 environment in place and the organization finally has time to take a breath and devote attention to the governance plan. The process will also be different for an organization that has SharePoint 2007 in place, has been using it for years, and is planning an upgrade to SharePoint 2010.

It is understood that the temptation to skip the documentation process is very strong, but to show how simple this can really be, here is a simple vision and scope of work statement that provide enough basic guidance to develop a governance plan:

▶ **Sample vision statement**—The goal of SharePoint 2010 at Company ABC is to provide a better alternative to our current intranet and file share while providing enhanced collaboration tools.

▶ **Sample scope of work summary**—SharePoint 2010 will be implemented by internal IT resources, with assistance from subject matter experts in a phased approach. The phases will be proof of concept (POC), pilot, implementation/migration, and finally governance and support. Best-of-breed backup, management, and add-on web parts will be identified in the POC phase. Documentation of server builds and recommended best practices for maintenance will be included, as will knowledge transfer to internal IT resources.

Guiding principles and steps such as these provide direction to the project and define basic milestones. Without at least a basic and agreed-upon foundation of vision and scope, the chances of a successful project are reduced; in fact, even determining whether the project was or was not successful will be difficult, because the success criteria and milestones were never set.

Visually Mapping the Governance Strategy

To prepare for the more formal documentation step, it is useful to visualize the overall plan, which will help provide shape to the plan of action and map the logical components of hardware, software, people, and processes to the different areas of functionality that will be implemented in the project. Figure 24.1 provides a sample visualization tool for a governance plan for a sample organization, Company ABC.

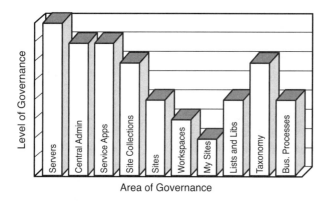

FIGURE 24.1   Equalizer diagram of governance for a sample company.

One way to define this diagram is to call it an "equalizer" chart, referring to the piece of audio hardware, not something more colloquial. This brings to mind the process of determining different "settings" for the components that comprise the SharePoint 2010 environment and then adjusting the individual settings as time goes by to "tune" the overall levels of governance. A distinction to make at this point in the governance process (brainstorming) is that the chart is driving the output rather than data driving the chart. For example, if the IT department is locked in a room working on this chart together, the CIO might simply say, "We don't have budget for new staff or any additional software and we're not supporting My Sites." That would immediately result in the removal of the My

Site component from the chart and "shorten" the bars across the board because the component of support resources is reduced.

To further understand how this chart can be useful, review Figure 24.1 in more detail. It is suggested that on the far left, the bar that represents governance of the servers that support the SharePoint environment (for example, Windows 2008 servers, including one or more SQL servers and one or more SharePoint 2010 servers) represents a maximal level of governance. Company ABC governs these servers very carefully, fully realizing that if they aren't stable, the entire environment will suffer. Therefore, the bar takes up the full height (or ranks an 8 of 8 in governance). To be more specific, there are standards for the operating system configuration in place, as well as for which version of Windows Server will be installed, how patches are applied, and antivirus use. Standards are also in place for backup software, maintenance plans for the SQL databases, as well as strict controls over which Active Directory (AD) groups and users have permissions to manage these servers.

Moving to the right in Figure 24.1, the Central Administration site will also be tightly controlled in terms of the configuration of the various components, such as web applications, jobs, reporting, and groups and accounts, that can make changes, and ranks a 7 out of 8. The service applications will be governed at a similar level. Site collections will be slightly less controlled and governed (6 of 8), sites still less (4 of 8), workspace still less (3 of 8), and My Site sites the least (2 of 8). The lists and libraries will be governed to a medium degree, while the overall taxonomy more highly managed and business processes (which include workflows) in the medium range.

> **NOTE**
>
> The level of governance for each area on this chart carries with it an element of cost and level of effort, both one-time (such as purchasing third-party software or hiring administrators) and over the long term (time to use the software, update policies, enforce procedures). It should be considered that the level of risk in each area grows inversely to the level of governance. Consider, for example, a SharePoint 2010 environment where the servers that house SQL Server and the SharePoint 2010 software are not managed, not backed up, and open for many users to modify the settings. Most people would agree that is a riskier configuration than the alternative.

Continuing with this visualization, each bar on the chart can be broken down into components, including the following:

- **Resources involved in the governance process**—This should include full-time and part-time resources as well as consultants and contractors.

- **Level of security and privilege constraints implemented**—A higher level of security translates to added governance, or control over the specific area that generally requires more time to manage than "looser" controls.

- **Templates used for creating the site collection, site, list, workflow, and other components**—Templates take time to create, manage, and update, as well as time to verify they are in fact being used.

▶ **Reporting and auditing to track events and activities**—This includes the built-in tools in the operating system, Internet Information Services (IIS), and SharePoint 2010, and can include third-party tools such as Microsoft System Center Operations Manager and products from AvePoint, Quest, or other third party.

▶ **Policies and procedures to define acceptable usage of the resources**—These can be enforced to a certain degree by the tools in place (SharePoint and third party, group policies, and so forth), but these also need to be documented and communicated to the user community and at some level enforced.

▶ **Third-party tools to add functionality**—Besides the possibilities mentioned previously, third-party tools can be used to add functionality to SharePoint 2010 in every conceivable area, or tools (such as new web parts) can be created internally.

Figure 24.2 gives an example of what generates the "height" of several sections of the chart, which should be translated as "cost and level of effort." In this example, starting at the right, the My Site environment will be minimally governed at Company ABC. Support staff is a fixed number, but no additional training will be provided to them on My Site support, the basic out-of-the-box templates will be provided, but no new ones created, and policies and procedures on My Site usage will be loosely defined, to essentially clarify that users can do what they want within the constraints of the software. Moving to the left, workspaces will be allowed, which translates to users having self-service site creation privileges, and the regular templates for meetings and document workspaces will be provided. The policies and procedures for using the sites will be loosely defined, and out-of-the-box auditing and reporting will be in place. However, IT will not be responsible for policing or cleaning up idle or abandoned workspaces. Moving to the Sites column shows a higher level of governance where the governance items security constraints and third-party tools have been added, increasing the level of governance. IT wants to strictly control privileges for the sites themselves that house the workspaces, lists, and libraries that users will be using. Finally, to the far left, the site collections will have additional constraints and auditing tools in place. IT will track carefully the different levels of usage of the site collections (as opposed to the sites themselves, which won't be as carefully managed) and have tools in place to manage the site collections.

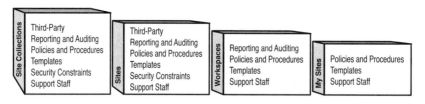

FIGURE 24.2   Detail of several regions of the equalizer diagram.

Defining Governance Roles and Responsibilities

One of the more important things to ensure success in SharePoint 2010 governance is to ensure that the roles and responsibilities of the parties involved are well defined not only in the rollout, but in the day-to-day processes in a SharePoint deployment and its maintenance. It is often underestimated what the day-to-day maintenance will be for the "steady-state" deployment of SharePoint.

Often, the emphasis is placed on the IT administrator, whereas little emphasis is placed on necessary business roles, designer roles, or even IT support structures. It's common to find entire roles undefined and failures can definitely happen as a result.

To start with, the organization should define the SharePoint farm administrator and site collection administrators. Key stakeholders, project managers, and business analysts can also add value to the governance process. For example, defining a "SharePoint steering committee chairperson" and "taxonomy tzar" can enhance the involvement of individuals in specific areas of the ongoing maintenance of the SharePoint 2010 environment. Members of the SharePoint steering committee may not be technical in nature, but will bring their individual perspectives to the process and help drive adoption of the technologies (and often, funding for specific initiatives).

Many organizations use a RACI charting strategy, which stands for responsible, accountable, consulted, and informed. A RACI chart is a simple and powerful vehicle for communication. It is used for defining and documenting responsibility. For each aspect of the project, both the initial rollout and the day-to-day management should have the people and their roles identified as well as the level of their involvement. This helps keep resources focused on their tasks and levels of involvement and typically enhances communications paths. Often, roles and responsibilities cross group and team lines. Figure 24.3 provides a sample RACI table for Company ABC.

SharePoint Governance	IT Mgmnt	Steering Committee	Business Analyst	Farm Admin	Site Collection Admin	Site Admin	Operations	Help Desk	Trainers
Governance Documentation, Policies and Procedures	A	C, I	C, I	R	R	C, I	C, I	C	
Hardware and OS Maintenance	A			I			R		
SQL Server Management	A			I			R		
Central Admin Site Management	A	I		R	C		I	I	
Service Applications Management	A	C	C	R	C		I	I	
Site Collection Management	A	I		C, I	R	I	I	I	
Site Management	A	I		C	R	R		I	
List, Library Management	A	I		C	C, I	R		I	
Taxonomy Management	A	C	R	C	C, I	C, I		I	
Business Process Design	I	C	R	C	C, I	C			
Change Control	A	C		C	C, I	I	R		
End User Support	A		C		C	R		R	
End User Training	A		C		C	R		C	R
Administrator Training	A		C		C	I			R
Communications	A	C	I	C, I	C, I	I		I	

FIGURE 24.3   Sample RACI table for roles and responsibilities.

Governing the Farm

This section concentrates on the tools provided in the Central Administration site, to provide an overview of the areas the governance plan should include. References are made to other chapters in the book that provide additional detail on specific areas, because each topic can be complex. For the purposes of this chapter, governing the farm can be seen to include the Central Administration site tools and settings combined with PowerShell and stsadm command-line tools and any third-party tools from companies such as AvePoint or Quest that assist the farm administrators with their jobs. The service application tools are embedded in the Central Administration site, and these settings should be clarified in this process.

To begin with, the organization should work through the different components of Central Administration. Chapter 6, "Managing and Administering SharePoint 2010 Infrastructure," gives a thorough walkthrough of the basic management categories that are broken out in Central Administration, as follows:

- ▶ Application Management

- ▶ System Settings

- ▶ Monitoring

- ▶ Backup and Restore

- ▶ Security

- ▶ Upgrade and Migration

- ▶ General Application Settings

- ▶ Configuration Wizards

The following is a partial list of important topics for which systemwide policies and standards should be defined:

- ▶ **Site collection creation standards**—Important items to cover in governance include which templates will be used, the use of managed paths, and the creation of different content databases for site collections. In addition, the use of site quotas, and their settings, is included. The site collection administrators need to be defined for each site collection and whether self-service site creation will be allowed.

- ▶ **"Standard" service application standards**—For the required service applications, the settings should be reviewed. For example, the Search Service application has a number of settings that need to be configured, such as Content Sources, Crawl Rules, File Types, Authoritative Pages, Federated Locations, and other settings. The User Profile Storage Service application performs a vital role in synching with Active Directory, and has numerous other capabilities that can be configured, such as compiling audiences. Usage and Health Data Collection is generally considered a vital component for IT to manage and monitor farm usage. Some less-familiar service applications like the Secure Store Service application and Managed Metadata Service application should also be reviewed and tested to see whether and how they will be used in the farm.

- ▶ **"Optional" service application standards**—If SharePoint Server 2010 Enterprise is being used, a number of additional Service applications can be rolled out, including Access Service application, Excel Services Service application, PerformancePoint Service application, PowerPoint Service application, Visio Graphics Service application, and the Word Viewing Service application. The organization needs to decide which of these will be deployed, to which users, and at what point in the project. Rolling out "everything" during the initial phases of a project is generally considered ill-advised unless both the user community and IT are fairly advanced in their SharePoint skills and training is provided for resources who will be managing these tools. Figure 24.4 illustrates the range of service applications available in the Enterprise edition of SharePoint 2010.

FIGURE 24.4   Service applications in Central Administration.

Chapter 22, "Managing Metadata and Content Types in SharePoint 2010," provides insight into the power of using managed metadata in SharePoint 2010. Chapter 26, "Extending SharePoint 2010 with Excel Services, Access Services, and Visio Graphics Services," and Chapter 27, "Office Web Apps Integration with SharePoint 2010," provide additional information about the configuration options for these service applications. Chapter 30, "Business Intelligence in SharePoint 2010 with PerformancePoint Services," provides information about and examples of PerformancePoint capabilities.

▶ **Managing services on servers**—For multiserver implementations, decisions should be made concerning which services will run on which server. This can impact performance and the user experience, since overloading servers will impact their responsiveness.

▶ **Monitoring settings**—Special attention should be given to the tools in this section of the Central Administration site as they allow the farm administrators to review problems and solutions, review rule definitions, review job definitions and job status, view administrative reports, configure diagnostic logging, review information management policy usage reports, view health reports, configure usage and health data collection, and view web analytics reports. Chapter 11, "Monitoring a SharePoint 2010 Environment," provides more information about these built-in tools and provides information about Microsoft's System Center Operations Manager (SCOM) 2007 R2.

▶ **Backup and Restore**—A high-level decision to be made here is whether the native SharePoint backup and restore tools will be used or if third-party backup tools from Symantec, Commvault, AvePoint, or others will be used. If the native SharePoint tools will be used, the farm administrators need to become familiar with the use of these tools and understand their strengths and weaknesses. Although a basic service level agreement (SLA) may be separate from the governance plan, the capabilities of the tools will affect the farm administrators' ability to meet end-user requests. Chapter 10, "Backing Up and Restoring a SharePoint Environment," provides additional information about this topic, including using PowerShell for backup and restore, and backing up IIS 7 configurations.

▶ **Security**—This page provides access to tools such as the farm administrators group and its members, web application security policies, managed accounts, service accounts, blocked file types, web part security, information rights management, and whether labels, barcodes, auditing, and retention will be available for use. Chapter 15, "Implementing and Validating SharePoint Security," gives additional information about this topic.

▶ **General Application Settings**—As shown in Figure 24.5, these settings include tools such as External Service Connections, InfoPath Forms Services, Site Directory, SharePoint Designer, Search, Reporting Services, and Content Deployment. Each of these tools should be reviewed and decisions made about their configurations.

Having reviewed this list, it may sound like an overwhelming task to define how each and every component will be configured. However, it might be sufficient, based on the organizational needs, to just create a grid of which features and tools will be made available during the initial phase and not delve too deeply into the individual configurations of the tools.

Chapter 18, "SharePoint Foundation Versus SharePoint Server 2010," provides a number of charts that can easily be adapted for use in the governance plan, to provide a summary of high-level organizational decisions about which tools and features will be used and supported. For example, Table 24.1 provides a sample grid that could be used to define the decisions that are made in the area of service applications with a minimal investment of time, and without delving too deeply into the details of the configuration of each service application.

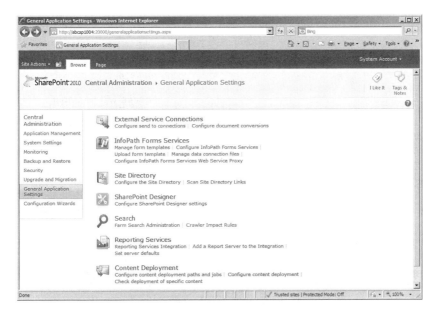

FIGURE 24.5   General Application Settings page in Central Administration.

TABLE 24.1   Governance Plan for Service Applications for Company ABC

Service Application	Provided in Phase 1	Provided in Future Phases	Notes
Access Services	No	Maybe	If it can be justified.
Application Discovery and Load Balancer Service application	Yes	Yes	
Business Data Connectivity Service	No	Maybe	If it can be justified.
Excel Services application	Yes	Yes	Finance department only.
Managed Metadata Service	Yes	Yes	This is key to the success of our SharePoint project.
PerformancePoint Service application	Yes	Yes	Easy to configure, and broadcast feature is nice.
Search Service application	Yes	Yes	
Secure Store Service	No	Yes	Need to better understand the benefits.

continues

TABLE 24.1   Continued

Service Application	Provided in Phase 1	Provided in Future Phases	Notes
Security Token Service application	Yes	Yes	
State Service	Yes	Yes	
Usage and Health Data Collection	Yes	Yes	Need to clearly define who will manage this.
User Profile Service application (including My Site)	Yes	Yes	Audiences will be important.
Visio Graphics Service	Yes	Yes	Easy to configure and use.
Web Analytics Service application	Yes	Yes	
Word Automation Services	No	No	
Word Viewing Service	Yes	Yes	Office web applications have value.

TIP

A recommended best practice for the development of governance documentation is to have a lab environment available where team members can gain experience with the Enterprise version of SharePoint 2010, where all service applications are enabled and configured. This can also be used when reviewing the site collection and site features that will be supported and also the list and library features and tools.

As mentioned previously, other chapters in this book review features at this level and can help designers and planners determine which features offer the most value to the organization and should therefore be governed.

For some organizations, the activity of reviewing the functionality can be done in the scope of a few hours; in others, this process may take months. In either case, the end result is a list of functionality that helps give shape to the governance plan in terms of which tools and features will be supported by IT and therefore need to be governed.

Another key element of the governance plan is defining the scope for which functionality will be governed. Whereas some settings are global to the farm, others are specific to the web application or the service application, and therefore can be made available to limited groups of users. This can, of course, complicate the governance process, but in most organizations, there is a demographic of users who are highly advanced and can be trusted to use more advanced functions, whereas a majority of users would simply get confused or not be interested. Being able to cater to the more advanced group is often where innovation and improvements come from. For additional granularity, features can be activated/deactivated at the site, site collection, web application, or farm level. Depending on how your organization decides to develop its taxonomy or information architecture, activate the features at the appropriate scope to simplify management. The web application and site collection level are typically a better place to manage most functions.

Governing Site Collections and Sites

Site collections and sites will require more governance than the Central Administration tools and environment because typically some of the day-to-day management of the site collections and sites is distributed to a wider group of IT staff and end users. Although some organizations do retain complete control over site and site collection settings, this is often seen to be overly heavy-handed and users, especially user with significant SharePoint experience, will push back. Furthermore, the workload will increase over time for the help desk performing menial tasks such as modifying views, tweaking .aspx pages, and changing user permissions.

Chapter 21, "Designing and Managing Pages and Sites for Knowledge Workers," provides a thorough exploration of the different tools available to the site collection administrator and the subset available to the site administrator. Figure 24.6 shows the Site Settings page when a site collection administrator logs in to a site collection where most of the site collection features have been enabled, which enable additional management tools. Not all the tools need to be included in a governance plan, but the governance plan should address several key areas:

FIGURE 24.6   Site Settings page as seen by a site collection administrator.

▶ To begin with, the question of which site collection features and site features should be enabled needs to be addressed. For example, IT may not want end users to use the legacy SharePoint 2007 workflows, PerformancePoint site collection features, Document ID Service, and in-place records management site collection features. IT might also want to turn off SharePoint Server Publishing and Hold and eDiscovery site features.

▶ Which site templates can be used to create new sites should be clarified, and "unapproved" templates should be removed so they are not used by accident. For example, the organization might want to discourage the use of the "web database" templates, such as the Assets Web Database and Charitable Contributions Web Database.

▶ Managing the site columns and content types in use can be critically important if the organization is serious about taking advantage of the metadata-oriented tools in SharePoint 2010. Ensuring that the different site collections stay in sync can be a challenge and often requires the use of custom scripts or third-party management tools.

▶ Providing an approved set of list and library templates can greatly facilitate governance because it allows site collection and site administrators to simply choose an approved template and set a couple of settings, and it can be used immediately. For example, this helps ensure that required columns are in place, managed metadata is properly leveraged, and versioning settings are consistent.

▶ Look and feel tools can dramatically affect the user experience and should also be governed to a certain extent. Approved master pages and page layouts should be set, as well as themes, navigation standards, and related standards.

▶ Site collection audit settings and report settings should be governed to ensure the appropriate events are tracked and audited and can be analyzed. Figure 24.7 shows the Configure Audit Settings page for the site collection. In this example, IT wants "everything on" so that user usage patterns can be analyzed, but they only need to retain the data for 90 days.

▶ Standards for the use of Web Analytics Reports should also be put in place. These provide reports of traffic and inventory for the site and site collection, and include search usage reports.

▶ Site collection policies provide options for enabling retention and retention stages, enabling auditing of opening or downloading documents, editing items, and checking out, moving, or deleting items. Barcodes and labels can also be enabled if used by some or all groups that use SharePoint.

▶ Record declaration settings can be important to define, as well. Once an item has been declared a record, additional restrictions and retention policies can be applied. The ability to manually declare a record can be enabled or disabled, and the declaration of records and undeclaration of records can be set to be performed by members of specific SharePoint groups.

▶ SharePoint Designer settings are used to enable SharePoint Designer 2010 use, enable detaching pages from the site definition, and enable customizing master pages and page layouts. IT might want to disable some or all of these tools.

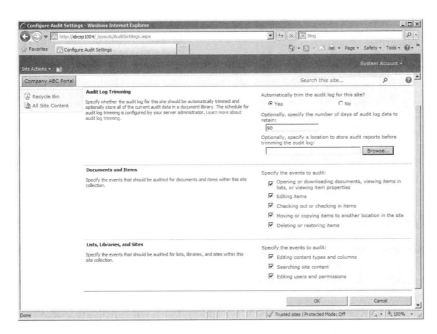

FIGURE 24.7   Configure Audit Settings page for the site collection.

These bullets give some suggestions as to areas that should be governed for sites and site collections, but this list is by no means exhaustive. Each project will be different, and each SharePoint 2010 environment will have unique purposes, so the governance plans should focus on the components and tools that are most important in the overall vision and scope of the project. Once again, without a defined vision and scope for the project, it becomes very difficult, if not impossible, to adequately govern the environment.

Records Management in SharePoint

Records management, like many of the acronyms associated with enterprise content management (ECM), can be executed in a number of different ways. SharePoint has continued to advance records management capabilities since the last release. Records management must truly begin at the business level and be carefully governed. Before determining how to use the Records Center, workflow, and notifications, the following questions should be answered:

▶ What is (and often more important, what is not) a record?

▶ What are the stages and lifecycle of the record?

▶ What are the critical requirements for the proper management of the record?

Only after these basic questions are understood at a detailed level can technology begin to enable records management within an organization. That said, once those questions have been answered, SharePoint can provide valuable tools to simplify and improve the management of business-critical records within the organization.

> **TIP**
>
> A useful exercise is to use a SharePoint list to build out a file plan that documents the types of records, lifecycle, access, and archive. Having a central file plan for key records is a proactive and strategic way to begin using SharePoint as part of a records management solution.

Records Declarations

With a new records management strategy, often a challenge for records that are not formally being managed is the declaration of when something becomes a record. The optimal situation is for the system to "know" when something is a record and then have a way to execute the proper requirements on that record. Whenever possible, look to automate the declaration of a record. Following are a few strategies for the automated, semi-automated, and manual declaration with SharePoint's records management capabilities.

Content types with associated workflows are the most flexible and likely to fit a specific requirement. The downside with this approach is that it is practical only when the declaration is something triggered in SharePoint, such as an approval or change in metadata field. Also, this approach is complex particularly if it requires integration with the systems initially generating the files that become records. Think of an ERP system that generates invoices. This method is particularly effective when there is not a person responsible for gathering, classifying, and stewarding records.

The Records Center is a site template that provides a way for users to declare records by uploading directly to the site and identifying the type of record. This method is good when a user or group of users is trained specifically on the record types and has a basic understanding of records management. The Records Center also provides a hold capability to facilitate eDiscovery.

eDiscovery can be a hugely resource-intensive activity for organizations, particularly if litigation is common for the organization. In addition to the hold capabilities with SharePoint, consider using SharePoint's search engine to search all repositories and enable select staff to then access these search results.

> **CAUTION**
>
> Indexing content of non-SharePoint content may not be able to properly prune results based on security. For eDiscovery, this may actually be beneficial because the organization is legally responsible to provide "everything," but when architecting your search environment, make sure to partition these search scopes so that they are available to only select members of the team who are gathering discoverable information.

The Governance Cycle

In the United States, Congress and the Supreme Court are constantly changing laws and passing bills in an attempt to improve the country. The government is constantly striving to improve how they govern our country. The best governance plan is one that changes and adjusts itself to the growing needs and pains. Figure 24.8 shows the cyclical nature of governance and suggests that each "component" of the plan should be regularly reviewed. A component might be taxonomy governance, for example, or site management, or service applications governance.

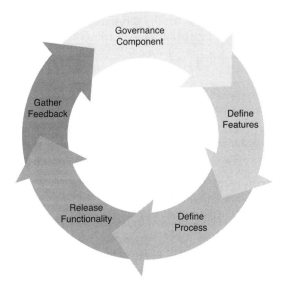

FIGURE 24.8   Cycle of governance.

Developing a mechanism to solicit user feedback and make refinements to the plan is a great way to proactively manage the application. Developing a governing board that includes application/system administrators and end users is a good way to discuss issues, requests, and build out new templates or expand features.

To be able to really take advantage of a governing board, an agenda needs to get built, and materials should be brought together. A good starting point for these meetings is a review of the usage trends, user feedback, and any issues that have arisen since the last meeting. Consider using a meeting workspace to capture agendas as well as tasks or takeaways.

Summary

A governance plan must carefully balance user innovation and freedom versus manage-ability and support. This requires that the organization "right size" the governance plan based on resources available to participate in the governance cycle and the vision and goals for the SharePoint 2010 project. Just configuring SharePoint initially is typically not sufficient. People need to review reports, gather input from end users, and perform spot checks to ensure that the rules and regulations are being followed and that they continue to map to end-user requirements. For example, the governance plan may require that IT make all changes to lists, libraries, and sites, but then find that this is stifling effective use of the SharePoint tools and so change the governance policy. And in closing, it is impor-tant to remember that taking away privileges and tools is generally more damaging than being restrictive to start with and just adding tools and capabilities over time.

Best Practices

▶ Governance includes maintenance of the SharePoint 2010 environment but extends to include policies and procedures, roles and responsibilities, and periodic review to ensure that the myriad SharePoint tools are being used in productive ways that meet the needs of management and end users.

▶ Any sized organization should have a SharePoint governance plan in place. It doesn't have to be hundreds of pages long, but should at least be defined from a high level, as suggested in this chapter, with specific roles and responsibilities defined for the tasks that should be performed.

▶ One key component of the governance plan should focus on the Central Administration site settings that will impact the tools and features made available to the site collection administrators, site administrators, and end users.

▶ An important subset of the Central Administration site settings are those that apply to the web applications that house the site collections and the service applications that IT chooses to provide to the user community.

▶ In addition, specific settings for site collections and sites should be governed, to ensure that the right combination of tools is provided to the user community. Just "turning everything on" is generally not an actionable governance plan, because many of the tools are complex to use and administer.

▶ If SharePoint is to be used for records management, the tools and processes made available by SharePoint should be governed closely.

▶ The governance plan should be reviewed periodically to ensure that it continues to meet the organization's requirements and those of the end-user community.

## CHAPTER 25

Using Office 2010 Applications with SharePoint 2010

This chapter examines key integration points between Office 2010 applications and SharePoint 2010, with a focus on using Word 2010, SharePoint Workspace 2010, and Outlook 2010 with SharePoint 2010 sites.

The intention of this chapter is to cover the topics of most interest to power users and administrators for several popular Office 2010 products, while also covering some of the enhancements available in these Office 2010 products.

Chapter 26, "Extending SharePoint 2010 with Excel Services, Access Services, and Visio Graphics Services," covers integration points between Excel 2010, Access 2010, and Visio 2010 from the same point of view of interaction with SharePoint 2010 sites. Chapter 27, "Office Web Apps Integration with SharePoint 2010," provides additional information on integration points between Office applications and SharePoint via the Office Web Apps feature.

Clearly, not all organizations will have adopted the new Office 2010 products, so this might be more informational than immediately practical, but by understanding some of the new features, organizations can better decide the pros and cons of upgrading to Office 2010 products.

A critical factor in adoption of SharePoint technologies is ease of use for end users, and a stumbling block for many end users is the process of saving documents to SharePoint document libraries. For this reason, this chapter covers several methods of adding shortcuts accessible from the Save As window. Methods are provided that will work for Windows 7 and Office 2010 users and for users of earlier versions of Office and earlier operating systems such as Vista.

Support for Earlier Versions of Office with SharePoint 2010

Microsoft has greatly enhanced the functionality and tools offered in SharePoint 2010, and it makes sense that the latest version of Office will provide the best level of integration with SharePoint 2010. This said, numerous organizations still use older versions of the Office products. This chapter provides examples of select Office 2007 product integration with SharePoint 2010 for reference purposes, but won't go further backward to older versions of the Office products (such as Office 2003, Office 2000, or XP) because of space limitations. And in keeping with its general practices, Microsoft offers a high level of support for the earlier version of Office, Office 2007. This level of support and integration will degrade as the version of Office gets older, so users of Office 2003 and earlier should test integration thoroughly with SharePoint 2010. This should also be said of support for non-Microsoft operating systems, such as the Mac OS, when using Office products.

Using Office 2007 Applications with SharePoint 2010

Microsoft offers a thorough guide on this topic, with 41 pages dedicated to the various versions of Office and the level of integration provided with SharePoint 2010: "SharePoint_2010_and_Office_2010_Business_Productivity_at_its_Best_Whitepaper.docx." This guide offers a detailed comparison of the user experience when Office 2007 products are used with SharePoint 2010 and when Office 2010 products are used with SharePoint 2010.

The following is a partial list from that white paper of the features that users *won't* get if using Office 2007 with SharePoint 2010. IT should find this useful to help determine whether any of these features would justify or help justify and upgrade to Office 2010 products.

Features available only with Office 2010 applications and SharePoint 2010 include the following:

▶ **Coauthor documents and presentations**—Word 2010 and PowerPoint 2010 offer the coauthoring capability that allows multiple people to work on one of these documents at the same time. Note that this is different from the ability in Office web applications to have multiple users work on the same spreadsheet at the same time.

▶ **Simultaneously edit spreadsheets and notebooks**—Excel 2010 and OneNote 2010 documents can be edited by multiple people simultaneously. This is discussed in more detail in Chapter 27. Excel 2010 takes advantage of Excel Services and Office web apps, whereas OneNote provides this functionality natively and doesn't require Office web apps.

▶ **Broadcast slide shows in PowerPoint 2010**—Another feature offered by Office web apps, this takes advantage of a SharePoint 2010 broadcast site, which is automatically created by Office web apps, which allows users to view a PowerPoint slide show without having PowerPoint on their desktops or using LiveMeeting, WebEx, or similar technology. This is covered in Chapter 27.

> ▶ **Office Backstage view**—This is available in Office 2010 applications when a user clicks the File tab and has access to the Backstage tools. This File tab is functionally the replacement for the Microsoft Office button.

> ▶ **Access SharePoint templates**—The New Document Wizard in Office 2010 applications enables users to select SharePoint templates that have been used previously.

> ▶ **Apply PowerPoint templates to SharePoint sites**—PowerPoint themes can be applied to SharePoint sites for basic customization and branding.

The following features are partially supported with Office 2007 applications:

> ▶ **Office Backstage view with Excel 2010**—This allows for selective publication of parts of a worksheet, to hide formulas, and "stage" data to SharePoint 2010. This can be done in Excel 2007, but the process is less intuitive.

> ▶ **Integration with Groove and SharePoint Workspace products**—SharePoint Workspace 2010 is the new version of the Groove product and provides powerful features for mobile workers, but Groove 2007 users will still have the ability to work offline with SharePoint 2010 document libraries.

25

The Basics of Saving a Word Document to a SharePoint Document Library

Users and administrators alike will want to become very familiar with the process of using Word in conjunction with SharePoint 2010 document libraries. Previous chapters have dealt in detail with the tools available in document libraries that provide users with a wide range of ways to interact with and manage their documents, specifically Chapter 19, "Using Libraries and Lists in SharePoint 2010." Although it might be somewhat repetitive, this section covers the basic steps a user needs to follow to create a new document in a document library and then populate the metadata fields and save the document.

In this example, the user has created a new document from a SharePoint 2010 document library and then accessed the File tab on the Ribbon to access Backstage. This document library has had several columns added to it that will be reviewed in the following steps.

Follow these steps to explore the capabilities of Backstage in more detail:

1. Click the new document from a document library that has had one or more choice columns added, and one or more managed metadata columns added. The assumption is that the document library uses a Word template.

2. When the new document opens, click Enable Editing if needed.

3. Enter some text in the document.

4. Click the File tab to access Backstage, which will default to the Info tab, and click the Show All Properties link in the lower-right corner. The results will look similar to Figure 25.1. The user has the option to enter metadata from the File tab or from the standard editing view of the document.

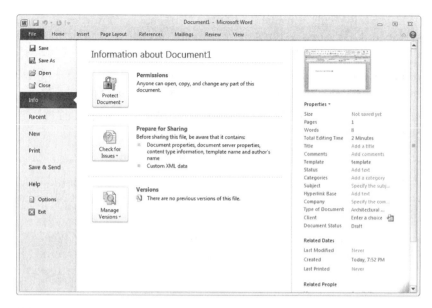

FIGURE 25.1   File tab showing the Backstage tools in Word 2010.

5. In this case, the user prefers to enter metadata from the regular editing view, so she accesses the drop-down menu titled Properties from the File tab and clicks Show Document Panel, and the Home tab opens, as shown in Figure 25.2.

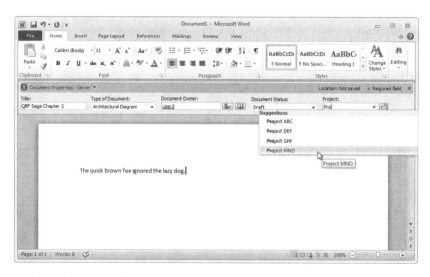

FIGURE 25.2   Populating the metadata fields in the Document Properties fields.

6. The user now enters data into the various metadata fields. In this example, those are Title (a default metadata field), Type of Document (a choice column added to the

document library), Document Owner (a person or group column added to the library), Document Status (a choice column added to the document library), and Project (a managed metadata column added to the document library).

7. In this example, when the user clicks the Type of Document drop-down menu, a message appears that informs the user "AutoComplete remembers entries in Document Information Panel and Web Forms.... Do you want to turn Autocomplete on?" She clicks Yes. This will make previously entered text available as suggestions for this and future documents.

8. She makes choices from the Type of Document drop-down, enters her own account as Document Owner, sets the Document Status at Draft, and then in the Project field, she starts typing the word **Project** and she is given options for the managed metadata values available to choose from, as also shown in Figure 25.2. She chooses Project MNO.

TIP

Depending upon the configuration of the managed metadata group, as well as the configuration of the managed metadata column, a user might be able to add values to the group from within the Office 2010 application. To try this from Word 2010, access the File tab, and click the icon next to the Managed Metadata field in the Properties section on the right side of the page (the property is Project in this example). The Select window opens, as shown in Figure 25.3. Then click Add New Item and enter the new term. For this to be functional, the term set Submission Policy must be set as Open in the Managed Metadata service application, and the column in the document library must have the Allow Fill-in setting set to Yes.

FIGURE 25.3   Adding a managed metadata entry from the File tab.

9. She then wants to save her work, so clicks the Save button.

10. The Save As window opens to the SharePoint document library where the document was created, and she enters a title and clicks Save.

Working with Backstage in Word 2010

Microsoft has repositioned the Office button and simply made it a part of the Ribbon interface, where it is now the File tab. The File tab now gives access to the Backstage page, which provides a number of tools: Save, Save As, Open, Close, Information, Recent, New, Print, Save & Send, Help, Options, and Exit. This section briefly summarizes the tools that pertain to SharePoint connectivity to help administrators and power users get a sense of how these will affect the user experience.

> **NOTE**
>
> Developers will be happy to know that the Backstage view is fully customizable by using XML to define the structure components and programming code.

A brief walk-through of the Info tab is as follows:

▶ **Protect Document drop-down menu offers a variety of tools**—Mark as Final, Encrypt with Password, Restrict Editing, Restrict Permissions by People, and Add a Digital Signature. Mark as Final, Encrypt with Password, and Restrict Editing are available without additional software, but Restrict Permissions by People requires Microsoft Information Rights Management Server, and Add a Digital Signature requires Digital Signature Services, which are available from different providers. Information Rights Management Server is covered in Chapter 17, "Safeguarding Confidential Data in SharePoint 2010." The Mark as Final tool sets the status property to Final, and typing, editing commands, and proofing marks are turned off. Users will still be able to edit the document at a future date; they just have to click the Edit Anyway button that appears under the Ribbon when the document opens.

▶ **Check for Issues menu offers three tools**—Provides the Inspect Document, Check Accessibility, and Check Compatibility tools. The Inspect Document tool checks for hidden properties or hidden information, whereas Check Accessibility looks for content that might be hard for a person with disabilities to read, and Check Compatibility checks for features not supported by earlier versions of Word. Check Compatibility will prove especially useful in environments that support multiple different versions of Office products.

▶ **Manage Versions offers up to five tools (depending on whether versioning is configured in the library that houses the document, and whether major versioning only or major and minor versioning are configured)**—These tools are Refresh Server Versions List, Check Out, Compare with Major Version, Compare with Last Version, and Recover Unsaved Documents. The Compare with Major Version and Compare with Last Version are extremely handy tools to have, and give the user a quick way to see recent changes in the document.

Additional tools that connect the Word document to the SharePoint document library can be found on the Save & Send menu. The Save & Send menu provides the Save to SharePoint tool and the Workflows section, which lists any workflows available to the document editor. The user can start a workflow listed here and then provide additional information required by the workflow.

Accessing SharePoint Templates from Word 2010

Word 2010 offers the new capability to select a template that lives in a SharePoint document library to create a document. The user must have already created a new document in a document library, which will download the template to their system, and then make the template available in Word 2010. Follow these steps to test the process:

1. Visit a SharePoint document library using an account that has contributor-level privileges. This assumes that the system has Office 2010 installed, and that the template for the document library is based on a Word document.

2. Click New Document from the Documents tab. Click OK to the warning message if needed, and Word will start using the document library template.

3. Enter some text, click Save from the File tab, and the Save As window opens.

4. Enter a document title and click Save.

5. Click the File tab, and click the New menu.

6. In the SharePoint Templates section under Available Templates, the template from the new document library should appear, as shown in Figure 25.4.

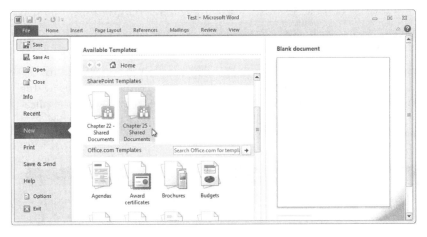

FIGURE 25.4   Choosing a template from a SharePoint document library in Word 2010.

7. Click the desired template (for example, Chapter 25 – Shared Documents), and then double-click the template icon. The template will have the metadata fields associated with the document library available.

Creating Shortcuts to SharePoint 2010

New users will be very happy if they find the process of saving documents to SharePoint easy and intuitive. And generally, users don't like always having to open a browser, find their favorite to get to SharePoint, navigate to the site they're using, find the document library, and then have to upload a document after saving it locally.

There are several ways to facilitate the process of saving documents to SharePoint by creating favorites and shortcuts. This first set of steps that follows shows how to create a shortcut by using the Connect to Office button in a document library, and the section that follows that describes how to manually create the shortcut from Windows Explorer.

Another method of creating shortcuts, which can be used on computers not using Office 2010, is to simply create a shortcut under Network Places, which is useful to know about if the SharePoint Sites folder isn't available for certain users.

> **NOTE**
>
> This section assumes Windows 7 is installed along with Office 2010

Using the Connect to Office Tool to Create Shortcuts

Users should be informed that the Connect to Office tool available on the Library tab is the easiest way to create shortcuts that will be available from Office 2010 applications via the Save As interface.

Follow these steps to use the Connect to Office feature in a SharePoint document library:

1. Visit a SharePoint document library using a computer with Office 2010 installed and an account with at least read permissions to the library.

2. Click the Connect to Office button from the Library tab, and the select Add to SharePoint sites. A message appears that states "In order to connect libraries in this site to Microsoft Office, your machine must register the user profile service application used by this site...." Click Yes; the SharePoint folder will be created under Favorites for the user, and the shortcut will be added.

> **NOTE**
>
> If Office 2007 or an earlier version of Office is installed, the Connect to Office button will be inactive.

3. Next, click the Connect to Office button again, but this time click Manage SharePoint Sites, and the MyQuickLinks page will display, showing the links available, as shown in Figure 25.5. Note that additional tools are available, including Add Link, Edit Link, Delete, and Create Tag from Link.

FIGURE 25.5   The MyQuickLinks page in Word 2010.

4. Verify that the new link appears in Word 2010 by opening Word 2010, and click the Save As button from the File tab.

5. Click SharePoint Sites from the Favorites section in the left pane, and the new SharePoint shortcut will appear. Double-click the new shortcut added in step 2, and the Save As window will now display the document library and existing contents, as shown in Figure 25.6.

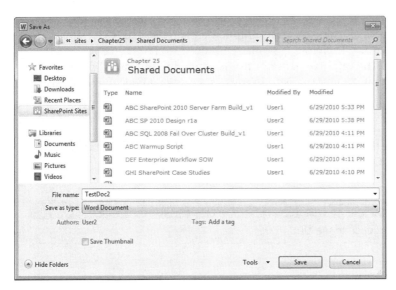

FIGURE 25.6   Accessing the SharePoint Sites folder in the Save As window in Word 2010.

6. Enter a valid filename and click Save.

NOTE

During testing, links added by using the Add Link tool on the MyQuickLinks page did not show up reliably in the SharePoint Sites folder. Let end users know that they can manually add these links by accessing the SharePoint Sites folder on their computer by following the steps in the section titled "Manually Add a Shortcut to the SharePoint Sites Folder."

Manually Add a Shortcut to the SharePoint Sites Folder

The previous section described how to add a shortcut from the Connect to Office button, but administrators might want to distribute shortcuts to end users either in bulk or on an as-needed basis. The following example assumes the SharePoint Sites folder exists under Favorites for the user, which is created when the user uses the Connect to Office button and clicks Yes to the warning that is provided (as described in the previous section):

1. Click the Start button and select Computer.

2. Double-click the SharePoint Sites folder under Favorites in the left pane.

3. Assuming there are already shortcuts in place, right-click an existing one (in this example, Chapter 25 – Shared Documents) and click Copy. Then click a blank portion of the right pane and click Paste.

4. This will paste a copy of the shortcut with the suffix - Copy. Right-click the copy and select Properties.

5. As shown in Figure 25.7, the path starts as follows: file://abcsp1004/ DavWWWRoot/sites/.... Therefore, a similar path needs to be entered for other shortcuts to work. The intuitive path of http://servername/sitename/libraryname won't work. Now, simply edit the path to the desired site and document library. In this example, the path is edited to Chapter 22 Shared Documents library or to the following complete path: file://abcsp1004/DavWWWRoot/sites/Chapter%2022/ Shared%20Documents. Then click the General tab and change the name of the shortcut to reflect the new path (in this example, to **Chapter 22 - Shared Documents**). Click OK.

NOTE

The %20 equates to a space in the URL.

6. Now double-click the new shortcut to make sure the SharePoint document library opens.

7. Open Word 2010, click the File tab, and then click Save As.

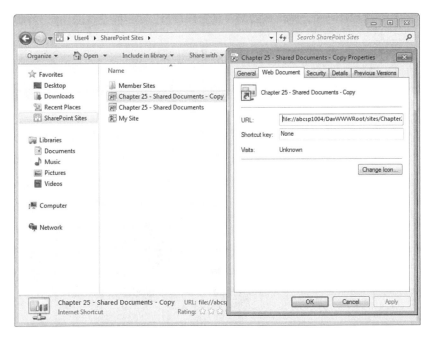

FIGURE 25.7   Manually creating a shortcut in SharePoint Sites in the Favorites folder.

8. In the Save As window, scroll down to the shortcut under Favorites, and then double-click the new shortcut (in this example, the new shortcut is Chapter 22 – Shared Documents), and verify that the file saves properly.

Manually Create a Network Location Shortcut

This method allows the end user or an administrator to create shortcuts in the My Computer Explorer Window. This is important for users who aren't on Office 2010 (for example, Office 2007 users) because they won't be able to use the Connect to Office tool from a document library—it will be inactive because Office 2007 doesn't support this level of interaction. By providing this shortcut, these users will still be easily able to save documents to SharePoint libraries.

Follow these steps to create a shortcut manually:

1. Access the Start button and click Computer.
2. Right-click in an empty section of the Explorer window in the right pane.
3. Click Add a Network Location.
4. Click Next.
5. Click Choose a Custom Network Location. Click Next.
6. Enter the URL for the SharePoint site and document library (for example, http://abcsp1004/sites/chapter25/shared documents, as shown in Figure 25.8).

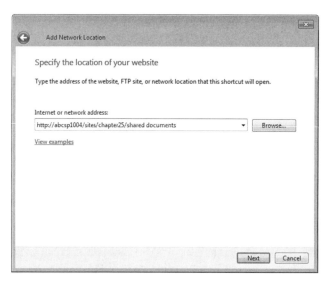

FIGURE 25.8   Manually creating a network location shortcut in Explorer.

7. Click Next and enter a name for the shortcut, such as **ABCSP1004 Chapter 25 Shared Documents**, and click Next, and then click Finish, leaving the box next to Open This Network Location When I Click Finish checked. Click Finish and verify that the document library opens.

8. Open Word and click access the Save As tool, click Computer from the left pane, and the shortcut should appear in the right pane. Double-click the shortcut and the SharePoint library will open. Provide a name for the document and click Save.

Coauthoring Word 2010 and PowerPoint 2010 Documents Stored in SharePoint 2010

End users have been clamoring for the ability to have multiple people working on the same document for many years, and SharePoint 2010 makes this possible in Word 2010 and PowerPoint 2010 with the coauthoring feature. As discussed in Chapter 27, Office Web Apps make this possible in Excel 2010, and OneNote 2010 allows this natively. Word 2010 enables users to simultaneously edit and save changes to a document that is stored on a SharePoint Foundation 2010 server or SharePoint Server 2010 server. File synchronization is accomplished via SOAP over HTTP (MS-FSSHTTP), which allows incremental upload or download of file changes and metadata changes.

To test coauthoring, two computers or virtual images with Word 2010 installed are required along with a document library housed in a SharePoint Foundation 2010 or SharePoint Server 2010 site collection. Make sure that Require Documents to Be Checked Out Before They Can Be Edited is *not* enabled in Document Library settings Versioning

Settings, because documents that are checked out cannot take advantage of coauthoring. Enable major and minor versioning to review the number of versions that were created once the exercise is complete.

Follow these steps to test coauthoring:

1. From Computer A (used by User1 in this example), navigate to the SharePoint 2010 document library (http://abcsp1004/sites/Chapter25/Shared Documents in this example). Hover over a document and select Edit in Microsoft Word from the drop-down menu. If needed, click OK to the standard warning.

2. After the document opens in Word, click the Enable Editing button under the Ribbon if needed.

3. From Computer B (used by User2 in this example), navigate to the same SharePoint document library, hover over the same document, and select Edit in Microsoft Word from the drop-down menu. If needed, click OK to the standard warning.

4. After the second document opens in Word, click the Enable Editing button under the Ribbon if needed.

5. Start editing the document from Computer A (for example, perform a find and replace of a word that appears multiple time in the document to make a number of changes) and notice that along the bottom of the Word document in the status bar, an icon will indicate that there are two people editing the document, as shown in Figure 25.9. Click the icon, and it will reveal the identities of the coauthors.

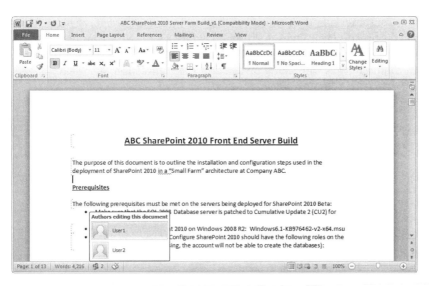

FIGURE 25.9   Viewing the identities of coauthors in Word 2010.

6. Switch over to Computer B and note that the sections that were changed by the other user are marked with the username (in this example, User1, as shown in Figure

25.10). Note in the status bar along the bottom that a message reads "This modification is not allowed because the selection is locked."

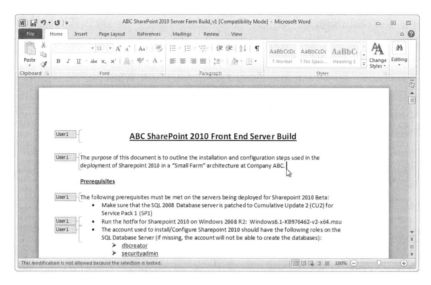

FIGURE 25.10   Error message if attempting to edit content modified by a coauthor in Word 2010.

7. Switch back to Computer A and click the Save button in the upper left, or if not available click the File tab and click Save, as shown in Figure 25.11. Note that the icon looks different than normal, and has a double arrow in it. This signifies that synchronization with multiple users will taking place upon the completion of the save.

FIGURE 25.11   Synchronizing changes by saving in Coauthor mode in Word 2010.

8. Switch to Computer B and try to edit a marked section, and note that the same message appears in the status bar.

9. Click Save from Computer B, and a message will appear stating "Word has refreshed your document with changes made by other authors. To compare the document with a previous version, click the File tab." Click OK to close the message. The changes made by the other user will be outlined in a different color to show the changes.

10. Close both documents.

11. Access the version history for the document and note that two versions were created as a result of these edits.

Additional testing with multiple users is recommended, for both Word 2010 and PowerPoint 2010. Users will soon learn that they need to perform a Save frequently to make sure they share their edits with their coauthors, and allow their coauthors to edit the sections they have changed.

Administrators should be aware that there are a number of settings that can be made with PowerShell that will perform the following changes. The following bullets list the page titles that provide the PowerShell code on the Microsoft TechNet site. Searching on these titles will bring up the pages and further instructions:

▶ **"Configure the Co-authoring Versioning Period"**—The coAuthoringVersionPeriod property determines how often SharePoint stores a version of a document that is being edited on a specific server. This is measured in minutes, and if set to zero, every change made by a new user in a different version of the document will result in a new version of the document. If the value is set to a number that exceeds the amount of editing time by a user, SharePoint Server will create just one version for the editing session.

▶ **"Configure the Maximum Number of Co-authoring Authors"**—The CoauthoringMaxAuthors property limits the maximum number of authors that can coauthor a Word or PowerPoint file at the same time on a specific server.

▶ **"Disable Co-authoring"**—The DisableCoauthoring server property disables coauthoring for Word and PowerPoint documents on a specific server.

Using SharePoint Workspace with SharePoint 2010

Formerly known as Microsoft Office Groove 2007, SharePoint Workspace 2010 provides support for existing Groove 2007 implementations and allows connectivity to SharePoint 2010 farms without any Groove infrastructure in place. SharePoint Workspace 2010 makes it easy for users to synchronize SharePoint content to the SharePoint Workspace 2010 client and have it accessible from their workstations, whether the SharePoint sites are available or not. Therefore, the product is a natural fit to the needs of "road warriors" and users who do not have continuously available connections to their SharePoint sites. This section reviews the process of loading and setting up SharePoint Workspace for the first time and the synchronization process and reviews several of the main tools available in the Workspaces and the Launchbar interfaces.

CAUTION

The term *workspace* can become confusing because "workspaces" can be created from SharePoint 2010 sites for meetings or document sharing and are specialized SharePoint sites. Workspaces created from the SharePoint Workspace 2010 tool are local filesets on the end users' computers that allow them to synchronize lists and libraries and work with the data offline. So, IT should be clear about the differences between the workspace sites that can be created from SharePoint 2010 and the "workspaces" that are created by using the SharePoint Workspace 2010 tool, because they are very different.

There are other ways of taking SharePoint 2010 content offline, including syncing to Outlook or to an Access database, but SharePoint Workspace provides the most versatility and tools specifically designed to manage the various situations that arise for mobile workers.

Follow these steps to synchronize a list to SharePoint Workspace 2010:

1. Access a SharePoint 2010 list or library with data in it. In this example, the list is titled Sales and Issues. Note that not all lists and libraries can be synchronized with SharePoint Workspace 2010.

2. Click the List tab, and then click Sync to SharePoint Workspace.

3. If this is the first time SharePoint Workspace has been used on the computer, the Account Configuration Wizard will open. Then follow steps 4 and 5. If not, skip to step 6.

4. In most scenarios, especially for testing, the user simply clicks Create a New Account, but the Restore an Existing Account option may be appropriate if the user already has an account created and doesn't want to end up with multiple accounts. The GRV file for the existing account will need to be available from this computer to perform the restore. For the purposes of testing, and this example, click Next.

5. Leave the circle next to Create the Account Using Your E-Mail Address checked and click Finish. SharePoint Workspace will open. The other option is to use the Create the Account Using an Account Configuration Code, but this is available only if Groove Server 2010 Manager is in use, because it creates and manages those codes.

6. Click OK on the Sync to SharePoint Workspace window, and the sync process will start. Click Open Workspace when the process completes.

7. Figure 25.12 shows the workspace where a number of tabs and tools are available that make it possible to interact with the data.

To synchronize a complete site with SharePoint Workspace 2010, follow these steps:

1. Access a SharePoint 2010 site with lists and libraries that have content. Access the Site Actions drop-down and click Sync to SharePoint Workspace.

2. A window opens, asking for confirmation to sync to your computer. Note that there is a Configure button that allows access to the specific settings to determine the

level of synchronization that will take place. The options are All Items, Headers Only, or No Content. Figure 25.13 shows an example where User1 clicked the Configure button and then selected several lists and libraries and selected No Content from the drop-down menu. Click OK to start the syncing process.

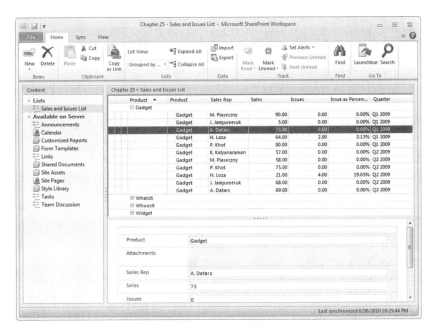

FIGURE 25.12   SharePoint Workspace showing data from a SharePoint list.

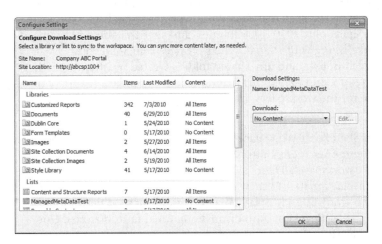

FIGURE 25.13   Configure Settings interface when synchronizing a whole site to SharePoint Workspace 2010.

> **NOTE**
>
> The Configure Settings window also lists the lists and libraries that cannot be synced, which include Calendars, Site Pages libraries and other specialty lists such as the Whereabouts list, and Phone Memos list.

3. A status window will show the sync progress for each list and library. There is also an Errors tab to consult if errors are encountered. Click Open Workspace when the process is complete.

> **NOTE**
>
> Errors are often the result of insufficient permissions on the SharePoint site, list, or library. For example, if a document is edited in a document library in SharePoint Workspace, and then the user clicks the Sync button from the Sync tab, an error will occur if the user account doesn't have the required permissions in the library. A Resolve tab will appear, and it provides tools to rectify the error.

A full complement of tools are now available for the lists and libraries, including adding new list items or documents, cut and paste capabilities, Copy as Link tool (which copies the URL of the item to include the SharePoint server name and location), Download tool (useful if only the headers of items have been synced initially), Save As, Properties, Versions, Check Out, Check In tools, Mark Unread, Set Alerts, Launchbar, and Search tools.

The Launchbar button loads the Launchbar interface, as shown in Figure 25.14, which is a smaller interface that allows access to workspaces and contacts. The Launchbar is an efficient interface to use for viewing the available SharePoint workspaces and shared folders the user has access to. Any SharePoint 2010 lists, libraries, and sites that are synchronized will show up in this interface, along with shared folders created from SharePoint Workspace 2010 by the logged-in user, and any shared folders created by other users that the logged-in user was invited to, and the confirmation process completed. A variety of different views are available for the workspaces, including Alphabetical, Folders, Last Unread Time, Status, and Type.

Alerts are quite powerful in SharePoint Workspace 2010 and offer some additional options to SharePoint alerts. Clicking the Set Alerts button allows the user to set an alert level for the list/library of the "tool" (workspace). These levels include Inherit (inherit the workspace settings), Off (don't display an alert for new or modified content), Medium (highlight unread content with an icon), High (display an alert for new of modified content), and Auto (similar to the high alert level but auto-dismisses ignored unread alerts). One complaint about SharePoint alerts is the fact that they result in emails, and busy users can find them irritating, so SharePoint Workspace provides an alternative to using SharePoint list- and library-based alerts, which some users find preferable. Users can also select the alert sound that plays or can upload their own.

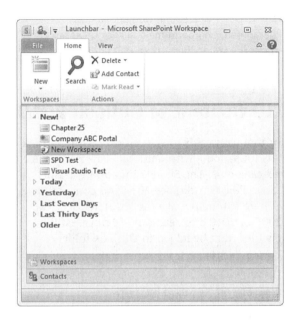

FIGURE 25.14   SharePoint Workspace Launchbar.

The Mark Unread tool allows the user to mark selected entries, an entire list or library, or a whole workspace as unread, which will place a green icon next to the unread items, and the Launchbar will reflect this status.

The Sync tab provides access to the Sync, Change Sync Settings, and Sync Status buttons. These tools make it very easy for the user to just sync one list or library (by clicking Sync Tool) or the whole workspace (by clicking Sync Workspace) and then see the sync status as the process takes place. The Change Sync Settings button provides an option to disconnect a list or library from the server if needed.

The View tab provides access to tools that allow the user to show or hide the Content pane, change the view being applied to the list data (assuming the SharePoint list or library has multiple views to use), and the New Window button. The New Window button allows access to the New Workspace tool, which opens a new instance of SharePoint Workspace, and New Selected Tool button, which opens the list or library in its own window. There is also a Reading Pane button for a list that makes it very easy to modify list items and properties.

NOTE

SharePoint Workspace 2010 also allows users to create Groove workspaces, if Groove Server is installed in the environment, and shared folders. Shared folders can be created on the user's desktop or other location, and once created the user can invite other users and manage the shared folders similarly to other SharePoint workspaces by adding and managing alerts, marking them as unread, and performing similar tasks. This enables users to quickly share files without uploading them to SharePoint libraries or creating SharePoint workspaces.

Connecting SharePoint 2010 Content to Outlook 2010

Another option for taking content offline for mobile users is to synchronize with Outlook 2010 or 2007. This section reviews the process for syncing with Outlook 2010 initially for document libraries and then for task lists and calendars. The SharePoint administrator should understand the differences between SharePoint Workspace 2010 and connecting content to Outlook, and the example shown here will help make these differences clear. For example, files downloaded to Outlook 2007 or 2010 are "read-only," but can still be edited by following the steps listed here. New files can't be added to Outlook folders synchronized with SharePoint document libraries, although tasks and calendar items can be added from Outlook.

To begin with, follow these steps to take a library offline in Outlook 2010:

1. Navigate to a document library in SharePoint 2010 that contains one or more Word documents using an account with at least contributor-level permissions and access the Library tab.

2. Click the Connect to Outlook button.

3. A message appears, asking "Do you want to allow this website to open a program on your computer?" Click Allow.

4. Outlook 2010 opens (if not open already), and a message appears, asking for confirmation to Connect This SharePoint Document Library to Outlook. Click Yes.

NOTE

There is an Advanced button available from the confirmation window. If clicked, it allows the user to change the folder name or add a description to the folder. Another option is to not display this list on other computers I use, and there is an option to update this subscription with the publisher's recommendation. Typically, these settings are left on their defaults.

5. The folder is then created in Outlook 2010 under the SharePoint lists node, and the content will synchronize. Assuming the documents are standard Office documents, previews will be available in the preview pane, as shown in Figure 25.15.

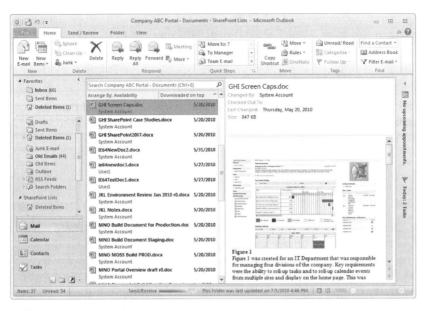

FIGURE 25.15   Results of using the Connect to Outlook tool from a document library in Outlook 2010.

NOTE

Outlook 2007 provides similar functionality with document library synchronization to SharePoint 2010.

---

6. Double-click one of the Word documents, and a message appears, asking "Would you like to open the file or save it to your computer?" Click Open.

7. The document opens in read-only mode. Click Edit Offline.

8. A window opens, informing the user that the document will be stored in the SharePoint Drafts folder. Click OK.

9. Make some edits to the document, and then click Save.

10. Next, access the File menu and click Exit. A message opens, stating "You are currently offline. Would you like to try to update the server with your offline changes?" Click Update.

11. Return to the document library in SharePoint 2010 and verify that the changes were saved to the document edited by clicking the document and viewing the document. Close the document.

12. Return to Outlook 2010, and with the SharePoint folder still active, click an item, and click Delete. A message appears, stating "This SharePoint list is read-only in Outlook."

13. Right-click the same document and select Remove Offline Copy. The document will then appear in a group titled Available for Download. After the next synchronization, the documents will be synchronized, so this is a temporary setting.

14. Next, try to drag and drop a document from a local folder to the Outlook 2010 folder, and note that it does not complete.

15. Try right-clicking the item on the local computer and clicking Copy, and then try right-clicking in the SharePoint connected folder, and note that the option to Paste is not provided. This illustrates that even if the account in use has owner-level privileges in the document library, items cannot be created in the connected Outlook folder.

Connecting Task Lists to Outlook 2010

Assuming that the user has completed the previous section, the process of taking content offline from a SharePoint document library should be clear. It is encouraged that the administrator or end user also test taking a Tasks list offline by following the previous steps, but on a Tasks list that has items in it. As shown in Figure 25.16, the list will show up along with other Tasks lists, not under the SharePoint Lists section from the Mail view. The user can interact with tasks, whether to Mark Complete, Remove from List, or change the data associated with the tasks. Tasks can also be dragged from the SharePoint Tasks list to the individual's Tasks list in Outlook and vice versa, which will make a copy of the task in the other task folder, and result in the task being added to the SharePoint Tasks list if a personal task is dragged to the SharePoint Tasks list in Outlook 2010.

FIGURE 25.16   Results of opening a Tasks list in Outlook 2010.

> **NOTE**
>
> Outlook 2007 provides similar functionality with task synchronization to SharePoint 2010 Tasks lists.

Connecting Calendars to Outlook 2010

Assuming that the user has completed the previous sections, the process of taking content offline from a SharePoint list should be clear, and as with Tasks lists, the administrator or end user should also gain experience with the process of connecting Calendar lists to Outlook 2010. The steps are similar to a Tasks list, and the ability of end users to drag a SharePoint calendar item to their personal calendar is the same, and to drag a personal event to the SharePoint calendar. This is an extremely useful capability because it enables end users to connect to SharePoint calendars and drag and drop their personal events, such as vacations, to a shared SharePoint calendar so the whole team will know about it. Likewise, the users can drag events from the SharePoint calendar to their personal calendar so that they can set reminders on those events and have them show up on personal calendars and mobile devices.

> **CAUTION**
>
> An important difference to point out between Outlook 2007 integration with SharePoint 2010 calendars and Outlook 2010 is the "glitch" in Outlook 2007, where an event can be dragged from one date to a different date. For example, an event scheduled for 7/19 could be dragged from a connected SharePoint 2010 calendar to an individual's personal calendar to a different date, such as 7/18, resulting in scheduling nightmares! Outlook 2010 has fixed this issue, but administrators and power users should be aware of it in Outlook 2007.

Creating Meeting Workspaces from Outlook 2007 and Outlook 2010

A feature loved by many users and disliked by many administrators in Outlook 2007 is the ability to create a meeting workspace from a meeting request. Savvy end users found this to be an easy way to create a workspace on a SharePoint site at the same time that they were setting the time and date, physical location, and inviting users to the event. This process is worth reviewing because it is still available in Outlook 2010, just hidden by default.

To create a meeting workspace from Outlook 2007, follow these steps:

1. Using an account that has appropriate permissions to create sites in SharePoint 2010, open Outlook 2007 (*not* Outlook 2010; that is covered in the next section).

2. From Outlook 2007, access the calendar and click the New menu, and select Meeting Request (*not* Appointment, because that doesn't provide the Workspace option).

3. Enter one or more users in the To field (in this example, **User1** and **User3** are entered because they are being invited to a meeting being scheduled by User2), and a Subject

(in this example, **Strategy**), and a Location (in this example, **Redwood Room**). Choose a start time and date in the future.

4. Click the Meeting tab if not active, and the Meeting Workspace icon should be available. Click the Meeting Workspace tab, and the Meeting Workspace tool pane will open on the right.

5. The Meeting Workspace pane may be populated with default workspace creation information if a workspace has been created by this user in the past. If so, click the Change Settings link to modify/review the settings. Alternatively, if no workspaces have been created by the user, there will be a different pane visible that allows the user to Select a Location and Select a Workspace, as shown in Figure 25.17.

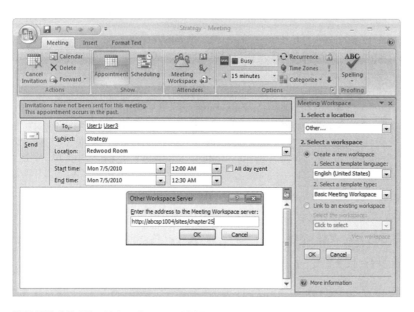

FIGURE 25.17   Using Outlook 2007 to create a meeting workspace in SharePoint 2010 (1 of 2).

6. In the Select a Location drop-down menu, choose Other, and then enter the URL of the site collection and site that will house the workspace, as also shown in Figure 25.17. Click OK.

7. In the Meeting Workspace pane, in the Select a Workspace section, make sure Create a New Workspace is checked, and then choose Basic Meeting Workspace. Then click OK.

8. The pane will change, and a Create button will be visible. Click the Create button, and the workspace will be created (assuming the user has sufficient rights), and the

invitation will now include the link to the workspace and some descriptive informa-tion, as shown in Figure 25.18.

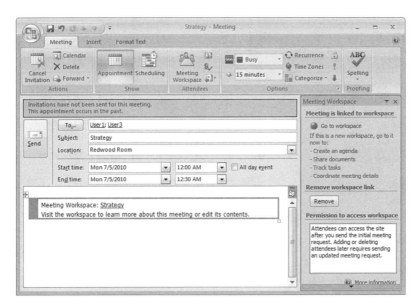

FIGURE 25.18   Using Outlook 2007 to create a meeting workspace in SharePoint 2010 (2 of 2).

9. Click Send to send the invite.

This workspace can now be accessed by the invitees, and will show whether they've accepted the invitations. It can be used to track objectives of the meeting, the agenda, and have supporting documents uploaded to it.

Modifying Outlook 2010 to Allow Creation of Meeting Workspaces

Oddly, this feature is harder to access in Outlook 2010, which no doubt is due to feedback that Microsoft received about hiding this feature by default, and then either having IT educate users on how to enable the feature or leave users to research the steps on their own.

Follow these steps to enable meeting workspace creation in Outlook 2010:

1. From Outlook 2010, click New Meeting.

2. The New Meeting window will open. Click the Customize Quick Access drop-down menu in the upper-left corner of the invitation. Click More Commands.

3. Locate Meeting Workspace in the list of commands, and click the Add button, and it will appear in the right pane, as shown in Figure 25.19. Then click OK.

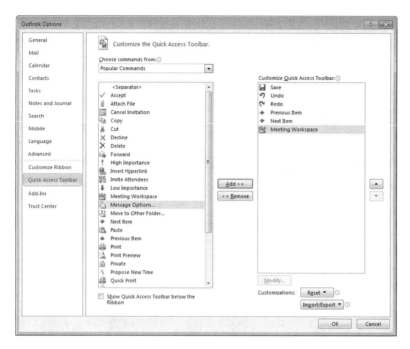

FIGURE 25.19   Configuring Outlook 2010 to allow the creation of meeting workspaces from the Quick Access toolbar.

4. Now the Meeting Workspace icon will be visible from the Quick Access toolbar at the top of the invitation. Follow the steps in the previous section to create a workspace from Outlook 2010 at this point.

Summary

This chapter covered a number of the key integration points between Office 2010 and SharePoint 2010. Not every feature could be covered in the space of one chapter, but a number of key topics were covered, such as the basics of using Word 2010 and SharePoint 2010, the newly branded Office Backstage tool, along with different methods of creating shortcuts that enable end users to quickly save documents to SharePoint document libraries. In addition, the coauthoring capabilities of Word 2010 and PowerPoint 2010 were covered, the basics of using SharePoint Workspace 2010, and finally a number of oft-used features in Outlook 2010 that allow users to connect lists and libraries to Outlook 2010. Some notes were provided about the 2007 versions of these products, but just from a high level, and power users and IT should test earlier versions carefully to ensure the end-user experience will be acceptable.

Best Practices

▶ The Backstage view is another name for the File tab on the Ribbon, but it provides access to an important set of tools for end users, as outlined in this chapter. Metadata can be applied from this area, workflows can be started, and the Backstage view can be customized to meet specific business requirements.

▶ It is important to make sure that the process of saving documents to the SharePoint 2010 document libraries is a smooth process, and several methods of adding shortcuts were provided: Using the Connect to Office button in document libraries for Office 2010 users, manually adding links to the SharePoint Sites folder in Favorites for Office 2010 users, and manually creating a network location for users of other versions of Office and other operating systems.

▶ Coauthoring is a feature available in Word 2010 and PowerPoint 2010 and allows multiple users to edit files at the same time. If a Word 2010 or PowerPoint 2010 file is checked out, coauthoring won't function, so checkouts can't be required in the document libraries.

▶ Coauthoring can be configured on a server basis by using PowerShell with several commandlets. The coAuthoringVersionPeriod determines how often SharePoint will save changes, whereas CoauthoringMaxAuthors determines the maximum number of simultaneous authors, and DisableCoauthoring will disable the functionality for the server.

▶ SharePoint Workspace 2010 provides powerful tools that allow users to decide which lists and libraries they want to be able to take offline and work with when they don't have SharePoint connectivity. Note that not all lists and libraries can sync to SharePoint Workspace 2010, so testing this should be taken into account when advising users on appropriate usage with the SharePoint 2010 environment.

▶ Outlook 2007 and 2010 can be connected to SharePoint 2010 in a number of ways. First, lists and libraries can be connected to Outlook when a user is accessing the list or library and clicks Connect to Outlook. Capabilities vary, as covered in this chapter, but this allows users to have copies of their list and library contents with them when they can't access SharePoint 2010 directly. Subtle variations in functionality between Outlook 2007 and 2010 are pointed out, and additional testing should take place to ensure that IT is ready to support the end users.

▶ Outlook 2010 and Outlook 2007 can be used to create meeting workspaces when a meeting is scheduled. Note that this is not available if the New Appointment tool is used. Also note that in Outlook 2010, the Quick Access toolbar must be modified to show the Meeting Workspace icon, which allows creation of the meeting workspace before the invitation is sent.

25

Extending SharePoint 2010 with Excel Services, Access Services, and Visio Graphics Services

The Service Applications covered in this chapter are available only in the SharePoint Server 2010 Enterprise edition, but provide a variety of tools and capabilities that will be of interest to organizations who are already familiar with the SharePoint "basics" and want to provide more powerful tools in the areas of managing spreadsheets and integrating Access databases and Visio diagrams with their SharePoint environment.

Note that this chapter focuses on Excel 2010, Access 2010, and Visio 2010, so organizations should test the capabilities of earlier versions of these products to ensure they meet the requirements of the application.

The "Excel Services" section provides examples that will give the administrator or power user a better sense of the capabilities and limitations of Excel Services. The "Access Services" section walks through the creation of a site using an Access Web Database template, and the "Visio Services" section provides a brief overview of the capabilities of the tool, which allows browser-based viewing of Visio diagrams.

Working with Excel Data in SharePoint 2010

Integration between Excel spreadsheets and SharePoint has been a hot topic for years, and Microsoft has provided a number of methods to integrate the two products. This section reviews some different basic methods of working with Excel data in SharePoint to prepare for additional discussions around Excel Services.

To begin with, a SharePoint list has many similarities with an Excel spreadsheet, so many organizations simply move the content from the spreadsheet to SharePoint by creating a list; replicating the column headings, order, and type of content; and then cutting and pasting from the worksheet into the SharePoint list. This is a fairly painstaking process, so many users instead use the Import Spreadsheet template. After the user specifies the spreadsheet to import and then selects the range of cells, SharePoint creates a list and does its best to choose column types to match the columns in the spreadsheet. Although not always perfect (and the administrator or power user should verify the column settings to make sure they do in fact match the type of content in the columns), this is a quick way to pull Excel content into SharePoint and then allow users to collaborate on the data.

In this situation, there is no connectivity between the SharePoint list and the source spreadsheet. And the SharePoint list doesn't provide all the "bells and whistles" that Excel provides, so the SharePoint list users might find themselves exporting content back out to Excel using the Export to Excel tool in the list. This process is a bit more "sticky" as a connection will be established between the SharePoint list and Excel 2010, but it is a one-way connection. The content in the spreadsheet can be updated by clicking Refresh All from the Design Tab, and any changes in the SharePoint list will be synced to the local copy of the spreadsheet.

These are certainly valid processes and are used frequently, and Excel Services offers an alternative that provides a different set of tools and features, which are discussed in the following sections.

Getting to Know the Excel Services Service Application

From a high level, Excel Calculation Services (Excel Services) is a shared service in SharePoint 2010 Enterprise that allows users to publish Excel workbooks to a document library. Excel Services can open workbooks from SharePoint libraries as well as from UNC paths and HTTP websites. For initial testing purposes, it is generally recommended to start with SharePoint library-based workbooks and then extend to other sources.

This is not meant to replace the other means of making Excel data available in SharePoint 2010 as outlined in the previous section, but is meant as a means of managing and securing the workbooks and publishing content through the SharePoint interface. For example, if Company ABC wants to make their Product Sales Spreadsheet available to all users in the organization so that they can input their personal sales information, Excel Services would not be the best way to do this. Rather, the manager, who wants to leverage SharePoint technologies, would ask users to update a SharePoint list (such as Product Sales List) and then review the information to ensure it was accurate. The manager would then export this content to create a spreadsheet, add graphs for ease of analysis, and then publish it using Excel Services. This example is shown in action later in this chapter.

Before the process of publishing using Excel Services is reviewed, the Excel Services service application will be reviewed from a high level because it is important for the farm administrator to understand the different tools available for configuring and managing the Excel Services service application before opening it up to users for testing purposes.

Excel Services was introduced in SharePoint 2007, and there are a number of new features in the product, including the following:

- Excel Services is now a service application, and as such is more manageable and customizable than it was in SharePoint 2007, where it was part of the shared services provider.

- Excel Services now leverages PowerShell for management instead of the stsadm tool.

- REST API: The REST API is a client/server software architecture/protocol that uses hyperlinks and lets the user access entities (such as ranges and charts) in workbooks using Excel Services through HTTP and also provides a method for users to set values in these ranges, including single cells.

- JSOM or ECMAScript (JScript or JavaScript object model): ECMAScript enables syndication, mash-ups, automation of Excel Services, and the extension of Excel Services by third parties. It also provides a subset of Microsoft Excel Web Access functionality that lets an administrator or developer insert JavaScript code on a web page to affect range navigation, cell values, and other grid operations.

Managing the Excel Service Application

Most SharePoint Server 2010 Enterprise installations will contain an Excel Services service application. If a new service application is needed, it can be created from the Manage Service Applications page on the Central Administration site. The details of each configuration will vary based on the needs of the organization, and the settings for the service application are discussed here from a high level.

A number of tools allow farm administrators to manage the instance of Excel Services, as shown in Figure 26.1. Each of these tools will be important for more complex Excel Services configurations, whereas the farm administrator can most likely leave them at their default settings for simpler implementations where the workbooks are stored in SharePoint libraries and don't contain connections to external content.

The Global Settings tool provides access to a number of settings that will be essential to have configured properly if content not stored in SharePoint libraries is being accessed. The configuration details will vary based on a number of factors, such as whether there is a dedicated Excel Services front-end server (in which case, more resources can be dedicated to the Excel Services service application) or if Excel Services is sharing a front-end server with numerous other services applications. Also the location of the data being connected to will affect these settings. For reference purposes, here are the items that can be configured:

- **Security settings**—File Access Method (Impersonation or Process Account), Connection Encryption (Not Required or Required), Allow Cross Domain Access (Yes/No). File Access Method settings have no effect when users try to access content stored in SharePoint 2010 libraries, only when the workbooks are stored in UNC or HTTP locations. Connection encryption supports Secure Sockets Layer (SSL) and IPsec.

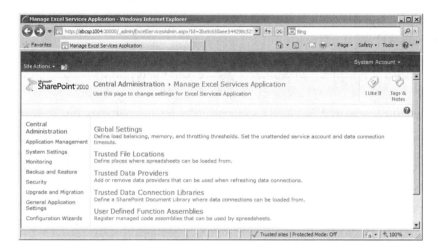

FIGURE 26.1 Excel Services service application management tools.

CAUTION

In most SharePoint 2010 deployments where front-end servers and Excel Calculation Services application servers run on different computers, impersonation will require Kerberos delegation.

▶ **Load-balancing options**—Workbook URL, Round Robin, with Health Check or Local.

▶ **Session management**—Maximum Sessions per User.

▶ **Memory utilization**—Maximum Private Bytes, Memory Cache Threshold, and Maximum Unused Object Age.

▶ **Workbook cache**—Location, Maximum Size of Workbook Cache, and Caching of Unused Files.

▶ **External data settings**—Connection Lifetime, and ability to specify an application ID for the Unattended Service Account.

The Unattended Service Account option allows the farm administrator to specify the Application ID of a Target Application ID that needs to be configured in the Secure Store service application. The Target Application ID is provided with credentials and a password, administrators are configured, and a key is generated for it. This Target Application ID is then used as a "get data" type of account when a workbook is loaded that contains a data connection for the unattended account, and it is required when a workbook connection specifies None for authentication.

Additional tools available from the Manage Excel Services Application page include the following:

▶ **Trusted File Locations**—These are the file locations that are considered "trustworthy," and Excel workbooks can be published to these locations. By default, the address http:// is considered trusted along with children sites, but this can be changed (for example, to only include the Accounting Department's site or other site or site collection).

▶ **Trusted Data Providers**—A number of data providers that can be used for external data sources in Excel workbooks are already provided, and new ones can be defined using the data provider types OLE DB, ODBC, or ODBC DSN.

▶ **Trusted Data Connection Libraries**—By default, there won't be any trusted data connection libraries, so a farm administrator will need to add them. First use the Data Connection Library template to create the library, and then click Add Trusted Data Connection Library, and then enter the URL of the library.

▶ **User Defined Function Assemblies**—The Microsoft.Office.Server.WebAnalytics.UI user-defined function assembly (UDF) is here by default, and is used to get Web Analytics report data.

26

Stsadm commands (such as Add-ecsfiletrustedlocation, Add-ecssafedataprovider) are no longer supported against Excel Services in SharePoint 2010. Fortunately, an error will be displayed in the command prompt if an administrator tries to run one of these commands. The error states: "Error. This stsadm command is no longer supported. Use PowerShell to modify Excel Services Application settings from the command line." The cmdlets are listed in full on TechNet: http://technet.microsoft.com/en-us/library/ee906545.aspx.

Publishing to Excel Services

This example provides a walk-through of exporting a SharePoint list to an Excel 2010 spreadsheet, and then publishing that content using Excel Services. This replicates the example offered in the previous section titled "The Excel Services Service Application," where a manager asks his employees to update a SharePoint list with sales data, and then he exports this to Excel 2010, edits it, and then publishes back to SharePoint 2010 using Excel Services. The home page for the site is then edited to include an Excel Web Access web part that links to the published content.

This example helps to clarify the full process of publishing using Excel Services and then exposing the data using the Excel Web Access web part, so administrators and power users can get a sense for what is and isn't possible using Excel Services. This is just "scratching the surface," and administrators and power users should feel free to then experiment with publishing other Excel workbooks using Excel Services and learning what is and isn't supported in the publishing process.

Prerequisites for this example include the following:

▶ SharePoint 2010 Enterprise must be installed and an Excel Services service application must be configured and working for the site where the lists live.

▶ A workstation with Excel 2010 must be available.

> **NOTE**
>
> Excel 2007 allows users to publish to SharePoint 2010 document libraries using Excel Services, but the steps will differ from this example and overall functionality will be different.

The site that will be used needs to have a custom list that will be described next, as well as a document library that doesn't need any special configuration settings. The site used in this example is http://abcsp1004/sites/Chapter26.

To walk through this example, follow these steps:

1. Create a Product Sales list with using the custom List template that contains the columns and settings described in Table 26.1.

TABLE 26.1   Product Sales List Columns and Settings

Column	Data Type	Require That This Column Contains Information
Title (change name of column to Invoice Number)	Single Line of Text (already present) Set Enforce Unique Values to Yes	Yes
Salesperson	Person or Group	Yes

TABLE 26.1   Continued

Column	Data Type	Require That This Column Contains Information
Product	Choice (enter choices of Widget and Gadget)	Yes
Quantity Sold	Number	Yes
Month of Sale	Choice (enter choices of January and February)	Yes

2. Add several items to this list so that there will be enough data to create charts from (for example, data for several different salespeople for different products sold in different months). An example of the resulting list is shown in Figure 26.2. This simulates a simplified tracking tool that salespeople use to enter their sales into a list that the manager will then verify, analyze, and publish in Excel Services.

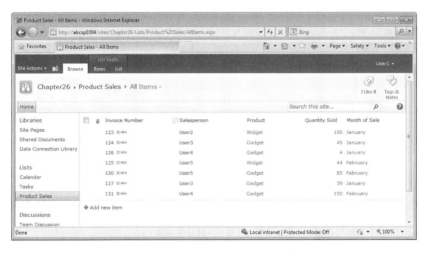

FIGURE 26.2   Custom list to use for Excel Services test.

3. Click the List tab on the Ribbon and select Export to Excel button.

4. Click Open when the File Download window opens.

5. Click Enable when the Microsoft Excel Security Notice window opens. This enables data connections between the computer and SharePoint 2010, which are required to update the content of the workbook at a later time.

6. Excel will open and display the content similar to what is shown in Figure 26.3. Actual values will vary based on what was entered in the SharePoint Product Sales list. At this point, there is still connectivity between the SharePoint list and the Excel workbook, as you can see on the Design tab on the Ribbon, which shows the Refresh button that will refresh the content from the SharePoint 2010 list.

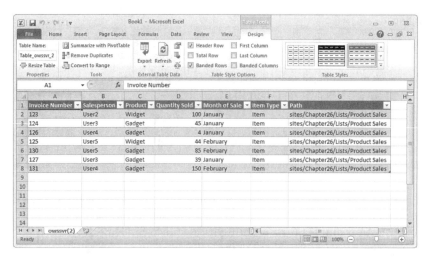

FIGURE 26.3   Product Sales list exported to Excel 2010.

7. Click the File tab in Excel, then Save As, and save the workbook to a local folder on the computer as **Product Sales Local Copy** and click Save. This reflects the manager's desire to save the workbook locally so that he can edit it before he publishes it using Excel Services.

8. Navigate back to the Product Sales list in SharePoint and change a value, such as the product sold for a specific entry. This simulates the manager spotting an error in the spreadsheet and fixing it in the list.

9. Return to the spreadsheet and make sure the Data tab is active and click the drop-down arrow under the Refresh All icon and select Refresh All. Verify that the spreadsheet changes to reflect the change in the SharePoint list.

10. Still in Excel, click the Design tab (if not visible, click any cell that contains data in the table) and check the value of the table name in the Table Name field in the Properties section of the Ribbon on the left. It will be something similar to Table_owssvr_3. Change this to **Table_1**.

11. Right-click the tab at the bottom of the screen and rename the active tab as **Sales Numbers**. These small changes make the workbook easier to deal with when it is published using Excel Services.

12. Next, a pivot chart will be added for more interactive analysis of the data. Click the Insert tab on the Ribbon and then the PivotTable drop-down menu and select PivotChart.

13. The Create PivotTable with PivotChart window opens. The Table/Range field should be active, and have the blinking text entry cursor in it. Click and drag to select the range of cells that includes the content under the Salesperson, Product, Quantity Sold, and Month of Sale columns, as shown in Figure 26.4. This selects a subset of the data contained in the table but leaves out the Invoice Number column, as well as Item Type column and Path column.

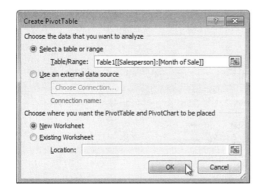

FIGURE 26.4   Selecting a data range for a PivotChart in Excel 2010.

14. Verify that New Worksheet is selected in the Choose Where You Want the PivotTable and PivotChart to Be Placed section. Click OK.

15. A new worksheet will open, and the PivotTable Field List tool pane will be open on the right side of the screen. Check the Salesperson, Product, Quantity Sold, and Month of Sale check boxes in the Choose Fields to Add to Report Field, as shown in Figure 26.5.

16. Close the PivotTable Field list pane.

17. Click the Save button to save the changes locally.

18. Now the manager is ready to publish the workbook to a SharePoint document library using Excel Services. To accomplish this, click the File tab on the Ribbon, and then click Save & Send.

19. Click Save to SharePoint from the Save & Send section, and then click Publish Options button on the right side of the screen, as shown in Figure 26.6.

20. The Publish Options window will open. From the Show tab, access the drop-down menu and choose Items in the Workbook.

21. From the list of items that appears, select the Chart (Chart1 in this example) and PivotTable (PivotTable2 in this example) and uncheck the table (Table 1) if checked, as shown in Figure 26.7. Click OK. These are the items in the workbook that will be published to Excel Services and be available for use in the Excel Web Access web part, whereas the table will not be.

22. Back on the Save & Send screen, scroll to the bottom of the page and click Save As.

26

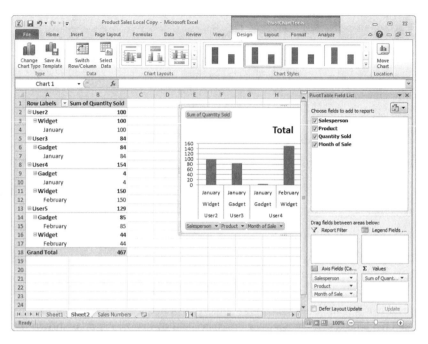

FIGURE 26.5   Selecting fields to add to the report.

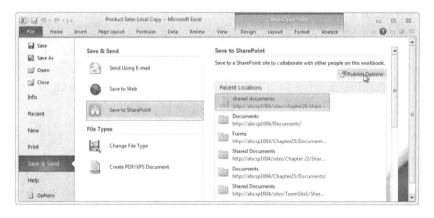

FIGURE 26.6   Save & Send page in Excel 2010.

23. The Save As window opens. Enter in the URL of the document library that the workbook will be published to, as shown in Figure 26.8. Change the name of the document to **Product Sales Q1**, verify that Open with Excel in the browser is checked, and then click Save.

24. A browser window will open and display the published items from the workbook in the browser, as shown in Figure 26.9. Access the drop-down menu next to View in the upper-right corner to switch to the PivotTable to validate both components have published.

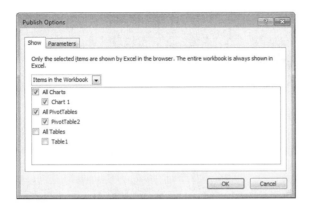

FIGURE 26.7   Setting the publish options for the worksheet.

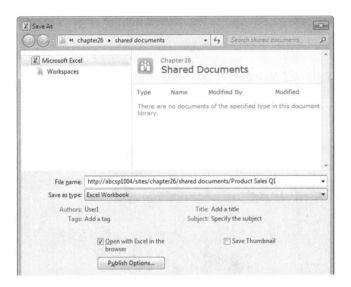

FIGURE 26.8   Saving the workbook to a SharePoint 2010 document library.

At this point in the example, components of the workbook have been published using Excel Services and they display properly in the browser. The manager, who happens to also manage the SharePoint 2010 site, now wants to display this content on the home page of the site, and so performs the following steps:

1. Assuming the previous steps have been completed successfully and the items specified previously we published to SharePoint using Excel Services, return to the home page of the site that houses the document and list (http://abcsp1004/sites/Chapter26/SitePages/Home.aspx in this example) and access the Site Actions drop-down and click Edit Page.

2. Click the Insert tab on the Ribbon and click the Web Part button.

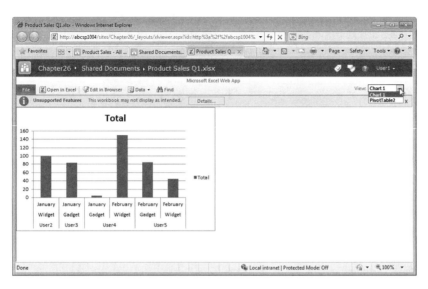

FIGURE 26.9   PivotChart open in the browser after publishing.

3. Click the Business Data icon in the Categories list of items, and then click Excel Web Access in the Web Parts section. Click Add and the Excel Web Access web part will be added to the page, as shown in Figure 26.10.

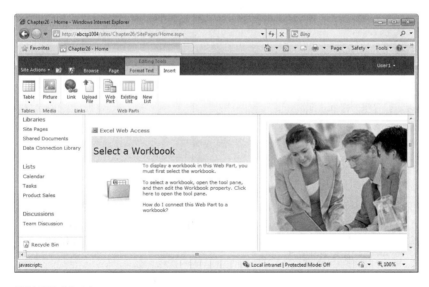

FIGURE 26.10   Excel Web Access web part added to a home page.

4. Next, the Excel Web Access web part needs to be edited to display data. Click the link inside the Excel Web Access web part that reads Click Here to Open the Tool Pane and the tool pane will open on the right.

5. Scroll to the right to expose the tool pane if needed, and click the button next to Workbook at the top. Then from the Select as Asset window, navigate to the document library that the Excel workbook was published to and select the workbook (Product Sales Q1 in this example) and click OK.

6. Click Apply and the page should look like Figure 26.11. In this example, the Chart 1 PivotChart is displayed, but the PivotTable can be displayed by changing the view from the drop-down menu in the Excel Web Access web part toolbar to PivotTable 2, as shown in Figure 26.12.

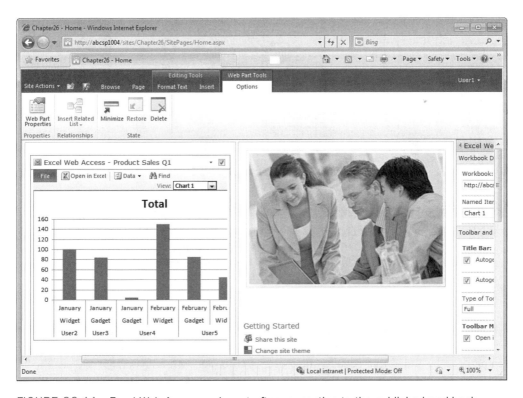

FIGURE 26.11   Excel Web Access web part after connection to the published workbook.

7. Click the Page tab on the Ribbon and click Save & Close. Perform additional tasks if needed to publish the page.

8. Finally, collapse the nodes in the PivotTable view and then switch to the Chart1 view and note that it reflects the change in the PivotTable and now only displays a single column per salesperson, as opposed to multiple columns per salesperson when the PivotTable nodes are expanded. Note that none of the cells can be edited in the Excel Web Access web part.

FIGURE 26.12   Excel Web Access web part showing the PivotTable.

NOTE

The Excel Web Access web part offers a handy tool in the File tab: the Reload Workbook tool. This will reload the workbook to Excel Services, which may sometimes be needed because content is cached and the version being viewed might not reflect all the most recent changes.

This exercise shows an example of how Excel Services can be used by a manager to publish certain items from a workbook a document library, and then the Excel Web Access web part can be added to a page to allow users to interact with a PivotTable and see the results on a PivotChart but not change the actual data itself.

Additional experimentation with the different tools provided in the Excel Web Access web part is encouraged, as well as additional modifications to the data in the SharePoint list, which is still connected to the spreadsheet, so can be refreshed when the SharePoint 2010 list changes and then republished to the SharePoint document library via Excel Services.

Allowing Parameter Input in Excel Web Access

Another feature to be familiar with is the ability to name a cell in Excel 2010, publish it using Excel Services, and users will then be able to input a value through the Excel Web Access interface. Although somewhat time-consuming to configure, it can allow for inter-activity through the Excel Web Access web part that might be very useful for encouraging end users to interact with the data. Bear in mind that any data input by end users in the

Excel Web Access web part is not saved to the published spreadsheet, so is really only for "what if" scenarios.

The following example reflects a situation where an IT manager wants to show senior management the impact of total number of help desk resources on average time to resolve the help desk tickets that come in based on numbers from the previous year. She creates a base spreadsheet with the months and number of help desk tickets per month and then creates an equation for the Average Time to Resolve (Hrs) column that divides the total number of tickets by the variable that will be input by the Excel Web Access web part users. This allows users of the published worksheet to enter in different numbers in the Number of Resources cell and see the results over the course of the year. She is hoping this will enable her to convince senior management that the organization needs more help desk staff at certain times of the year if they want to meet their SLA of no more than four hours average time to revolve help desk tickets. This example also allows the IT manager to show off her Excel Services skills to show senior management another capability of SharePoint 2010.

Follow these steps to test the process:

1. Create a new spreadsheet in Excel 2010.
2. Provide the heading **Month** to column A in cell A1.
3. Enter the text **January** in cell A2. Grab the lower-right corner of the cell while high-lighting cell A2 and drag downward, until all the fields are populated with the months up to December.
4. Enter **Help Desk Tickets** as the header in cell B1. Enter random numbers between 0 and 200 for cells B2 through B13.
5. Enter **Average Time to Resolve** as the header in cell C1.
6. Enter the text **Number of Resources** in cell A15.
7. Select cell B15 and access the Formulas tab.
8. Click Define Name in the Defined Names section of the Ribbon. Enter a name of **NumberofResources** and click OK. The results should look like Figure 26.13, with the exception of the actual values entered in cells B2 through B13.
9. Select cell C2 and enter the following formula, which will use the named cell:

    ```
    =B2/(NumberofResources*4)
    ```
10. The error #Div/0 error will display because there is no value in cell B15.
11. Click cell C2 and drag down to cell C13, and all cells should display the #Div/0 error.
12. Click the File tab, click Save & Send, and then click Save to SharePoint in the Save & Send column.
13. Click the Publish Options on the right side, above the Recent Locations list.
14. Click the Parameters tab, click Add, and select the box next to NumberofResources. Click OK, and the results should resemble Figure 26.14.
15. Click the Show tab and access the drop-down menu and select Sheets. Select Sheet1 and click OK.

26

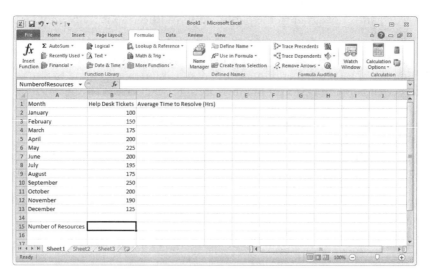

FIGURE 26.13   Naming a cell in an Excel 2010 worksheet.

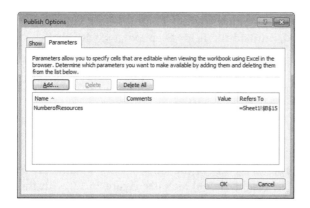

FIGURE 26.14   Setting the publish options when publishing using Excel Services.

16. Back on the Save & Send page, scroll down if needed and select Save As.

17. Enter the full path for the SharePoint site and document library in the Filename field and include the filename of HelpDeskTickets (so in this example, it is `http://abcsp1004/sites/chapter26/shared documents/HelpDeskTickets`). Verify that Open with Excel in Browser is checked. Click Save.

18. A browser window will open, and will display the worksheet, with a field on the right side titled Parameters, with a field next to the label NumberofResources. Enter a number such as 5 in the field and click Apply. The results will look like Figure 26.15.

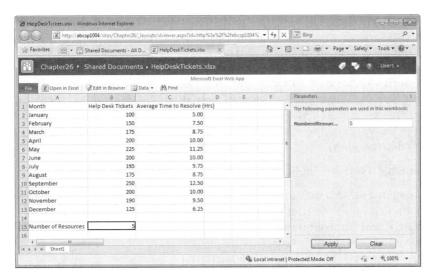

FIGURE 26.15   Results of entering a parameter value in the browser.

26

This example shows the steps involved with defining the name of a specific cell and then including that cell in the publishing process using Excel Services, as well as showing the interface that results. Multiple named cells can be defined in a workbook, which can then essentially be used as variables in the resulting content that is surfaced in the Excel Web Access web part. Combine this with tools such as charts and pivot tables and conditional formatting, and the results can be very powerful.

Access Services Overview

Access Services is designed to allow connectivity between SharePoint and Access 2010 databases for business applications where out-of-the-box lists and libraries may not fully meet the business needs. Several site templates are available that can be used to create sites with specific purposes: Assets Web Database, Charitable Contributions Web Database, Contacts Web Database, Issues Web Database, and Projects Web Database. Skilled Access DBAs can also create tables, forms, queries, and reports and then publish them to the SharePoint 2010 environment. This section gives an example of creating a Projects Web Database from a template to give an idea of the out-of-the-box templates that are available, but won't cover a new build in Access.

Access Services is also only available with SharePoint Server 2010 Enterprise, and if the wizard is used to configure the farm, and Access Services is left checked, an Access

Services service application should already be present in the farm. If a new service application is needed, it can be created from the Manage Service Applications page on the Central Administration site. The details of each configuration will vary based on the needs of the organization, and the settings for the service application are discussed here from a high level.

Compared to an Excel Services service application, the Access Service service application is relatively simple, and only includes one page of settings, as follows:

▶ **Lists and Queries**—Maximum Columns per Query (limit 255), Maximum Rows per Query (limit 200,000), Maximum Sources per Query (limit 20), Maximum Calculated Columns per Query (limit 32), Maximum Order by Clauses per Query (limit 8), Allow Outer Joins (yes/no), Allow Non Remotable Queries (yes/no), Maximum Records per Table (no limit)

▶ **Application Objects**—Max Application Log Size (no limit)

▶ **Session Management**—Maximum Request Duration (limit 2073600 seconds [24 days]), Maximum Sessions per User (no limit), Maximum Sessions per Anonymous User (no limit), Cache Timeout (limit 2073600 seconds [24 days]), Maximum Session Memory (maximum 4095MB)

▶ **Memory Utilization**—Maximum Private Bytes (limit of 50 percent of the physical memory on the machine)

▶ **Templates**—Maximum Template Size (no limit)

One prerequisite is important if the reporting features of these sites are going to be used (which users will almost certainly request if they are given one of these sites): The installation of Microsoft SQL Server 2008 R2 Reporting Services add-in for SharePoint Technologies 2010 (SSRS) is required. Additional instructions are available from Technet (http://technet.microsoft.com/en-us/library/ee662542.aspx) and should be reviewed because this can be a nontrivial installation. It should be noted that there are two modes in running Reporting Services with SharePoint Server: connected mode and local mode. Connected mode requires SharePoint Server 2010, the SSRS add-in, and a SQL Server 2008 R2 Report Server. Local mode only requires SharePoint Server and the SSRS add-in.

Creating an Access Web Database Site

This section looks at the process of creating one of the web databases from a template provided with SharePoint Server 2010 Enterprise. The Projects Web Database will be used, and then explored to see the different components of this new kind of site.

To create a web database using the Projects Web Database, follow these steps:

1. Using an account with sufficient privileges from a workstation that has Access 2010 installed, access the Site Actions drop-down menu and click New Site.

2. Select Projects Web Database from the list. Provide a title for the site (in this example, **Projects Database**) and a URL name (in this example, **ProjectsDatabase**) and click Create.

3. The site opens with an interface that looks very different from a typical SharePoint 2010 site, as shown in Figure 26.16. The Getting Started tab is open, which provides access to a video that users can view. Other tabs include Open Projects, Closed Projects, Users, Customers, and Report Center.

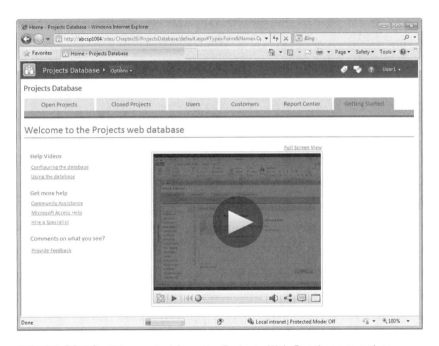

FIGURE 26.16   Site created from the Projects Web Database template.

4. Click the Options drop-down menu to reveal additional tools: Open in Access, Site Permissions, Settings, and Navigate Up.

5. Note that there is no tool available to view all site content. Change the URL of the current page by deleting the code after the site name (in this case, .../ProjectsDatabase/) and pasting it in _layouts/viewlsts.aspx so the full URL looks like the following (substitute in the appropriate path for your server and site):

```
http://abcsp1004/sites/Chapter26/ProjectsDatabase/_layouts/viewlsts.aspx
```

6. Press Enter, and the Viewlsts.aspx page opens, showing the contents of the site, as shown in Figure 26.17. This page helps to demystify the site by showing that there are in fact document libraries and lists that make up the site, even though they are "hidden" from easy access.

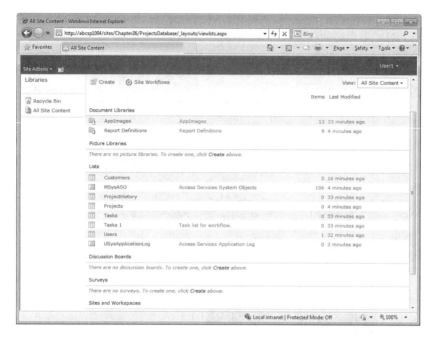

FIGURE 26.17   Hacking the URL to access the Viewlsts.aspx page.

7. Return to the home page of the site by clicking the site name in the breadcrumb.

8. Click the Options drop-down menu and click Settings.

9. The ModifyApplication.aspx page opens, showing the different tables, forms, reports, and queries that are available on the site, as shown in Figure 26.18.

10. Experienced Access developers can make changes to the individual tables, forms, reports, and queries from this interface.

CAUTION

It is very easy to make a change that will damage the site and result in a "site is down" error, so use caution when making edits to components of the site, such as the tables.

---

11. Click the Options drop-down menu, and click Site Permissions to open the user.aspx page. Notice that the Site Actions drop-down menu is available from this page. Note that the tools are the same as for other SharePoint 2010 sites in terms of granting permissions to the Access Web Database site.

12. Return to the home page and click the Open Projects tab. Enter information for a project in the top row. Note when the Category drop-down is open, there is a link to Edit List Items, so customized categories can be entered rather than the generic ones.

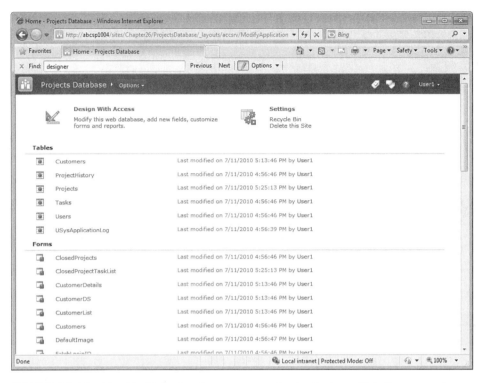

FIGURE 26.18   The ModifyApplication.aspx page for the Projects Web Database site.

13. Next, click New Project, and a window will open where more complete information can be entered about a project, as shown in Figure 26.19. Complete the form by entering in project information, and creating a new customer by clicking Edit List Items in the Customer drop-down menu. In this example, click Save & Close when complete.

14. Next, click the Tasks link on the toolbar, and select the project just created. Enter the task information on this screen, as shown in Figure 26.20, in the process adding another user by clicking the Edit List Items link from the Assigned To drop-down menu. Click in the next row down to save the entry.

Visio Graphics Services Overview

As with the Excel Services service application and the Access Services service application, the Visio Graphics Services service application is created by default in SharePoint Server 2010 Enterprise via the wizard in most cases. If a new service application is needed, it can be created from the Manage Service Applications page on the Central Administration site.

Visio Graphics Services allows Visio Web drawings published in VDW format to be shared with other users who may not have Visio 2010 installed on their computers. VDW formats can be created only by Visio Professional 2010 or Visio Premium 2010. Standard Visio drawings (VSD files) are not rendered by Visio Services and require Visio to be viewed.

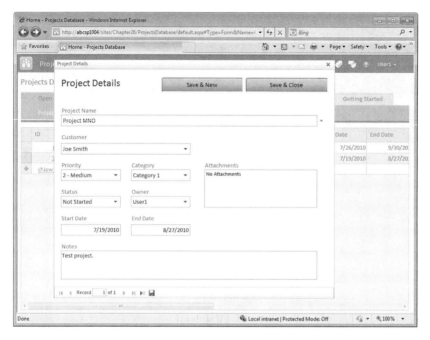

FIGURE 26.19   Creating a new project in the Projects Web Database site.

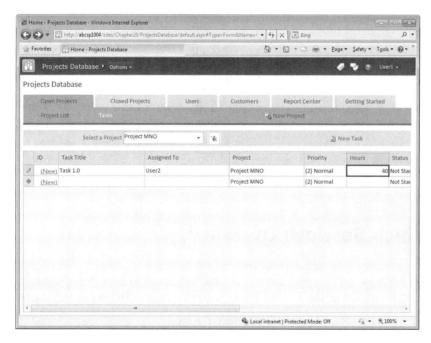

FIGURE 26.20   Creating a new task for a project in the Projects Web Database.

An example is shown in Figure 26.21 of a Visio diagram published using Visio Graphics Services. The standard options of Open in Visio and Refresh are available, as well as the ability to view different pages, zoom in or out, and show the Shape Information Pane visible in the lower-right section of Figure 26.21. The publishing process is accomplished by accessing the Save & Send tool from the File tab, selecting Save to SharePoint, and then choosing the Web Drawing format.

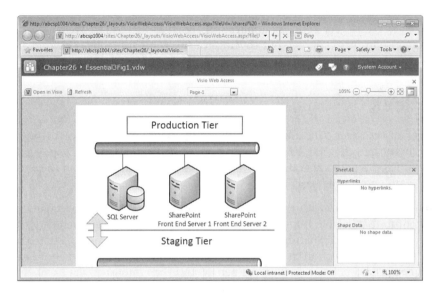

FIGURE 26.21   Example of a Visio file viewed in the browser.

The settings for the Visio Graphics Services service application are as follows:

▶ **Global Settings**—Include Maximum Web Drawing Size (50MB limit), Minimum Cache Age (number of minutes, 34560 maximum), Maximum Cache Age (number of minutes, 34560 maximum), Maximum Recalc Duration (120 seconds maximum), Unattended Service Account Application ID.

▶ **Trusted Data Providers**—A number of data providers are already provided, or new ones can be added, using the following types: 1 for OLEDB, 2 for SQL, 3 for ODBC, 4 for ODBC with DSN, 5 for SharePoint Lists, and 6 for Visio Custom Data Providers.

Summary

This chapter spends a bulk of its time reviewing the integration of Excel and SharePoint, especially using the Excel Services tools because this is such an important capability of SharePoint 2010. Many knowledge workers and managers still "live" in Excel and manage much of the most critical information in workbooks, so understanding what Excel Services can and can't do is important for SharePoint power users and administrators. A brief overview of Access Services and Visio Graphics Services was provided. Access Services can be used to create very complex applications, such as the Project Web Database that is reviewed in this chapter, but coverage of this topic in depth is beyond the scope of this chapter.

Best Practices

▶ Excel Services allows Excel 2010 users to publish components of a workbook to a SharePoint library, and then the Excel Web Access web part can be used to connect to a published Excel workbook and display tables, charts, and other items in the web part, typically on a read-only basis.

▶ Many users want to interact with the data presented by Excel Web Access web part, so the different tools available from the File tab in the Excel Web Access web part (Open in Excel, Download a Snapshot, Download a Copy) should be demonstrated to users. In addition, the section in this chapter titled, "Allowing Parameter Input in Excel Web Access," shows how a cell can be named and then published via Excel Services to allow input to the Excel Web Access web part.

▶ Access Services site templates provided some functional examples of how Access Services can be leveraged in a SharePoint 2010 environment. For example, the Projects Web Database template creates a complex and powerful "site" for managing customers, users, projects, and tasks.

▶ Although all the components of an Access Services site (tables, forms, queries, and reports) can be customized in Access 2010, an experienced Access DBA should lead these efforts due to potential of damaging site functionality.

▶ The installation of Microsoft SQL Server 2008 R2 Reporting Services add-in for SharePoint Technologies 2010 (SSRS) is required for users to access reports from sites created using Access Services.

▶ Visio Graphics Service allows users to publish Visio documents in the VDW format, which can only be created by Visio Professional 2010 or Visio Premium 2010.

## CHAPTER 27

Office Web Apps Integration with SharePoint 2010

Office Web Apps provide a browser-based viewing and editing experience for SharePoint 2010 users who need to collaborate on Word, Excel, PowerPoint, or OneNote documents. Office Web Apps provide a subset of functionality and should be tested thoroughly so the organization understands the capabilities and limitations of the browser-based editing tools.

This feature will be of special interest to organizations that support non-Microsoft operating systems such as Linux, UNIX, and Macintosh, or support other browsers such as Firefox and Safari, which provide a lower level of compatibility than IE 7 and 8.

Office Web Apps also provide some innovative features explored in this chapter, such as enabling multiple users to edit an Excel document simultaneously and enabling the broadcast of PowerPoint slide decks using the browser. Yet, there are complexities to consider when implementing Office Web Apps, which are also discussed in this chapter and should be considered by IT decision makers before making the feature widely available, especially in environments that use heterogeneous browsers, desktop OS, and Office versions.

Microsoft is also making this functionality available from its Windows Live service, but that will not be covered in this chapter, which focuses on integration and features available when Office Web Apps are used with SharePoint 2010 products.

Planning for Office Web Apps Use

This section provides some "food for thought" for organizations interested in implementing the Office Web Apps functionality to allow end users another vehicle for collaborating on Word, Excel, PowerPoint, and OneNote documents. Prerequisites, licensing issues, and limitations by browsers are covered in this section, although from a fairly high level due to the wealth of information provided by Microsoft on these topics (for which links are given).

Server Prerequisites and Licensing Considerations

SharePoint Foundation 2010 or SharePoint Server 2010 Standard or Enterprise is required to use Office Web Apps. As discussed later in this chapter, in the section "Installing and Configuring Office Web Apps for SharePoint 2010," a separate set of installation files need to be downloaded. Server prerequisites are listed in Table 27.1.

TABLE 27.1   Server Prerequisites

System Requirements	Details
Supported operating systems	Windows Server 2008 Windows Server 2008 R2 and Windows Server 2008 with Service Pack 2 (SP2)
Hardware	Processor: 64-bit; dual processor: 3GHz RAM: 4GB for stand-alone; 8GB for farm Hard disk: 80GB
Software	SharePoint Foundation 2010 or SharePoint Server 2010
Browser support	Internet Explorer 7.0 or later on Windows Safari 4.0 or later on Mac Firefox 3.5 or later on Windows, Mac, and Linux

As defined by Microsoft on TechNet in the "Deploy Office Web Apps (Installed on SharePoint 2010 Products)" article (http://technet.microsoft.com/en-us/library/ff431687.aspx): "Office Web Apps are available to business customers with Microsoft Office 2010 volume licensing and document management solutions that are based on Microsoft SharePoint 2010 Products."

Organizations interested in using Office Web Apps in their environments still need to comply with Microsoft licensing policies, which can be found on the following site: http://www.microsoftvolumelicensing.com/userights/default.aspx. The legalese used makes a full understanding of appropriate usage difficult; however, several statements in the Excel Web App 2010 section shed light on some key concepts:

▶ "If you comply with your volume license agreement, including these product use rights and the Product List, you may use the software and online services only as expressly permitted in these product use rights."

▶ "You may not host the products for commercial hosting services."

From an organization standpoint, it is clear that existing product use rights (such as use of other Office products) still apply to the Office Web App (in this case, Excel Web App 2010) and some homework may be required to ensure that the organization is meeting the terms of the volume license agreement.

> **NOTE**
>
> In plain English, for a properly licensed organization to use Office 2010 core applications, including Word, Excel, and PowerPoint, and have appropriate licenses for SharePoint 2010, there should not be an extra cost to use Office Web Apps. However that organization cannot allow external users to use the Office Web Apps feature without incurring liability on the licensing side, which would most likely include having to purchase any SharePoint CALs and Office 2010 CALs for these external users. For this reason, IT decision makers should carefully consider whether to enable the Office Web Apps feature, and if so, for which libraries and site collections.

Browser Support of Office Web Apps

For organizations that decide to support Office Web Apps, it is important to test the various browsers in use because the browser will become a primary tool used for editing documents. Office Web Apps can also fill the functionality gap that appears when organizations support browsers other than Internet Explorer 7 and 8 32-bit version, and operating systems other than the newest Microsoft operating systems, such as Linux, UNIX, and Mac OSX.

Microsoft offers a more in-depth review of limitations at the following URL: http:/ /technet.microsoft.com/en-us/library/cc288142.aspx. This list should be reviewed in detail by organizations that officially support browsers other than the 32-bit versions of IE 7 and 8. In this article, Microsoft defines three levels of compatibility:

- ▶ **Supported (the highest level of compatibility)**—IE 8 (32-bit) and IE 7 (32-bit) fall into this category.

- ▶ **Supported with known limitations (most features and functionality work)**—IE 8 (64-bit), IE 7 (64-bit), Firefox 3.6 (on Windows operating systems and on non-Windows operating systems), and Safari 4.04 (on non-Windows operating systems) fall into this category.

- ▶ **Not tested (there may be issues when using a browser in this category)**—Any browser not listed in the previous two sections fall into this category (such as Google Chrome).

A partial list of limitations is as follows:

- ▶ **Internet Explorer 8 (32-bit)**—There are no known limitations for Internet Explorer 8 (32-bit).

- ▶ **Internet Explorer 7 (32-bit)**—There are no known limitations for Internet Explorer 7 (32-bit).

27

▶ **Internet Explorer 8 (64-bit)**—There are a variety of known limitations for Internet Explorer 8 (64-bit). See the previously mentioned link for more information on Microsoft's TechNet website.

NOTE

An example of IE 8 64-bit limitations include the following: When accessing a SharePoint 2010 document library from an IE 8 64-bit browser, if the user clicks on Edit in a Microsoft Office Word entry from the drop-down menu for a Word document in the lib, an error message will appear that states, "The document could not be opened for editing. A Microsoft SharePoint Foundation compatible application could not be found to edit the document."

▶ **Internet Explorer 7 (64-bit)**—There are a variety of known limitations for Internet Explorer 7 (64-bit). See the previously mentioned link for more information on Microsoft's TechNet website. Limitations are similar to IE 8 64-bit.

▶ **Mozilla Firefox 3.6 (on Windows operating systems)**—There are a variety of known limitations for Firefox 3.6 on Windows operating systems. See the previously mentioned link for more information on Microsoft's TechNet website.

NOTE

A Firefox plug-in is required to open and edit Microsoft Office applications. However, testing showed that this plug-in is included with Firefox for Windows version 3.6.3, as shown in Figure 27.1, so use of Firefox 3.6.3 to open and edit Microsoft Office Word 2010 was seamless.

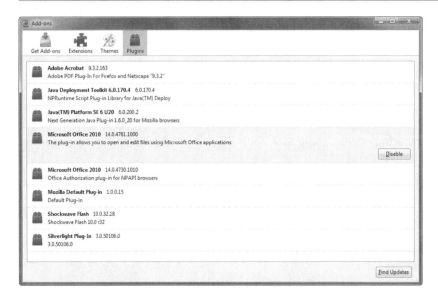

FIGURE 27.1   Microsoft Office 2010 plug-ins installed by default with Firefox 3.6.3.

▶ **Mozilla Firefox 3.6 (on non-Windows operating systems)**—There are a variety of known limitations for Firefox 3.6 on non-Windows operating systems (Mac OSX and UNIX/Linux). See the previously mentioned link for more information on Microsoft's TechNet website.

▶ **Safari 4.04 (on non-Windows operating systems)**—There are a variety of known limitations for Safari 4.04 on non-Windows operating systems (Mac OSX (Version 10.6 and Snow Leopard)). See the previously mentioned link for more information on Microsoft's TechNet website.

NOTE

Per the Microsoft document, "Plan browser support (SharePoint Foundation 2010)" for Firefox 3.6 Windows and non-Windows operating systems and Safari 4.04 on non-Windows operating systems: "If you install and configure the Office Web Apps on the server, the Edit functionality works and you can modify Office documents in your browser."

Planning to Support Multiple Versions of the Office Rich Client

Even though Office Web Apps enable users to edit Word, Excel, and PowerPoint documents in their browsers, the features made available are limited and pared down from what the full Office applications provide, as discussed and demonstrated later in the chapter. Therefore, users will still often work in the full clients, assuming the organization uses the Microsoft Office application suite. Initial testing of Office Web Apps reveal the importance of thorough testing for an organization interested in implementing this functionality. These examples are just examples of the issues that can be encountered and should be taken into account in the planning process.

If Word 2003, Excel 2003, or PowerPoint 2003 were used to create documents that were saved to SharePoint 2010 and users want to edit those documents in the browser, they will get an error message. The error message will state, "To Edit This File in Word Web App It First Must Be Converted to the Newest File Format. This Will Also Create a Backup of The Original File. To Edit This File Without Converting It, Open It in Microsoft Word." If the user proceeds with the editing process, a new version of the document will be saved in the same document library with "- Converted" attached as a suffix to the document title. Although not a "show stopper," this behavior could lead to confusion, so the SharePoint administration team may require that files be converted to the newer .docx, .xslx, and .pptx formats before being uploaded to SharePoint 2010 document libraries that will be enabled for use with the Office Web Apps feature and browser-based editing.

Another example pertains to organizations that may be standardized on the Office 2007 suite, but users may still save files using the older, backward-compatible file types. In this case, a user created a spreadsheet in Excel 2010 but then saved the document in Excel 97–2003 format because she needed to send it to an external partner who she believe had

27

an older version of Excel. She then uploaded the spreadsheet to a SharePoint 2010 document library enabled for browser editing using Office Web Apps. One of her coworkers accesses the library from his netbook that doesn't have the full Excel client on it and clicks on the title of the spreadsheet, expecting to edit it in the browser. Instead, the coworker sees an error, "Do You Want to Save This File, or Find a Program Online to Open It." If the coworker had Excel installed locally, he would be asked to open the document in Excel in Read Only or Edit mode, which again was not what he was expecting.

Mobile Device Support

Many organizations are intrigued by the ever-present concept of further enabling productivity between mobile users and office-bound employees. Office Web Apps offer a toolset that can be investigated for this purpose and provide a reduced set of tools that are better suited for devices with small screens. Of course, the SharePoint environment needs to be accessible from the outside world for this functionality to be useful, and the organization needs to thoroughly test the different supported devices.

A primary limitation is the small size of the screens on the mobile devices, but new features such as panning and zooming and more powerful processors in the devices make the experience more tolerable than in the past.

The following devices provide mobile "support" for Office Web Apps in SharePoint according to Microsoft, but the organization needs to test thoroughly to establish if the level of functionality provided is adequate:

▶ Windows Mobile

▶ BlackBerry

▶ iPhone, iPod Touch

▶ Nokia S60

▶ Japan feature telephones, including NTT DOCOMO, SoftBank, and au by KDDI

The organization should make an initial decision whether mobile devices will be supported, and if so which specific makes and models, and then engage in thorough testing.

As an example of this testing, the iPhone is listed in the preceding list of compatible devices, but when Office Web App access was tested from an iPhone (operating system version 3.1.3) the documents were viewable but not editable using the built-in version of Safari nor could new documents be created. Over time, Microsoft may change their support, or other browser could become available that enable more interactive access to Office Web Apps from mobile devices.

TIP

A good way to test mobile device access to Office Web Apps is to use the Microsoft Live service. Simply visit http://home.live.com/ and then either log in with an existing account or sign up for a new account and provide the information requested. Then click Office in the top menu, and then click one of the icons under the heading "Create a New Online Document" to test Office Web Apps and create a Word, Excel, PowerPoint, or OneNote document, as shown in Figure 27.2.

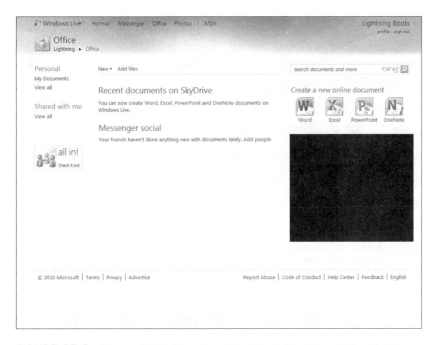

FIGURE 27.2   Microsoft Windows live site with online document options.

Installing and Configuring Office Web Apps for SharePoint 2010

When Office Web Apps are installed in a SharePoint Foundation 2010 or SharePoint Server 2010 farm, the Word Viewing Service, PowerPoint Service, and Excel Calculation Services are created in as service applications. No OneNote service application is created, because OneNote is capable of sharing documents natively.

The Word Viewer Service and PowerPoint service applications use worker processes to then convert documents and presentations into PNG images or into XAML (if Silverlight is installed), which are stored in a cache, which can be used for future requests for the same content. The Excel Web Application uses DHTML and JavaScript to render and enable sharing and editing of content, and Excel Calculation Services is used to load the workbook, perform Excel calculations, and maintain the session.

This section gives instructions for installing Office Web Apps for SharePoint 2010 on a two-server farm, where SharePoint Server 2010 Enterprise is in use and has been fully configured. This section also outlines several areas where the default behavior for opening documents in the browser (that is, using Office web applications) or in the Office application (for example, Word, Excel, or PowerPoint) can be modified by the farm or site collection administrators.

Microsoft provides a detailed document titled, "Deploy Office Web Apps (Installed on SharePoint 2010 Products)" at http://technet.microsoft.com/en-us/library/ff431687.aspx, and this article also provides the PowerShell scripts that can be run to shortcut the manual process presented in this section. It is important to note that there are four installation scenarios that this document covers, whereas the following steps cover only a single common scenario. The Microsoft document covers the following different configurations:

▶ Install and configure Office Web Apps on an existing stand-alone SharePoint server

▶ Install and configure Office Web Apps on a new stand-alone SharePoint server

▶ Install and configure Office Web Apps on an existing SharePoint server farm

▶ Install and configure Office Web Apps on a new SharePoint server farm

The following steps apply to the third scenario, that of installing and configuring Office Web Apps on an existing SharePoint server farm. Assuming your environment meets that requirement, perform the following steps to configure Office Web Apps:

1. Insert the CD/DVD or mount the .iso image (in this example, en_web_apps_2010_x64_dvd_515376.iso was used) and run Setup.exe.

2. Enter the product key on the Enter Your Product Key page, and click Continue.

3. Check the box next to I Accept the Terms of This Agreement, and click Continue.

4. On the Choose a File location page, leave the defaults unless there is a specific reason for changing the file locations. If the existing server build, for example, stores the index files on the D:\ drive, then it makes sense to also store the Office web applications search index files on the same volume. Click Install Now.

5. When the Run Configuration Wizard window opens, leave the box next to Run the SharePoint Products Configuration Wizard Now checked and click Close.

6. The Welcome to SharePoint Products window opens; click Next.

7. Click Yes when the window opens, mentioning that several services might have to be started or reset during configuration.

8. On the Completing the SharePoint Products Configuration Wizard window, click Next.

9. When the process completes, the Configuration Successful window appears; click Finish and adminconfigintro.aspx page from Central Administration opens.

10. Click Start the Wizard.

11. Assuming the farm has already been configured, which was an assumption for this section, the Service Account section should already be filled in, and a number of the services should already be checked and grayed out because they will already be configured. Verify that Excel service application, PowerPoint service application, and Word Viewing service are checked and then click Next.

12. Next, the createsite.aspx page appears. Because the assumption is that the farm was already configured, and a default site collection was already created, click Skip.

13. The next page shows the results of the farm configuration and lists the configured and available service applications. Click System Settings in the Quick Launch.

14. From the Servers section, click Manage Services on Server to ensure that the relevant services are enabled.

15. Verify that Excel Calculation Services, PowerPoint Service, and Word Viewing Service are all started. If not, click Start for any that need to be started and complete any additional configuration if needed.

16. Next, click Application Management from the Quick Launch.

17. From the Service Applications section, click on Manage Service Applications. Verify that there is an Excel Services Application, a PowerPoint Service Application, and a Word Viewing service application. Figure 27.3 shows a portion of this page with the Excel service application and the PowerPoint service application visible.

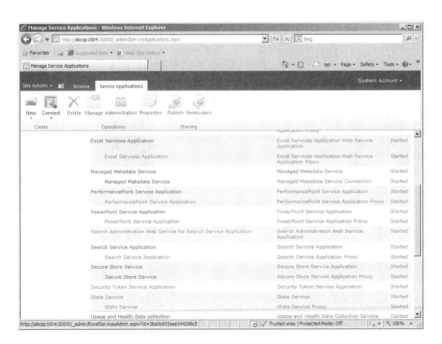

FIGURE 27.3   Service applications from the central administration site showing Excel services and PowerPoint service applications.

Steps at this point can vary based on the base farm configuration and the preferences of the administrator. For example, for testing purposes, the administrator may choose to create new service applications for one or more of the Office Web Apps. To create a new service application for Excel Services, follow these steps:

1. From the Manage Service Applications page, on the Service Applications tab of the Ribbon, click the New drop-down menu, and select Excel Services Application.

2. From the Create New Excel Services Application page, enter a name for the service application, such as **Excel Services Application 2**.

3. Check the box next to Use Existing Application Pool, and choose SharePoint Web Services Default, as shown in Figure 27.4.

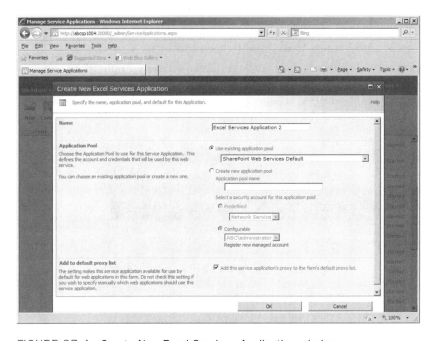

FIGURE 27.4   Create New Excel Services Application window.

4. Verify that the check box next to Add This Service Application's Proxy to the Farm's Default Proxy List is checked, and click OK.

5. When this process completes, verify that the new service application appears in the list of service applications on the Manage Service Applications page.

A similar process should be followed to create additional PowerPoint service applications or Word Viewing service applications.

Reviewing Central Administration Settings for the PowerPoint Service Application and Word Viewing Service Application

Farm administrators should familiarize themselves with the range of options available for the different Office Web Apps. The Excel Office web app functionality is embedded in the Excel Services web app, so the settings available for the Excel services application are more complex than those for the PowerPoint service application or the Word Viewing service application. The Excel Services configuration is covered in Chapter 26, "Extending SharePoint 2010 with Excel Services, Access Services, and Visio Graphics Services."

To review the PowerPoint service application, follow these steps:

1. Navigate to the central administrator site, and from the home page under the Application Management section, click Manage Service Applications.

2. Click the top-level PowerPoint Service App link (not the link indented under it), and the Manage PowerPoint Service Application page opens, as shown in Figure 27.5.

FIGURE 27.5   Manage PowerPoint Service Application page.

3. In the Supported File Formats section, note the options for file format support include Open XML Presentations in the .pptx and related formats (.pptm, .potx, and .potm), and PowerPoint 97–2003 Presentations in the .ppt and related formats (.pot).

4. The Broadcast Site section lists a default broadcast site with a URL (http://abcsp1004/sites/broadcast in this example) and a link to the New Site

Collection page, where an additional Broadcast Sites can be created. Click the URL to visit the Broadcast Site and verify that it loads. Figure 27.6 shows the home page for the broadcast site, which lists instructions for using the broadcast site that will be covered later in this chapter.

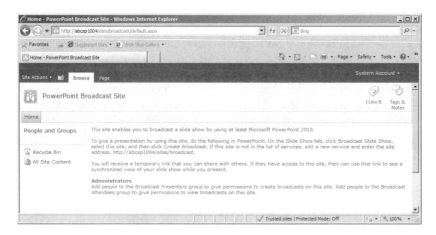

FIGURE 27.6   PowerPoint Broadcast Site.

5. Click the back arrow for the browser to return to the Manage PowerPoint Service Application page.

6. Finally on this page, the PowerPoint 97–2003 Presentation Scanning section allows the option to disable PowerPoint 97–2003 presentation scanning, a process that checks for malicious content in the document but can slow down performance. A best practice is to leave Presentation Scanning enabled, unless performance issues are encountered, in which case it can be disabled.

TIP

You can set maximum worker processes for the PowerPoint Viewing service application by using Windows PowerShell, which can also affect server performance. See the Microsoft document "Configure PowerPoint service application settings" (http://technet.microsoft.com/en-us/library/ee837424.aspx) for the instructions and the PowerShell script.

---

7. Review the settings to ensure that they meet the organization's requirements, and click OK if changes were made or Cancel if no changes were made.

To review the Word Viewing service application, follow these steps:

1. Navigate to the Central Administrator site, and from the home page under the Application Management section, click on Manage Service Applications.

2. Click the top-level Word Viewing Service Application link (not the link indented under it), and the Word Viewing Service Application page opens, as shown in Figure 27.7.

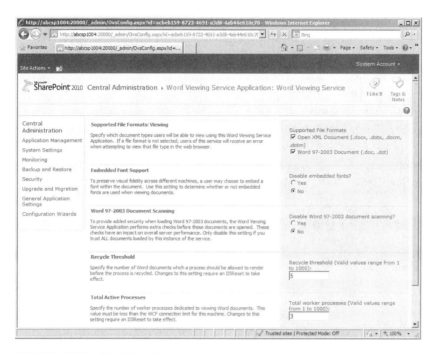

FIGURE 27.7   Word Viewing Service Application settings page.

3. In the Supported File Formats: Viewing section options are provided to enable support for Open XML (.docx, .dotx, .docm, .dotm) and Word 97–2003 (.doc, .dot) file types.

4. The Embedded Font Support section is set to not Disable embedded fonts, but embedded fonts support can be turned off if needed.

5. The Word 97–2003 Document Scanning is enabled by default but can be turned off if needed.

6. The Recycle Threshold is set to 5 by default and refers to the number of Word documents that a process should be allowed to render before the process is recycled. Changes require an IISreset to take effect.

7. Total Active Processes specified the number of worker processes dedicated to viewing Word documents and is set to 3 by default. Changes require an IISreset to take effect.

Verifying the Site Collection Features Are Enabled for Office Web Apps

Assuming the previous steps were followed and the Office Web Apps installed, the site collection features need to be reviewed to make sure the appropriate ones are enabled. Follow these steps to verify that the feature is enabled on site collection where the Office Web Apps feature will be used:

1. Navigate to the site settings page for the site collection that houses the documents that will be accessed via Office Web Apps using an account that is a site collection administrator.
2. In the Site Collection Administrator section, click Site Collection Features.
3. Locate the Office Web Apps entry and click the Activate button.
4. Test that viewing Word, Excel, PowerPoint, and OneNote documents in the browser and editing in the browser is functioning properly.
5. If the functionality is not working properly, check the settings for the document library and default behavior in Central Administration covered in the next two sections.

Verifying the Settings in the Document Library

An additional step to take in an existing SharePoint 2010 environment is to validate the settings of the document library or libraries that house the documents that the administrator wants to support the Office Web Apps access method. Follow these steps to make sure the document library is configured to support Office Web Apps use:

1. Navigate to the document library with an account that has Owner-level permissions on the site and click on the Library tab on the Ribbon, and then click the Library Settings button.
2. Click Advanced Settings in the General Settings section.
3. In the Opening Documents in the Browser section, select the option next to Open in the Browser or Use the Server Default (Open in the Browser). Click OK.
4. Test that viewing Word, Excel, PowerPoint, and OneNote documents in the browser and editing in the browser is functioning properly.
5. If the functionality is not working properly, check the settings for the site collection, as covered in the previous section, and default behavior in central administration covered in the next section.

Set the Default Open Behavior for Site Collections in Central Administration

This following method is also available for setting preferences for how documents are handled in document libraries:

1. From Central Administration, click Site Actions, and then from the drop-down menu, click Site Settings.
2. On the Site Settings page, in the Site Collection Administration section, click Site Collection Features.

3. On the Features page, scroll down to locate the Open Documents in Client Applications by Default feature, click Activate to open documents in the client application by default, or click Deactivate to open documents in the browser by default.

4. Test that viewing Word, Excel, PowerPoint, and OneNote documents in the browser and editing in the browser is functioning properly.

5. If the functionality is not working properly, check the settings for the site collection and document library, as covered in the previous two sections.

Testing Office Web Apps Functionality

Now that the service applications are configured and the configurations for the site collection, the library, and the central administration site are reviewed, it is time to test the functionality of accessing and editing documents in the browser.

The following sections assume the following:

1. **On the PC:** Word 2010, Excel 2010, and PowerPoint 2010 are installed on the PC, which is using Windows 7 and IE 8, 32-bit version.

2. **For the document library:** The Advanced Settings page is set to Open in the Browser in the Opening Documents in the Browser section. Documents are not required to be checked out before they are edited, nor is Content Approval required for submitted items.

3. **For the document library (optional):** Versioning can be on or off for the document library at the discretion of the administrator.

4. **For the site collection:** The Office Web Apps feature is set to Active for the site collection that houses the site that houses the document library.

5. **For the farm:** The Open Documents in Client Applications by Default feature is not activated in Site Collection Features in the Central Administration site.

Testing Word Access via Office Web Apps

Assuming the conditions listed at the beginning of the "Testing Office Web Apps Functionality" section are met, follow these steps to test Office Web Apps with a Microsoft Word 2010 Document. These steps are high level, and additional testing from different browsers, operating systems, and versions of Office should be performed:

1. Using an account with Contribute-level permissions, navigate to the document library that meets the prerequisites listed in the previous section and that contains one or more file created in Word 2010.

27

2. Hover over the Name field of a Word document and click it. The file should open in the same browser session, as shown in Figure 27.8. Note that the toolbar provides a File tab, Open in Word, Edit in Browser, Find icons, and a Zoom drop-down menu, page forward and page backward arrows, and help and pop-out buttons.

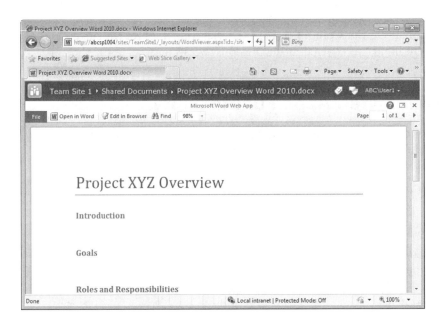

FIGURE 27.8   Word 2010 document viewed in the browser.

NOTE

Clicking on the pop-out button (on the right side of the toolbar between the help and X buttons) opens the Word document opens in a new window, and the browser session can revert back to the previous view of the document library. Pop-ups need to be enabled for the browser for the specific SharePoint site for pop-out functionality to work.

3. Click the Edit in Browser button on the toolbar, and the Open Document window opens. Select Edit and click OK.

4. A limited Word ribbon now appears, which provides File, Home, Insert, and View tabs. The File tab provides Save, Open in Word, and Close tools. The Home tab

provides Clipboard, Font, Paragraph, Styles, Spelling, and Office sections with corresponding tools. The Insert tab provides Table, Pictures, and Links tools. The View tab provides Editing View, and Reading View tools.

NOTE

Multiple users cannot edit a Word document via Office Web Apps. To test this, with the Word 2010 document open for editing as one user (User1), access the same document using another PC and different user account (User2) so that it opens in the browser, and click on Edit in Browser. Note that a message appears to User2, stating "Word Web App Cannot Open This Document Because It Is Currently Being Edited by Another User." If the Open in Word button is clicked, and the Edit option is chosen, the user will be informed that the document Is Locked for Editing by domainname\username."

5. Add some text and an image to the document, as shown in Figure 27.9. Note that a new tab appears when the image is added and selected that provides limited image editing tools.

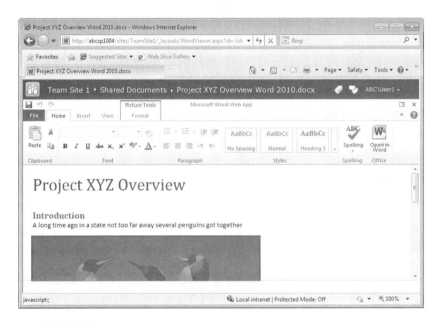

FIGURE 27.9   Word 2010 document edited in the browser.

6. Click the Find button in the toolbar, and search for text in the document to verify functionality of the find feature.

7. Click the Save button to save the changes.

8. Then click the Close button, and the browser returns to the document library.

CAUTION

If a document is checked out by a user and saved to the local drafts folder, it cannot be edited in the browser. An error message appears, stating "Word Web App Cannot Open This Document for Editing Because It Is Checked Out to Your Local Drafts Folder."

Testing Excel Access via Office Web Apps

Assuming the conditions listed at the beginning of the "Testing Office Web Apps Functionality" section are met, Excel document access via Office Web Apps should be functional. This section reviews a sampling of features available when a user chooses to edit an Excel 2010 spreadsheet in SharePoint 2010, and also tests two users accessing and editing the same spreadsheet in Office Web Apps.

Follow these steps to test the Excel services application:

1. Using an account with contribute-level permissions, navigate to the document library that meets the prerequisites listed at the beginning of this section and that contains one or more file created in Excel 2010. The Excel 2010 file should have some equations and at least one graph in it ideally.

2. Hover over the Name field of an Excel document and click it. The file should open in the same browser session. Note that the tools offered for Excel are subtly different than those for Word (as covered in the previous section). The toolbar provides a File tab, Open in Excel, Edit in Browser, Data drop-down menu, and Find tool. If there are multiple worksheets in the Excel file, the tabs will be visible at the bottom on the browser. The File tab is actually a drop-down menu and provides the following tools: Open in Excel, Save a Copy, Download a Snapshot, Download a Copy, and Reload Workbook.

NOTE

The Download a Snapshot option opens the Excel document in Excel but does not include any formulae, just the values of the cells, but can be useful if a user simply wants to capture the state of the document at a particular point in time.

---

3. Click Edit in Browser and the file will be editable and provide File, Home, and Insert tabs, as shown in Figure 27.10. Note that the tools available on the Home tab are somewhat limited but still allow a moderate level of editing capability. For example, the Insert tab enables only the insertion of a Table or a Hyperlink. Also, for example, the graph shown in Figure 27.10 is not editable.

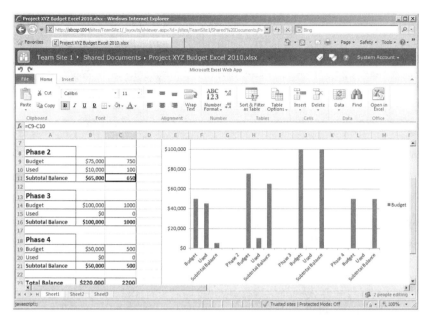

FIGURE 27.10   Excel 2010 document edited in the browser.

> **NOTE**
>
> There is no Save button when Excel is edited in the browser. Instead, all changes are saved when they are made.

4. Test multiple people editing the spreadsheet in the browser by logging on to the same SharePoint site with a different user clicking the same spreadsheet filename and clicking Edit in Browser.

5. When two different users edit the same spreadsheet in the browser, click the drop-down arrow in the lower-right corner that is labeled X People Editing (where X is an integer) and review the results. It shows the names of the users who are editing the spreadsheet. Test modifying the spreadsheet with two users to see the results.

NOTE

If versioning is enabled for the document library containing the spreadsheet, a version is saved only when the last user exits the document by navigating away from the spreadsheet after editing. So, for example, User1 and User2 are editing the same spreadsheet at the same time in their browsers, and each makes a handful of changes. User1 navigates away first by clicking the document library name in the breadcrumb. Then User2 makes additional changes and then navigates away from the page using the breadcrumb. Only after User2 navigates away from the spreadsheet is a new version saved.

CAUTION

If two or more people edit a spreadsheet in the browser, none of the users can click Open in Excel; instead, a message displays, stating "You Are Currently Collaborating on This Workbook with Other People. You Cannot Edit This Workbook in Excel While Other People Are Also Editing It in the Browser." Users can Download a Snapshot or Download a Copy, however. Also note that the undo and redo features are not enabled when multiple users edit a spreadsheet in the browser.

Testing PowerPoint Access via Office Web Apps

Assuming that the conditions listed at the beginning of the "Testing Office Web Apps Functionality" section are met, PowerPoint document access via Office Web Apps should be functional. This section reviews a sampling of features available when a user wants to access a PowerPoint document via Office Web Apps.

Follow these steps to test the PowerPoint services application:

1. Using an account with contribute-level permissions, navigate to the document library that meets the prerequisites listed previously and that contains one or more files created in PowerPoint 2010.

2. Click the name of the PowerPoint file, and it opens in the browser. A File tab is visible, and it provides the options Open in PowerPoint, Outline View, and Close. Additional tools provided on the toolbar are Open in PowerPoint, Edit in Browser, Start Slide Show, and in the upper-right corner, help, pop-out, and Close buttons. Slide navigation arrows are available at the bottom.

3. Click Edit in Browser, and the document should be editable. Again the tools provided are fairly limited, so for anything but basic changes, the full version of PowerPoint may be required. For example, slide layouts cannot be changed; instead, a new slide with a different layout needs to be added. Graphics can't be edited, except for the Format that is limited to the shape of the graphic and the borders, as shown in Figure 27.11.

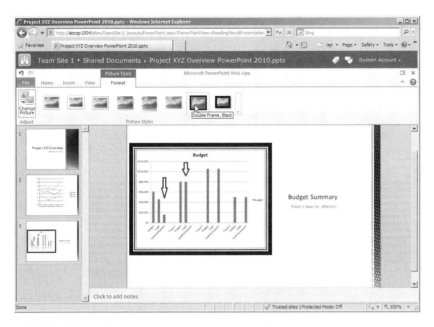

FIGURE 27.11   PowerPoint 2010 document edited in a browser.

4. From the Home tab on the Ribbon, click Open in PowerPoint to open the full version of PowerPoint 2010 and create a slideshow.

5. When the file is open in PowerPoint 2010, click the Slide Show tab, and then click Broadcast Slide Show.

6. The Broadcast Slide Show window opens, and shows the Broadcast Service it will use. If the incorrect Broadcast Service is shown, click the Change Broadcast Service button in the lower-left portion of the window. Then click Add a new service, and enter the URL of the Broadcast Service. The URL of the Broadcast Service was provided in the Manage PowerPoint Service Application page accessible from the Central Administration site home page by accessing Manage Service Applications and then clicking on the PowerPoint service application.

7. When the correct Broadcast Service is listed, click Start Broadcast.

8. When the processing has completed, the window displays the link that remote viewers can use to access the broadcast, and Copy Link and Send in Email links and Start Slide Show button, as shown in Figure 27.12.

27

FIGURE 27.12   Broadcast Slide Show window in PowerPoint 2010.

9. Click the Send in Email link, and email the link to a test user or coworker. Note that the attendee can view the slide show in full screen mode if wanted.

10. Then click Start Slide Show and access the provided URL as the test user, or ask a coworker to access the URL to test. Advance from slide to slide as the presenter by clicking the slide.

11. The slide show broadcast is ended by the presenter from PowerPoint 2010 by clicking the End Broadcast button underneath the Ribbon. Any attendees will then see a notice saying "The Broadcast Is Over."

Testing OneNote Access via Office Web Apps

OneNote was designed with document sharing in mind, and does not require a dedicated service application but still requires Office Web Apps to be installed to enable browser-based viewing and editing of OneNote documents. Several other recommendations for configurations should be kept in mind when using Office Web Apps with OneNote documents:

1. OneNote 2010 stores versioning information in the files, so in general it is recommended not to enable minor versioning in the document library that will be storing OneNote 2010 documents.

2. In addition, if major versions are enabled for the document library storing OneNote 2010 files, it is recommended that a limit is set to the number of major versions stored by using the Keep the Following Number of Major Versions feature and setting it to a number below 10.

3. For OneNote 2010 documents to be accessible via Office Web Apps, they need to be shared to a SharePoint 2010 document library that is Office web app-enabled.

Follow these steps to share a OneNote 2010 notebook with a SharePoint 2010 document library:

1. Open OneNote 2010 and click on File, then New, and My Computer.

2. Provide a name for the new Notebook, such as New Project. Keep the location information for the new notebook on the local computer, and click Create Notebook.

3. Add some text and graphics to the new notebook; then click File, Share, and select Network from the Share On field. Then either enter the URL for the SharePoint 2010 document library that is Office web app-enabled, or choose the URL if it is shown in the Network Locations section, as shown in Figure 27.13.

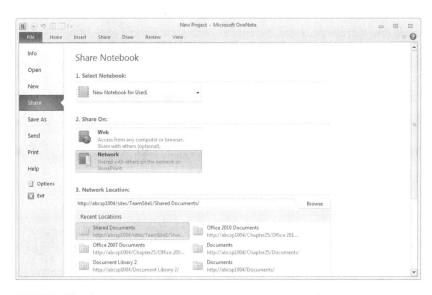

FIGURE 27.13   Sharing a OneNote with SharePoint 2010.

4. Then click Share Notebook at the bottom of the screen. A note appears stating, "The Notebook Is Now Accessible to Anyone with Permissions at That Network Location. Do You Want to Email Someone About the Notebook?" Click Email a Link and send an email to a coworker or test account.

5. Then ask the coworker to access the new Notebook or access the new Notebook using the test account. Instead of clicking the Notebook name, access the drop-down menu, and click View in Browser.

6. Figure 27.14 shows User2 accessing a Notebook published by User1 to SharePoint 2010. The graphics added to the Notebook are not visible, and a message is shown under the Ribbon that states, This Page Contains Items That Cannot be Displayed in OneNote Web App. Open This Notebook in Microsoft OneNote to See All Content. The Show Authors button on the toolbar is active, and the authors of the different sections of the page are listed.

7. Click Edit in Browser and experiment with the tools available.

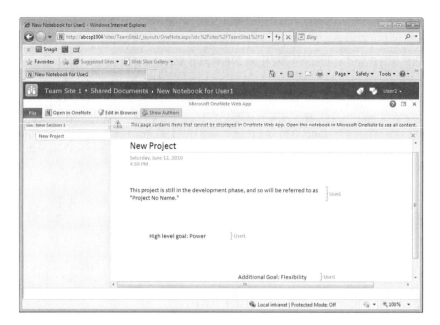

FIGURE 27.14   Viewing a OneNote Notebook in SharePoint 2010 Office Web Apps.

Summary

This chapter covers prerequisites for Office Web Apps and topics to consider when planning to support Office Web Apps, such as browser support, support of older versions of Microsoft Office documents, and mobile device support. The configuration of Office Web Apps on a two-server farm is provided, and a walkthrough of the service application configuration options. Accessing Word, PowerPoint, Excel, and OneNote documents via Office Web Apps is covered to give an overview of the main features of each and some indication of limitations. In summary, Office Web Apps provide some potentially invaluable tools for organizations wanting to provide Word, Excel, PowerPoint, and OneNote content to users through supported browsers, but there are also caveats and limitations to the editing and collaboration tools made available in the browser.

Best Practices

▶ Office web app features and functionality vary based on the operating system and browser in use, so the different permutations supported by the organization should be thoroughly tested prior to a production implementation of Office Web Apps.

▶ Organizations interested in using Office Web Apps in their environments still need to comply with Microsoft licensing policies, which can be found on the following site: http://www.microsoftvolumelicensing.com/userights/default.aspx.

▶ Due to limitations in support for older Office 2003 file formats, such as .doc., the SharePoint administration team may require that files be converted to the newer .docx, .xslx, and .pptx formats before being uploaded to SharePoint 2010 document libraries that will be enabled for use with the Office Web Apps feature and browser-based editing.

▶ It is generally recommended to leave the PowerPoint service application and Word Viewing service applications settings at their defaults unless the organization does not want to support legacy document types for Word and PowerPoint.

▶ Using the PowerPoint Broadcast service, as outlined in this chapter, is an easy way to share PowerPoint presentations with users on the network or accessing SharePoint 2010 remotely, and combined with a conference bridge can replace more expensive and complex options, such as WebEx.

▶ Compatible Excel documents and OneNote notebooks accessed by Office Web Apps are the only types of documents that can be edited by more than one user simultaneously.

▶ OneNote 2010 stores versioning information in the files; in general, it is recommended not to enable minor versioning in the document library that will be storing OneNote 2010 documents. Furthermore, if major versions are enabled for the document library, it is recommended that a limit is set to the number of major versions stored by using the Keep the Following Number of Major Versions tool and setting it to a number below 10.

27

## CHAPTER 28

Out-of-the-Box Workflows and Designer 2010 Workflows

SharePoint 2010 offers a variety of different types of workflows that can be used to enhance business processes and replace legacy business workflows that involve time-consuming manual processes and may not be well defined. This chapter provides information about a number of different workflows available in the SharePoint 2010 product line and is intended to whet the appetite of users and administrators alike to delve deeper into the out-of-the-box workflows as well as capabilities of SharePoint Designer 2010 to create complex workflows to meet everyday user requirements.

Alerts are discussed briefly as an introduction to the concept of workflows in SharePoint 2010 products, and then a detailed look at a Three-State workflow in action is provided, which is a complex enough process to give a solid introduction to the processes involved with starting and interacting with a workflow in SharePoint 2010. An overview of the other standard workflows is given from a high level, as well as the process of installing and using SharePoint Designer 2010 to create a custom workflow. Along the way, tips are given for farm administrators and site collection administrators about the tools and settings available to manage workflows and the use of SharePoint Designer 2010.

Defining Workflows in the Business Environment

In a business environment, workflows exist throughout the organization in formal and informal incarnations, and organizations of all sizes are increasingly concerned with formalizing and streamlining processes critical to the business. A key challenge in workflows is the combination of forms, the human element, time, and lack of defined processes. Consider the prototypical workflow involving an expense report form filled out by hand by User5, who then puts it in the mail slot of User2, who signs it, and puts it into the HR mail slot for processing. Consider then that User5 doesn't get the reimbursement and the steps that need to be taken for him to try and figure out what happened.

SharePoint-based workflow is one of the enterprise-level features that many users began to adopt in the SharePoint 2007 product line, and will continue to leverage in SharePoint 2010 products. This is especially true as users come to embrace the SharePoint storage modules of libraries and lists, where the ability to leverage workflows is immediately available.

Several advantages of creating and managing workflows in a SharePoint 2010 environment include the following:

▶ An easy-to-use design interface in SharePoint 2010 that quickly enables site administrators and power users to translate informal processes into well-defined, automated, and audited processes

▶ A structure that contains and manages the workflow engines, leveraging the hardware and software investment already made in SharePoint

▶ Interaction with SharePoint lists such as the Tasks list to facilitate the use and management of workflows and reduce the learning curve for end users

▶ The option of using SharePoint Designer 2010 to create different types of workflows than in the SharePoint user interface that offer more options, flexibility, and intelligence

▶ The option to use Visio 2010 to make the workflow design process more intuitive for less-technical users

Considering Alerts as Basic Workflows

As discussed in Chapter 19, "Using Libraries and Lists in SharePoint 2010," and specifically in the section titled "Reviewing the E-mail a Link and Alert Me Tools," alerts are powerful and simple to use, and can be seen to provide a type of workflow functionality. Alerts are triggered by certain activities or changes, and they result in an email being sent immediately, or at a later time, to one or more end users. The end users can then take action based on the alert, as they see fit.

This is a form of workflow because an automated process is pushing information to end users via email, which is similar to one component of the workflows that will be discussed in this chapter, such as the Three-State workflow. Although alerts are limited in terms of configuration options, certain lists add customized alerts to the list of what's available. For example, in an issues list, an alert option is added in the Send Alerts for these Changes section: Someone changes an item that appears in the following view. As shown in Figure 28.1, an alert in this type of list can be triggered by a change in a specific view. Because views are extremely customizable, and could, for example, just include items where the column values match certain criteria, this capability can be very powerful. For example, a view could be created in an issues list called My Active High Priority Issues that only displays items where the Assigned To value equals [Me], the Priority is set to (1) High, and where the Issue Status is set to Active. Then if any changes happen in this very specific view, the user will be notified.

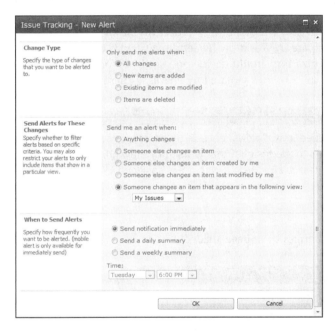

FIGURE 28.1   Alert options in an issues list.

> **TIP**
>
> Review the different alert options available in lists such as Calendar, Tasks, and Issues to see the unique alerts provided and think about how they might be leveraged to enhance the usefulness of the alerts for users of the lists.

Reviewing the Workflow-Related Settings in Central Administration and Site Settings

Workflows do not have a service application they rely on because they are built on the Windows Workflow Foundation, but there are several areas where the farm administrator can find tools related to workflow configuration.

To begin with, each web application has workflow-related settings that should be reviewed. Follow these steps to review the workflow settings for a web application:

1. Click the Application Management link from the Central Administration home page, and then click Manage Web Applications.

2. Select the web application of interest (for example, SharePoint – 80), so that the row is highlighted, and click General Settings on the Web Applications tab on the Ribbon. Select Workflow, and the Workflow Settings window will open.

3. Review the settings and make sure they meet the organization's standards. User-defined workflows are created in tools such as Designer 2010 or Visual Studio 2010, so the farm administrator needs to decide whether to allow the use of these tools in the specific web application. The other two options are to Alert Internal Users Who Do Not Have Site Access When They Are Assigned a Workflow Task (Yes/No) and Allow External Users to Participate in Workflow by Sending Them a Copy of the Document (Yes/No). The organization should decide on standards for these settings to ensure that the security of the site isn't violated by enabling these options.

NOTE

If nonsite members are to be included in workflows, each of those users needs a minimum of contribute-level permissions to the task list that is used by the workflow. Otherwise, they won't be able to interact with the tasks that are assigned to them, limiting the usefulness of the workflow.

4. Click OK after any required changes have been made.

NOTE

PowerShell cmdlets are available to complete these tasks: Get-SPWorkflowConfig returns workflow settings for the specified web application, and Set-SPWorkflowConfig configures the workflow settings for the specified web application.

There are also workflow-related jobs that can be found by clicking the Monitoring link from the Central Administration site, and then clicking Review Job Definitions. These are as follows:

▶ **Bulk Workflow Task Processing**—This job processes bulk workflow tasks, and by default is set to occur once a day.

▶ **Workflow**—This job processes workflow events and by default is set to occur every 5 minutes.

▶ **Workflow Auto Cleanup**—By default, set to occur every 15 minutes. This deletes tasks and workflow instances that have been marked complete longer than the expiration specified in the workflow association.

▶ **Workflow Failover**—By default, set to occur every 15 minutes. This processes events for workflows that have failed and are marked to be retried.

Reviewing the Site Settings Tools for Workflows

A quick place for a site collection administrator to check on which workflows are enabled is from the Site Settings page, in the Site Administration section, and clicking the link for Workflows. Note that this link isn't available for site owners, however. The site collection administrator can then see which workflows are available for use on the site. Figure 28.2 shows the Workflows page, where a number of workflows on a SharePoint Server 2010 Enterprise site collection have been enabled.

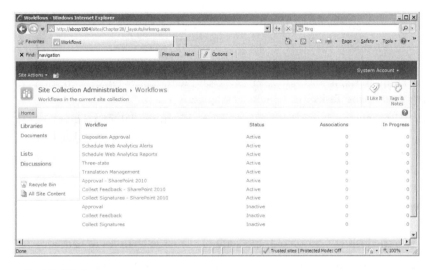

FIGURE 28.2   Workflows page from Site Settings.

> **NOTE**
>
> The Schedule Web Analytics Alerts and Schedule Web Analytics Reports are enabled or disabled by the site collection feature Advanced Web Analytics. These are not accessible to end users, but are used to compile management reports.

The Site Collection Features link should be accessed to make change to the workflows that will be available to the user community. A general best practice is to not enable the SharePoint 2007 workflows unless there is a specific need for them (for example, to support workflows that are migrated in various states of completion from a SharePoint 2007 environment, or to allow SharePoint 2007 workflow users to transition to the new SharePoint 2010 workflows gradually). Likewise, the Publishing Approval workflow should be enabled only in sites where Content Approval is going to be used in document libraries (this is turned on from Document Library Settings, Versioning Settings page). This workflow will then trigger when documents are saved as major versions in document libraries with Content Approval enabled, which can annoy end users if they don't see specific value in it and are not trained in the process.

Next check the Workflow Settings link to see whether there are existing workflows associated with the site collection and remove any that aren't desirable.

Testing the Three-State Workflow

The Three-State workflow is a good choice for initial testing because it is available in both SharePoint Foundation 2010 and SharePoint Server 2010 environments. It is also somewhat complex and takes a number of steps and at least two user accounts to complete. The main steps involved with this workflow are as follows:

1. An issue is created in an Issues list by a manager (User1), where an assignee is specified (User2) and the issue saved.
2. The workflow is manually started by the manager (User1).
3. After the workflow starts, it notifies User1 and User2 with a brief email, and then creates a new task in the Tasks list, which is assigned to User2.
4. The assignee (User2) gets a more detailed email 1 to 5 minutes later that gives instructions on what to do. These instructions tell the assignee to review the issue and then update the task.
5. After the assignee (User2) updates the task and sets it to complete, the state of the issue changes to Resolved and the manager/initiator (User1) is assigned a new task.
6. The manager (User1) receives an email with instructions to review the issue and then update the task.
7. After User1 sets the task to Completed, the state of the issue changes to Closed.

There are several key concepts to understand in this process. One is that this workflow is created in a specific list, and won't be available from other lists in the site or site collection. Another key concept is that tasks are generated in a separate Tasks list by the workflow—first when the workflow is started, and then when the first task is marked as complete, which then changes the value of a column in the list and creates a second task. Each of these actions makes entries into the History list, which is not visible to users or even site administrators directly, but then provides audit history of the workflow.

It is also important to realize that there are multiple points of interaction with the issue and the task items, and users can change more than just the minimal fields discussed in the example. So in other words, there is margin for error, and users need to be clear which fields they should and shouldn't modify.

The prerequisites for this testing are as follows:

▶ The Three-State workflow is enabled for the site collection.

▶ Two accounts are available for testing, each with an active email account in Outlook, and preferably Outlook 2010. Although this workflow can be completed by using just one account, it is harder to interpret the activities taking place and less useful as a training exercise.

▶ The account that creates the workflow should be a site owner, whereas the other account can just be a site member.

Follow these steps to test the workflow:

1. Create a new list using the Issue Tracking template and name it **Issue Tracking.**

2. Click the List tab on the Ribbon from within the Issue Tracking list, and then click List Settings.

3. Click the Issue Status link in the Columns section. Scroll down on the Change Column page to the choices and note that there are three choices for this column: Active, Resolved, and Closed.

4. Click Cancel to return to the List Settings Page. Click Workflow Settings in the Permissions and Management section.

5. The Add a Workflow page will open. Select Three-State from the list of workflows.

6. Name the workflow **Issues-ThreeState.**

7. Verify that the Task list is set to Tasks (New) and that the History list is set to Workflow History (New). These settings indicate that a new tasks list will be created to track tasks associated with this workflow and a new workflow history list created to track workflow auditing information.

8. In the Start Options section, verify that the Allow This Workflow to Be Manually Started option is selected. Click Next.

9. The Customize the Three-State Workflow page will open. Verify that the Choice field is set to Issue Status, and the Initial State is set to Active, the Middle State is set to Resolved, and the Final State is set to Closed, as shown in Figure 28.3.

10. Scroll down to the next section titled Specify What You Want to Happen When a Workflow Is Initiated. Leave these settings at their defaults, as also shown in Figure 28.3, but review the different components of this section. Note that the task that will be created can be customized, the individual the task is assigned to can be modified, as can the fields that are included on the email. Note that the task will be assigned to the individual in the Assigned To field.

11. Scroll down to the next section titled Specify What You Want to Happen When a Workflow Changes to Its Middle State. After again, leave the settings at their defaults. Note that the Task Assigned to is set to the Created By column for this stage. Click OK to complete the workflow definition process and return to the Issue Tracking list.

12. Verify that you are logged in to the SharePoint site as a user who will be considered to be the manager for this test (User1 in this example). This user will create the Issue, and then assign it to another user for completion.

13. Click Add New Item, and create a new issue title **Test Issue 1**, assign it to a test user who will be charged with completing the task (User2 in this case). Leave the Issue Status to Active, Priority to (2) Normal, as shown in Figure 28.4. Enter a brief description for the issue, such as Test issue for workflow testing. Leave the other settings on the page at their defaults and click Save.

28

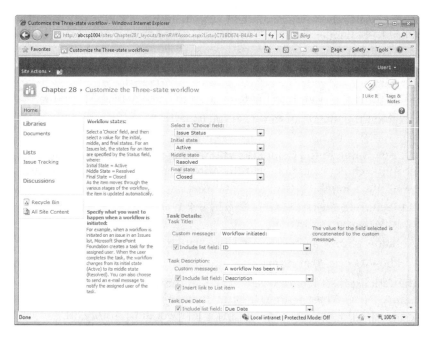

FIGURE 28.3   The Customize the Three-State Workflow page.

FIGURE 28.4   Creating a new issue to test the Three-State workflow.

14. Navigate to the tasks list that was defined in step 7 (in this case, Tasks) and note that no tasks have been created at this point. This is because the workflow has not been started.

15. The manager (User1) next manually starts the workflow, which assigns it to the user in the Assigned To column (User2 in this example). To do this, access the drop-down list for the Issue (Test Issue 1 in this example) and click Workflows.

16. The Workflow.aspx page opens. Click the Issues-ThreeState link in the Start a New Workflow section.

17. The workflow starts and the user (User1) is returned to the Issue Tracking list, as shown in Figure 28.5. Note that a new column will be visible that is titled Issues-ThreeState and shows the In Progress status for the workflow. The user also receives an email with a subject that reads "Workflow initiated" with the ID number of the workflow include. This email also provides a link to the Issues list. This helps remind the manager that he did in fact start the workflow.

FIGURE 28.5   Issue list after the Three-State workflow is started.

18. Next, log off as the manager (User1) and log in as the assignee (User2) and open Outlook. This user should have received both a copy of the "Workflow initiated" email and shortly thereafter an email that informs them that they have been assigned a task, and are given other information about the task, as shown in Figure 28.6. A URL is given to the issue in the Issue Tracking list, as well as instructions on how to complete the task: Review the issue, perform specific activities required for this task, and then edit the task and mark it as completed.

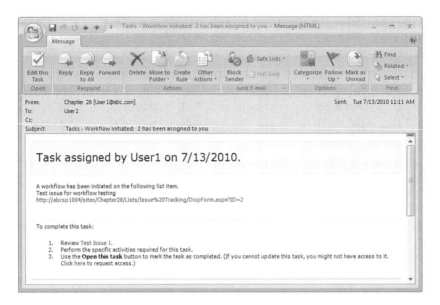

FIGURE 28.6   Email received by issue assignee once the Three-State workflow is started.

CAUTION

This is a key point in the workflow where users forget to edit the task! They click the link to the issue, update the issue, and then think they are done, but unless the task is updated the workflow won't move on to the next step. So, the training process should emphasize the importance of updating the task as well as the issue.

19. At this point in the process, the assignee (User2) now knows he has an issue to work on, and he clicks the URL to open the issue and get to work on it, and update the issue. After the issue has been resolved, he needs to then edit the task to indicate the issue has been resolved. To do this, while still logged in as the assignee (User2), click the Open This Task button on the Ribbon to edit the task that was created by the workflow.

NOTE

In this example, User2 is using Outlook 2007, so the button on the Ribbon is titled Edit this Task as opposed to Open this Task (as shown in Figure 28.6), as it is labeled in Outlook 2010.

20. The task will open as shown in Figure 28.7. Change the Status to Completed, and enter 100 in the % Complete field. Then click Save.

21. The assignee (User2) will then be returned to the Tasks list and will see that a new task has been created, which is assigned to the initiator (User1).

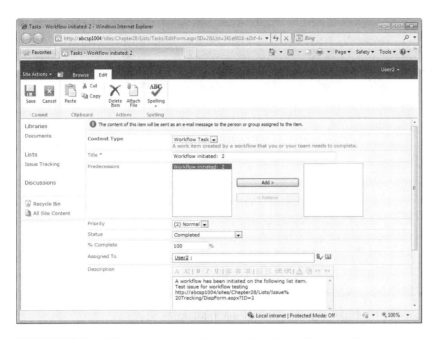

FIGURE 28.7   Editing the task assigned by the Three-State workflow.

22. Log back in as the manager/initiator (User1) and open Outlook. An email should have been received with a subject line "Review task X" (where X is the ID of the task created in the Issue Tracking list). Click the URL to review the issue, which the assignee (User2) claims to have completed. Note that the issue is now set to the status of Resolved, as shown in Figure 28.8.

23. Shortly after (up to five minutes), the manager receives another email with the subject line "Tasks – Review Task 2 has been assigned to you." Open the email and click the link to the issue, which should have been updated by the assignee (User2). If this were a real-world situation, the manager would now review the issue, and any notes added by the assignee (User2), to make sure it was appropriately updated.

24. After the manager is satisfied the issue has been taken care of, the task can be marked as complete. To do this, as the manager (User1), click the Open This Task button and close the task by setting the Task Status to Completed and the % Complete field to 100 and then clicking Save.

25. The Tasks list will then be visible, as shown in Figure 28.9, and shows both the original task where User2 was assigned a task, and marked it as complete, and the second task where User1 was assigned a task and marked it as complete.

26. Still logged in as the manager (User1), navigate to the Issue Tracking list, and verify that the status of the issue is now set to Closed and the field under the column titled Issues-ThreeState shows the value of Completed.

28

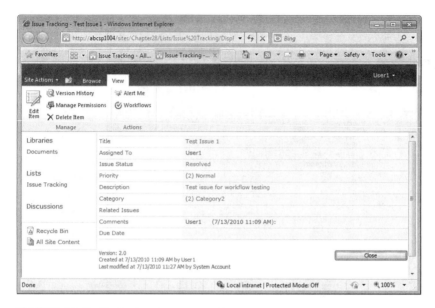

FIGURE 28.8   Reviewing the status of the issue in the Three-State workflow.

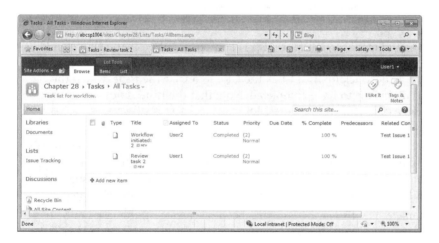

FIGURE 28.9   Viewing the tasks created by the Three-State workflow.

27. Click the work Completed in the Issues-ThreeState column to view more details about the workflow, as shown in Figure 28.10. This page shows information about the initiator (User1), start time, status, which tasks were created and their outcomes, and the workflow history, which shows details of the event types that make up the workflow.

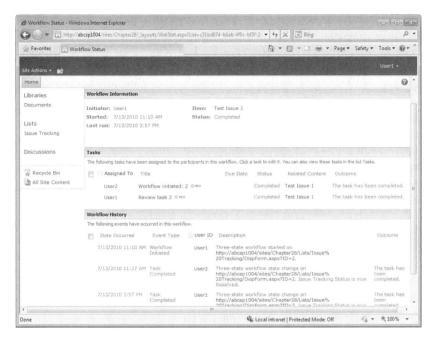

FIGURE 28.10   Viewing the workflow information for the Three-State workflow.

An Overview of Other Standard Workflows

The previous example of the Three-State workflow could be considered a form of "tough love" because it is a fairly complex workflow in terms of end-user interactivity require-ments. Microsoft's decision to make this available in SharePoint Foundation 2010 but not the other standard SharePoint Server 2010 workflows is somewhat mysterious. For organi-zations using SharePoint Server 2010, the following additional workflows should be tested and may well prove to be more useful than the Three-State workflow:

▶ **Approval**—An Approval workflow routes a document for approval. Approvers can approve or reject the document, reassign the approval task, or request changes to the document.

▶ **Collect Feedback**—This routes a document for review to reviewers who can provide feedback, which is compiled and sent to the person who initiated the workflow.

▶ **Collect Signatures**—This workflow routes a Microsoft Office document to a group of people to collect their digital signatures and must be started in an Office application that is part of the Office 2007 or 2010 family. Figure 28.11 shows an example of a Word 2007 document that was included in a Collect Signatures workflow after User1 has opened it and added a signature to the document by executing the task which then provides the interface for adding the signature. The signature is a graphic image User1 created and then added to the document. The process of signing the document also marks it as Final, and any changes will invalidate the signature, so the signing process is more complex than simply adding a graphic image to the Word document.

FIGURE 28.11   Adding a signature to a document in a Collect Signatures workflow.

▶ **Translation Management**—This workflow manages the manual document translation process by creating copies of the document to be translated and assigning translation tasks to translators. This workflow is available only for Translation Management libraries.

▶ **Disposition Approval**—This manages document expiration and retention by allowing participants to decide whether to retain or delete expired documents.

The Approval, Collect Feedback, and Collect Signatures workflows are available for editing when Designer 2010 is used to open a site, and listed in the Globally Reusable Workflow section. Figure 28.12 shows the settings page for the Approval workflow. Note that there is an Edit Workflow link available, as well as the ability to disable different Start Options, and the actual InfoPath forms can be accessed and edited. Using SharePoint Designer 2010 with SharePoint 2010 workflows is covered later in this chapter, as well as in Chapter 29, "Application Development with SharePoint Designer 2010 and Visual Studio 2010."

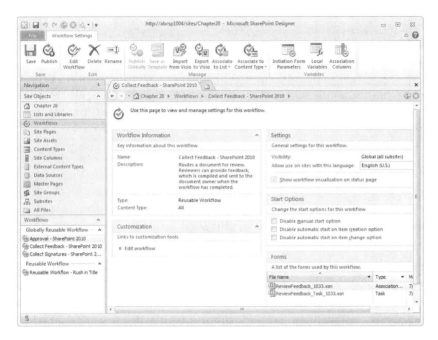

FIGURE 28.12   Modifying a Collect Feedback workflow in Designer 2010.

Verifying the Web Application Settings for SharePoint Designer 2010 Use

Organizations often find that the standard out-of-the-box workflows simply do not provide enough flexibility to meet their requirements and want to be able to access additional tools to create these workflows, and the logic that drives them. SharePoint Designer 2010 can be used to create a wide variety of workflows, to include list workflows, reusable workflows, and site workflows. SharePoint Designer 2010 also allows interactivity with Visio 2010 as well as InfoPath 2010 and a host of other tools to facilitate the overall design and implementation process.

Power users and developers who will be using SharePoint Designer 2010 should verify that it is supported by IT, even though the software can be downloaded for free, to ensure that it will function properly. Often, due to configurations in SharePoint or on the desktop, SharePoint Designer 2010 will not function properly if IT is not prepared to "officially" support it.

28

In addition, the farm administrator may have chosen to not allow the use of SharePoint Designer from the Central Administration site. This should be verified to avoid possible confusion or issues during the development process.

To configure SharePoint Designer settings for a web application, follow these steps:

1. Open SharePoint 2010 Central Administration and click Manage Web Applications from the Application Management Section.

2. Select the web application to manage (such as SharePoint – 80), and then click the General Settings button on the Ribbon bar and choose SharePoint Designer from the drop-down menu that appears. The Configure SharePoint Designer Settings are typically all checked. If one or more are not enabled, that will limit the level of SharePoint Designer 2010 customizations possible.

3. Click OK when finished.

The options are as follows:

▶ **Allow SharePoint Designer to be used in this Web Application**—If this option is not checked (enabled), SharePoint Designer can't be used in the web application.

▶ **Allow Site Collection Administrators to Detach Pages from the Site Template**—"Old timers" in the SharePoint world will remember this as the "unghosting" process.

▶ **Allow Site Collection Administrators to Customize Master Pages and Layout Pages.**

▶ **Allow Site Collection Administrators to see the URL Structure of their Web Site.**

Downloading and Installing SharePoint Designer 2010

SharePoint Designer is available free of charge from Microsoft who wants to encourage power users and developers to customize the SharePoint 2010 environment to meet a wide variety of business needs. The workstation or server needs to have .NET 3.5 installed, and as discussed in the previous section, the web application needs to be configured to allow the use of SharePoint Designer 2010.

SharePoint Designer 2010 is available in both 32- and 64-bit versions, so developers should be sure to download the version that corresponds to their workstation's operating system version. The main decision point between 32- and 64-bit development machines comes down to the 4GB limit for 32-bit Vista and XP workstations.

To Install SharePoint Designer 2010, follow these steps:

1. If it is not already installed on the workstation that will house SharePoint Designer 2010, install .NET 3.5 from the following link:

http://www.microsoft.com/downloads/details.aspx?familyid=333325FD-AE52-4E35-B531-508D977D32A6&displaylang=en

2. Download the 32- or 64-bit version of SharePoint Designer from http://www.microsoft.com/downloads/en/results.aspx?freetext=SharePoint+Designer+2010.

3. Run the SharePointDesigner.exe and complete the install by selecting either the standard or custom options.

With SharePoint Designer 2010 downloaded and installed, development can begin immediately as long as the user has a minimum of designer-level rights to a SharePoint 2010 site.

Creating a Reusable Workflow from SharePoint Designer 2010

To create a reusable workflow, the site that will house the workflow must be opened from SharePoint Designer 2010, and then the workflow is designed, tested, and published to the site. It can then added to a list or library on that site and is then ready for use. The following example creates a reusable workflow that is triggered whenever the word "rush" is found in the title field of a document. The application in this example is a collaboration site where managers (User1 and User2) need to review and provide feedback on documents in different libraries before they can be released to marketing. Complaints had occurred before when User1 and User2 weren't responsive enough, so the workflow was created. If a user thinks his or her document deserves "rush" status, he or she simply needs to add that text to the title field, and the workflow will initiate, and User1 will be informed of the task, and once he completes it, User2 will be assigned a task. Auditing information will track the responsiveness of both User1 and User2.

This workflow takes advantage of the Start Feedback Process action in SharePoint Designer 2010, which contains the logic and functionality of the Collect Feedback workflow that is a standard workflow in SharePoint Server 2010. So, this is an example of a workflow within a workflow that enables even relatively novice workflow designers to take advantage of the standard workflows provided out of the box.

Follow these steps to open a SharePoint 2010 site and create this site workflow:

1. Open SharePoint Designer 2010 by clicking the Start button, click All Programs, SharePoint, and then click Microsoft SharePoint Designer 2010.

2. From the File tab, the Sites node should be open; if it does not open, click Sites. Then click the Open Site icon.

3. Type the URL of the site (for example, http://abcsp1004/sites/Chapter28) or select the site from the list of available sites if it has been accessed before, as shown in Figure 28.13. Note: Do not include a page name such as default.aspx or /pages/home.aspx.

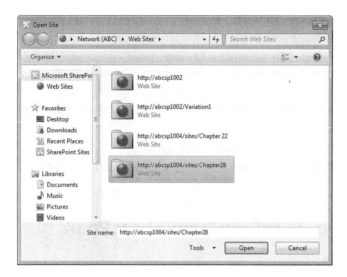

FIGURE 28.13   Opening a site from Designer 2010.

4. Click Workflows from the Site Objects list in the navigation pane.

5. Click Reusable Workflow from the Workflows tab, and the Create Reusable Workflow window will open, as shown in Figure 28.14.

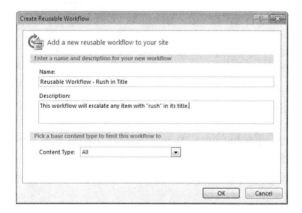

FIGURE 28.14   Naming the Reusable workflow in Designer 2010.

6. Provide a title for the workflow, such as **Reusable Workflow - Rush in Title**, and a description if desired. In this case, the description is entered as follows: This work-flow will escalate any item with 'rush' in its title. Leave Content Type set to All, and click OK.

7. Click the flashing line in the Step 1 box and type **if current** and press Enter; Designer will determine that you want to enter If current item field equals value. Alternatively, you can click the Condition button and choose If Current Item Field Equals Value.

8. Click the link labeled Field in the Step 1 box, and select Title from the drop-down menu.

9. Click the link labeled Equals in the Step 1 box, and select Contains from the drop-down menu.

10. Click the link labeled value in the Step 1 box, and type **rush** and press Enter. The results will look like Figure 28.15.

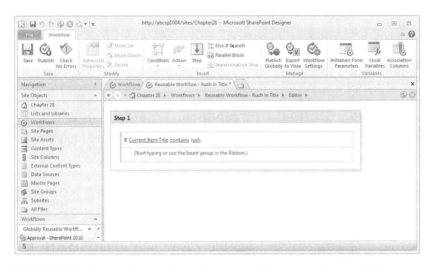

FIGURE 28.15   Setting conditions for the workflow in Designer 2010.

28

NOTE

Before making changes to a production system, test your code on a development server or, at a minimum, in a different site collection.

---

11. Click the area directly below the line where data was just entered and type **Start feedback** and press Enter. Designer 2010 will interpret this to mean Start Feedback Process. The results will be the same as Figure 28.16. This action effectively imbeds a Collect Feedback workflow within this Reusable Workflow, which provides significant functionality within the workflow, as will be demonstrated upon completion of the workflow.

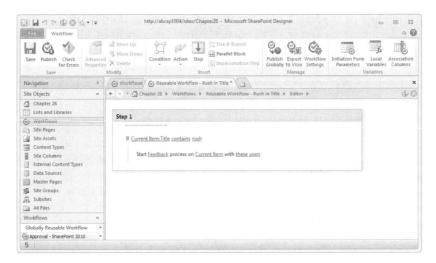

FIGURE 28.16   Workflow action after adding Start Feedback process in Designer 2010.

12. Click the These Users link, and the Select Task Participants window will open.

13. In the Participants field, enter two valid usernames separated by a semicolon (;) (**User1;User2** in this example). Leave One at a Time (Serial) selected in the field to the right of Participants.

14. In the CC field, click the Select Users icon on the right, and click User Who Created Current Item, and then click the Add button. Click OK.

15. In the Title field, enter the text **Rush Item Escalated.**

16. In the Instructions field, enter text describing the activity, such as, **This item's title contained the word 'rush' and so has been escalated for review and processing.**

17. In the Duration per Task field, enter 1 and verify that Days is selected to the right. The window should look like Figure 28.17. Click OK.

18. Click the Check for Errors button on the Ribbon and the message "The workflow contains no errors" should display.

19. Click the Publish button on the Ribbon, and the workflow will publish to the site.

In this next section, the workflow will be initiated, and started, to display the functionality without completing the entire workflow. To test the workflow, follow these steps:

1. Log in to the site as an account with owner-level privileges (http://abcsp1004/sites/Chapter28/documents in this example).

2. Add the Reusable workflow to the library by accessing Library Settings and clicking the Workflow Settings link in the Permissions and Management section.

3. The Reusable workflow should appear in the Select a Workflow Template list, as shown in Figure 28.18. Click the workflow.

FIGURE 28.17   Defining participants in the Start Feedback Process action in Designer 2010.

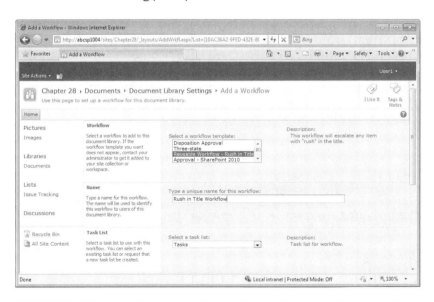

FIGURE 28.18   Choosing and configuring the workflow from Library Settings.

4. Enter a name for the workflow in the Name section (for example, **Rush in Title Workflow Automatic**).

5. Leave the Task list and History list settings at their defaults.

6. Under Start Options, verify that the Allow This Workflow to Be Manually Started by an Authenticated User with Edit Item Permissions is checked, and check the Start This Workflow When a New Item Is Created and Start This Workflow When an Item Is Changed boxes. Click OK.

7. Now, log in as a user who is not involved in the feedback process but has contributor-level privileges in the library (for example, User3).

8. Access the document library on the site and upload a sample document. For this example, the document title is "User3's super-important document.docx."

9. Next, edit the properties of the document and add the term **rush** to the Title field, and save.

10. The column titled Rush in Title Workflow will appear in the library and the document should be set to a status of In Progress in that column.

11. Open Outlook for this user (User3) and an email will be there, announcing the start of the Feedback workflow, as shown in Figure 28.19.

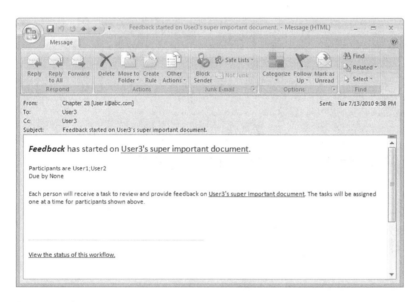

FIGURE 28.19   Email informing document owner of workflow start.

12. Log out, and then log back in as the first approver (User1 in this example). Open Outlook and note that an email has been received, as shown in Figure 28.20.

The rest of the workflow won't be covered here, but it gives User1 a change to provide feedback on the document and then once approved, a task will be created for User2 and that user will be given a chance to provide feedback.

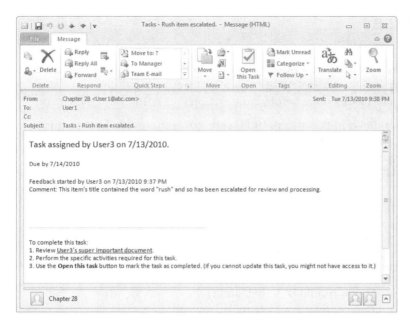

FIGURE 28.20   Email informing workflow participant of workflow

Summary

This chapter touches on many of the different types of workflows provided in the SharePoint 2010 product line, and gives two detailed examples to familiarize readers with the process of creating and using workflows. Information is also provided to administrators pertaining to the management of workflows and for controlling SharePoint Designer 2010 use. Testing workflows can be challenging due to the requirements of having multiple user accounts involved in the process, but having a solid foundation on the out-of-the-box workflows and an understanding of what can be accomplished in SharePoint Designer 2010 will help administrators and power users more efficiently create useful workflows.

28

Best Practices

▶ As a starting point for encouraging end users to use SharePoint workflows, train them on the range of capabilities of list and library alerts, and educate users about some of the unique alerts available in lists such as the calendar, issues, and tasks lists. This is a good starting place before more complex workflows are implemented.

▶ Before testing workflows in the organization, verify the settings outlined in this chapter in the Central Administration site, as well as for the Site Collection where they will be used, to ensure that the settings meet the organization's needs and the appropriate workflows are enabled.

▶ As a general rule, don't enable the SharePoint 2007 workflows unless they are specifically required.

▶ The Three-State workflow is available in both SharePoint Foundation 2010 and SharePoint Server 2010 and is useful for testing and training purposes because there are multiple tasks generated and several points of interaction for end users.

▶ Other standard workflows should be tested, and IT should decide which, if any, of the additional workflows will be available for use by end users.

▶ IT should decide whether to allow the use of SharePoint Designer 2010 in the environment and can control its use via the Central Administration site.

▶ SharePoint Designer 2010 allows the creation of new workflows as well as modification of out-of-the-box workflows and provides access to many powerful conditions and actions that can create complex workflows, as shown in this chapter.

## CHAPTER 29

Application Development with SharePoint Designer 2010 and Visual Studio 2010

Application development is a weighty topic, and this chapter seeks to communicate to architects, administrators, and developers some of the new and exciting features for developing with SharePoint 2010 using Designer 2010 or Visual Studio 2010. This chapter also provides exercises designed to give users of varying levels of expertise experience with Designer 2010 application design and create a Visual Studio 2010 Visual Web Part.

SharePoint Designer 2010 will be used to create a workflow that interacts with several SharePoint lists to serve as the foundation for an "application" that can be created by a power user within the organization that doesn't require the use of Visual Studio. This workflow enables a user to convert a sales lead into a customer by executing a workflow that creates a new item in a different list and leverages lookup columns to populate the new list.

The example using Visual Studio 2010 demonstrates the development of a Visual Web Part that uses many new development features that SharePoint 2010 supports, including LINQ, a .NET feature normally reserved for database development, and the ListView user interface component that improves upon the .NET repeating section.

Deciding Whether Development Is Required to Meet Business Needs

When embarking on a development project in Microsoft SharePoint 2010, there are several important criteria to consider so that the developer has the proper tools to complete the task at hand. An initial question to ask is whether SharePoint 2010 offers tools out-of-the-box that might provide the functionality required. Some investigation in this area might save the developer many hours of needless labor.

For example, some of the lesser-known web parts (such as the Content Query Web Part, Content Editor Web Part, or Page Viewer Web Part) provide functionality that can be leveraged and extended to meet more complex business needs. Many tips exist for pasting JavaScript into the Content Editor Web Part to perform a wide variety of tasks.

SharePoint web parts can be connected to each other, enabling one list to filter the contents of another list. Connected web parts enable a selection in one list to filter the contents that display in another list. Although the functionality is limited to single column joins, the relative ease of connecting web parts should not be overlooked as a possible solution and is leveraged in many dashboard configurations to enable a user interaction with the data displayed.

In SharePoint 2010, to support the connected web part features, the underlying lists and libraries can now maintain enforced relationships among each other using the lookup column, as covered in Chapter 22, "Managing Metadata and Content Types in SharePoint 2010." New in SharePoint 2010, lookup columns can spawn additional columns from the source list into the host list that contains the lookup column. Calculated columns allow SharePoint administrators and developers alike to complete many of the same calculations that Excel supports, including advanced string, date, and number operations. Although the functionality is fairly limited, this just might satisfy the business owner's requirements.

Content types are another overlooked and often misunderstood feature in SharePoint that, when used properly, can reduce the need for custom programming. Content types are in use throughout SharePoint from lists and libraries to article pages and are heavily used under the hood by InfoPath Forms Services. Creative use of content types is a powerful way of providing enhanced behavior, metadata, and workflows, ultimately providing the user with a rich and intuitive experience.

There are also many possibilities provided by features such as alerts, tasks, project tasks, or out-of-the-box workflows that push information to users of the SharePoint environment. Creative SharePoint administrators have long used alerts as simple workflows, because they push a limited amount of information to end users based on changes that take place in lists and libraries.

> **TIP**
>
> In addition to out-of-the-box SharePoint tools, features, and capabilities, make sure to research whether third-party retail products may provide the required functionality. Developers don't like explaining why they have spent weeks developing a web part that could be purchased for $500 and comes with updates, technical support, and other benefits.

Assuming this due diligence has been performed, and the desired functionality was not readily attainable, it is time to look into SharePoint Designer 2010 and Visual Studio 2010. This chapter demonstrates several different methods to harness the features provided by the two very different applications.

Planning the Development Project

A recommended best practice is always to document the goals for the application development project to ensure that the scope of work is clearly defined and there are clear milestones for the development process. Simply writing up a list of bullets of the reason for the project and the success criteria that will prove that the project has been successfully completed can be extremely valuable at a later date.

A simple development project—for example, a workflow for an expense report or the creation of a web part that displays data from a website—might require only a few minutes to summarize. However, a more complex project—for example, a purchase order application development project—can require several days and numerous meetings to thoroughly define.

Typically SharePoint development projects involve out-of-the-box SharePoint components and the creation of workflows in SharePoint Designer 2010, forms in InfoPath 2010, and Solutions in Visual Studio 2010, and putting together a list of the components expected from the final project can help guide the development process. The following list provides a number of high-level tasks that should not be forgotten when planning a more complex development project:

- ▶ Define the Statement of Work (SOW).
- ▶ Configure/update the development environment.
- ▶ Configure the base SharePoint 2010 site/sites/site collection.
- ▶ Configure required lists and libraries to support the application.
- ▶ Create mock-ups of forms and visual components.
- ▶ Develop the required components and functionality in Designer 2010 and/or Visual Studio 2010.
- ▶ Ensure auditing functionality is in place as needed.
- ▶ Ensure that security for the objects involved in the application (lists, libraries, forms, and so on) is in place.

29

▶ Ensure that the application is fault tolerant and scalable enough to meet the needs of the organization.

▶ Ensure that exception handling and logging is in place.

▶ Document key steps in the development process.

▶ Test functionality and "prove the concept" of the application.

▶ Make sure the application is portable and can be moved from the development environment to the staging or production environment.

▶ Allow time for User Acceptance Testing (UAT) and Pilot Phases before a full rollout.

▶ Allow time for end users and administrator training to use and support the application.

▶ Include sign-offs along the way to ensure management approval of progress.

▶ Establish change control practices for changes after the application is in production use.

Following these steps for even simpler projects will enhance the success, and sometimes even more importantly, the perception of success by managers and stakeholders who may not be technically savvy enough to appreciate the elegance of the code of stability of the code.

Evolutions in the SharePoint Platform for Developers

SharePoint 2007 grew in leaps and bounds over SharePoint 2003 and became recognized as a versatile and powerful development platform, but there were still limitations in the areas of security, portability, performance, reliability, and features. With SharePoint 2010, the bar has been raised yet again. The latest iteration of the SharePoint platform has too many enhancements to cover in a single chapter, but some of the highlights are covered in this section, along with a summary of enhancements in Designer 2010 and Visual Studio 2010.

SharePoint 2010 provides a powerful new client object model that is formally defined as the SharePoint Foundation 2010 Managed Client Object Model, or simply the client object model. The client object model allows code that runs remotely or directly on the server to consume SharePoint objects, methods, lists, and libraries using a referenced DLL instead of referenced web service calls. Previously, web services needed to be used to remotely interact with SharePoint lists and other features, or server-side code such as console applications or timer jobs would need to be written.

The new client object model enables the development of rich client applications based on the Microsoft .NET Framework providing for feature-rich web parts, console applications, Microsoft Silverlight applications, and ECMAScript (JavaScript, JScript) applications that run client-side or in a SharePoint Web Part. An added value of the new client object model is the inclusion of the familiar intellisense in Visual Studio that developers have grown used to. This allows developers to rapidly develop applications and utilities that remotely access SharePoint, and developers will quickly recognize the benefit of having the object-aware intellisense that allows for familiar interactions with SharePoint objects without having to learn the complicated web service endpoints included with SharePoint 2003 and SharePoint 2007. Furthermore, web service endpoints of SharePoint 2003 and SharePoint 2007 required more of a steady hand for dealing with failed events.

When using the client object model, applications can use CAML or LINQ to query content from SharePoint lists and libraries, create client objects, and persist those objects back to SharePoint. In addition, items may be deleted, updated, and checked in/out as needed. Lists, library sites, and even the farm can be queried for schema information, and many administrative tasks can be carried out using the object model.

SharePoint 2010 also supports a powerful feature that used to be reserved only for data-base applications: LINQ. LINQ enables developers to access SharePoint fields in lists and libraries as if they are strongly typed objects. An example later in the chapter demon-strates how to use LINQ to query data for a visual web part. In addition to the base features of the .NET Framework, SharePoint 2010 also leverages Windows Workflow Foundation, a powerful business process management engine seamlessly integrated into SharePoint for the development of advanced state applications. Visual Studio 2010 provides the project templates necessary to create sequential and state machine workflows and now supports their full development life cycle from development, to testing, to deployment, to packaging.

NOTE

A state machine workflow is a workflow associated with a SharePoint list item or docu-ment that can enter different states in any order. For example, a purchase order may have five states, such as Not Submitted, Submitted, Pending, Approved, and Completed. A state machine workflow, unlike a sequential workflow, enables the item to be routed and rerouted to each state as needed.

To make the development process more seamless and intuitive, Visual Studio 2010 now contains a variety of templates built in with no need to install the Visual Studio Extensions for SharePoint to start with SharePoint development. Some of the new templates include site definitions, business data connectivity models, event receivers, and modules. Coupled with the new deployment features, developers are provided with the entire framework and are simply required to produce the code for the desired solution.

REST (Representational State Transfer) APIs included in SharePoint 2010 are standard web service interfaces that enable the development of HTTP-based applications. REST is essen-tially a client-server request using HTTP to retrieve or send information and can be lever-aged in Visual Studio projects.

Finally, because development servers are not always available and code often needs to be tested in a staging environment, SharePoint 2010 now supports sandboxed solutions. A sandboxed solution is deployed directly to SharePoint 2010 and trusted to run within the context of a web application without having to trust the assembly in the web.config. This

29

has important implications for SharePoint customers whose SharePoint implementation is
running in a hosted environment.

Designer 2010 Enhancements

Designer 2010 has a large number of enhancements over Designer 2007 that include a
redesigned interface, Visio 2010 integration, extensive use of InfoPath forms, capability to
create External Content Types and External Lists, and many other features. For developers
who are familiar with SharePoint Designer 2007, some of the highlights of SharePoint
Designer 2010 include the following:

▶ **Impersonation steps**—Enable workflows to run under the context of another user
   other than that of the executing user. This enables a user with lesser privileges to
   start a workflow that can then perform actions that the author of the workflow has
   permissions to perform. This eliminates a major challenge in workflow design in
   which the initiator's privileges often limited the tasks that could be performed.

▶ **Reusable and exportable workflows**—A workflow created at the top level of a site
   collection can be used by any subsite, whereas a workflow created in a specific
   subsite can be reused within that subsite. Workflows can also be exported from one
   site collection and then uploaded and activated in another site collection.

▶ **Association columns**—If the reusable workflow requires certain columns to exist in
   the list or library that it is associated to, those columns can be added as association
   columns and will get added automatically to a list or library when a reusable workflow is associated to that list or library.

▶ **Associate workflows with content types**—Reusable workflow can be filtered to a
   specific content type and be associated either to that specific content type or to any
   content type that inherits from that content type. If a workflow is associated to a
   site content type, that workflow becomes available for all items of that content type
   in every list and library to which that site content type has been added.

▶ **Site workflows**—Associated to a site, rather than to a list, library, or content type.
   Clicking Site Workflows on the Site Actions menu shows the status of these types of
   workflows.

▶ **Edit the workflows included with SharePoint Server**—Approval, Collect
   Feedback, and Collect Signatures workflows are now "declarative workflows," which
   means they are customizable in SharePoint Designer 2010.

Visual Studio 2010 Enhancements

Visual Studio 2010 offers many enhancements in Visual Basic, Visual C#, Visual C++, and
Visual F#, Office system development, and leverages improvements in .NET Framework 4
that are beyond the scope of this chapter. For developers familiar with Visual Studio 2010

or other integrated development environments that might access SharePoint, some highlights are as follows:

▶ A new client object model allowing for code to be run on a client that was once relegated to running only on the SharePoint server.

▶ REST APIs for standards-based XML over HTTP communication with SharePoint.

▶ LINQ support for integrated, object-like access to SharePoint data from familiar .NET languages such as C# and VB.Net.

▶ Sandboxed solutions are solutions safely deployed to a SharePoint site and limited from doing harm to the farm through code access security (CAS). This has obvious implications for multitenancy hosting environments.

▶ Improved monitoring through timer jobs, which can be scheduled to run as often as every minute for a specified time span.

▶ New service application framework designed to support applications that were once reserved only for the components of the SSP.

▶ Import, modify, and extend solution packages (.wsp).

▶ Develop SharePoint solutions with SharePoint project type templates and SharePoint project item templates.

▶ Design association and initiation forms for sequential and state workflows.

▶ Aggregate and integrate backend data by using Business Data Connectivity (BDC) models.

▶ Create web parts and application pages for a SharePoint site.

Considering SharePoint Designer 2010 for Development

SharePoint Designer has evolved from SharePoint FrontPage 2003 to SharePoint Designer 2007 and is now in its latest manifestation as SharePoint Designer 2010. Microsoft has decided to make it available free of charge to encourage its use by SharePoint power users and developers.

SharePoint Designer 2010 provides a wide range of tools for power users, site administrators, farm administrators, and developers, which become immediately obvious when opening a website, as shown in Figure 29.1. In contrast to SharePoint Designer 2007, SharePoint Designer 2010 has a streamlined look and feel, a customizable ribbon, and broader access to functionality that was reserved to the browser in SharePoint 2007. The most notable change in functionality includes a larger repertoire of workflow actions and conditions, expanded page design capabilities, and simplified check-in/out and publishing functions.

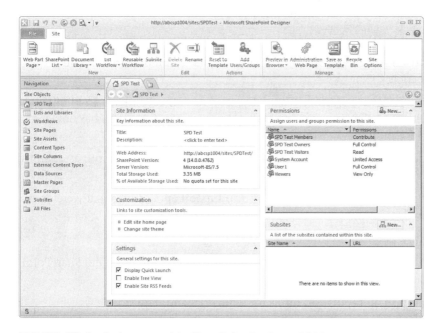

FIGURE 29.1 A site opened in SharePoint Designer 2010.

Common Development Tasks

SharePoint Designer 2010 supports a variety of development tasks including but not limited to the following items:

▶ Extending upon the basic workflows provided out-of-the-box with SharePoint 2010. These were covered in more detail in Chapter 28, "Out-of-the-Box Workflows and Designer 2010 Workflows."

▶ Although basic branding can be done with the standard UI tools in SharePoint 2010, more extensive branding in SharePoint 2010 requires SharePoint Designer 2010. The WYSYWIG editor and integrated CSS editor support extensive branding options.

▶ Custom ASPX and .Net pages extend the functionality of SharePoint and enable the development of custom .Net web pages within SharePoint that take advantage of powerful components such as the DataView.

▶ Custom forms to extend the functionality of the built-in SharePoint 2010 forms.

▶ Basic web parts can be developed using SharePoint Designer 2010; however, not all the features supported by Visual Studio 2010 are available.

Creating a Workflow-Based Application in SharePoint Designer 2010

Although Chapter 28 provides an introduction to the basic types of workflows available in SharePoint 2010 and covers some of the capabilities of SharePoint Designer 2010 when working with workflows, this section takes the process further and covers the creation of a basic application that involves multiple lists and a customized workflow that creates a new item in a new list and leverages lookup columns.

The following instructions describe the process of creating a workflow that interacts with multiple SharePoint lists when items are created and modified. The workflow is based on three lists: a Region list, a Sales Lead list, and a Customer list. When a user marks a sales lead as SaleClosed, a manager can trigger the workflow and create a customer based upon the data in the Sales Lead list. This workflow also demonstrates how to work with SharePoint lookup columns by copying the salesperson from the Region list and adding the value to the customer list.

Although limited, this example demonstrates the steps necessary to develop a relatively simple application using SharePoint Designer. The functionality is limited because the processes are asynchronous, and the lists can only be joined by a single column, but the general concept could be reused for a variety of business purposes. Generally, a quickly developed application built in SharePoint is an easier sell to business owners than a stand-alone .NET application that requires everything from an IIS site, security, documentation, and even its own database. Furthermore, the following example can be extended with list item security, custom views, custom forms, and email notifications to make the application more fully featured.

Follow these steps to create the application using SharePoint Designer 2010:

1. In a nonproduction site collection, create three SharePoint lists with a Standard View (Do not use Datasheet View) using the Custom List template with the columns and data types, as shown in Tables 29.1, 29.2, and 29.3. Unless specified in these tables, leave the other settings for the columns and the list on their defaults. Table 29.1 provides the columns needed for the Region list, Table 29.2 provides the columns needed for the Sales Leads list, and Table 29.3 provides the columns needed for the Customer list. Several of the columns are specified as Required to maintain data integrity within the application; if fields are allowed to be left blank, the application may not function properly.

TABLE 29.1   Region List Columns and Settings

Column	Data Type	Require That This Column Contains Information
Title	Single Line of Text (Already Present)	Yes
Salesperson	Person or Group	Yes

TABLE 29.2   Sales Leads List Columns and Settings

Column	Data Type	Require That This Column Contains Information
Title	Single Line of Text (Already Present)	Yes
Region	Lookup Column—Link to Region List's Title Column	Yes
SaleClosed	Yes/No with Default Value set to No	No

TABLE 29.3   Customer List Columns and Settings

Column	Data Type	Require That This Column Contains Information
Title	Single Line of Text (Already Present)	Yes
Region	Lookup Column—Link to Region List's Title column	Yes
Salesperson	Person	No
Customer ID	Single Line of Text	No

NOTE

Leave the lists blank at this point. They will be populated after the workflow is created and full instructions are provided.

2. Browse to the home page of the site housing these lists, and from the IE File menu, click Edit with Microsoft SharePoint Designer. If this option doesn't exist, open SharePoint Designer manually, and then select Open Site and enter the URL for the site that houses these lists (such as http://abcsp1004/sites/spdtest). Provide credentials if asked.

3. Next, select the Workflows entry from the Navigation pane, Site Objects section on the left side of SharePoint Designer, and then select the drop-down menu under List Workflow in the Workflows tab that should be active. Click Sales Leads list, as shown in Figure 29.2.

4. Name the workflow **Sales Leads-On Change.** Click OK.

TIP

When creating a workflow, it is good practice to provide a name that identifies the underlying list and if the workflow is triggered On Change, Manually, or On Create.

5. Upon creation of a new workflow, the workflow editor screen appears with a blank canvas containing a single step named Step 1. Click within the Step 1 editor box in

the section under the title bar to ensure it is active, and then click the Condition button on the Workflow Ribbon and choose the Condition If Current Item Field Equals Value. Step 1 will now reflect this change and display If Field Equals Value.

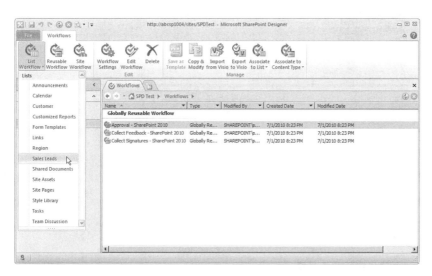

FIGURE 29.2   Creating a workflow for the Sales Leads list.

6. Click the field link that now appears in Step 1, and select SaleClosed from the drop-down list.

7. Then click the value link, and select Yes from the drop-down list. Figure 29.3 shows the contents of the step at this point.

8. Next add an action just below the condition created. Click in the Step 1 box below the row where the Condition was just defined. Type **Create** and press Enter, and choose Create List Item from the options.

9. Click the This List link that will now be visible to open the Create New List Item window.

10. Choose Customer from the drop-down menu List field at the top of the window. Figure 29.4 shows the results.

11. In the Create New List Item window, double-click the field Title to open the Value Assignment window.

12. In the Value Assignment window that opens, click the fx button and the Lookup for Single Line of Text window opens.

13. In the Lookup for Single Line of Text window, select Title in the Field from Source field, as shown in Figure 29.5.

14. Next, click OK to close the Lookup for Single Line of Text window, and click OK to close the Value Assignment window. The Create New List Item window should be active. The Title (*) entry in the Field column now has a Value entry of Current Item:Title.

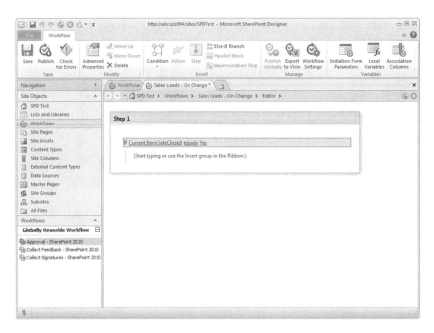

FIGURE 29.3   Creating a workflow condition.

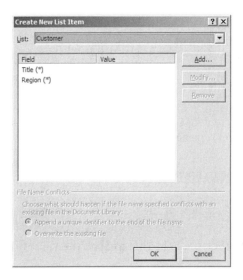

FIGURE 29.4   Create a New List Item window.

15. In the Create New List Item window double-click the field Region to open the Value
Assignment window.

16. In the Value Assignment window, click the fx button to open the Lookup for Integer
window. Verify that the Data Source field has Current Item in it.

17. Change the value for the Field from Source to Region.

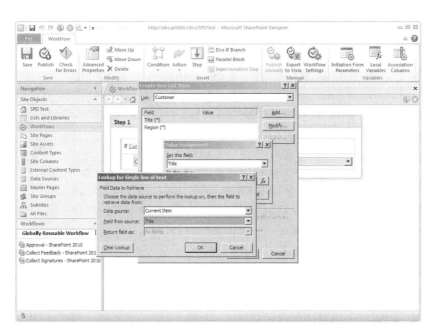

FIGURE 29.5   Complete the Lookup for Single Line of Text window.

18. Choose Lookup Id (as Integer) for the Return Field As field. The completed Lookup for Integer window looks like Figure 29.6.

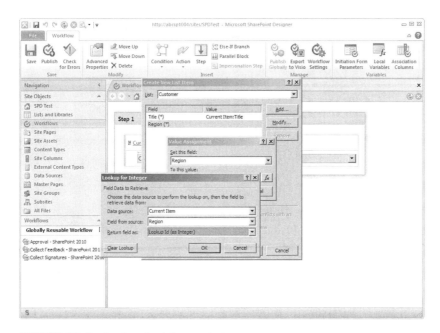

FIGURE 29.6   Lookup for Integer window.

19. Click OK in the Lookup for Integer window and again in the Value Assignment window to return to the Create New List Item window. Now the Create New List Item window has a value assigned to the Region (*) field of Current Item:Region.

20. In the Create New List Item window, click the Add button to open the Value Assignment window.

21. In the Value Assignment window, specify Salesperson for the Set This Field drop-down list.

22. Click the fx button to open the Lookup for Person or Group window.

23. Change the value in the Data Source field to Region and additional fields appear.

24. In the Field from Source field, select Salesperson from the drop-down menu.

25. In the Return Field As drop-down menu, verify that As String is selected.

26. In the Find the List Item section of the Lookup for Person or Group window, select Title in the Field drop-down list, as shown in Figure 29.7.

27. To complete the Lookup for Integer window, click the fx button for the Value field to open the Lookup for Single Line of Text window.

28. In the Data Source field, leave Current Item selected.

29. In the Field from Source field, choose Region from the drop-down menu.

30. In the Return Field As drop-down, choose Lookup Value (as Text) from the drop-down menu. Click OK.

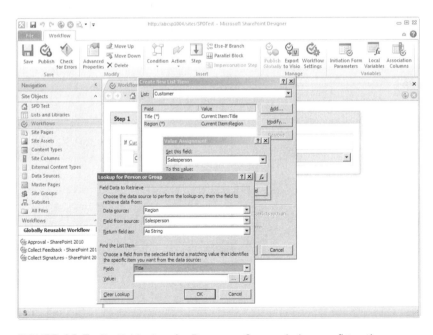

FIGURE 29.7   Partial lookup for Person or Group window configuration.

31. The Lookup for Person or Group window will now be complete and look like Figure 29.8.

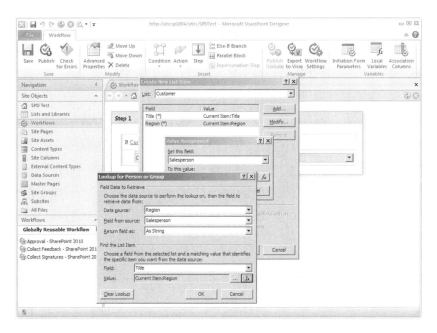

FIGURE 29.8   Completed Lookup for Person or Group window configuration.

32. Click OK to close the Lookup for Person or Group window, and click Yes when the message The Lookup You Defined Is Not Guaranteed to Return a Single Value appears. Click OK to close the Value Assignment window.

33. The Create New List Item window should now look like Figure 29.9 and include a Salesperson field with a value of Region:Salesperson.

34. Click OK to close the Create New List Item window.

35. Save the workflow by clicking the Save button on the Workflow tab of the SharePoint Designer Ribbon.

NOTE

Unlike SharePoint 2007 workflows that were immediately active upon save, SharePoint 2010 workflows are only available for use after they are published.

29

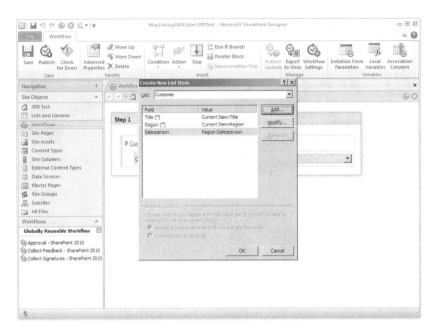

FIGURE 29.9   Completed Create New List Item window.

To publish the SharePoint Designer workflow designed so far, follow these steps:

36. Click the Workflow Settings tool on the Ribbon, and the display changes to show the workflow settings.

37. Verify that Allow This Workflow to Be Manually Started is selected from the Start Options section in the lower-right side.

NOTE

The workflow can be configured to start automatically, but the logic in this example is that the list item may be changed many times, and a user might accidentally set the item to Closed; a manager should be the only one starting the workflow, after the manager has confirmed that the lead is closed.

38. Click the Publish button on the Workflow tab on the Ribbon to deploy and activate the workflow on the list.

TIP

A form will be visible on the Workflow Settings page that should be titled "Sales Leads – On Change.xsn." Clicking this link opens InfoPath 2010 if installed on the computer and enables customization of the initiation form.

Testing the Workflow

Immediately after saving and publishing the workflow it's ready for testing. To test the Sales Lead workflow, follow these steps to populate the necessary lists and start a workflow:

1. Return to the SharePoint site where the workflow was published and the three custom lists are present. (In this example, the site is http://abcsp1004/sites/spdtest.)

2. Access the Region list and add two items. The first item should be titled **Region A** and have a salesperson assigned who is a valid AD user account (such as User1 in this example). The second item should be titled **Region B** and have a different salesperson (such as **User2** in this example).

3. Next, access the Sales Leads list on the SharePoint site. Click Add New Item; fill in the title with **Customer ABC** and select Region A. Click Save. This simulates the process of a field being created for a sales prospect in a specific region. In a production situation, additional fields could be added to track conversations with the client or upload proposals and other documents to the list item.

4. Next, edit the Sales Lead item created in the previous step, and check the SaleClosed check box; then click Save. This simulates the event where the sale is closed and the lead is ready to be converted to a customer.

5. Next, access the drop-down menu for the item, and click Workflows.

6. The Sales Leads – On Change workflow should appear next to the workflow icon and should display as shown in Figure 29.10. Click the link next to the workflow icon to access the initiation page.

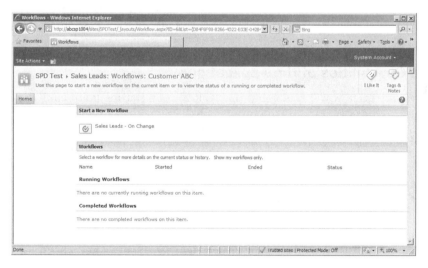

FIGURE 29.10   Initiating the workflow from the Sales Leads list item.

7. The IniWrkflIP.aspx page loads. Click the Start button.

8. You return to the Sales Leads list and a column appears titled Sales Leads – On Change, which indicates that the workflow is In Process and then Completed.

9. Navigate to the customer list and verify that a new item has been created, as shown in Figure 29.11.

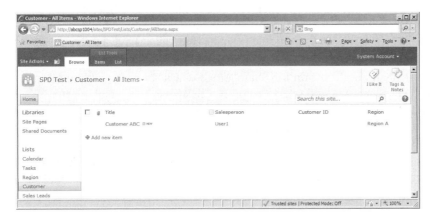

FIGURE 29.11 New item created in the customer list as a result of the workflow.

10. Return to the Sales Leads list, and click the value that appears in the workflow column to view the workflow history for that particular list item. The workflow history window opens and displays the status for the latest instance of the workflow.

Extending the Capabilities of the Application

Although the previous workflow will function properly, it is just a starting point and would not generally be considered to be "enterprise ready." Following are some items to consider as ways of enhancing the functionality of the application:

▶ Create custom list views to show and hide the sales leads depending on whether the lead is actually closed.

▶ Create an alert in the Sales Leads list that alerts a manager when an item that is set to SaleClosed equals Yes.

▶ Create a new workflow that starts when an item is added to the Customer list that sends an email to the assigned salesperson to alert her that she has a new client.

▶ For testing purposes, add the workflow action Log to History List to output debug or informational messages to the workflow history screen.

▶ Logically, the application has flaws because if a sales lead were reopened and then marked as Closed again, the workflow would trigger and create a duplicate customer; therefore, a condition should be added to step 1 that checks for the existence of the customer through the use of a lookup on the customer's title column.

Using Visual Studio 2010 with SharePoint 2010

Development for SharePoint 2010 using Visual Studio 2010 requires the developer to take caution and adhere to more stringent standards for the project to be a success. Although an aggressive approach may allow the developer to make great strides in a short period of time, .NET and SharePoint 2010 development is both a science and an art. Code can still cause memory leaks, applications can enter near endless loops, and simple mistakes may drastically affect SharePoint 2010's performance. However, the resulting applications can meet a great range of business requirements, making Visual Studio 2010 the choice of many developers.

Now in its fourth generation, Visual Studio 2010 is the de facto standard for development on the Windows platforms. Although developers can take advantage of Visual Studio 2010 to develop C++ applications and other applications that are compiled down to machine code, the typical developer creates applications on top of the .NET Framework, the same framework that SharePoint is built upon. SharePoint's use of the .NET Framework is apparent in the ASP.NET controls, layout pages, master pages, ascx controls, and aspx pages visible throughout the system's C:\Program Files\Common Files\Microsoft Shared\Web Server Extensions\14 directory.

When developing applications for SharePoint 2010, developers typically code using familiar languages such as VB.Net or C#. Although the syntax of these two languages is different, Visual Studio 2010 compiles the code down to an intermediate language called MSIL where the code, regardless of the originating syntax, behaves roughly the same. Furthermore, code developed in different .NET projects using different languages can reference code developed in another .NET language. For more information about the .NET Framework, see http://www.microsoft.com/net/.

Visual Studio 2010 has now standardized and streamlined packaging and deployment of solution packages (WSP), an area in which the preceding versions of Visual Studio fell short. A solution package is a cabinet file with a .wsp extension that contains the application code, a manifest, and one or more directories containing application specific files. Visual Studio 2010 can deploy, activate, deactivate, and un-deploy solution packages without requiring the developer to open a command prompt or PowerShell.

29

> **NOTE**
>
> Before starting development in SharePoint 2010 with Visual Studio 2010, a developer should have familiarity with the Microsoft.NET Framework and familiarity with VB or C# because most code samples available on the web are provided in one or both of these common languages.

Getting Started with Visual Studio 2010

This section introduces some basics in getting Visual Studio installed and the basics of creating a new project. Experienced users may want to skip this section and move to the next section, which covers creating a web part.

If needed, Visual Studio Professional or Ultimate can be downloaded from Microsoft at http://www.microsoft.com/visualstudio/ for a 60-day trial. The Professional, Premium, and Ultimate versions of Visual Studio 2010 all contain the SharePoint add-in that makes it possible to develop for SharePoint 2010. Although Visual Studio 2010 supports development and deployment of SharePoint components on a remote server, most templates cannot be developed or deployed unless SharePoint is installed on the same system as Visual Studio 2010.

Downloading and Installing Visual Studio 2010

Follow these steps to download and install Visual Studio Professional. These steps may vary slightly on different system configurations. Note that the full installation requires ~7GB of space:

1. Access the Microsoft Downloads site (http://www.microsoft.com/downloads/details.aspx?FamilyID=26bae65f-b0df-4081-ae6e-1d828993d4d0&displaylang=en or search on "Microsoft Visual Studio 2010 Professional Trial - Web Installer" on Microsoft's website) and click the Download button.

2. Click Run to run the downloader application vs_proweb.exe.

3. Click Run when this application downloads.

4. The Installation Wizard opens and starts. If desired, uncheck the box next to Yes, Send Information About My Setup Experiences to Microsoft Corporation, and then click Next.

5. The wizard then informs that it will install: Microsoft Application Error Reporting, VC 9.0 Runtime (x86), VC 10.0 Runtime (x86), VC 10.0 Runtime (x64), Microsoft .Net Framework 4, Microsoft Visual Studio 2010 64-bit Prerequisites, Microsoft Visual Studio 2010 Professional. Click the box next to I Have Read and Accept the License Terms, and click Next.

6. Leave the Full option selected and click Install.

7. The items mentioned in step 5 will then download and install. This process takes a while, but the wizard lists which step it is on and the download speed, which is more helpful than the average progress bar.

8. When the installation is complete, a reboot is required, so click Restart Now.

9. Upon reboot the installation process completes, which again takes a while.

10. After the setup completes, the option is provided to Install Documentation that is recommended for less-experienced users of Visual Studio. Click Install Documentation to start the process.

11. Accept the default Library location or enter a new one. Click OK.

12. The Help Library Manager window then provides a directory of content to choose from. For example, click Add next to SharePoint Development in the Visual Studio 2010 section, and click on Update.

13. Click Finish; then click Exit to exit the Help Library Manager.

14. Finally, click Finish to close the Visual Studio installation wizard.

Developing a Visual Web Part

The most commonly developed components for SharePoint are web parts. SharePoint 2010 now contains project templates that contain all the functionality that supports the immediate deployment of a variety of objects including but not limited to workflows, event receivers, web parts, business data connectivity objects, and even list definitions. SharePoint 2007 developers will be pleased to note that the packaging of these components as a SharePoint solution (.wsp) is automatic.

Follow the next steps to create a Visual Web Part that renders a SharePoint announcements list in a custom format. To show some of the more recent advancements of both .NET and SharePoint 2010, this example uses LINQ and a ListView control. LINQ is an advanced query tool that enables developers to reference database objects directly as native types. The ListView control is a powerful new UI component that allows for complete control of the HTML output based upon developer-defined templates.

To create a Visual Web Part, follow these steps on a system with SharePoint Server 2010 Standard or Enterprise installed and Visual Studio 2010 Professional or Ultimate:

1. Choose a site in a development SharePoint site collection. In this example, the site used is a site collection created beneath a top-level portal site collection (http://abcsp1004/sites/VSTest). It needs an announcements list and a picture library. If these do not exist, they need to be created. The announcements list needs to be named Announcements for the code included in this exercise to work. The image library can be named anything because it is not directly addressed in the code. For this exercise, the picture library is named Images.

2. The announcements list needs to have several columns added, but otherwise settings should be left at their default. Table 29.4 shows the columns that need to be added and relevant settings.

TABLE 29.4   Add These Columns to the Announcements List

Column	Data Type
Author	Person or Group
Start Date	Date and Time
Picture	Hyperlink or Picture (Choose the Picture Option under Format URL As)

3. The picture library should have an image uploaded to it. When the image is uploaded, capture the URL for the image; then create an announcement and paste

the URL for the image in the Picture field. Figure 29.12 shows the Announcements
list with an entry in it that references a picture.

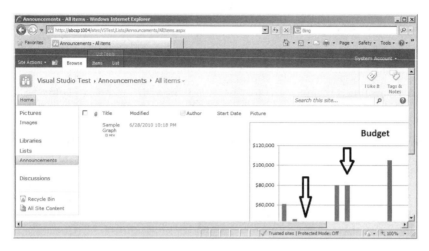

FIGURE 29.12   Preparing an Announcements List prior to the creation of the web part.

Before continuing with the web part development, verify that the account used to run
Visual Studio 2010 has the following rights:

▶ Local administrator rights to the development machine

▶ Farm administrator rights (not necessary if a sandboxed solution is created, but
  always helpful to have if possible)

▶ Site collection administrator rights to the site collection where the solution will be
  deployed during debugging

To create a project in Visual Studio 2010, which will be used in the following exercise,
follow these steps:

1. Open Visual Studio 2010 by clicking the Start button, then All Programs, SharePoint,
   and click Microsoft Visual Studio 2010.

2. The first time it is opened, the default environment settings need to be set. Different
   developers have their preferences, but for the exercises in this chapter, the first
   setting, General Development Settings, is sufficient.

3. When Visual Studio is open, access the File menu, then click New then Project.

4. In the New Project window, choose Visual C#, and choose the SharePoint node from
   the list of choices in the left pane. Expand the SharePoint node and select the entry
   2010, as shown in Figure 29.13.

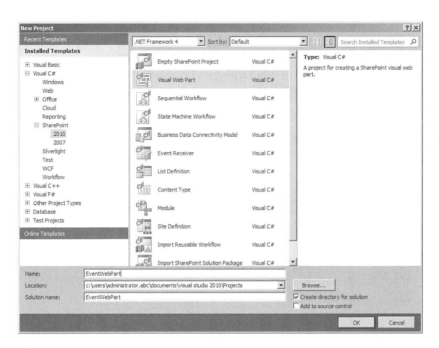

FIGURE 29.13   Creating a SharePoint project using Visual Studio 2010.

5. Then select the Visual Web Part template from the center pane. Name the Visual
   Web Part project **EventWebPart**, and it will be auto-populated in the Solution name
   field. Verify the location where Visual Studio 2010 creates the project folder structure
   is suitable. Click OK.

CAUTION

If SharePoint 2010 is not installed on the machine, an error message displays. In addition, if the account used does not have sufficient permissions, an error message
appears. It may be necessary to restart Visual Studio 2010 by right-clicking it from the
Start menu and choosing Run as Administrator.

NOTE

Templates include Empty SharePoint Project, Visual Web Part, Sequential Workflow,
State Machine Workflow, Business Data Connectivity Model, Event Receiver, List
Definition, Content Type, Module, Site Definition, Import Reusable Workflow, and Import
SharePoint Solution Package for both the Visual C# and Visual Basic languages.

---

6. The SharePoint Customization Wizard dialog then opens. Enter the URL for the
   target SharePoint site with the Announcements list configured in the previous
   section running on the server where Visual Studio 2010 deploys the code. In this

example, the URL is http://abcsp1004/sites/vstest. Press the Validate button, and Visual Studio 2010 verifies that the URL responds properly and runs the appropriate version of SharePoint 2010 and should display a Connection Successful message. Click OK to close the message. Verify that Deploy as Farm Solution is checked, as shown in Figure 29.14, and click Finish. The resulting view should be similar to Figure 29.15.

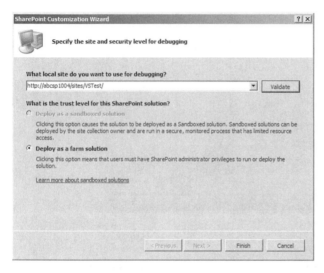

FIGURE 29.14   Choosing the local site that will be used for debugging.

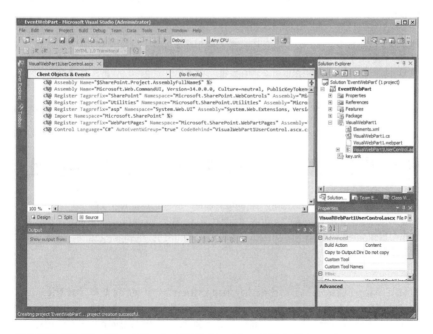

FIGURE 29.15   Visual Studio 2010 New Visual Web Part project.

NOTE

Sandboxed solutions are "safer," because they can be deployed to a site collection, instead of deployed to the whole farm. Also they are run in a more secure fashion by using a combination of features, solution galleries, solution monitoring, and a validation framework. In addition, the sandboxed solution's assembly is not loaded into the IIS process (w3wp.exe); it is loaded into a separate process (SPUCWorkerProcess.exe) that is more closely monitored and managed by SharePoint 2010. Sandboxed solutions have some limitations, such as a not offering site definitions and workflows, and only types in the Microsoft SharePoint Foundation 2010 assembly Microsoft.SharePoint can be used in sandboxed solutions.

There is a Boolean project property called Sandboxed Solution that can be changed in the project. However, changing the Sandboxed Solution property of a project after it is created may cause validation errors. Farm solutions require higher-level privileges to run or deploy the solution.

7. By default, Visual Studio creates the web part with the name VisualWebPart1, as shown in the Solution Explorer to the right of Figure 29.15. (Click the View menu and choose Solution Explorer if it is not already visible.) To give the web part a more meaningful name, open the VisualWebPart1.webpart file by double-clicking it, and a new tab will open.

8. In the new tab in the code editor, under <properties>, replace the Title text VisualWebPart1 with the text **Event Web Part**; then in the next line, replace the text My Visual Web Part with the text Web Part to Display Events with an Image and click the Save icon. The results are shown in Figure 29.16 where the two modified lines of code are highlighted. Now click the Save icon to save the project.

9. Before adding any code or UI components to the Visual Web Part, debug the web part by clicking the Debug menu, and then click Start Debugging. Debugging the web part before adding code or UI components allows the developer to verify that the project and development environment work as expected, and in this case, packages and deploys the solution, and then removes the solution when it is complete.

29

NOTE

An error message may appear after Start Debugging is clicked. This message states The Project Cannot Be Debugged Because Debugging Is Not Enabled in the Web.config file. If this message appears, select Modify the Web.Config File to Enable Debugging or Run Without Debugging. A note in this window also suggests that debugging should be disabled in production SharePoint 2010 environments, so this is a judgment call. Debugging is generally considered to be essential in most development efforts, so in general the option to Modify the Web.Config File to Enable Debugging needs to be enabled.

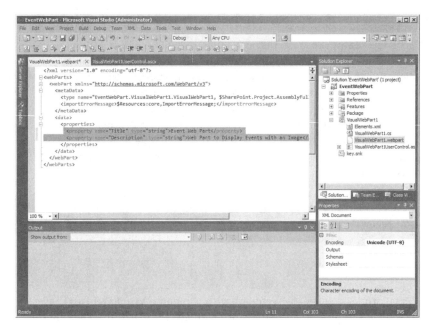

FIGURE 29.16   Changing the title and description of the web part.

NOTE

Installing a solution into SharePoint 2010 using Visual Studio 2010 by deploying or
debugging the solution can complete an IISReset that automatically forces all http
requests to be temporarily unavailable.

10. A browser window opens to the SharePoint site as part of the debugging process,
    because manual intervention is required to add the web part to the SharePoint site.
    From this window, click Site Actions, Edit Page.

11. Click the Add a Web Part link in a zone on the page.

12. Click the Custom folder in the Categories list under the Ribbon, and then select
    Event Web Part. Click the Add button and the web part should be added to the zone
    selected. Figure 29.17 shows the result (other contents of the page may vary) where
    the web part title Event Web Part is visible on the page.

13. If needed, depending upon the type of site being edited, click Save and if necessary
    publish the page. Then close the browser and return to Visual Studio.

14. In Visual Studio, the debug process completes, and the Output window shows the
    activities taking place, ending with the solution being retracted.

15. Next, to take advantage of the LINQ feature in this project, a reference to
    Microsoft.SharePoint.Linq needs to be added. In the Solution Explorer, right-click
    References, and click Add Reference.

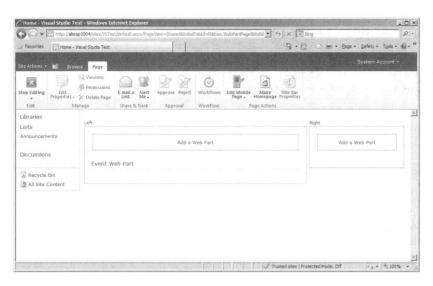

FIGURE 29.17   New web part added to the page as part of the debugging process.

16. Click the .NET tab, scroll roughly halfway down, and find and click Microsft.SharePoint.Linq. Click OK to save this reference, and it appears under the References node.

17. Next, the SPMetal program will be run from the command prompt to generate a LINQ class file. Open a command prompt by clicking the Start button and entering **cmd** in the Search field and pressing Enter.

18. Navigate to the c:\Program Files\Common Files\Microsoft Shared\Web Server Extensions\14\BIN folder.

19. Run the following command to generate a LINQ class file, EventLinq.cs, that the web part can use to read the announcements list created previously. Be sure to update the following command by replacing the text in bold to reference the project directory where SPMetal will place the EventLinq.cs file. Figure 29.18 shows a sample of code with the servername and site collection name included (http://abcsp1004/sites/vstest), and the username to set the correct EventWebPart directory location (administrator.abc). Type the following code and press Enter, and SPMetal will run:

```
spmetal.exe /web:http://servernameandsitename
➥/code:"c:\Users\username\Documents\Visual Studio 2010\Projects\
➥EventWebPart\EventWebPart\EventLinq.cs" /namespace:EventWebPart
```

> **NOTE**
>
> LINQ enables developers to access data using strongly typed .NET objects. A program shipped with SharePoint 2010 called SPMetal.exe generates the LINQ class file that enables these strongly typed .NET components to be used.

FIGURE 29.18   Running SPMetal.exe to create the EventLinq.cs file.

20. No message appears, but a new line appears when the process finishes. Close the command prompt and return to Visual Studio.

21. After successfully generating the EventLinq.cs code file, the code can now be consumed by the EventWebPart project. In Visual Studio 2010, in the Solution Explorer, right-click the project's title EventWebPart. A context menu appears; click Add, and then choose Add Existing Item.

22. In the dialog box that opens, locate and select the EventLinq.cs file created previously and click Add, as shown in Figure 29.19. The EventLinq.cs should now appear in the Solution Explorer.

23. Click Save in Visual Studio to save the progress.

24. In the Solution Explorer, locate the VisualWebPart1UserControl.ascx file, and open it by double-clicking it.

25. Click the Split button under the active tab for VisualWebPart1UserControl.ascx.

26. Access the View menu, and click Toolbox to display the Toolbox. Locate the ListView component in the Data node, and drag it to the Design pane (which opened when the Split button was pressed), as shown in Figure 29.20, where the ListView can be seen in the Design pane.

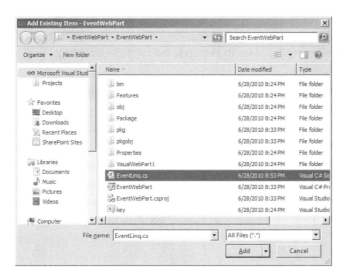

FIGURE 29.19   Adding the EventLinq.cs item to the project.

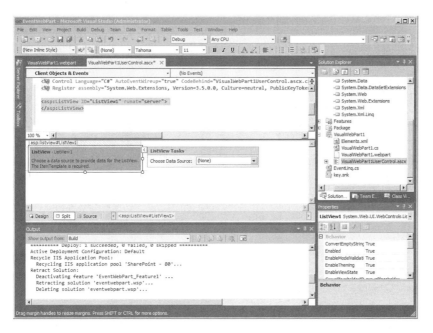

FIGURE 29.20   Adding the Listview component to the Design pane.

27. Return to the Source view by clicking the Source button on the WebPart1UserControl.ascx editing window. Position the cursor after the code:

```
<asp:ListView ID="ListView1" runat="server">
```

28. Then paste in the following code, and the results will look like Figure 29.21. Be sure to modify the href so that the *sharepointservernameandsitename* portion of the code refers to the test site collection and site in the code below before pasting:

```
<LayoutTemplate>
<asp:PlaceHolder runat="server" ID="itemPlaceholder"></asp:PlaceHolder>
</LayoutTemplate>
<ItemTemplate>
<div style="width:100%;float:left">
<a href="http://sharepointservernameandsitename/lists/announcements/
➥DispForm.aspx?id=<%#Eval( "ID")%>"><%#Eval("Title")%></a>
<br />
<img src="<%#((String)Eval("Picture")).Substring(0,((String)Eval("Picture")).
IndexOf(" ")-1)%>"style="width:160px; height:120px; padding:3px"
➥align="left" alt="">
<%#Eval("Body")%>
</div>
</ItemTemplate>
<ItemSeparatorTemplate>
<hr />
</ItemSeparatorTemplate>
```

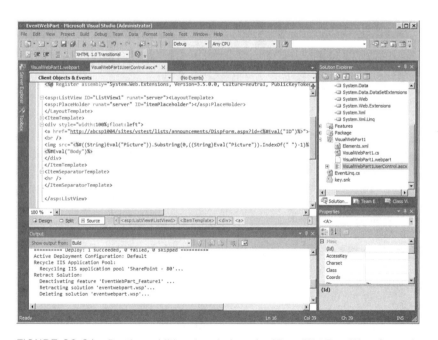

FIGURE 29.21   Pasting additional code into the VisualWebPart1UserControl.ascx code.

NOTE

Adding the ListView component using the Design view enables Visual Studio 2010 to update the import and tag prefixes as needed.

NOTE

Using the `Eval()` statement with LINQ objects provides a relatively easy way to insert code directly into the web part; however, in some cases, the result of the `Eval()` statement needs to be modified. The code inside the `<img` tag demonstrates the use of standard .NET string operations against the results of an `Eval()` statement.

29. In the Solution Explorer, click the plus button next to the VisualWebPart1UserControl.ascx; a child file appears named VisualWebPart1UserControl.ascx.cs. Double-click this file and paste the following code within the Page_Load method (between the brackets under the line that starts with "protected void"). Make sure to update sharepointservernameandsitename with the appropriate site name, as done previously. Figure 29.22 shows the results, with the new lines of code highlighted:

```
EventLinqDataContext dsEvent = new
➥EventLinqDataContext("http://sharepointservernameandsitename");
ListView1.DataSource = dsEvent.Announcements.GetEnumerator();
ListView1.DataBind();
```

30. Click the Save button to save the work done so far.

31. To debug the solution, click the Debug menu, and choose Start Debugging or simply click F5.

32. Again, a browser opens to the site home page. If the web part doesn't display, edit the page as done before, and add the Event Web Part to a zone on the page. Figure 29.23 shows a sample result.

33. Close the browser and return to Visual Studio where the debugging process completes.

Although the results may not appear to be earth shattering, this web part is quite different from a normal list view web part, an example of which is shown in Figure 29.24. In this regular list view, note that the image has not been resized, which was accomplished in the WebPart1UserControl.ascx code. Of course, a contributor to the images library could simply go in and resize the image, but that gets time-consuming. Also note that in Figure 29.23, the column headers are not included, making the web part more esthetically pleasing. This is a common request and an example of making a page look "less SharePointy."

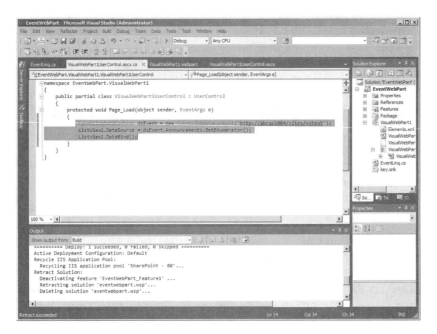

FIGURE 29.22   Adding code to VisualWebPart1UserControl.ascx.cs file.

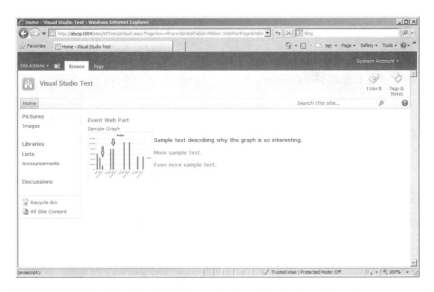

FIGURE 29.23   The Event Web Part displayed during the debugging process after completion.

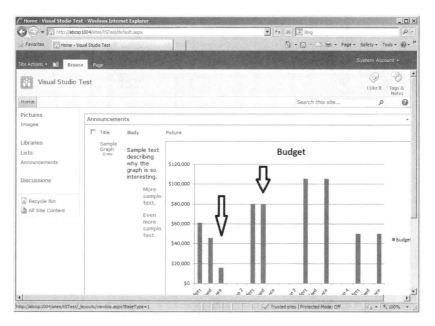

FIGURE 29.24   Normal announcement list view.

Packaging a Visual Web Part

This section assumes that the previous section was completed successfully and the web part displays, as shown in Figure 29.23 (with the exception that most likely a different image displayed). To deploy the solution to a staging or production machine, follow these steps:

1. With the SharePoint 2010 solution open in Visual Studio 2010, access the Solution Configuration drop-down menu on the Standard toolbar, as shown in Figure 29.25, visible just beneath the top menu bar, and change the configuration to Release. The next time the project is built, Visual Studio 2010 generates each project's binaries (DLLs) without the debug symbols, making them optimized for deployment to production environments.

2. Next, rebuild the solution by clicking the Build menu and choosing Rebuild Solution.

3. Open the Solution Explorer and right mouse key on the project name, and choose Package, as shown in Figure 29.26. Packaging the solution creates a SharePoint solution file with the familiar .wsp extension. The solution file is a compressed cab file that contains the web part's DLL, its visual components, and a manifest.

4. After packaging the project, a solution file with the .wsp extension appears in the project's bin/release directory. To locate this directory, open Windows Explorer from the Start menu, and navigate to \Documents\Visual Studio 2010\Projects\ EventWebPart\EventWebPart\bin\Release. Within the release directory, the .wsp file should appear, as shown in Figure 29.27.

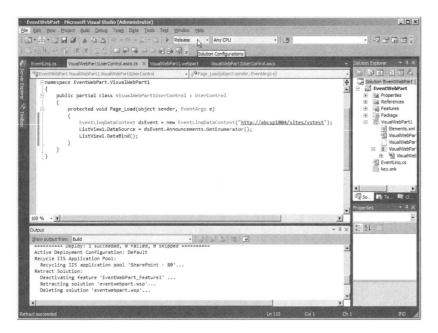

FIGURE 29.25   Change the project to Release Configuration for Production-Ready Code.

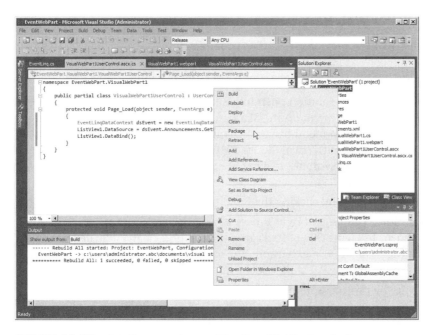

FIGURE 29.26   Creating a package of the EventWebPart project.

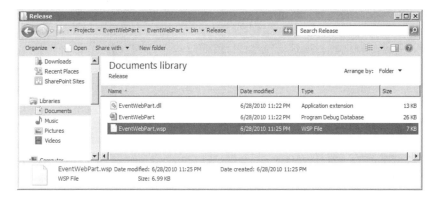

FIGURE 29.27   Locating the .wsp file.

5. On the Start menu, click All Programs, Microsoft SharePoint 2010 Products, and SharePoint 2010 Management Shell.

6. At the Windows PowerShell command prompt, type the following command, where `<SolutionPath>` is replaced by the full path to the .wsp file, including the .wsp filename, as shown in the top part of Figure 29.28, and press Enter:

```
Add-SPSolution -LiteralPath <SolutionPath>
```

FIGURE 29.28   Using PowerShell to add the solution.

7. The PowerShell screen should then show the name of the solution, the SolutionID, and the Deployed state, which is false at this point.

8. Next, navigate to the Central Administrator site; click System Settings. In the Farm Management section, click Manage Farm Solutions.

9. On the Solution Management page, click the solution eventwebpart.asp.

10. On the Solution Properties page, click Deploy Solution, as shown in Figure 29.29.

29

FIGURE 29.29   Deploying the solution from the CENTRAL ADMINISTRATION site.

11. On the Deploy Solution page, in the Deploy When section, leave the Now option selected.

12. In the Deploy To section, select a specific web application. In this example, http://abcsp1004 is selected. Click OK.

The web part should now be available to add to the test site (http://abcsp1004/sites/test), as it was during the debugging process.

Summary

This chapter starts with some cautionary information about taking time to understand what SharePoint 2010 can do out-of-the-box before deciding to use SharePoint Designer 2010 or Visual Studio 2010 to develop windows SharePoint 2010 applications, web parts, event handlers, and workflows. In addition, developers should have experience with the .NET platform and preferably C# or VB.NET before delving into Visual Studio 2010 development.

An example of creating a workflow-based application in Designer 2010 is provided that showed how to create a workflow that interacts with several SharePoint lists. The workflow, while demonstrating basic functionality, shows how a power user can quickly develop SharePoint workflows supporting basic needs using a variety of predefined actions and conditions.

The next example using Visual Studio 2010 demonstrates the development of a Visual Web Part. The Visual Web Part uses many new development features that SharePoint 2010 supports including LINQ, a .NET feature normally reserved for database development, and the ListView user interface component that improves upon the .NET repeating section.

Best Practices

▶ A developer should make sure that out-of-the-box SharePoint 2010 features do not provide capabilities that can meet end user requests before diving into Designer 2010 or Visual Studio 2010. This is no easy task because SharePoint 2010, as shown throughout this book, has many new and powerful features, such as calculated columns, lookup columns, external data, workflows, alerts, and other tools that might be good enough for end users to start with, rather than over-building a solution.

▶ When working with Designer 2010, it is recommended to not install Designer 2010 on production servers but to install it on a workstation or on a development or test SharePoint 2010 server.

▶ Always use a nonproduction server to develop and test code. When a development server is not available, use sandboxed solutions in a nonproduction web application or site collection.

▶ When possible, use a development, staging, and production deployment scenario to minimize the impact on the production environment.

▶ When developing code for SharePoint 2010 using Visual Studio 2010, you need both Visual Studio 2010 and SharePoint 2010 installed on the same machine.

▶ Many new features in SharePoint 2010 make it better suited to use as a development platform, including the sandboxed solution deployments, client object model, LINQ integration, and enhanced development environments. However, not all projects require direct integration with SharePoint. Take care to evaluate all contingencies because SharePoint may not be the optimal platform to support the desired solution for many reasons, including licensing, storage requirements, throughput, record count, and security, to list a few.

## CHAPTER 30

Business Intelligence in SharePoint 2010 with PerformancePoint Services

Business intelligence can be thought of in broad terms as the key pieces of information used to support business decisions. Business intelligence can take many forms: analytical, measurable data, anecdotal information, or factual details. It can be used by people at many different levels of an organization. Senior executives may use high-level analytical sales data to make key decisions about hiring. Mid-level managers may make budget allocation decisions based on available budget and departmental objectives. And project managers may shift project resources based on project-specific factors. Different types of decisions can be made at many distinct times. Regional sales information may be used mid-year to support an increase or decrease in advertising dollars for a particular region. Year-end performance metrics can be used to justify disbursements of end-of-year bonuses. And a customer service agent may use customer or product history information during a customer service call.

For information consumers to make the correct decisions, the information they use must fulfill three criteria. First, it must be the correct information. Second, it must be current information. Having either inaccurate or out-of-date information leads to bad decisions. Finally, it must be available to the people who need the information.

In short, the making of informed decisions is all about the right information being available to the right people at the right time. Although a number of systems exist to produce, store, consolidate, or aggregate data, the set of tools available for "surfacing" the information—making it readily available to the information consumer—are historically lacking. SharePoint provides a rich suite of tools whose intended purposes are to bring the information out of their discrete systems and into the hands of the decision makers.

The next two chapters focus on two key business intelligence components of SharePoint 2010. PerformancePoint Services (PPS) is intended more for top-down views of information; it starts with high-level enterprise metrics but provides the capability to break down numbers by region, county, product line, time period, or other key measures. Business Connectivity Services, which will be covered in the next chapter, is intended for bottom-up views of information, such as details on a product or an order.

PerformancePoint Services Overview

PerformancePoint Services is relatively new even to veteran SharePoint users and administrators. The 2010 version of SharePoint is the first to include PerformancePoint Services as a base part of the installation. The product was born from a merger of Microsoft's Business Scorecard Manager and products acquired from ProClarity. The first version of PerformancePoint was launched in 2007 and was initially sold under a separate license.

In early 2009, Microsoft announced plans to roll it into the SharePoint product. Effective in 2009, owners of the SharePoint Enterprise CAL became licensed for PerformancePoint; however, it remained a separate installation. With SharePoint 2010, PerformancePoint Services is now rolled into the SharePoint installation.

Despite being the "new kid" on the SharePoint block, the product is one of the more heavily anticipated components of SharePoint 2010. This is due primarily to its capacity to place rich report creation capabilities into the hands of power users. Users who are interested in seeing real-time analytical metrics can create reports that they can see updated whenever the data changes. No longer will they have to wait on a reporting tool or another department to generate a monthly or quarterly report. Additionally, some reports provide interaction for report consumers, which will enable them to more deeply analyze specific metrics of greater interest. Thus, they are no longer limited to the information they can glean from predefined report formats. Following are three example scenarios:

▶ A company's advertising department is trying to target its advertising based on a number of factors. One objective is to help the company achieve its regional and product sales goals. At the same time, a limited advertising budget requires it to make appropriate decisions on where to place advertisements. Every month, advertising dollars are designated to specific television spots with all the major networks. To make the right decisions, the brand managers need to be able to determine which product lines are on track to sell above the target levels, and which ones are falling short. By having sales data available immediately, they can make more rapid decisions about where to and how often to place advertisements.

▶ A sales executive is reviewing sales data for the last quarter. In reviewing a graph of sales, he notices that one product line had lower sales during the period. With one click of the mouse, he can reform the chart by drilling down into that one product line to view individual products within the product line. He then notices that sales of most products within the product line remained steady during the quarter; however, one specific SKU underperformed. He could also see how the same data looks on a regional basis. With no individual region standing out as a problem area, he can return to the previous graph. From there, he can once again drill down to see sales for the one product, broken down by monthly or weekly timely periods. Having this power to regenerate graphs on demand enables people to isolate a problem area, which in turn enables them to make the decisions necessary to correct the problem.

▶ A product manufacturing company has several plants that have been producing below target levels. Several factors could help drive this, including frequency of safety incidents, capacity utilization, availability of just-in-time materials, and several other components. At the same time, other plants may be producing above their target levels. By having the appropriate metrics available to them, executives can strategically shift resources as appropriate to help the plants that are underachieving.

In the coming sections of this chapter, we look at some examples of how the various reports are built and distributed to help drive some of these decisions. We also explore examples of the types of dashboards users might create with the tools available.

Getting Started with a PerformancePoint Service Application

Before building a PerformancePoint Service application, a few initial setup steps are required. The first step of setting up is to configure the web application to use PerformancePoint Services. Chapter 1, "Introducing SharePoint 2010," talks about the services-oriented architecture, and how services can be enabled only where and when they are needed. One of these services is PerformancePoint Services.

> **NOTE**
>
> To configure a PerformancePoint Service application, you must have SharePoint Server 2010 Enterprise installed and configured. Neither SharePoint Foundation 2010 nor SharePoint Server 2010 Standard offers the PerformancePoint Service application.

Before getting started with a PerformancePoint Services site, you need to have a service application established for PerformancePoint Services. It is recommended that a new service application be created for testing purposes, which is done by following these steps:

1. Open SharePoint Central Administration by clicking the SharePoint 2010 Central Administration link from All Programs, Microsoft SharePoint 2010 Products menu.

2. Under Application Management, click Manage Service Applications.

3. In the Service Applications Ribbon, select New and then PerformancePoint Service Application from the list. The New PerformancePoint Service Application Wizard opens.

4. Enter a name for the service application, which is the name of the PPS service application and needs to be unique. It is helpful to start the name with PerformancePoint so that it appears at a logical place in the list of other service applications on the ServiceApplications.aspx page, and it is immediately clear what the purpose of this service application is in the future. A unique GUID, assigned at creation time, can distinguish this service application from any other service application. Figure 30.1 shows a sample of the wizard.

   You can optionally choose to make this service application part of the Default settings for all future web applications. If you later create additional SharePoint web applications on your SharePoint farm—that is, for additional URLs, such as http://external.mycompany.com and http://projects.mycompany.com—the default set of service applications can be shared among those web applications.

5. Next choose to use an existing application pool, or create a new one. A general best practice is to create a new application pool, keeping in mind that server performance can degrade if too many application pools run at one time. Then determine whether to use a predefined security account for the application pool or to use a configurable account, or click the Register new managed account if wanted.

6. Click Create to create the new service application.

The next step in the process is to create a new custom web application by following these steps:

1. Return to the home screen of Central Administration. Under the Application Management section, click Manage Web Applications.

2. In the Web Applications Ribbon, click New. When the New Web Application dialog opens, leave Classic Mode Authentication selected, and enter an IIS Web Site name and Port Number, such as **PerformancePoint1**, and enter **25000** in the field under Port.

3. In the Security Configuration section, leave NTLM selected, and No for Allow Anonymous, and No for Use Secure Sockets Layer (SSL), unless your test environment is configured differently. For example, Kerberos is often used for business intelligence configurations because it enables impersonation to take place, and SSL is often implemented to ensure that all data is encrypted.

4. In the Public URL section, leave the default (http://servername:portnumber) unless a different Public URL is wanted, or if SSL is used.

5. In the Application Pool section, select Create New Application Pool if not already selected, and create an application pool that matches the web application name (for example, **PerformancePoint1 - 25000**) and select a security account or register a new managed account.

6. Validate the database server and database name to meet your requirements. A best practice is to make the database name simpler, readily identifiable, and still include the term Content. So instead of the randomly generated name, something such as **PerformancePoint1_Content** could be used.

7. Enter a failover server if there is a failover database server in the farm.

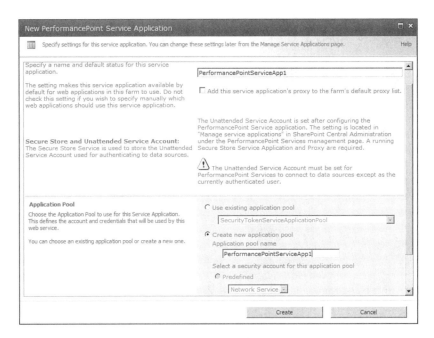

FIGURE 30.1   The new PerformancePoint Service Application Wizard.

8. In the Service Application Connections section, ensure that the correct service application is selected by choosing [custom] from the drop-down list, and then selecting the service application just created (in this example, PerformancePointServiceApp1), as shown in Figure 30.2.

9. Review your settings to make sure they meet your requirements, and click OK.

The next step is to create a new site collection using the Business Intelligence Center site template. To do so, complete the following steps:

1. On the SharePoint 2010 server, select Start and SharePoint 2010 Central Administration.

2. Under the Application Management section, click Create Site Collections.

3. In the upper-right corner of the Create Site Collection page, verify that the Web Application setting is the same name and port number that you used when you created a new Web Application earlier in the chapter. If not, click the down arrow in the Web Application box, and select Change Web Application. Then change the web application to the one created earlier.

4. In the Title box of the Create Site Collection page, type **PPS Sample Site.**

5. In the URL section, select the /sites/ option in the drop-down box, and type **PPSSample** in the text box.

6. Enter one or two login accounts to serve as the site collection administrator(s).

30

7. In the Template Selection section, click the Enterprise tab, and choose the Business Intelligence Center site template.

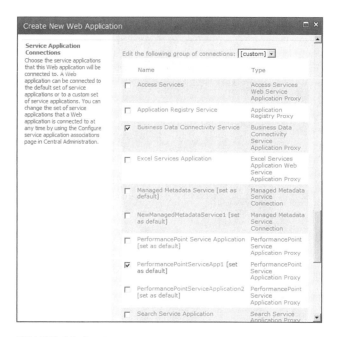

FIGURE 30.2   Service Application Connection window.

When this site is created, you can begin building a PerformancePoint Services dashboard.

Understanding Dashboard Designer

A key to understanding PerformancePoint Services is to know how to use Dashboard Designer. Dashboard Designer is the client interface for building PerformancePoint reports and scorecards. It provides a drag-and-drop interface for creating the dashboards, scorecards, reports, and Key Performance Indicators (KPIs) that bring a company's business intelligence and analytical metrics to life. Equally significant is that it enables business users to build reports without having to do any programming.

Many veterans of SharePoint are familiar with SharePoint Designer as one of the tools that enables power users to create SharePoint sites. Dashboard Designer can be thought of as the SharePoint Designer of the PerformancePoint world. However, unlike SharePoint Designer, which is not required for creating and setting up SharePoint sites, Dashboard Designer is a necessary component to creating PerformancePoint dashboards.

You can launch Dashboard Designer from two places. The first method is to complete the following steps:

1. Go to the SharePoint site built from the Business Intelligence Center site template in the previous section. The URL should be http://servername:portnumber/sites/PPSSample/.

2. Click the PPS Sample link in the main navigation.

3. From this page, click the Run Dashboard Designer button, shown in Figure 30.3, and the executable will download and run.

After running Dashboard Designer for the first time, a menu option will be added to the Programs menu on the local desktop in a Programs group called SharePoint. Thus, all future designing sessions can be launched from the desktop. However, it should be noted that no application is actually stored on the desktop, because the shortcut that is added to the Programs menu actually points to the executable that lives on the SharePoint 2010 server.

It is helpful to understand the four main components of Dashboard Designer: the Office button, the Office Ribbon, the Workspace Browser, and the working area, as shown in Figure 30.4.

▶ **File button**—Dashboard Designer contains the File button in the upper-left corner. Clicking this button reveals the usual menu options for New, Open, Save, and Close and provides access to a button at the bottom to set specific Designer Options.

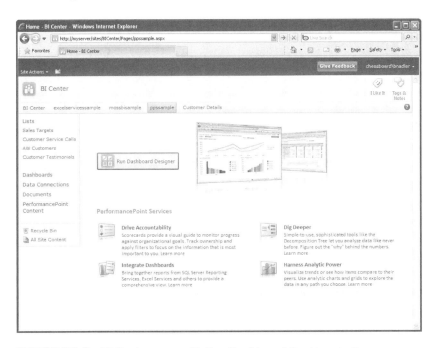

FIGURE 30.3   BI Center page with Run Dashboard Designer button.

▶ **Dashboard Designer Ribbon**—Also like other Office 2007/2010 products, Dashboard Designer contains the Ribbon interface across the top, as shown in Figure 30.4. Ribbon options include Home, Edit, and Create.

▶ **The Home Ribbon**—Allows for operations such as Cut/Copy/Paste, Adding Items and Lists from the SharePoint server to the workspace, and a Delete button to remove items from the server and workspace. There are also a few buttons for comparing server and workspace versions of components. The Home Ribbon also contains an Import button that allows for pulling items from one workspace into a new SharePoint site.

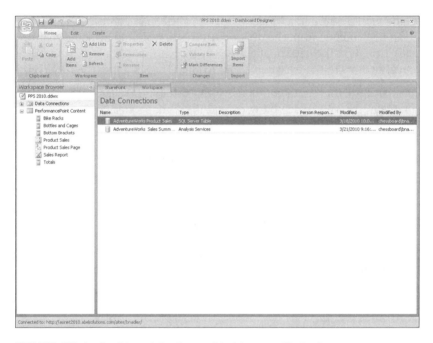

FIGURE 30.4   Dashboard Designer with AdventureWorks Data connections.

▶ **The Edit Ribbon**—Provides the ability to apply bulk changes to several items at once.

▶ **The Create Ribbon**—Contains icons to instantiate each of the different PPS components that make up a PerformancePoint dashboard. Each of these components will be discussed in more detail.

▶ **Workspace Browser**—The Workspace Browser, displayed along the left sidebar of Dashboard Designer, shows all the components in use in the current workspace. The Workspace Browser is divided into two groupings. Data Connections are the different sources of data that will determine how the visuals are displayed. PerformancePoint Content, the second grouping, lists the various visual elements used by the workspace.

▶ **Working area**—The last section of Dashboard Designer is the working area, which consumes the majority of the Dashboard Designer window. The working area displays two different views: SharePoint and Workspace. As you create new components, copies are stored on both the local computer and the SharePoint Server.

The local, or workspace, versions are bundled together and saved to a local file with a .ddwx extension. The server components are stored in a SharePoint site in a PerformancePoint Content list.

As you browse through Dashboard Designer, notice a pair of tabs in the PerformancePoint Content section for SharePoint and Workspace, as shown in Figure 30.5. The SharePoint tab lists all the content currently stored in the linked SharePoint site. The Workspace tab shows the items that are utilized in the current workspace.

The reason for having both a local and a server copy of the various PPS components is that multiple individuals or departments may use some common KPIs but would be interested in seeing the data grouped together in many different ways. This fits into the notion of PerformancePoint Server providing a framework where individuals and teams can easily build the reports of interest to them.

Consider, for example, shoe sales based on both brand and region, where there are four different geographic regions and six unique brands. Factoring in both brand and region, there are 24 unique combinations of measurements. A brand manager may be interested in seeing just the four KPIs derived from his brand. The manager of the east region, on the other hand, may be interested in all six brands, but only how they sold within the East

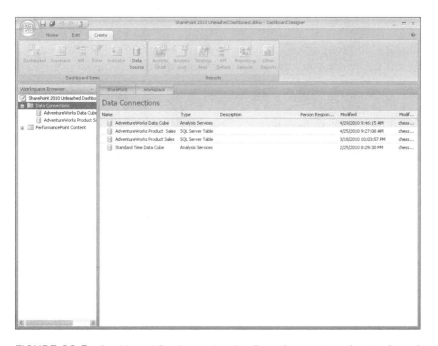

FIGURE 30.5   Dashboard Designer showing Data Connections for the SharePoint tab.

30

region. Although the same figures are being measured, they each have their own set of measurements that they want to monitor. Having the components stored on the server enables reuse of commonly used items, whereas having the workspace copies for individuals to consume prevents the clutter of unwanted components.

Additionally, storing PerformancePoint content in a central SharePoint list allows for many of the same benefits offered by other SharePoint lists. Approval routing, categorization based on metadata, and the application of security to various components are all standard functionality provided to PerformancePoint content.

NOTE

If there is a server component, such as a KPI, that you want to include in your workspace, simply locate it under the Server tab and double-click it. Switch back to the Workspace tab, and you notice that it has been added to the Workspace components. This saves the designer the time of having to otherwise re-create an existing component.

Creating Dashboards in Dashboard Designer

When you have loaded Dashboard Designer, as described in the previous section, you are ready to start creating dashboards in your local workspace.

To begin adding components to be stored on the SharePoint server, a connection to a specific SharePoint site needs to be established. To do so, complete the following steps:

1. Click the Office button, and then click the Designer Options button.

2. In the Options dialog box, click the Server tab.

3. The Server settings tab prompts for a URL, as shown in Figure 30.6. Enter the name of the SharePoint site where you intend to store your dashboard components.

NOTE

The SharePoint site to which you connect does not necessarily have to be based on the Business Intelligence Center site template. As long as the site to which you connect has the PerformancePoint Services Site Features feature activated, you can use this site in the SharePoint URL box of Dashboard Designer.

In the upcoming sections, we talk about the different components available to create dashboards.

Data Connections Defined

The first thing to design and plan out when building dashboards in PerformancePoint is which data connections to use. The data connections are links to any externally generated and maintained set of data on which the dashboard components will be based. Data can come from any of the following types of sources:

- ▶ SQL Server Analysis Services

- ▶ Excel components from either Excel Services or Excel Workbooks

- ▶ SharePoint Lists

- ▶ SQL Server tables

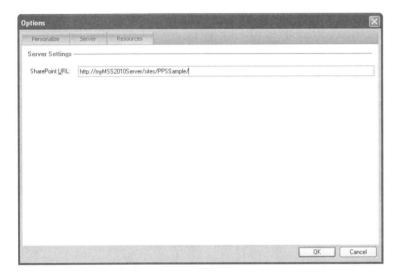

FIGURE 30.6   Set the URL for the SharePoint site in Dashboard Designer Options.

Recall that Business Intelligence in SharePoint is not about creating data or determining how to organize it. SharePoint's focal point is about surfacing the data, making it available, presentable, and consumable for those who need to make key business decisions. Therefore, a key prerequisite to doing anything with PerformancePoint Services is to have the right data repositories already in place.

In Dashboard Designer, you can create all new components from either of two places. The Create Ribbon contains a series of icons for the various components. Additionally, from the Workspace Browser, you can right-click on the Data Connections grouping and select the appropriate option.

KPIs Defined

A Key Performance Indicator (KPI) is a measurement against a specific, measurable objective. It is one specific numeric measurement, comparing an actual result to a target result.

When creating a new KPI, the subsequent KPI Details screen presents two rows: an actual and a target value. Both fields can be input manually in this screen. Alternatively, the values for these items will come from one of the predefined external data sources.

For example, consider a multidimensional data source Annual Shoe Sales. The data source may have dimensions for product line, region, and size, and measures for dollar sales and unit sales. Results from this data source can be used as the actual value.

Consider also a SharePoint list that contains a set of target values for each product line in the various regions. Each KPI can be configured to point to items in the SharePoint list as its target values.

As either the target or the actual value changes in the data source, the resulting KPI is automatically updated.

Indicators Defined

KPIs are typically presented in a graphical fashion, using visual indicators. An indicator can be any type of visual display that represents the degree to which the target measurement has been achieved or exceeded. Examples of indicators include fuel gauges, thermometers, stop lights, and many others.

Each indicator is divided into multiple levels, each of which displays differently. A stoplight indicator, for example, might have three indicators: red, yellow, and green. A green-level would visually demonstrate that the target measurement has been achieved or exceeded. A yellow indicator would show that the actual result is slightly off-target. And a red indicator would mean that the actual result is farther off-target.

They say a picture is worth a thousand words, and KPIs make this adage a reality. When viewing multiple KPIs on a single scorecard, a manager can quickly scan through the KPIs to quickly identify and root out those that are off-target and focus on those that warrant additional investigation.

When creating a new indicator, a number of different visual indicators are available, as shown in Figure 30.7.

Different indicators serve different purposes and visually convey different messages. For example:

> ▶ The various "trending" indicators display arrows in various colors—red, yellow, and green—and pointing in various directions. These indicators would be useful for KPIs that compare the results of a previous period to the current one.

> ▶ Some indicators, such as Stoplights and Smiley Faces, are helpful in demonstrating targets versus actual at the end of a measurable period of time. Use these indicators to show how sales figures at the end of a year or quarter compare to their corresponding target measurements.

> ▶ The sets of Bar, Cylinder, Gradient, and Gauge indicators might be appropriate for showing progress during the middle of a measurable period of time. They might be appropriate in scenarios where you want to present things such as the amount of

budget exhausted or month-to-date or year-to-date figures versus the corresponding targets for the month or year. Because the measure would continue to change over the course of the measurable period, this set of indicators would convey the amount of progress toward a specific goal. Halfway through the month or quarter, you would expect to see progress of halfway (or better) toward the goal.

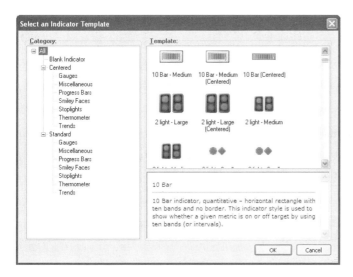

FIGURE 30.7   Different indicator template styles available for KPIs.

Besides the display style for indicators, you can apply a couple of other settings to make the indicator set unique. KPIs can have both positive and negative measurements. With targets such as sales volumes, the more the better. Thus, with a positive KPI, exceeding the target result is good. On the other hand, for a measurement such as number of safety incidents, the fewer the better. Thus staying at or below the target level is preferable. When defining indicators, designers can specify whether more is better or less is better.

In addition, for each level within a set of indicators, you can specify the percentage toward the actual goal that applies to each level. For some goals, 75% of the total may be considered "slightly off target," whereas for other measurements, 75% would be considered "way off target."

Scorecards Defined

KPIs are the individual measurable goals. A set of KPIs are grouped together to form a scorecard. For example, on a Capacity Utilization scorecard, each factory would represent a unique KPI. All the company's factories would be grouped together to display a single scorecard.

A scorecard is an example of a report about the achievement of measurable goals. The scorecard shows a series of measurements, along with the target amount, and the degree to which the target has been reached. The scorecard can provide either a visual or numeric indication to show to what degree the goal has been attained.

In the PerformancePoint world, a scorecard represents the same thing: a set of measurable goals and their corresponding levels to which those goals have been attained. Ultimately, a scorecard will be displayed as a web part on a SharePoint page.

Each scorecard will contain a set of KPIs. Examples of scorecards might include the following:

- Sales volumes, with specific KPIs for each region

- Capacity utilization, with factories making up the individual KPIs

- Number of safety incidents, with per-plant line items

- Customer service complaints, based on product line

Alternatively, a plant manager's scorecard might show a number of disparate measurements that demonstrate the overall performance of his plant. The following KPIs, when grouped together on a scorecard, might be useful in determining the plant manager's compensation:

- Number of safety incidents

- Capacity utilization

- Units manufactured

When provisioning a new scorecard, there are three categories of scorecards from which to choose, as follows:

- **Microsoft**—Enables creation of a scorecard based on Analysis Services, which requires that you have a corresponding data source based on SQL Server Analysis Services.

- **Standard**—Enables you to create either a blank or fixed value scorecard. These two options enable you to add KPIs created and manually added to your workspace.

- **Tabular**—Contains several options for creating KPIs based on various table-centric data sources. Like the Analysis Services scorecard, selection of any of the scorecards in this category requires you to have a data source based on the corresponding KPI type.

Some of the scorecard types enable you to define additional KPI measurements as part of the creation process. In addition, when the scorecard is created, you can drag additional KPIs onto the scorecard.

Figure 30.8 shows a scorecard for sales per product line. Notice that some KPIs are on-target, whereas one is slightly off-target. Notice also that KPIs on a scorecard can be rolled up into a parent KPI (All Products), to show how the grouping as a whole is performing.

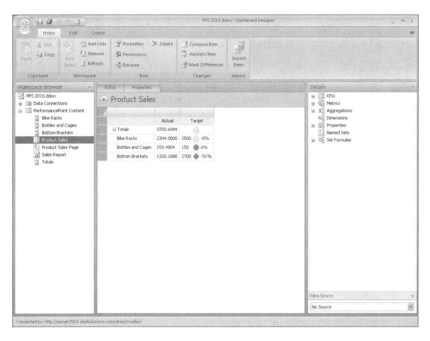

FIGURE 30.8   Sample Product Sales scorecard.

Reports Defined

Like scorecards, Reports in PerformancePoint will ultimately be displayed as a web part on a SharePoint page. Reports can be of several different varieties, each of which requires you to have a corresponding data source of the same type:

- ▶ **Analytic Chart**—Interactive charts, based on OLAP cube data, such as SQL Server Analysis Services, can be in bar, line, and pie chart format.

- ▶ **Analytic Grid**—Also based on data from OLAP cubes, Analytic grids display rows and columns of processed data.

- ▶ **Excel Services**—Allows for views of any components from Excel Services.

- ▶ **KPI Details**—View detailed information about any KPI line item.

- ▶ **ProClarity Analytics Server Page**—Create a reference to an existing ProClarity Analytics server page.

- ▶ **Reporting Services**—Reference an existing report from SQL Server Reporting Services.

30

▶ **Strategy Map**—Create a strategy map report that is connected to a scorecard by using Microsoft Office Visio 2007 or 2010.

▶ **Web Page**—Create a reference to an existing web page

Of all the report types, the Analytic Chart is one of the most interesting and most often used by organizations. When connecting to a well-defined Analysis Services OLAP data source, you can drag any combination of relevant measures and dimensions to the series and Axis sections to quickly spin up various charts.

Even more interesting, however, is the ability to click any data point within the chart and drill down to see how the chart changes based on the selected factor. Imagine the power of an executive viewing corporate sales data to re-create the chart, on-the-fly, based on any of the following:

▶ Salesperson

▶ Region

▶ Product line

▶ Year, month, quarter, week, or day

▶ Customer

Figure 30.9 shows a simple report showing the progression of sales on a quarterly basis. Notice that the user, when viewing the chart, has several options. He can drill down to view the chart based on one of the other dimensions. Additionally, he can sort, filter, pivot, and perform a number of other additional actions.

Dashboards Defined

A dashboard is loosely defined as having a lot of visual information, displayed in a number of different ways, on a screen for a user to quickly assess the current state of affairs. A car's dashboard, for example, provides the driver with important information about the current state of the car—how fast the car is going, the current engine temperature, the amount of fuel in the tank, and many other things.

Similarly, a web dashboard provides a manager with several key pieces of information about the current state of affairs. The previous sections discussed how Reports and Scorecards are ultimately displayed as web parts on SharePoint pages. In the SharePoint and PerformancePoint world, a dashboard can also be thought of as a web part page. When creating a new dashboard in PerformancePoint Server, a new page is added to the SharePoint Pages library, which, when published, can be viewed by authorized users.

Like all the other PerformancePoint components discussed, a new Dashboard page can be created from one of two places: the Create Ribbon or the Workspace Browser. If you're accustomed to creating new pages in SharePoint from the various layout pages available, the first screen of the New Dashboard interface should be familiar. On this screen, you are presented with a set of dashboard page templates, each of which provides a unique combination of web part zones. Select the zone that is right for you for the data you want to display.

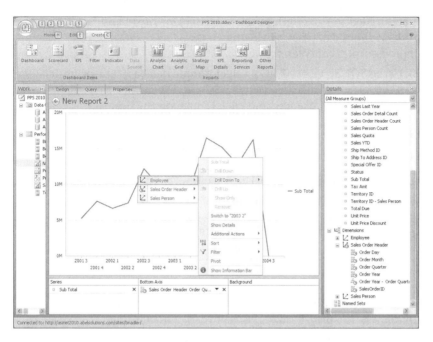

FIGURE 30.9   Drilling into information data using key data dimensions.

Users are not ultimately tied to the page layout that was initially selected. If the user right-clicks on any existing dashboard page zone, she can add new zones, split a zone into two, delete the zone, or change the existing zone's settings. Using these options, she can essentially change the whole layout of the page she started with.

After selecting a template, a Details pane is displayed on the right side of Dashboard Designer (as shown in Figure 30.9). As you create scorecards and reports, or grab existing ones from your SharePoint site, those elements become available for you to drag—essentially as web parts—onto your dashboard page. Simply drag the appropriate ones to the various zones available.

Building a Sample Dashboard in Dashboard Designer

Now that each of the components of Dashboard Designer has been presented, we're ready to walk through setting up a sample dashboard. The first step in this exercise is to download and install the AdventureWorks sample databases by following these steps:

You need a server running SQL Server 2008 and SQL Server Analysis Services to proceed with this exercise.

1. Data sources are needed to work with in this exercise. Download and install the AdventureWorks samples databases by visiting http://msftdbprodsamples.codeplex.com/.

2. Click the link to the SQL Server 2008R2 product sample databases (http://msft-dbprodsamples.codeplex.com/releases/view/45907), and then click the AdventureWorks2008R2 RTM.exe link and click I Agree on the licensing page; then click Save and save the installation file to a machine running SQL Server 2008 and SQL Server Analysis Services.

CAUTION

The sample product databases for AdventureWorks will change over time, so the link might be replaced by a newer version. If possible, locate the specific .exe file listed in this section because using an updated file may invalidate certain steps in this or future sections.

---

3. When the file finishes downloading, double-click the executable, and the self-extracting zip unloads the files. Read and accept the license terms.

4. On the next screen, select the AdventureWorksLT and the AdventureWorks Data Warehouse 2008 databases to install, plus any additional ones you would like to use.

Preparing the Data Sources

Next, compile and build the AdventureWorks data warehouse by completing the following steps:

1. On the SQL Server 2008 machine, open c:\Program Files\Microsoft SQL Server\100\Tools\Samples \AdventureWorks 2008 Analysis Services Project\ Enterprise (or \Standard, depending on the version of your SQL Server installation), and open the Adventure Works.sln file.

2. From the Build menu, select Deploy project.

Next, create a new view in the AdventureWorksLT database by following these steps:

1. Launch SQL Server Management Studio from the Programs area.

2. Connect to the SQL Server instance where you installed the AdventureWorksLT database.

3. In the Object Explorer, expand the databases node and then the AdventureWorksLT node.

4. Right-click the Views node and select New View.

5. Close the Add Table dialog box, and enter the following directly in the text box, as shown in Figure 30.10:

```
SELECT DISTINCT PC.Name AS ProductCategory,
SUM(SOD.UnitPrice * SOD.OrderQty) AS TotalSales
```

```
FROM SalesLT.SalesOrderDetail AS SOD
INNER JOIN SalesLT.Product AS P ON SOD.ProductID = P.ProductID
INNER JOIN SalesLT.ProductCategory AS PC
ON PC.ProductCategoryID = P.ProductCategoryID
GROUP BY PC.Name
```

6. Save the view with the name vw_ProductCategorySales.

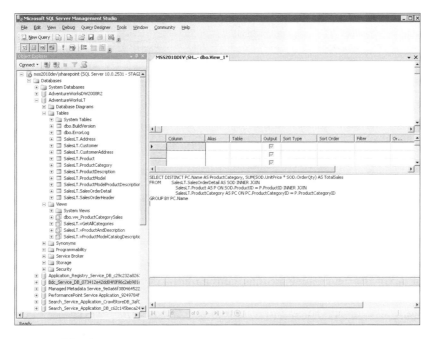

FIGURE 30.10   Create a new view on the AdventureWorksLT database.

Creating Data Connections

At this point, a lot of the initial "plumbing" is in place, and you are ready to start building a dashboard.

Start by creating at least two data sources to be used by the PerformancePoint Content you create by following these steps:

1. In the Workspace Browser of Dashboard Designer, click Data Connections.

2. On the Create Ribbon, click Data Source, as shown in Figure 30.11. Note that when Data Connections is selected in the Workspace Browser on the left pane, Data Source will be enabled and all other items disabled. When PerformancePoint Content is selected, Data Source will be disabled, and all other items enabled.

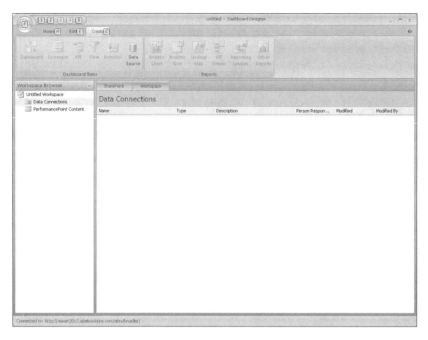

FIGURE 30.11   Create tab on the Ribbon for Dashboard Designer.

3. In the Select a Data Source Template dialog box, select SQL Server table and click OK.

4. In the Editor tab of the data source settings, configure the data source. In the Server text box, enter the name of your SQL Server instance where you installed the AdventureWorksLT database. For example, enter **mySQLServer.myDomain.com.**

5. After entering the server name, the Databases list box will be enabled. Click the down arrow for the Databases list box. A list of databases on the server load. Select AdventureWorksLT.

6. Click the down arrow for the Tables list box. Note that both SQL Server tables and views appear in this list, sorted alphabetically. Select dbo.vw_ProductCategorySales, as shown in Figure 30.12.

7. Click the Test Data Source Connection button.

8. Switch to the Properties tab in Dashboard Designer, and change the Name of the Data Source to AdventureWorks Product Sales. Click the Save icon (located in the top-left corner of Dashboard Designer, next to the Office button) to add the new Data Source to your SharePoint site.

9. Preview the data by selecting the View tab of the Data Source properties. Click the Preview Data button, and the data loads in two columns: ProductCategory and TotalSales, as shown in Figure 30.13.

Next, you need to create a second data source, this time connecting to a SQL Server Analysis Services data cube. To do so, complete the following steps:

1. In the Create Ribbon, click the Data Source icon.

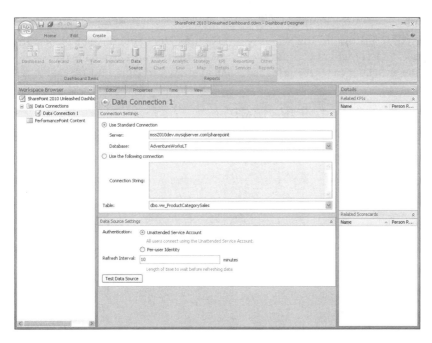

FIGURE 30.12   Connection settings for the AdventureWorks Product Sales data connection.

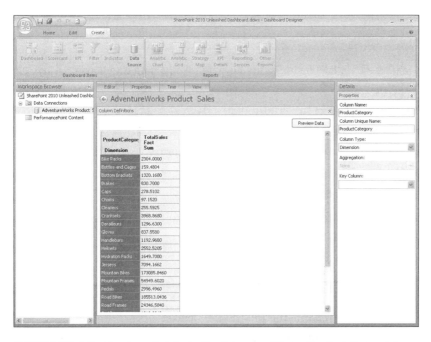

FIGURE 30.13   Preview of data in the AdventureWorks Product Sales data connection.

2. In the Select a Data Source Template dialog box, this time select Analysis Services.

3. In the connection settings, in the Server text box, enter the name of the SQL Server Analysis Services server where you installed the AdventureWorks DW cube. For example, enter **mySQLServer.myDomain.com\SSAS** as shown in Figure 30.14.

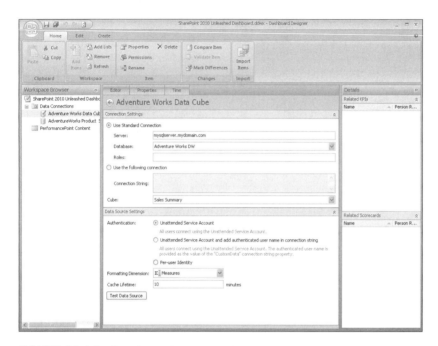

FIGURE 30.14   Creating a data connection to the AdventureWorks data warehouse.

4. In the Database list box, select Adventure Works DW.

5. In the Cube list box, select Sales Summary.

6. Click the Properties tab, and change the Name to Adventure Works Data Cube.

Creating Key Performance Indicators

Now that the data connections are in place, the next step is to begin creating a few KPIs. To do so, complete the following steps:

1. In the Workspace Browser, click on PerformancePoint Content.

2. In the Create Ribbon, click KPI.

3. In the Select a KPI Template dialog box, select Blank KPI and click OK.

4. In the Workspace Browser, rename the KPI to **Bike Racks.**

5. Next, configure the actual value for the KPI to use the database. In the Actual row, click 1 (Fixed Values) under the Data Mappings column. In the Dimensional Data Source Mappings dialog box, click the Change Source button. In the Select a Data

Source dialog box, click AdventureWorks Product Sales and click OK, as shown in Figure 30.15.

FIGURE 30.15   Configuring the Bike Racks KPI.

6. In the Dimensional Data Source Mapping dialog box, click the arrow for the Select a Measure list box, and select TotalSales.

7. In the Select a Dimension section, click the New Dimension Filter icon.

8. In the select a Dimension dialog box, select ProductCategory and click OK.

9. In the Default column, click the Default link, and select Bike Racks in the Select Members dialog box. Click OK.

10. Next configure the target value against which the KPI will be measured. In the Target row for the KPI, click 1 (Fixed Values), Enter **2500** for the Value and click OK. When complete, your KPI settings should look like Figure 30.16.

11. When selecting the Target row of the KPI settings, in the bottom half of the KPI settings, you can optionally select a different indicator by clicking the Set Scoring Pattern and Indicator button. Step through the wizard, but do not make any changes.

12. Repeat steps 1 through 10 for a second KPI. For the KPI name, use **Bottles and Cages.** For the KPI Actual value, again use **Bottles and Cages** as the selected member in the dimension filter. For the target value, use **150**.

13. Repeat steps 1 through 10 for a third KPI. For the KPI name and for the dimension filter select member, use **Bottom Brackets**. For the target value, use 2700.

Finally, you need to create a rollup KPI, which will use the aggregate of the three previous KPIs, by following these steps:

1. Create a new KPI, but this time in the Select a KPI Template dialog box, select Objective.

2. Rename the KPI to **Totals.**

30

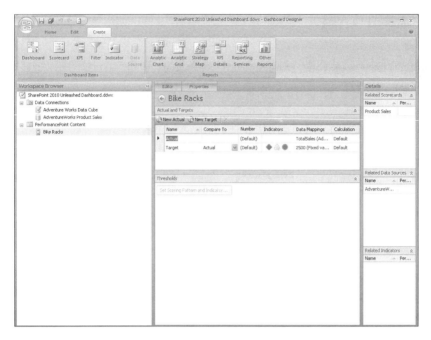

FIGURE 30.16   Configuration for the Bike Racks KPI.

3. In the Calculation column of the KPI settings, click No Value.

4. Select the Sum of Children option. Apply this setting for both the Target and the
   Actual values. The Totals KPI is shown in Figure 30.17.

Creating a Scorecard

Now that the KPIs have all been created, you can combine them into a single scorecard.
To do so, complete the following steps:

1. In the Create Ribbon of Dashboard Designer, click Scorecard.

2. In the Select a Scorecard Template dialog box, select the Standard category, and
   select Blank Scorecard.

3. Click the Properties tab, and change the Name for the scorecard to **Product Sales.**

4. In the Details pane on the right side of Dashboard Designer, expand KPI, and
   expand PerformancePoint Content.

5. Drag the Totals KPI to the working pane on top of the Drop Items Here label.

6. Drag the Bike Racks KPI to the working pane. While holding the left mouse key, drag
   the Bike Racks KPI to the right edge of the label for the Totals label. You should see the
   Total KPI highlighted, with gray borders on the left, top, and bottom edges. The right
   edge of the Totals KPI should be blue. In addition, a blue arrow should be pointing at
   the right edge of the Totals KPI. Release the mouse key, and the Bike Racks KPI should
   display beneath the Totals KPI, slightly indented. This is shown in Figure 30.18.

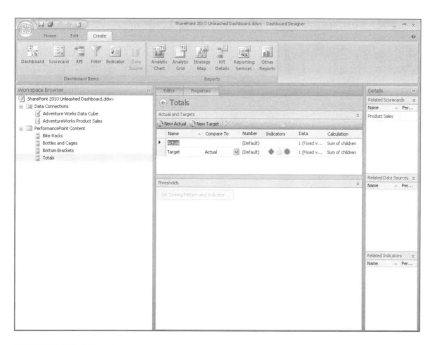

FIGURE 30.17   KPI Using the sum of children calculation, to be used for aggregation.

7. Repeat step 6 for the Bottles and Cages KPI, and again for the Bottom Brackets KPI. Bike Racks, Bottles and Cages, and Bottom Brackets should all display on the scorecard beneath the Totals KPI, and all three should be indented.

Creating a Report

Reports are the life blood of many companies, and Dashboard Designer provides a variety of chart options to facilitate the process. The following steps walk through the process of creating an Analytic Chart:

1. In the Create Ribbon, select Analytic Chart.

2. In the Select a Data Source dialog box, select AdventureWorks Data Cube.

3. In the Workspace Browser, the new report will be selected, with the name highlighted. Change the name to **Adventure Works Sales Chart**. Alternatively, you can change the name by clicking the Properties tab in the working area.

4. The report Details pane loads on the right side of Dashboard Designer. Expand the Measure grouping, and drag Sales Amount to the Series pane.

5. Expand the Dimensions grouping, the Date subgrouping, and the Calendar subgrouping. Drag the Calendar Quarter of Year dimension to the Bottom Axis section.

6. Expand the Named Sets grouping and the Sets subgrouping. Drag the Core Product Group named set to the Bottom Axis section. The report should look like Figure 30.19.

7. Click the Save All icon (or select Ctrl-Shift-S) to save all items.

30

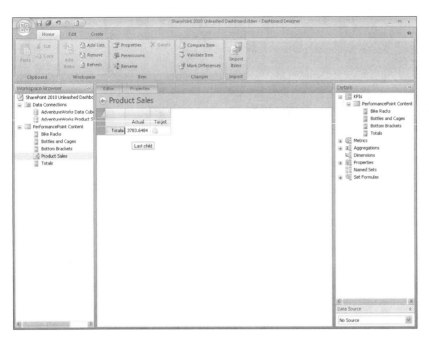

FIGURE 30.18   Adding a child KPI to a scorecard.

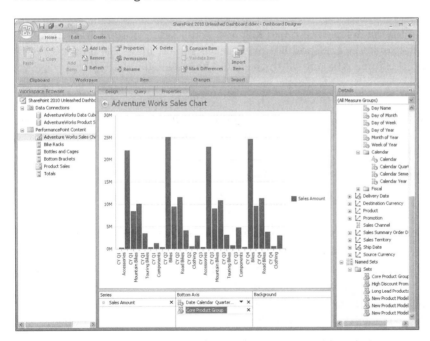

FIGURE 30.19   Completed Analytical Chart of Sales Amounts by quarter for each Core
Product Group.

Creating a Dashboard

The previous sections walked through the process of creating KPIs, scorecards, and reports. As noted earlier in the chapter, scorecards and reports are examples of web parts that appear on dashboard web pages. The final steps of the process demonstrate how to make these contents viewable on dashboard pages in SharePoint:

1. In the Create Ribbon, select Dashboard. You can select any of the Dashboard page templates.

2. In the Workspace Browser, rename the dashboard to **Product Sales Dashboard.**

3. In the Pages section of the working area, click Page 1, and rename it to **Product Sales.**

4. In the Details pane, expand Scorecards, and expand PerformancePoint Content. Drag the Product Sales scorecard into one of the dashboard zones.

5. In the Details pane, expand Reports, and expand PerformancePoint Content. Drag AdventureWorks Sales Chart onto the other zone.

6. In the Workspace Browser, right-click on Product Sales Dashboard, and select Deploy to SharePoint.

7. Select one of the master page options, and click OK.

8. After the deployment is complete, the dashboard page launches in Internet Explorer, as shown in Figure 30.20.

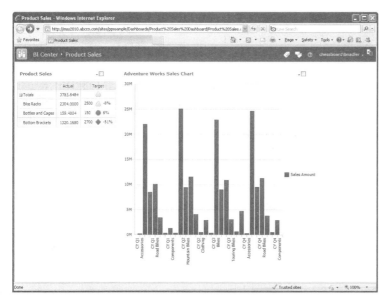

FIGURE 30.20   PerformancePoint Dashboard page.

30

Summary

The age of waiting for periodic reports to be generated by IT is over. The day has arrived in which reports no longer need to be predefined and preformatted before delivering them to the person who needs to see them. With PerformancePoint Services, included in the Enterprise version of SharePoint Server 2010, and in particular with the power of the Analytical Reports, the right business intelligence is truly placed in the hands of the right people at the right time.

This chapter walks through the process of configuring a PerformancePoint Service Application, working with Dashboard Designer and creating a dashboard, using Data Connections, KPIs, Indicators, Scorecards, Reports, and Dashboards. It also walks through the process of creating a dashboard so that the PerformancePoint tools will no longer be mysterious, and the process of creating a dashboard less intimidating.

Best Practices

▶ When connecting to a data source, use the Unattended Service Account option for authentication. If using the other option, Per-User Identity, you may find that the dashboard components that use the data source load when you log in but fail to connect for other users visiting your page.

▶ With PerformancePoint Services, the quality of the dashboard is all about the data. To that end, some additional planning needs to go into the types of data sources you want to leverage. Well-designed transactional databases and data cubes are key to a successful BI implementation.

▶ Give some thought to which indicator sets you want to use for each KPI. Different image sets convey different messages. Comparisons of metrics from one time period to those from another warrant use of one of the trending indicators. Some indicators are appropriate to show at the end of a measurable time period, whereas others make more sense in the middle of a measurable time period.

▶ If starting a new Dashboard Designer workspace, check the SharePoint tab of Dashboard Designer to see which dashboard components have already been defined. If one exists that you want to use, simply double-click the component to include it in your workspace.

▶ It is not necessary to create a site using the Business Intelligence Center site template to use PerformancePoint Services. Simply activating PerformancePoint Site Features will be sufficient.

## CHAPTER 31

Business Intelligence in SharePoint 2010 with Business Connectivity Services

Business Connectivity Services (BCS) provides an interface for surfacing detailed information about an entity in SharePoint. As noted in Chapter 30, "Business Intelligence in SharePoint 2010 with PerformancePoint Services," Business Intelligence in SharePoint is about bringing the right information to the right people at the right time. Chapter 30 focused on PerformancePoint Services, which emphasizes the presentation of analytical data—numbers that can be totaled, averaged, or analyzed in other mathematical ways. With BCS, the information that is surfaced is typically more anecdotal, presenting detailed information about a specific entity, such as a customer, a product, or an individual sale.

Consider, for example, a customer service department for an online retailer. The company receives an average of 200 calls and online chats per hour. With recent staff cuts, the customer service agents are under increasing pressure to address calls as quickly as possible, without sacrificing the quality of the customer service. For the various types of customer interactions, the customer service representative needs to quickly and easily access information about the customer, the order, and the products included in the order.

The company has a variety of applications that serve various business functions. There is an order fulfillment system based on a SQL Server database. A customer database, owned by the marketing department, contains information about previous customers and is used for direct marketing initiatives. Finally, the customer service department has started using a SharePoint team site and a SharePoint issues list to track customer service issues.

Using BCS features of SharePoint 2010, the company can tie all this information together so that its customer service representatives can quickly and easily access key information about orders and customers when handling calls. The department's goal is to provide one single, seamless user interface. The vision is to create a customer service dashboard, where anyone in the department can quickly record, view, and address customer service issues in the shortest amount of time.

External Content Types

SharePoint 2010 adds the notion of external content types. The content type, first introduced in SharePoint 2007, is a way of describing an entity of information stored in SharePoint. Document content types can be items such as contracts, policies, and forms. Nondocument content types can be items such as announcements, tasks, or contacts. All these are content types whose information is physically stored within the SharePoint taxonomy. Each would have its respective set of attributes, known as columns, properties, or metadata.

An external content type is just what it sounds like: an entity whose underlying data exists external to SharePoint. Just like a SharePoint content type, an external content type will also have its set of attributes or columns. Using BCS, external content types can be defined and made available for consumption within SharePoint.

Options for Building BCS Entities

In the 2007 version of the BCS—known at the time as the Business Data Catalog (BDC)—definitions of entities required third-party tools. A few competing tools were available, but they provided only functionality for building BDC entities. Two such products are BDC Metaman from Lightning Tools and MOSS BDC Design Studio from Simego.

However, the 2010 versions of Visual Studio and SharePoint Designer, both of which provide functionality for developing a wide range of other SharePoint features, introduce built-in BCS design and development. This can enable an easy definition of external content types for later consumption in SharePoint. The ability to build BCS functionality using the SharePoint tools already used for other SharePoint extensions is one improvement in the capabilities offered by the 2010 suite of products.

Developing external content types in Visual Studio 2010 requires a machine running SharePoint 2010. This can be either a 64-bit Windows Server 2008 machine running as a SharePoint server, or a Windows 7 machine, which is capable of running a development version of SharePoint. Details of how to develop external content types through Visual Studio 2010 is beyond the scope of this chapter.

Installing SharePoint Designer

SharePoint Designer 2010 also includes built-in capabilities for developing external content types. SharePoint Designer 2010 is a free tool that can be used to extend and customize SharePoint sites. To download and install SharePoint Designer 2010, complete the following steps:

1. In Internet Explorer, go to http://www.microsoft.com/downloads.

2. In the Bing Search box on the Downloads page, type **SharePoint Designer 2010.**

3. Select either Microsoft SharePoint Designer 2010 (32-bit) or Microsoft SharePoint Designer 2010 (64-bit), depending on your desktop operating system.

4. On the subsequent page, click the Download button. When prompted with Do You Want to Run or Save This File? select Save, and save the file to your Desktop. The total size of the download is 254MB for the 32-bit version and 279MB for the 64-bit version.

5. When the download is complete, double-click the SharePointDesigner.exe file on your desktop. This begins the installation process.

6. After the file extraction process completes, read the Microsoft Software License Terms, and accept the terms of the agreement; then click OK. Click the Install Now button. When the installation completes, you will be ready to start using SharePoint Designer.

Preparing to Build External Content Types

Prior to building External Content Types in SharePoint Designer, a few preparation steps are necessary. First, a SharePoint site is required. To create a new SharePoint site, complete the following steps:

1. On the SharePoint 2010 server, select Start and SharePoint 2010 Central Administration.

2. Under the Application Management, click Create Site Collections.

3. In the Title box of the Create Site Collection page, type **BCS Sample Site.**

4. In the URL section, select the /sites/ option in the drop-down box, and type **BCSSample** in the text box.

5. Enter one or two login accounts to serve as the site collection administrator(s).

6. In the Template Selection section, choose the blank site template, as shown in Figure 31.1.

Additionally, external content types require a SQL Server database to connect to. Chapter 30 includes a set of steps to install the AdventureWorksLT database. If you completed

those steps in the previous chapter, it is not necessary to do so again; if not, these steps
are repeated here:

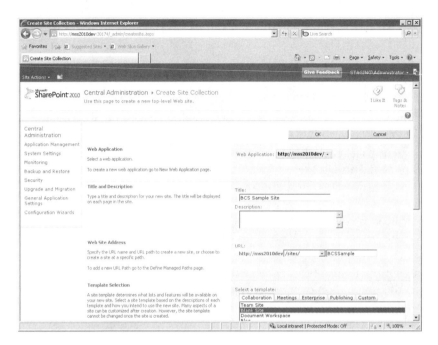

FIGURE 31.1   Create a blank SharePoint site.

NOTE

You need a server running SQL Server 2008 and SQL Server Analysis Services to proceed with this exercise.

1. Download and install the AdventureWorks samples databases by visiting
   http://msftdbprodsamples.codeplex.com/.
2. Click the link to the SQL Server 2008R2 product sample databases (http://
   msftdbprodsamples.codeplex.com/releases/view/45907), and then click the
   AdventureWorks2008R2 RTM.exe link; click I Agree on the licensing page. Click Save
   and save the installation file to a machine running SQL Server 2008.

CAUTION

The sample product databases for AdventureWorks will change over time, so the link
above might be replaced by a newer version. If possible, locate the specific .exe file
listed in this section because using an updated file might invalidate certain steps in
this or future sections.

3. When the file finishes downloading, double-click the executable, and the self-extracting zip unloads the files. Read and accept the license terms.

4. On the next screen, select the AdventureWorksLT database to install, plus any additional ones that you would like to use.

Defining the External Content Type

The next set of exercises step through how to create the most basic External Content Type. The example uses the Customers table of the AdventureWorks database.

There are several operations available for an External Content Type; however, two specific ones—Read List and Read Item—are required before it can be consumed by SharePoint.

A Read List operation provides all the rows of the table that meet the criteria defined in the operation. In the Customer example, a Read List operation can enable viewing of all the records from the Customers table in one SharePoint list, with it looking and acting like a SharePoint list. Although the data continues to live in the AdventureWorksLT database on SQL Server, it can be consumed in SharePoint, with the benefit of SharePoint views, and column sorting and filtering.

A Read Item operation allows for the isolation of an individual record from the list, based upon some unique identifier, such as a Customer ID. The Read Item operation also enables you to join together a regular SharePoint list with the records of the Customer table. In the forthcoming examples, a Customer Service Issues list, stored in SharePoint, can capture data about calls fielded by the Customer Service department. The list contains a mixture of SharePoint data and external data.

There are other operations available as well for External Content Types, including

▶ **Create Operation**—Add a new record to a table.

▶ **Update Operation**—Modify an existing record.

▶ **Delete Operation**—Remove a record from a table.

▶ **Association**—Define a relationship between two related tables.

Each of these operations is discussed in later sections of this chapter.

To begin building the external content types, complete the following steps:

1. Open SharePoint Designer 2010. Following installation, the application should be added to a SharePoint grouping on your computer's Programs menu.

2. In SharePoint Designer 2010, click the Open Site button from the File Ribbon. Enter the web address for the site created in the previous section. For example, enter `http://mss2010.mydomain.com/sites/BCSSample/`.

3. In the Site Objects window, shown on the left side bar in Figure 31.2, select External Content Types.

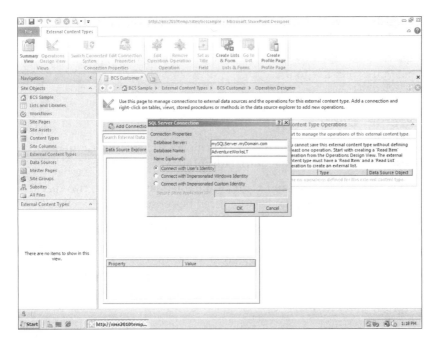

FIGURE 31.2   Connect to the Adventureworkslt database.

4. In the External Content Types Ribbon at the top of the screen, select New External Content Type.

5. In the External Content Type Information section, click the link next to Name called New External Content Type. The link will be replaced with a text box to enter the name. Type **BCS Customer.** The Display Name updates automatically.

6. Next to the External System header, click the Click Here to Discover New External Data Sources and Define External Content Types link.

7. In the Data Source Explorer view, click the Add Connection button.

8. In the External Data Source Type Selection dialog box, select SQL Server as the Data Source Type and click OK.

9. In the SQL Server connection dialog box, enter the SQL Server connection information. The Database Server should be the name of the SQL Server and instance where you installed the AdventureWorks LT database. For example, type **mySQLServer.myDomain.com.** For Database Name, type **AdventureWorksLT.** For the connection options, select Connect with User's Identity. Click OK.

10. After a connection to the AdventureWorksLT database is established, the database schema loads under the Data Source Explorer. Expand the AdventureWorksLT node. Note that tables, views, and Routines (SQL Server stored procedures) are all available for use. Expand the Tables node as well.

11. Right-click the Customer table, and a list of available operations loads. Begin by selecting New Read Item Operation.

31

12. The Read Item Wizard is divided into three parts. In the first part—Operation Properties—type **Customer Read Item** as both the Operation Name and the Operation Display Name. Click Next.

13. In the Input Parameters, the CustomerID field, by virtue of it being defined as a unique identifier for the table in the database, is automatically recognized as the identifier for the external content type. Notice when the CustomerID field is selected, the Map to Identifier box is selected. No changes are necessary on this screen. Click Next.

14. The last portion of the wizard—Return Parameter—defines which columns from the database will be available for consumption and is shown in Figure 31.3. No changes are necessary on this screen. Click Finish.

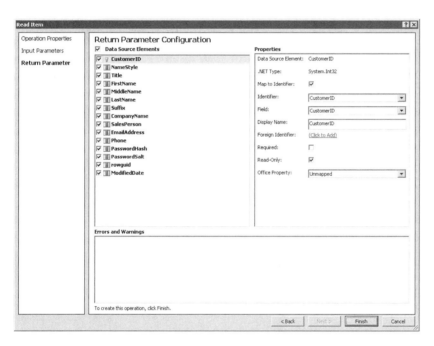

FIGURE 31.3   Creating the external content type read item operation.

15. In the Data Source Explorer of SharePoint Designer, right-click the Customer table and select New Read List Operation.

16. In the Operation Properties portion of the wizard, type **Customer Read List** as the Operation Name and the Operation Display Name. Click Next.

17. In the Filter Parameters section, no changes are necessary. Click Next.

18. In the Return Parameters section, select CustomerID field in the Data Source Elements section, and select the box in the Properties section labeled Show in

Picker. Repeat this for the FirstName, LastName, EmailAddress, and Phone fields. Click Finish.

19. Click the Save icon in the upper-left corner of SharePoint Designer (or use the CTRL-S keys) to save the External Content Type.

> **NOTE**
>
> Saving the external content type uploads the information to the BCS service application in SharePoint Central Administration. The external content type can later be removed or modified by going to Central Administration, Application Management, Manage Service Applications, and Business Data Connectivity.

Creating an External Content Type for a Related Item

Most normalized databases have several tables with relationships to other tables, which are models for real-world information. A customer, for example, can place one or more orders with a company. An order can contain one or more products, and a single order may be delivered in one or more shipments.

A normalized database, to accurately model this information, can define relationships between these tables. A one-to-many relationship would exist between a Customers table and an Orders table. Both tables would contain a CustomerID field. In the Customers table, each individual record would have a unique CustomerID. In the Orders table, there might be several records with the same CustomerID. This represents that one customer has placed multiple orders.

The AdventureWorksLT database contains this exact relationship between the Customers and Orders tables. With Business Data Connectivity, there is an extra step involved with defining an External Content Type with this type of relationship.

The following steps address how to create an External Content Type for Orders, where a relationship to another content type exists:

1. In SharePoint Designer, in the Site Objects pane on the left side, click the External Content Types option.
2. In the External Content Types Ribbon, click the New External Content Type button.
3. In the External Content Type Information, type **BCS Order** for both the Name and the Display Name.
4. In the External System field, click the Click Here to Discover External Data Sources and Define External Content Types link.
5. The AdventureWorksLT data source should already be available from having completed the previous set of steps. Expand the AdventureWorksLT node and the Tables node. Expand the SalesOrderHeader node and the Columns node to view the columns in the SalesOrderHeader table. Notice the CustomerID column.

6. Right-click SalesOrderHeader, and select New Read Item Operation.

7. In the first part of the Read Item Wizard—Operation Properties—type **Sales Order Read Item** as both the Operation Name and the Operation Display Name. Click Next.

8. As with the CustomerID field for the Customer external content type, the SalesOrderID field is automatically recognized as the identifier for the external content type. No changes are necessary on this screen. Click Next.

9. The last portion of the wizard—Return Parameters—defines which columns from the database will be available for consumption. No changes are necessary on this screen. Click Finish.

10. Next, right-click on SalesOrderHeader, and select New Association. This is the operation necessary to establish the relationship between a customer and an order.

11. The Association Creation Wizard is divided into four sections, as shown in Figure 31.4. In the first, Association Properties, type **SalesOrder Customer Association** as both the Name and the Display Name.

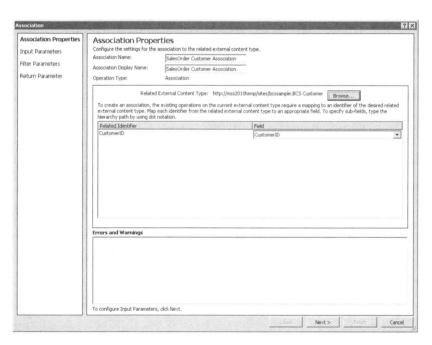

FIGURE 31.4   Create an association between related external content types.

12. Next to Related External Content Type, click the Browse button. The BCS Order (the current one) and BCS Customer (created earlier) external content types should both

be available. Select BCS Customer and click OK. Below, the field CustomerID is automatically selected because both tables have the field with the same name. Thus
SharePoint Designer recognizes that this is the likely field on which to establish the
relationship. Click Next.

13. In the second part of the wizard—Input Parameters—click the CustomerID field
    under Data Source Elements. Then check the box to the right labeled Map to
    Identifier and click Next.

14. In the Filter Parameters section, no changes are necessary. Click Next.

15. In the Return Parameters section, no changes are necessary. Click Finish.

16. In the Data Source Explorer of SharePoint Designer, right-click the SalesOrderHeader
    table and select New Read List Operation.

17. In the Operation Properties portion of the wizard, type `SalesOrder Read List` as the
    Operation Name and the Operation Display Name. Click Next.

18. In the Filter Parameters section, click Add Filter Parameter. In the Properties section
    for the new filter, change the Data Source Element to CustomerID. For the Filter
    parameter, click the Click to Add link. Make no changes in the Filter Configuration
    dialog box, and click OK. For the Default Value property, enter 1. Click Next.

19. In the Return Parameters section, select SalesOrderID field in the Data Source
    Elements section, and select the box in the Properties section labeled Show in Picker.
    Repeat this for the OrderDate, ShipDate, and TotalDue fields. Click Finish.

20. Click the Save icon in the upper-left corner of SharePoint Designer (or use the Ctrl-S
    keys) to save the External Content Type.

At this point, there are now two external content types in the BCS Metadata Store in
SharePoint central administration. These external content types are now available for use
in the SharePoint sites.

Consuming External Content Types

When all the heavy lifting is complete, and the external content type has been built and
saved into SharePoint, it is ready for consumption. There are three main ways that you
can leverage the external content type in SharePoint: External Lists, External Data, and
BCS web parts.

External Lists

An external list looks and acts just like a SharePoint list. Contents are displayed in rows
and columns. You can also leverage the columns by sorting and filtering on them and by
creating custom views. The main difference between an external list and a regular

SharePoint list is that the actual contents of the external list live outside of SharePoint, hence the name.

To create an external list, complete the following steps:

1. In Internet Explorer, open the SharePoint site created earlier in the chapter. The URL will be something like http://mss2010.mydomain.com/sites/BCSSample/.

2. Select Site Actions and View All Site Content.

3. In the All Site Content page, click Create.

4. In the Create page, select External List, and click Create.

5. In the new list page, enter Customers as the list name.

6. Leave the Display This List on the Quick Launch option set to Yes.

7. For the External Content Type field, an External Content Type picker is available. Click the Select External Content Type icon. Select BCS Customer, as shown in Figure 31.5, and click OK.

FIGURE 31.5   Settings for creating a new external list.

8. BCS Customer (AdventureWorksLT) should display as underlined. Click Create.

The resulting display is the entire Customers table from the AdventureWorksLT database looks and acts like a standard SharePoint list. Notice that the following capabilities are available on the list, as shown in Figure 31.6:

▶ **Sorting**—Hover over any of the column headers to sort the list in either Ascending or Descending order.

▶ **Filtering**—Any column—for example, SalesPerson—can be used for refining the number of records shown in the list.

▶ **Views**—As with any other SharePoint list, site owners can create custom views.

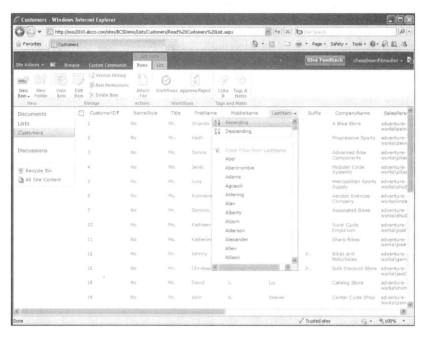

FIGURE 31.6   Sorting and filtering columns on an external list.

External Data

The second means by which external content types can be consumed in SharePoint sites is through External Data columns. An External Data column basically provides a hybrid between a SharePoint list and an external list. External Data starts with any basic SharePoint list. The following steps use the SharePoint issues list with an external column to connect each issue to one of Adventure Works' customers:

1. In the SharePoint site, select the View All Site Content option from the Site Actions menu.

2. In the All Site Content page, click Create.

3. In the Create page, select Issues Tracking. In the Name box, type **Customer Complaints** and click Create.

4. Once the list is created, click the List Ribbon, and click the Create Column icon.

5. Type **Customer** as the Column Name, and select External Data as the column type.

6. In the External Content Type picker, type the word **Customer** into the text box, and click the checkmark icon to Check if External Content Type Exists. BCS Customer (AdventureWorksLT) should display as underlined, as shown in Figure 31.7.

7. Select CustomerID from the Select the Field to be Shown on This Column list box.

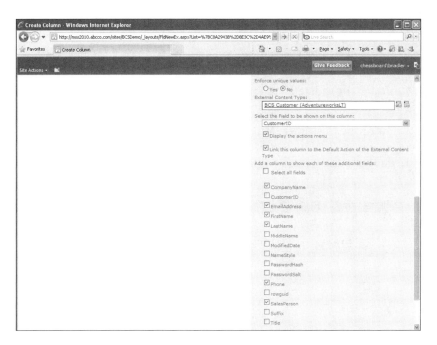

FIGURE 31.7   Applying the External Data column settings.

8. Under Add a Column to Show Each of These Additional Fields, select CompanyName, EmailAddress, FirstName, LastName, Phone, and SalesPerson, as shown in Figure 31.7. When these selections have been made, all the fields selected will be dynamically added to the custom SharePoint list. Click OK.

When all this is complete, you can begin entering data into the Customer Complaints list.

1. In the Customer Complaints list, click the Add New Item link.

2. Type **Order received was incomplete** as the Title.

3. The Customer field, displayed at the bottom of the New Item form, provides an External Item picker utility. Click the Select External Item icon (the second icon). Select the record with CustomerID of 3, Donna Carreras, and click OK.

NOTE

Recall that, earlier in the chapter, when creating the Read List operation on the
Customers table, the Return Parameters portion of the wizard included a Show in
Picker check box for each field listed. The exercise called for checking this box for the
CustomerID, FirstName, LastName, EmailAddress, and Phone fields. These are the
fields displayed in the Choose BCS Customer lookup.

   4. Click Save to commit the new item to the Customer Complaints list.

   5. Repeat steps 1 through 4 to add a second record. Type **Order included broken
      parts** as the Title. Select the record with a CustomerID of 4, Janet Gates.

   6. Repeat steps 1 through 4 to add a third record. Type **Order is three weeks overdue**
      as the Title. Select the record with a CustomerID of 1, Orlando Gee.

Figure 31.8 shows a view of the Customer Complaints list that has the three records
entered in the preceding exercises. Notice that, in addition to the traditional Issue
Tracking columns, there is also the Customer (External Data) column.

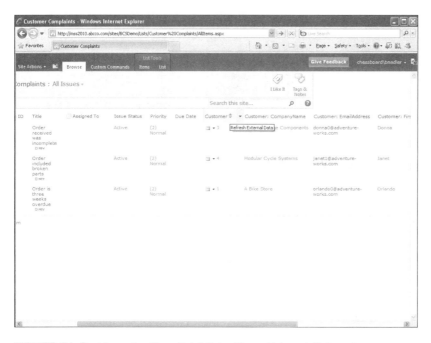

FIGURE 31.8   View of a SharePoint list with an External Data column.

The view also includes several additional columns relating to the customer. These columns
are prefixed with Customer:, which indicates that they are columns based on the
Customer External Content Type.

Periodically, data in the source SQL Server database may change. The BCS database contains cached versions of this data. In Figure 31.8, the Customer column header is highlighted, the result of hovering the mouse over this header. The column includes a double-arrow icon next to it. Clicking this arrow initiates a refresh of the data stored in SQL Server. If using External Data columns, periodically click this icon to ensure that the most current data is displayed in your SharePoint lists.

Writing to External Content Types

In SharePoint 2007's Business Data Catalog, interaction with external data was read-only. There were no means by which authorized users could write back to the external data source. The other major change with BCS in SharePoint 2010 is that external content types can be defined with full CRUD (Create, Read, Update, and Delete) capabilities.

For many scenarios, writing to an external content type is going to be beyond the scope of what you can do within the confines of SharePoint Designer. It's likely that the database to which you are connecting will have columns with more sophisticated data requirements. For example, many database tables will have some internal fields whose values are generated by the code in whatever application the database connects to.

The following steps walk you through the process of creating these operations and subsequently demonstrate why there are limitations to using SharePoint Designer for write-back operations:

1. Click Start, and open SharePoint Designer 2010 from the SharePoint group.
2. In SharePoint Designer 2010, from the File Ribbon, click Open Site. Type the web address for the site created in the early parts of this chapter. For example, type **http://mss2010.mydomain.com/sites/BCSSample/**.
3. In the Site Objects window, select External Content Types.
4. BCS Customer and BCS Order should be listed in the External Content Types pane in the bottom-left corner of SharePoint Designer. Click BCS Customer.
5. In the External Content Types Ribbon, click the Operations Design View icon.
6. In the Data Source Explorer, right-click the Customer table, and select New Create Operation, as shown in Figure 31.9.
7. In the Operation Properties section of the Create Wizard, type **Create Customer** as both the Operation Name and the Operation Display Name. Click Next.
8. In the Input Parameters section, no changes are necessary. Several fields from the File Ribbon (PasswordHash, PasswordSalt, and ModifiedDate) will be discussed in more detail shortly. Also notice the opportunity to enter a default value for each of the fields below. Finally, observe that each field can be unchecked; however, doing so results in an error message being added to Errors and Warnings, which will block instantiation of the Create operation. Click Next.
9. In the Return Parameter portion of the wizard, no changes are necessary. Click Next.
10. Click Save, or enter CTRL-S to save the changes.

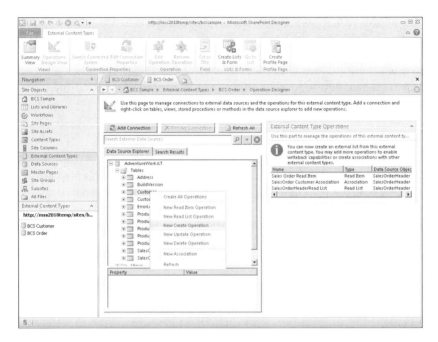

FIGURE 31.9   Building a create operation for an external content type.

Although this exercise provided a simple set of steps to build a Create operation on the Customers table, some of the fields previously mentioned—Password Hash, Password Salt, and ModifiedDate—present specific problems.

These fields all perform important functions on the database. Yet, at the same time, they aren't the types of fields meant to be provided by end users. The PasswordHash and PasswordSalt fields, for example, are managed by other applications and provide encryption on the actual password entered by a system user. Finally, the ModifiedDate field, also intended to be system-generated, is used to capture when the field was actually entered.

For fields such as these, SharePoint Designer is only sophisticated enough to allow you the following options: Ignore the Fields on Write Operations, Specify a Default Value, or Leave It Up to the User to Enter a Value. The resulting outcomes of these options would be that a) the field was left blank on the new entry, b) useless data was entered, or c) an invalid entry resulted in an error that prevented the entire record from being added.

So although BCS provides the capability to write back to SQL Server from SharePoint, and although this can be a powerful business tool, it is only realistic for small, simple databases. For most line-of-business database systems, this is most likely going to be a practice best left to a more advanced BCS authoring tool, such as Visual Studio 2010.

Delete operations can pose similar problems on many database applications. A well-designed, normalized database is likely going to have records in one table that depend on records in another table. An Orders table, for example, might have a CustomerID foreign key field, which depends on a related record in the Customers table. In the database, if you try to delete a Customer record when there are dependent records in the Orders table,

SQL Server might issue an error message and block the deletion. The error message would be returned to the user and indicate the existence of such a dependency.

A simple Delete operation, however, can be created with the following steps:

1. In the Data Source Explorer of SharePoint Designer, right-click the Customer table, and select New Delete Operation.

2. In the Operation Properties section of the Create Wizard, type **Delete Customer** as both the Operation Name and the Operation Display Name. Click Next.

3. In the Input Parameters section, no changes are necessary. Note that the CustomerID field is automatically selected, with the Map to Identifier check box automatically checked. Click Finish.

4. Click Save or press Ctrl-S to save the changes.

To see how these additional operations would be used in SharePoint, and how the problems previously described manifest themselves, complete the following set of exercises:

1. In Internet Explorer, open the SharePoint site used by all previous examples in this chapter. The URL, for example, would be http://mss2010.mydomain.com/sites/ BCSSample/.

2. Click the Customers list from the Quick Launch Bar on the left side.

3. Click the List Ribbon, and click the List Settings icon.

4. Click Delete this List, and confirm the deletion.

NOTE

When including Create or Update operations on an external content type, it is important to create these operations before creating the external list in SharePoint. The reason the operations need to be defined first is that, when SharePoint creates a new list, it creates the form pages as needed for Edit Item and New Item. If no operation is defined, no corresponding form pages will be created when the list is instantiated. If the list is created first, and operations for Create or Update are then retroactively defined, the Add/Edit options show up on the item's Actions menu. However, selecting one of these options on the external list will result in an error message. This is corrected by deleting and re-creating the external list.

---

5. Select Site Actions, View All Site Content.

6. In the All Site Content page, click Create.

7. In the Create page, select External List, and click Create.

8. In the new list page, type **Customers** as the list name.

9. For the External Content Type field, an External Content Type picker is available. Click the icon for Select External Content Type. Select BCS Customer, and click OK. BCS Customer (AdventureWorksLT) should display as underlined. Click Create.

10. After the list is re-created, click the Item Ribbon, and click New Item.

11. Fill in the New Item record, as shown in Figure 31.10, and click Save.

FIGURE 31.10   New item screen for the Customers external list.

Notice a few things about the New Item screen. First, the PasswordHash and PasswordSalt
fields provide no guidance to the user completing the form on how to fill in the fields.
Additionally, the fields are required, because they are required in the AdventureWorksLT
database. Thus, leaving the fields blank is not an option for the user. Also, the
ModifiedDate field enables the user to directly input a date, even though it is intended to
be controlled by the system.

The record will indeed get added to the AdventureWorksLT database. However, certain data
points, crucial to the database and other dependent systems, will end up with invalid data.

To observe the issue with the delete operation, complete the following steps:

1. In the Customers SharePoint list, click the link for 1 in the CustomerID column,
which corresponds to the record for Orlando Gee.

2. In the Customers – View Item screen, click Delete. Confirm the deletion.

3. The error message displayed in Figure 31.11 should result. This is because the
Orlando Gee record has records in one or more related tables on the database.

4. On the resulting error screen, click the Go Back to Site link.

5. Hover over the CustomerID column. Click the yellow arrow, and select Descending
to sort the list in reverse order.

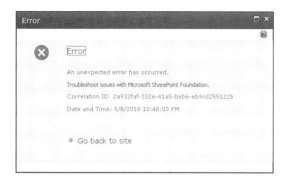

FIGURE 31.11   Error deleting external item with related records.

6. The James Smith entry, added in the recent set of exercises, should appear first.

7. Repeat steps 1 and 2 to attempt to delete the James Smith record. Because this record has no related rows in any other database table, the deletion attempt should succeed.

Creation of the Delete Operation against the Customer table using SharePoint Designer was relatively simple and straightforward. And there were no issues when attempting to delete Customer records through SharePoint when they had no related Order records. But when attempting to delete one that did have a related record, the database protected the integrity of the related data. However, the resulting error message was not indicative of the issue.

Business Connectivity Services Web Parts

Up until this point, all the functionality covered in this chapter is available with SharePoint Foundation 2010, the unlicensed version of SharePoint. The Enterprise version of Microsoft SharePoint Server offers some additional functionality.

Specifically, a set of Business Data web parts are available. These web parts provide a third way that BCS external content can be consumed in SharePoint and can be useful for building dashboard pages.

Consider, for example, a Customer Details page, which would show profile information— Name, Phone Number, Company, and Email Address—about the customer in one web part. Another web part could show recent orders—including Order Date, Total Amount, and Order Status. A last one would list a set of recent customer service calls. Having all this information available in one screen would make it easier for a Customer Service Representative to quickly access all relevant information, without having to go from one application to another. It doesn't even matter that all this information would live in a series of different SharePoint lists and database tables, or even in separate databases. The power of BCS is the capability to pull it all together into one location.

Before using these web parts, however, SharePoint Server Enterprise Site Collection Features needs to be activated. Activating this feature will add the web parts previously described to the site collection's web part gallery. Complete the following steps:

1. In Internet Explorer, open the SharePoint site used throughout this chapter. The URL will be something like http://mss2010.mydomain.com/sites/BCSSample/.

2. From the Site Actions menu, select Site Settings.

3. Under the Site Collection Administration heading, click the Site Collection Features link.

4. Locate SharePoint Server Enterprise Site Collection Features, and click the corresponding Activate button.

The following sets of examples show how to use three main web parts to build this dashboard: Business Data Item, Business Data Related List, and Query String URL Filter.

Business Data Item Web Part

The first web part of interest is the Business Data Item web part, which can be used to show the details of a single BCS record. The following example will use this web part to show the main profile information about a customer—Name, Phone Number, Email Address, and so on:

1. In Internet Explorer, return to the home page of the SharePoint site used throughout this chapter.

2. From the Site Actions menu, select Edit Page. The web page should show Left and Right web part zones.

3. In the Left Zone, click the Add a Web Part link.

4. In the Categories section, select the Business Data category. In the Web Parts section, select the Business Data Item web part. Click Add.

5. The Business Data Item web part should display in the Left web part zone. Click the link in the web part that says, Open the Tool Pane to modify the web part settings.

6. For the Business Data Item section of the settings, enter the word Customer in the Type field, and check the Check Mark icon to locate the BCS Customer external content type. After the external content type is located, it should display in the Type box as underlined.

7. In the View list box, select Default (Read Customer Item).

8. In the Item field, enter the number 1, and click the Check Mark icon to locate the record with CustomerID of 1. When the record is located, it should also display in the box as underlined.

9. Under the Fields heading, click the Choose box to change which fields are displayed. Deselect the NameStyle, Suffix, PasswordHash, PasswordSalt, rowguid, and ModifiedDate fields, leaving the remaining fields selected. Click OK.

10. Click OK in the web part settings to save the changes to the web part. When the page reloads, the record for Orlando Gee should be displayed, as shown in Figure 31.12.

Business Data Related List Web Part

Another important component of the Customer Dashboard page is the Recent Orders web part. As the name implies, this web part will show recent orders associated with the given customer. This web part will use the Business Data Related List web part.

The Business Data Related List web part uses associations defined between two external content types. Recall the earlier set of exercises to create the BCS Order external content type, which included an association to the BCS Customer external content type. The Business Data Related List web part will leverage this association to display only the orders that relate to a selected customer:

1. From the Site Actions menu, select Edit Page.

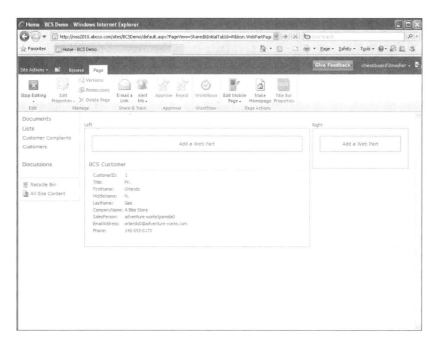

FIGURE 31.12   Configured Business Data Item web part.

2. In the Left Zone, click the Add a Web Part link.

3. In the Categories section, select the Business Data category. In the Web Parts section, select the Business Data Related List web part. Click Add.

4. The Business Data Related List web part should display in the Left web part zone, just above the BCS Customer web part. Move the new web part below the BCS Customer web part by clicking on the Business Data Related List header, holding the mouse button down, and dragging it beneath the BCS Customer web part. Release the left mouse button.

5. Click the link in the web part that says Open the Tool Pane to modify the web part settings.

6. In the Type box, click the Select an External Content Type icon. Notice that only the Sales Orders content type appears in the selection list. This is because Sales Orders was the only external content type for which an association was defined. Select Sales Orders and click OK.

7. In the Relationship list box, select Sales Order Customer Association that should be the only option in the list. Click OK to save the web part settings.

8. All the columns from the Sales Order table should display. To reduce the columns displayed, use Internet Explorer's horizontal scroll bar to move to the right. Click the Edit View link, which appears just above the right-most column.

9. In the Columns section of the view settings page, deselect all EXCEPT the following columns: OrderDate, ShipDate, SalesOrderNumber, CustomerID, SubTotal, TaxAmt, and TotalDue. Click OK.

10. Next, a connection must be established between the two web parts so that the value used in the BCS Customer web part (Business Data Item web part) is passed to the Sales Orders List web part (Business Data Related list web part).

11. From the Site Actions menu, select Edit Page.

12. Hover over the BCS Customer web part header. Click the down-arrow that appears at the right of the web part header. Click Connections, select Send Selected Item To, and select Sales Orders List, as shown in Figure 31.13.

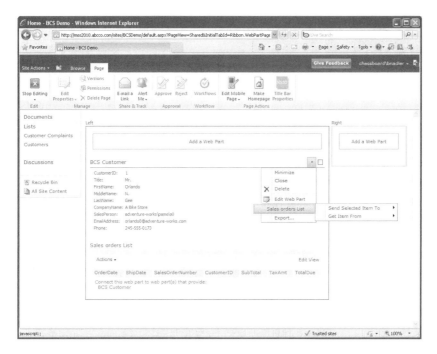

FIGURE 31.13 Establishing a connection between two web parts.

Query String Filter Web Part

Recall that the operations assigned to both the Customer and SalesOrderHeader operations contain filters for CustomerID. Rather than try to view all customers and all sales order on one web page, the orders information is most usable when viewing it one customer at a time To isolate the records to just those for a single customer, a filter can be used.

Furthermore, it would be inefficient to create a separate page for every customer in the database and have to design it the exact same way each time, changing only the CustomerID in each web part. Instead, it would obviously make more sense to create a single page, and simply differentiate between customers via a single parameter.

A query string parameter provides this capability. A query string parameter is the portion of a website address that appears after the question mark. For example, a query string parameter might be something like CustomerID. The web address to a page might look something like http://mss2010.abcco.com/Pages/CustomerDashboard.aspx?CustomerID=227. This URL will pull up the page called CustomerDashboard.aspx and reference the customer whose ID is 227.

The Query String Filter web part is designed to read the designated query string parameter and then send that value to connected web parts. To see this web part in action, complete the following steps:

1. From the Site Actions menu, select Edit Page.
2. In the Left zone, click the Add a Web Part link.
3. Select the Filters category and the Query String Filter web part. Click Add.
4. Click the Open the Tool Pane link to edit the web part settings.
5. In the Filter Name property, type **CustomerID.**
6. For the Query String Parameter Name, type **CustomerID.**
7. Finally, assign 1 as the default value. This last parameter is not critical but will assign an ID to be used if the user lands on the page without the CustomerID being specified.
8. Under the Appearance heading, change the web part title to **CustomerID Query String Filter.**
9. Click OK to save the web part settings.
10. Finally, connect the web part to the BCS Customer web part. To do so, hover over the CustomerID Query String Filter web part header. To the right, click the arrow, select Connections, Send Filter Values To, and select BCS Customer.
11. In the Configure Connection dialog box, select BCS Customer, and click Finish.
12. In the Page Ribbon at the top of the SharePoint page, click Stop Editing to complete all changes.
13. In the address bar of Internet Explorer, change the address removing everything that appears after default.aspx. In its place, type **?CustomerID=1** and press Enter. Notice that the page shows the default data for Orlando Gee and any related orders.
14. Repeat step 13, but use 61 for the CustomerID. Notice that the data changes to show the customer details and orders for Jeffery Kurtz, as shown in Figure 31.14.

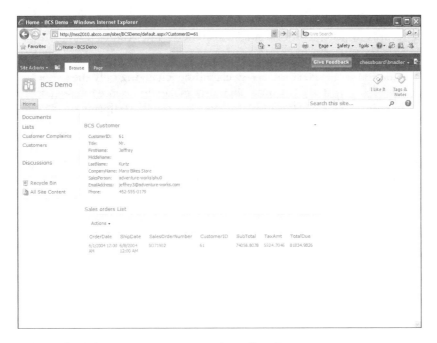

FIGURE 31.14   Customer dashboard for Jeffrey Kurtz.

15. Repeat step 13, and instead use 151. Observe how the data changes again, this time
showing the records for Walter Brian.

Summary and Conclusion

Business Connectivity Services provides a unique way of making information available for
widespread consumption. A successful implementation is all about the data. However,
assuming that the proper data repositories are available, the tool provides a means of
quickly and easily presenting the data for consumers to access the information.

For years, powerful tools have made it possible to generate reports based on large volumes
of data. Nevertheless, the traditional problems have been related to making the reports
available to the right people and having the reports available at the time that they were
most useful.

Like PerformancePoint Services in the previous chapter, Business Connectivity Services
solves these problems in several ways. First, the ability to publish information to pages in
SharePoint brings the information to the fingertips of anyone who might need it. Second,
the client tools in SharePoint Designer make it possible for nondevelopers to build relevant, meaningful reports and to establish their own connections to the data. Finally,
having a single location to where the information is published means that only one
version of the truth is available for consumption.

For all these reasons, SharePoint 2010's new Business Connectivity Services functionality helps make the right information available to the right people at the right time.

31

Best Practices

▶ Use any site template, including the Blank Site template, for creating external content types.

▶ Define associations for external content types that have relationships with others, such as the relationship between customers and orders.

▶ If using External Data columns in SharePoint lists, periodically click the Refresh icon to ensure that the most current data is displayed in your SharePoint lists.

▶ For simple databases with little or no logic on various columns or tables, SharePoint Designer may be a useful tool for creating write-back operations. However, for larger or more complex databases, use a more advanced tool, such as Visual Studio 2010 for building write-back operations.

▶ When including Create or Update operations on an external content type, it is important to create these operations before creating the external list in SharePoint.

Index

A

AAM (alternate access mappings)

configuring, external URL, 345-346

extranets, 321

access

Excel, testing, 781

servers, restricting, 363

Access Services, 31, 741, 757-762

Access Services application, 439

Foundation and Server, 443

Access View button (Library tab), 529-530

Access Web Database site, creating, 758-762

Activity Feed, My Site, 684-686

Activity Monitor, SQL Server, 217-218

AD (Active Directory)

Exchange Server 2010, planning for, 391-394

profile fields, mapping to, 681-684

AD CS (Active Directory Certificate Services), servers, 375-376

AD RMS (Active Directory Rights Management Services)

document libraries, 424-430

installing, 424-427

IRM (Information Rights Management), enabling, 429-431

limitations, 424

prerequisites, 424

RMS certification pipeline, modifying, 428

Add and Customize Pages permission, 591

Add Items permission, 591

Add/Remove Personal Web Parts permission, 591

administration, 147

automating, PowerShell, 162-169

extranets, mobile administration, 321

STSADM tool, 143-145

B

backend systems, managing, PowerShell, 174

backing up, IIS 7 configuration, 260-261

Backstage, Word 2010, 717-719

backup settings, SPCA (SharePoint Central Administration) tool, reviewing, 129-135

backup software, 38

backups, 15-16

    Administration Management Shell, 242

    Central Administration tool, 242-246

        granular backups, 246-252

    components, 241-242

    environments, 241

    IIS backup, 242

    PowerShell, 158, 257-258

    SQL Server, 242, 261-264

    validating, 286

    verifying, 282

Bar indicators, 865

Basic Meeting Workspace template, 581

Basic Search Center template, 581

BCS (Business Connectivity Services), 881-882, 903-905

    entities, building, 882

    external content types, 882-890

        building, 883-884

        consuming, 890-904

        defining, 884-888

        external data, 892-895

        external lists, 890-892

        operations, 884

        related items, 888-890

        writing to, 895-898

    Foundation and Server, 443-445

    web parts, 898-904

        Business Data Item web part, 898-901

        Business Data Related List web part, 898-902

        Query String Filter web part, 902-904

BDC (Business Data Catalog). *see* BCS (Business Connectivity Services)

Best Bets, Search, 193-194

binaries, installing, 66-68

Blank Meeting Workspace template, 581

Blank Site template, 581

BLOG storage, externalizing, 231-239

Blog template, 11, 581

bookmarklets, My Site, 689-691

Browse Directories permission, 591

Browse User Information permission, 591

browser support, Office Web Apps, 767

business applications, SharePoint 2010 versions, 436

Business Connectivity Services (BCS). *see* BCS (Business Connectivity Services)

Business Data Connectivity Services, 31-439

Business Data Item web part, 898-901

Business Data Related List web part, 898-902

business environments, workflows, 791-793

business intelligence

    BCS (Business Connectivity Services), 881-882, 903-905

        external content types, 882-904

    PPS (PerformancePoint Services), 853-854

    tools, leveraging, 24

business needs

    customer extranet portal, 51

    development projects, analyzing, 815

    functionality, mapping, 89

    team collaboration, outlining, 47

business requirements, extranets, 307

C

How can we make this index more useful? Email us at indexes@samspublishing.com

J

K

L

How can we make this index more useful? Email us at indexes@sampublishing.com

W

UNLEASHED

Unleashed takes you beyond the basics, providing an exhaustive, technically sophisticated reference for professionals who need to exploit a technology to its fullest potential. It's the best resource for practical advice from the experts, and the most in-depth coverage of the latest technologies.

Microsoft SharePoint 2010 PerformancePoint Services Unleashed
ISBN-13: 9780672330940

OTHER UNLEASHED TITLES

Windows PowerShell Unleashed
ISBN-13: 9780672329883

Windows Small Business Server 2008 Unleashed
ISBN-13: 9780672329579

ASP.NET 3.5 AJAX Unleashed
ISBN-13: 9780672329739

WPF Control Development Unleashed
ISBN-13: 9780672330339

Microsoft Exchange Server 2010 Unleashed
ISBN-13: 9780672330469

Windows Server 2008 Hyper-V Unleashed
ISBN-13: 9780672330285

System Center Operations Manager (OpsMgr) 2007 R2 Unleashed
ISBN-13: 9780672333415

System Center Configuration Manager (SCCM) 2007 Unleashed
ISBN-13: 9780672330230

Microsoft Dynamics CRM 4.0 Unleashed
ISBN-13: 9780672329708

Microsoft Dynamics CRM 4 Integration Unleashed
ISBN-13: 9780672330544

LINQ Unleashed
ISBN-13: 9780672329838

Silverlight 2 Unleashed
ISBN-13: 9780672330148

Windows Communication Foundation 3.5 Unleashed
ISBN-13: 9780672330247

Microsoft System Center Enterprise Suite Unleashed
ISBN-13: 9780672333194

Microsoft Expression Blend Unleashed
ISBN-13: 9780672329319

Microsoft SQL Server 2008 Reporting Services Unleashed
ISBN-13: 9780672330261

WPF 4 Unleashed
ISBN-13: 9780672331190

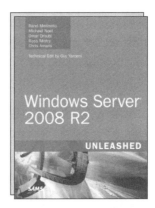

Windows Server 2008 R2 Unleashed
ISBN-13: 9780672330926

Microsoft SQL Server 2008 R2 Unleashed
ISBN-13: 9780672330568

SAMS

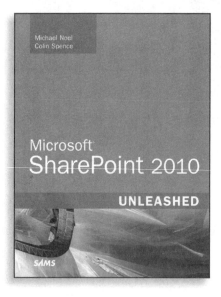

FREE Online Edition

Your purchase of **Microsoft SharePoint 2010 Unleashed** includes access to a free online edition for 45 days through the Safari Books Online subscription service. Nearly every Sams book is available online through Safari Books Online, along with more than 5,000 other technical books and videos from publishers such as Addison-Wesley Professional, Cisco Press, Exam Cram, IBM Press, O'Reilly, Prentice Hall, and Que.

SAFARI BOOKS ONLINE allows you to search for a specific answer, cut and paste code, download chapters, and stay current with emerging technologies.

Activate your FREE Online Edition at www.informit.com/safarifree

> **STEP 1:** Enter the coupon code: JEVIPXA.

> **STEP 2:** New Safari users, complete the brief registration form.
> Safari subscribers, just log in.

If you have difficulty registering on Safari or accessing the online edition, please e-mail customer-service@safaribooksonline.com